Ultimate Guide to
Mastering FamilySearch

by

Dana Ann Palmer, CG®, CGL®

Genealogical Publishing Company

2025

Paperback book ISBN: 9780806322094

eBook ISBN: 9780806372631

Published by:

Genealogical Publishing Company
3600 Clipper Mill Rd. Suite 229
Baltimore, Maryland 21211

Cover design by Kate Boyer, Heron Creek Press, LLC

Table of Contents

PREFACE

This book was created as a guide for those who are just getting started with finding their family and using the resources on FamilySearch. The layout design for the website on a cell phone varies significantly from the layout on a desktop or laptop computer. The majority of the examples in this book are based on the layout design of the FamilySearch website for a desktop or laptop computer.

The best way to learn is to practice. Web links have been provided so you can more easily find the examples shown. Follow the examples to see how to do the various tricks shown throughout this book, then implement the same techniques for your family lines.

Many of the examples in the MEMORIES are from my personal photos. You will not be able to see my GALLERY in MEMORIES and the photo example that is marked "private" on the FamilySearch website, which is why I did not provide the links for them. The other MEMORIES example is marked public, and the link to the image was provided in the example in this book.

It is recommended that you scan and upload your own photos to your GALLERY and follow the steps shown in the MEMORIES chapter using the photos from your GALLERY.

ACKNOWLEDGEMENTS

This book has been many years in the making and would not be possible without the support of my loving husband and seven wonderful children. A shout out to them for allowing me time to work and providing feedback and suggestions for improvement over the years.

Thank you to my parents and grandparents for instilling in me a love of family and seeking out my roots. Thank you especially to my mother who encouraged me to take over for her typing our family information into the old Personal Ancestral File (PAF) program when it was first introduced and then supporting me as I explored my family roots and visited family history centers as a teenager.

Thank you to my husband, Andy Palmer; my mom Kris Croft; my friends, Lori Esch, Karynne Moses, and Katie Leishman, and Joe Garonzik and Tamara Wise; for proof reading and editing this book and for their valuable insight and comments.

Thank you to Rhett Dabling, the team at RootsTech, and the many historical and genealogical societies across the country for allowing me to present on various FamilySearch topics over the years. Many of the examples in this book come from the examples shown in my FamilySearch lectures.

A special thank you to Joe Garonzik and all those at Genealogical.com for making this book a possibility.

And thank you to the readers for your support and encouragement.

Dana Palmer
2025

INTRODUCTION

My love of family history is in my blood. As members of the Church of Jesus Christ of Latter-day Saints, my ancestors left a rich legacy and love of family that was passed down through the ages. Spending time together as a family was valued and super important in my life. As the oldest grandchild on my father's side and the fourth oldest grandchild on my mother's side, I had the opportunity to be close to my grandparents and remember some of my great-grandparents, great-aunts, and great-uncles.

Even though we lived in a different state than my extended family, we always made time around the holidays to visit my grandparents and spend time getting to know them better. I cherished the time we spent with family during the Christmas holidays and the family parties where we could visit and play. I chose to attend college close to where my grandparents lived and was able to visit with them on the weekends when time allowed a trip to see them.

At an early age, my extended family would take time to tell me stories and explain who the people were in the photographs on my great-grandmother's wall during our Christmas dinner party. I loved to hear their stories and learn more of where I came from and who went before me. My maternal grandmother had a wall up to the second floor of her home also filled with photographs. I remember sitting on the stairs and looking at the photos. Of course, I always checked to see if she had a picture of me on the wall, then I often looked at those of my mother, and then the others. I loved when my grandparents told me stories, especially the ones where my mom or her siblings got into trouble as kids.

My journey using FamilySearch started when I was about nine years old, after my parents got the new Personal Ancestral File (PAF) software and I started typing information from their old family group records into the database. Computers were still very new at this time, and it was an exciting time to be able to organize information using a machine instead of typing it on a typewriter or recording the information by hand onto papers. Eventually, busyness of life made it so my parents did not have a lot of extra time to finish typing the information into PAF, so I took over shortly after they started.

As time passed and I finished typing in all the information, I wanted to know more about my family and started visiting at what was then the local family history center. It was always exciting when something new was released digitally.

As a teenager, I made all the mistakes common to beginners, but I wanted to learn about my roots and taught myself what was needed. Back then, I didn't have much of my own money to pay for copies of records, so instead I visited many libraries and cemeteries. I was always excited when I found things relating to my family. When I started, census records were only available on microfilm, and it was exciting news when Soundex was started. Digitization of these records came much later. Once census records were digitized, I remember spending two weeks searching the online records and was able to find census records for all of my relatives in my first few generations, which was so much faster than the four years I spent as a teenager looking for just a portion of my family in the same collection on microfilm.

I married at the young age of 20 and joined my first lineage society (Daughters of the Utah Pioneers) around that time. After graduating from college, I spent two years researching weekly at the Brigham Young University library in Provo and driving to Salt Lake City to research at what was then known as the Family History Library several times a month. After my husband graduated in 1998, we moved several times in multiple states and cities. Of course, I visited repositories in those locations and nearby all over the country.

The FamilySearch website was launched in 1999. At the time, we lived in Indiana while my husband attended graduate school. Since we didn't have any children, I volunteered at the local family history center in my spare time.

In 2000, we moved to Ohio after my husband graduated and got a job in Cincinnati. Part of that year, we lived in Mehoopany, Pennsylvania while my husband finished his job training. I continued to research at the family history center in Norwood until we moved to Lebanon in the summer of 2001. Our first child was born in the fall of 2001.

I served as a family history consultant in Middletown for more than a decade and started teaching genealogy classes during that time. I also helped our local genealogical society create a website where people could find their ancestors in the various indexes we created from the records contained in that society's collection, with the idea they would come research in person and find their family in the records or write to the society and request a copy of the record. Not many online indexes existed at this time, so this was a very inventive advancement for the society. The idea was to help both the researcher and the society to be more efficient.

FamilySearch continued to release new features on their website. Over the years, I often was asked to teach genealogy and technology topics to volunteers and patrons for our local and surrounding genealogical societies. I also taught genealogy classes at the Warren County Career Center for about 7 years and at Sinclair Community College for over 10 years until the pandemic caused my Sinclair classes to be cancelled. I served as a Stake Family History Consultant in our Church for several years until the Stake boundaries were adjusted and our ward was moved to a new Stake. One of my responsibilities as a Stake consultant during this time was to plan our Stake's annual Family History Jamboree, kind of like the RootsTech conference for this area. I served in this leadership capacity for about seven years but was a speaker at the event just about every year since 2004. I often was asked to teach how to effectively use the FamilySearch website and tricks finding records on it.

When I was pregnant with our third child, I decided to become a certified genealogist and completed the process in the spring of 2009 after giving birth to my daughter in the summer of 2008. I became a certified genealogical lecturer in 2019. I submitted my first proposal to speak at RootsTech for the 2020 conference and have spoken there every year since.

My family doesn't travel out west very often, but when we do, I always take time to spend time researching at the FamilySearch Library in Salt Lake City. FamilySearch has so many amazing collections and are so willing to help you find your family. I hope you are as successful finding your family using FamilySearch's resources as I have been.

Dana

Chapter 1: Overview

FAMILYSEARCH OVERVIEW

FamilySearch is a non-profit genealogy organization of The Church of Jesus Christ of Latter-day Saints devoted to helping individuals connect their family by providing free genealogical and historical resources online. At the end of 2024, FamilySearch had over 20.5 billion records from over 170 countries and principalities with more than 2.5 billion new records added that year alone. They currently collaborate with over 10,000 organizations in more than 100 countries to provide free access to genealogy records onsite in Salt Lake City, online, and in more than 6,500 FamilySearch centers or affiliates world-wide.[1] They are affiliated with other genealogy giants such as Ancestry.com, My Heritage, Find My Past, and Geneanet.

It is remarkable the amount of information they have gathered over time, considering this world-wide genealogy giant started as the Genealogical Society of Utah in 1894 with just 300 books.[2]

By 1998, the society began digitizing their genealogical and historical records. To date they have over 2.4 million rolls of microfilm and 742,000 microfiche[3] stored in archive-safe conditions in the Granite Mountain vault. Only a few of these microfilms, not available digitally, are still available on-site at the FamilySearch Library in Salt Lake City. In addition, FamilySearch has over 630,000 books and serials and 4,500 periodicals.[4] Each month, millions of new records are added to their growing digital image collection available on their website.[5]

In 1999, the name of FamilySearch was introduced and the website launched on 24 May 1999. The first digital images were released on their website in 2007. In 2010, FamilySearch's new Record Search was launched. By 2017, web-based indexing began opening remarkable access to records difficult to find otherwise.[6] In 2024, FamilySearch labs introduced Full-Text Search, which uses Artificial Intelligence (AI) to read handwritten records and convert the image to a searchable and transcribed text format, providing access to ancestors not easily found.[7]

FamilySearch's plans of further implementing AI technology continue to astound the genealogy community. Computer-Assisted Indexing with volunteer correction and input will yield access to countless records. Oral genealogies, more digitized books, and new tree features will further help individuals connect their kin and find their loved ones.[8]

To access their blog, go to www.familysearch.org/en/blog.

---

[1] "FamilySearch 2024 Genealogy Highlights," blog post, *The Church of Jesus Christ of Latter-day Saints* (https://newsroom.churchofjesuschrist.org/article/familysearch-2024-genealogy-highlights : posted 2 January 2025).

[2] "24 Fun Facts about FamilySearch You May Not Know," blog post, *FamilySearch* (https://www.familysearch.org/en/blog/24-fun-facts-about-familysearch-you-may-not-know : posted 11 December 2019).

[3] Ibid.

[4] Ibid.

[5] "New Free Historical Records from 8 Countries July 2025 Update," blog post, *FamilySearch* (https://www.familysearch.org/en/blog/new-records-july-2025 : posted 1 July 2025).

[6] "24 Fun Facts about FamilySearch You May Not Know," blog post, *FamilySearch* (https://www.familysearch.org/en/blog/24-fun-facts-about-familysearch-you-may-not-know : posted 11 December 2019).

[7] "FamilySearch 2024 Genealogy Highlights," blog post, *The Church of Jesus Christ of Latter-day Saints* (https://newsroom.churchofjesuschrist.org/article/familysearch-2024-genealogy-highlights : posted 2 January 2025).

[8] "FamilySearch Shares Plans for 2025," blog post, *The Church of Jesus Christ of Latter-day Saints* (https://newsroom.churchofjesuschrist.org/article/familysearch-shares-plans-for-2025 : posted 8 January 2025).

FINDING A FAMILYSEARCH CENTER OR AFFILIATE

FamilySearch has over 6,500 FamilySearch centers or affiliate sites world-wide that provide access to resources on the FamilySearch website and partner sites, including some restricted records not available to patrons logged in to their own personal devices.

To find the closest FamilySearch center or affiliate, go to https://www.familysearch.org/en/search/ and ether scroll to the bottom of the main page and click CONTACT US or click the question mark icon in the upper-right corner from the HELP menu and choose CONTACT US. Both will take you to the same page, https://www.familysearch.org/en/fieldops/familysearch-support-contact-us.

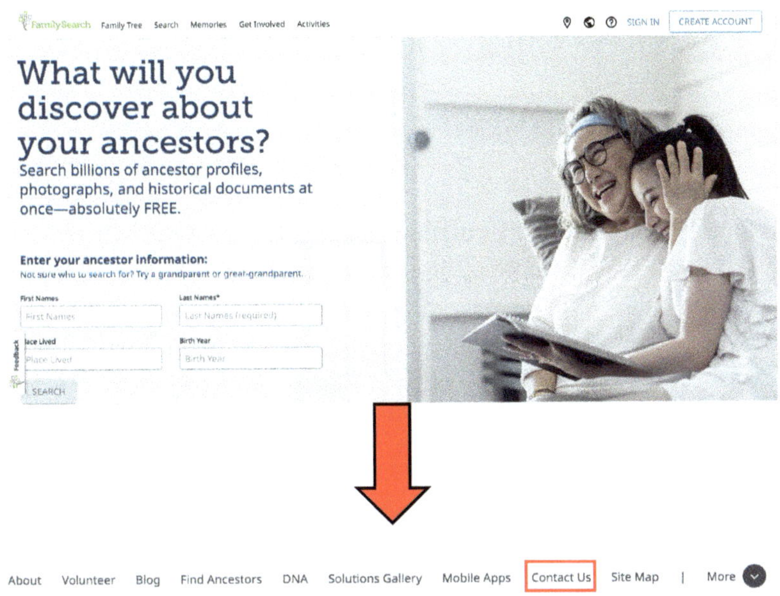

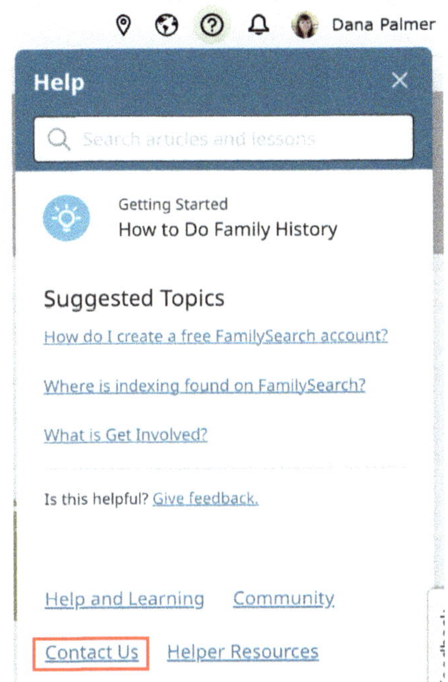

Click on the country where you reside to find the phone number or email of the support team for that region or scroll down to the bottom of the page for more options.

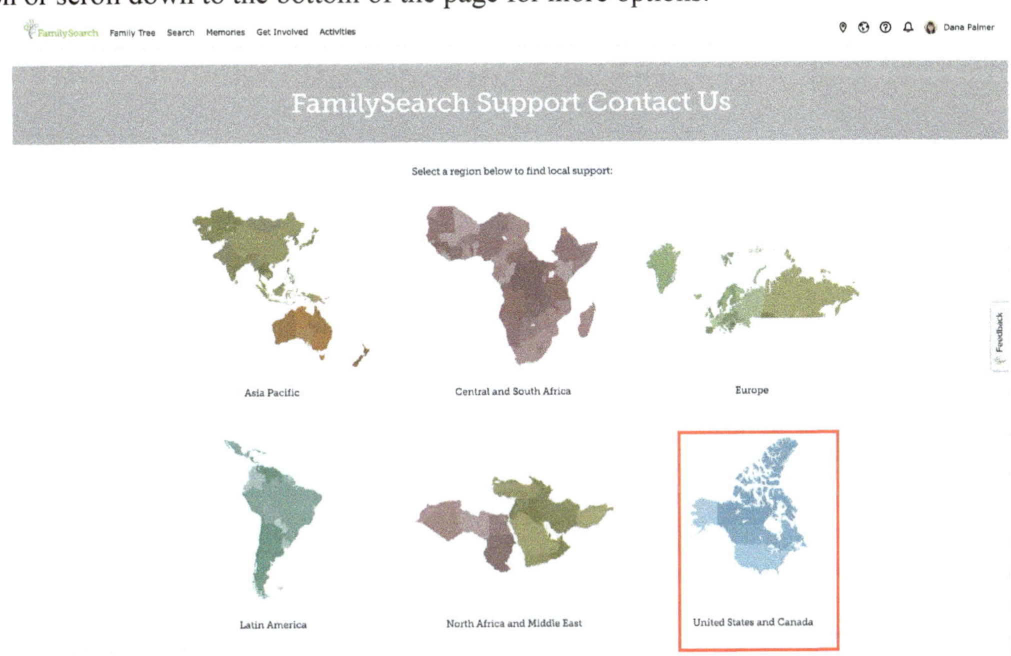

https://www.familysearch.org/en/fieldops/united-states-and-canada-contact-us

Scroll down to find the location to the FamilySearch center or affiliate closest to you and click on FIND IN-PERSON HELP.

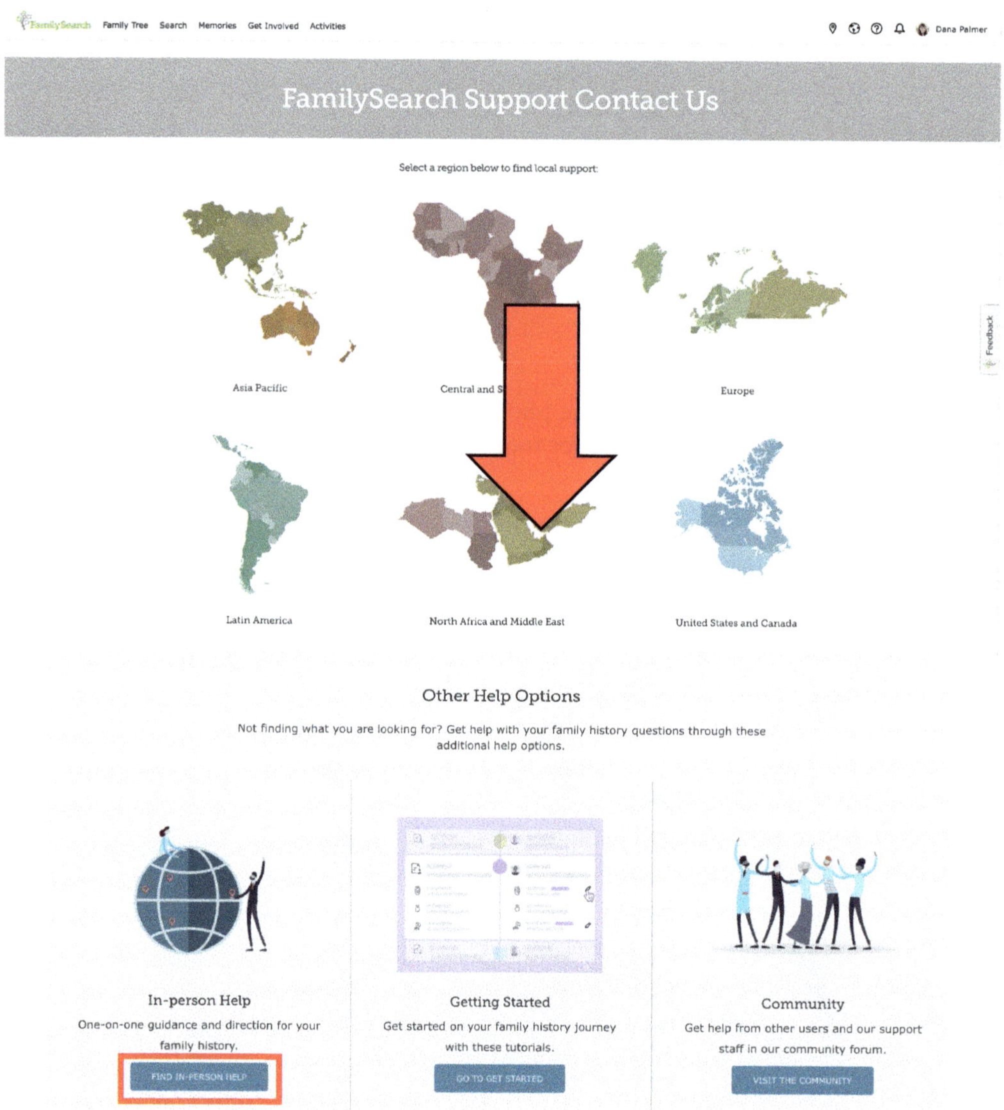

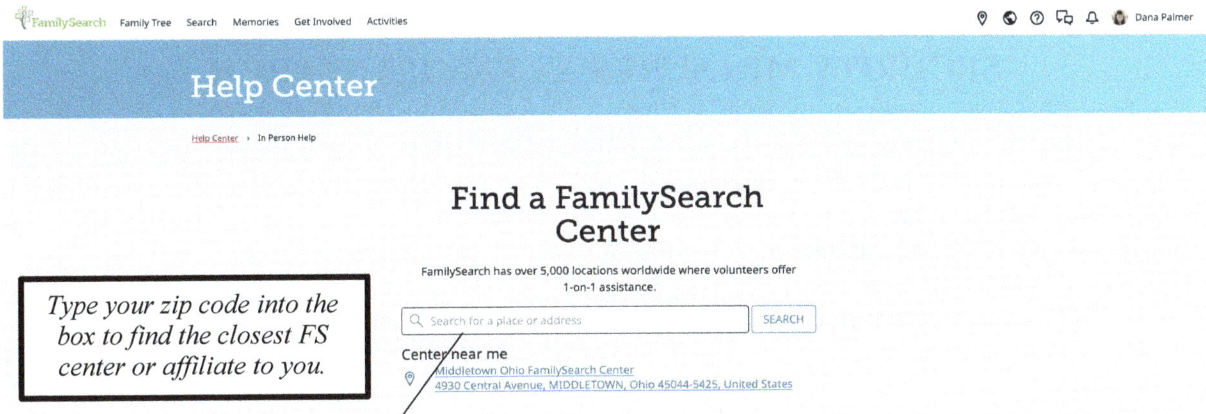

Type your zip code into the box to find the closest FS center or affiliate to you.

Since you are logged in to your account, it should show you the closest FamilySearch center or affiliate to the zip you have on file in your account. To see other locations, type in your zip code or the zip code where you want to locate a FamilySearch center or affiliate in the search box and click SEARCH.

It will show you all the FamilySearch centers (in green) or affiliates (in orange) located near the address, zip, city, or region entered. Click on the icon to see details about that location including the address, phone number, hours of operation, and a link for directions to it.

Keep in mind that if a FamilySearch center is located in one of the church buildings, check to see if it will be open before you travel there since it is staffed by volunteers, and some are only available by appointment.

For more help or details on how to find a FamilySearch center or affiliate using a smart phone, go to https://www.familysearch.org/en/help/helpcenter/article/find-a-familysearch-center.

SECURITY MEASURES AT FAMILYSEARCH

Protecting the information of users of the FamilySearch website is paramount. Not only is the information about living individuals entered in the tree only viewable by the person who entered it, but login is now required for daily use on the website. Over the past few years, FamilySearch has significantly increased security measures to make it harder for unauthorized users to hack the system.

You can still use the traditional sign in with your login name and password, or you can add additional security by adding in the multi-factor authentication (MFA) feature in the Settings feature of your profile image and account tab. The multi-factor authentication (MFA) will send a code to your email account on file, which must be entered to finish logging in. After you type in the code, you will need to log back in.

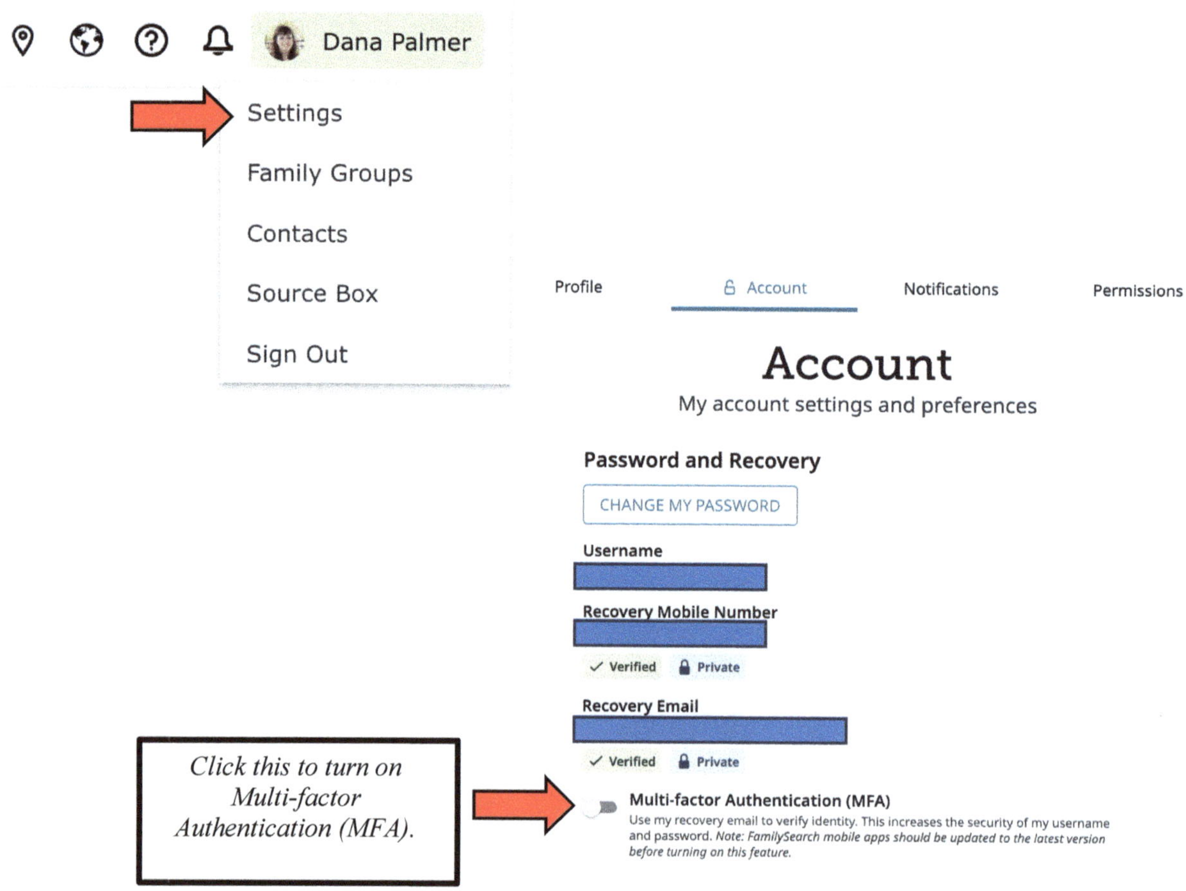

For more details go to https://www.familysearch.org/en/blog/familysearch-multi-factor-authentication

Chapter 2: Finding Records

GETTING STARTED

The FamilySearch.org website (http://www.familysearch.org/ or https://www.familysearch.org/en/home/portal/ for English speakers) has many free resources available to researchers. Using filters and other advanced search techniques can help you find those elusive ancestors.

There are five main places on FamilySearch that have record collections:

1. **RECORDS**:
   - *Search Collections by Name* – This is a good way to search if you don't know what collection your person is in, and you have basic facts about the person.
   - *Browse All Collections* – This is my favorite way to search and allows you to browse to a location or topic, then choose the applicable record collection. This way to search is really good for names that are misspelled or mis-indexed.
   - *Browse Places* – This is helpful to see what records are available for a specific region in both the indexed and un-indexed records. It usually has links to free webinars and is very useful for people researching internationally.
2. **IMAGES**: This is where the newly digitized collections are organized. Some microfilms are restricted due to the content and dates contained within them, so they will not be available for viewing. Searches are done by location. Once the location is selected, life events and locations within the selected place can narrow down search results. Click on the collection and view the images like you would in the catalog.
3. **CATALOG**: Search by location, then choose the appliable category of record you want to search. Microfilms that have been digitized will have a camera icon to the far right. If there is a lock above it, you will need to go to a FamilySearch Center or FamilySearch affiliate to view the records. If there is a magnifying glass on the far right, you can use a name to search the collection. Keep in mind that the magnifying glass may not cover all the dates or facts on the microfilm, so if you don't find it using the magnifying glass search feature, check the record manually by clicking on the camera icon and searching the pages of the digitized collection. Catalog is a very good place to find vital records, deeds, probates, tax records, and maps for specific localities. In the United States, search by county and state, unless your location is in New England, then search by the town. For locations outside the USA, search by the town or parish name unless you are looking for civil registration records kept at the county or state level.
4. **RESEARCH WIKI**: Click the blue online records to see what records are available on other websites. Some record collections also may be found by clicking on the applicable archives or repository links. This is where you will find word lists and other useful tools for languages other than English. Topical searches such as specific Civil War companies or immigration can also be used. Be sure to check if the Guided Research has tools for the area you are researching.
5. **BOOKS**: This is where you will find books from FamilySearch's vast collection as well as those from contributing libraries. This is a good place to find books about your family, county histories, and other published books for various locations.

RECORDS

The historical record collection (https://www.familysearch.org/en/search/) has both indexed and unindexed collections from the massive microfilm, microfiche, and digital records of FamilySearch. More digitized records are being added every day, so check back often for updates. The screen below is what will appear if you are not logged in. Once you are logged in, the main page will be customized based on your unique information.

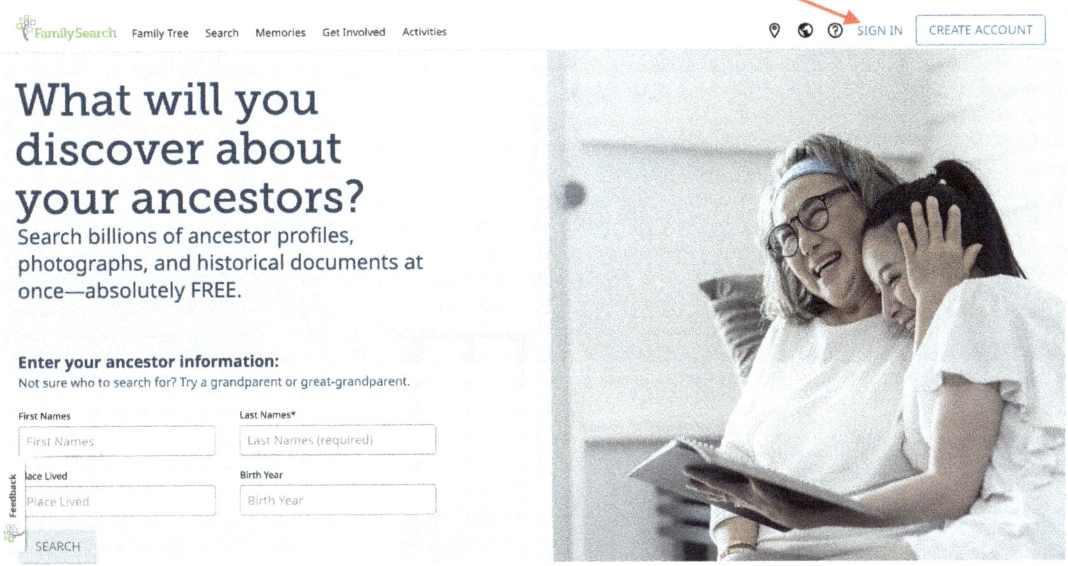

To start searching for your family, click on the SEARCH tab and then RECORDS in the dropdown menu.

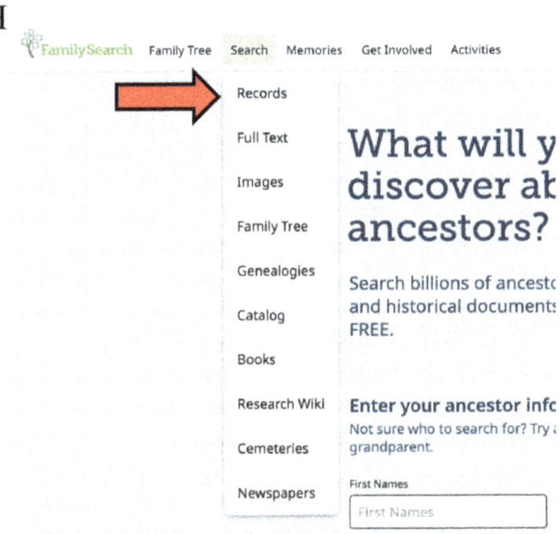

There are three ways to search:

- general search in the big search box in the center of the page
- browse all collections
- browse places

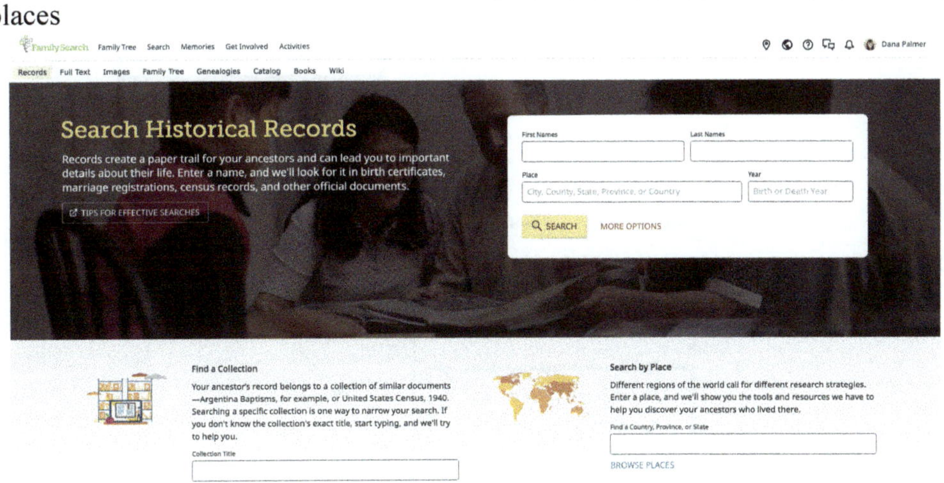

https://www.familysearch.org/en/search/

Searching Historical Records – Basic Search

Searching the historical record collection is an excellent way to find your family in the records on the website. It is generally more efficient to browse all collections, then choose the database you want to find people misspelled or mis-indexed, but searching in the general search box can be useful if your ancestor's location is unknown or they may be in records in multiple locations / states.

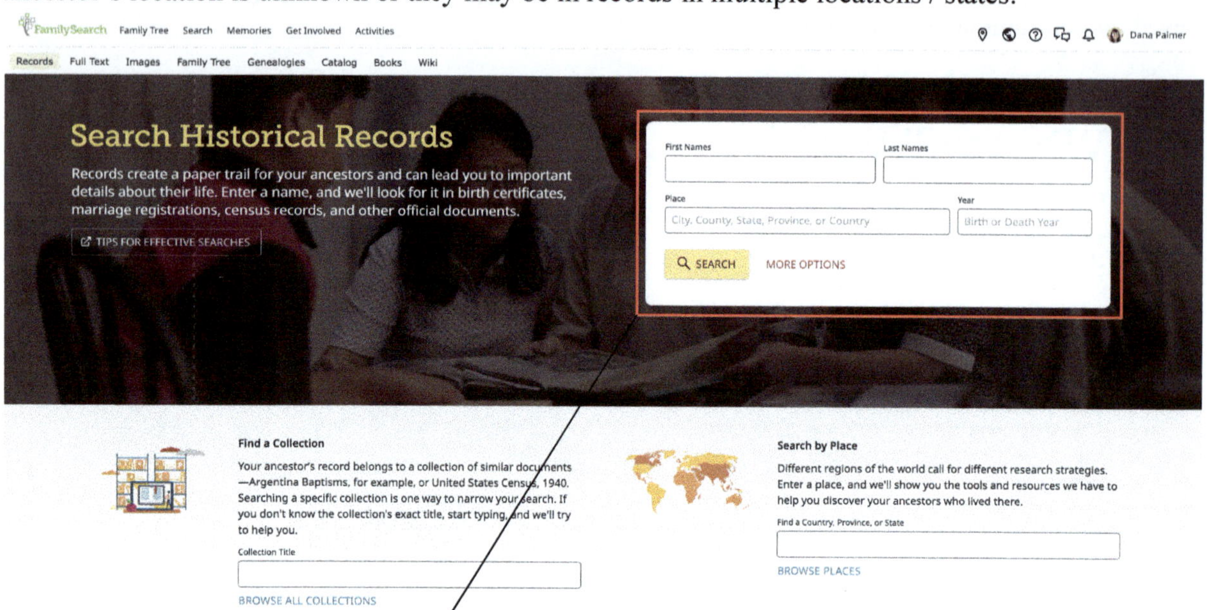

https://www.familysearch.org/en/search/

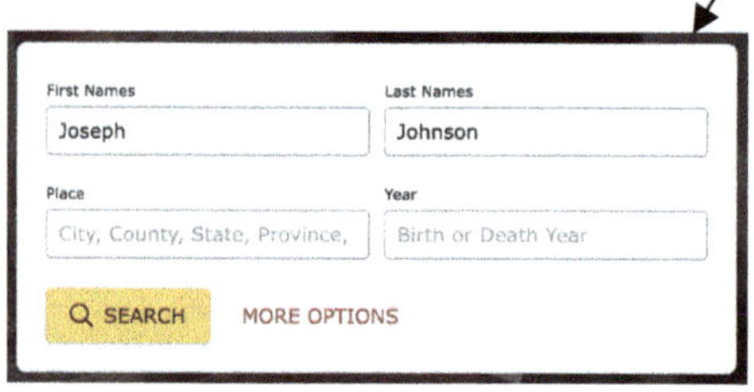

To search for your ancestor, type their name in the box. You can add more details to help reduce the search results but be careful. If you add too many details, it may eliminate the record you want to find. Also, if your ancestor has a common name, like Joseph Johnson, you may get millions of search results.

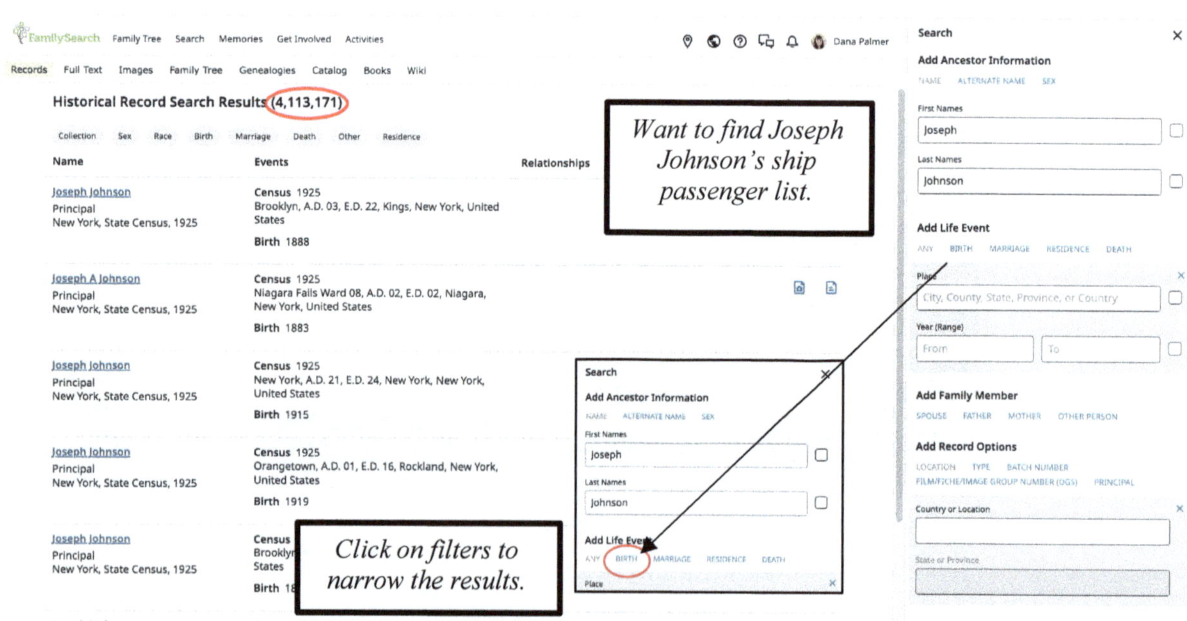

https://www.familysearch.org/en/search/record/results?q.givenName=Joseph&q.surname=Johnson

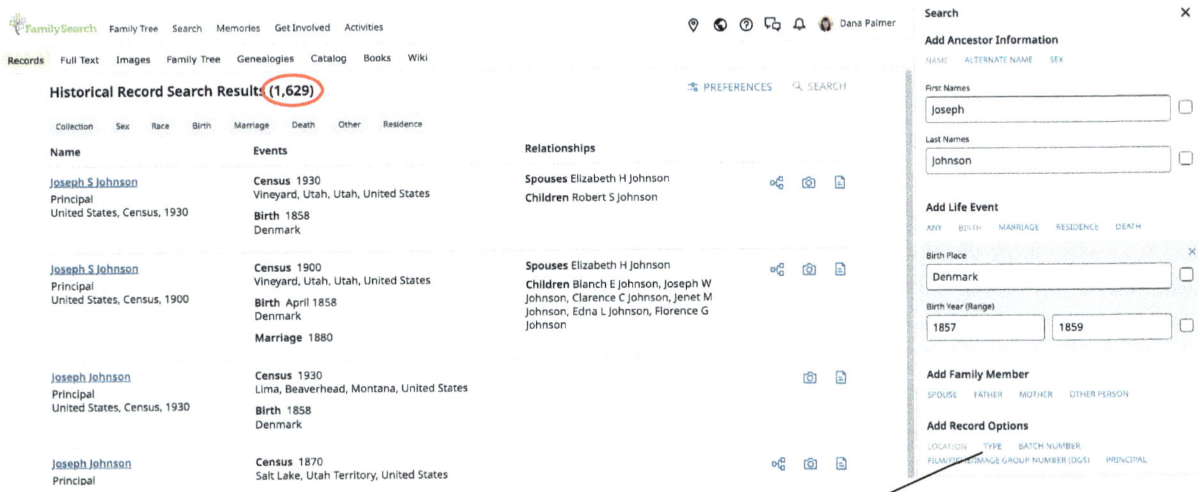

https://www.familysearch.org/search/en/record/results?count=20&q.birthLikeDate.from=1857&q.birthLikeDate.to=1859&q.birthLikePlace=Denmark&q.givenName=Joseph&q.surname=Johnson

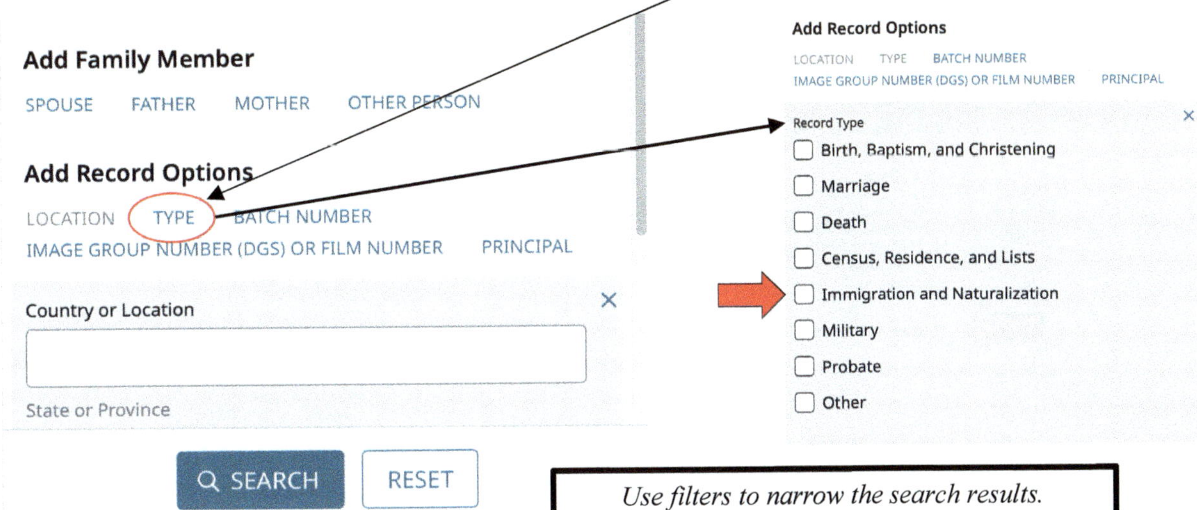

Use filters to narrow the search results.

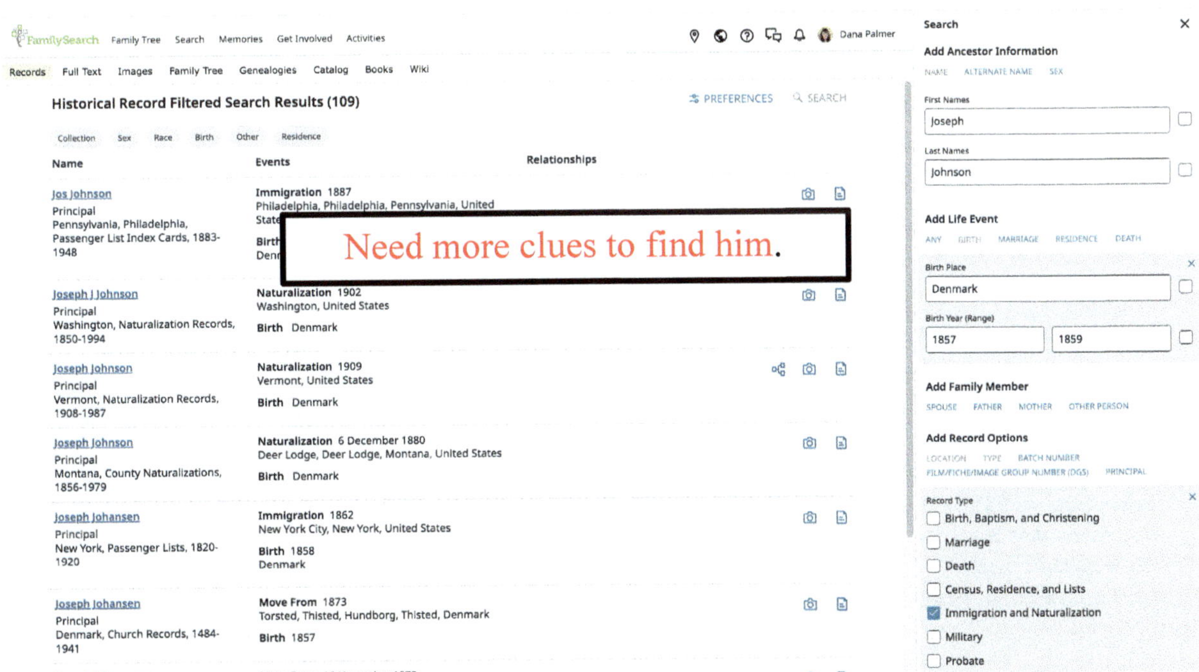

https://www.familysearch.org/en/search/record/results?count=20&f.recordType=4&q.birthLikeDate.from=1857&q.birthLikeDate.to=1859&q.birthLikePlace=Denmark&q.givenName=Joseph&q.surname=Johnson

Browse All Collections

If you can't find your family by typing their information into the general historical record search box, click on BROWSE ALL COLLECTIONS to go directly to the database. You can also type the name of the database you want (e.g. "Find a Grave") into the COLLECTION TITLE box to find it more quickly. This is probably the easiest way to find misspelled or mis-indexed individuals in the various collections in this part of FamilySearch.

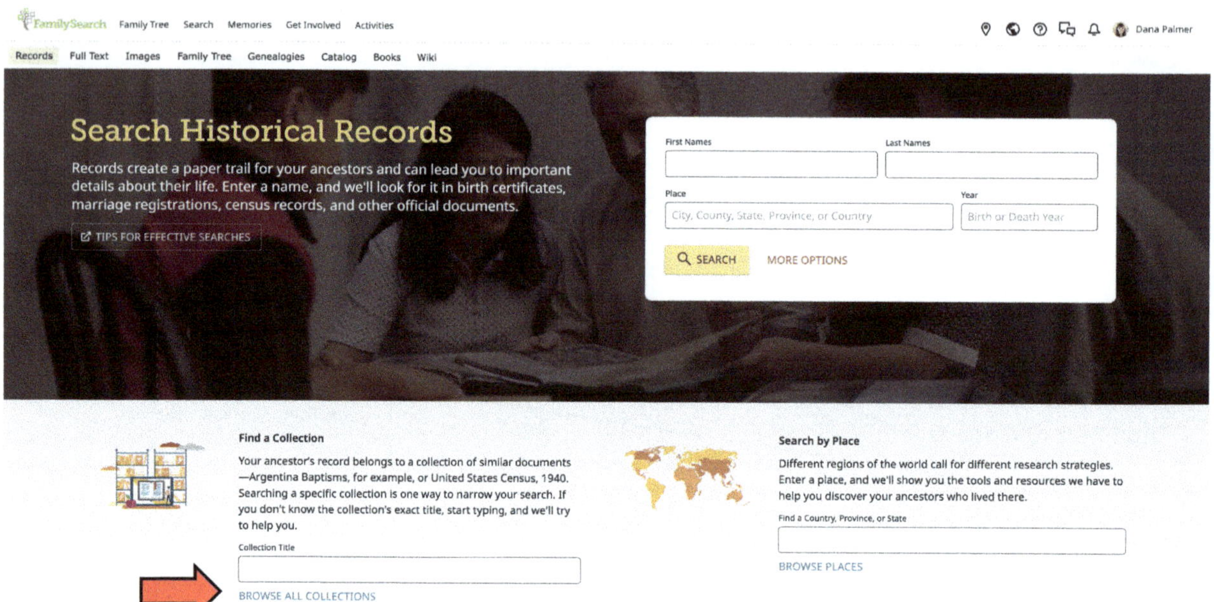

https://www.familysearch.org/en/search/

Click on the database for that specific locality. You can also type the name of the database in the COLLECTION TITLE box if you forgot to type it in the prior screen. To narrow down the selections for your location, add filters from the far-right side of the screen.

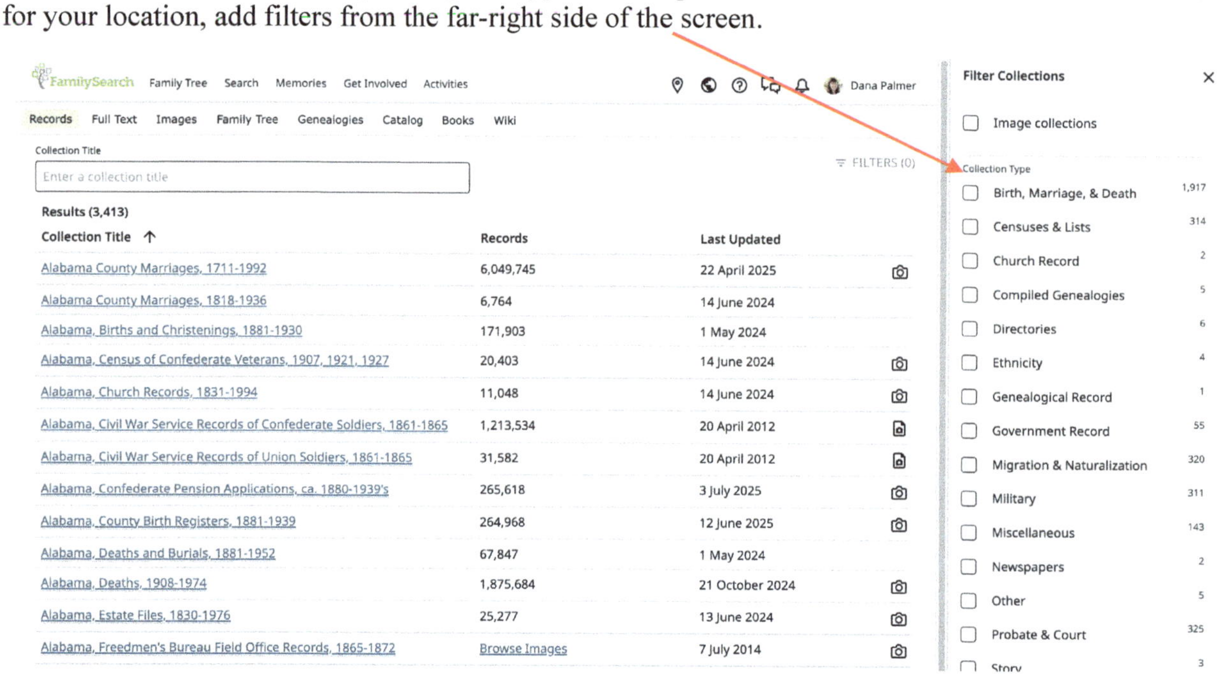

https://www.familysearch.org/en/search/collection/list?count=20

To find ship passenger lists, choose the MIGRATION AND NATURALIZATION category, then the UNITED STATES OF AMERICA country, and the state, in this case NEW YORK.

This will then give you a list of all the databases on this part of the FamilySearch website. Choose the specific database you want to search. For passenger lists, be sure you choose the database with the original lists, not just the index to the lists.

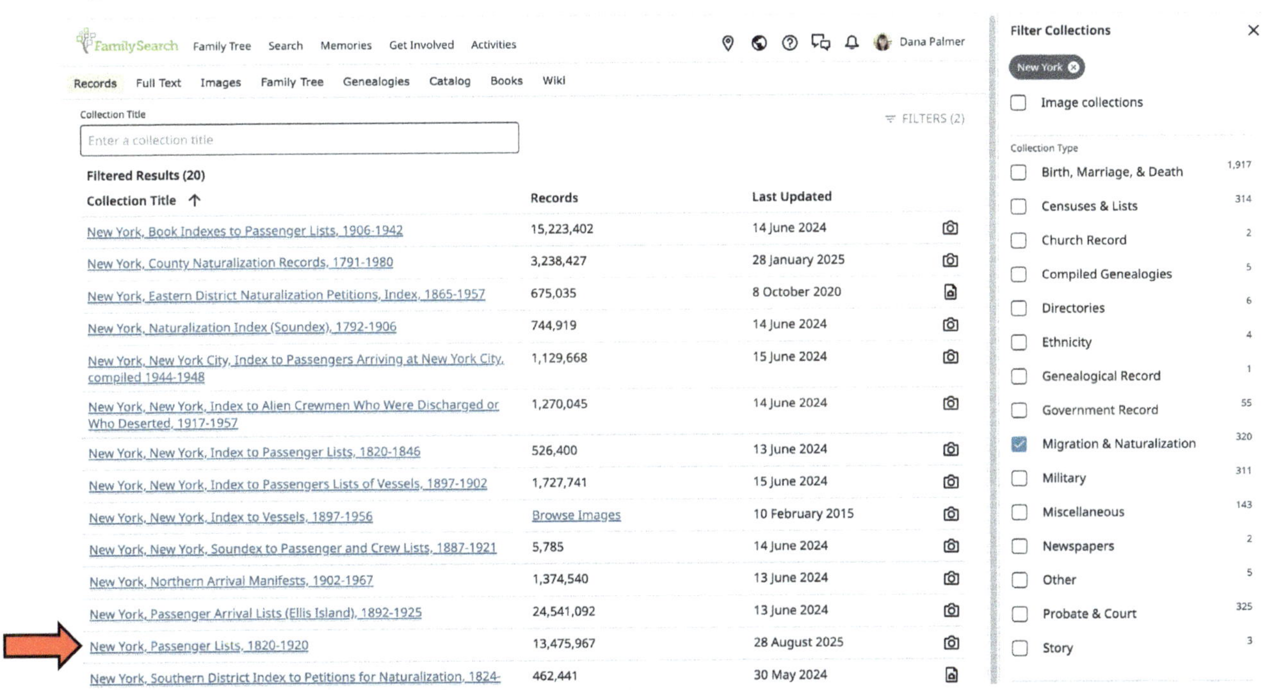

https://www.familysearch.org/en/search/collection/list?count=20&ec=region%3AUNITED_STATES%2CplaceID%3A22%2CrecordType%3AMIGRATION&fcs=placeID%3A22%2CrecordType%3AMIGRATION

Collections with a camera icon to the far right have images associated with that collection you can view. If you see a camera icon with a warning symbol next to it, you will have to view that collection at a FamilySearch center or FamilySearch affiliate. Collections that state BROWSE IMAGES for the record size columns are those that have not been indexed by FamilySearch, and you will need to search for your person page by page digitally, just like you would if you visited the repository in person.

When you get to the collection with the yellow background, you can finally search for your person.

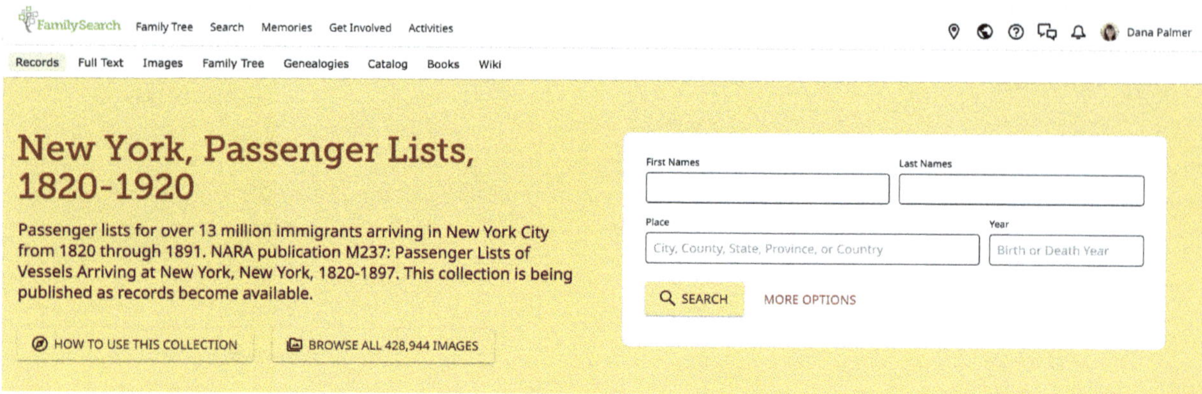

https://www.familysearch.org/en/search/collection/1849782

Click on MORE OPTIONS to add additional filters. Try various searching tricks until you find them.

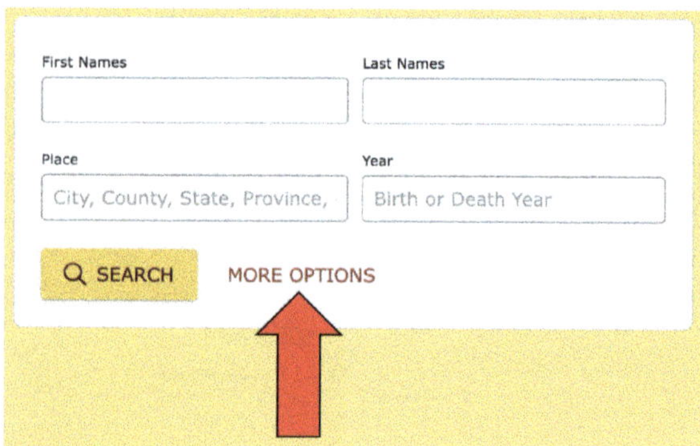

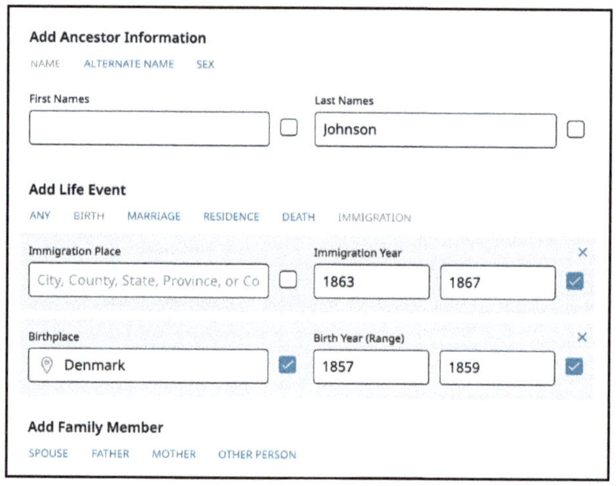

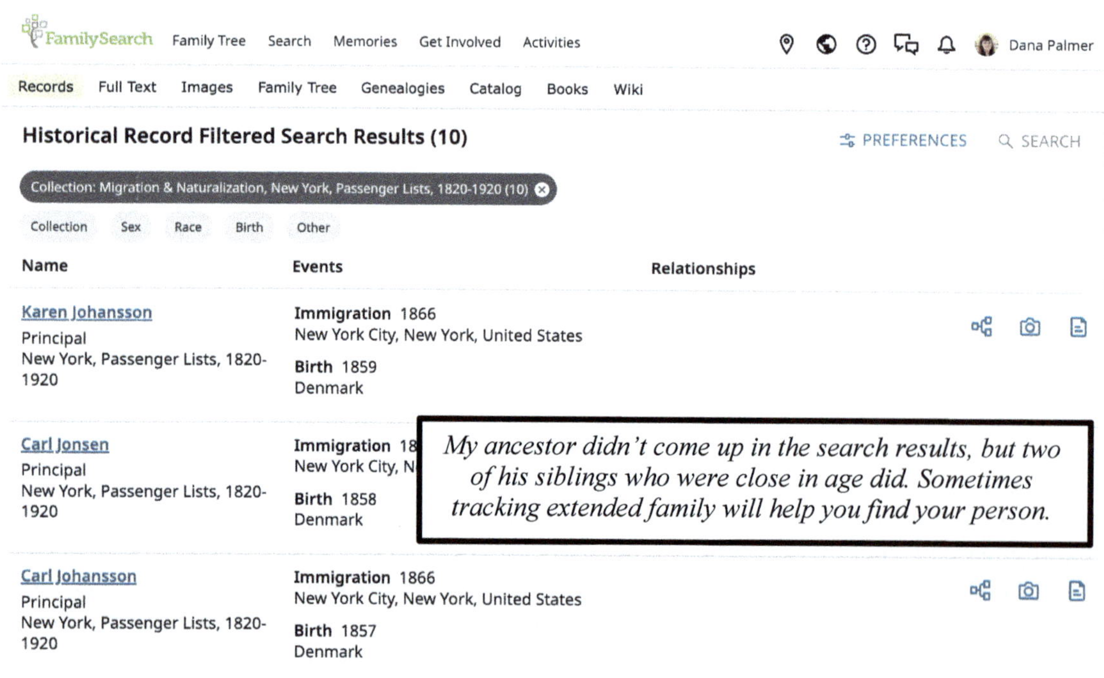

My ancestor didn't come up in the search results, but two of his siblings who were close in age did. Sometimes tracking extended family will help you find your person.

Once you click on the link for the person in the database, you will be redirected to that person's transcription page. If the name or other details have been mis-indexed and the EDIT button is blue instead of grey, you can submit a correction. To see the record image, click on the picture above the source details section. Sometimes you will need to browse through the collection to find it.

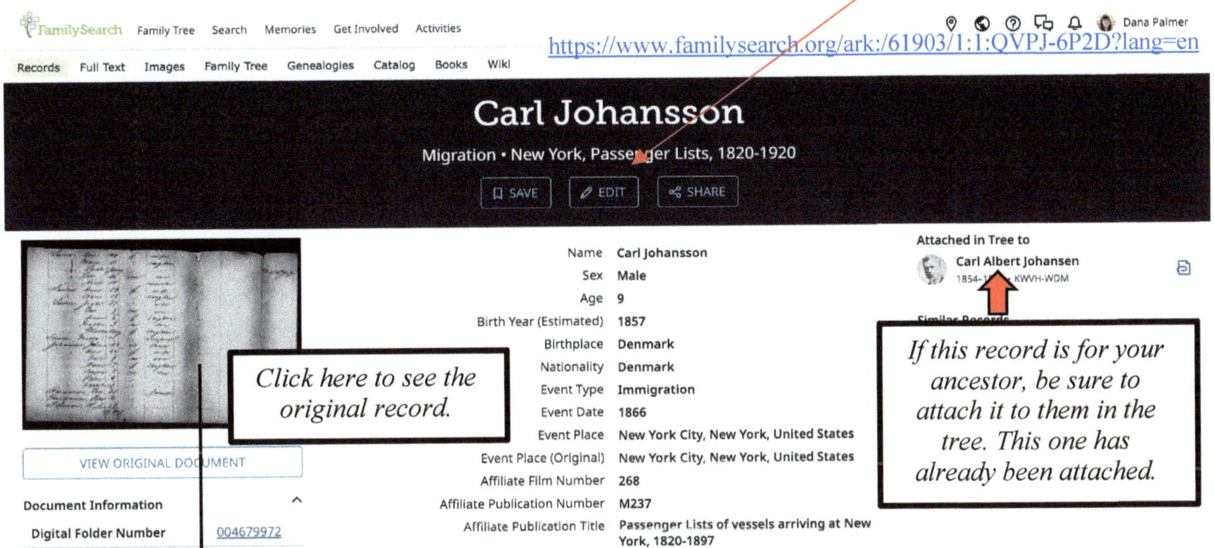

"New York, Passenger Lists, 1820-1920," digital images, *FamilySearch* (https://www.familysearch.org/ark:/61903/1:1:QVPJ-6P2D?lang=en : accessed 28 Apr 2025), Carl Johansson, 16 July 1866, Kenilworth, citing *Passenger Lists of vessels arriving at New York, 1820-1897*, National Archives microfilm publication M237.

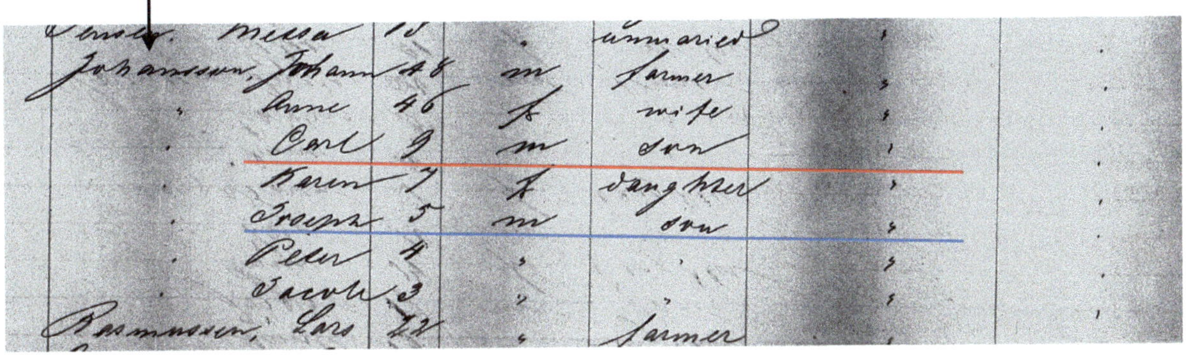

Johansson, Johann, 48, M, farmer
" , Anne, 46, F, wife
" , Carl, 9, M, son
" , Karen,7, F, daughter
" , Jrseph, 5, M, son
" , Peter, 4, M, son
" , Jacob, 3, M, son

"New York, Passenger Lists, 1820-1920," digital images, *FamilySearch* (https://www.familysearch.org/ark:/61903/1:1:QVPJ-6P2D?lang=en : accessed 28 Apr 2025), Carl Johansson, 16 July 1866, Kenilworth, citing *Passenger Lists of vessels arriving at New York, 1820-1897*, National Archives microfilm publication M237.

Often, if the second letter was mis-indexed, as in this example where "o" was mis-indexed for "r," the name won't come up in the search engine without using a wildcard. Joseph was found by searching for the surname using a birth date range and place and immigration date filter until his siblings appeared as search results. Keep in mind, the letter "L" is also often mistaken for the letter "S."

Finding BMDs

U.S. birth, marriage, and death records are found in RECORDS in the BIRTH, MARRIAGE, & DEATH topical category, and then country category of UNITED STATES OF AMERICA, and the sub-category of whatever state you want to search.

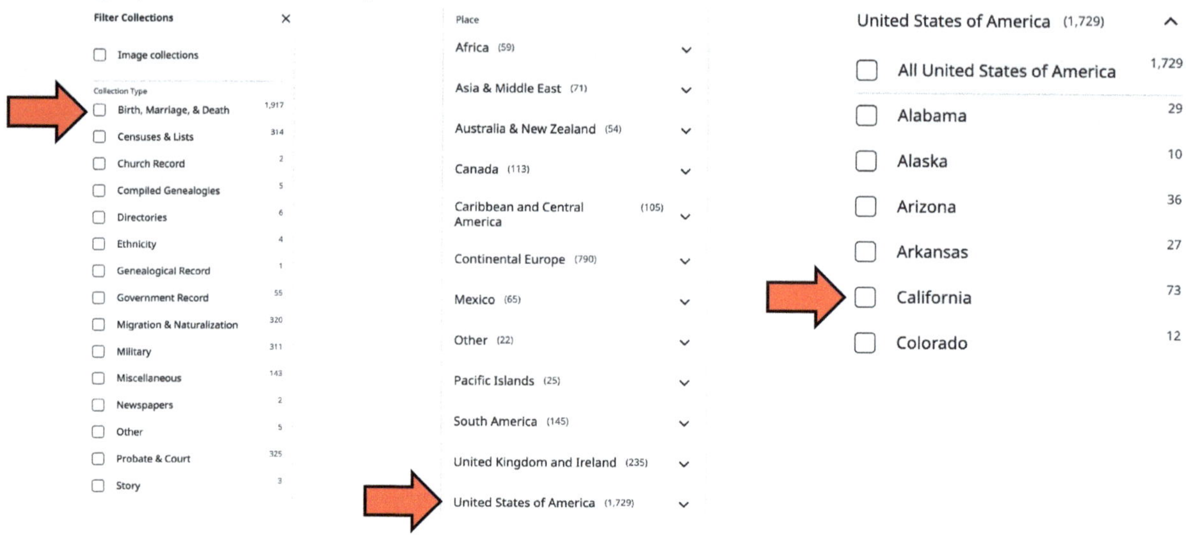

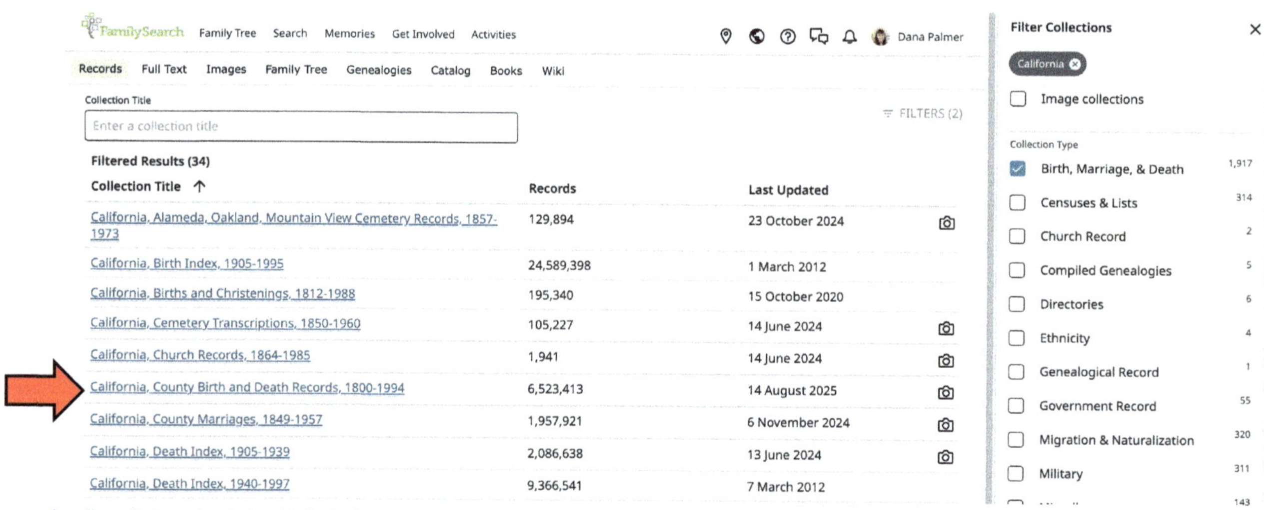

https://www.familysearch.org/en/search/collection/list?count=All&fcs=recordType%3AVITAL%2CplaceId%3A11&ec=recordType%3AVITAL%2CplaceId%3A11%2Cregion%3AUNITED_STATES

Finding Federal U.S. Census Records

There are two types of census records for the United States on FamilySearch: (1) the decennial Federal census records of the United States and territories enumerated every ten years by the Federal government; and (2) state census records enumerated by many, but not all states independently in the intervening years. To find U.S. Federal census records first select the RECORDS tab, then BROWSE ALL COLLECTIONS. In the far-right column, select CENSUS & LISTS, then choose UNITED STATES OF AMERICA for the country, and UNITED STATES in the state list as shown below.

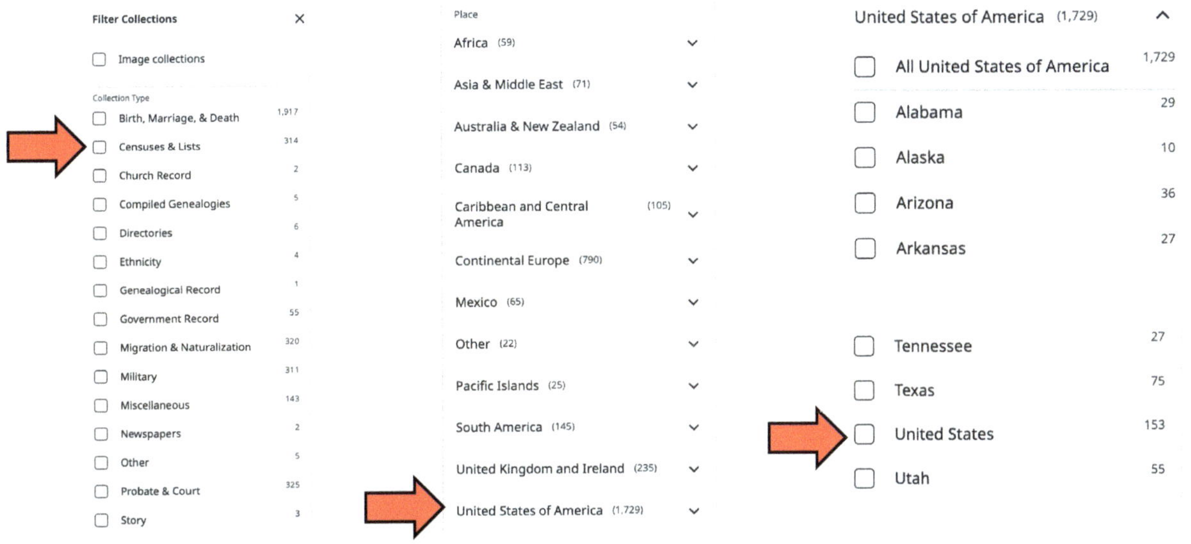

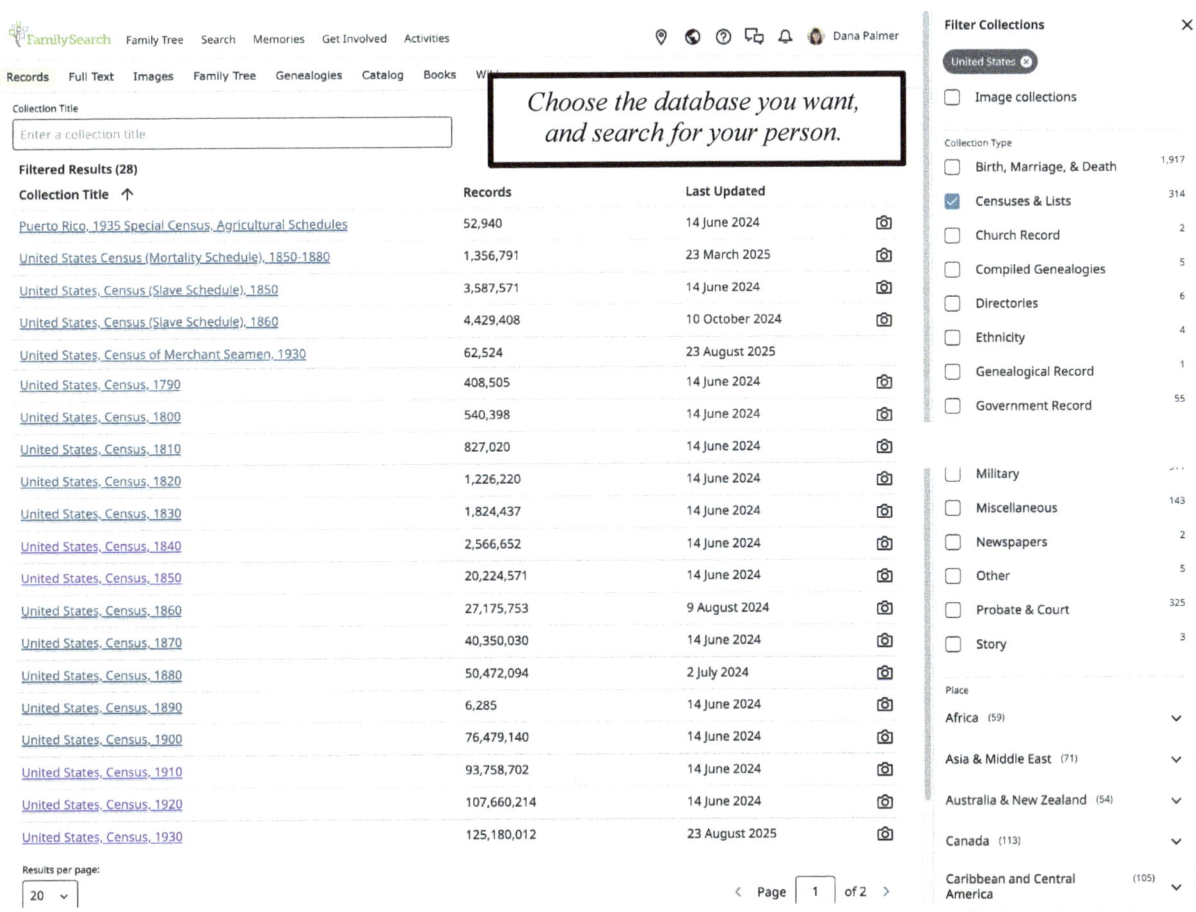

https://www.familysearch.org/en/search/collection/list?count=20&fcs=recordType%3ACENSUS%2CplaceId%3A1&ec=recordType%3ACENSUS%2Cregion%3AUNITED_STATES%2CplaceId%3A1

Finding State Census Records

State census records can be found under the RECORDS tab, then BROWSE ALL COLLECTIONS. In the far-right column, select CENSUS & LISTS, then choose UNITED STATES OF AMERICA for the country, and then the specific state you want to search for state census records.

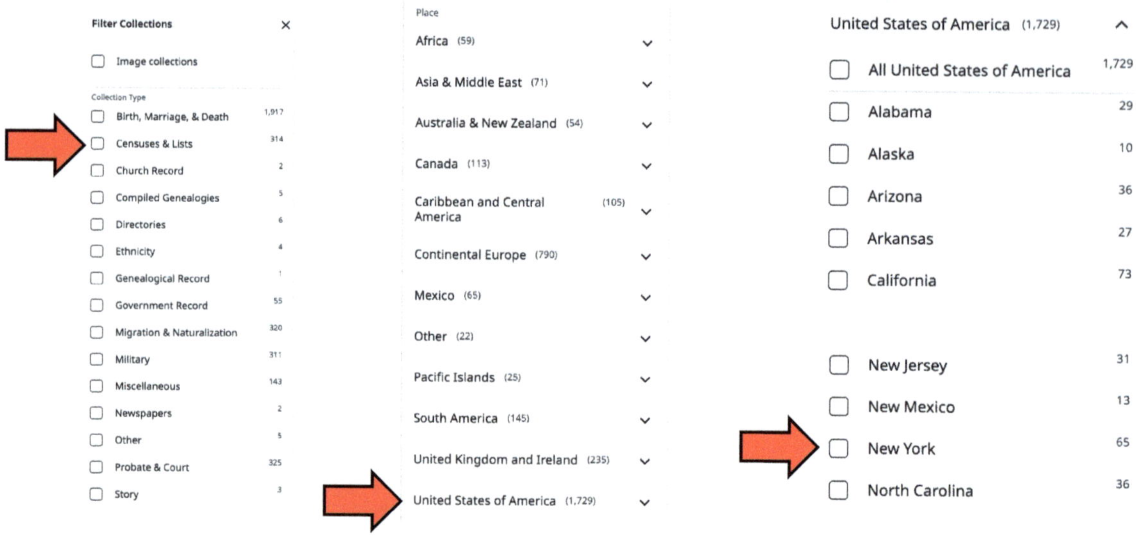

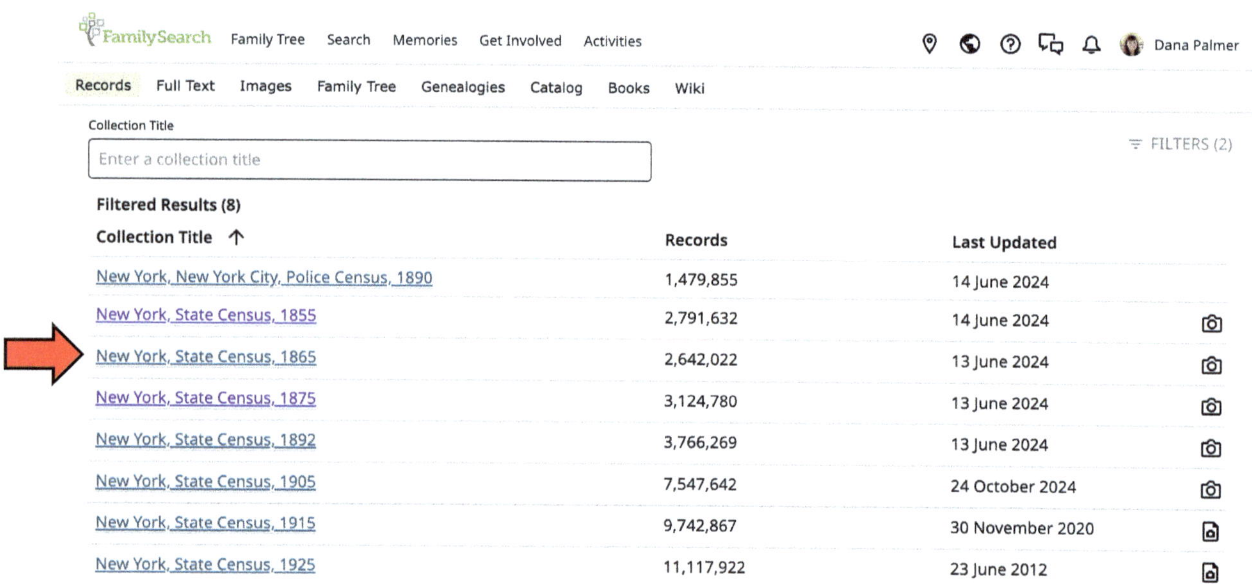

https://www.familysearch.org/en/search/collection/list?count=All&fcs=recordType%3ACENSUS%2CplaceId%3A22&ec=recordType%3ACENSUS%2Cregion%3AUNITED_STATES%2CplaceId%3A22

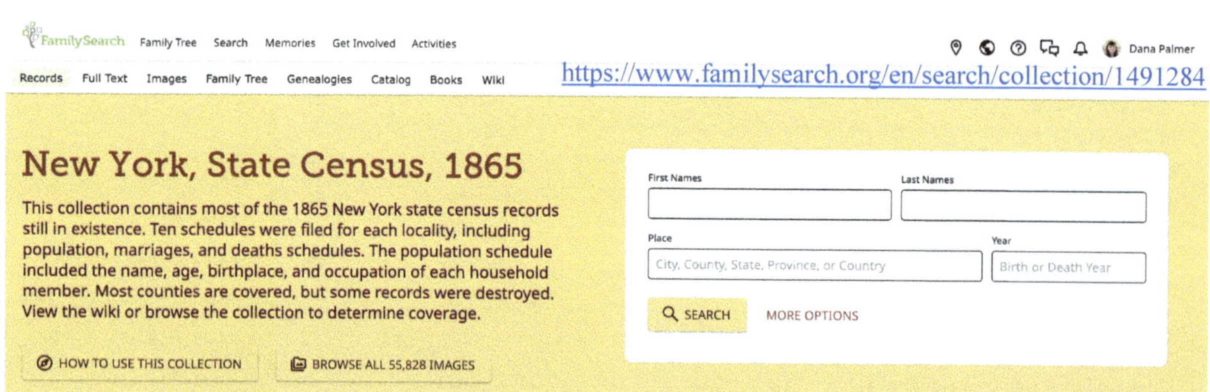

United States Bureau of Land Management Tract Books

One of my favorite and often underutilized databases is the United States, Bureau of Land Management Tract Books (https://www.familysearch.org/en/search/collection/2074276), which can be used in conjunction with the Bureau of Land Management website (https://glorecords.blm.gov/default.aspx).

These tract books on FamilySearch contain the original digitized version of the land transaction from the United States government in one of the twenty-seven states or territories using the section, township, range system of an individual(s). The name of the individual receiving the land and their origin prior to purchase is noted, as is the date of the transaction, type of payment, and a physical description of the property. These are invaluable for those wanting to trace a person from one location to another or prove early residence in the area.

To access these tract books, go to the SEARCH tab, and click on RECORDS. Click on BROWSE ALL LOCATIONS, then select UNITED STATES OF AMERICA as the country, and UNITED STATES as the sub-location from the side filters. You can then choose the United States Bureau of Land Management Tract Books database (https://www.familysearch.org/en/search/collection/2074276).

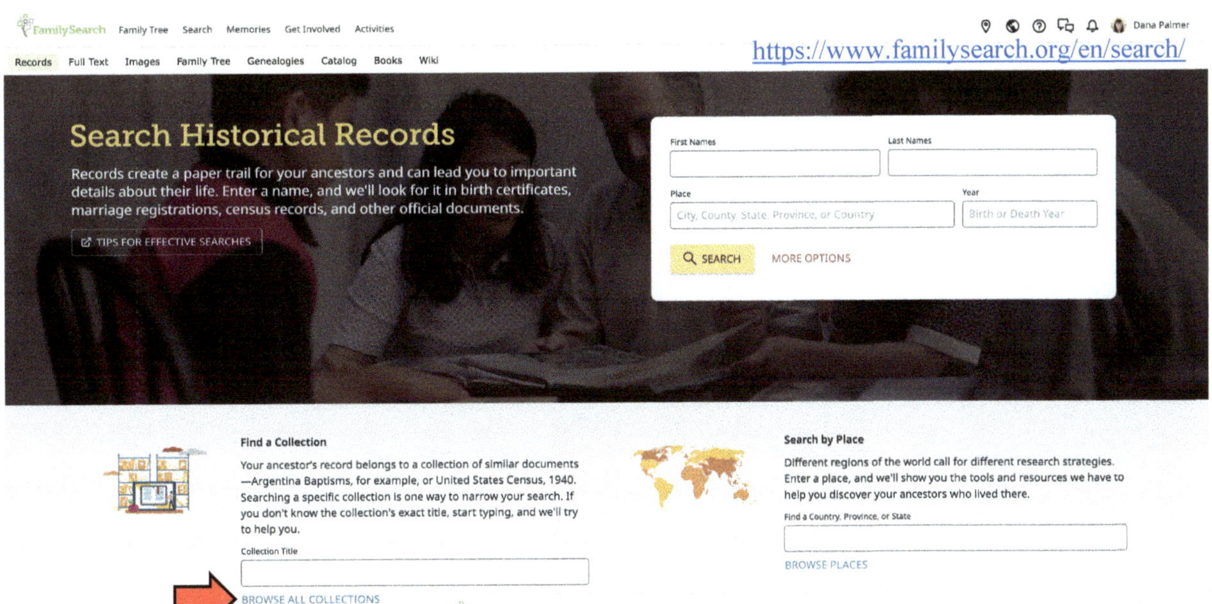

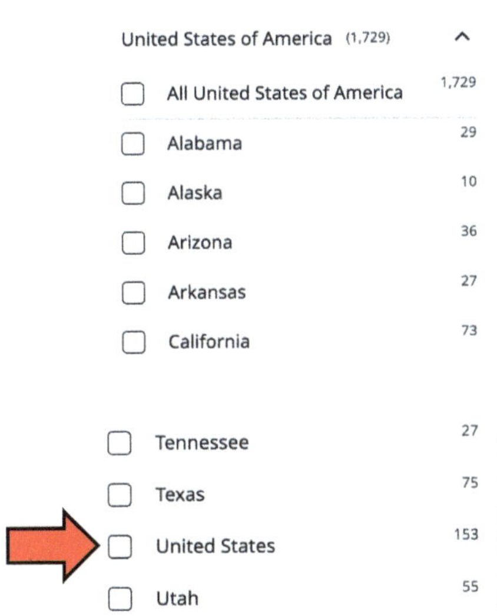

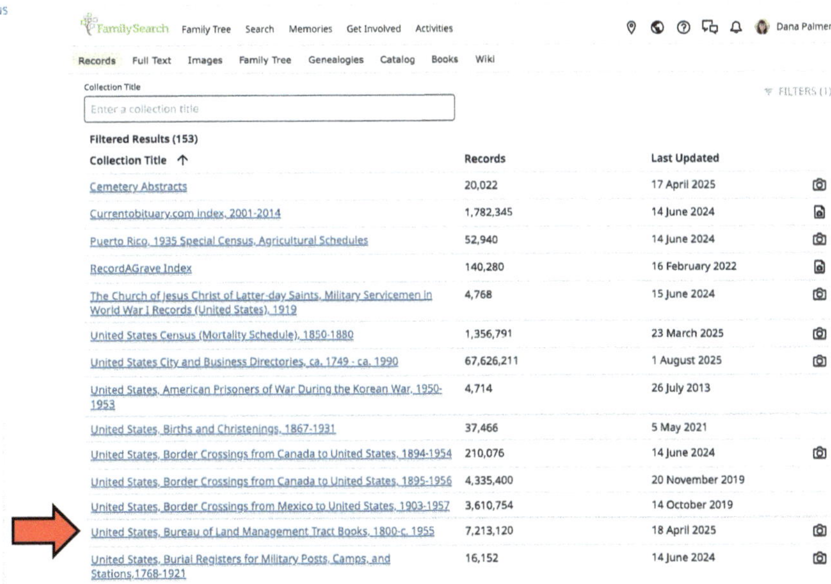

https://www.familysearch.org/en/search/collection/list?count=20&cc=region%3AUNITED_STATES%2CplaceId%3A1&fcs=placeId%3A1

If you have never used the tract books before, it's best to first click on the link HOW TO USE THIS COLLECTION. Most of the early records in this collection have not been indexed yet, so it's better to search manually for your person, and this link will help you do that.

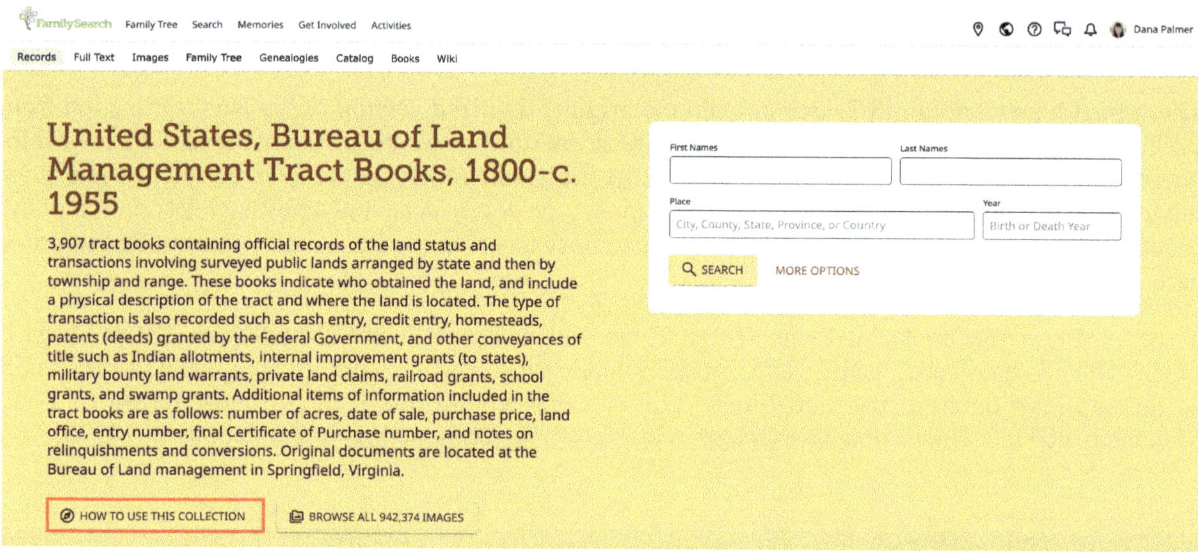

https://www.familysearch.org/en/search/collection/2074276

This will take you to a page that describes the collection and how to use it. Scroll down to the INVENTORY subsection.

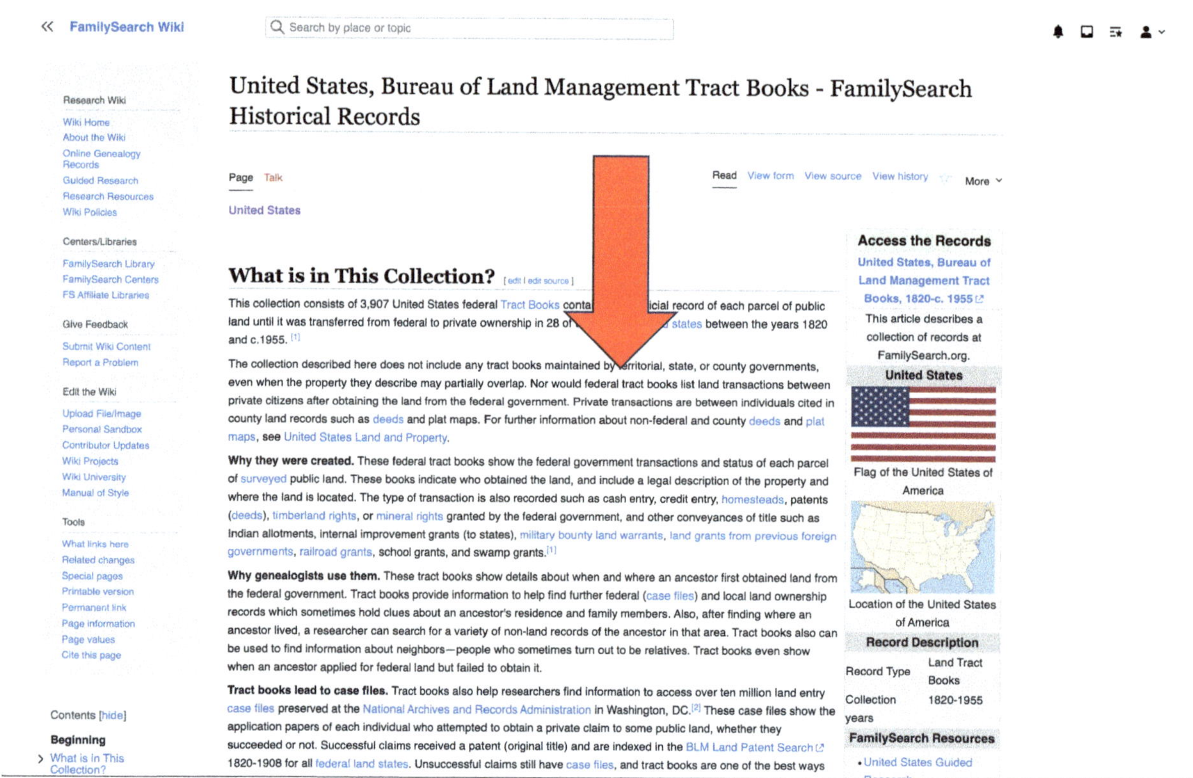

https://www.familysearch.org/en/wiki/United_States,_Bureau_of_Land_Management_Tract_Books_-_FamilySearch_Historical_Records

Click on the UNITED STATES BUREAU OF LAND MANAGEMENT TRACT BOOKS – INVENTORY link.

Inventory [edit | edit source]

These articles provide a more detailed description of the tract books included in this collection.

- United States Bureau of Land Management Tract Books - Inventory
- United States, Bureau of Land Management, General Land Offices (NARA Finding Aid)

How Do I Search the Collection? [edit | edit source]

To begin the search it is helpful to know:

- The name of your ancestor who filed the claim, officially known as the *entryman*
- The state where the land was located
- The land description (Township (T), Range (R) and Section (S)) **See Rectangular surveys** for an explanation of these terms
- The volume covering the land entry
- It is also helpful to know the Land Office where the claim was filed and the county the land is in

Search the Index [edit | edit source]

Search by name on the Collection Details Page.

1. Enter the information in the fields in the **Search Collection** section or click **More Options** to see additional fields
2. Click **Search** to show possible matches

https://www.familysearch.org/en/wiki/United_States,_Bureau_of_Land_Management_Tract_Books_-_FamilySearch_Historical_Records

On the INVENTORY page, scroll down to the state or territory of interest. Each state has scrolling capability to show the Land Office and applicable description for each.

Choose the one that matches the description from the Bureau of Land Management website (https://glorecords.blm.gov/search/default.aspx?searchTabIndex=0&searchByTypeIndex=0).

« FamilySearch Wiki   Search by place or topic

Research Wiki
Wiki Home
About the Wiki
Online Genealogy Records
Guided Research
Research Resources
Wiki Policies

Centers/Libraries
FamilySearch Library
FamilySearch Centers
FS Affiliate Libraries

Give Feedback
Submit Wiki Content
Report a Problem

Edit the Wiki
Upload File/Image
Personal Sandbox
Contributor Updates
Wiki Projects

United States Bureau of Land Management Tract Books - Inventory

Page Talk   Read View form View source View history More

FamilySearch

This article contains an inventory of the microfilm/digital folders found in a FamilySearch Historical Records Collection.
Not all content listed here may have been included or indexed in this collection.
To learn how to use the collection and to access the records see:
United States Bureau of Land Management Tract Books - FamilySearch Historical Records

Tip: Please Note: Not all records in each film or folder in this collection may be indexed.

These tables can be resorted by clicking on any column heading. The default sort is by **State**, **Land Office/ Volume Number**, and **Description**. For additional information on these records see the United States Tract Books article.

Ohio [edit | edit source]

State	Land Office/ Volume Number	Description
OHIO	Vol. NUMBER INDEX	
OHIO	Vol. 1 BUCYRUS	Township 1-2N, Range 9-10
OHIO	Vol. 1 BUCYRUS	Township 5-8N, Range 9
OHIO	Vol. 1 BUCYRUS	Township 4-7N, Range 10
OHIO	Vol. 1 BUCYRUS	Township 1-6N, Range 12
OHIO	Vol. 1 BUCYRUS	Township 1-3N, Range 13-14
OHIO	Vol. 1 BUCYRUS	Township 1-6N, Range 15
OHIO	Vol. 1 BUCYRUS	
OHIO	Vol. 1 BUCYRUS	
OHIO	Vol. 1 BUCYRUS	
OHIO	Vol. 1 BUCYRUS	

Find the correct state and land office, then write down the applicable volumes based on the description that matches what was on the BLM website.

https://www.familysearch.org/en/wiki/United_States_Bureau_of_Land_Management_Tract_Books_-_Inventory

Find the volume for your land office that matches the physical description from the Bureau of Land Management website. Go back to the Land Management main page and click on BROWSE ALL 942,374 IMAGES.

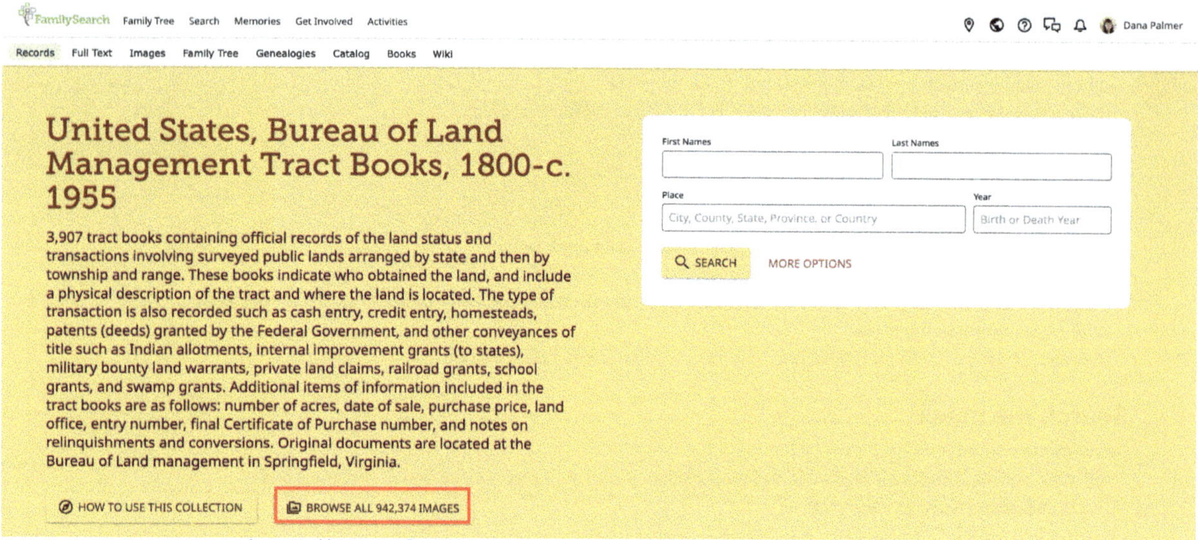

https://www.familysearch.org/en/search/collection/2074276

Select the state or territory you want and click on the link.

https://www.familysearch.org/en/search/image/index?owc=https://www.familysearch.org/service/cds/recapi/collections/2074276/waypoints

Find the appliable tract book volume and click on the link.

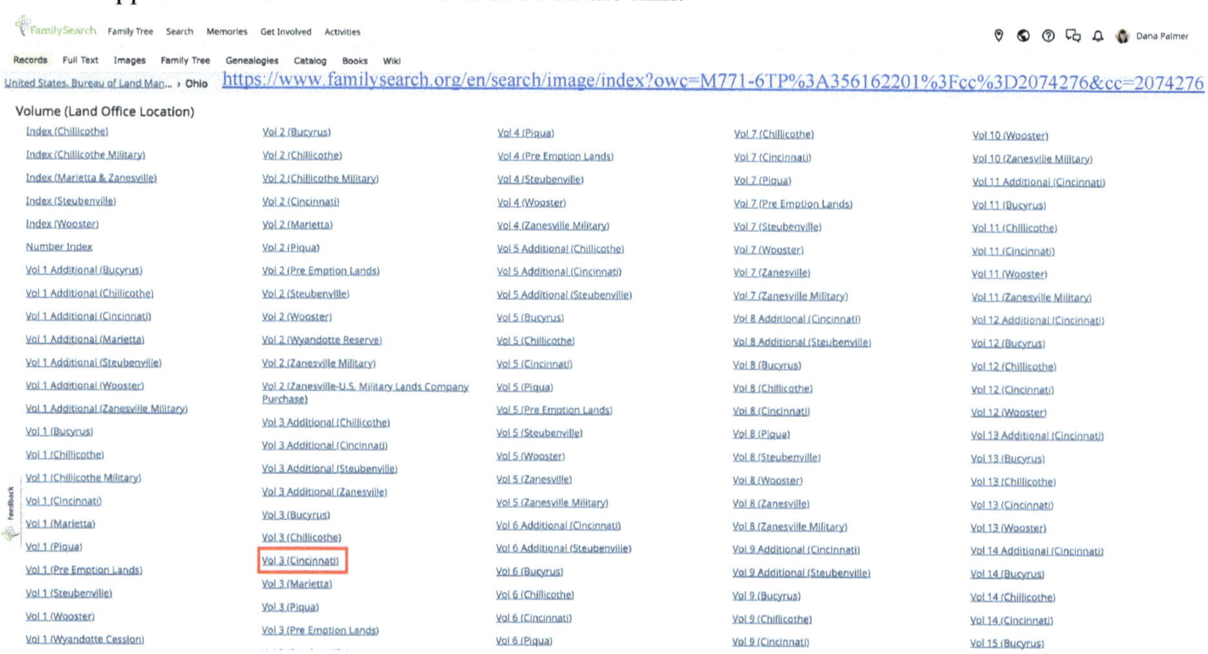

https://www.familysearch.org/en/search/image/index?owc=M771-6TP%3A356162201%3Fcc%3D2074276&cc=2074276

Browse the pages and match the physical land description exactly then search for your person.

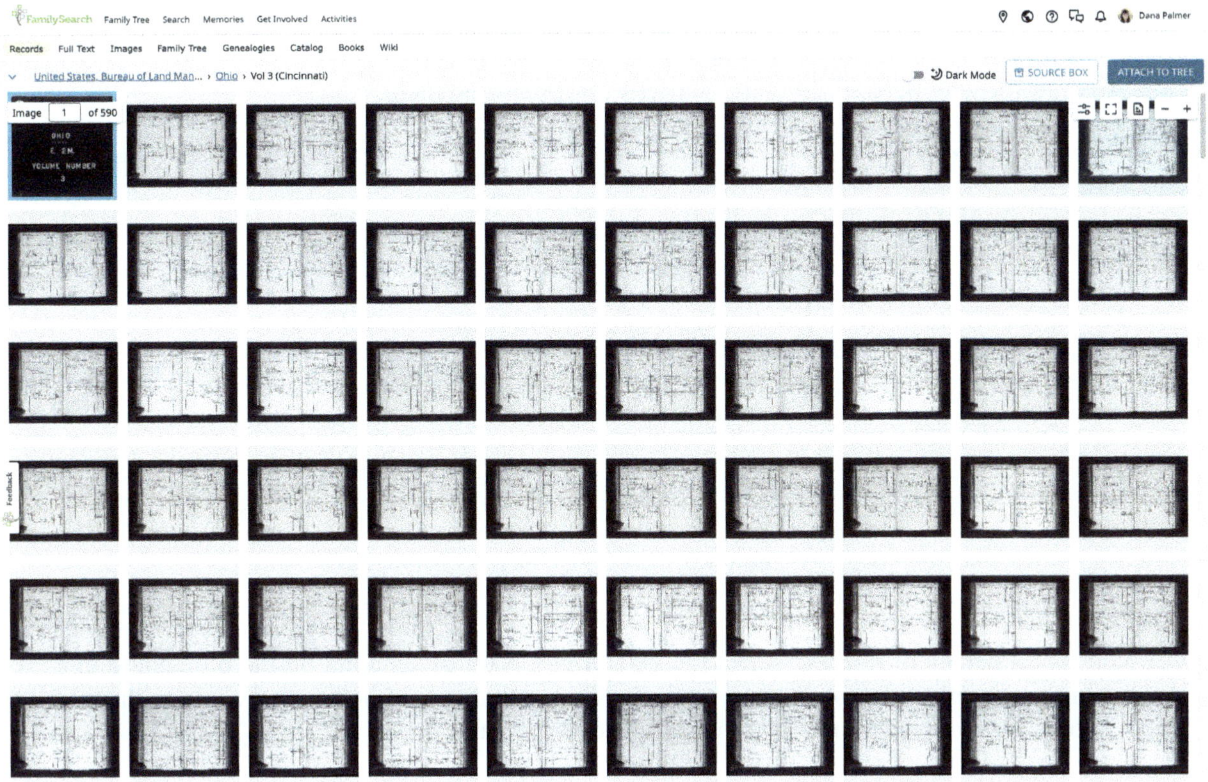

https://www.familysearch.org/ark:/61903/3:1:3QS7-99W3-SK2W?wc=M7WQ-VZC%3A356162201%2C356296001%26cc%3D2074276&cc=2074276&lang=eng&i=0&mode=g

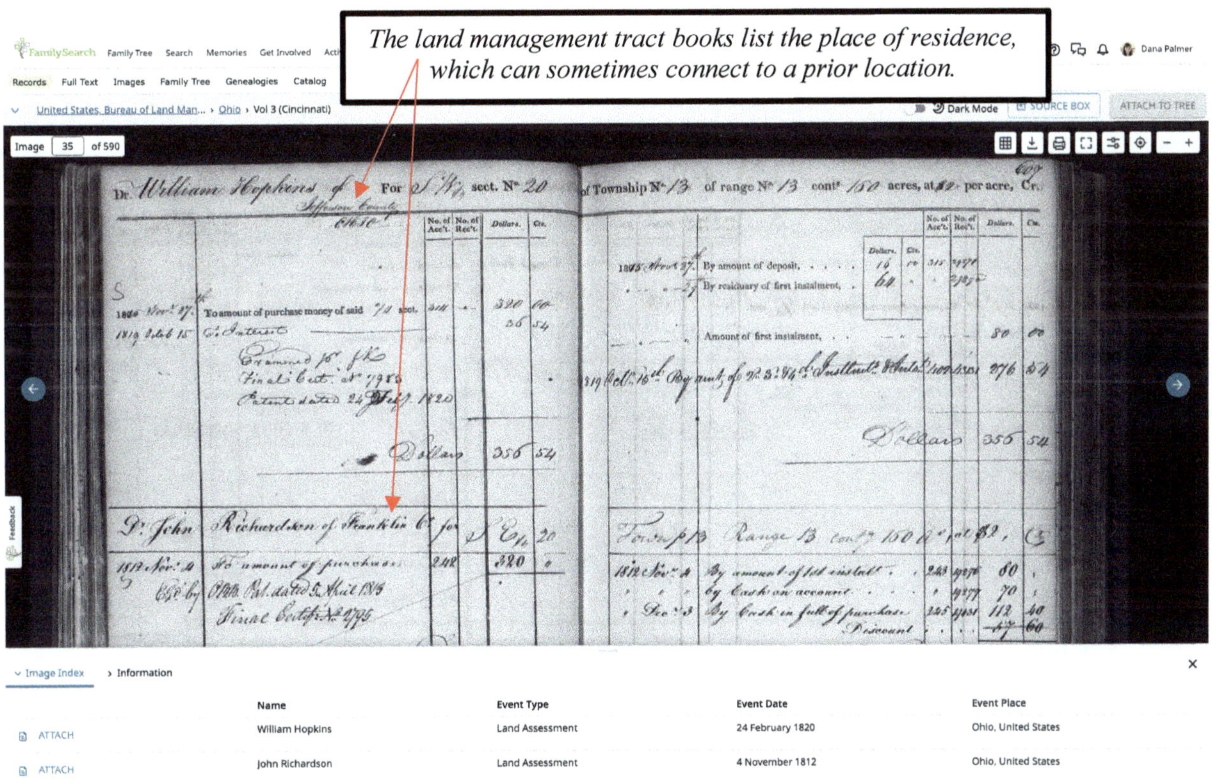

https://www.familysearch.org/ark:/61903/3:1:3QS7-99W3-SK2W?wc=M7WQ-VZC%3A356162201%2C356296001%26cc%3D2074276&cc=2074276&lang=eng&i=34

Searching the Historical Records

Browse to the specific collection you want. When you get to the screen with the yellow background, start searching for your person. Try various tricks until you find them.

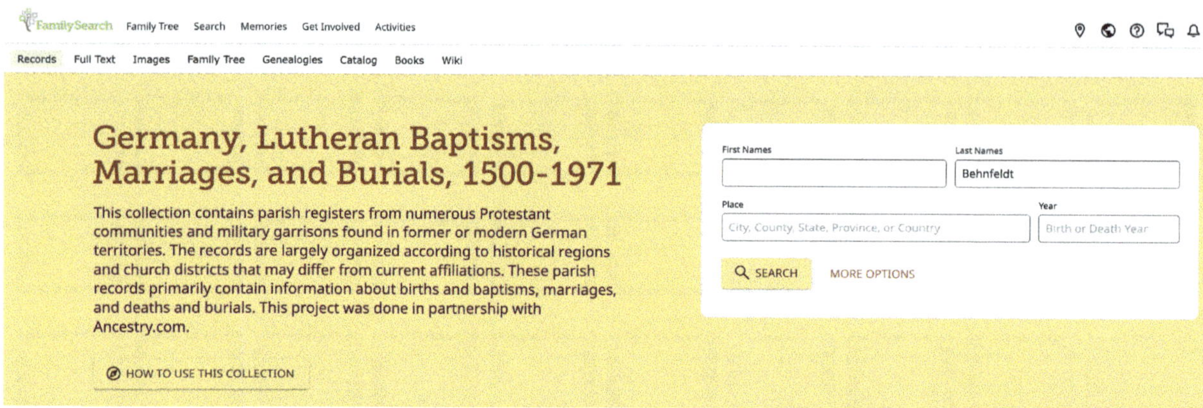

https://www.familysearch.org/en/search/collection/3015626

Once you find a person of interest, select the person you want by clicking on the blue name link. To view the image directly, click on the camera icon. To see that person in the tree, click on the tree icon if there is one. To go to the transcription page, click on the paper icon.

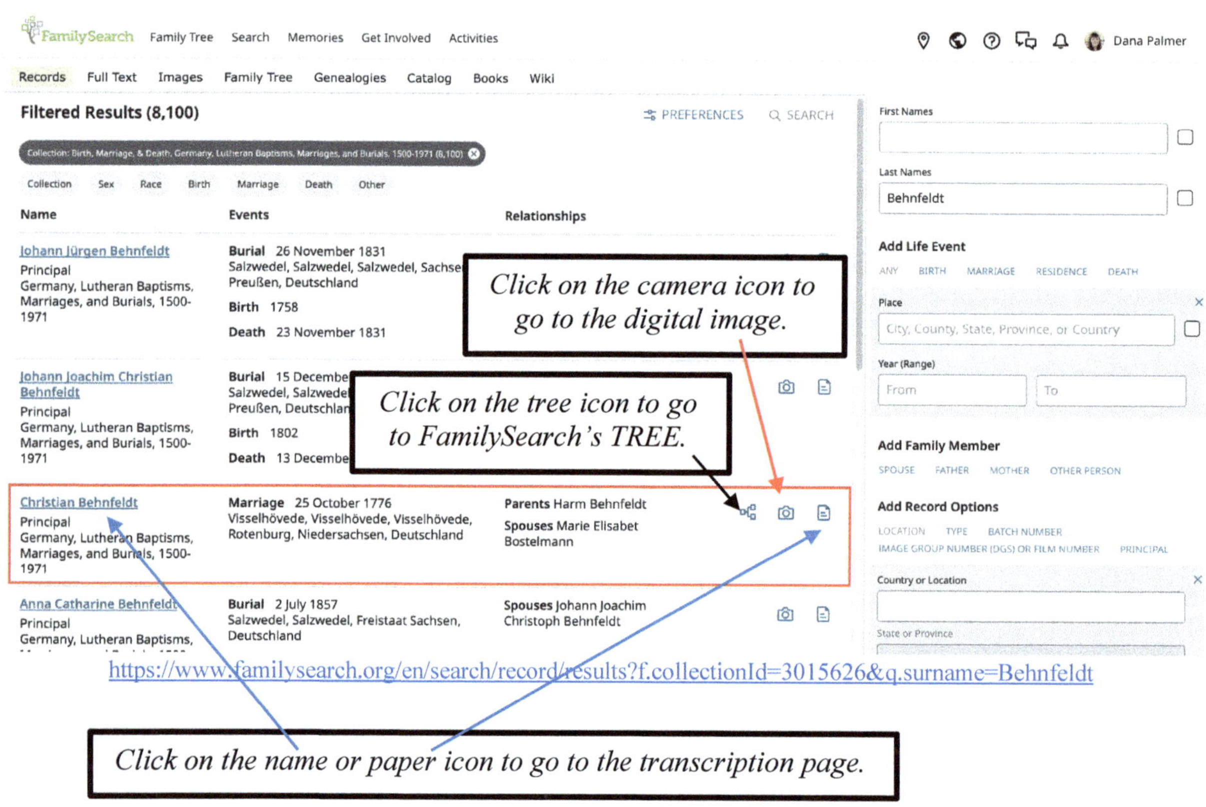

https://www.familysearch.org/en/search/record/results?f.collectionId=3015626&q.surname=Behnfeldt

Click on the name or paper icon to go to the transcription page.

If the image of the document is not visible, click on the arrow next to DOCUMENT INFORMATION to get the microfilm number or Digital Folder Number. Often the image can be seen in the CATALOG if it isn't online in RECORDS.

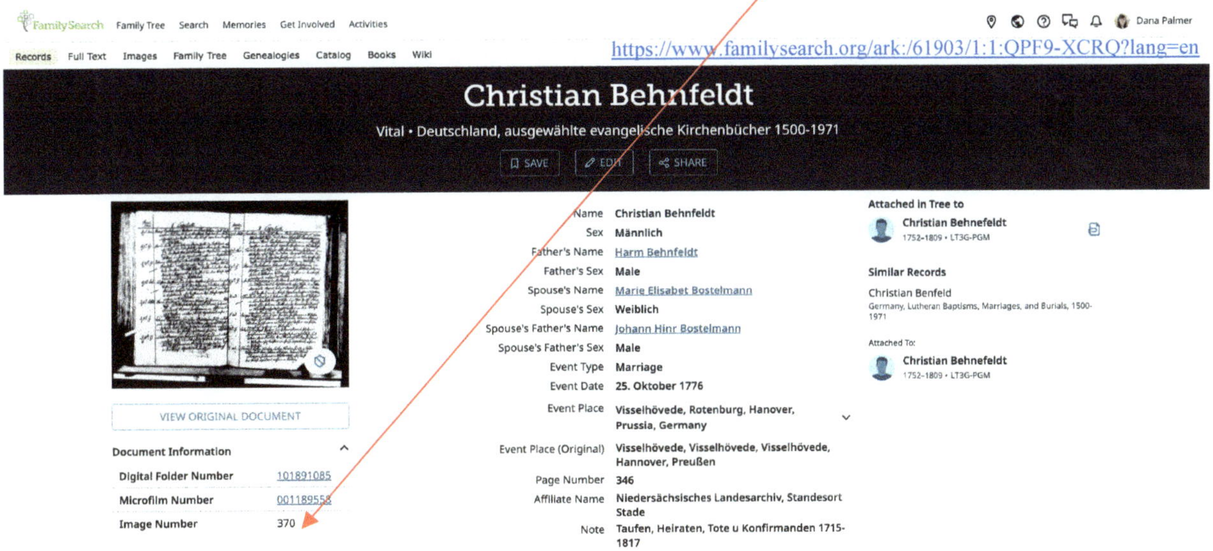

"Deutschland, ausgewählte evangelische Kirchenbücher 1500-1971," database with images, *FamilySearch* (https://www.familysearch.org/ark:/61903/1:1:QPF9-XCRQ?lang=en : accessed 28 Apr 2025), p. 346, Christian Behnfeldt, 25 Oct 1776, citing Marriages, Visselhövede, Rotenburg, Niedersachsen, Deutschland, FS microfilm 1,189,558.

If you click on the microfilm number or digital folder number, you can search that specific microfilm by surname or given name in the search filter box. This can save a lot of time, especially in record collections with difficult or foreign handwriting.

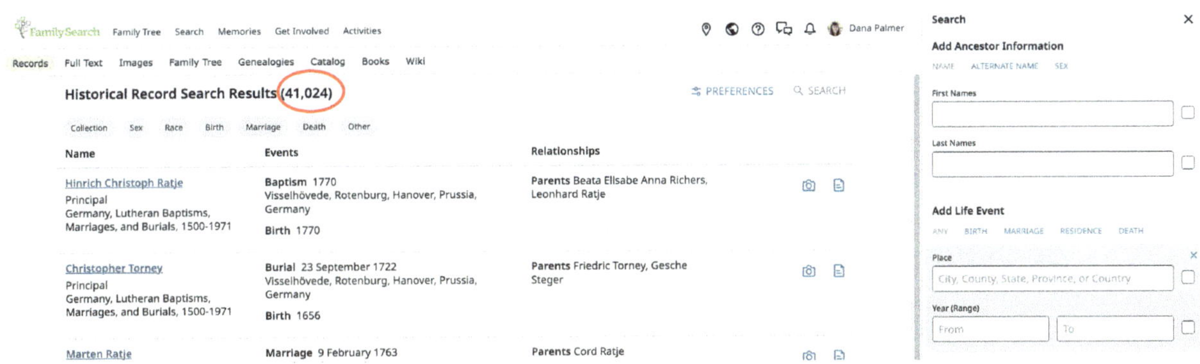

https://www.familysearch.org/en/search/record/results?count=20&q.filmNumber=001189558

Filters reduce search results.

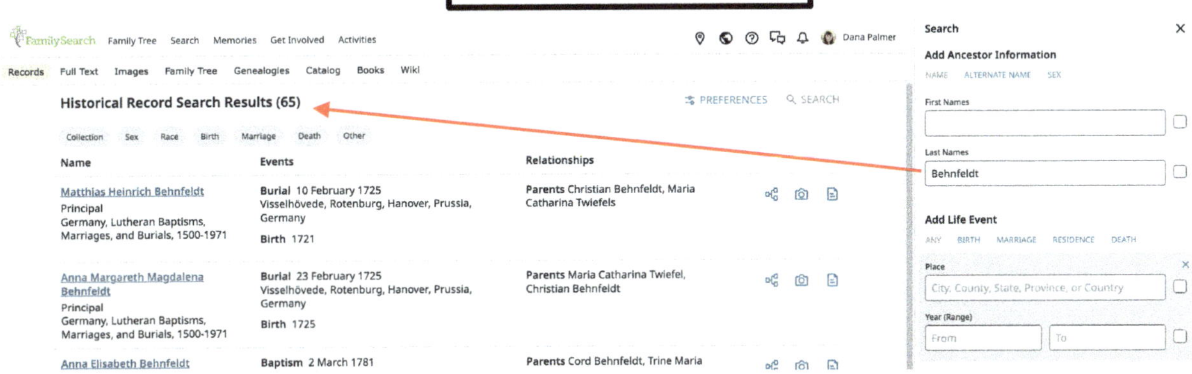

https://www.familysearch.org/en/search/record/results?count=20&q.filmNumber=001189558&q.surname=Behnfeldt

Browse Places

Searches can also be done by BROWSE PLACES, which provides many useful tools and resources for those with international ancestors. Go to the SEARCH tab and click RECORDS from the dropdown menu. On the RECORDS page, scroll down and click on BROWSE PLACES.

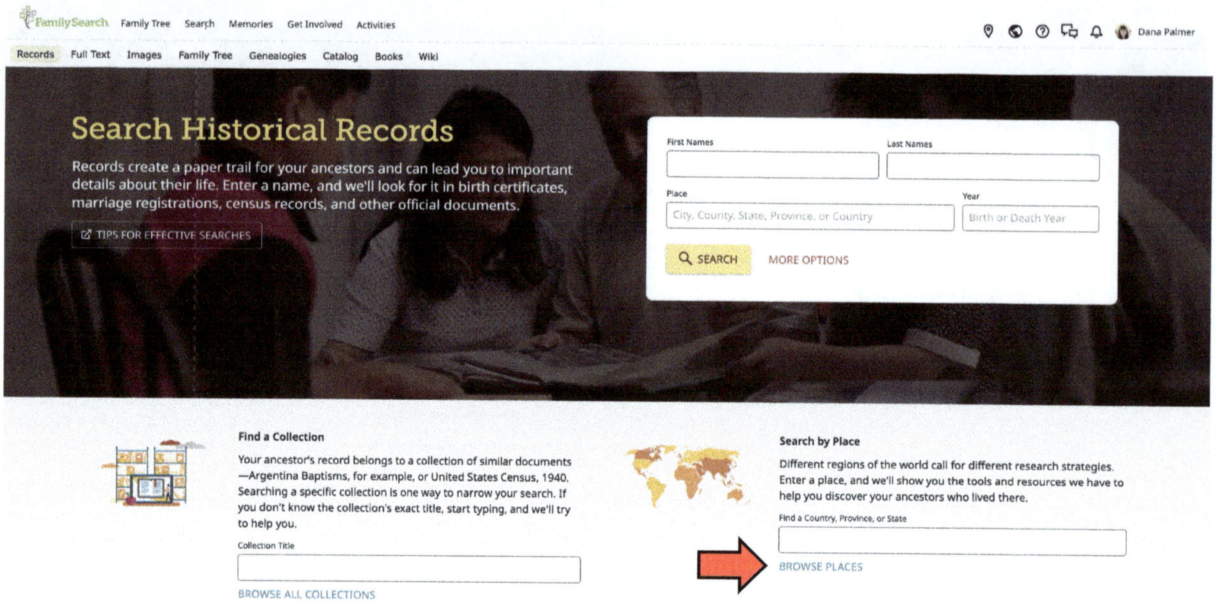

https://www.familysearch.org/en/search/

On the map page, you can click on the country you want, type the name of the country in the box, or select the name from the options to the far right.

https://www.familysearch.org/en/search/location/list

If you click on the map, you will see a list of countries within that region to the far right. Choose the one you want, and you will be redirected to the page for that country.

https://www.familysearch.org/en/search/location/list

https://www.familysearch.org/en/search/location/list

BROWSING PLACES will allow you to see at a glance the resources that may exist for your location. Often there will be links to that location's RESEARCH WIKI page, or sometimes, a link to the GUIDED RESEARCH page. Many countries have links to free webinars and other resources in the LEARNING CENTER. The collections found in the INDEXED HISTORICAL RECORDS are the same ones found if you used the BROWSE ALL COLLECTIONS in RECORDS.

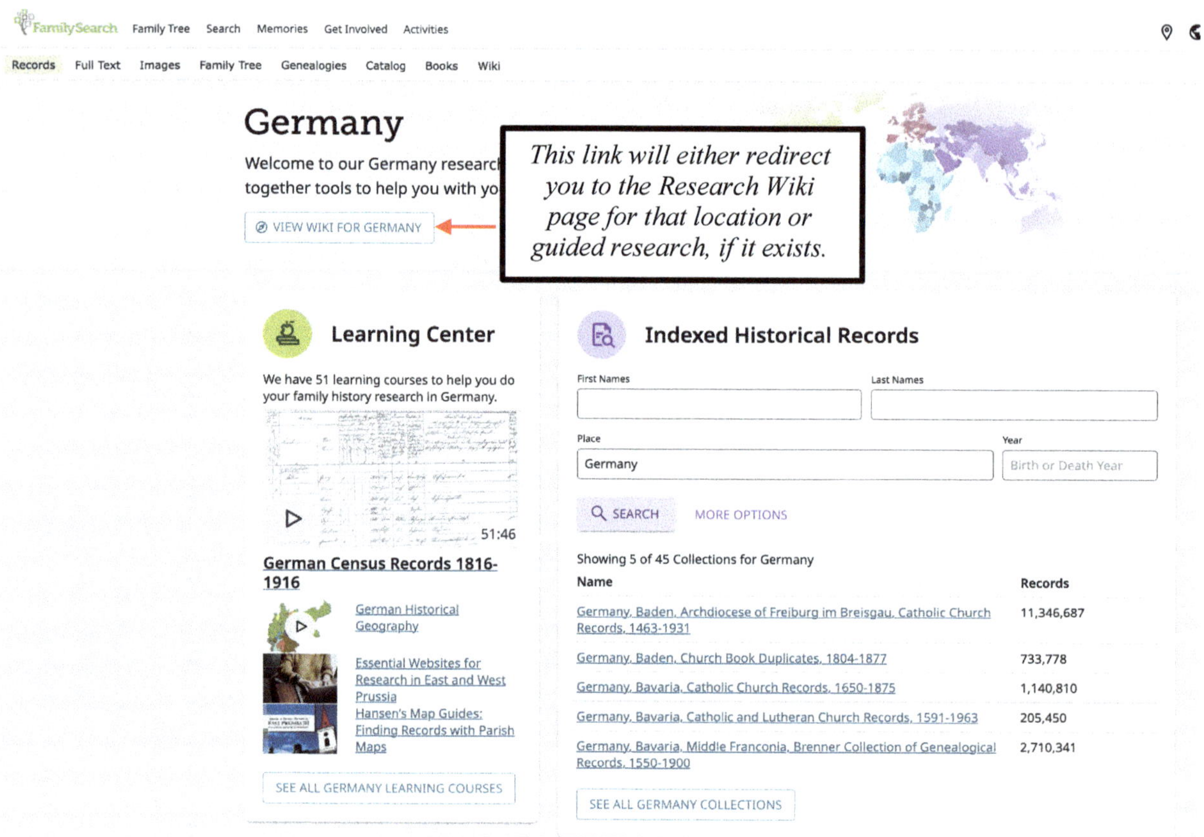

https://www.familysearch.org/en/search/location/continental-europe/germany

Some locations will have links to genealogies, image-only historical records, and other catalog material. There are some hidden gems in these resources.

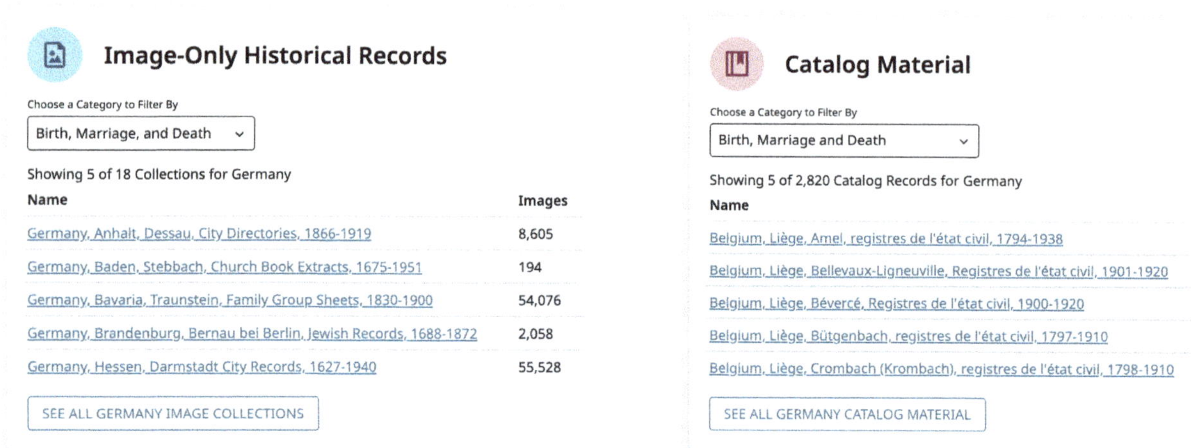

https://www.familysearch.org/en/search/location/continental-europe/germany

IMAGES

FamilySearch's IMAGES (https://www.familysearch.org/en/records/images) has the newly digitized record collections, which are expanding continually (versus the microfilm images in the CATALOG). IMAGES are currently only searchable by location, instead of by keywords, topics, authors, etc. as available in the CATALOG.

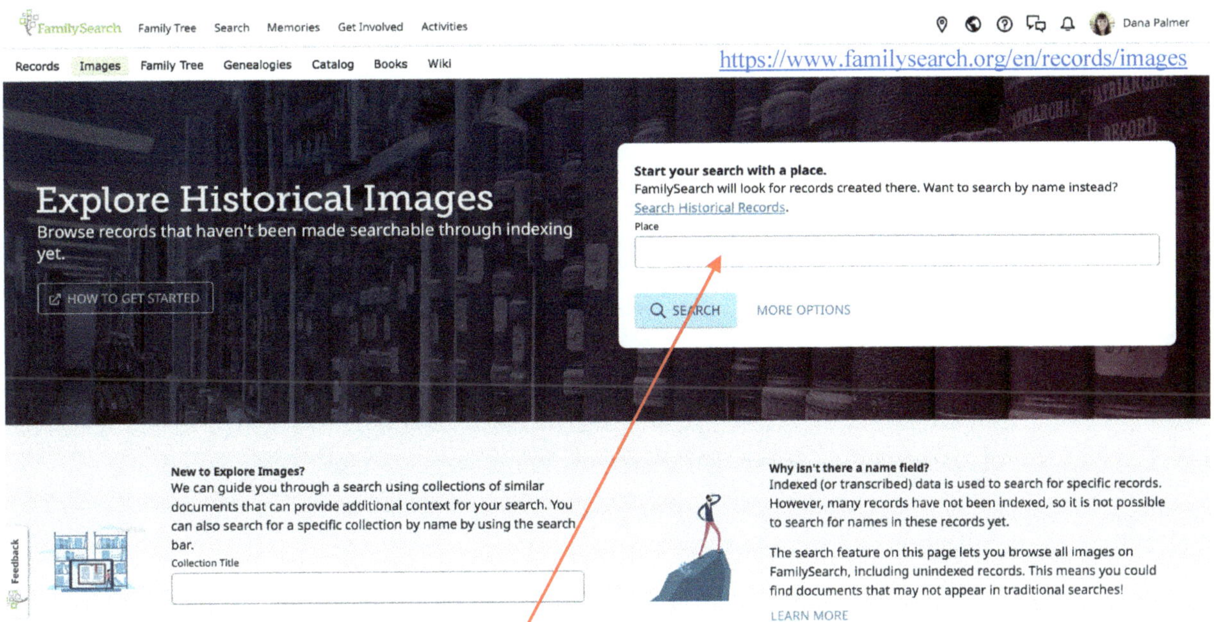

https://www.familysearch.org/en/records/images

Type the location you want into the PLACE search box and select the applicable choice. You will then get a dropdown list of collections available for that area.

To refine the search results, select a sub-location from the filters to the right, type in a date or date range in the DATE filter box, or narrow by selecting LIFE EVENT.

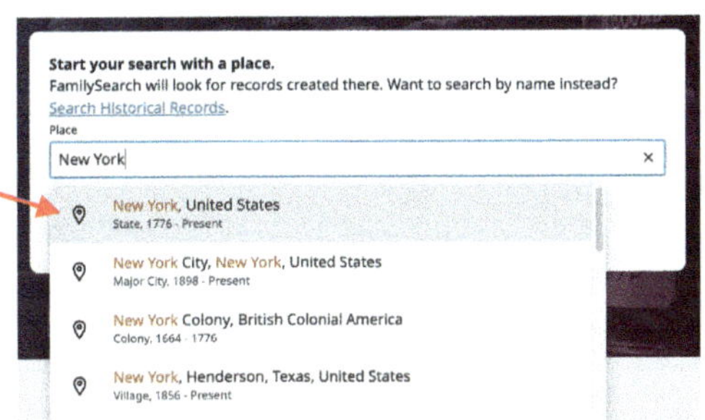

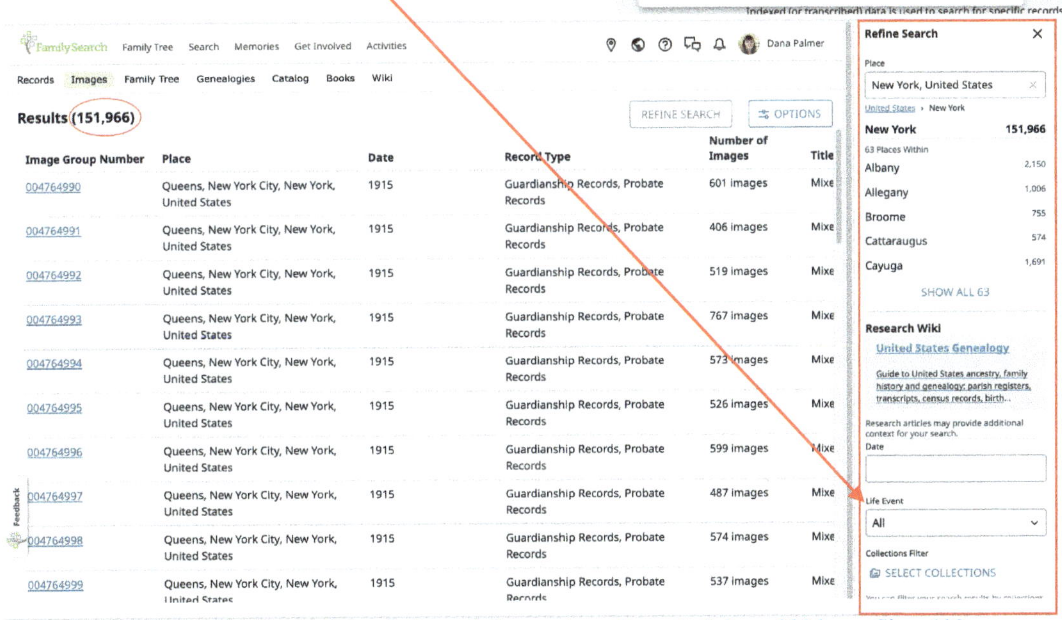

https://www.familysearch.org/en/records/images/search-results?place=339&pageSize=100

Use LIFE EVENTS and the location filters to further narrow down the databases.

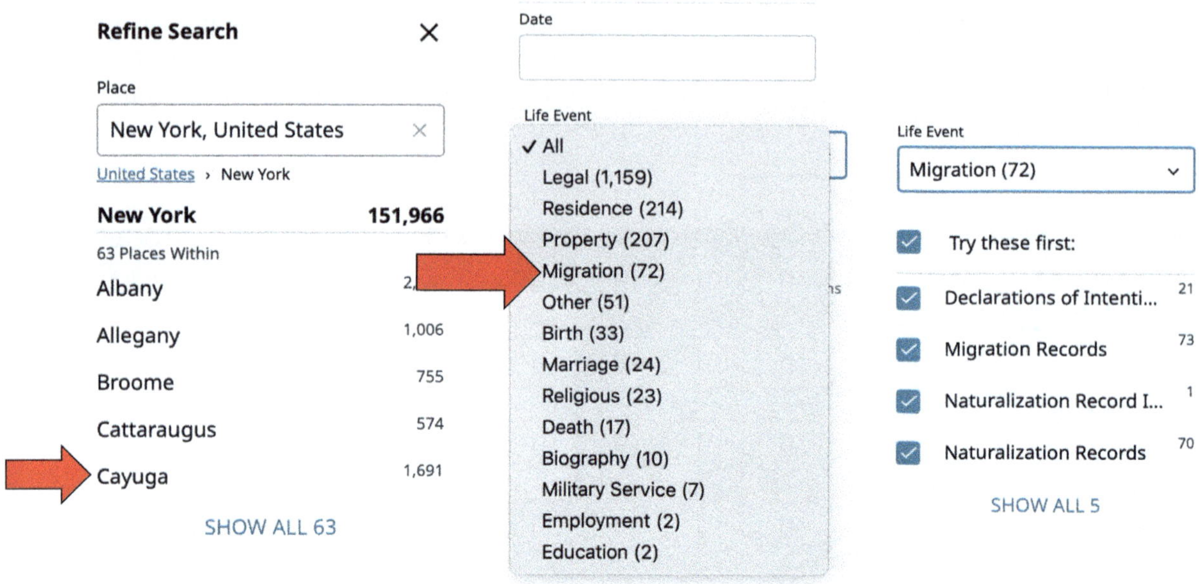

https://www.familysearch.org/en/records/images/search-results?place=339&pageSize=100

Select the record collection you want to search.

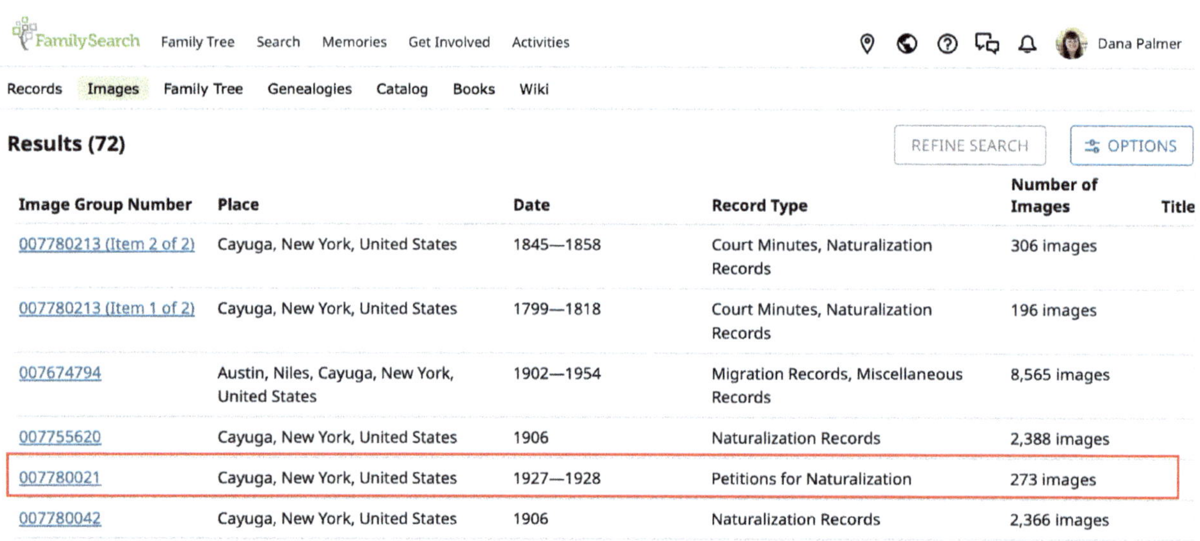

Image Group Number	Place	Date	Record Type	Number of Images	Title
007780213 (Item 2 of 2)	Cayuga, New York, United States	1845—1858	Court Minutes, Naturalization Records	306 images	
007780213 (Item 1 of 2)	Cayuga, New York, United States	1799—1818	Court Minutes, Naturalization Records	196 images	
007674794	Austin, Niles, Cayuga, New York, United States	1902—1954	Migration Records, Miscellaneous Records	8,565 images	
007755620	Cayuga, New York, United States	1906	Naturalization Records	2,388 images	
007780021	Cayuga, New York, United States	1927—1928	Petitions for Naturalization	273 images	
007780042	Cayuga, New York, United States	1906	Naturalization Records	2,366 images	

https://www.familysearch.org/en/records/images/search-results?place=393019&lifeEvent=127180&lifeEventRecordTypes=123218%2C123940%2C124162%2C124245%2C127023&page=1&pageSize=100

If the record collection has an index at the beginning or end of the images, be sure to use this first as it will save you time finding your person. If it doesn't have an index, you will need to search page by page to find your person.

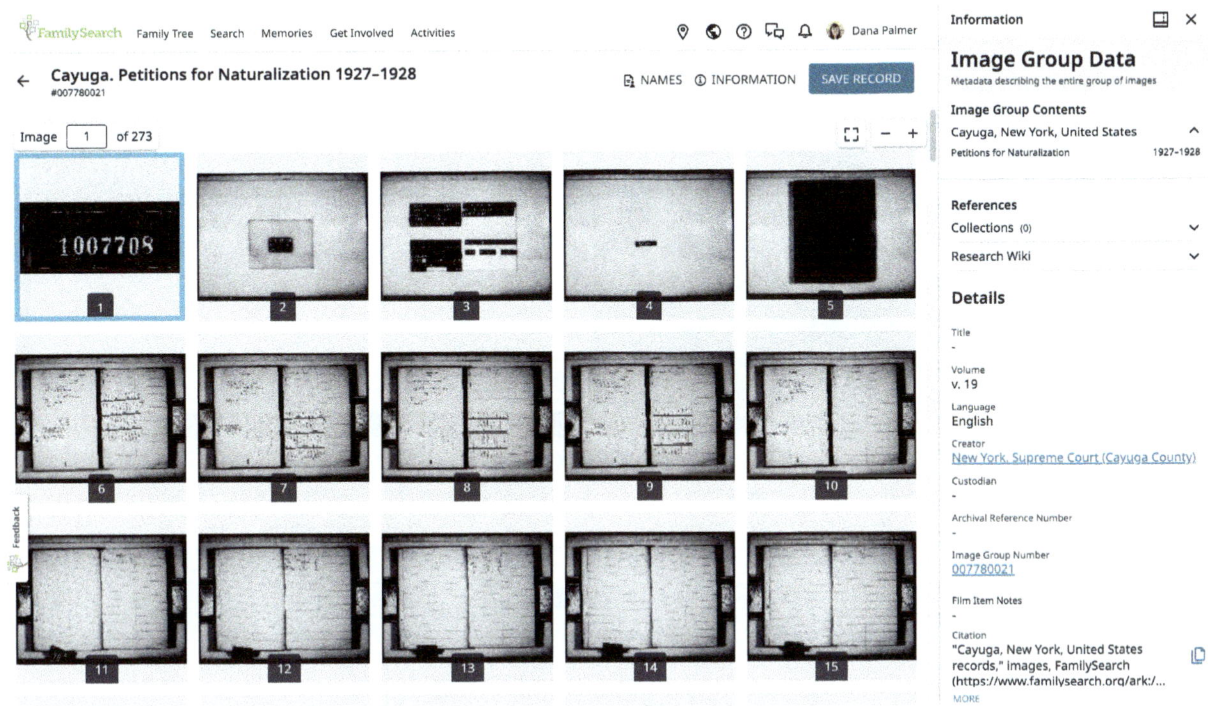

https://www.familysearch.org/ark:/61903/3:1:3Q9M-CSML-N44S-3?view=explore&groupId=TH-909-54646-193624-53&grid=on&lang=en

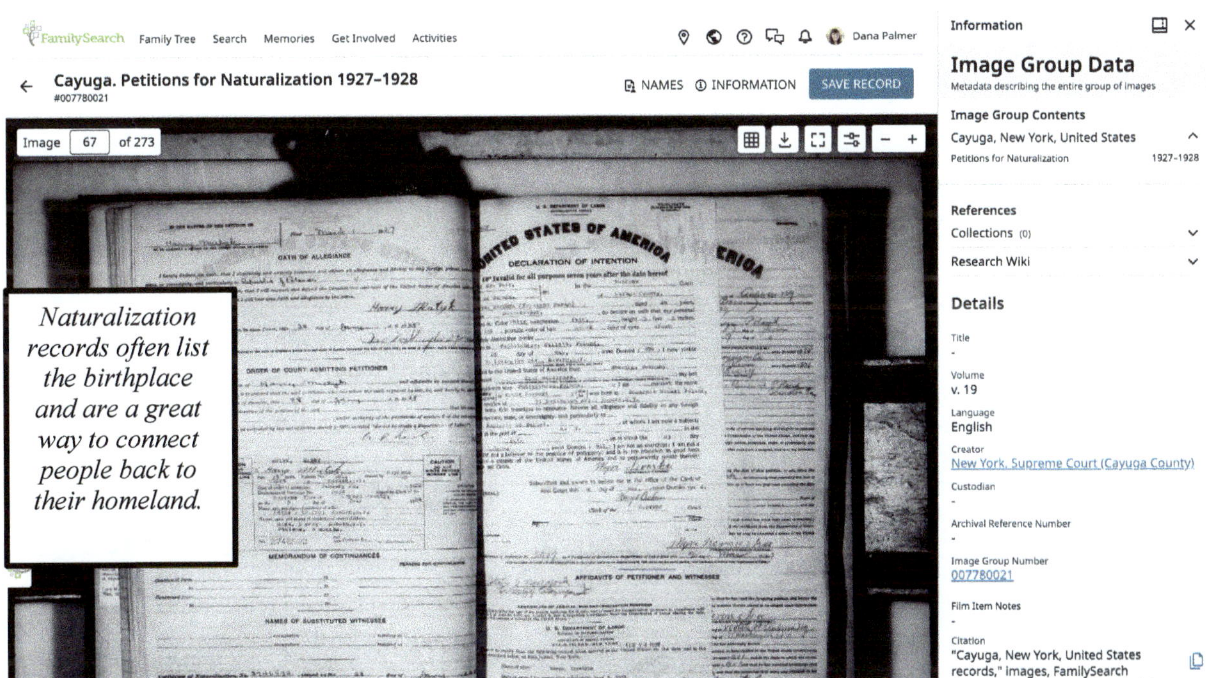

Naturalization records often list the birthplace and are a great way to connect people back to their homeland.

https://www.familysearch.org/ark:/61903/3:1:3Q9M-CSML-N4W3-P?view=explore&groupId=TH-909-54646-193624-53&lang=en

"Cayuga, New York, United States," images, FamilySearch (https://www.familysearch.org/ark:/61903/3:1:3Q9M-CSML-N4W3-P?view=explore&groupId=TH-909-54646-193624-53&lang=en : accessed 28 Apr 2025), Myri Neroska, declaration of intent; citing New York Supreme Court, image 67 of 273, FS image group 007780021.

Getting Help Finding a Collection in Images

Since FamilySearch's IMAGES only allows for a location search, it can be tricky finding the needed record, especially for locations with changing boundaries. Be sure to check out HELP ME FIND A COLLECTION for additional tools to help you find the needed collection.

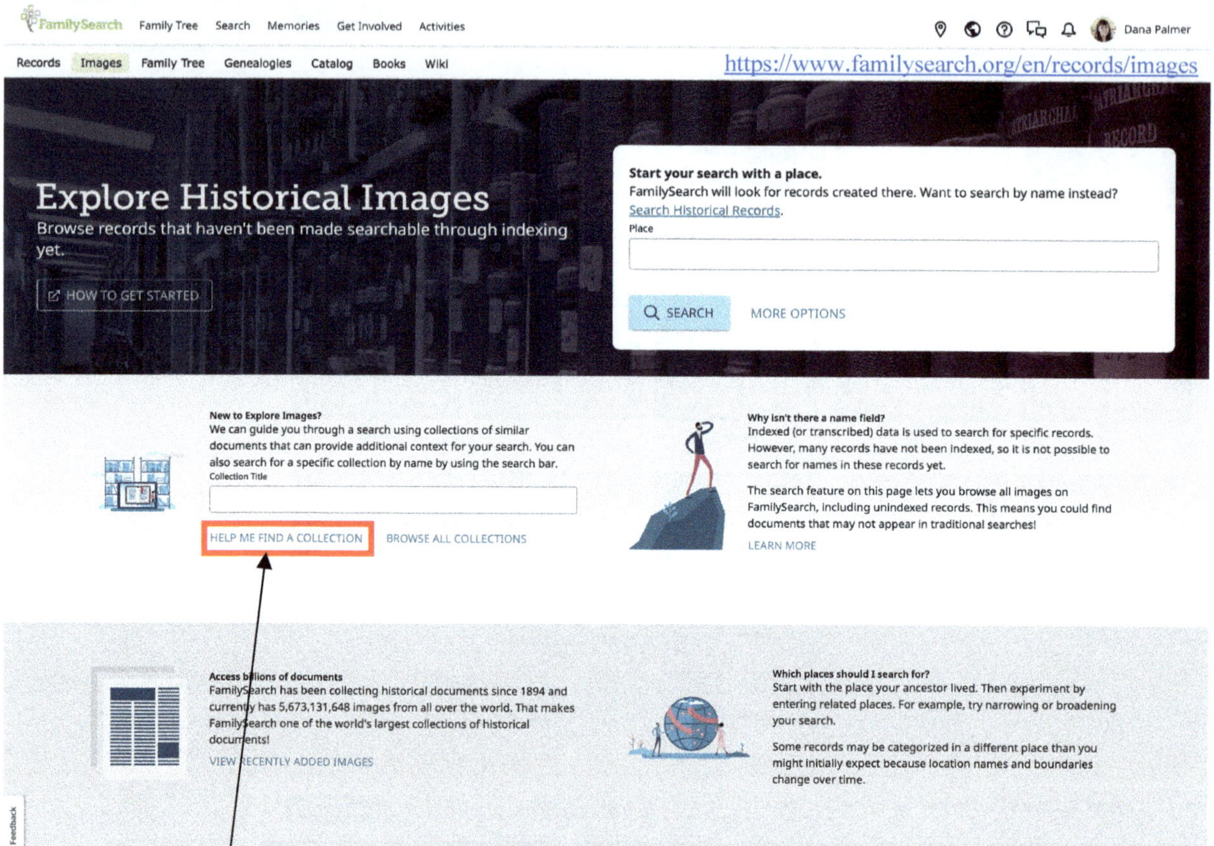

https://www.familysearch.org/en/records/images

Click on HELP ME FIND A COLLECTION, then type your location in the search box, and choose your location.

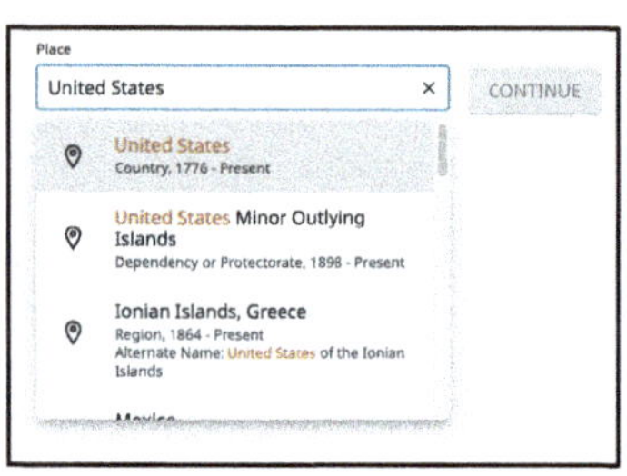

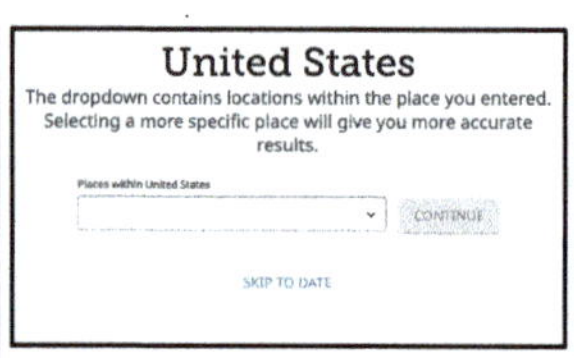

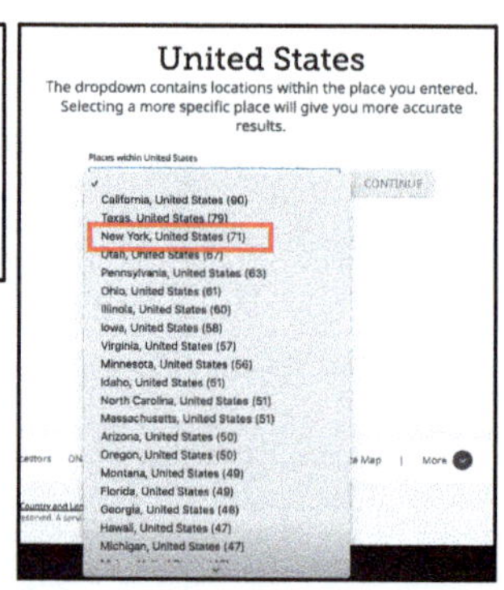

https://www.familysearch.org/en/records/collections/search

You will then be prompted to answer questions to further narrow the results.

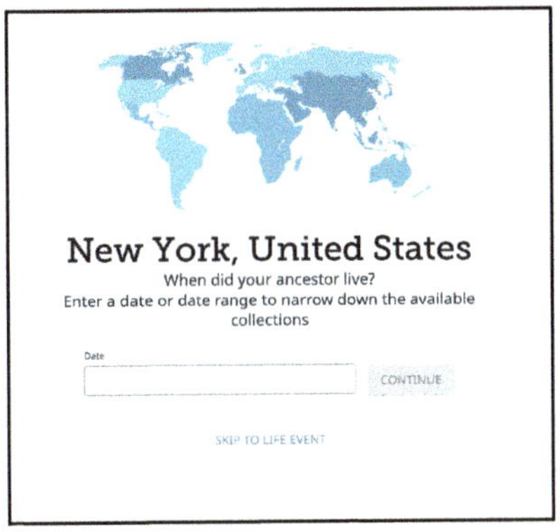

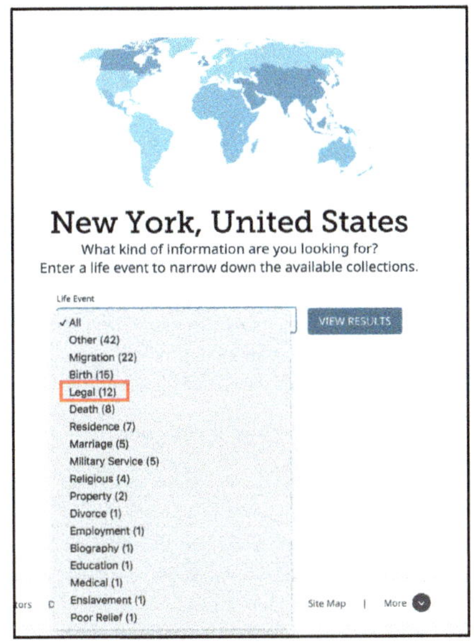

https://www.familysearch.org/en/records/collections/search

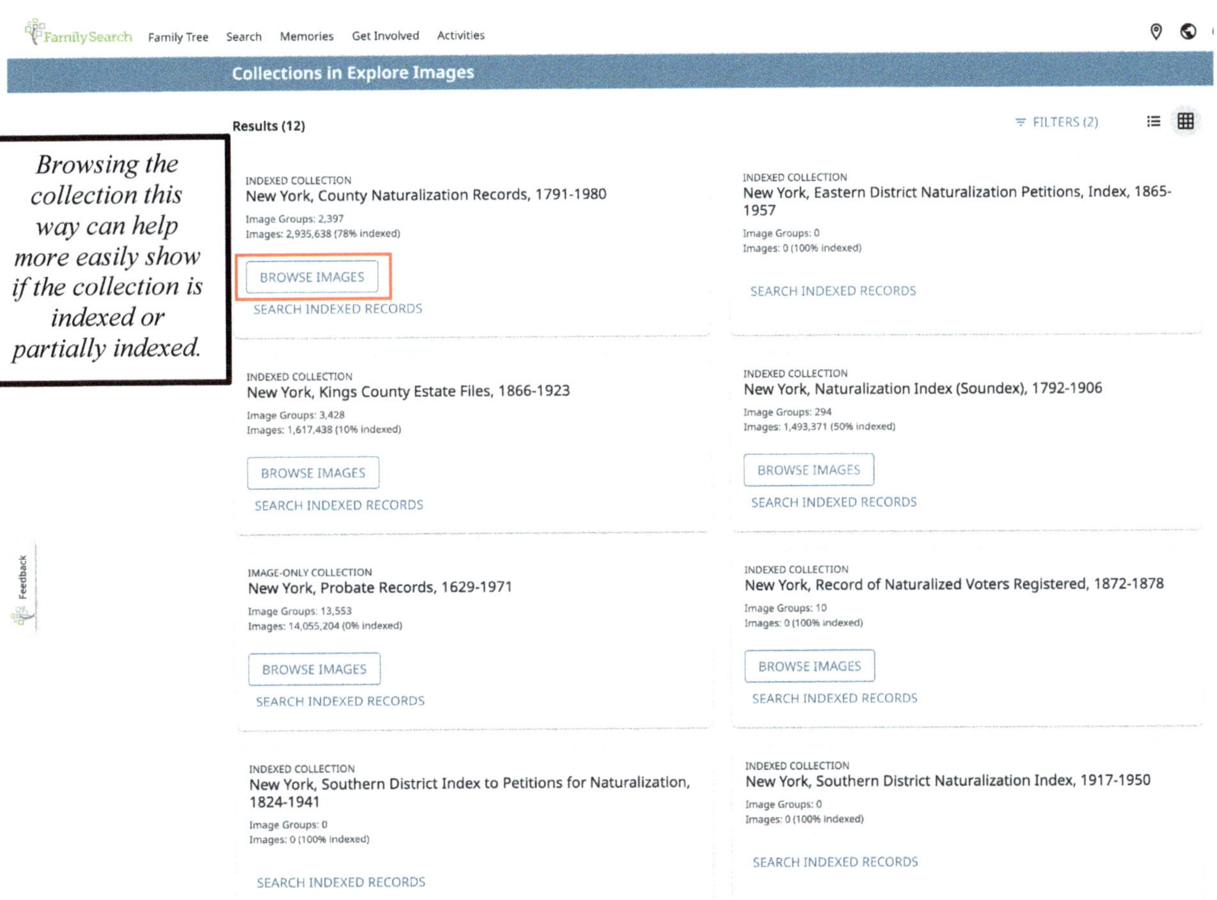

Browsing the collection this way can help more easily show if the collection is indexed or partially indexed.

https://www.familysearch.org/en/records/collections/results?place=339&lifeEventIds=127179&page=1

Select the collection you want to view, or narrow more using the filters to the right.

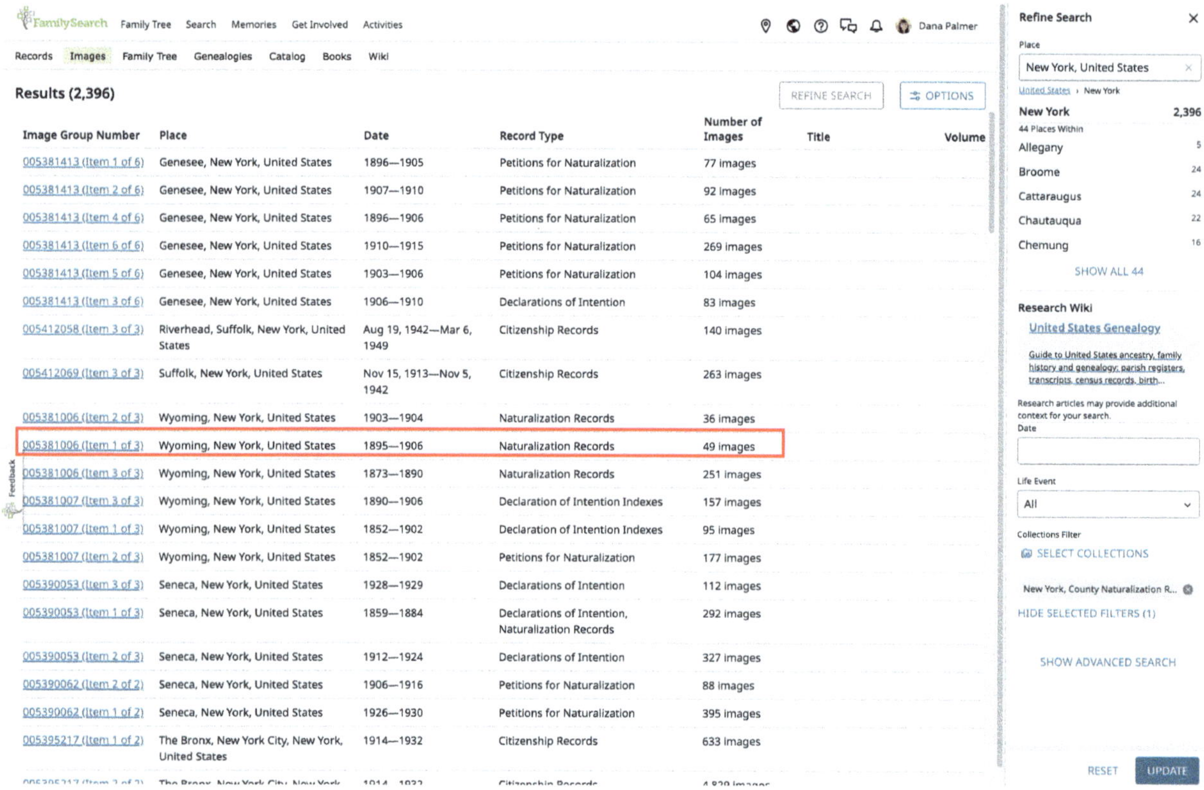

https://www.familysearch.org/en/records/images/search-results?collectionIds=M944-RSF&place=339&pageSize=100

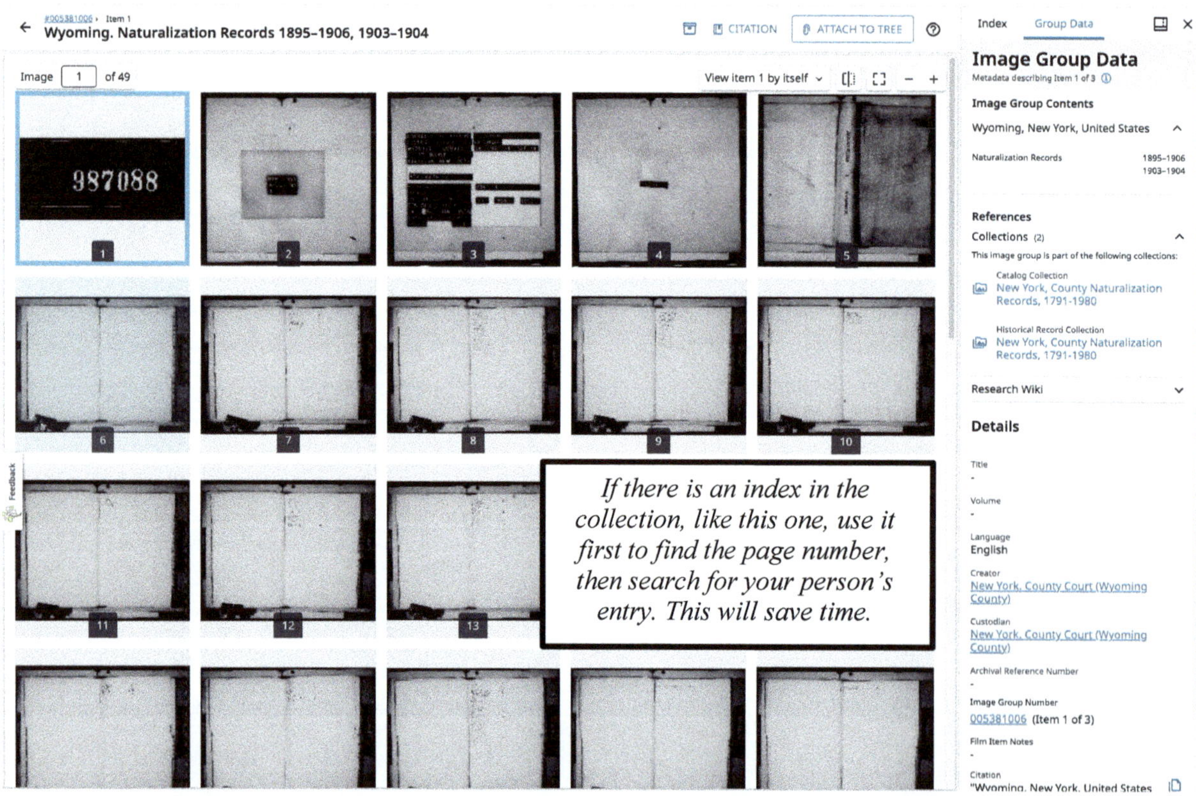

https://www.familysearch.org/ark:/61903/3:1:3QS7-L9M7-49M1-3?view=explore&groupId=M99X-PBD&grid=on&lang=en

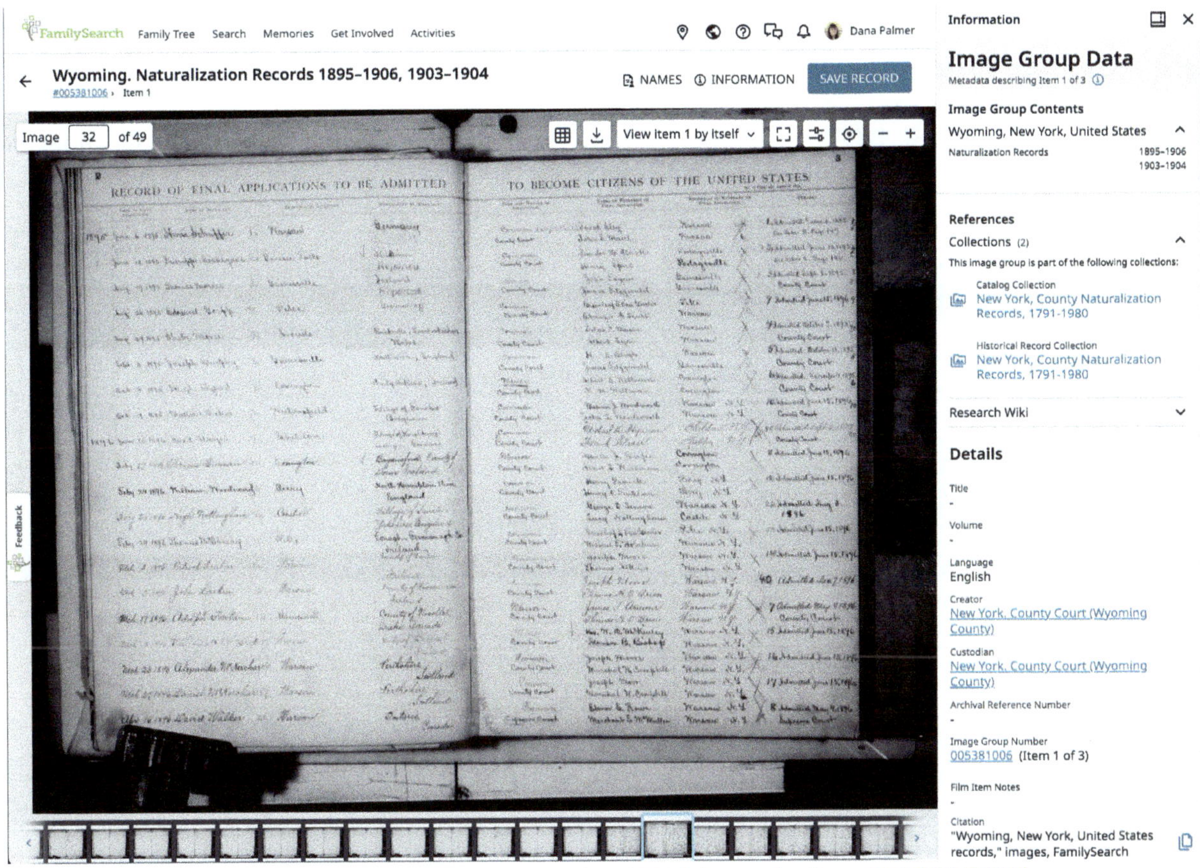

https://www.familysearch.org/ark:/61903/3:1:3QS7-89M7-4BLK?view=explore&groupId=M99X-PBD&lang=en

Searching the indexed records will take you to the database in RECORDS like this one.

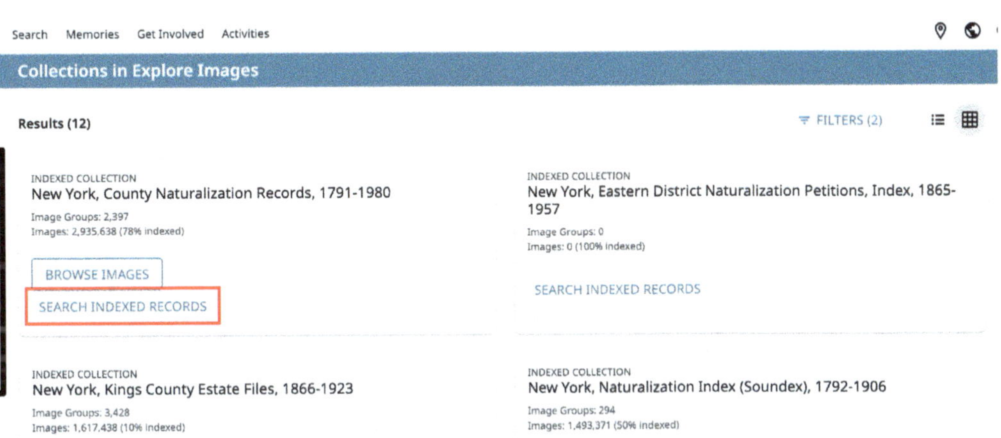

https://www.familysearch.org/en/records/collections/results?place=339&lifeEventIds=127179&page=1

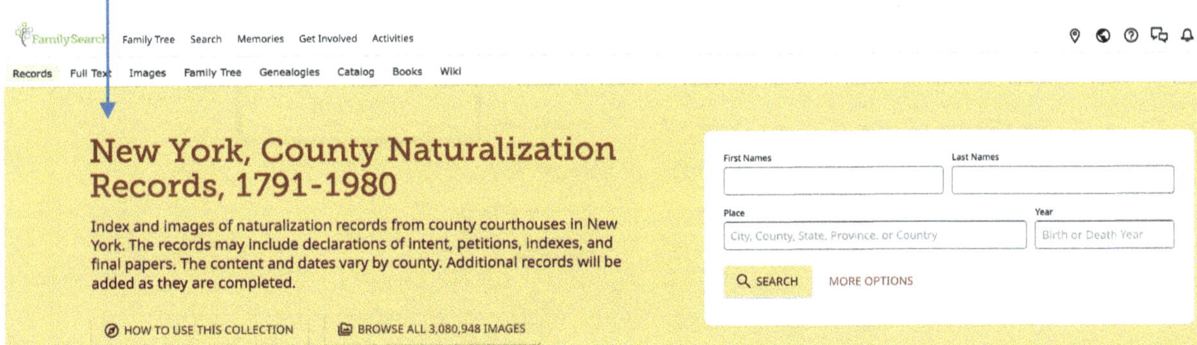

https://www.familysearch.org/en/search/collection/1999177

Browsing the Collections in Images

BROWSE ALL COLLECTIONS allows you to view the digitized collection, size of the collection, and percent indexed. This is a helpful way to find collections that don't appear in PLACE search results.

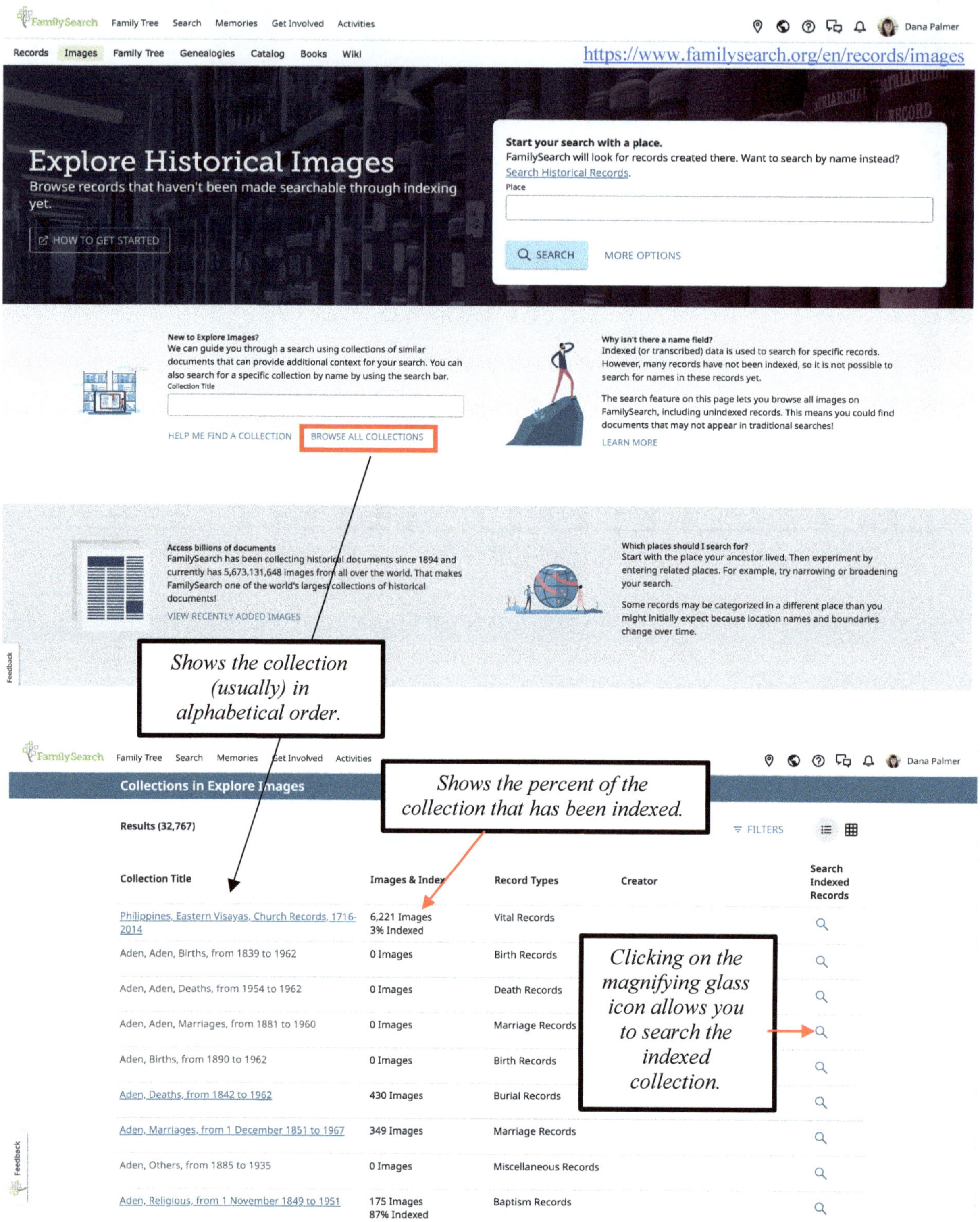

https://www.familysearch.org/en/records/collections/results?page=1&view=list

https://www.familysearch.org/en/records/collections/results?page=1&view=grid

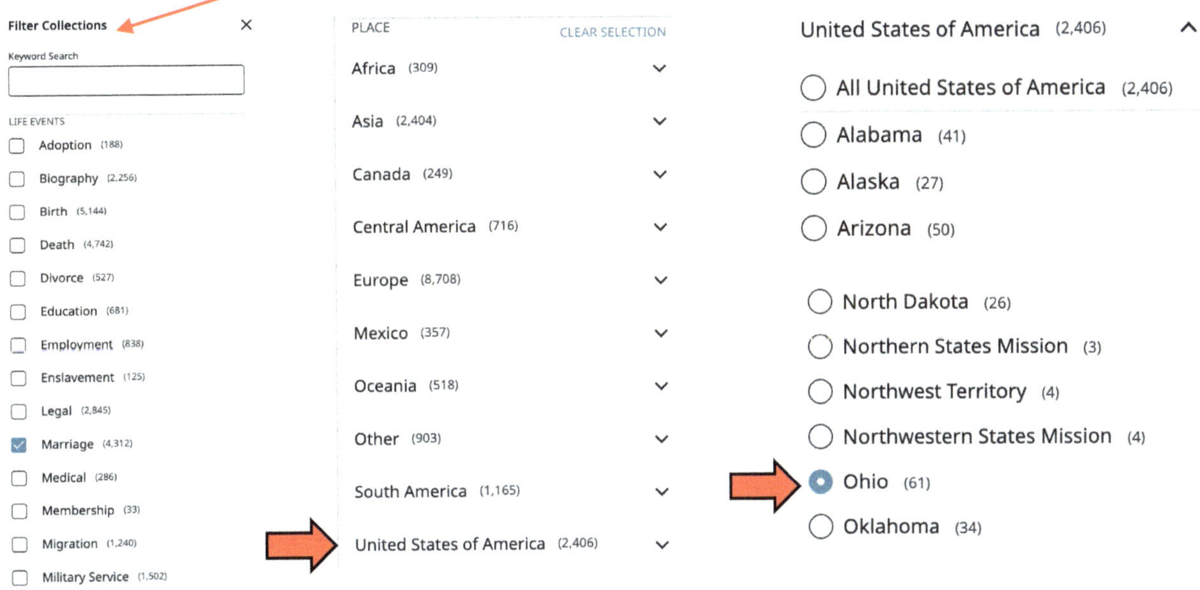

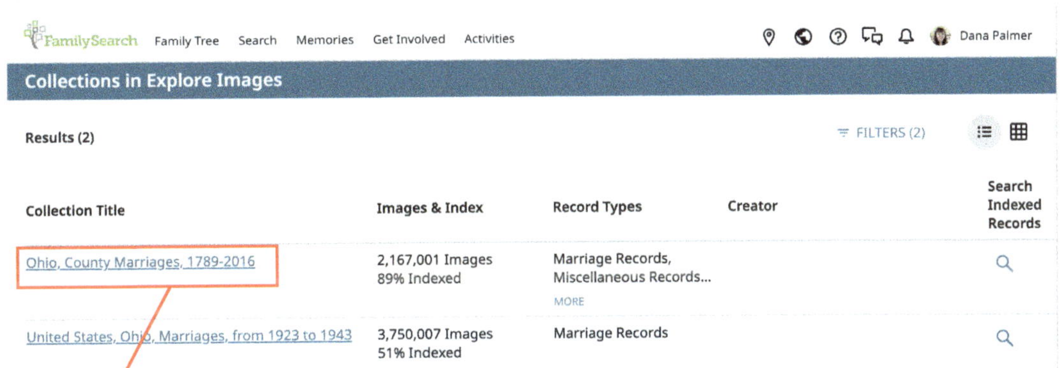

https://www.familysearch.org/en/records/collections/results?page=1&view=list&place=357&lifeEventIds=102860

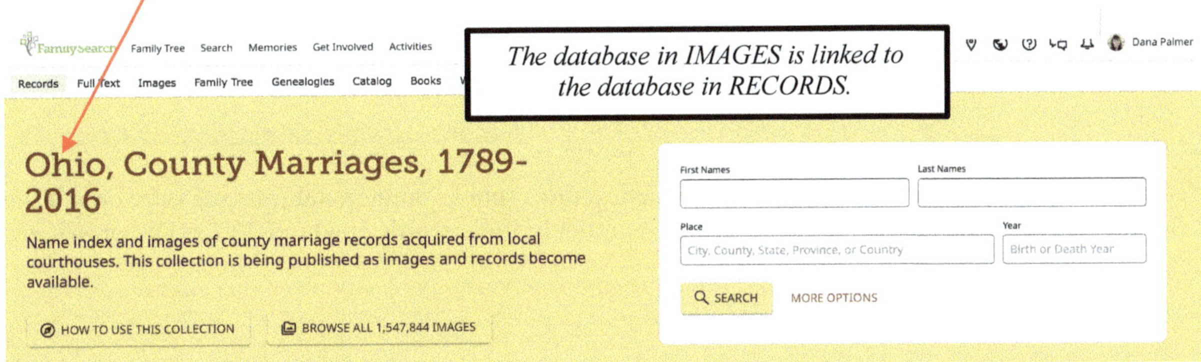

https://www.familysearch.org/en/search/collection/1614804

CATALOG

The CATALOG (https://www.familysearch.org/en/search/catalog) is a compilation of all the books, microfilms, microfiche, etc. that are available at the FamilySearch Library in Salt Lake City, Utah. These records are copies of original records (vitals, census, church, tax, court, etc.) from around the world.

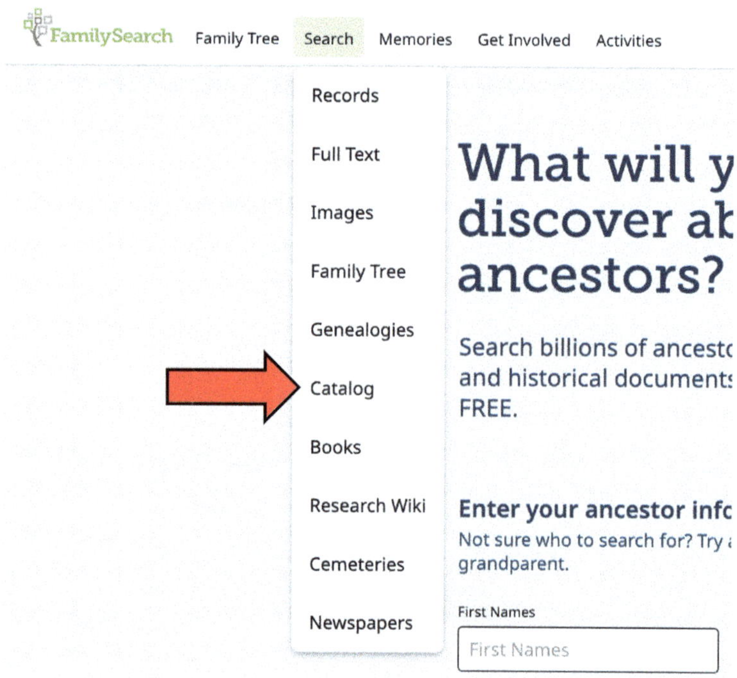

If the needed record is not found in RECORDS, the next place to search is CATALOG.

FamilySearch has a massive amount of information in their catalog that can't always be found using the search engines or full-text search feature.

Sometimes, searching the collection directly from the catalog allows you to find your record. This is especially true for mis-indexed or misspelled records.

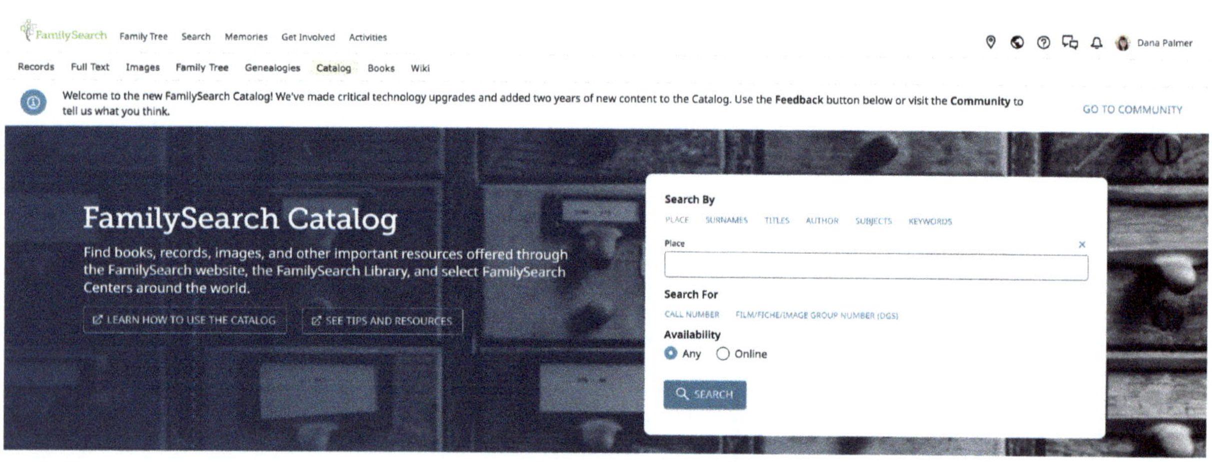

https://www.familysearch.org/en/search/catalog

Searches can be done by location (place), surnames, titles (book), author, subjects, or keywords. Film / fiche/ digital image searches can also be done to quickly find records cited in RECORDS, or in some cases, other organization partner websites.

Finding Records by Location

The CATALOG can be searched by location (place), surnames, titles, authors, subjects, and keywords. The PLACE search provides a list of collections within the typed location. Most records in the United States are organized and found at the county level, except for New England, which often has records at the town level and sometimes also the county level. Many states in the United States also have records at the state level. International records are often recorded at the town or parish level. Searching for keywords such as Quaker, Draper Manuscript, territorial papers, Northwest Territory, etc. can provide additional sources that may be difficult to find otherwise.

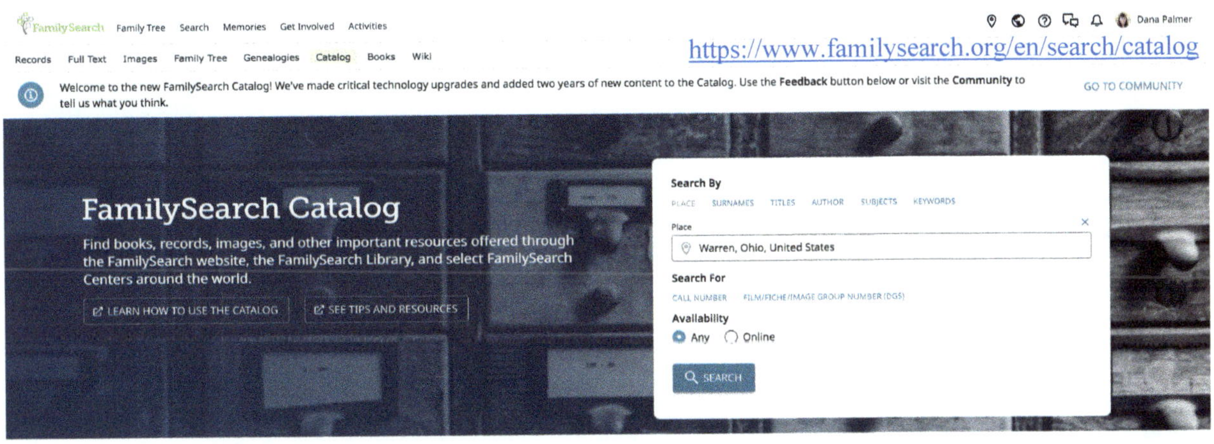

Type your location in the PLACE box and click SEARCH. You will get a list of categories for that specific location. Scroll down, then click on the dropdown arrow for the category you want to search.

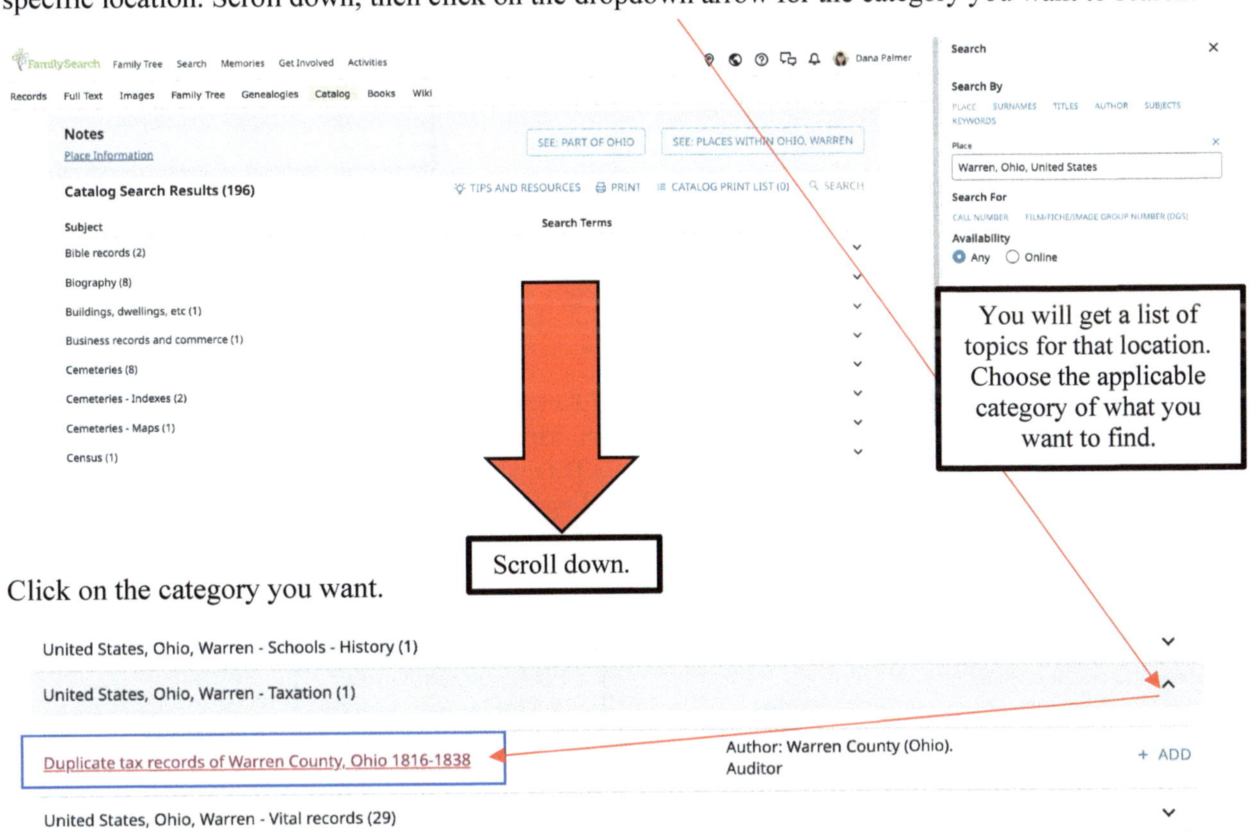

https://www.familysearch.org/en/search/catalog/results?q.place=Warren%2C%20Ohio%2C%20United%20States

Once you are on the page describing the collection, scroll down to view details on the collection. Click on the camera icon to view the digital image. If there is no camera icon, then it is not digitized on this part of FamilySearch. If the camera icon looks like a movie reel, then it is ONLY available for viewing in the FamilySearch library in Salt Lake City. If there is a warning symbol near the camera icon, then that record can only be viewed at a FamilySearch center or affiliate. All microfilms have been digitized and most are available online, but there are a few that are only available for viewing in person because of the agreement FamilySearch has with the participating record donor.

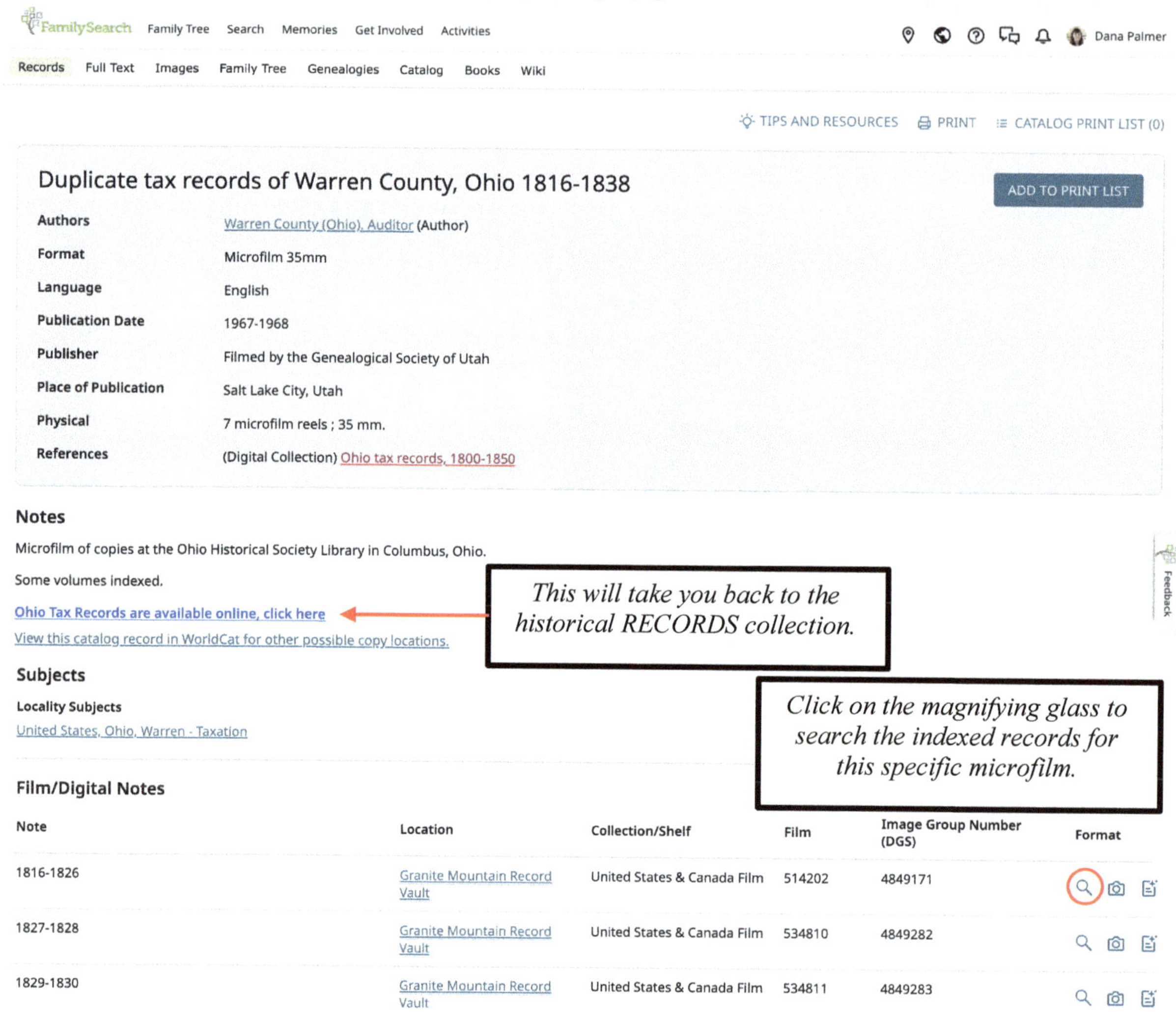

https://www.familysearch.org/en/search/catalog/237578

One of my favorite tricks for finding people in the digitized records in CATALOG is to first click on the magnifying glass icon next to the camera icon. This will show you how many names have been indexed for that specific microfilm / digital record. Type your surname in the LAST NAMES box to narrow the search results.

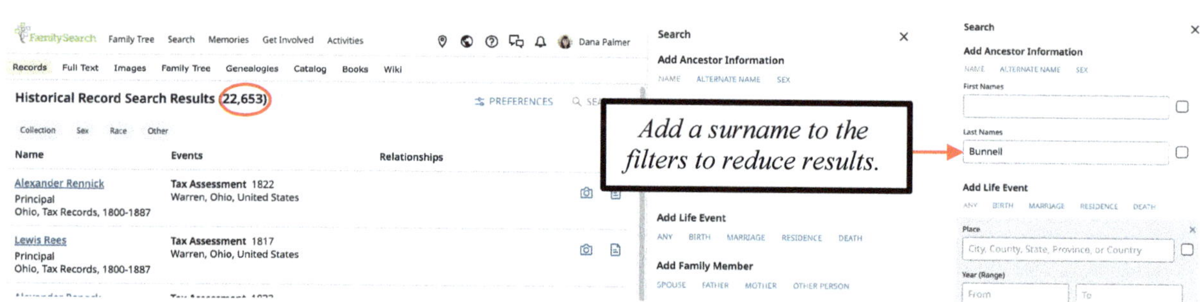

https://www.familysearch.org/en/search/record/results?q.filmNumber=4849171

To further narrow search results, add a given name or the name using wildcards.

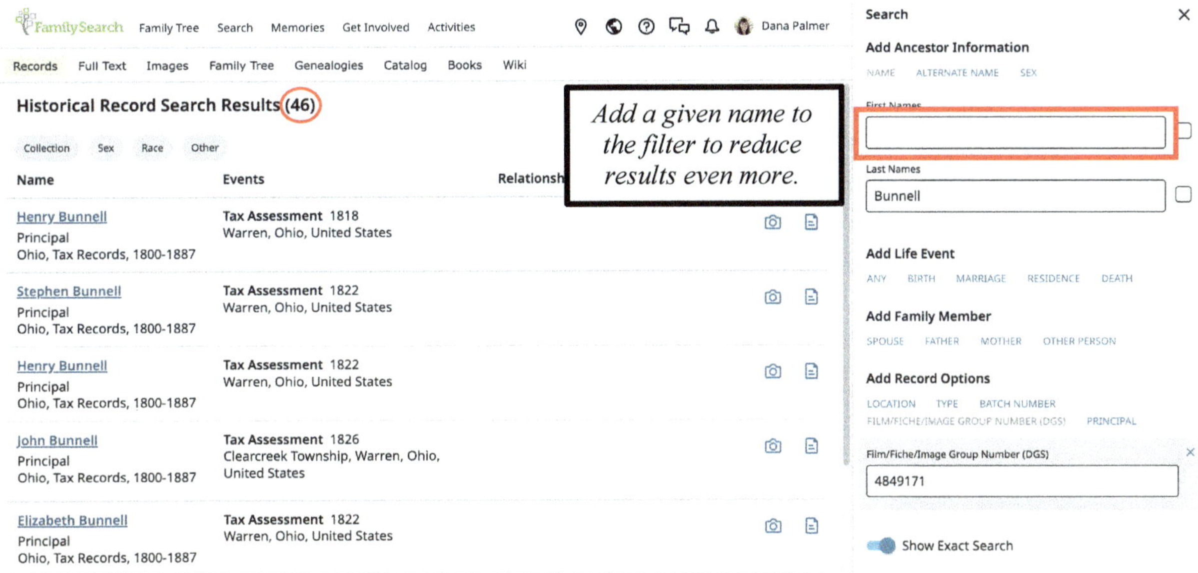

https://www.familysearch.org/en/search/record/results?count=20&q.filmNumber=4849171&q.surname=Bunnell

Adding in the given name, or in this case using a wildcard search to find variations on the name, further reduces the search results from 46 matches to 6 matches and shows Anna Bunnell with lots of spelling variations. (In wildcard searches, you can replace a single letter by using the question mark (?) or multiple letters by using the asterisk (*), or a combination of the two. For more examples of wildcard searches, see chapter 3, trick 3, starting on page 73.) To see a specific record, click on the blue name and you will be redirected to the description page.

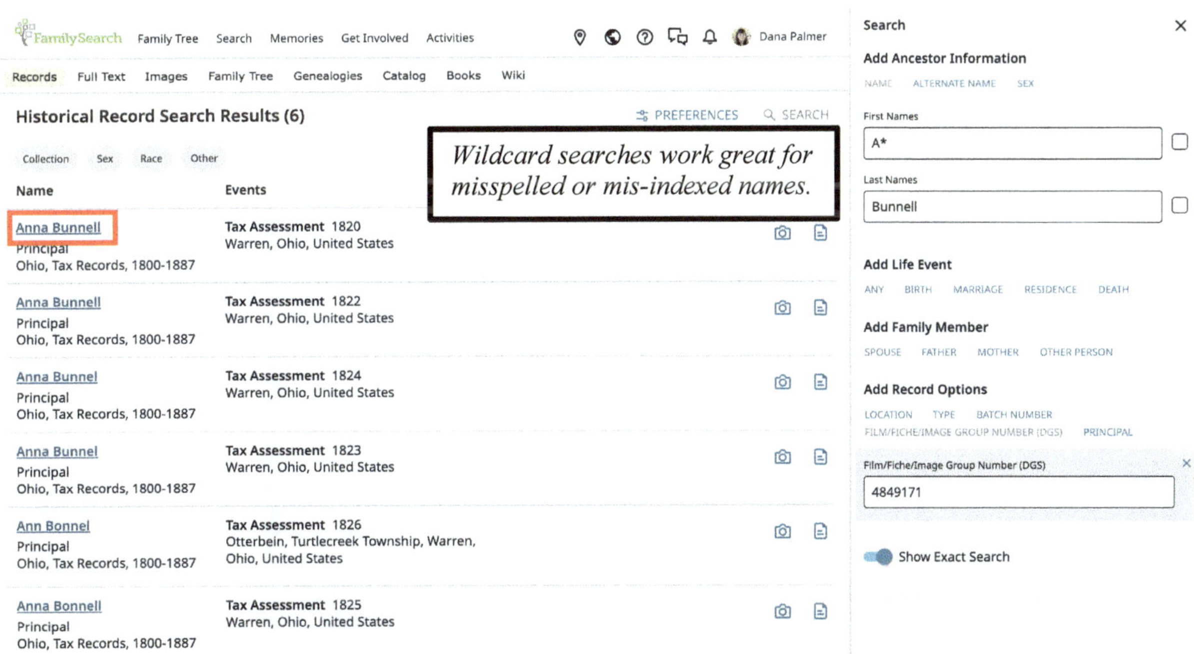

https://www.familysearch.org/en/search/record/results?count=20&q.filmNumber=4849171&q.givenName=A%2A&q.surname=Bunnell

Click the image icon to see the digitized record. Be sure to attach the record to the tree if this is the correct person.

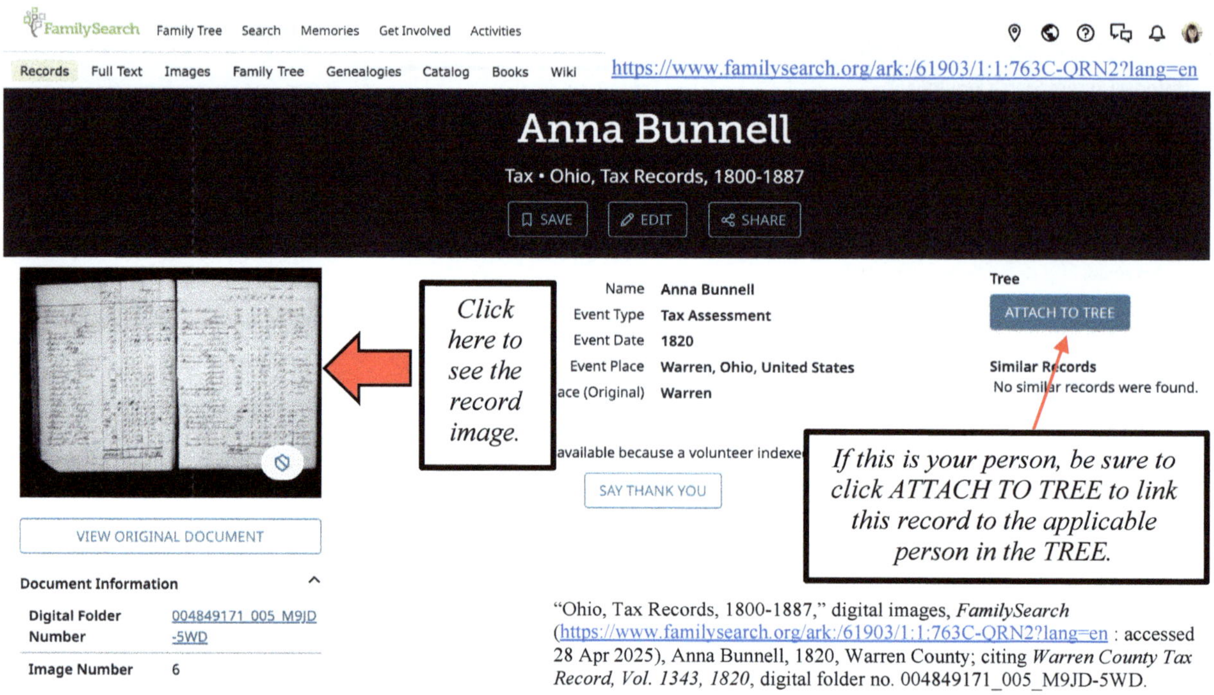

If any of the indexed information for your person is incorrect, it can be edited by clicking on the pencil icon next to the fact. The record can also be downloaded if desired or saved to the tree by clicking SAVE RECORD.

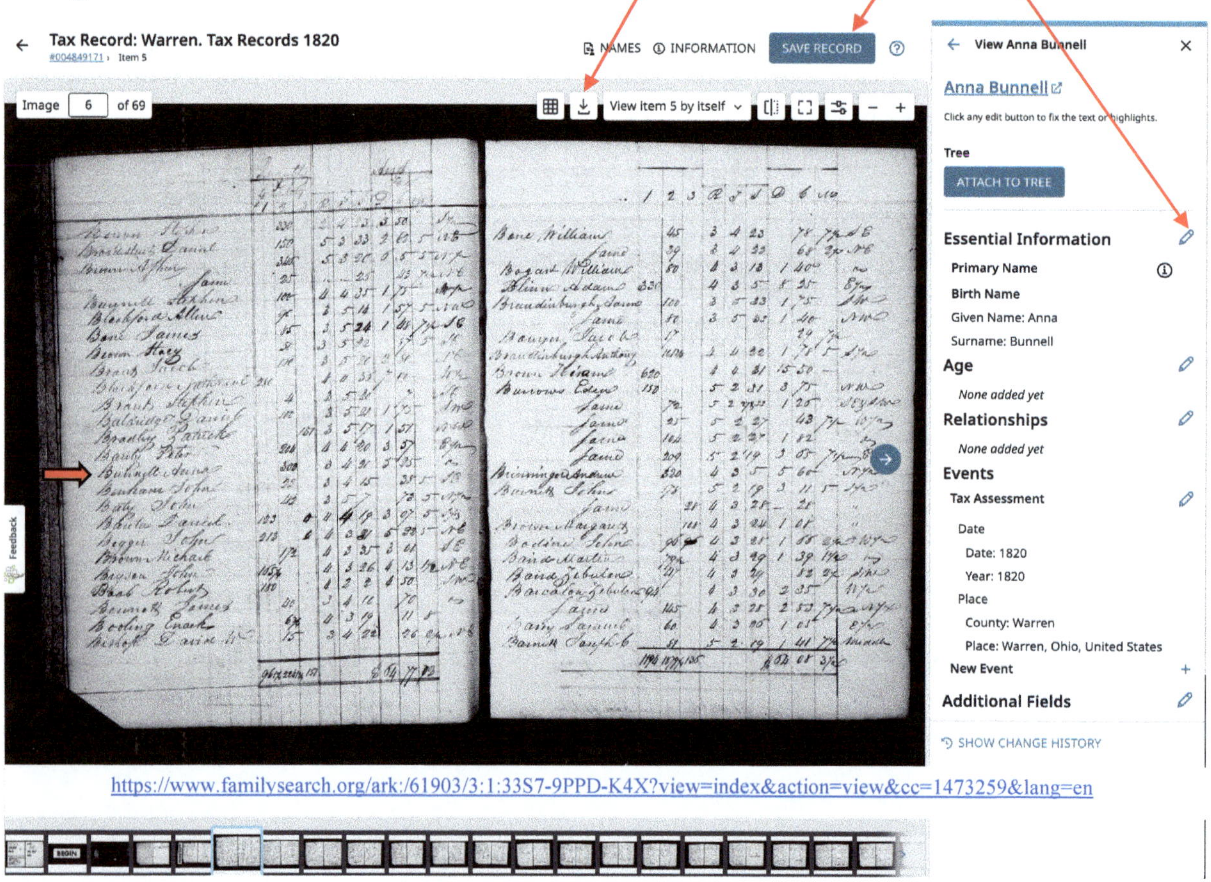

Accessing Locked Records

The agreement FamilySearch has with some participating organizations' results in their records only viewable at FamilySearch centers or FamilySearch affiliates. If the collection you want to view is in this category, find the closest center or affiliate and make arrangements to use their facility. Once you are there and logged in, you will be able to view the collection. Be sure to bring a USB drive along so you can save any records you find for viewing later.

Locked records can be attached to people in the tree, but they will only be viewable to those logged in using the tree at a participating FamilySearch center or affiliate.

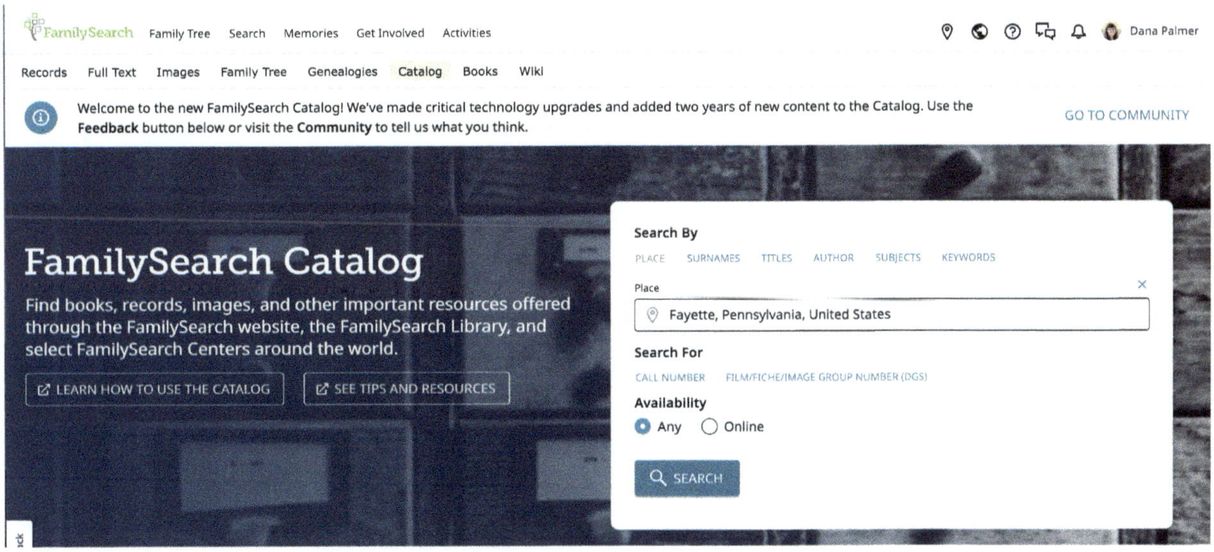

https://www.familysearch.org/en/search/catalog

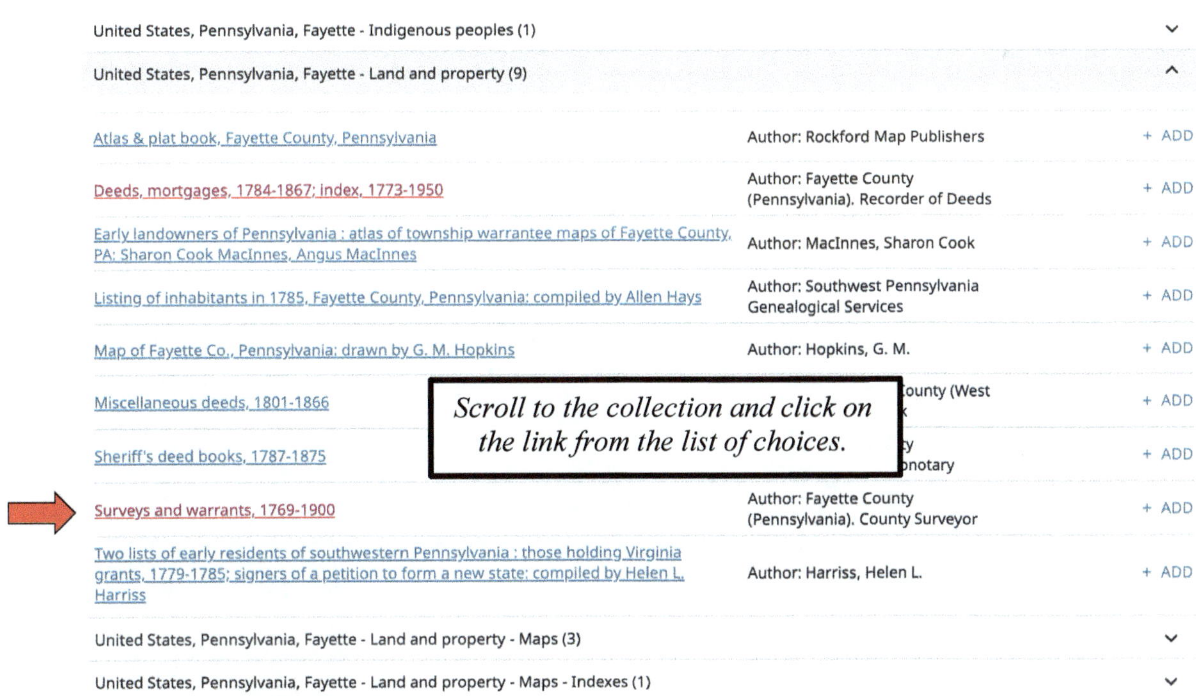

https://www.familysearch.org/en/search/catalog/results?q.place=Fayette%2C%20Pennsylvania%2C%20United%20States

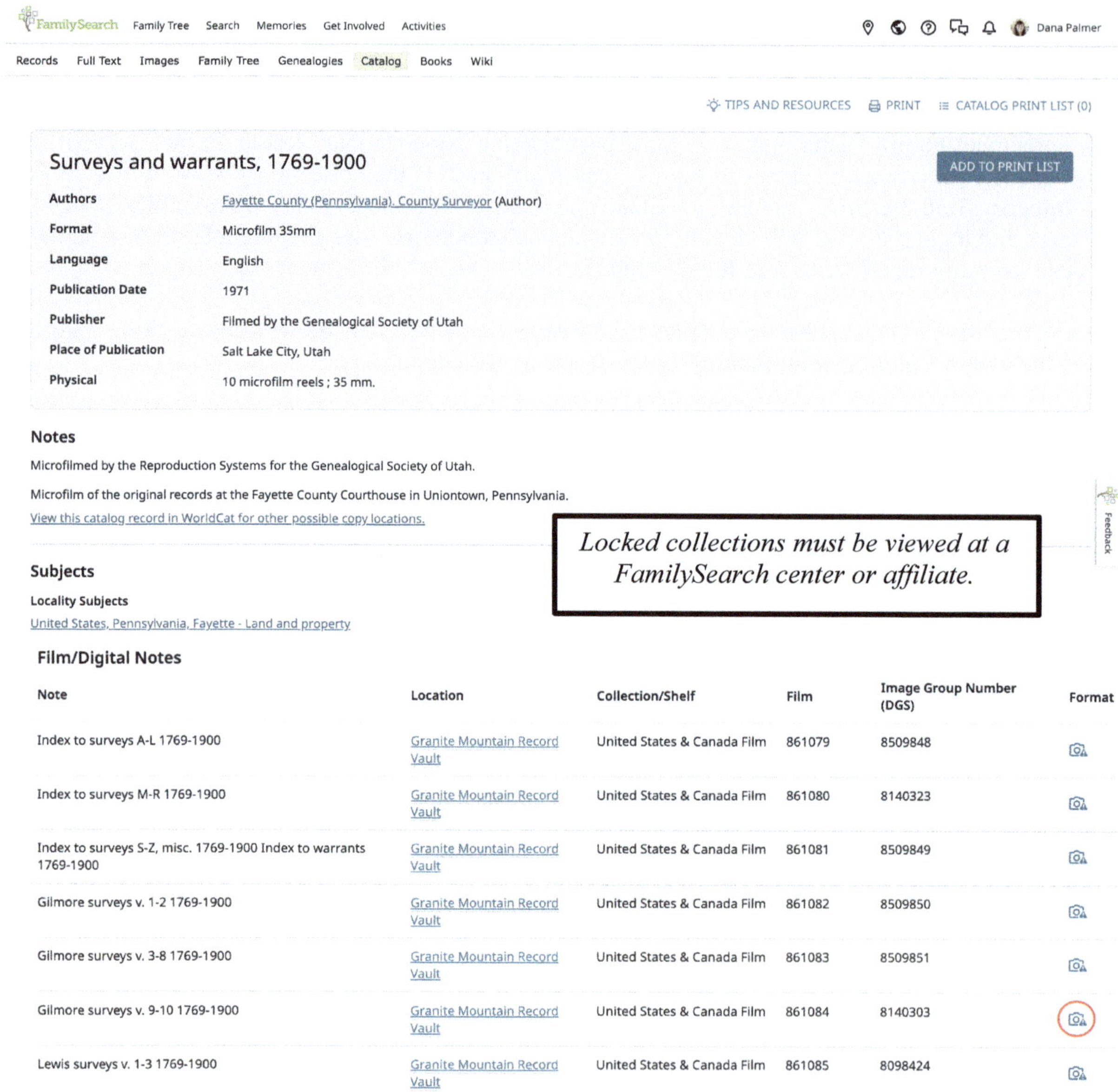

Locked collections must be viewed at a FamilySearch center or affiliate.

https://www.familysearch.org/en/search/catalog/291760

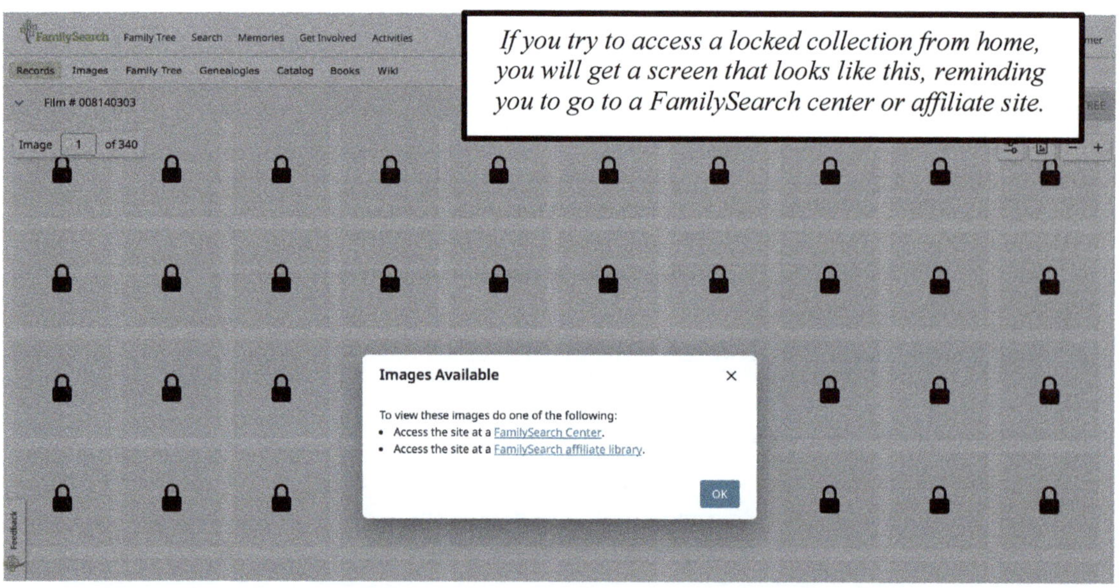

If you try to access a locked collection from home, you will get a screen that looks like this, reminding you to go to a FamilySearch center or affiliate site.

https://www.familysearch.org/en/search/film/008140303?cat=291760&i=0

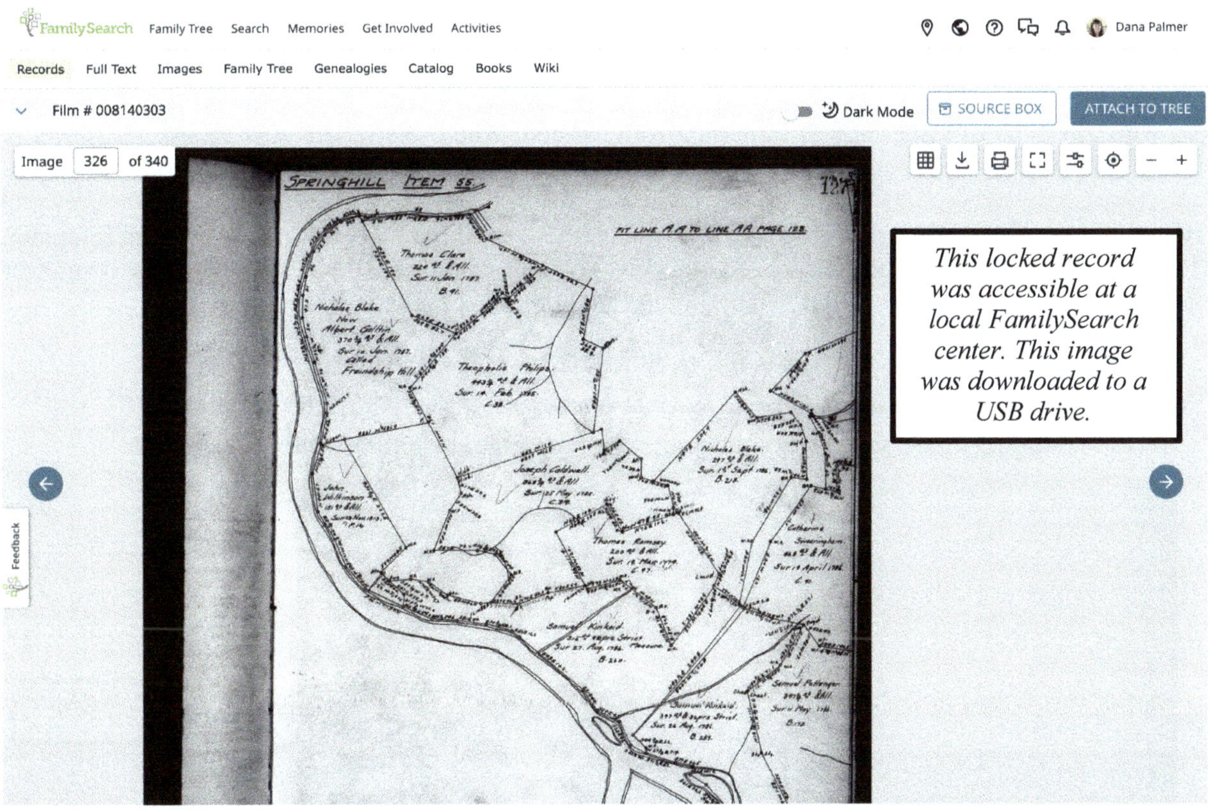

Fayette County, Pennsylvania. *Surveys and warrants, 1769-1900,* Catherine Swearingham [sic], Springhill, Bk 10, p. 127; imaged in "Surveys and warrants, 1769-1900," *FamilySearch* (https://familysearch.org : accessed 28 Apr 2025); citing Pennsylvania, Fayette County > Land and property > Gilmore surveys v. 9-10 1769-1900 > image 326 of 340; citing Fayette County Courthouse; FS microfilm 861,084.

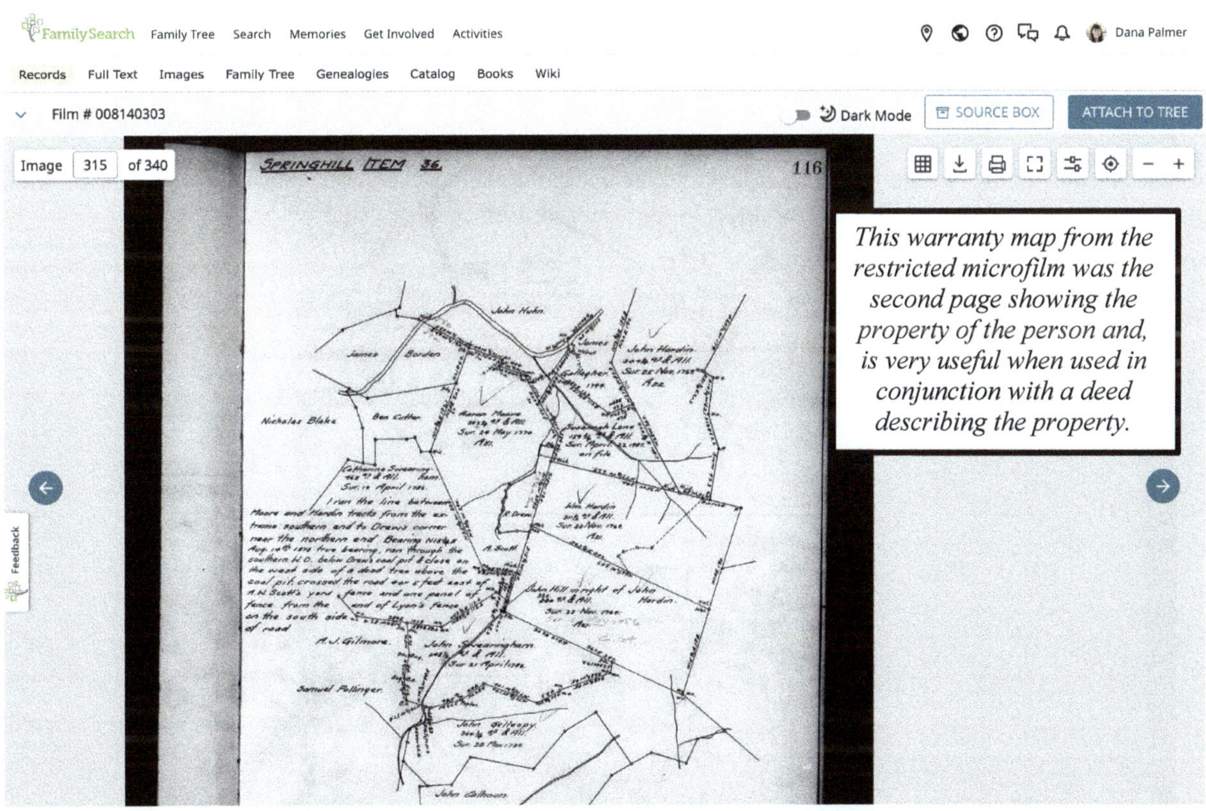

Fayette County, Pennsylvania. *Surveys and warrants, 1769-1900,* Catherine Swearingham [sic], Springhill, Bk 10, p. 116; imaged in "Surveys and warrants, 1769-1900," *FamilySearch* (https://familysearch.org : accessed 28 Apr 2025); citing Pennsylvania, Fayette County > Land and property > Gilmore surveys v. 9-10 1769-1900 > image 315 of 340; citing Fayette County Courthouse; FS microfilm 861,084.

Finding the Record Origin

As with any type of research it is important to document where the record was found. This can be tricky when using online sources. FamilySearch makes it fairly easy to find the citation for your source.

If you find your ancestor in a source while browsing, there are three ways to find the original reference. The easiest is to see if the entry has been indexed. To do this be sure the NAMES category is selected in the far-right panel, then scroll down until you find your person's name.

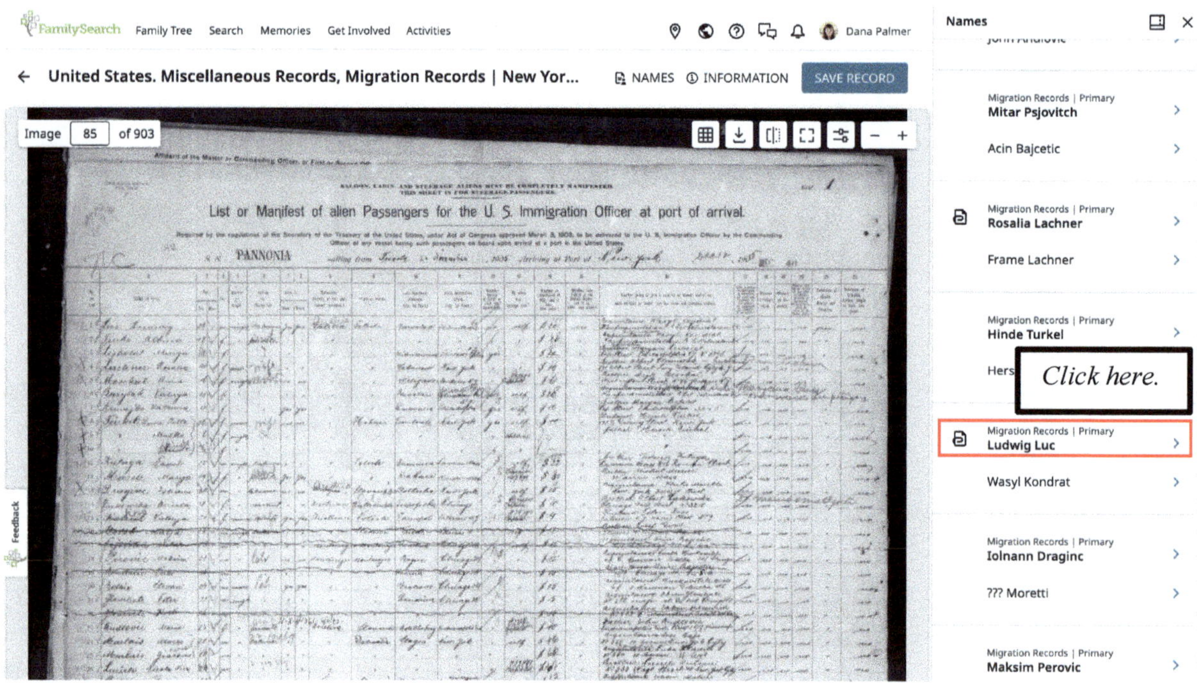

https://www.familysearch.org/ark:/61903/3:1:3Q9M-C9PT-NLYR?view=index&action=view&cc=1368704&lang=en&groupId=TH-909-48496-19394-26

Click on their name. In the far-right side panel, you should see details about that person. Click on their name at the top and you will be redirected to the transcription page for that record.

https://www.familysearch.org/ark:/61903/3:1:3Q9M-C9PT-NLYR?view=index&action=view&cc=1368704&lang=en&groupId=TH-909-48496-19394-26&personArk=%2Fark%3A%2F61903%2F1%3A1%3AJFH9-R22

The transcription page not only provides details about what is contained in the record, but it lists the microfilm or digital image collection that contained that record. Sometimes the record will even note the page and entry number or file number (fn).

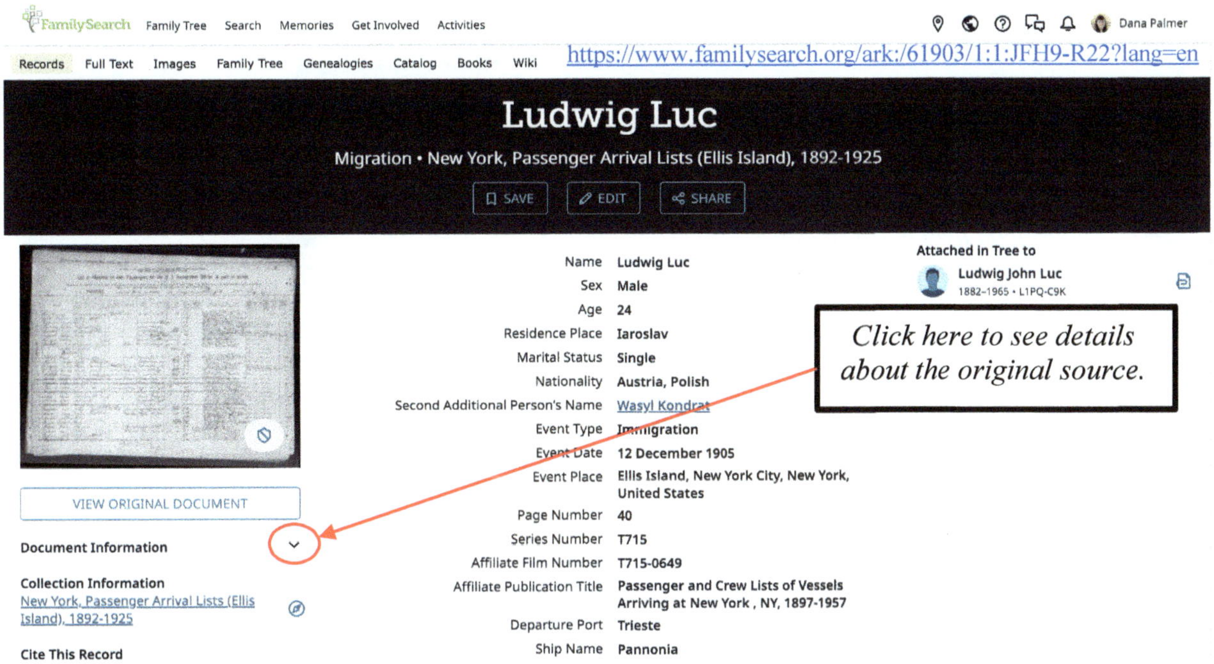

"New York, Passenger Arrival Lists (Ellis Island), 1892-1925," *FamilySearch* (https://www.familysearch.org/ark:/61903/1:1:JF-H9-R22?lang=en : accessed 2 May 2025), Ludwig Luc, 12 Dec 1905, ship *Pannonia*; citing Passenger and Crew Lists of Vessels Arriving at New York, NY, 1897-1957, National Archives microfilm publication T715, roll 649; FS microfilm 1,399,333.

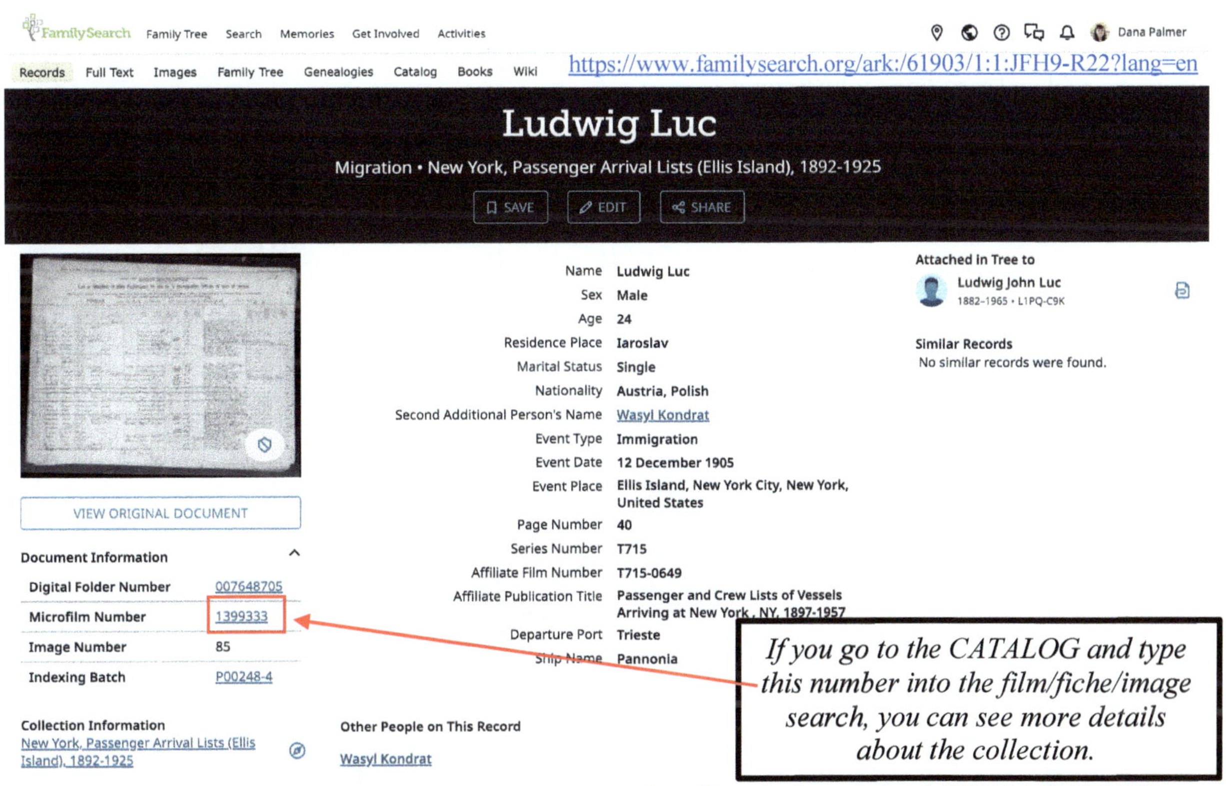

"New York, Passenger Arrival Lists (Ellis Island), 1892-1925," *FamilySearch* (https://www.familysearch.org/ark:/61903/1:1:JF-H9-R22?lang=en : accessed 2 May 2025), Ludwig Luc, 12 Dec 1905, ship *Pannonia*; citing Passenger and Crew Lists of Vessels Arriving at New York, NY, 1897-1957, National Archives microfilm publication T715, roll 649; FS microfilm 1,399,333.

The second method to find the original source is to click on INFORMATION at the top of the screen.

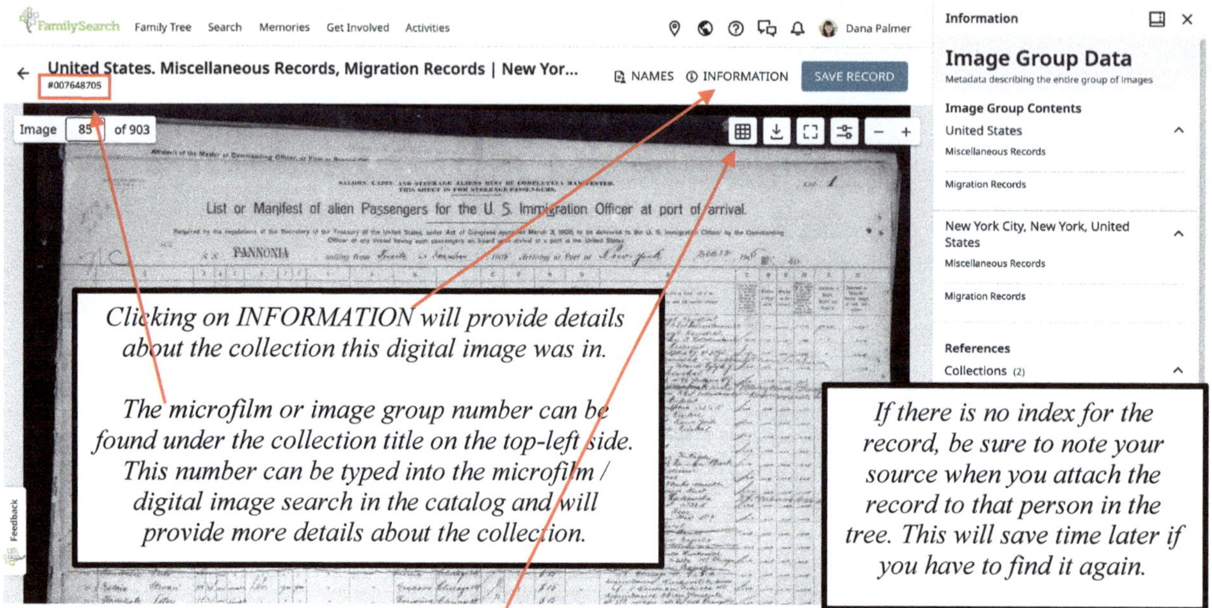

Clicking on INFORMATION will provide details about the collection this digital image was in.

The microfilm or image group number can be found under the collection title on the top-left side. This number can be typed into the microfilm / digital image search in the catalog and will provide more details about the collection.

If there is no index for the record, be sure to note your source when you attach the record to that person in the tree. This will save time later if you have to find it again.

https://www.familysearch.org/ark:/61903/3:1:3Q9M-C9PT-NLYR?view=index&action=view&cc=1368704&lang=en&groupId=TH-909-48496-19394-26

The third method is to click on the grid icon and then see if the record is contained within a book or microfilm in that collection by browsing the images. If it is from a microfilm, the number will be on the first or second images in that collection. You can browse to it by using the grid and scrolling, or by typing the number 1 into the box at the top.

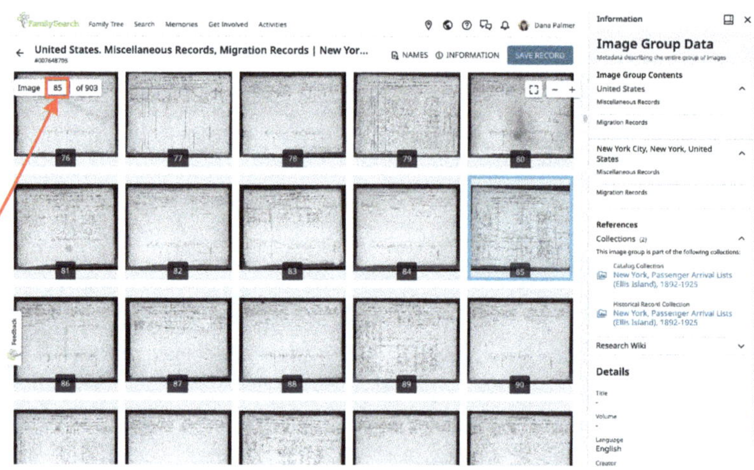

Browse to the beginning of the images to find the microfilm number.

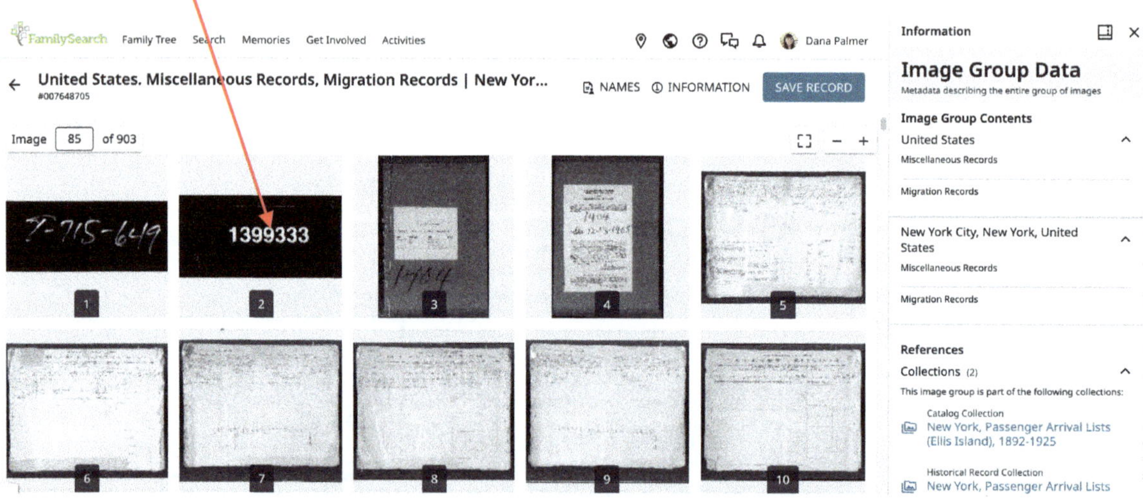

https://www.familysearch.org/ark:/61903/3:1:3Q9M-C9PT-NLYR?view=index&action=view&cc=1368704&lang=en&groupId=TH-909-48496-19394-26&grid=on

Finding Records from an Image or Film Number

To find records for a specific locality, type in the county (for the U.S.) or town/ parish (for international countries). Click the drop-down arrow from the available categories.

Choose a link from the available records and see if there is a camera icon next to the microfilm. If so, then the records can be viewed online. If there is a camera icon with a lock above it (or warning icon), then the records can only be viewed at a local FamilySearch center or FamilySearch affiliate.

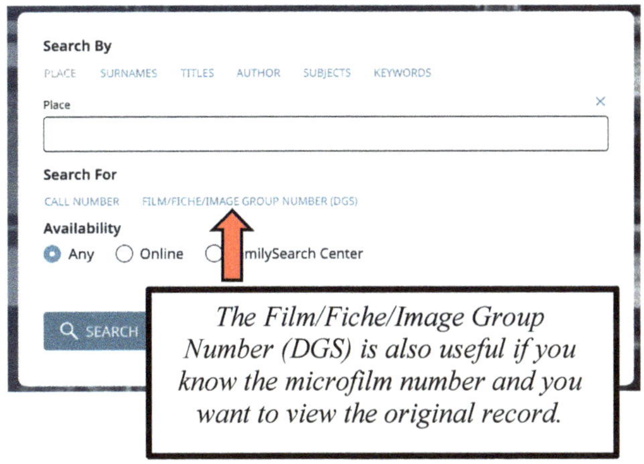

https://www.familysearch.org/en/search/catalog

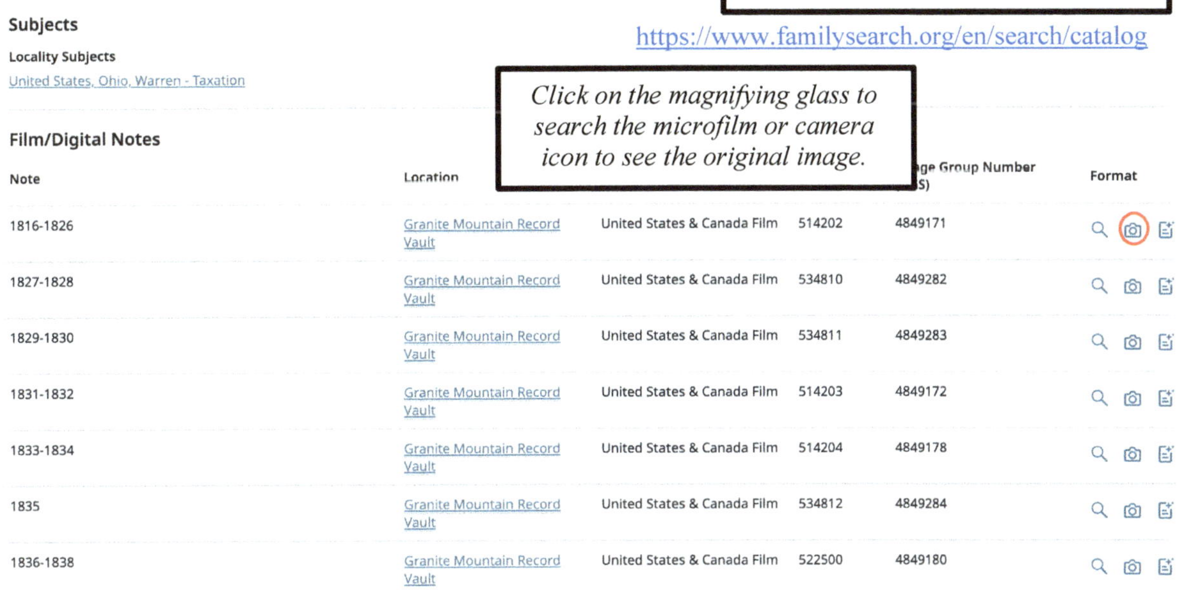

https://www.familysearch.org/en/search/catalog/237578

Unless the record has an index at the beginning, you will need to search for it.

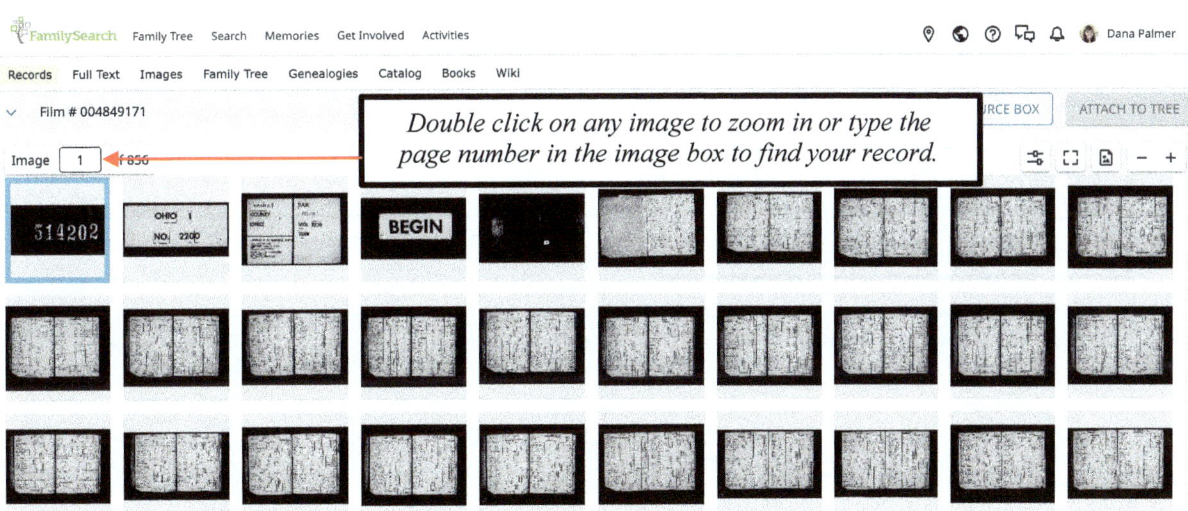

https://www.familysearch.org/en/search/film/004849171?cat=237578&i=0

Finding Nearby Places by Browsing the Levels

If you search a town / parish and are unable to find your person in that location, and are unsure where else to look, you need to use a circular search to check records in other nearby locations. To find nearby locations, click on the PART OF or PLACES WITHIN to view other places near the location you are searching.

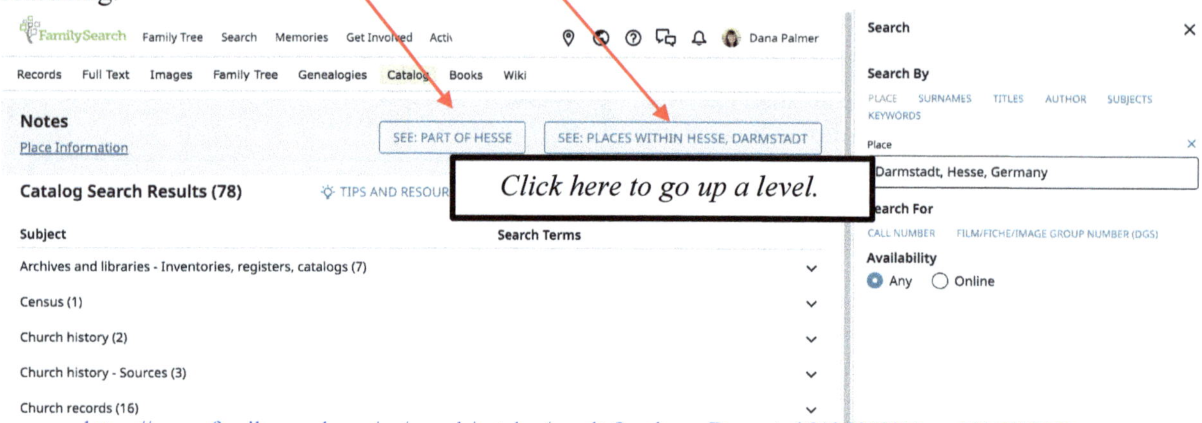

https://www.familysearch.org/en/search/catalog/results?q.place=Darmstadt%2C%20Hesse%2C%20Germany

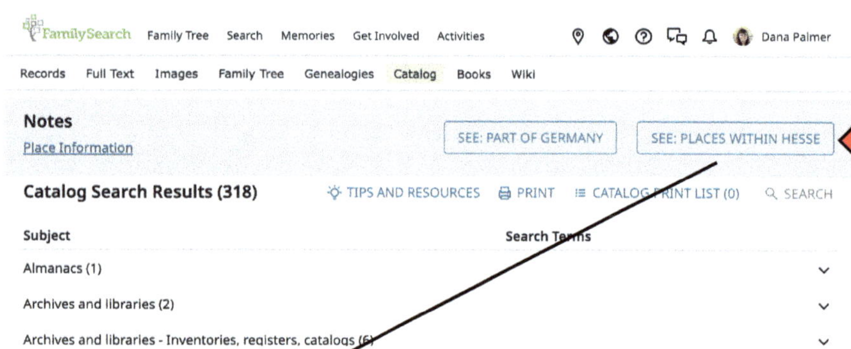

If you click on the PLACES WITHIN, you can see a list of the locations within that region. In this case, it shows the locations within Hesse that allow quick access to those records.

https://www.familysearch.org/en/search/catalog/results?count=20&q.place=Germany%2C%20Hesse

Click on the new location from the drop-down menu to see more locations within that region.

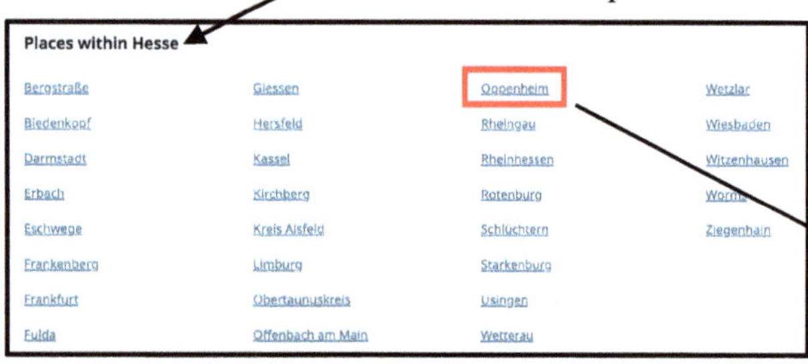

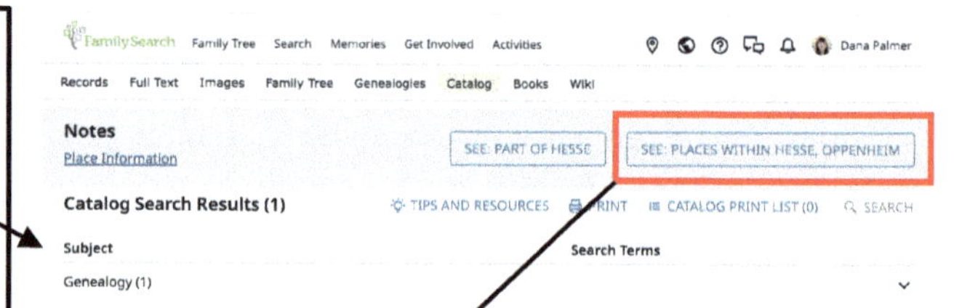

https://www.familysearch.org/en/search/catalog/results?count=20&q.place=Germany%2C%20Hesse%2C%20Oppenheim

Clicking the Oppenheim link in the image above shows the towns within it, to the right.

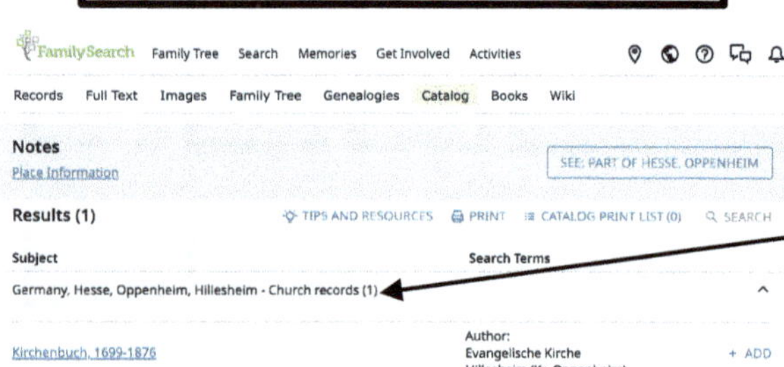

https://www.familysearch.org/en/search/catalog/results?count=20&q.place=Germany%2C%20Hesse%2C%20Oppenheim%2C%20Hillesheim

Finding Original Images of Index-Only Collections

Many records have been indexed by FamilySearch but do not have the original images attached in the RECORDS category. These records are still invaluable since the index may provide details on where to find the original record in the CATALOG. Search by location and then the collection type to find the record collection you want. Then search the digitized microfilm until you find your entry.

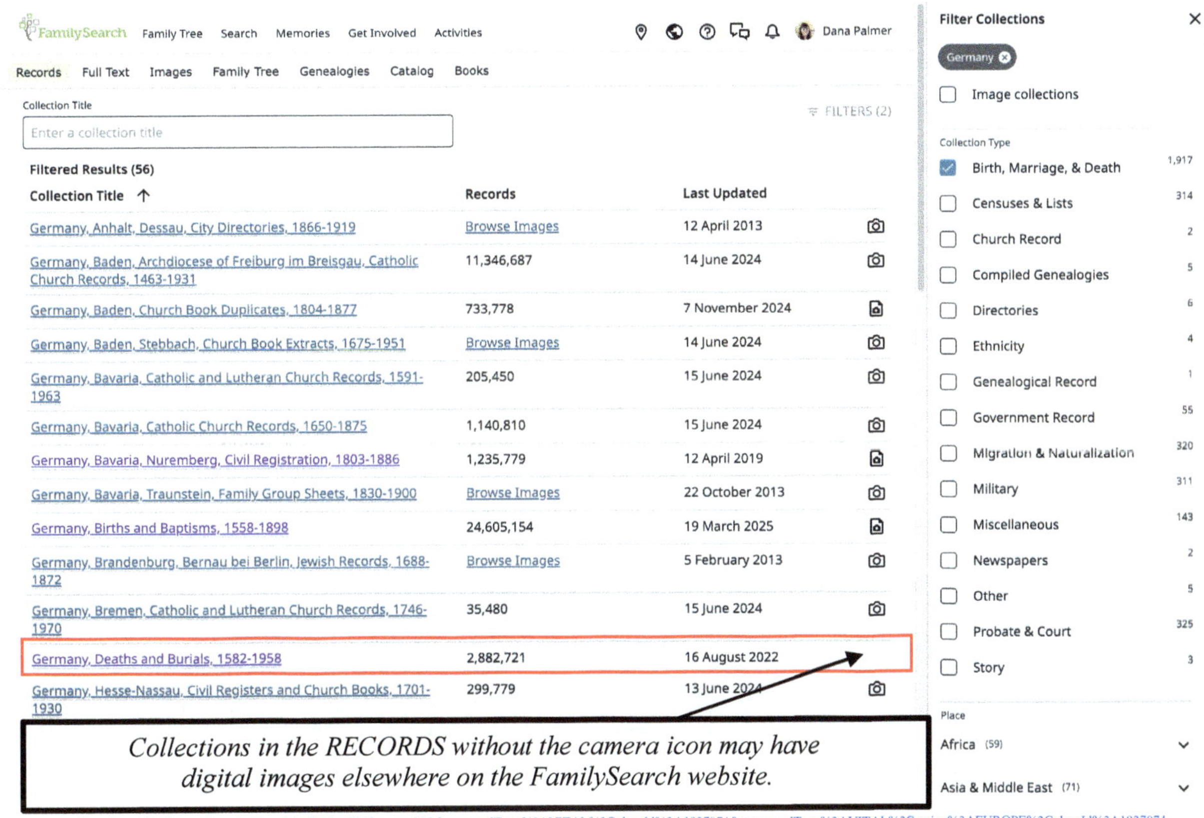

Collections in the RECORDS without the camera icon may have digital images elsewhere on the FamilySearch website.

https://www.familysearch.org/en/search/collection/list?count=20&fcs=recordType%3AVITAL%2CplaceId%3A1927074&ec=recordType%3AVITAL%2Cregion%3AEUROPE%2CplaceId%3A1927074

Even though the database camera icon does not show in the above list, the database can still be searched. Sometimes the images are on FamilySearch, but because of the agreement they have with their partner organization, they are not allowed to display all the records.

Searching these databases can still be invaluable as they often provide details on where the original was stored by FamilySearch or at the partner site.

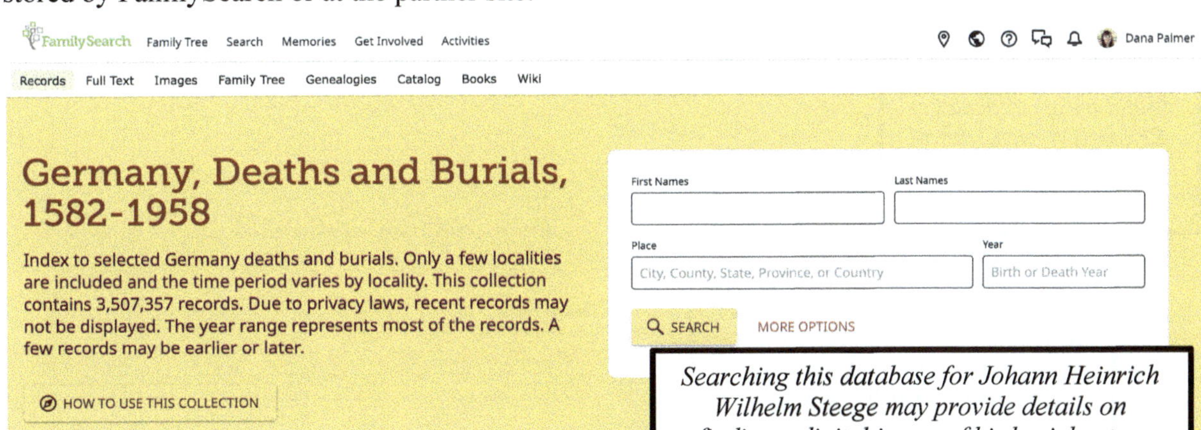

https://www.familysearch.org/search/collection/1494474

Searching this database for Johann Heinrich Wilhelm Steege may provide details on finding a digital image of his burial entry, even if it's not on this part of FamilySearch.

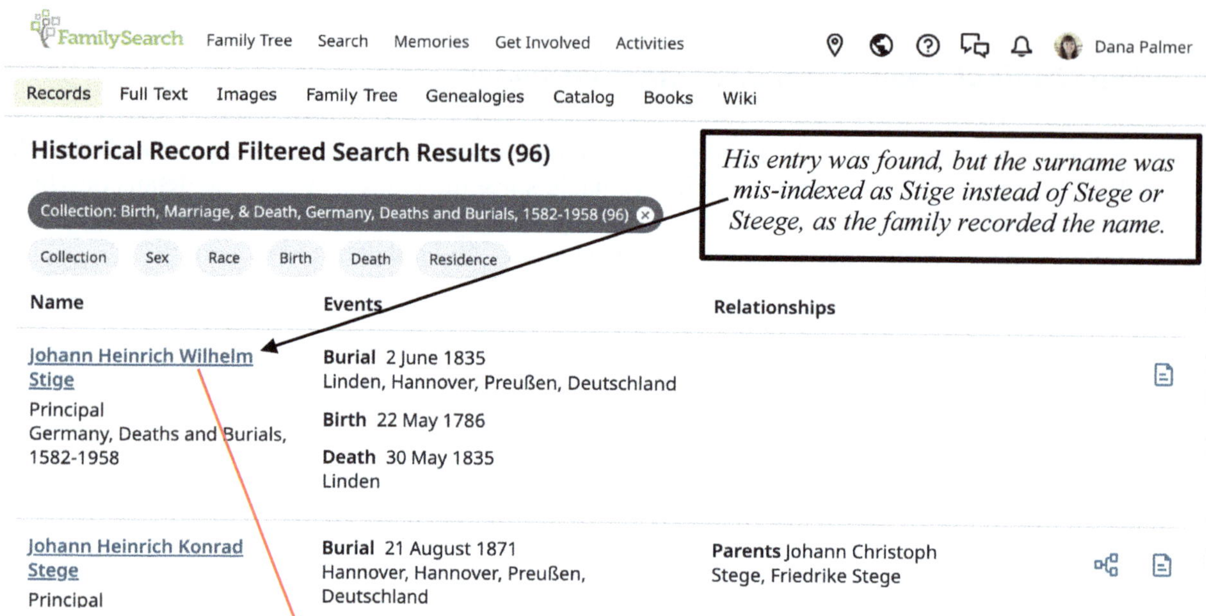

His entry was found, but the surname was mis-indexed as Stige instead of Stege or Steege, as the family recorded the name.

https://www.familysearch.org/en/search/record/results?f.collectionId=1494474&q.givenName=Johann&q.surname=Steege

Click the person's blue link to go to their record description page. The record details page often provides information on where to find the original record in the microfilm or digital folder collections.

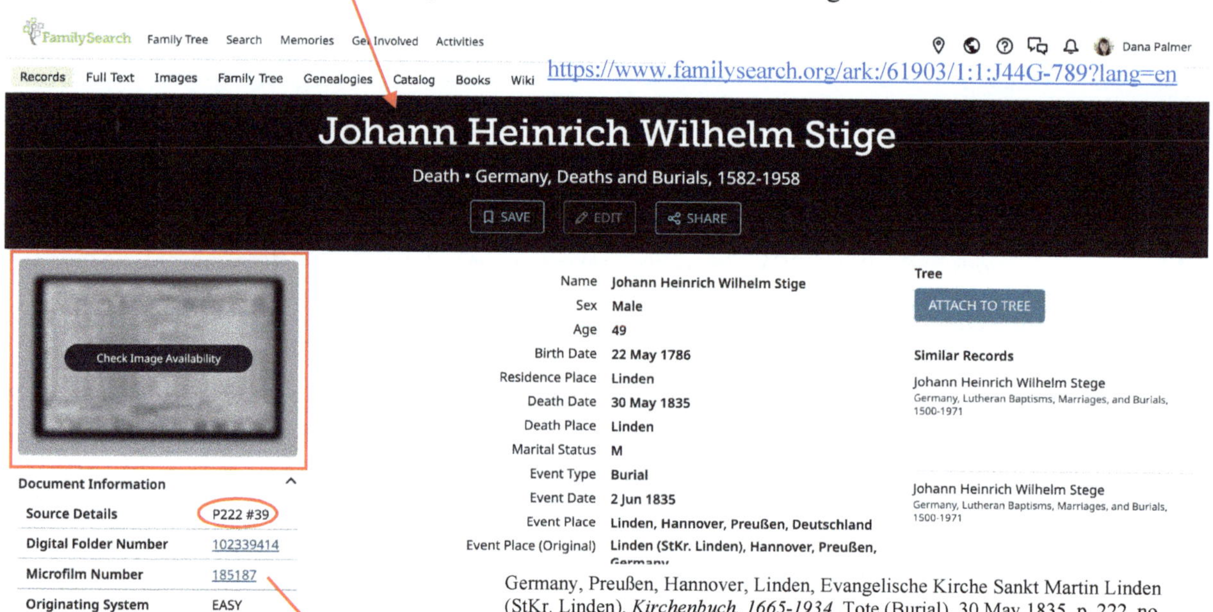

Germany, Preußen, Hannover, Linden, Evangelische Kirche Sankt Martin Linden (StKr. Linden), *Kirchenbuch, 1665-1934*, Tote (Burial), 30 May 1835, p. 222, no. 39, Johann Heinrich Wilhelm Stege; Kirchenbuchamt Hannover, *FamilySearch* (https://www.familysearch.org/ark:/61903/1:1:J44G-789?lang=en : accessed 28 Apr 2025), FS microfilm 185,187.

For records without the digital image attached in RECORDS, write down the microfilm or digital folder number.

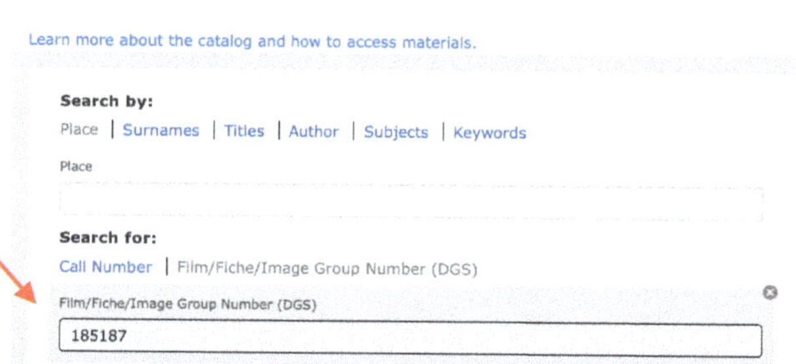

Go to the CATALOG and type the microfilm or digital folder number into the FILM/FICHE/IMAGE GROUP NUMBER (DGS) box.

https://www.familysearch.org/en/search/catalog

Click on the blue link for the collection that relates to the microfilm you typed in.

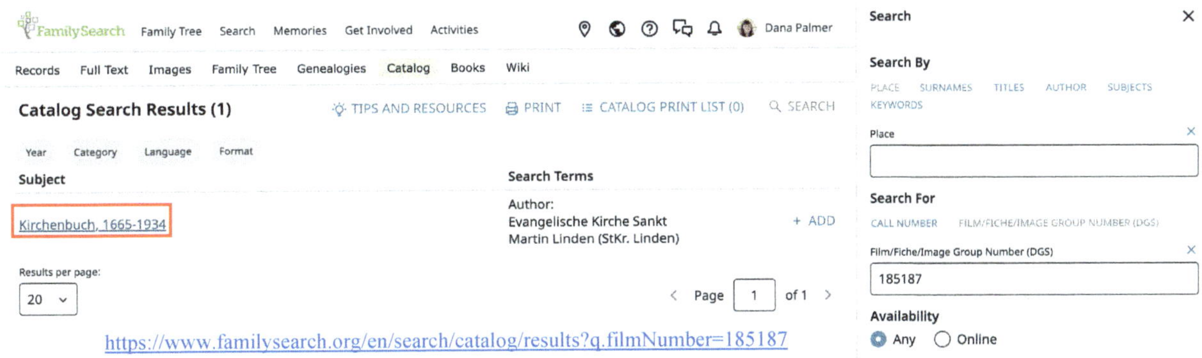

On the description page, scroll down to the section with the film details and choose the collection with the matching microfilm. Click on the camera icon.

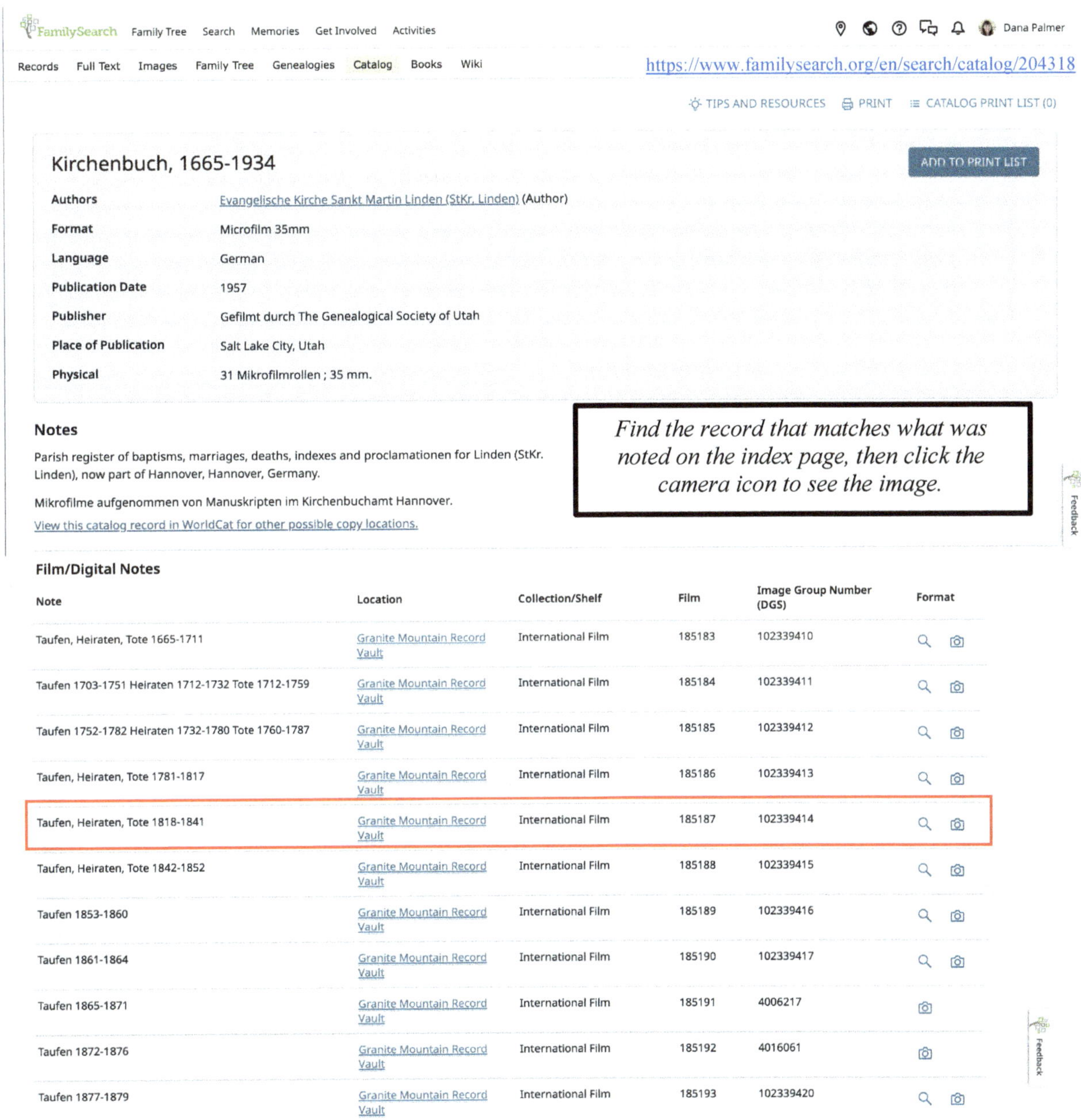

Note	Location	Collection/Shelf	Film	Image Group Number (DGS)	Format
Taufen, Heiraten, Tote 1665-1711	Granite Mountain Record Vault	International Film	185183	102339410	
Taufen 1703-1751 Heiraten 1712-1732 Tote 1712-1759	Granite Mountain Record Vault	International Film	185184	102339411	
Taufen 1752-1782 Heiraten 1732-1780 Tote 1760-1787	Granite Mountain Record Vault	International Film	185185	102339412	
Taufen, Heiraten, Tote 1781-1817	Granite Mountain Record Vault	International Film	185186	102339413	
Taufen, Heiraten, Tote 1818-1841	Granite Mountain Record Vault	International Film	185187	102339414	
Taufen, Heiraten, Tote 1842-1852	Granite Mountain Record Vault	International Film	185188	102339415	
Taufen 1853-1860	Granite Mountain Record Vault	International Film	185189	102339416	
Taufen 1861-1864	Granite Mountain Record Vault	International Film	185190	102339417	
Taufen 1865-1871	Granite Mountain Record Vault	International Film	185191	4006217	
Taufen 1872-1876	Granite Mountain Record Vault	International Film	185192	4016061	
Taufen 1877-1879	Granite Mountain Record Vault	International Film	185193	102339420	

Search through the microfilm until you find your entry.

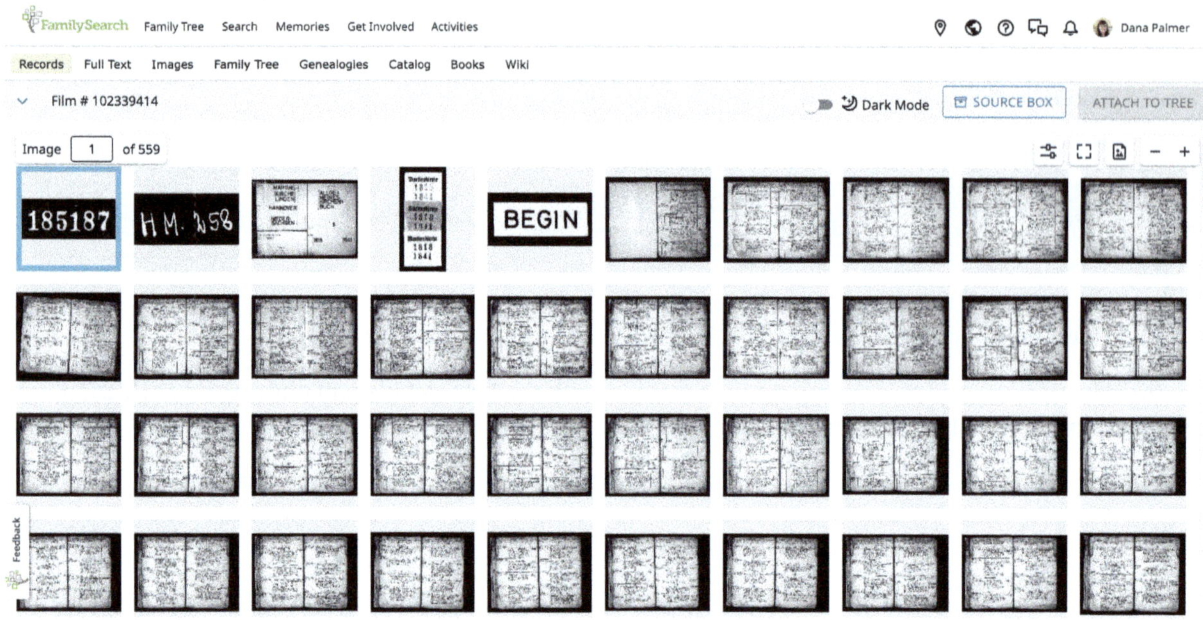

https://www.familysearch.org/en/search/film/102339414?cat=204318&i=0

If the page was noted in the index, double click on the image to zoom into the specific page and then search until you find the matching reference. If the page was not specified in the index, you will need to search each page until you find the entry.

If you need help reading the handwriting, go to the FamilySearch Research Wiki.

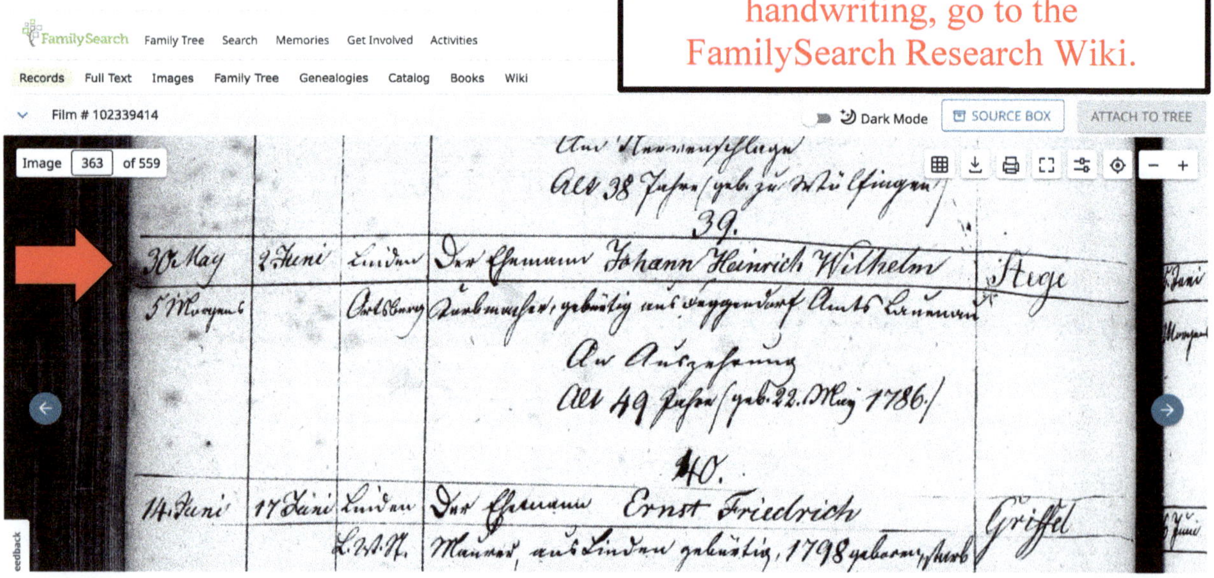

Germany, Preußen, Hannover, Linden, Evangelische Kirche Sankt Martin Linden (StKr. Linden), *Kirchenbuch, 1665-1934*, Tote (Burial), 30 May 1835, p. 222, no. 39, Johann Heinrich Wilhelm Stege; Kirchenbuchamt Hannover, *FamilySearch* (https://www.familysearch.org/en/search/film/102339414?cat=204318&i=362 : accessed 28 Apr 2025), FS microfilm 185,187.

Finding Original Images of Indexed Records without an Image Attached

Searching for original records found in indexes in RECORDS, or attached sources in the TREE, works the same whether it is for an international record or a United States one. Below is an example found from a source in the TREE that did not have the original image attached to it.

https://www.familysearch.org/ark:/61903/1:1:X8JF-LM4?lang=en

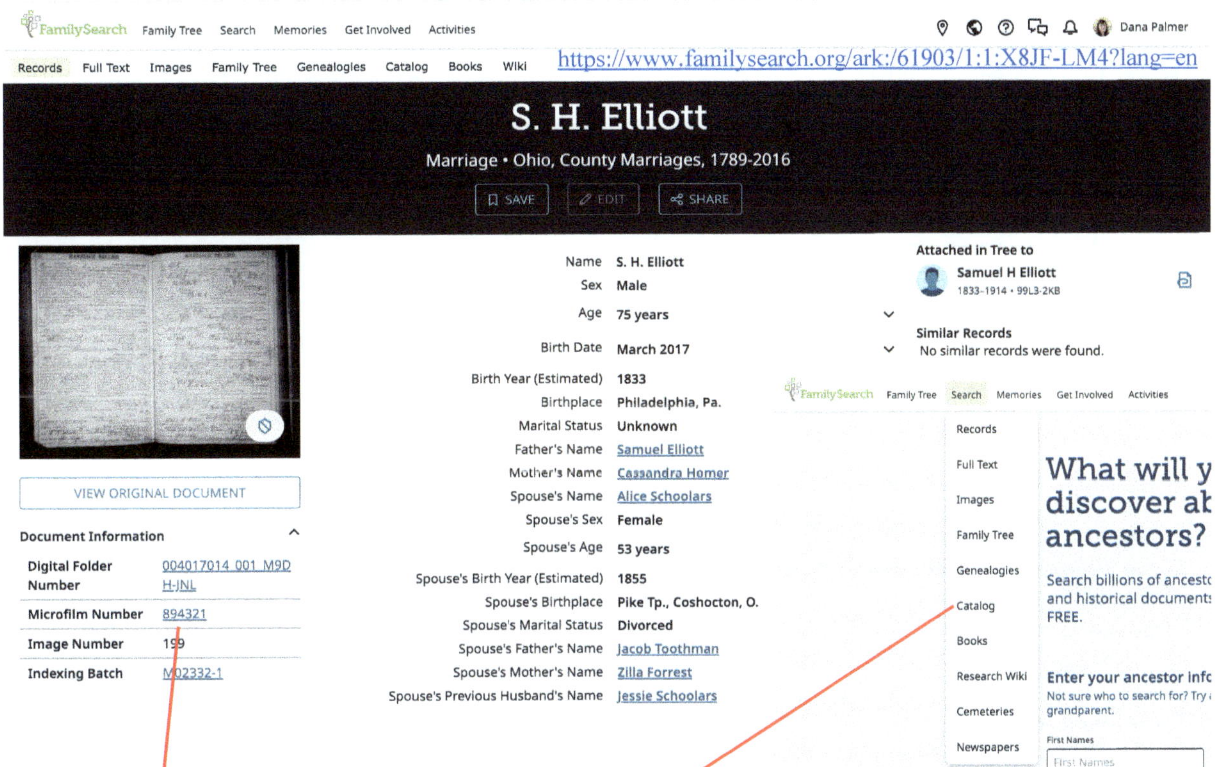

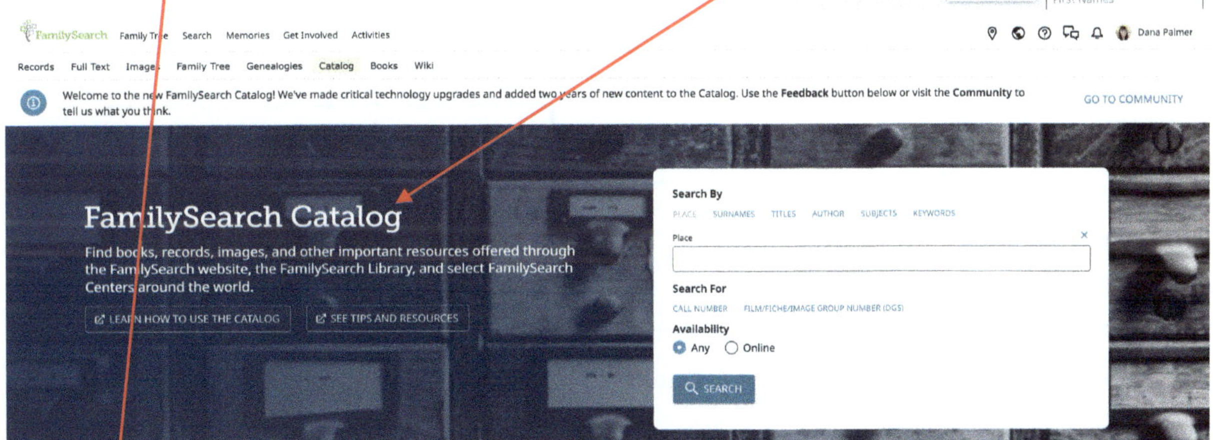

https://www.familysearch.org/en/search/catalog

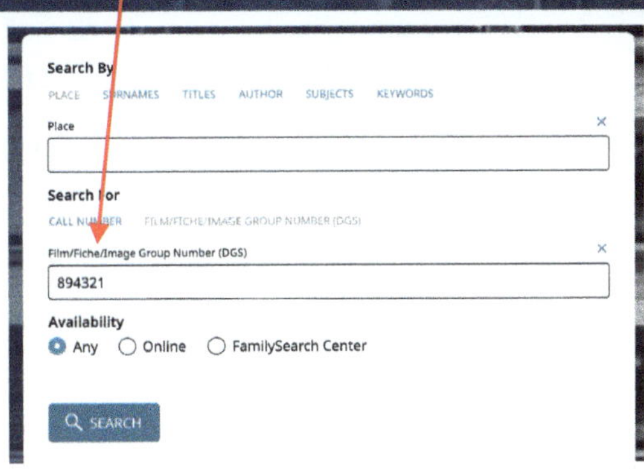

Type the microfilm / microfiche / or digital image number into the box and click SEARCH. This will take you precisely to that collection.

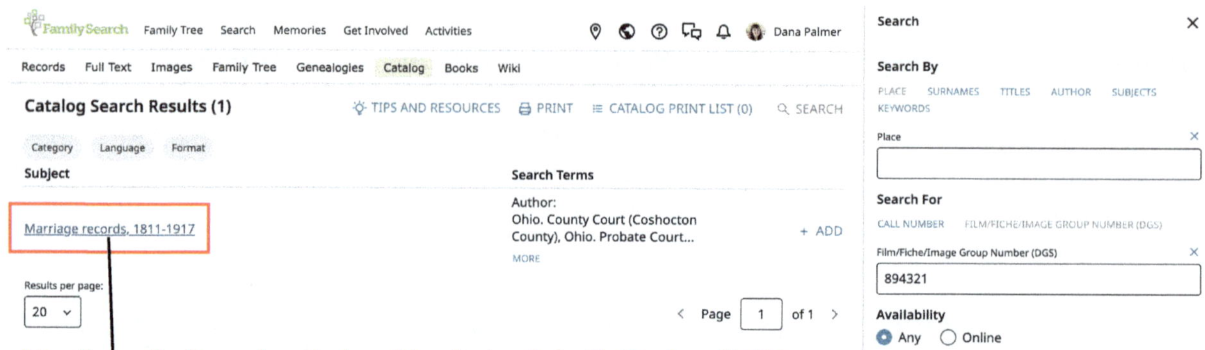

https://www.familysearch.org/en/search/catalog/results?q.filmNumber=894321

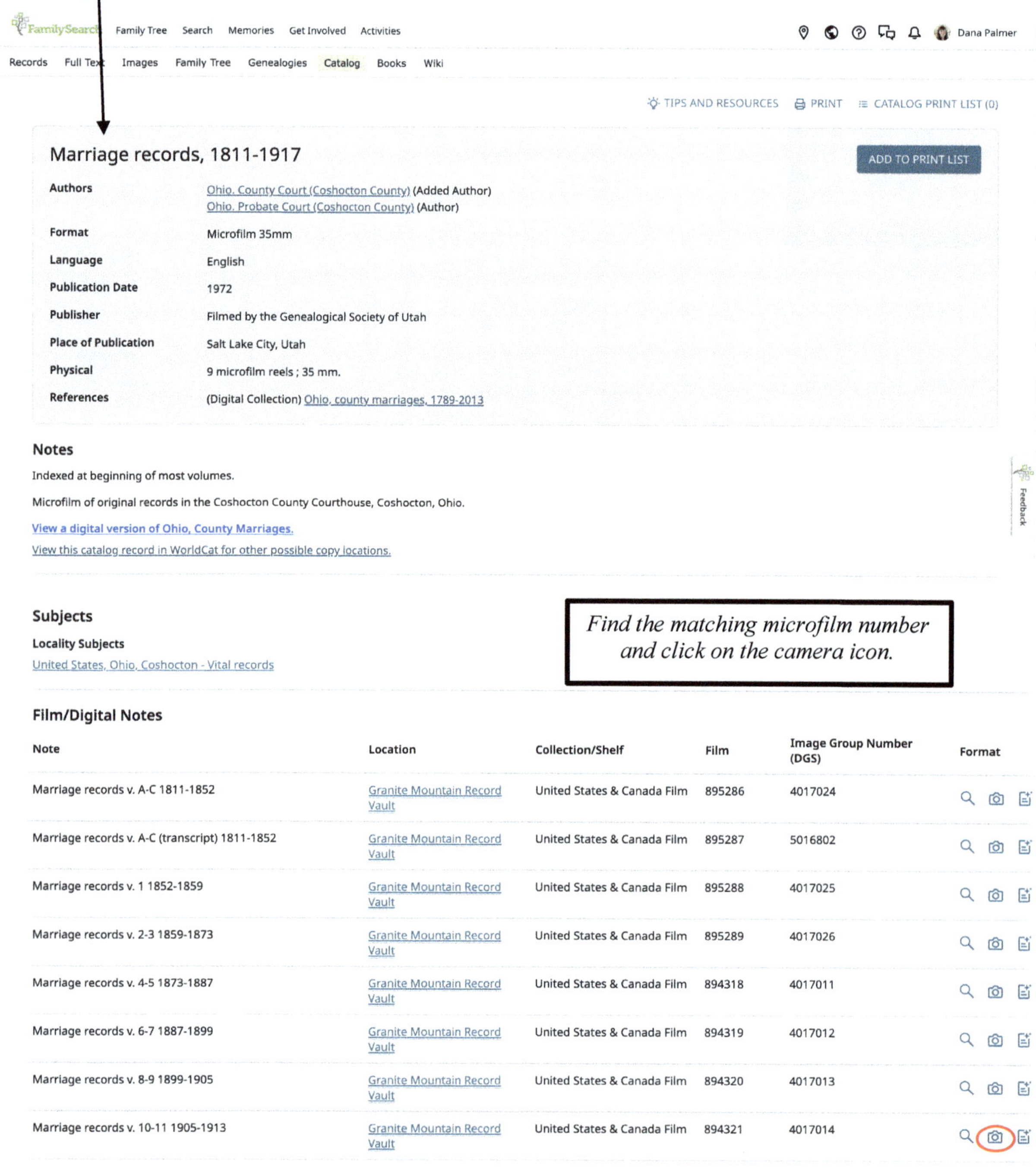

Find the matching microfilm number and click on the camera icon.

https://www.familysearch.org/en/search/catalog/84799

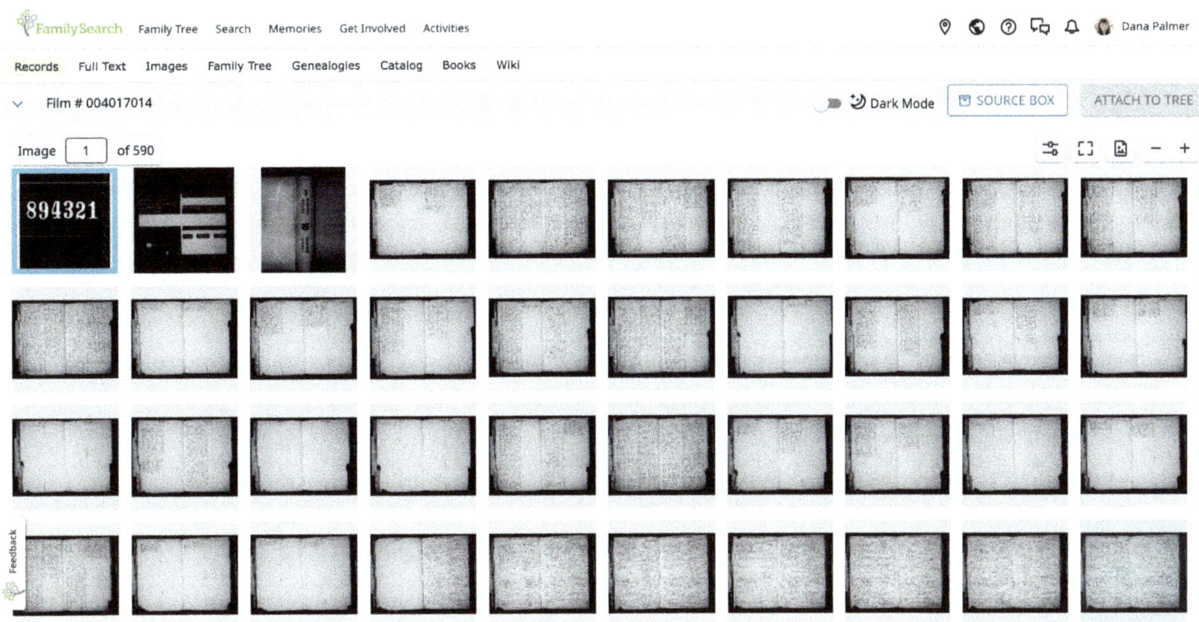

https://www.familysearch.org/en/search/film/004017014?cat=84799&i=0

This collection has an index at the start of it, like many others. If there is an index, consult it first to find your person, so you can navigate and find the original entry more quickly. This is especially important if the handwriting is hard to read or misspelled.

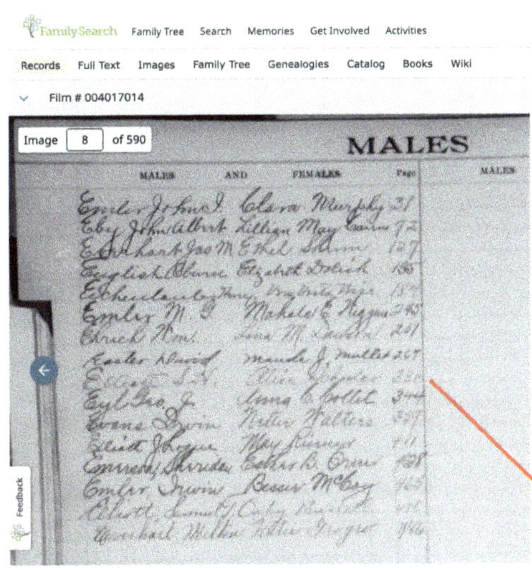

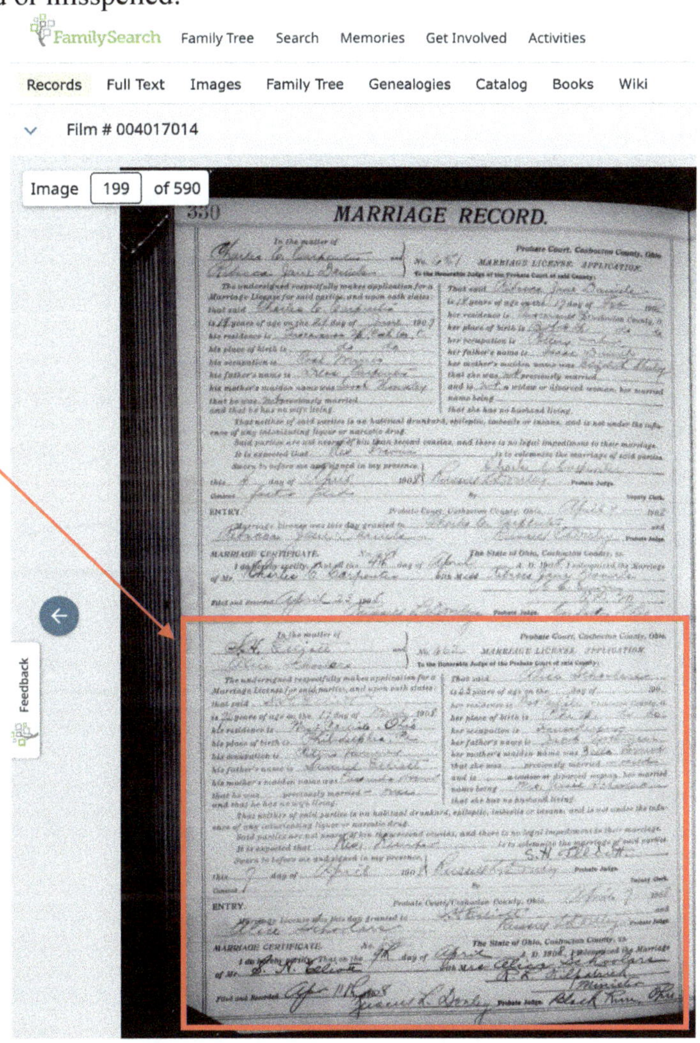

Once the groom's name was found in the males (grooms) marriage index, and page noted, the record was found on that specified page.

Microfilm / Batch / Digital Folder Searches

Microfilm or batch searches allow you to find all the given names or surnames in a specific indexed batch of records or microfilm. This saves a lot of time because this type of search allows the user to find all the surnames on that microfilm or batch very quickly. Click on microfilm/microfiche/image group number or icon.

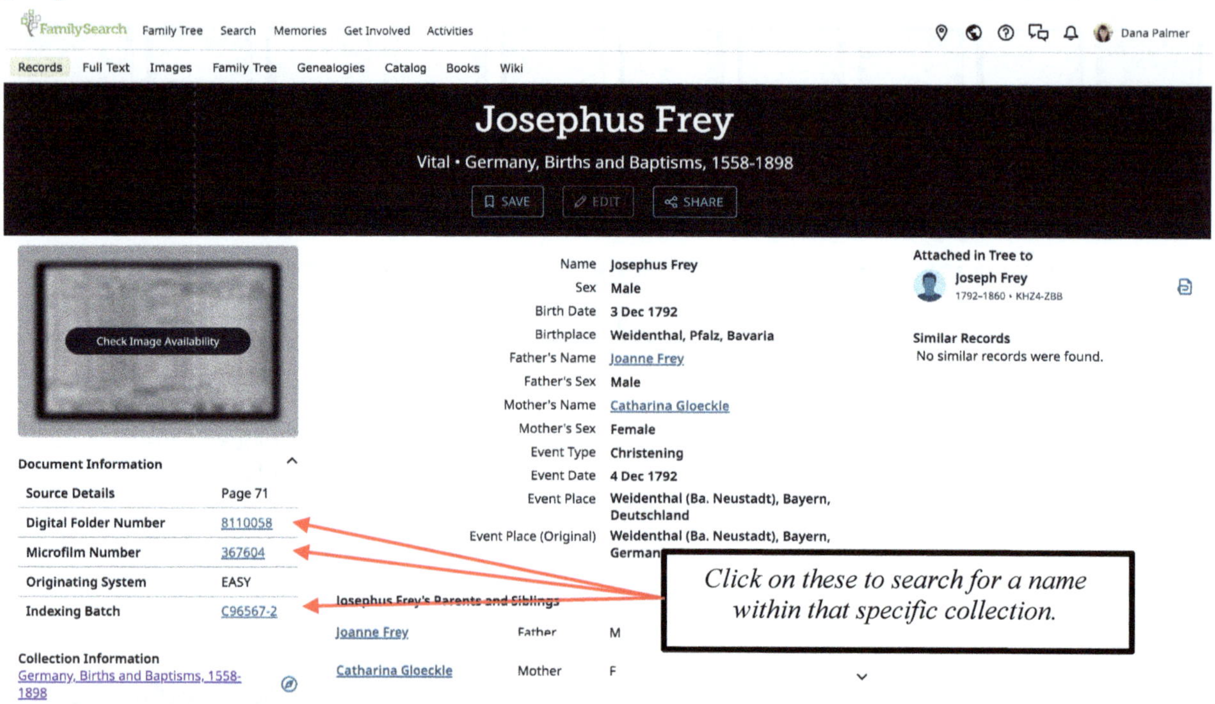

"Deutschland Geburten und Taufen, 1558-1898," database, FamilySearch (https://www.familysearch.org/ark:/61903/1:1:NCBQ-R7Q?lang=en : accessed 2 May 2025), Josephus Frey, born 3 Dec 1792, Weidenthal; citing FS microfilm 367,604.

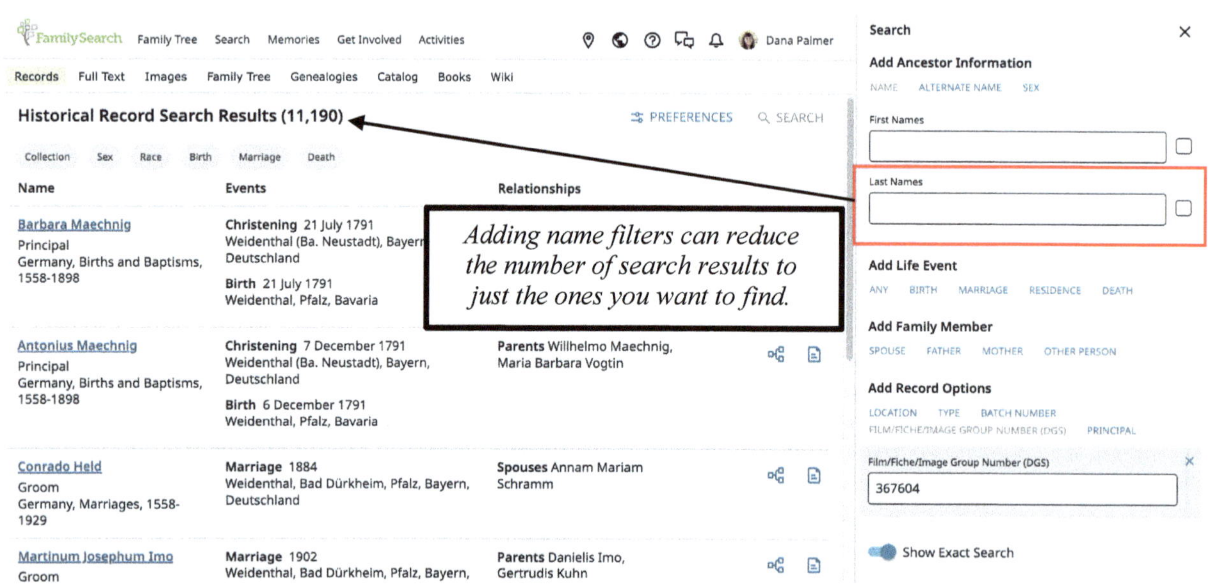

https://www.familysearch.org/en/search/record/results?q.filmNumber=367604

Type the name in the given name, surname field, or both. This should reduce the number of search results you get. Add more filters as needed to reduce the search results. If you are having trouble finding your person, use wildcards. (An asterisk can replace multiple letters and a question mark can be used for single letter replacements. See chapter 3, trick 3, starting on page 73 for more wildcard tricks.)

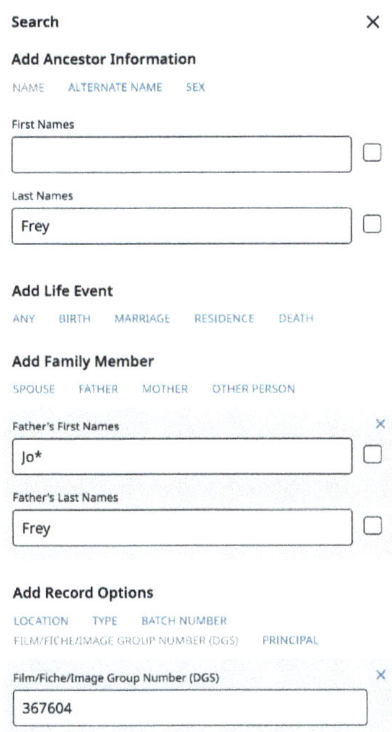

Click on the blue name link to see more information about that person.

You will get a list of people that match your search parameters. Write down the matches and group the family members together with relevant information into an excel spreadsheet. Note if the index page provides the microfilm with the page and entry number for that person.

If the original image is not attached to the transcription page for that person, write down the microfilm/microfiche/image group number and go to the CATALOG. Type in the number in the microfilm / digital image search field. Click on the appropriate record collection and scroll down to the film / digital notes section describing the collection. Find the matching number and click on the camera icon to go directly to the record. Find the entry that matches what you found in the index.

Using a wildcard for parents' names can greatly narrow the search parameters and make it easier to find other family members when you go back and search the original records.

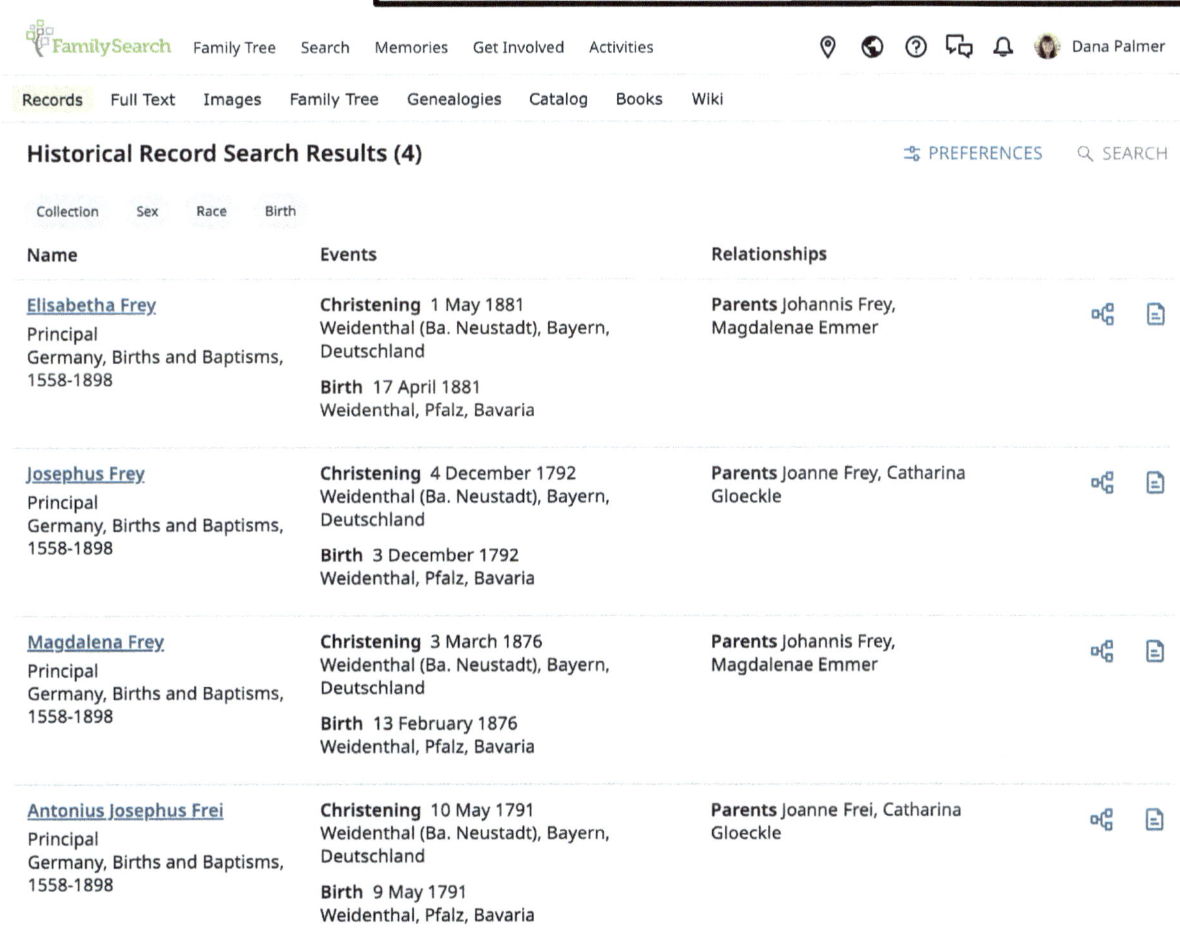

https://www.familysearch.org/en/search/record/results?count=20&q.fatherGivenName=Jo%2A&q.fatherSurname=Frey&q.filmNumber=367604&q.surname=Frey

Unindexed Records

Unindexed records in the RECORDS category under the SEARCH tab are generally listed as BROWSE IMAGES, instead of indicating how many records are in the collection. These have not been indexed in RECORDS yet, but you may find the same records in the FULL-TEXT SEARCH. Unindexed records in the CATALOG will not have a magnifying glass next to the camera icon. These too will need to be searched page by page until you find your entry, if you didn't find it in FULL-TEXT SEARCH. These are the same records you will find if you visit the local repository. Remember to also attach the record to the applicable person in the tree.

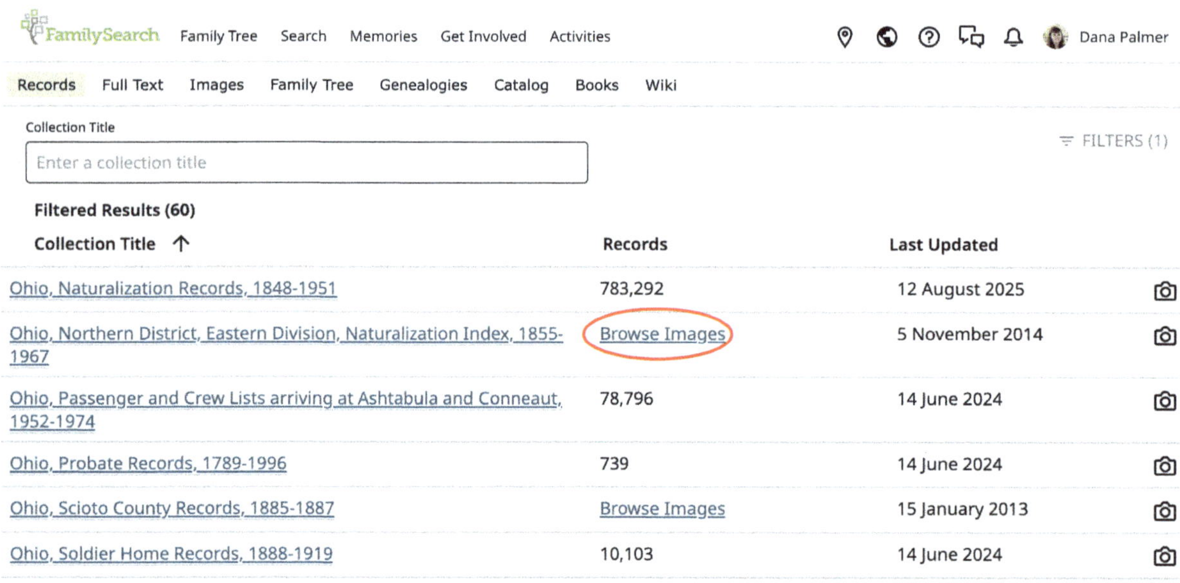

https://www.familysearch.org/en/search/collection/list?count=20&ec=region%3AUNITED_STATES%2CplaceId%3A43&fcs=placeId%3A43

Those who only use the main search box under the SEARCH tab instead of BROWSE ALL COLLECTIONS would miss out on records in the BROWSE IMAGES collection that are not indexed. To view these records, click RECORDS under the SEARCH tab, then BROWSE ALL COLLECTIONS. Narrow the results by choosing filters to the side. Click on the applicable database you want to search.

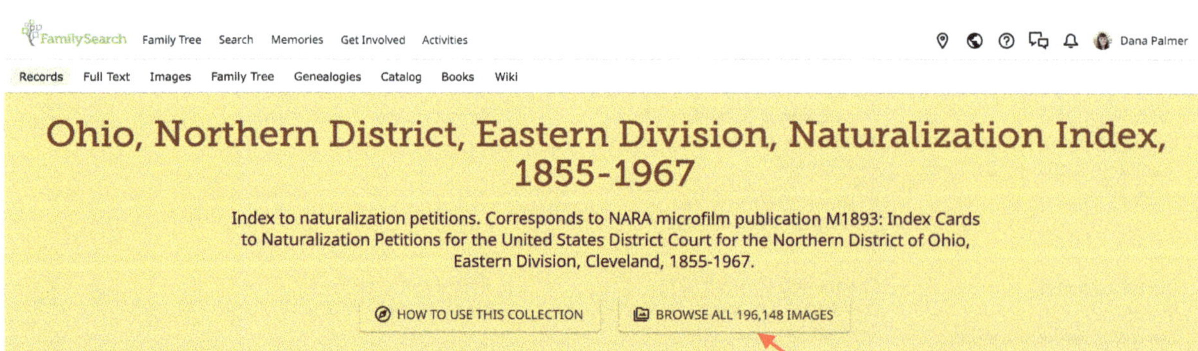

https://www.familysearch.org/en/search/collection/2110746

For this unindexed record collection, click on
BROWSE ALL 196,148 IMAGES
to see what records are contained in it.

Choose the location or topic you want to search for this collection.

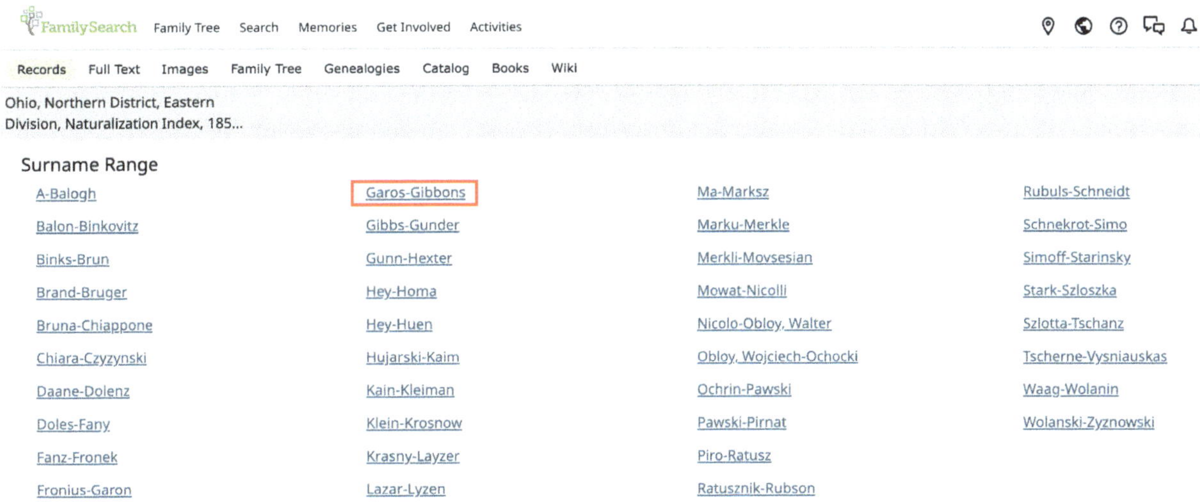

https://www.familysearch.org/en/search/image/index?owc=https://www.familysearch.org/service/cds/recapi/collections/2110746/waypoints

Choose the desired record collection.

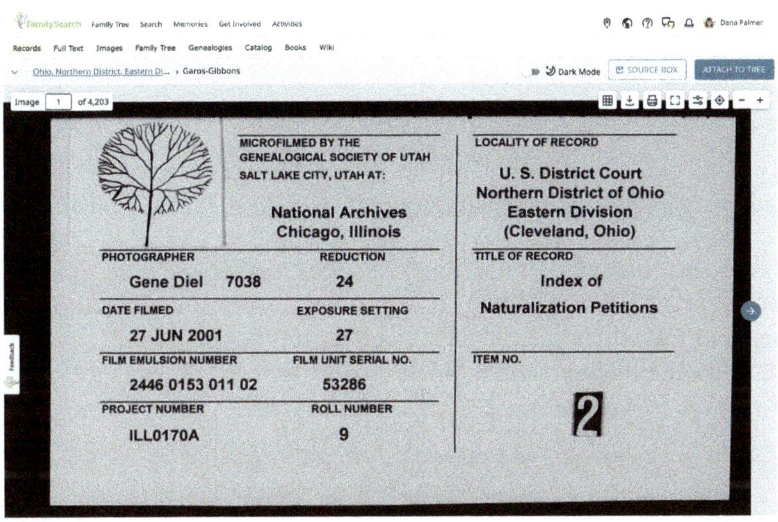

This is the first page of the digital images. To find your person, you'll need to scroll through the images until you find them.

https://www.familysearch.org/ark:/61903/3:1:3QS7-99HV-NVPC?wc=SJHF-VZS%3A361710101%26cc%3D2110746&cc=2110746&lang=en&i=0

Navigate by clicking the side arrows, typing a different number in the Image box, or by clicking the grid icon and then choosing a different image and then double clicking.

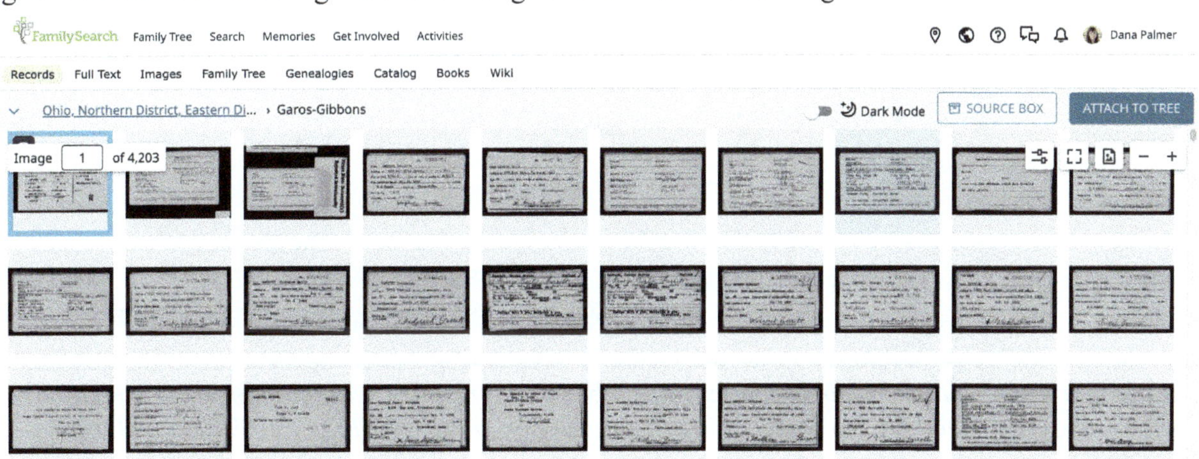

https://www.familysearch.org/ark:/61903/3:1:3QS7-99HV-NVPC?wc=SJHF-VZS%3A361710101%26cc%3D2110746&cc=2110746&lang=en&i=0&mode=g

Partially Indexed Records

Some collections in RECORDS are not fully indexed. It can be hard to tell the actual dates and locations included in the indexed records from just glancing at the name of the collection. Most collections have an ABOUT THIS COLLECTION page that describes what is included in the set. Be sure to check this out.

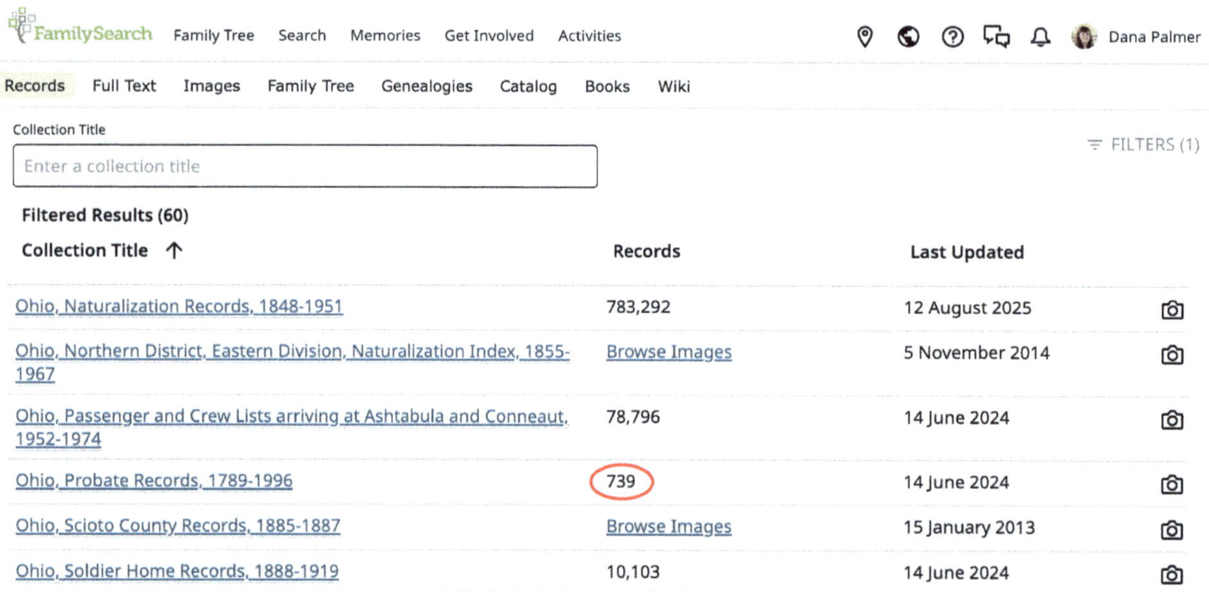

Collection Title	Records	Last Updated
Ohio, Naturalization Records, 1848-1951	783,292	12 August 2025
Ohio, Northern District, Eastern Division, Naturalization Index, 1855-1967	Browse Images	5 November 2014
Ohio, Passenger and Crew Lists arriving at Ashtabula and Conneaut, 1952-1974	78,796	14 June 2024
Ohio, Probate Records, 1789-1996	739	14 June 2024
Ohio, Scioto County Records, 1885-1887	Browse Images	15 January 2013
Ohio, Soldier Home Records, 1888-1919	10,103	14 June 2024

https://www.familysearch.org/en/search/collection/list?count=20&ec=region%3AUNITED_STATES%2CplaceId%3A43&fcs=placeId%3A43

RECORDS notes that the Ohio Probate Record collection here only has **739 people indexed**, making it seem like a very small database, but this is very misleading. If you click on the actual database, it notes there are **almost 7 million images** in the collection. This is a collection that is probably part of FULL-TEXT SEARCH, and you would likely find them much quicker using that search strategy rather than searching page by page for your person.

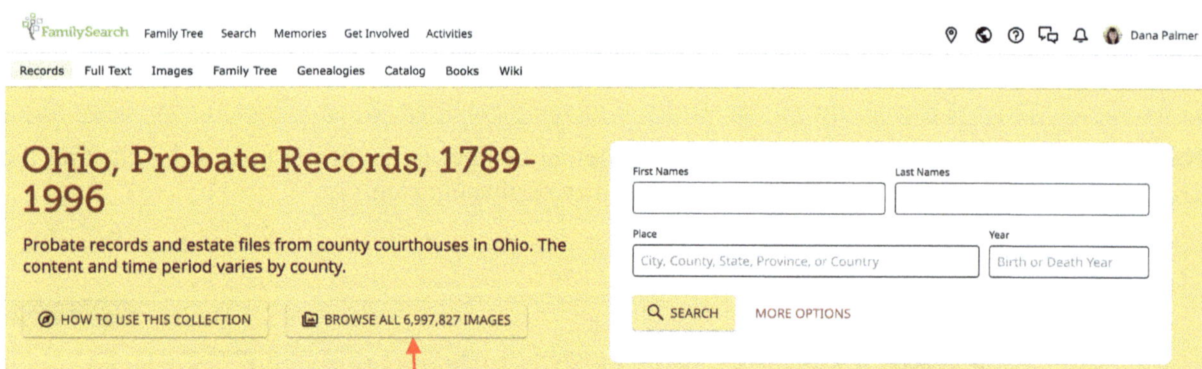

https://www.familysearch.org/en/search/collection/1992421

If you can't find your person by using the search box and filters, try searching for them directly by browsing the collections. To search this collection, click on BROWSE ALL 6,997,827 IMAGES.

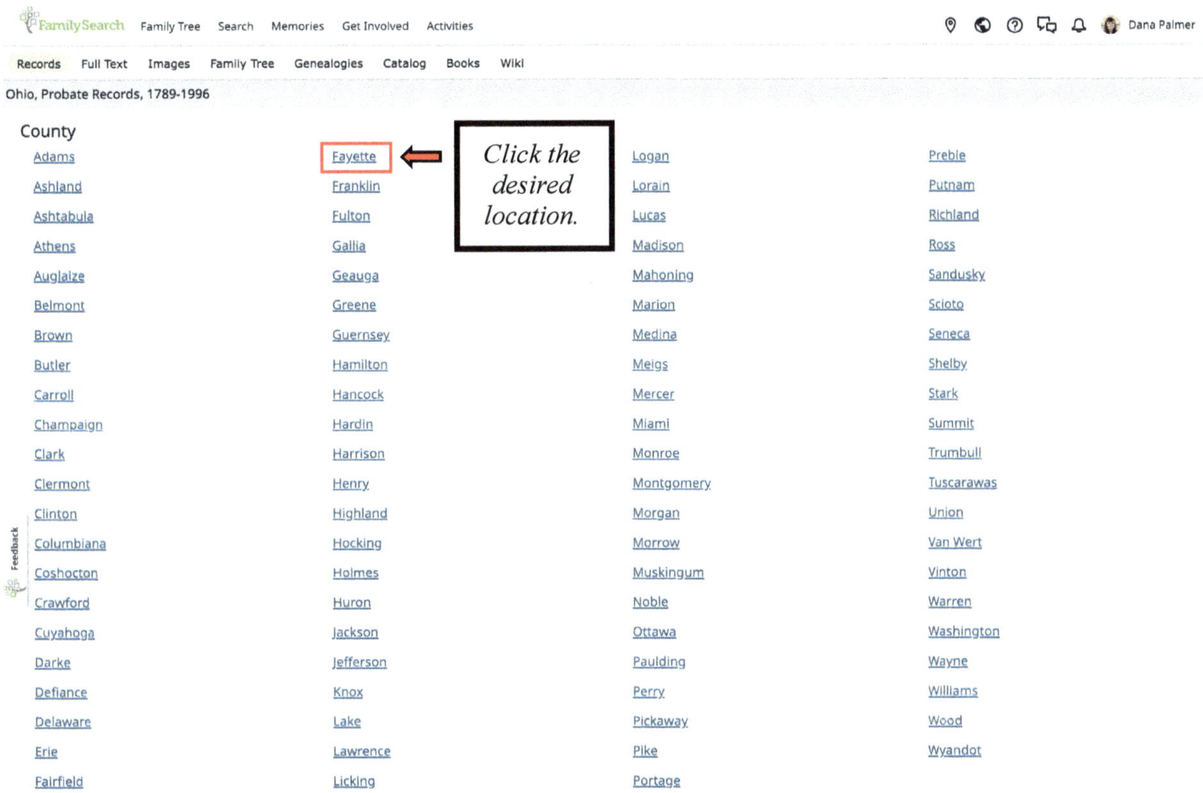

https://www.familysearch.org/en/search/image/index?owc=https://www.familysearch.org/service/cds/recapi/collections/1992421/waypoints

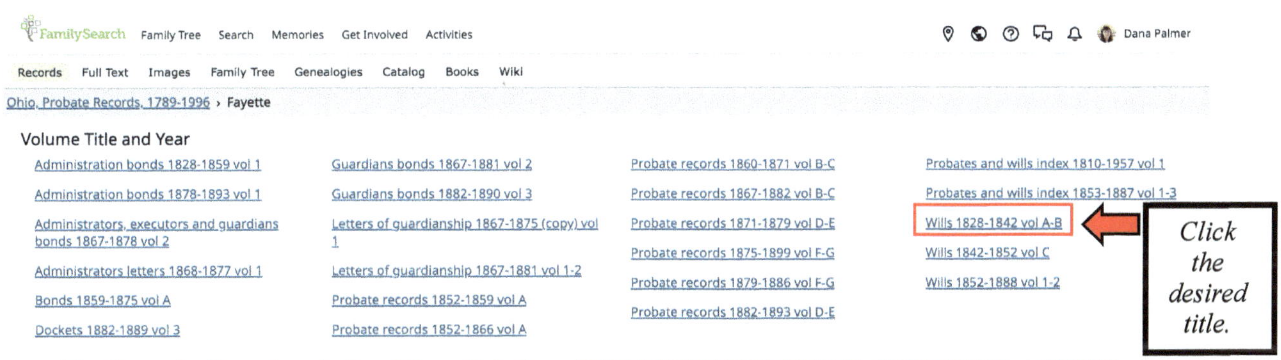

https://www.familysearch.org/en/search/image/index?owc=S24W-N3N%3A266276701%3Fcc%3D1992421&cc=1992421

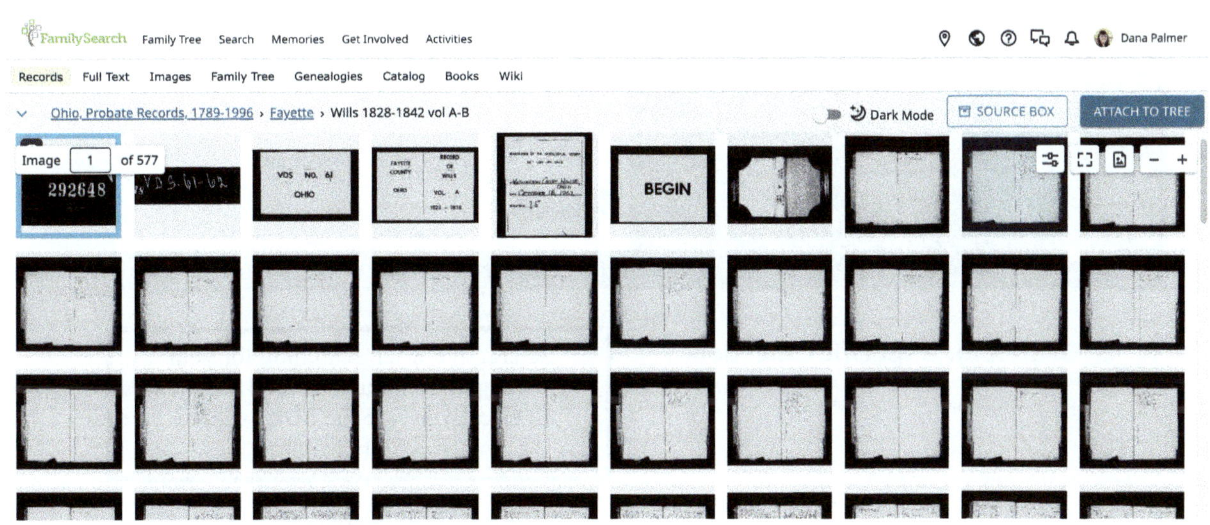

https://www.familysearch.org/ark:/61903/3:1:3QS7-L9MK-G9M6-C?wc=S24W-N3J%3A266276701%2C266421201%26cc%3D1992421&cc=1992421&lang=en&i=0&mode=g

FULL-TEXT SEARCH

FULL-TEXT SEARCH is one of FamilySearch's newest features on their SEARCH dropdown menu. Users can search for names or words in records (https://www.familysearch.org/search/full-text). In this type of search, all names, locations, dates, or keywords that are included in the search fields appear in the search results. This is helpful to find parents, neighbors, witnesses, or others who appear in the document of the primary person and those who are not generally indexed. Many of the included records are from deeds, court records, and vital records in the United States.

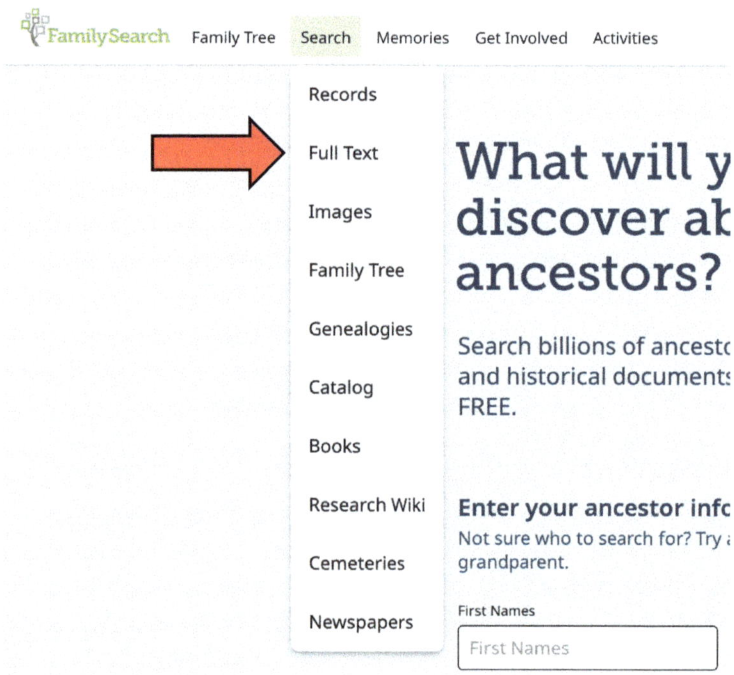

Click on SEARCH and then choose FULL-TEXT to use this feature.

To narrow search results, try various search tricks, including using exact search words or phrases, names with keywords or names and keywords that exclude words or phrases, along with locations and dates.

For a more focused search, include the IMAGE GROUP NUMBER (DGS) as well as the name or keywords.

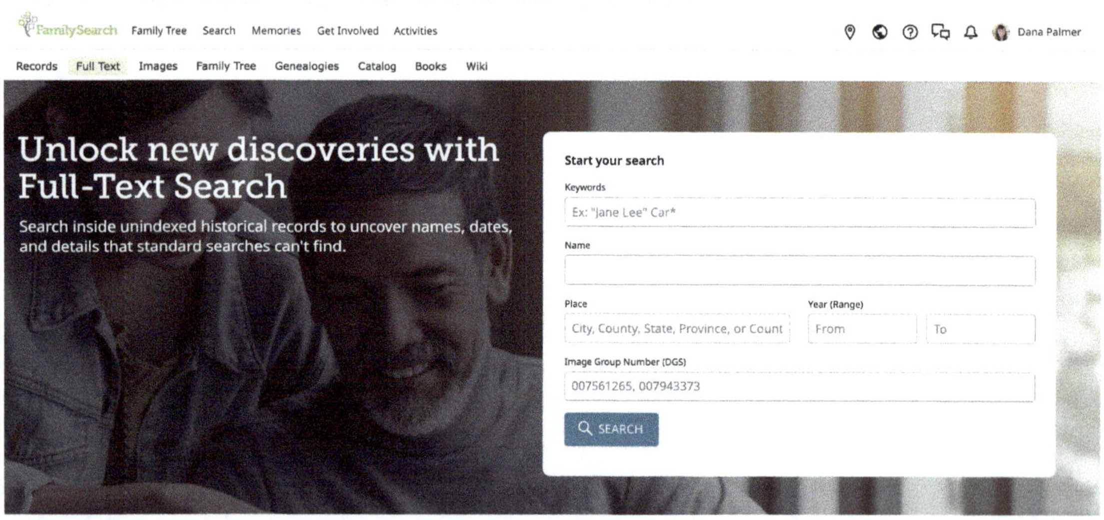

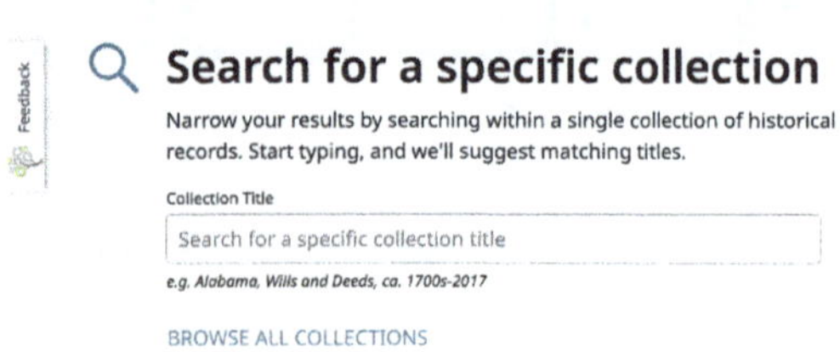

Be creative when searching for your person and check out chapter 4 for tricks to effectively use the FULL-TEXT SEARCH feature.

https://www.familysearch.org/search/full-text

RESEARCH WIKI

FamilySearch's RESEARCH WIKI (https://www.familysearch.org/en/wiki/Main_Page) is a free website resource database similar to Wikipedia, but its focus is on genealogy research and sources. It can be searched by key word for specific articles or by browsing topics or locations. Many articles and how-to instructions about family history can be found or posted on this site.

The page can be displayed in several languages for people who are from countries other than the United States. The page layout is similar throughout all countries and often has details on the history of the location, tools for getting started with research, a button with links to online collections, and a map showing the jurisdictions. There is often a link to pages about specific research topics and other tools.

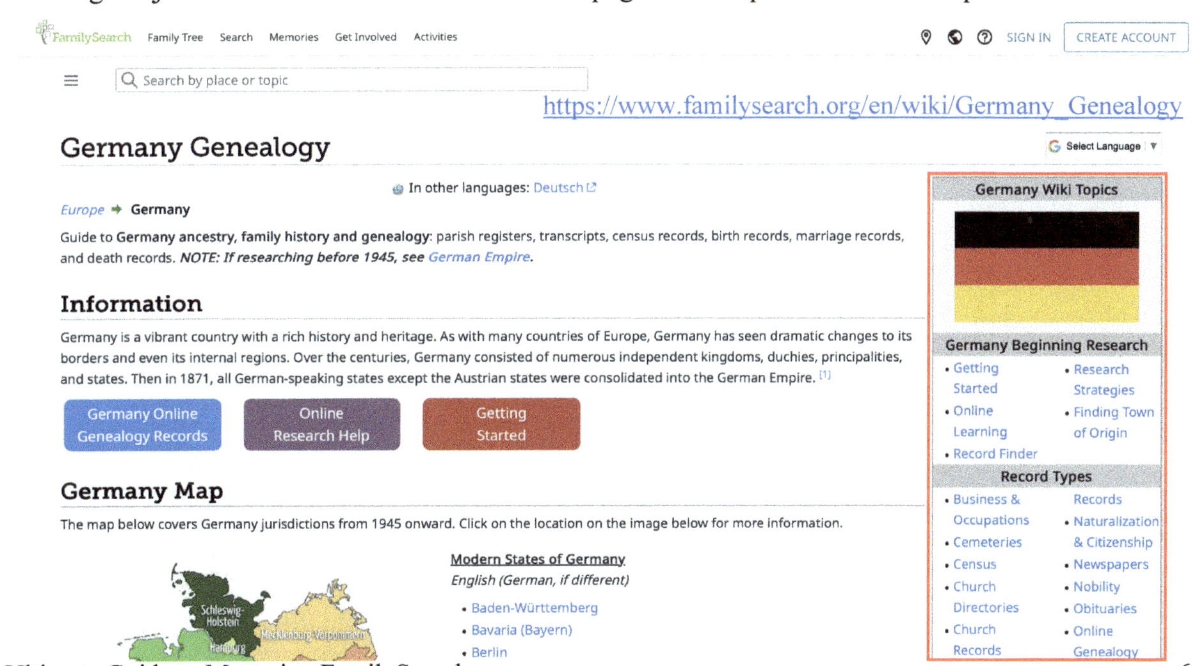

External website links to databases and other records can often be found using the RESEARCH WIKI for a specific locality. Here's an example from the German handwriting wiki page if you are looking for handwriting helps.

FamilySearch Family Tree Search Memories Get Involved Activities SIGN IN CREATE ACCOUNT

Search by place or topic

Germany Handwriting

Select Language

Contents [hide]

Beginning
- Handwriting Examples and Tools
  - Script Generator Tool
  - Transkribus
- Downloadable Handouts
  - Tutorials and Classes
- German Word Lists
- Books

In other languages: Deutsch

Germany ➜ Handwriting

Handwriting Examples and Tools

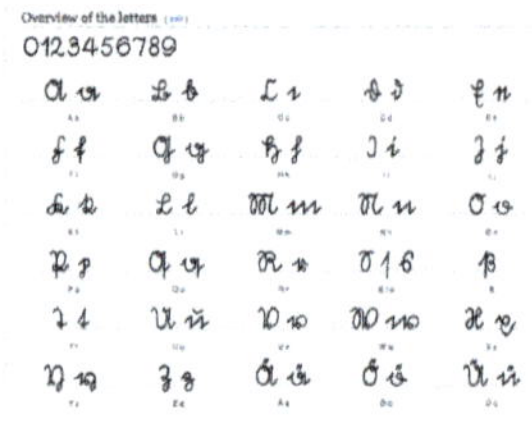

Germany Wiki Topics

Germany Beginning Research
- Getting Started
- Research Strategies
- Online Learning
- Finding Town of Origin
- Record Finder

Record Types
- Business & Records

Old German gothic handwriting and print are very different from the Roman script most English- speaking genealogists use.

- For examples of old German Gothic handwriting see the PDF file Handwriting Guide: German Gothic.
- A short handy reference guide with an alphabet, reading tips, and record samples is found here.
- A list of given names with handwritten examples from records is found here: German given names handwriting examples

Sütterlin or Suetterlin writing ("old German hand") is a practiced style of writing similar to earlier styles. This is a script, created by the Berlin graphic artist Ludwig Sütterlin (1865-1917), which was taught from 1915 to 1941 in German schools. It is also called the "deutsche Schrift". The website suetterlinschrift.de allows you to type any word and see what it would look like in that script. This is a very useful learning tool. This comparison page for the alphabet gives multiple examples of each letter.

Script Generator Tool [edit | edit source]

See your family names in the script of the era. Type your name o... using "alte deutsche Handschriften" website. Click on the 8 different fonts. Save the image to your computer and us...s.

- **List of Names in Old German Script** A comprehensive lis...ript, with possible variations.
- **Old German Script Transcriber (alte deutsche Handschr...** ...ipt of the era. Type your name or other word into the font generator tool. Click on the 8 different fonts. Save th...u work with old Germanic records.

Links to some of my favorite free German handwriting tools.

Transkribus [edit | edit source]

Transkribus is an artificial intelligence (AI) tool trained on historic script. Watch the instructional video on the website for details on how to use this tool for a rough transcription of documents.

Note: This tool is AI, and can regularly make mistakes. Transcriptions obtained through Transkribus should be taken with a grain of salt, and always double-checked by a handwriting expert.

https://www.familysearch.org/en/wiki/Germany_Handwriting

Many countries found in the Wiki also have free word list and language tools such as these for Germany.

Language Aids [edit | edit source]

- FamilySearch Wiki has genealogical **word lists** for:
  - German Word List
  - Danish Word List Danish is used in some records of Schleswig-Holstein.
  - French Word List French is used in some records of Alsace-Lorraine (Elsass-Lothringen).
  - Polish Genealogical Word List
  - Portuguese Genealogical Word List
- The German Word List includes symbols commonly used in German genealogical sources.
- **List of Names in Old German Script** A comprehensive list of German given names, written in old script, with possible variations.
- **Old German Script Transcriber (alte deutsche Handschriften):** See your family names in the script of the era. Type your name or other word into the font generator tool. Click between the 8 different fonts. Save the image to your computer and use it as you work with old German records.
- **Schreibübung [writing practice]** Type a name or other word into one of the blank text boxes (note: if an "s" is at the end of a syllable, type # instead in order to generate the ending "s"). Fill out one to five of the boxes with text. Click on the "umwandeln" button. Scroll down to see the word(s) written in Kurrent. To see other words in Kurrent, click on "löschen" or delete the text in a box, write something new, and click on "umwandeln" again.
- **WordMine** If the website language is not in English, click on "Language" at the top right and change it to English. (To look at a word in a language other than German, from just above the search box click on "German" and select a different language.) Check the box next to "Number of letters" underneath the search box, and change the range to fit the word you are looking for. Then click on "Select search type" from above the search box and select an option, such as "Words starting with," "Words ending in," or "Words containing." Type the letter sequence you see (from the German word you're trying to decipher) into the search box and click on the search button. Then browse through the results, which may be listed on multiple pages, to potentially locate the correct full German word.

https://www.familysearch.org/en/wiki/Germany_Languages

BOOKS

FamilySearch has collaborated with libraries worldwide to digitize their family histories, yearbooks, biographies, county histories, maps, atlases, and other useful genealogy reference books. They currently have over 500,000 books in their digital collection (https://www.familysearch.org/en/library/books/).

To find a book go to the SEARCH tab and click BOOKS from the dropdown menu. Type a surname, location, or keyword into the search box. You will then get a list of topics that relate to your search parameters. If you need to narrow your parameters, you can use exact searches, Boolean search terms, or wildcards. Use quotation marks for more exact searches such as "Tippecanoe County." Boolean searches use the capitalized words AND, NOT, and OR. Wildcards use an asterisk (*) to replace several letters and a question mark (?) to replace a single letter. (See page 73 for more wildcard search tricks.)

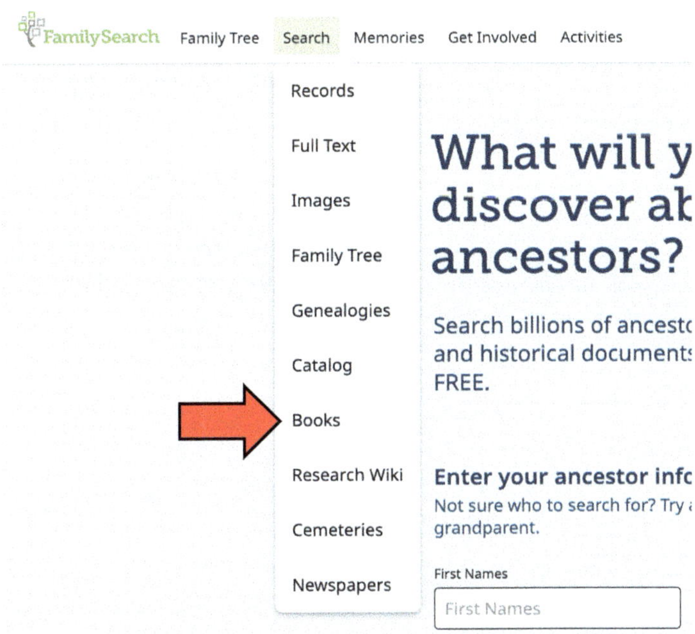

FamilySearch has over 650,000 digitized books from their own collection, and from partnering organizations all over the country, that you can access for free. Check it out!

Maybe you'll find a story or photo of your relative.

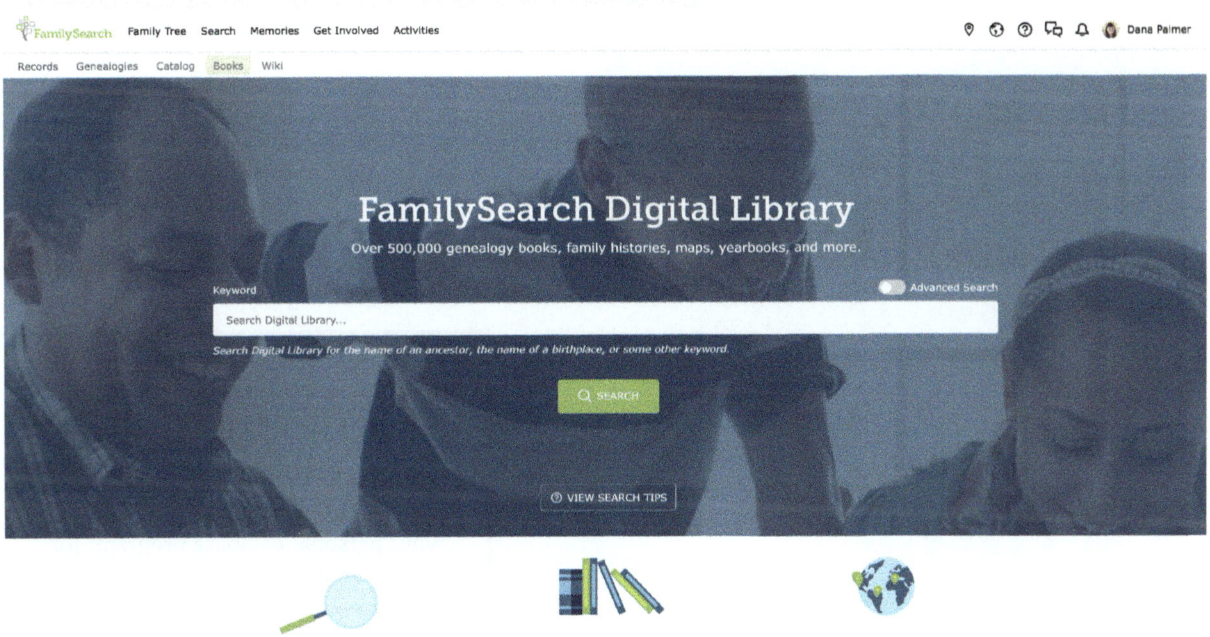

https://www.familysearch.org/en/library/books/

FAMILY TREE

Clicking on FAMILY TREE under the SEARCH dropdown menu takes you to the same place as if you clicked the FAMILY TREE icon next to the SEARCH icon, then selected FIND. This is a fast way to find people in the TREE (https://www.familysearch.org/en/search/tree/name?from=search/). You can find people by their name or by their ID.

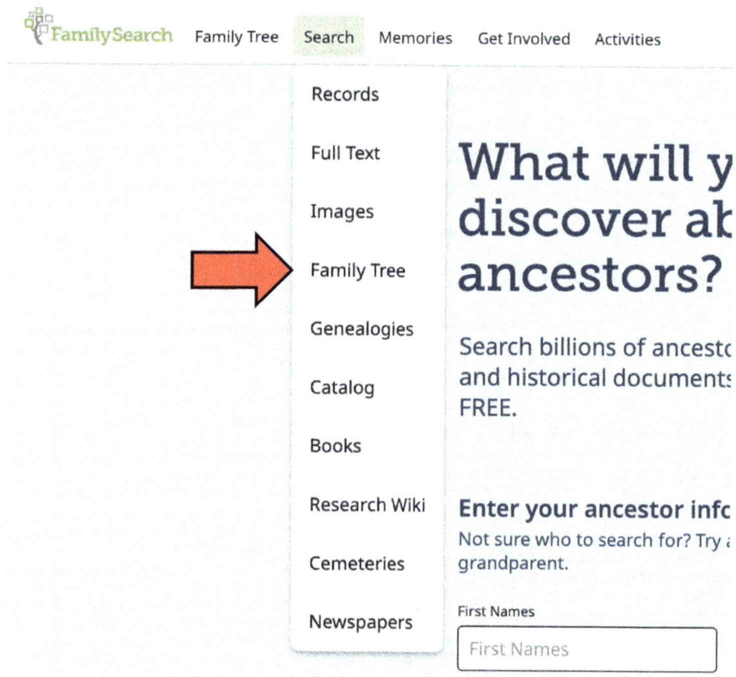

To find your family in the TREE, click on SEARCH, then choose FAMILY TREE.

Type the name of the person you want in the name fields. Include a place or year to further narrow the results.

Use MORE OPTIONS to add a spouse or parents' names. Often, this will find your family more quickly than by adding in any other search parameters.

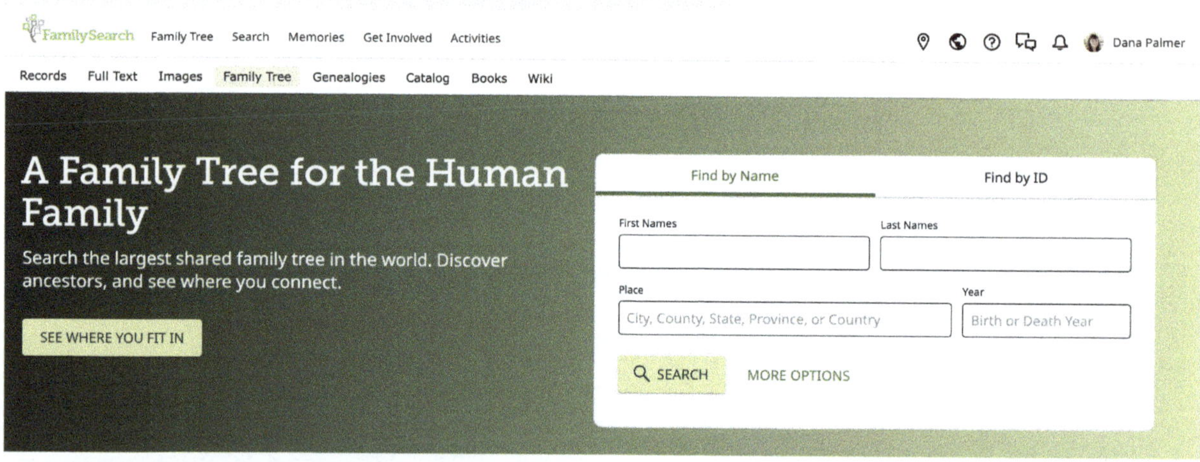

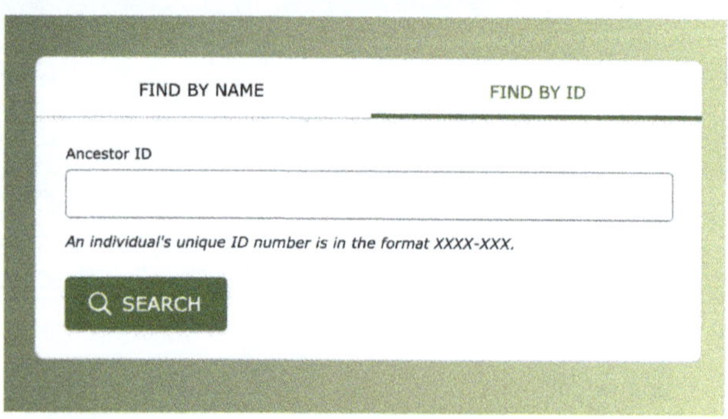

https://www.familysearch.org/en/search/tree/id?from=tree

FIND BY ID is best used when you know the ID assigned to your person and you want to find them quickly.

It's helpful to record these IDs on a printed pedigree chart or note them in your personal database program, for quick reference.

GENEALOGIES

GENEALOGIES is a database of thousands of family trees submitted by individuals or created for people residing in specific towns or communities, whereas in TREE, there is just one database that is interlinked. Many of the older trees from Ancestral File and Pedigree Resource File can be found here as well as newly added personal trees (https://www.familysearch.org/search/genealogies/).

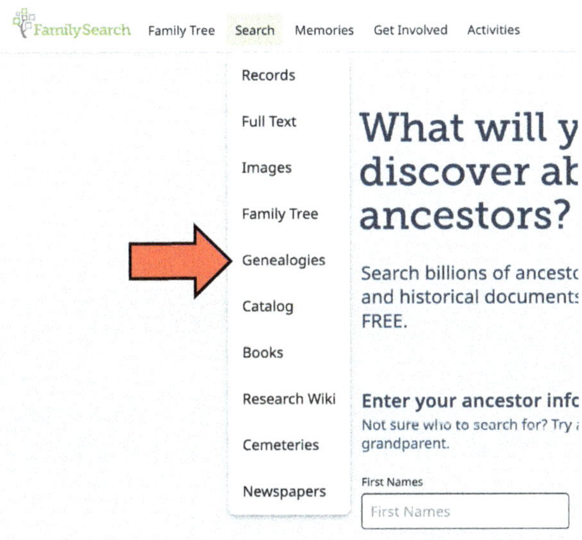

Some spoken lineages and oral histories can be found here.

Click on SEARCH, then choose GENEALOGIES to use this feature.

You can search for your family in GENEALOGIES just like in the other databases on the website. Use MORE OPTIONS to add additional filters to narrow your search results.

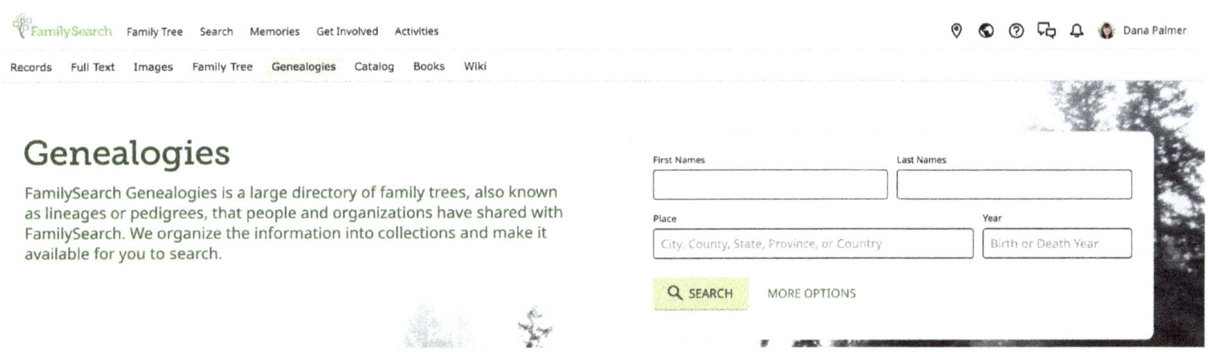

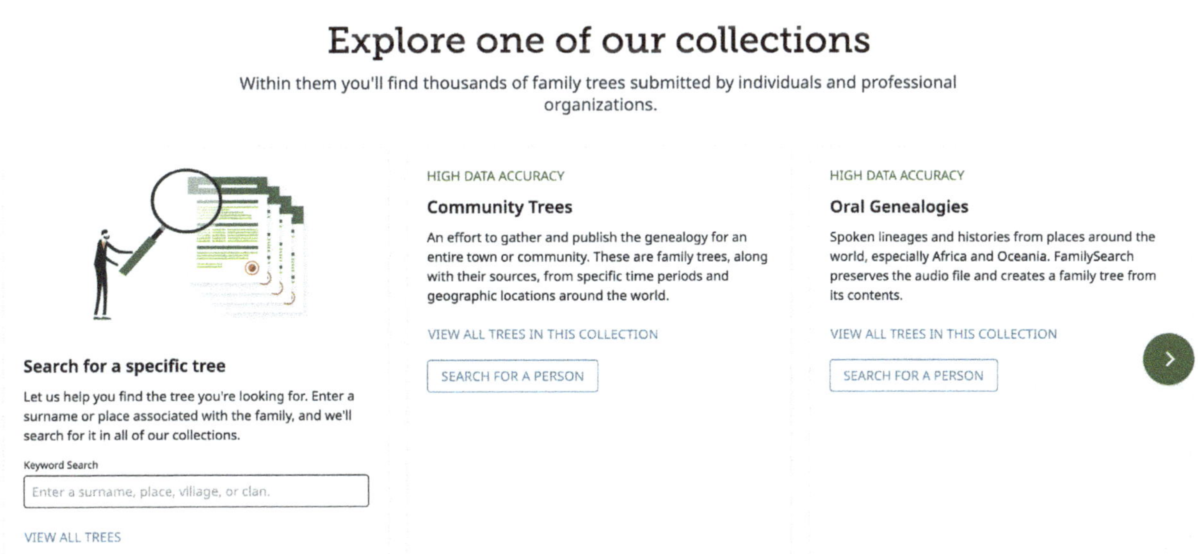

CEMETERIES

CEMETERIES helps you locate a graveyard by name, or by browsing, to find your family (https://www.familysearch.org/en/cemeteries/).

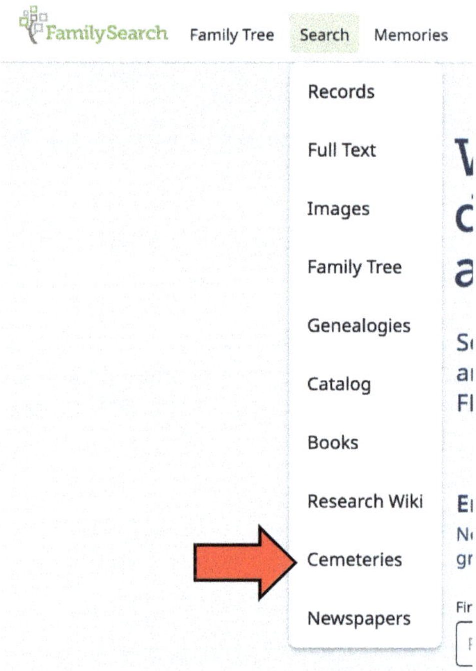

Each cemetery page provides details about that specific burial site (those buried therein), and general information about its address, and hours, as well as a link to the cemetery home page.

Click on SEARCH and then choose CEMETERIES to use this feature.

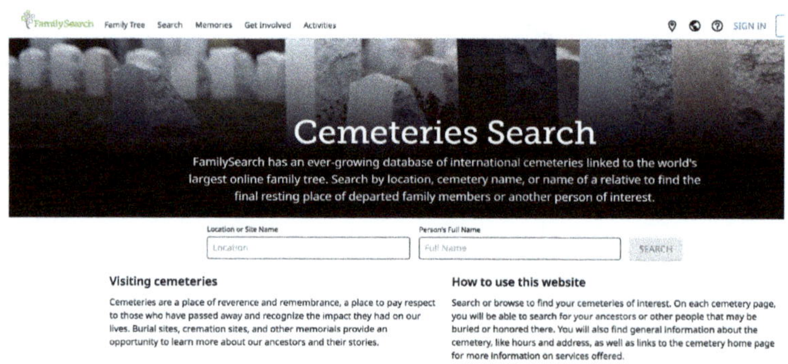

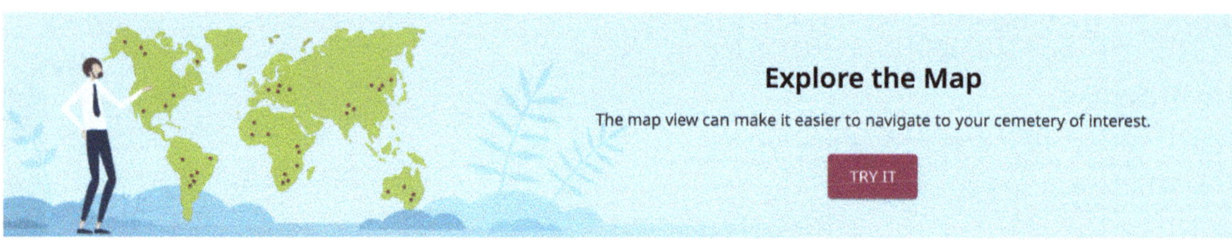

This map shows the larger cemeteries located near the entered location.

Zoom in for even more cemeteries and links.

Click on any red pin icon to be redirected to its page where you can search for family buried in that cemetery.

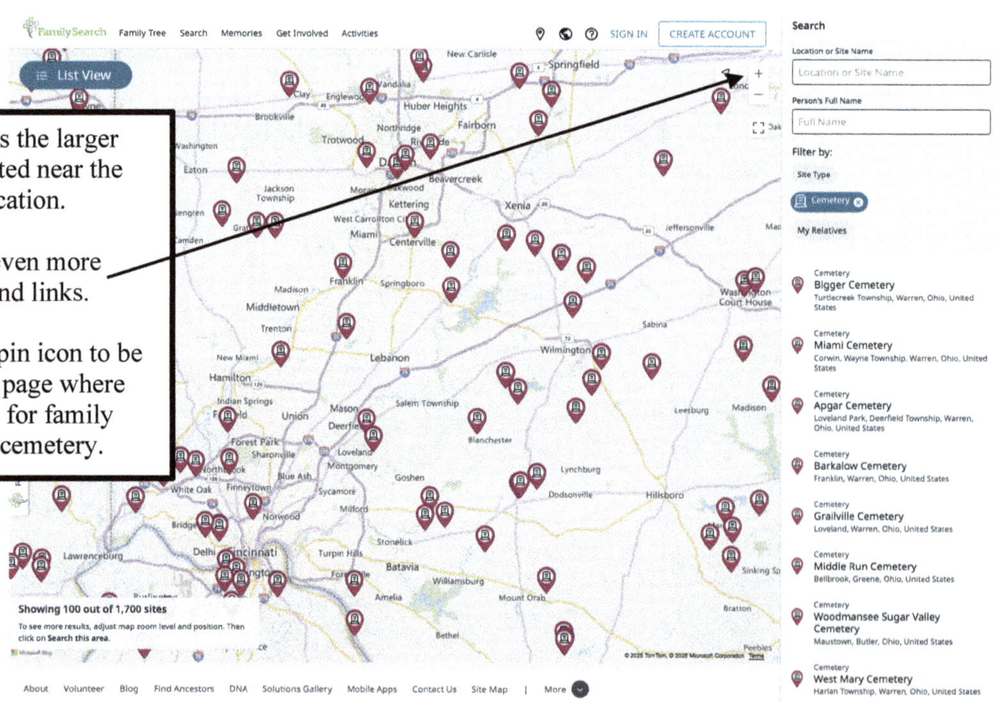

FamilySearch Family Tree Search Memories Get Involved Activities
SIGN IN
CREATE ACCOUNT
Return to Map > Pioneer Cemetery
Pioneer Cemetery
Lebanon, Warren, Ohio, United States
Sign in to access additional features and see if you are related to the people in the cemetery.
Site Information and Links
Get driving directions
Find a nearby site
Find a different site
Additional Links
Visit the Find a Grave website
Visit the BillionGraves website
Click here to go to Find a Grave or BillionGraves
Find someone in this site:
Here is a list of people from Family Tree that are connected to this place. Sign in, or create an account to see if any are your relatives.
Search for a specific person
REFINE SEARCH
Only show my relatives
241 people found
Click here to go to that person's DETAILS page in the TREE.
Click here to add or move the pin to mark the burial site for this person.
Add Person
Thomas Anderson
1768–1839 • K6QQ-L8D
Susanna Catherine Augustine
1786–1865 • M1GX-YLK
Jane Janeke Barkalow
1778–1844 • LCF8-5JH
Josiah H. Barton
1801–1848 • MHY7-VNM
George Enos Benford
1844–1844 • M3BY-H47
Peter Benham
1829–1833 • LZW7-D17
Peter O. Benham
1830–1833 • M7TT-8HR
Ann Benham
1793–1861 • LHPP-RD9
Maria Jane Bercaw
Rachel Biggs
Sarah Bone
PERSON
ADD GRAVESITE
Family Tree Search Memories Get Involved Activities
FamilySearch Tree Tree Recents Find Following Person List My Contributions
Thomas Anderson
25 November 1768 – 3 September 1839 • K6QQ-L8D
VIEW TREE
VIEW RELATIONSHIP
FOLLOW
About Details Sources (4) Collaborate (0)
Vitals
Detail View
Name • 4 Sources
Thomas Anderson
Birth • 1 Source
25 NOV 1768
, Essex, NJ
Death • 1 Source
3 SEP 1839
Turtle Creek, Warren, OH
Sex • 1 Source
Male
Christening
+ ADD
Burial • 1 Source
Lebanon Cem., Warren, OH
https://www.familysearch.org/en/tree/person/details/K6QQ-L8D
Add a Gravesite for Thomas Anderson
Drag the pin to mark the correct location
Aerial
W Main St
Turtle Creek
SAVE

NEWSPAPERS

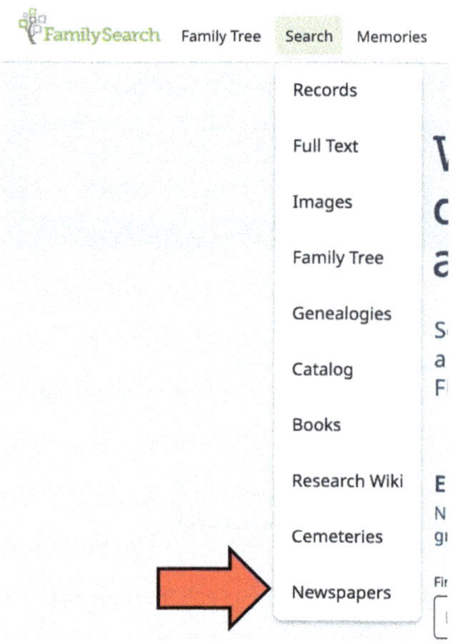

NEWSPAPERS helps you find your family in historic newspapers using Storied.com (https://www.familysearch.org/en/search/newspapers/). Click on SEARCH and then choose NEWSPAPERS to use this feature.

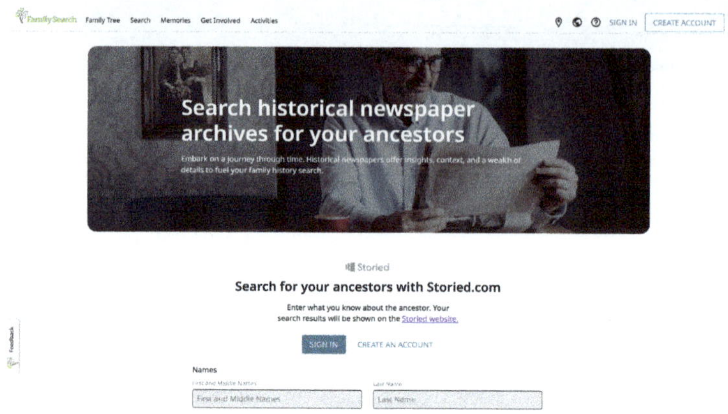

Search for Newspapers in FamilySearch Databases

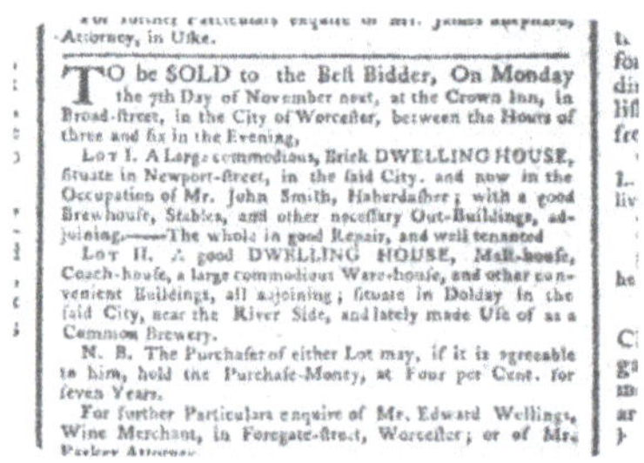

Searchable Record Collection - Newspapers

Find newspapers using predefined search fields, making it easier to locate particular documents related to your ancestors.

Search Newspaper Collections >

Full Text Search

Search through machine readable images using keyword and the machine will sort through the entire content of newspapers.

Search Text in Image Collections >

FamilySearch Library Catalog

Lists physical items available at the Library, as well as links to items in the FamilySearch Digital Library.

Search the Catalog >

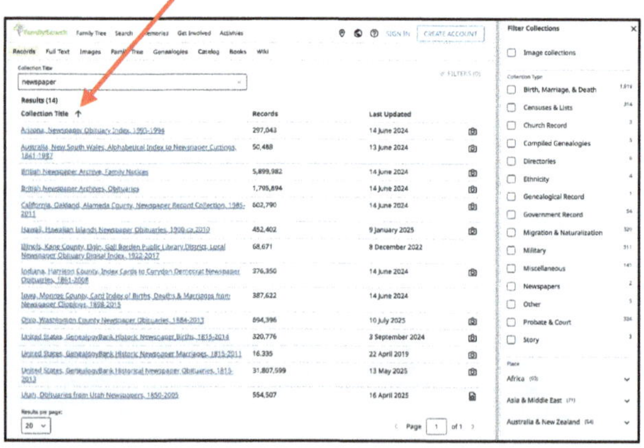

https://www.familysearch.org/en/search/collection/list?count=20&cqs=newspaper

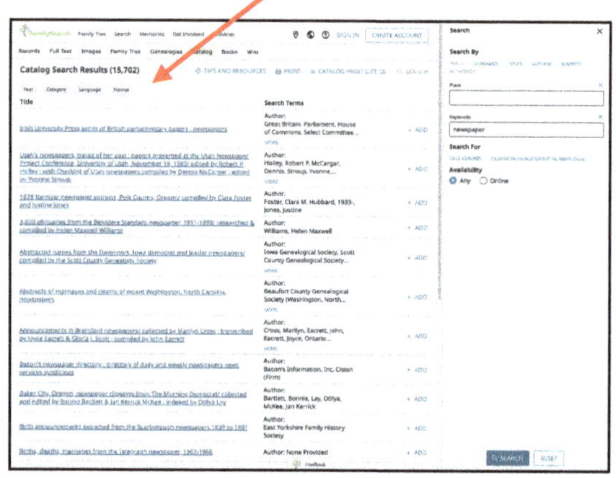

https://www.familysearch.org/en/search/catalog/results?q.keywords=newspaper

Chapter 3: Searching Tricks

SEARCH STRATEGIES FOR SUCCESS

The (www.familysearch.org) website has many free resources available to researchers. Knowing how to use the website effectively can help you find those elusive ancestors. If you can't find your family by typing their information into the search box, click on **BROWSE ALL COLLECTIONS**, then choose the specific database you want to search and try various search tricks until you find them.

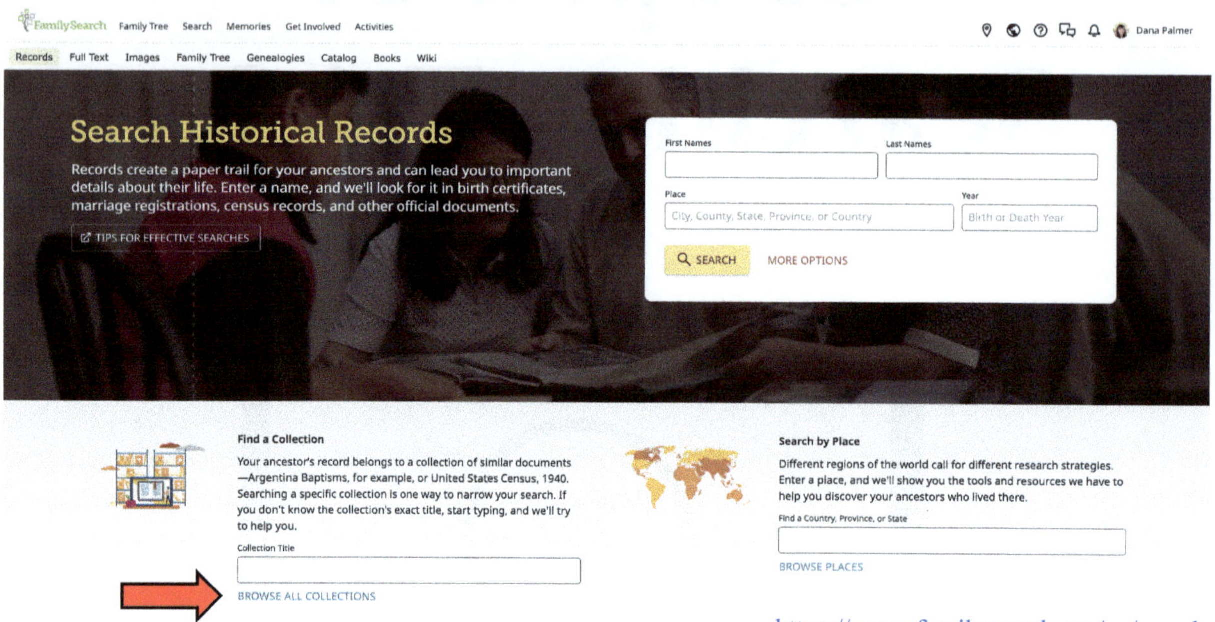

https://www.familysearch.org/en/search

Keep in mind that not everything is indexed and part of the historical record collection (**RECORDS**). If you can't find them in **RECORDS**, you'll need to search other parts of the website such as the CATALOG, IMAGES, or RESEARCH WIKI.

The **CATALOG** allows you to search by location, topic, keyword, author, or title to find specific collections. Most records in the United States are organized at the county level, except in New England, which is often by the town. Once you choose your location and specific record collection in the CATALOG, see if there is a camera icon next to the collection title. If so, you can search for your ancestors online just as if you were onsite at that repository. Some of these records are indexed, many are not.

Using **IMAGES** is similar to the CATALOG, but searches can only be done by location.

The **RESEARCH WIKI** will help you find online collections on FamilySearch and on other websites, as well as contact details for local repositories whose records might not be online.

TRICK 1: General Search

To do a general search, choose the collection you want from the BROWSE ALL COLLECTIONS category, then type the name of the person in the name field for a specific database. Many times, you will find your person easily.

- Select your specific database.
- Type in the surname and given name.
- If you get too many hits, add in a birth/death/marriage date depending on the database you are using +/- 5 years.

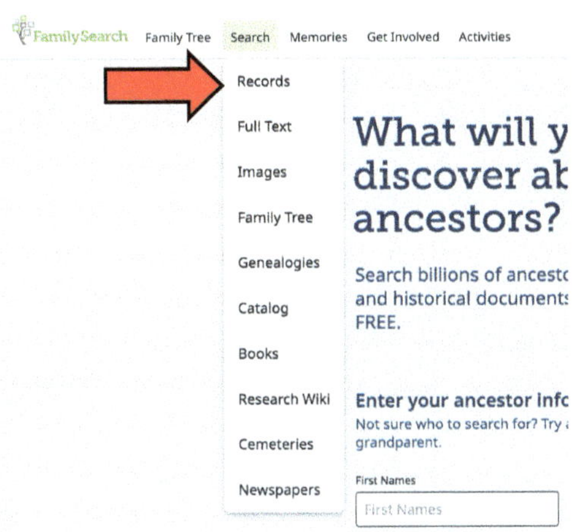

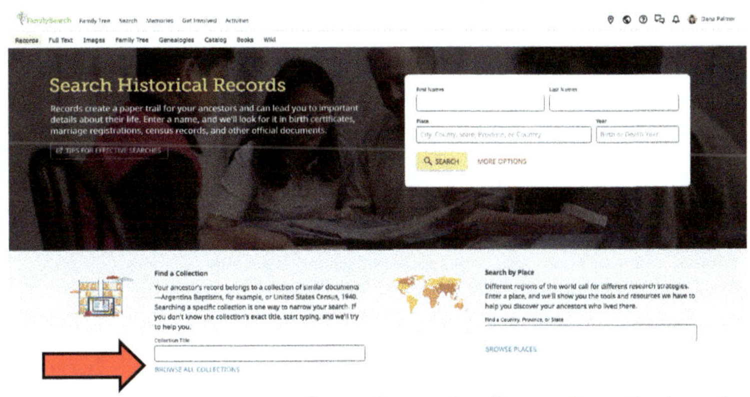

https://www.familysearch.org/en/search

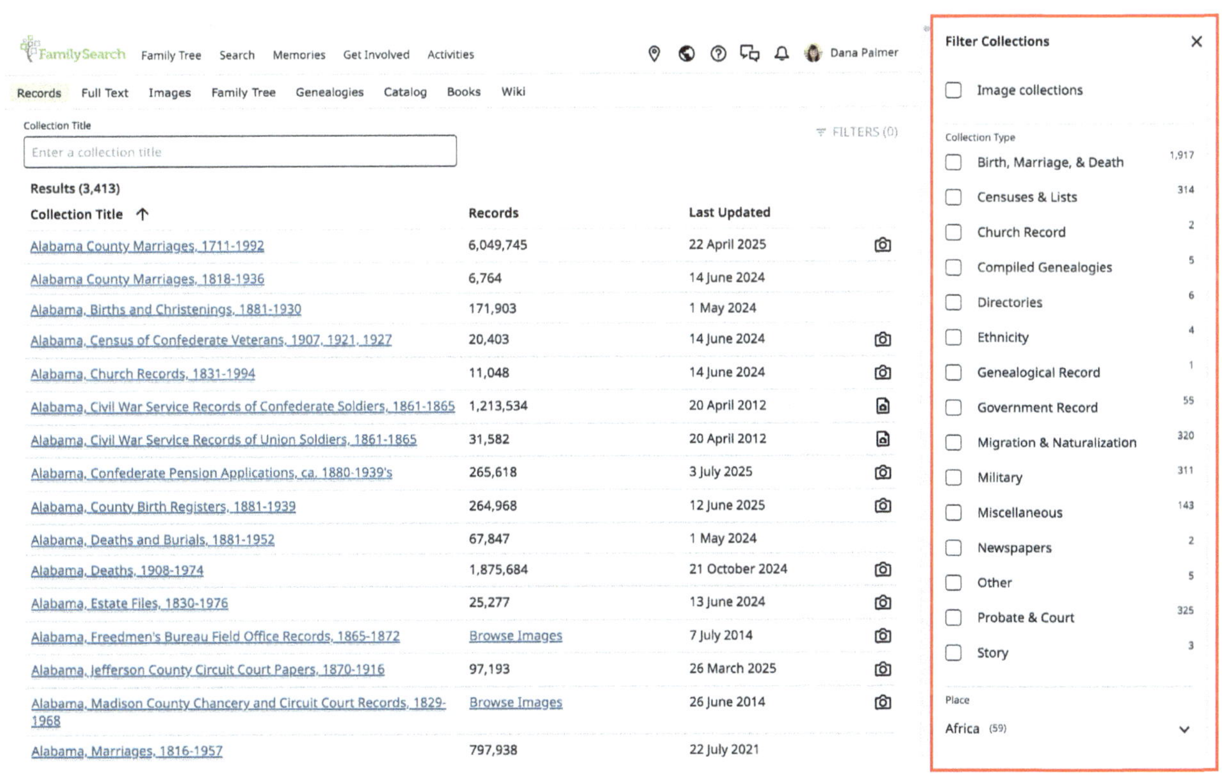

https://www.familysearch.org/en/search/collection/list?county=20

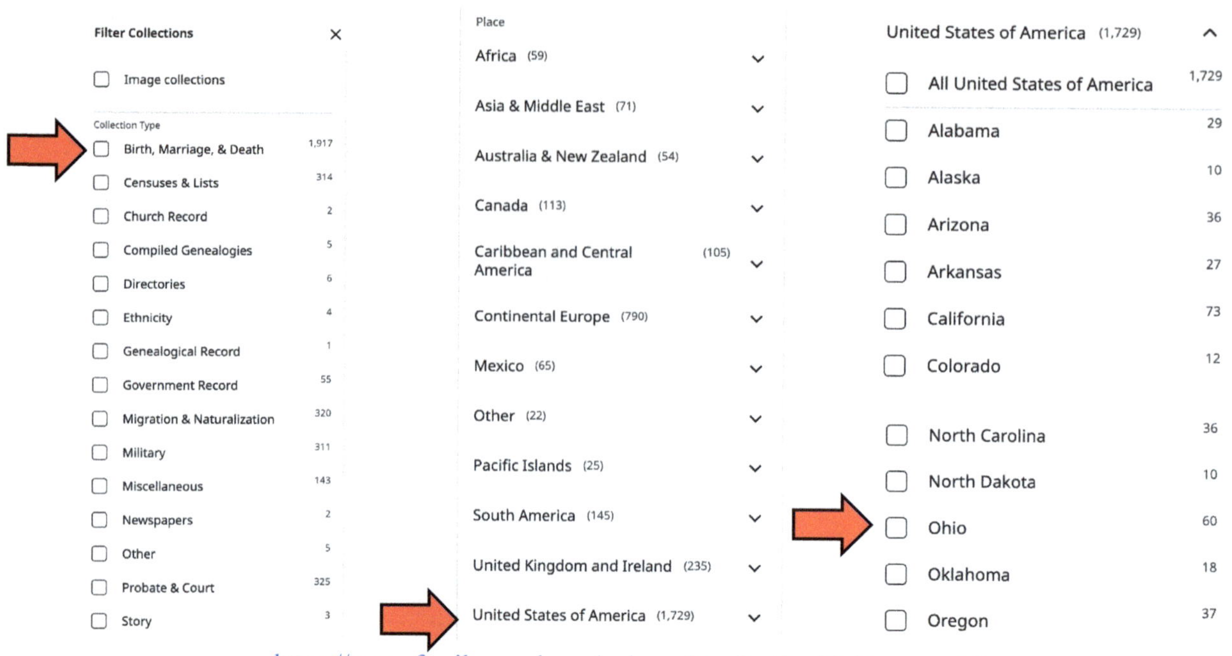

https://www.familysearch.org/en/search/collection/list?county=20

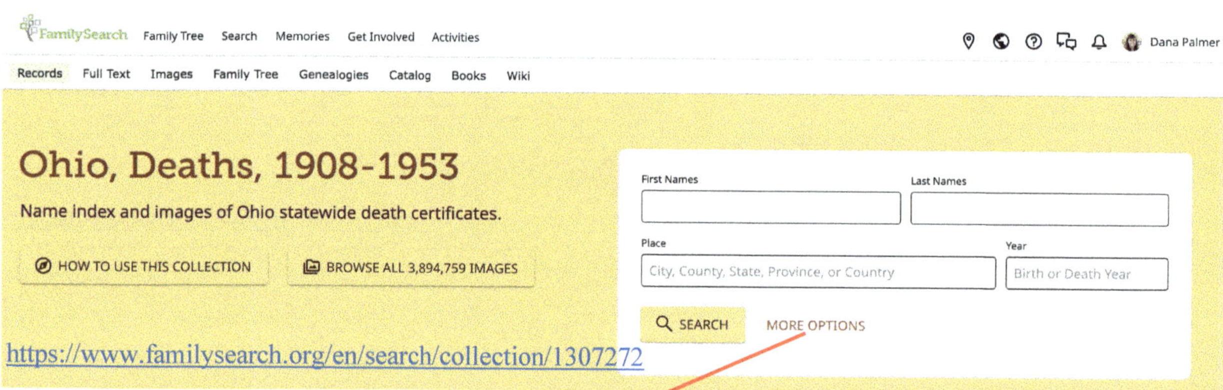

https://www.familysearch.org/en/search/collection/1307272

This is the main search field for this specific collection. Type the name and place here for a basic search. MORE OPTIONS allows for better search options when names are misspelled, mis-indexed, or hard to find.

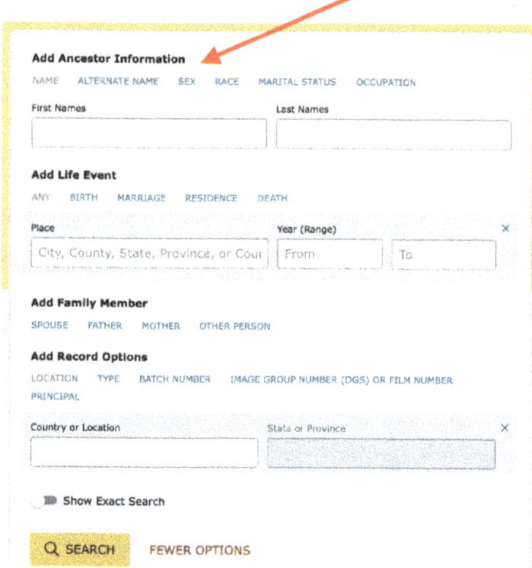

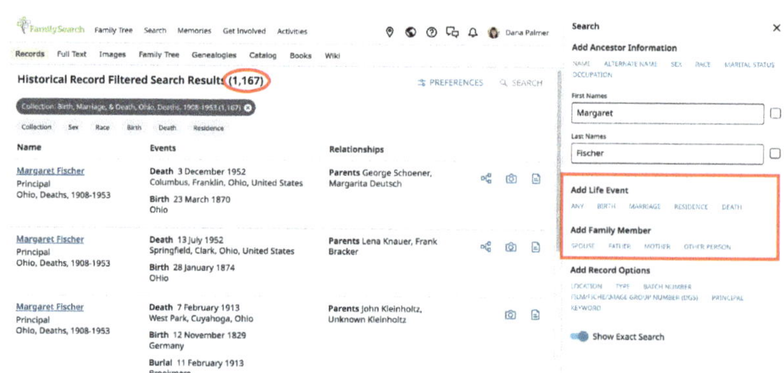

https://www.familysearch.org/en/search/record/results?f.collectionId=1307272&q.givenName=Margaret&q.surname=Fischer

Often, the name you want will appear towards the top of the search results. If not, add more filters to narrow the results.

TRICK 2: Date Search

To do a date search, add in a date or date range in the filters for a specific collection. You can search for a person by using the date filter by itself without a name, but you will get a lot of search results. You'll have better success if you use this trick in conjunction with the surname or location filter. The date filter is really helpful to track people with common surnames in a specific location for specific dates.

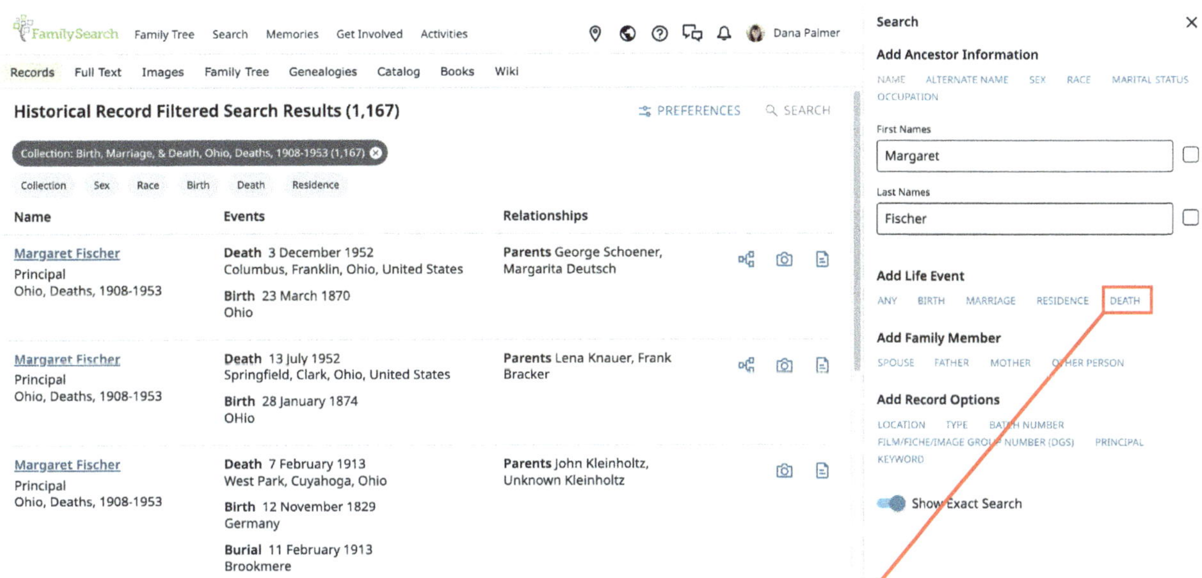

https://www.familysearch.org/en/search/record/results?f.collectionId=1307272&q.givenName=Margaret&q.surname=Fischer

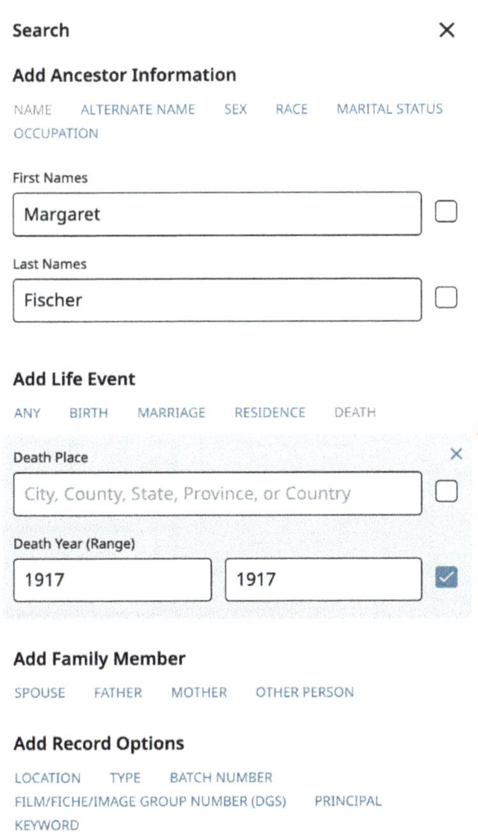

Using an exact filter (box is checked next to a name, date, or location) will significantly reduce the number of search results. If you choose a date range, the exact search filter can be used with or without a location. Adding a location will reduce the search results, but if the location is not listed in the index, and you've selected it as an exact filter, or the location is slightly different, as with census records, it may eliminate the record you want. So be creative when searching this way.

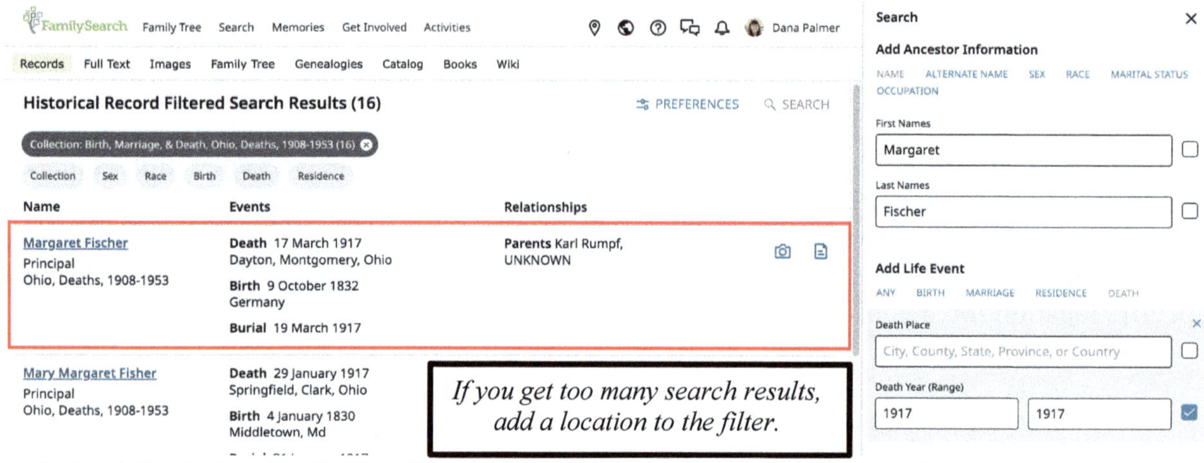

If you get too many search results, add a location to the filter.

https://www.familysearch.org/en/search/record/results?count=20&q.deathLikeDate.from=1917&q.deathLikeDate.to=1917&q.givenName=Margaret&q.surname=Fischer&f.collectionId=1307272

https://www.familysearch.org/ark:/61903/1:1:XZVN-NB9?lang=en

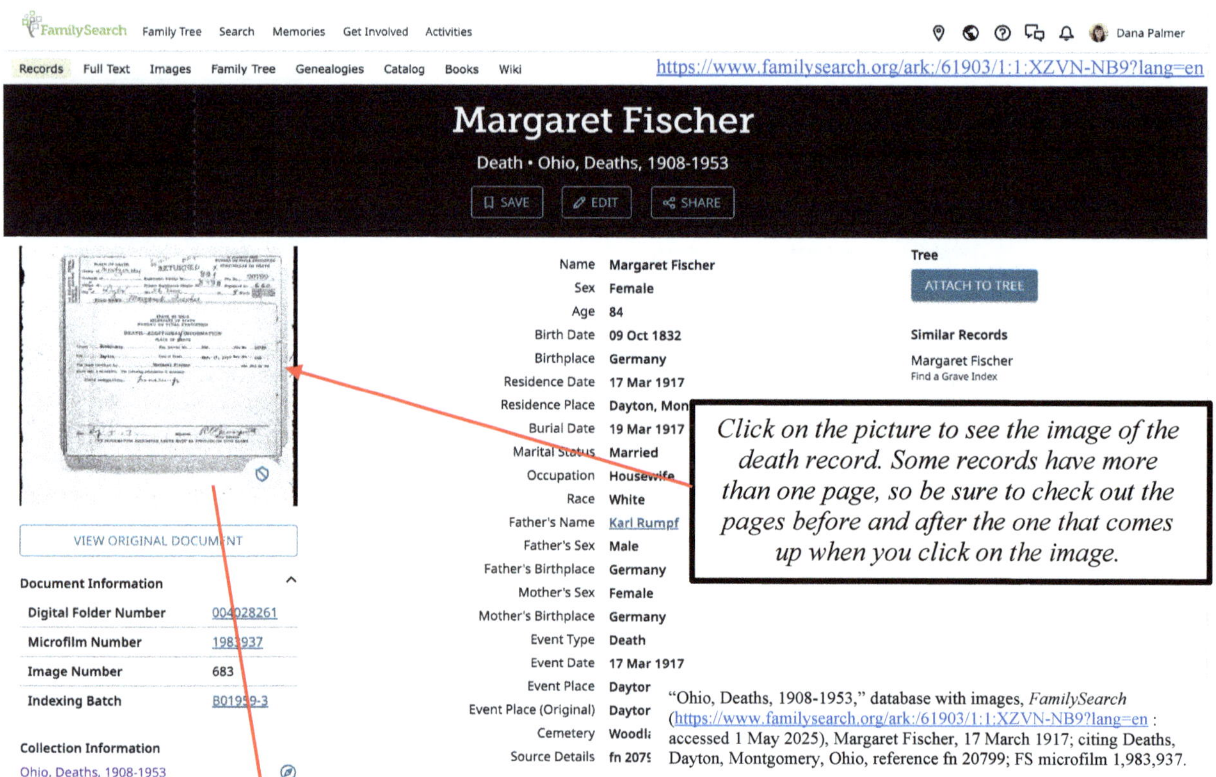

Click on the picture to see the image of the death record. Some records have more than one page, so be sure to check out the pages before and after the one that comes up when you click on the image.

"Ohio, Deaths, 1908-1953," database with images, *FamilySearch* (https://www.familysearch.org/ark:/61903/1:1:XZVN-NB9?lang=en : accessed 1 May 2025), Margaret Fischer, 17 March 1917; citing Deaths, Dayton, Montgomery, Ohio, reference fn 20799; FS microfilm 1,983,937.

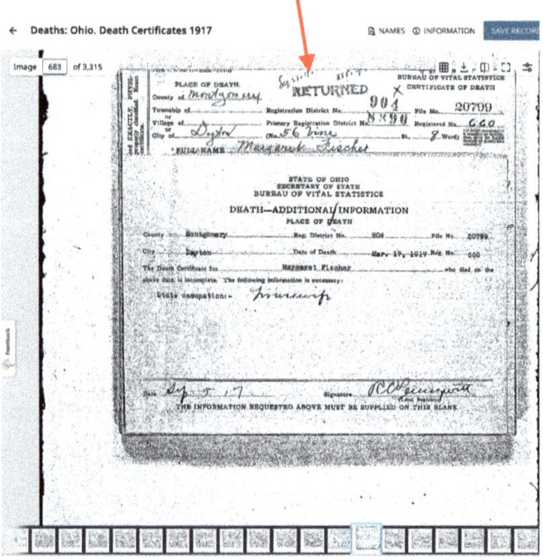

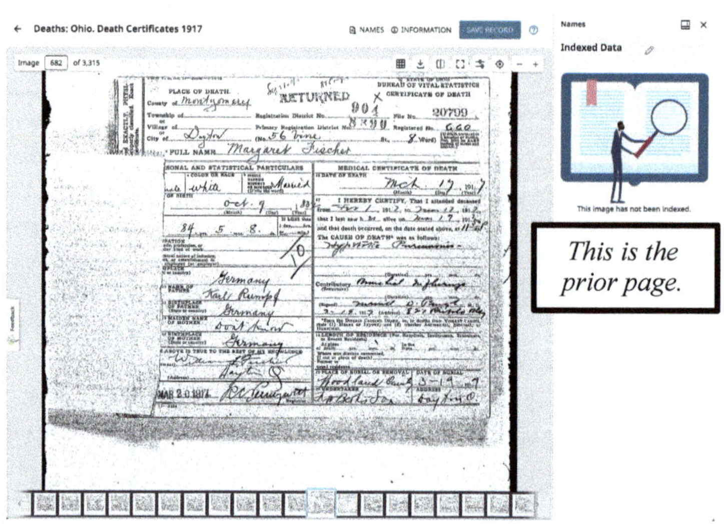

This is the prior page.

https://www.familysearch.org/ark:/61903/3:1:33S7-95WL-9ZCS?view=index&action=view&cc=1307272&lang=en&groupID=TH-1942-21801-24520-91

TRICK 3: Wildcard Search

Sometimes your general search won't work because your person's name is abbreviated, misspelled, or listed as a nickname. Wildcard symbols can aid in your search.

- Use the **question mark** (?) symbol to replace a single letter within the word.
  - So, **Eli?abeth** would result in searches for Elizabeth and Elisabeth.
  - This is especially useful if the second letter is indexed or recorded other than expected (Jrseph versus Joseph).
  - It can be used multiple times in a word when you are only replacing individual letters (such as **Pe?ers?n** for Pederson, Petersen, Pedersen, Pederson, etc.).
- Use the **asterisk** (*) symbol to replace multiple letters.
  - On FamilySearch you only need 1 letter before the * wildcard feature.
  - If you used **ROS*** as a given name, you would get Rosa, Rose, Ross, Rossina, Rosina, etc. and all variations on the given name starting with Ros.
  - If you used **JOH*SON**, you would get Johanson, Johansson, Johnson, Johannsson, etc.
- **Combinations** – you can also use the asterisk and question mark wildcards in combination such as:
  - **T?r*** (Torok, Török, Turk, etc.)
  - **N*ls?n** (Neilsen, Neilson, Nielsen, Nielson, Nelson, Nelsen, etc.)
  - **H?l*day** (Holliday, Holiday, Holyday, Halyday, etc.).
  - This is really helpful if you have letters that are often interchanged with others or an ending that is not consistent.

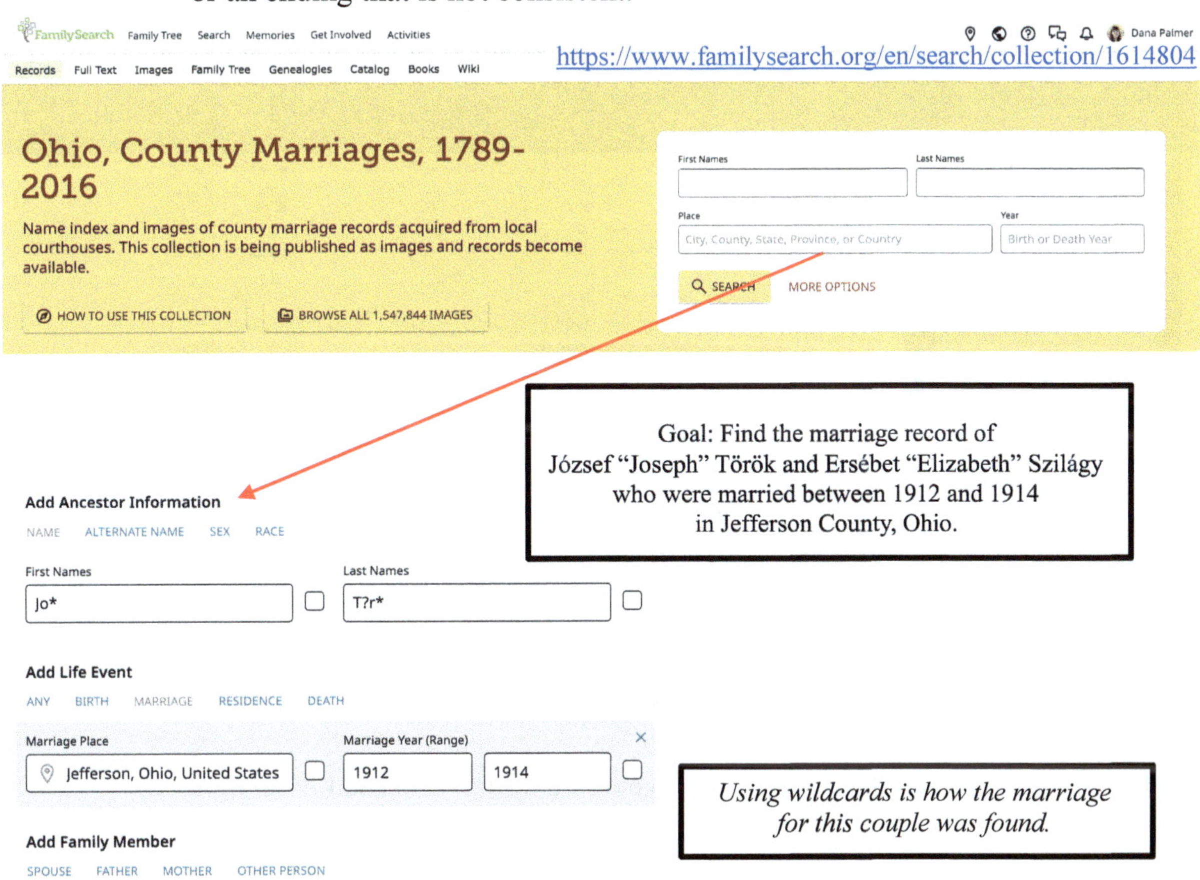

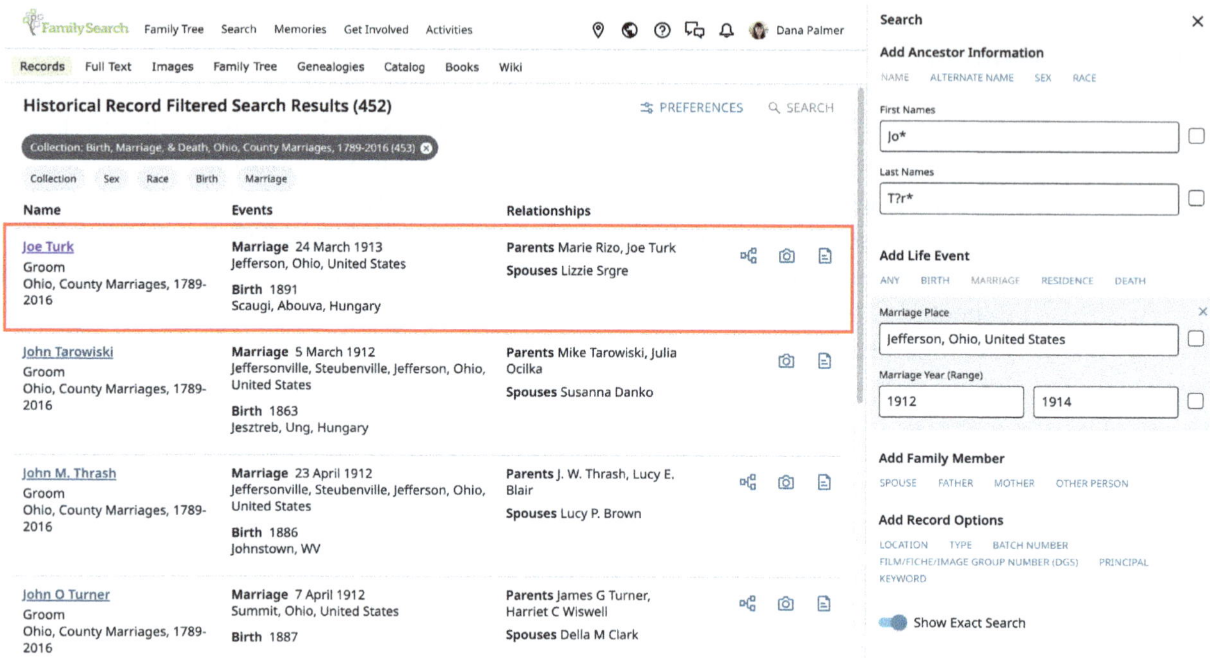

https://www.familysearch.org/en/search/record/results?f.collectionId=1614804&q.givenName=Jo%2A&q.marriageLikeDate.from=1912&q.marriageLikeDate.to=1914&q.marriageLikePlace=Jefferson%2C%20Ohio%2C%20United%20States&q.surname=T%3Fr%2A

Click on the blue name link to go to the transcription page.

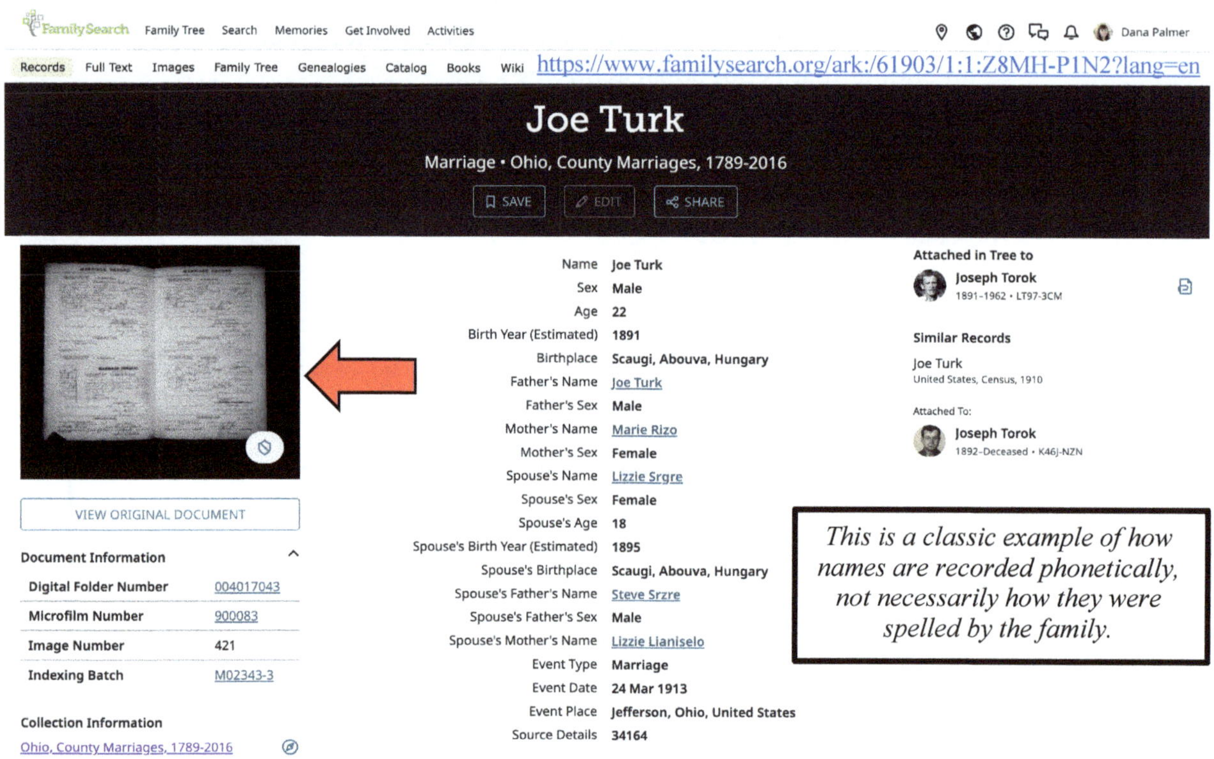

"Ohio, County Marriages, 1789-2016," database with images, *FamilySearch* (https://www.familysearch.org/ark:/61903/1:1:Z8MH-P1N2?lang=en : accessed 1 May 2025), Joe Turk and Lizzie Srgre, 24 March 1913; citing Marriages, Jefferson County, Ohio, p. 523, no. 34164; FS microfilm 900,083.

Click on the picture to see the digitized marriage record for Joe Turk and Lizzie Srgre.

This is the marriage record of Joe Turk and Lizzie Srgre, the same as what you would find if you visited the local probate court in Jefferson County, Ohio, and asked to see their marriage books. This one is digital and available online for free. Their entry is the one in the bottom right corner marked with a red box.

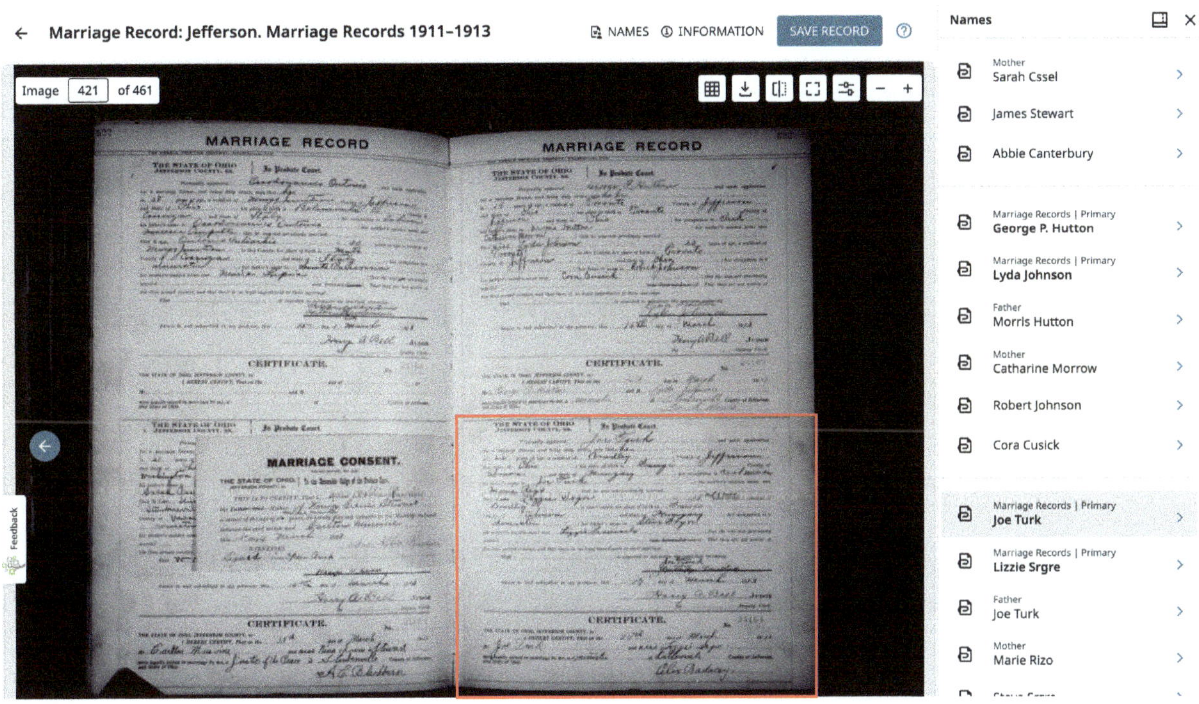

https://www.familysearch.org/ark:/61903/3:1:9392-S596-L3?view=index&action=view&cc=1614804&lang=en&groupId=TH-1-18084-36551-31

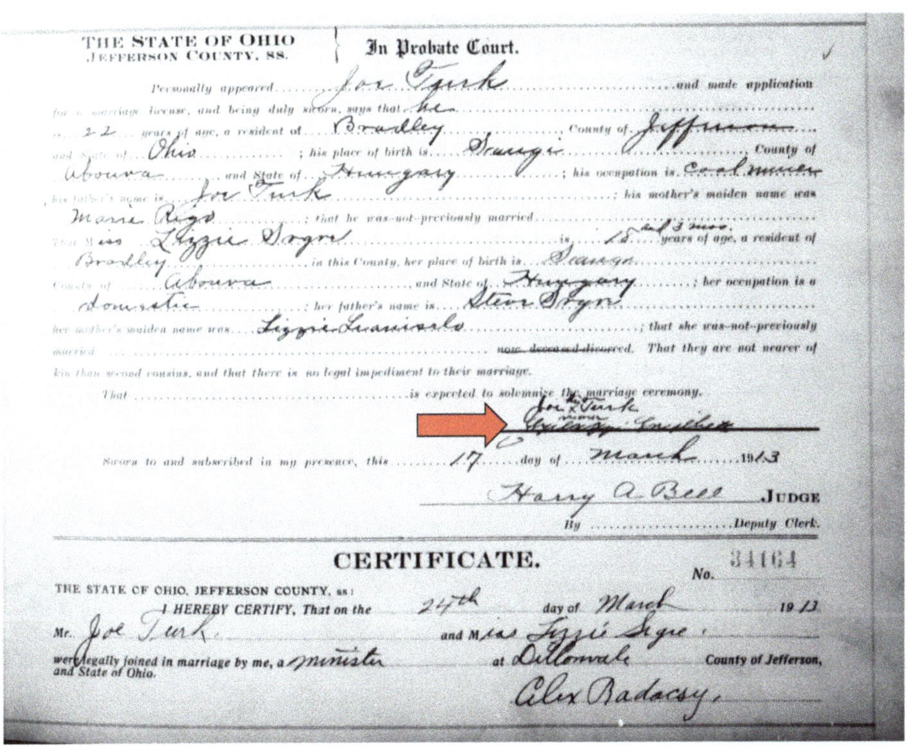

THE STATE OF OHIO, JEFFERSON COUNTY, SS. In Probate Court.

Personally appeared Joe Turk and made application for a marriage license, and being duly sworn, says that he [is] 22 years of age, a resident of Bradley County of Jefferson and State of Ohio; his place of birth is Sranugi[?] County of Abouva[?] and State of Hungary; his occupation is Coal miner; his father's name is Joe Turk; his mother's maiden name was Marie Rizo; that he was not previously married. That Miss Lizzie Srgre is 18 and 3 mos. years of age, a resident of Bradley in this County, her place of birth is Sranugi[?] County of Abouva[?] and State of Hungary; her occupation is a domestic; her father's name is Steve Srgre; her mother's maiden name was Lizzie Leanicoke[?]; that she was not previously married, now deceased and divorced. That they are not nearer of kin than second cousins, and that there is no legal impediment to their marriage.

That ... is expected to solemnize the marriage ceremony.

Joe Turk
Szilagyi Ersebet

Sworn to and subscribed in my presence, this 17 day of March 1913

Harry A. Bell Judge

By ..... Deputy Clerk.

CERTIFICATE. No. 34164

THE STATE OF OHIO, JEFFERSON COUNTY, ss:

I HEREBY CERTIFY, That on the 24th day of March 1913 Mr. Joe Turk and Miss Lizzie Srgre were legally joined in marriage by me, a minister at Dillonvale County of Jefferson, and State of Ohio.

Alex Badacsy

This zoomed in version of their marriage record shows that "Joe Turk" signed by his mark, indicating he probably couldn't read, while "Lizzie Srgre" signed her name as "Szilagyi Ersebet," which is the Hungarian version of her name.

The clerk wrote her name as he heard it, not as she spelled it when she signed it.

"Ohio, County Marriages, 1789-2016," database with images, *FamilySearch* (https://www.familysearch.org/ark:/61903/1:1:Z8MH-P1N2?lang=en : accessed 1 May 2025), Joe Turk and Lizzie Srgre, 24 March 1913; citing Marriages, Jefferson County, Ohio, p. 523, no. 34164; FS microfilm 900,083

TRICK 4: Surname Search

For a surname search, leave off the given name and just search by the surname with or without a date or location for a specific collection. This is helpful if their given names are abbreviated, misspelled, or they are using a middle name or nicknames. This is a great trick for finding marriage records.

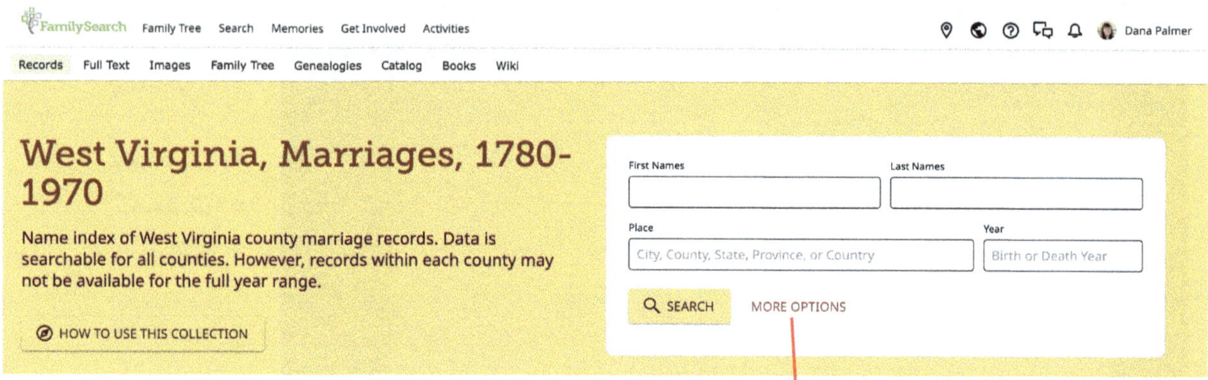

https://www.familysearch.org/search/collection/1408729

Goal: Find the marriage record of Lorenzo Dow Ramsey and Laura Belle Janney who married about 1903 in West Virginia.

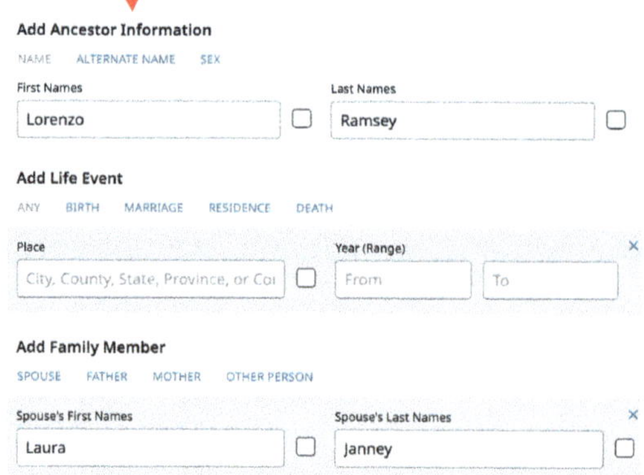

If you don't get search results for the couple you want, try removing the given names and try various combinations of tricks until you find them.

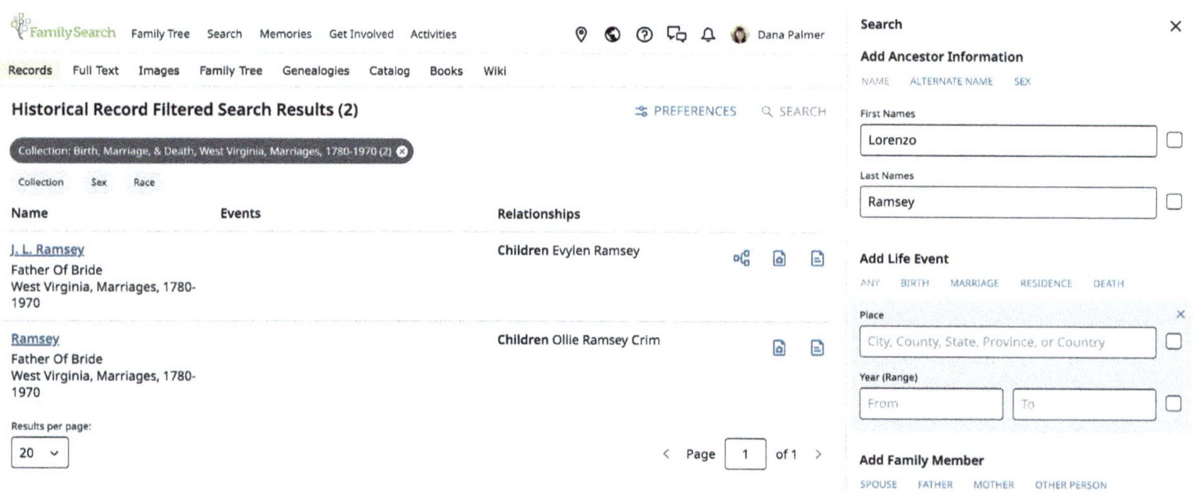

https://www.familysearch.org/en/search/record/results?f.collectionId=1408729&q.givenName=Lorenzo&q.spouseGivenName=Laura&q.spouseSurname=Janney&q.surname=Ramsey

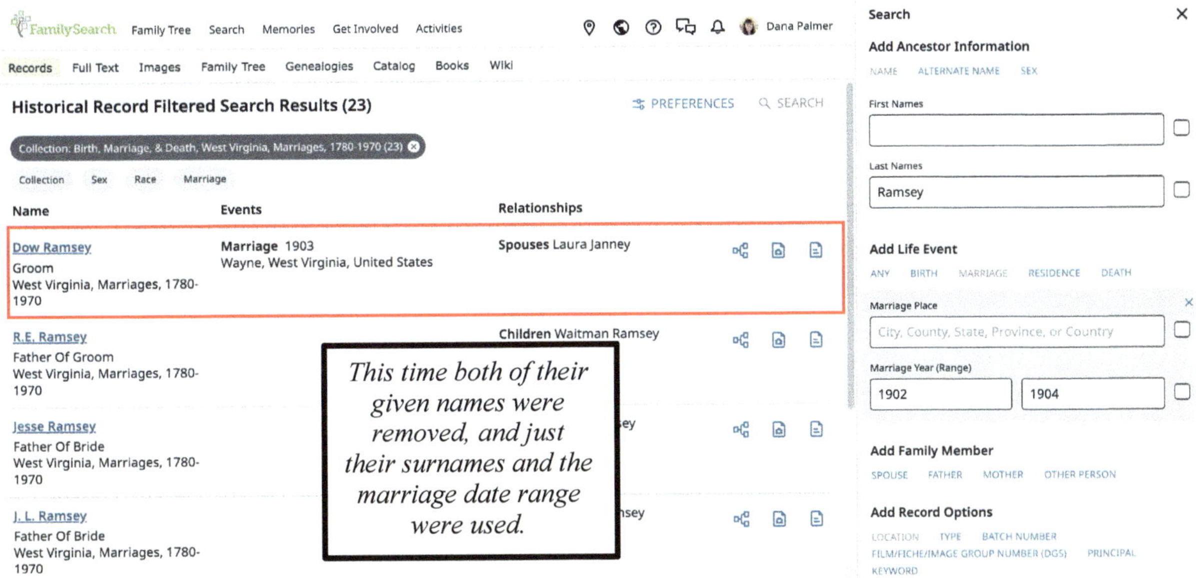

This time both of their given names were removed, and just their surnames and the marriage date range were used.

https://www.familysearch.org/en/search/record/results?count=20&q.marriageLikeDate.from=1902&q.marriageLikeDate.to=1904&q.spouseSurname=Janney&q.surname=Ramsey&f.collectionId=1408729

https://www.familysearch.org/ark:/61903/1:1:FTNY-G2B?lang=en

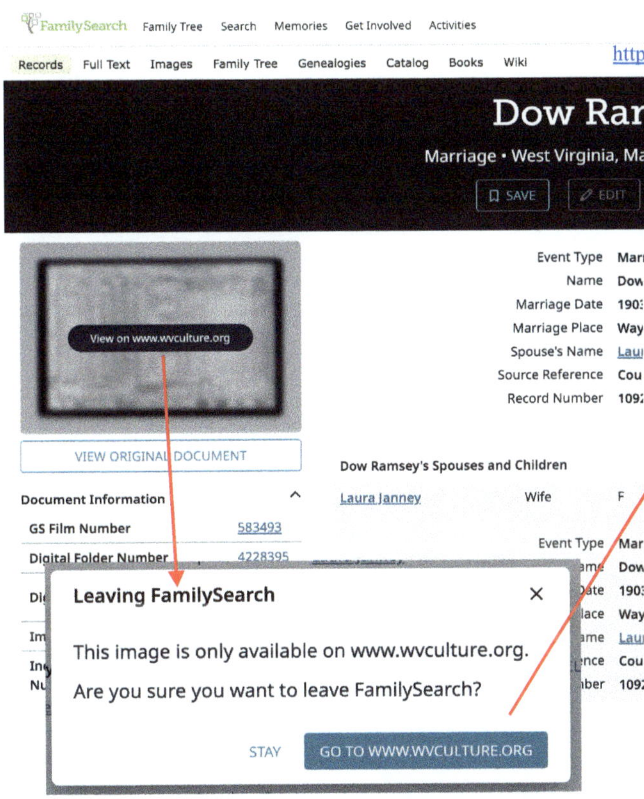

The transcription page for this couple's marriage entry indicates that these records come from the West Virginia partner website.

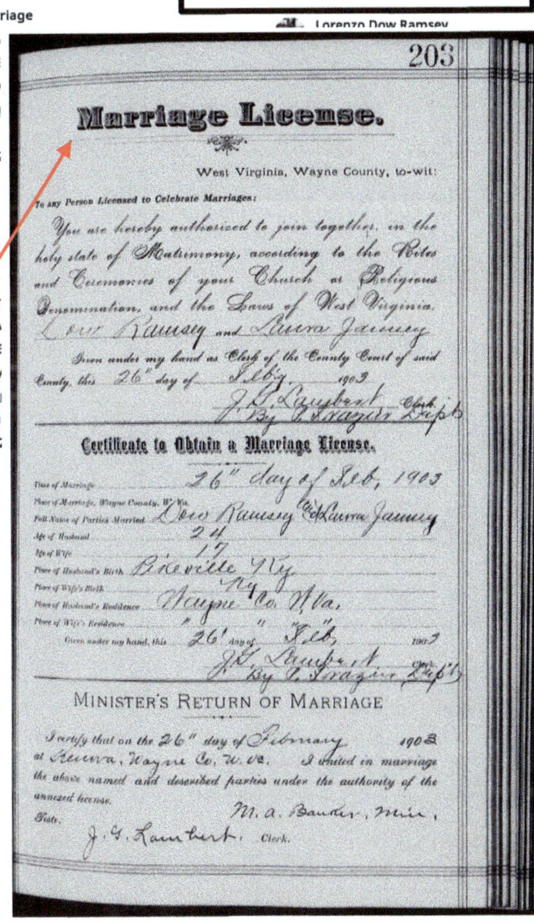

The copy of their digitized marriage record found on the WV Culture website shows he went by his middle name Dow. These partner websites along with the FamilySearch indexes make it much easier to quickly find your person's original records.

"West Virginia, Marriages, 1780-1970," database with images, *West Virginia Archives & History* (https://archive.wvculture.org/vrr/va_view2.aspx?FilmNumber=583493&ImageNumber=474 : accessed 4 Jan 2025), Dow Ramsey and Laura Janney, 26 Feb 1903; citing Marriages, Wayne County, West Virginia, no. 1092, West Virginia Vital Records Office.

TRICK 5: Given Name Search

For a given name search, leave off the surname and search by the given name with or without dates and locations for a specific collection. You will get a lot of search results with this type of search, so be sure to use the date or location filters to narrow the results. This trick is especially helpful for misspelled or mis-indexed surnames. It is especially effective for finding married women's surnames when you don't know their spouse, but you do know their parents' names.

- Type in the given name and give an approximate birth date +/- 5 years.
- If the name is common, add more filters to reduce the search results.

Be sure to check the information in the tree for your family. Sometimes there are clues to household members and residence that can help you find them. If you are really lucky, the desired record will appear in the hints or already be attached in the tree. If not, try this type of trick to find them.

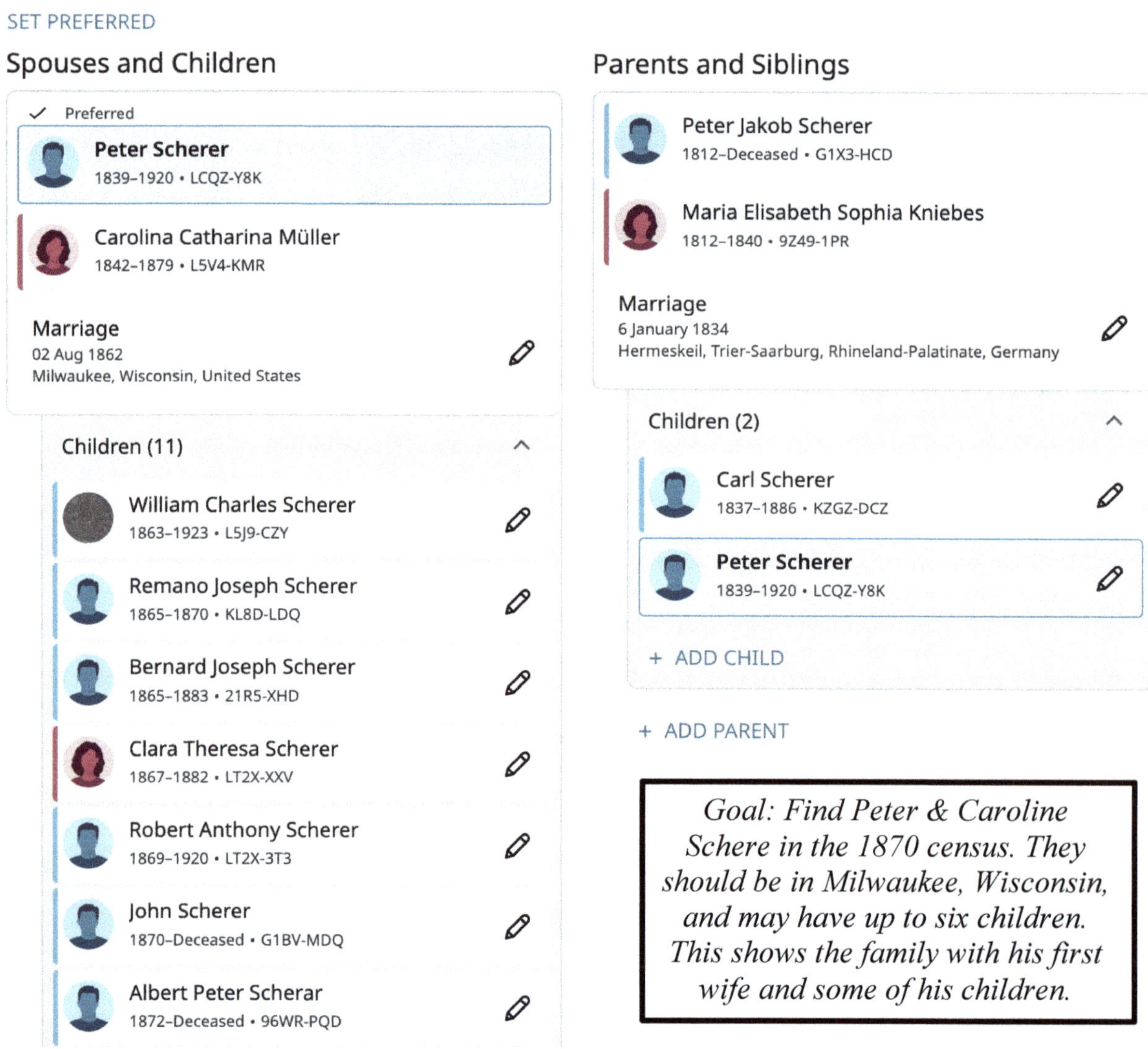

Goal: Find Peter & Caroline Schere in the 1870 census. They should be in Milwaukee, Wisconsin, and may have up to six children. This shows the family with his first wife and some of his children.

https://www.familysearch.org/en/tree/person/details/LCQZ-Y8K

Go to the SEARCH tab, and choose RECORDS, then select BROWSE ALL COLLECTIONS. Narrow by selecting the CENSUS & LISTS filter and UNITED STATES OF AMERICA as the country and UNITED STATES as the sub-location to view all the census records. You can also type the name of the census "i.e., 1870 census" in the COLLECTION TITLE box to find it faster.

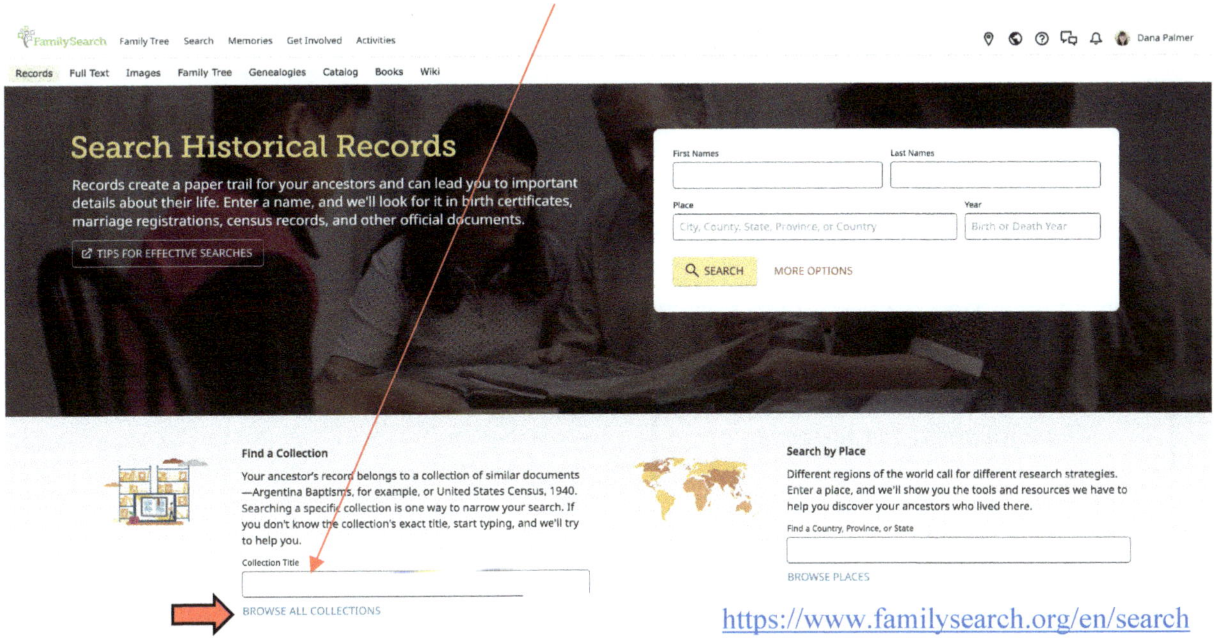

https://www.familysearch.org/en/search

Select the desired census collection and click on the blue link, **UNITED STATES, CENSUS, 1870**, to search for your person.

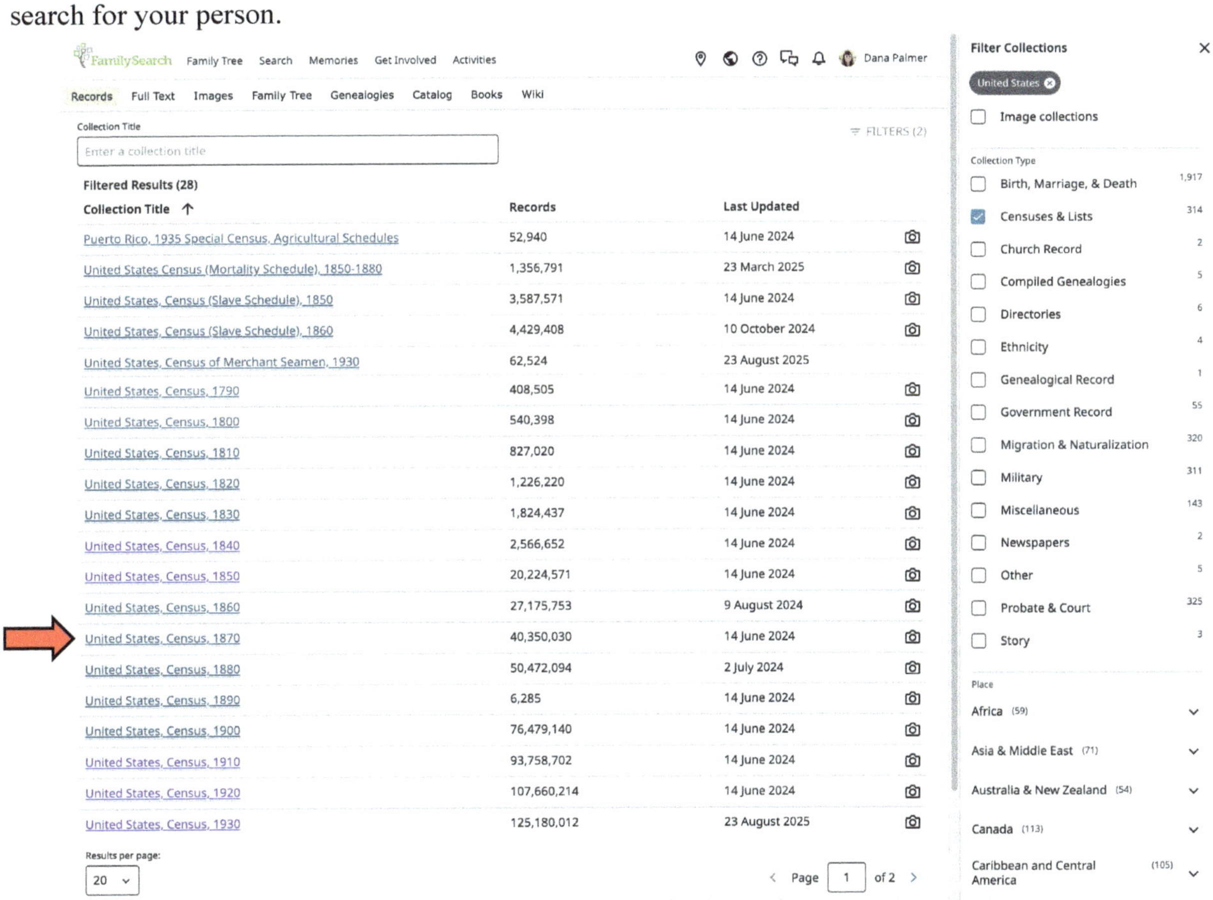

https://www.familysearch.org/en/search/collection/list?count=20&fcs=recordType%3ACENSUS%2CplaceId%3A1&ec=recordType%3ACENSUS%2Cregion%3AUNITED_STATES%2CplaceId%3A1

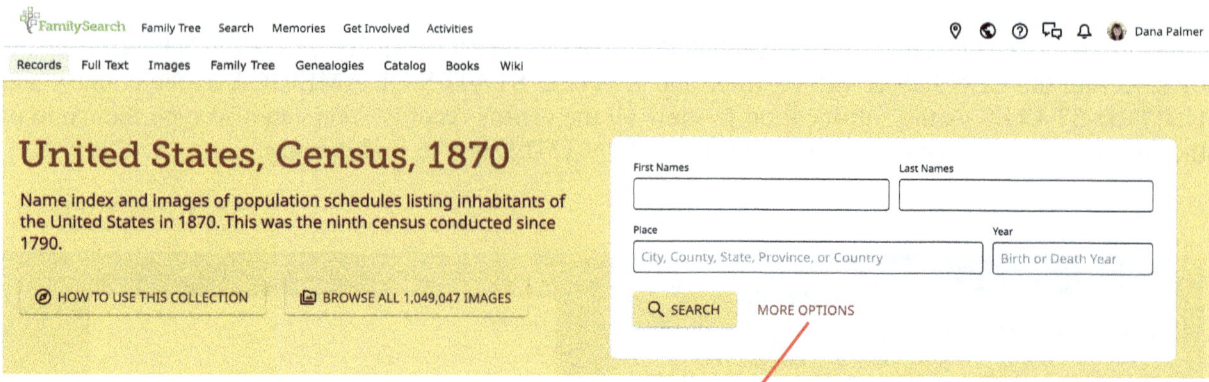

https://www.familysearch.org/search/collection/1438024

A search using his surname did not result in any good matches for Peter Scherer, so a given name search was done removing his surname.

To reduce the search results, exact filters were included for his birth location and range and his residence.

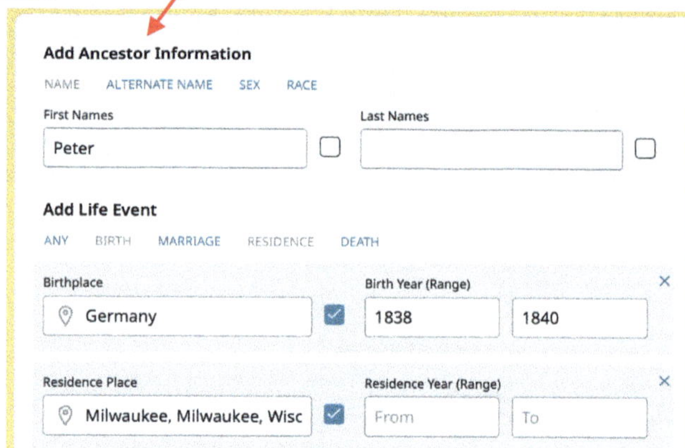

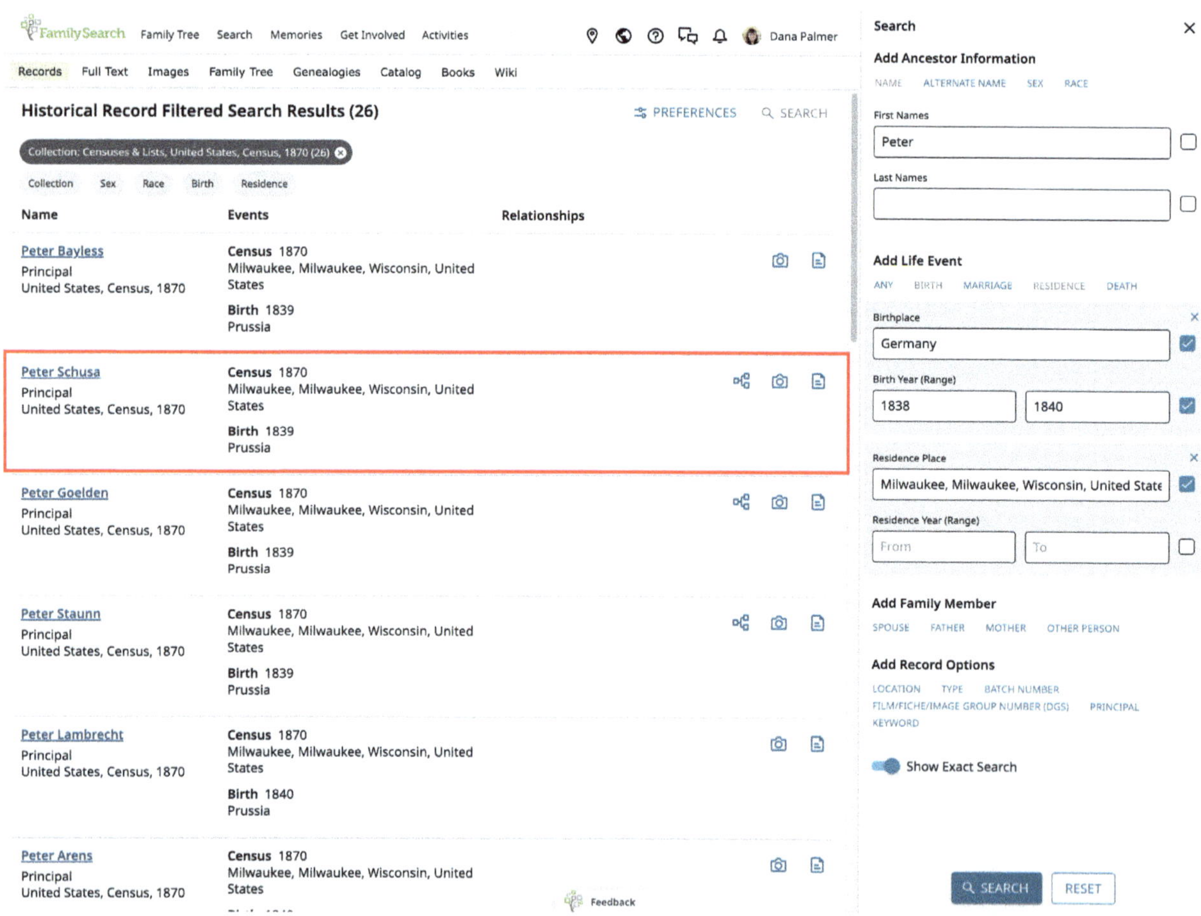

https://www.familysearch.org/en/search/record/results?count=20&q.birthLikeDate.from=1838&q.birthLikeDate.to=1840&q.birthLikePlace=Germany&q.birthLikePlace.exact=on&q.givenName=Peter&q.residencePlace=Milwaukee%2C%20Milwaukee%2C%20Wisconsin%2C%20United%20States&q.residencePlace.exact=on&f.collectionId=1438024

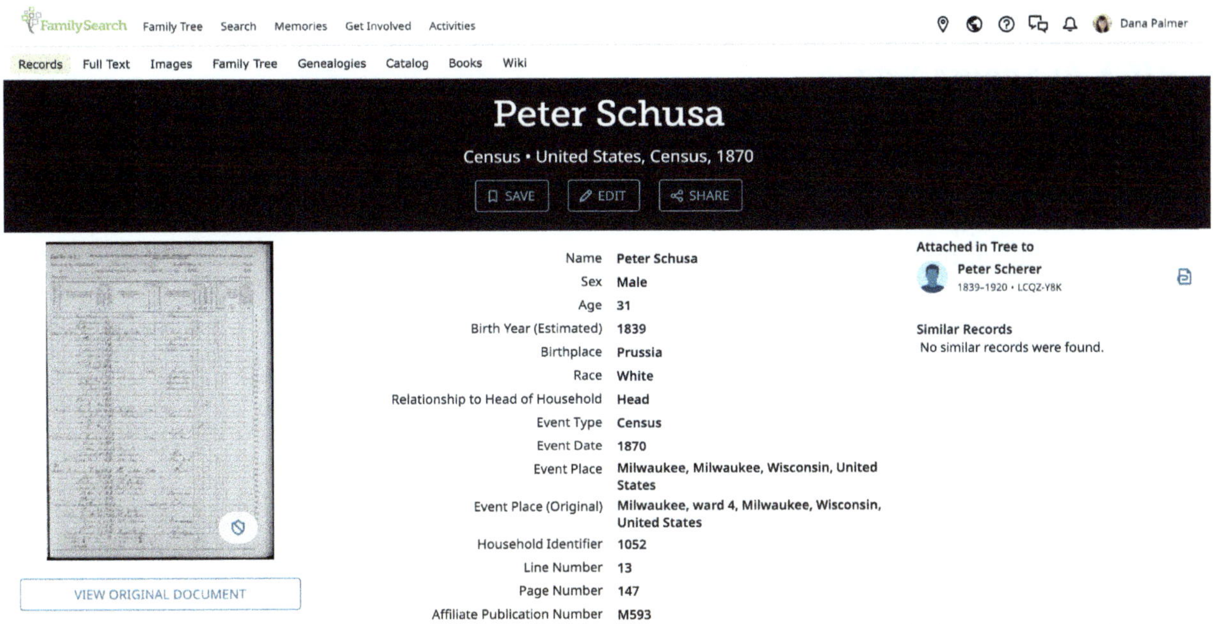

1870 U.S. Census, Milwaukee County, Wisconsin, population schedule, Milwaukee, p. 147 (handwritten), p. 525 (stamped), dwelling 1237, family 1052, Peter Schusa [sic], imaged, "United States, Census, 1870," *FamilySearch* (https://www.familysearch.org/ark:/61903/1:1:MN9Y-RJY?lang=en : accessed 1 May 2025), citing National Archives microfilm publication M593, roll 1727.

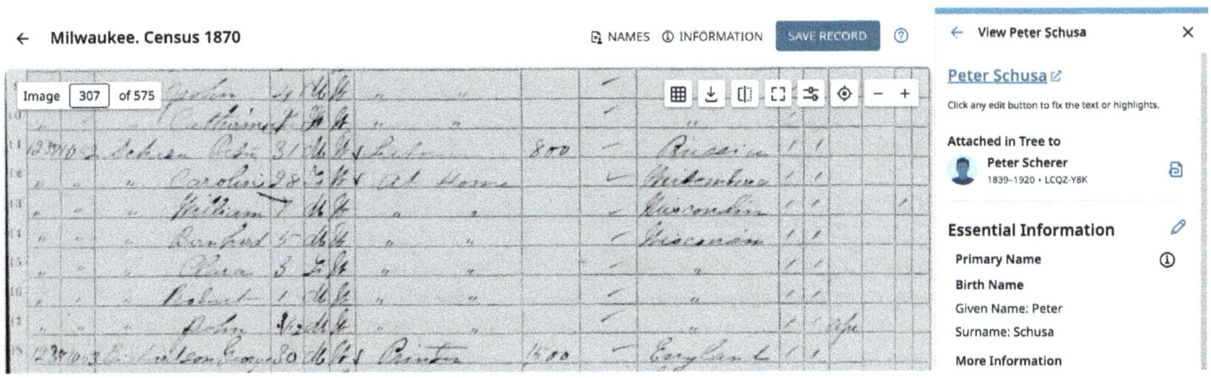

This handwriting is very hard to read, which could be why it was indexed differently.

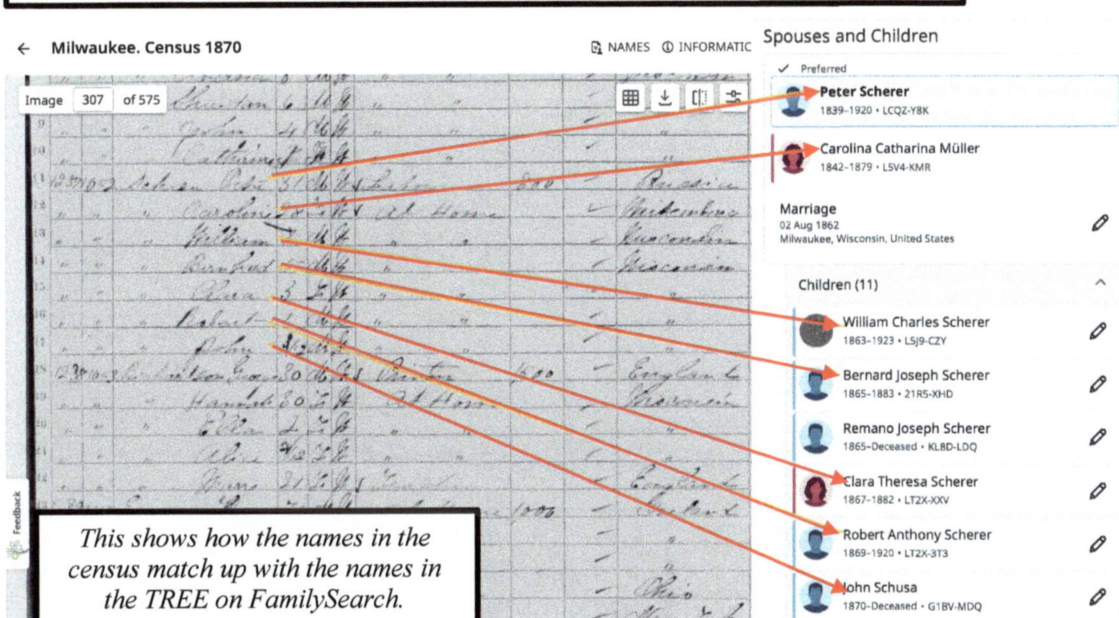

This shows how the names in the census match up with the names in the TREE on FamilySearch.

https://www.familysearch.org/ark:/61903/3:1:S3HT-6S7H-H1?view=index&action=view&cc=1438024&lang=en&groupId=TH-266-11765-5815-92

TRICK 6: Spouse Search

For a spouse name search, you can search by his / her full name, just the surnames of the couple, just the given names of the couple, or a combination. You will get a lot of search results with this type of search, so be sure to use the date and location filters to narrow the results. Try the following:

- Use given name and surname of both bride and groom.
- Use the given name and surname of just one spouse with just the surname of the other.
- Only use the surnames of the groom and bride.
- Only use the given names of the couple. (This will give a lot of search results, so it is best done if you also use the marriage date or location filters.)
- Leave off the names completely except for either one surname or one given name and search using the location filter and a date range. (This will give you a lot of search results, but you will usually be able to find them this way, if their record was part of the indexed records.)

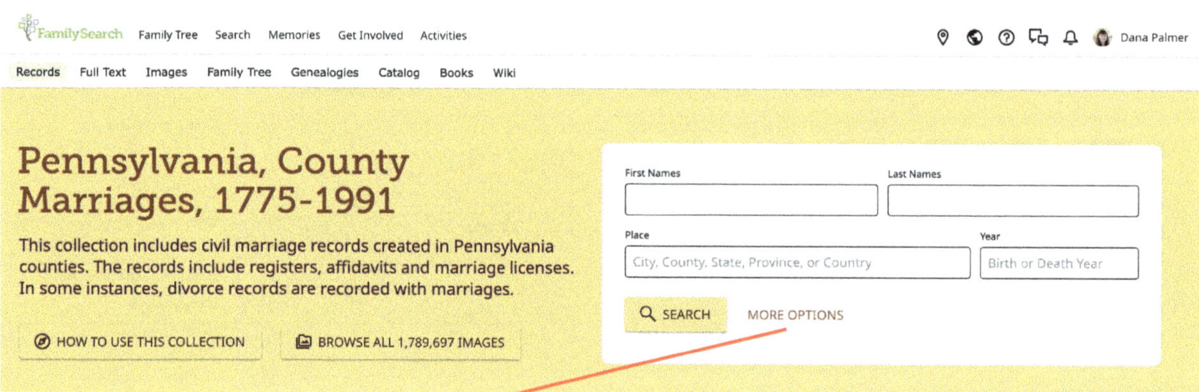

https://www.familysearch.org/search/collection/1589502

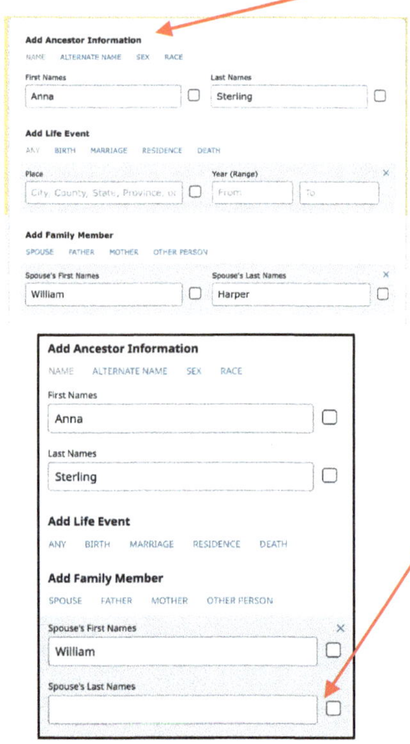

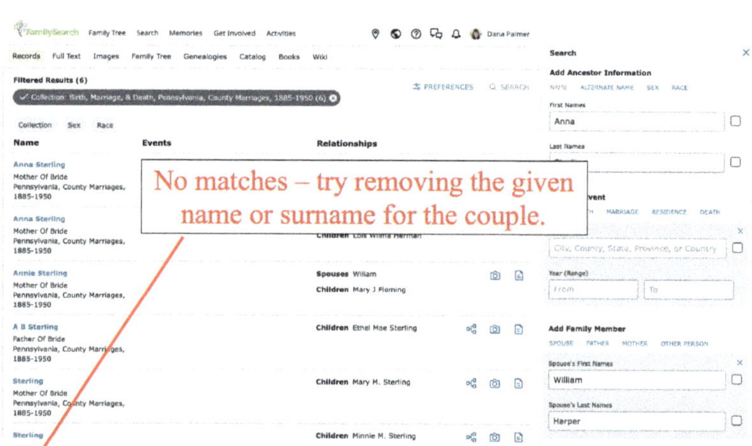

https://www.familysearch.org/en/search/record/results?f.collectionId=1589502&q.givenName=Anna&q.spouseGivenName=William&q.spouseSurname=Harper&q.surname=Sterling

If you can't find your couple when their given names are typed in the search boxes, try removing names in various combinations until you find them. Also try wildcards and nicknames. Be creative!

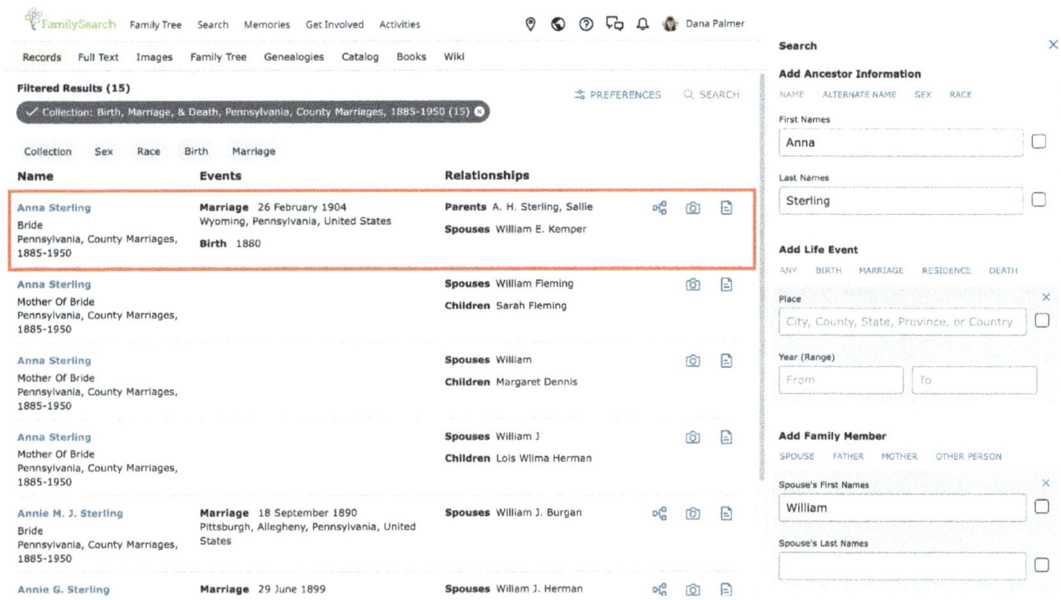

https://www.familysearch.org/en/search/record/results?count=20&q.givenName=Anna&q.spouseGivenName=William&q.surname=Sterling&f.collectionId=1589502

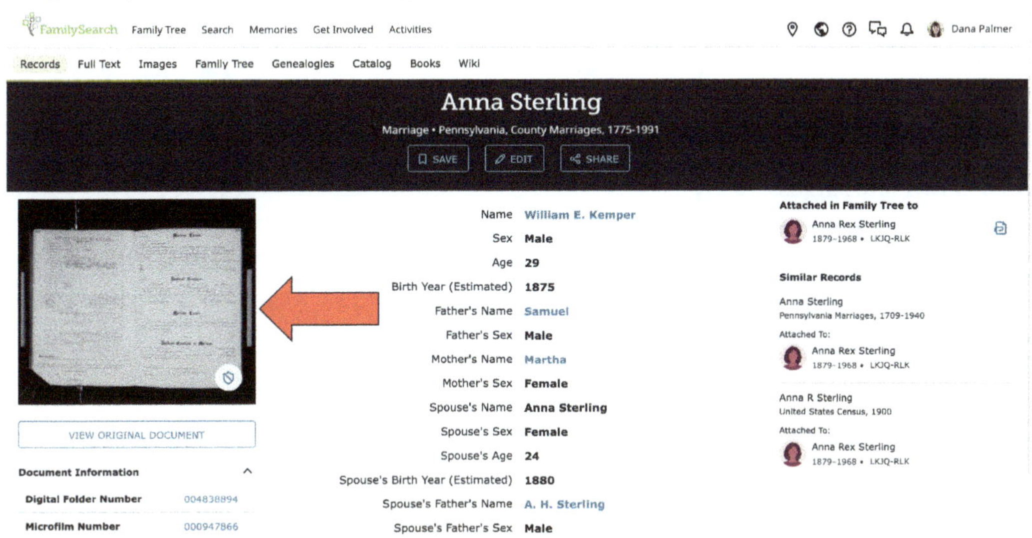

"Pennsylvania, County Marriages, 1775-1991," database with images, *FamilySearch* (https://www.familysearch.org/ark:/61903/1:1:VF4Q-BB9?lang=en : accessed 1 May 2025), citing Marriages Wyoming County, Pennsylvania, p. 178, no 2230, FS microfilm 947,866.

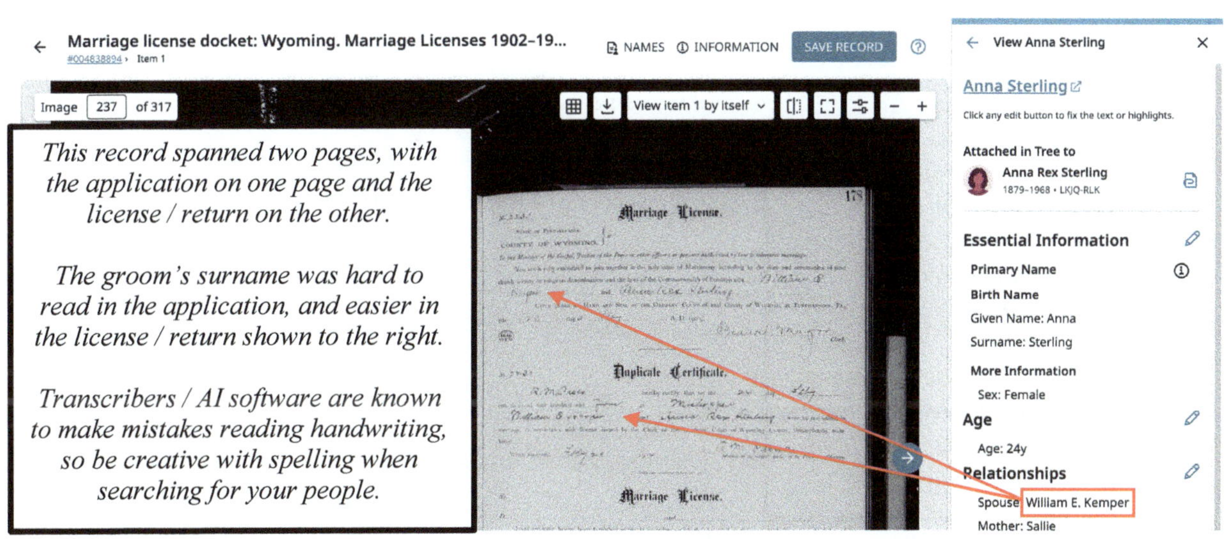

https://www.familysearch.org/ark:/61903/3:1:33S7-9PX6-VR1?view=index&action=view&cc=1589502&lang=en&groupId=M9Z5-PQF

TRICK 7: Other Family Members

By searching for other people who may be on the record for the person you are searching, you may be able to locate the record for your person. This is especially true when using census or death records. Be sure to use a location filter to narrow down the residence if using census records.

Goal: Find Dama Bertha Henderson, age 18, in the 1870 U.S. Census.

Her residence was unknown at that time. Her mother was married twice. She may be on the census with her mother Elizabeth Lilly, stepfather Henry Lilly, two siblings (Alzira and William Henderson), and half-sister Alice Lilly.

The tree to the right shows the family composition with her mother's two marriages.

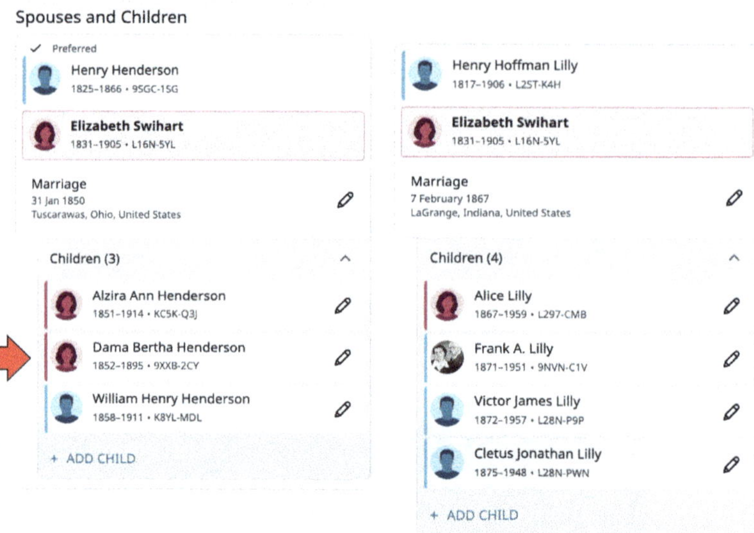

https://www.familysearch.org/en/tree/person/details/L16N-5YL

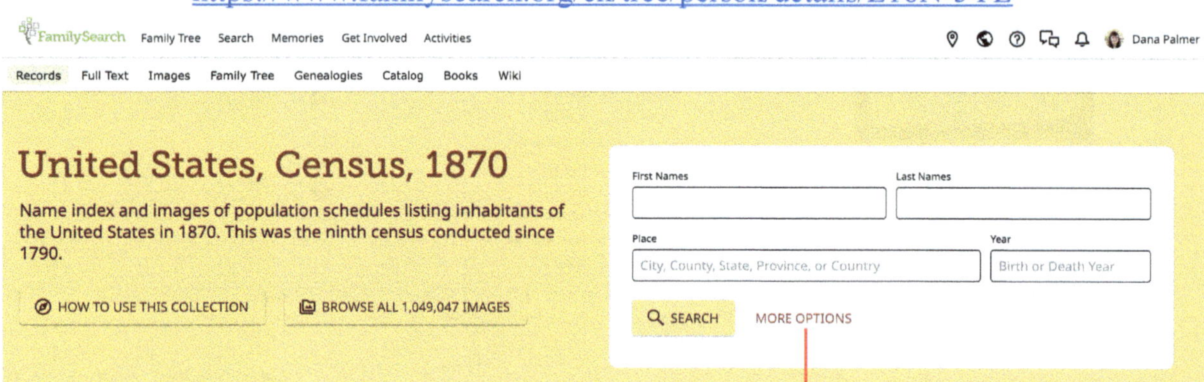

https://www.familysearch.org/en/search/collection/1438024

Searching for Dama's brother William Henderson and half-sister Alice, led to the discovery of Dama Henderson's whereabouts in the 1870 census.

If you can't find your ancestor, search for others who may be on the record or in the household with them at that time.

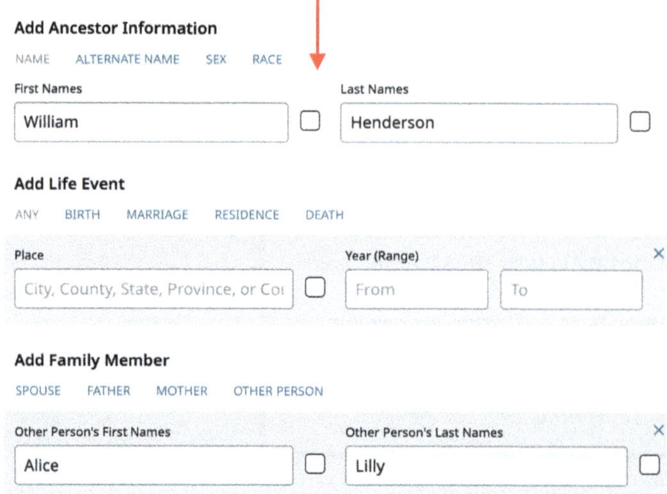

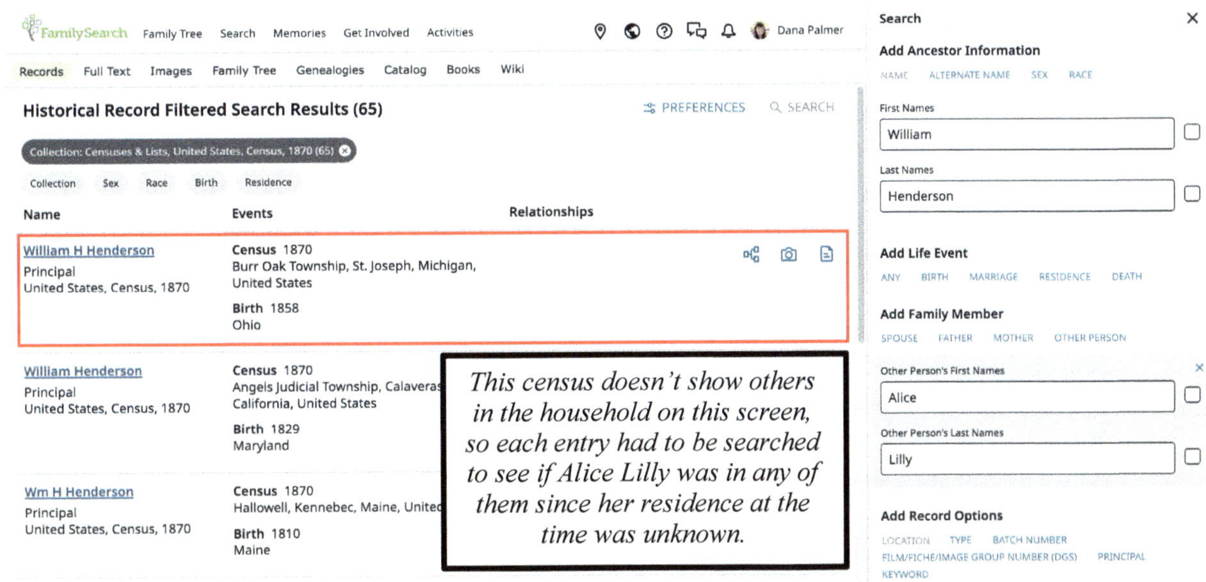

This census doesn't show others in the household on this screen, so each entry had to be searched to see if Alice Lilly was in any of them since her residence at the time was unknown.

https://www.familysearch.org/en/search/record/results?count=20&q.givenName=William&q.otherGivenName=Alice&q.otherSurname=Lilly&q.surname=Henderson&f.collectionId=1438024

https://www.familysearch.org/ark:/61903/1:1:MHCF-QTK?lang=en

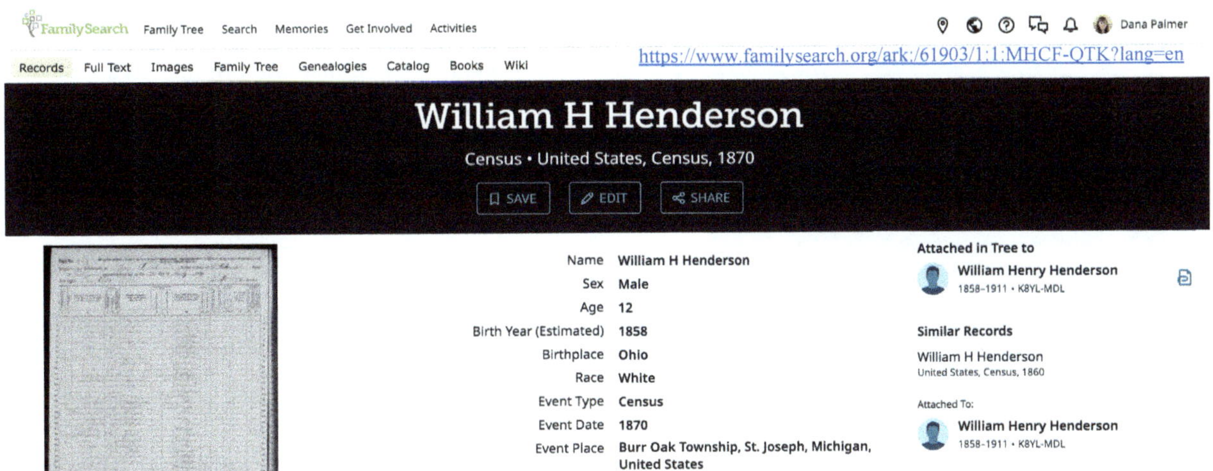

1870 U.S. Census, St. Joseph County, Michigan, population schedule, Burr Oak, p. 14 (handwritten), p. 7B (stamped), dwelling 116, family 116, William H Henderson in the household of Henry Lilly (indexed incorrectly as Selly), imaged, "United States, Census, 1870," *FamilySearch* (https://www.familysearch.org/ark:/61903/1:1:MHCF-QTK?lang=en : accessed 1 May 2025), citing National Archives microfilm publication M593, roll 700.

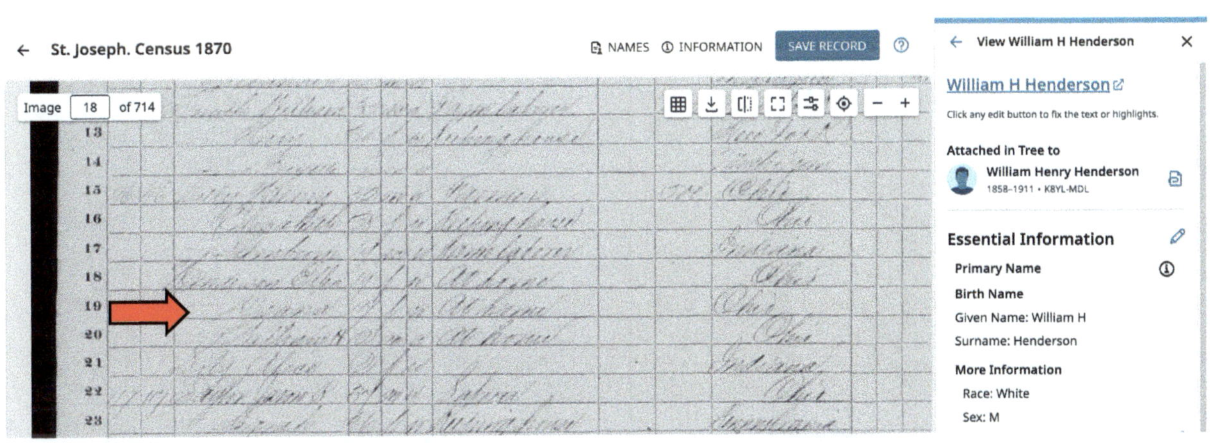

https://www.familysearch.org/ark:/61903/3:1:S3HY-XX89-ZKJ?view=index&cc=1438024&lang=en&groupId=TH-267-13031-31561-76&personArk=%2Fark%3A%2F61903%2F1%3A1%3AMHCF-QTK&action=view

Dama Henderson was listed as Diana on the census page, which is why she wasn't initially found. Searching for her siblings resulted in finding her in this blended family during the 1870 census.

TRICK 8: Parent Search

A parent search is useful if you want to find children of specific parents. This search will only work if the parents are listed on the record. Using a parent search by adding the father's or mother's surname or given name, along with the child's given name and other date or location filters, can help you find the elusive child. This is immensely helpful for misspelled children or married daughters when you don't know their married name.

- Leave the child's surname in the regular search field and add the parent's name in the search filter below. This should give you all the children listed for those parents with the names you typed.
- You can also type the parents' names in the regular search field and list the mother's name as the spouse.

Goal: Find the death record of Elizabeth (Brown) Irwin who died in or near Clermont County, Ohio.

It was initially hard to determine her death date from the tombstone because the photo was so blurry, making it difficult to narrow down her death year needed for the search filters.

Find a Grave, database with images (https://www.findagrave.com/memorial/127905873/elizabeth-c-irwin : accessed 1 May 2025), memorial 127905873, "Elizabeth C Brown Irwin" (1864-1919), memorial created by "Joseph", with tombstone image by "Joseph" citing Goshen Cemetery, Goshen, Clermont County, Ohio.

Because her death year and her married surname were unknown, the search was done by using her given name, birth range, and father's surname, since her parents were known.

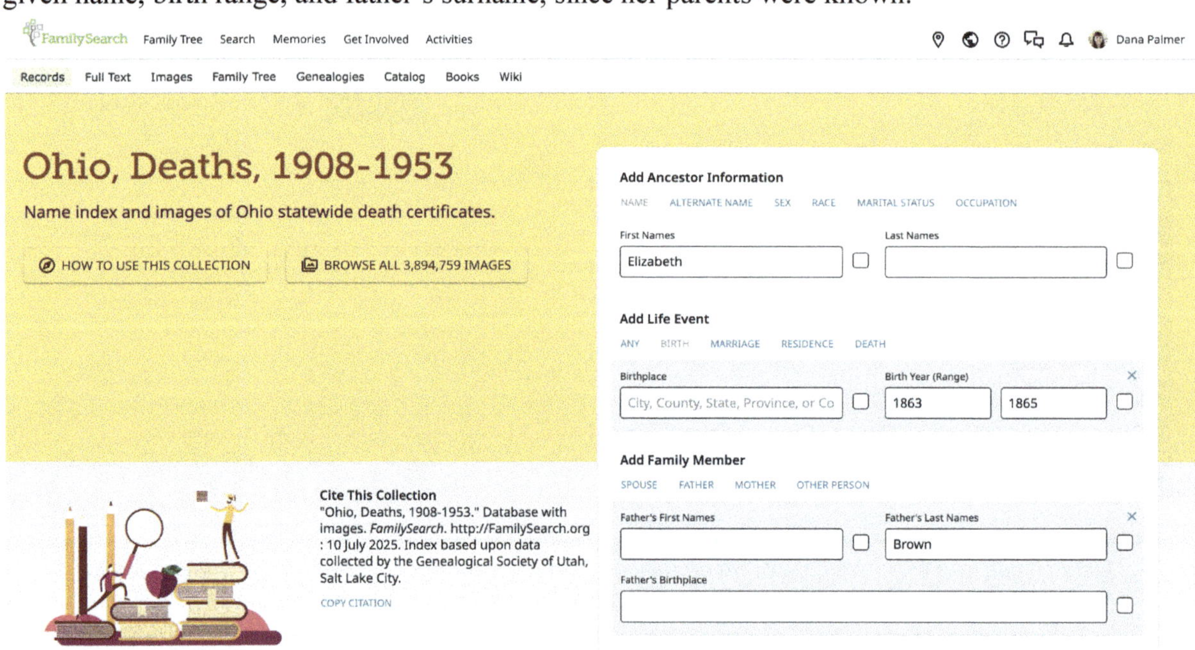

https://www.familysearch.org/en/search/collection/1307272

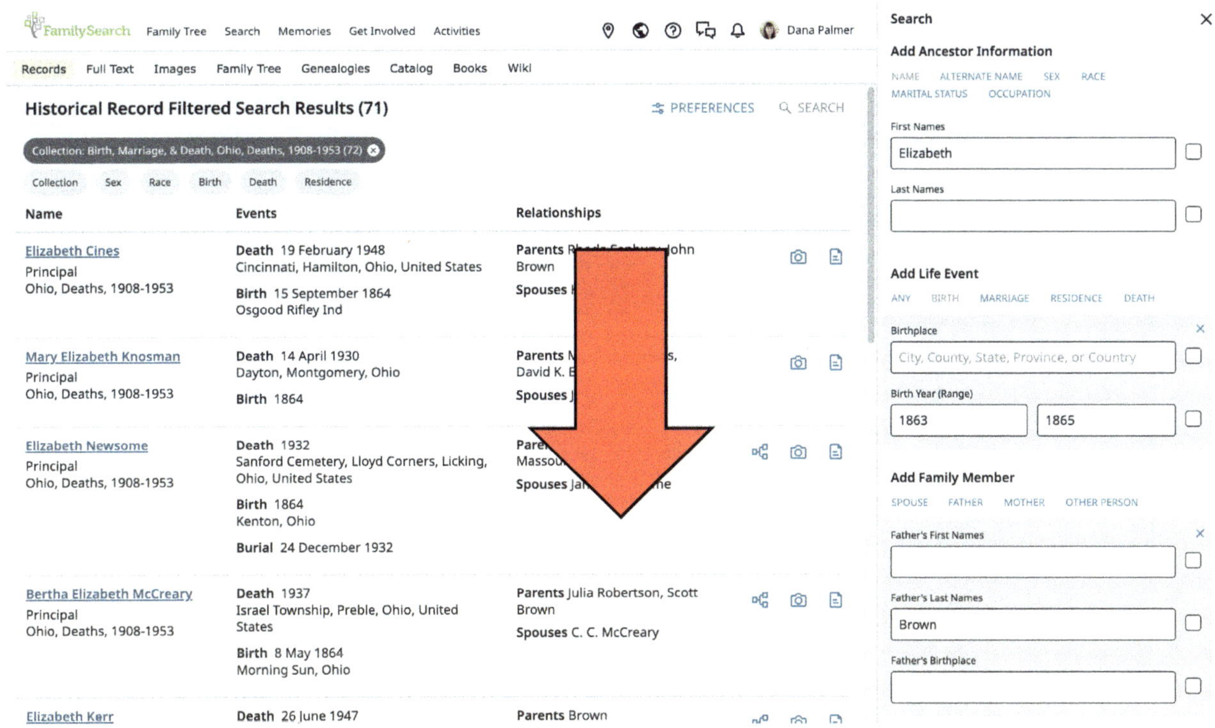

https://www.familysearch.org/en/search/record/results?f.collectionId=1307272&q.birthLikeDate.from=1863&q.birthLikeDate.to=1865&q.fatherSurname=Brown&q.givenName=Elizabeth

Scrolling down through the results yielded the entry for Elizabeth Irwin, who was listed incorrectly under the surname Truin.

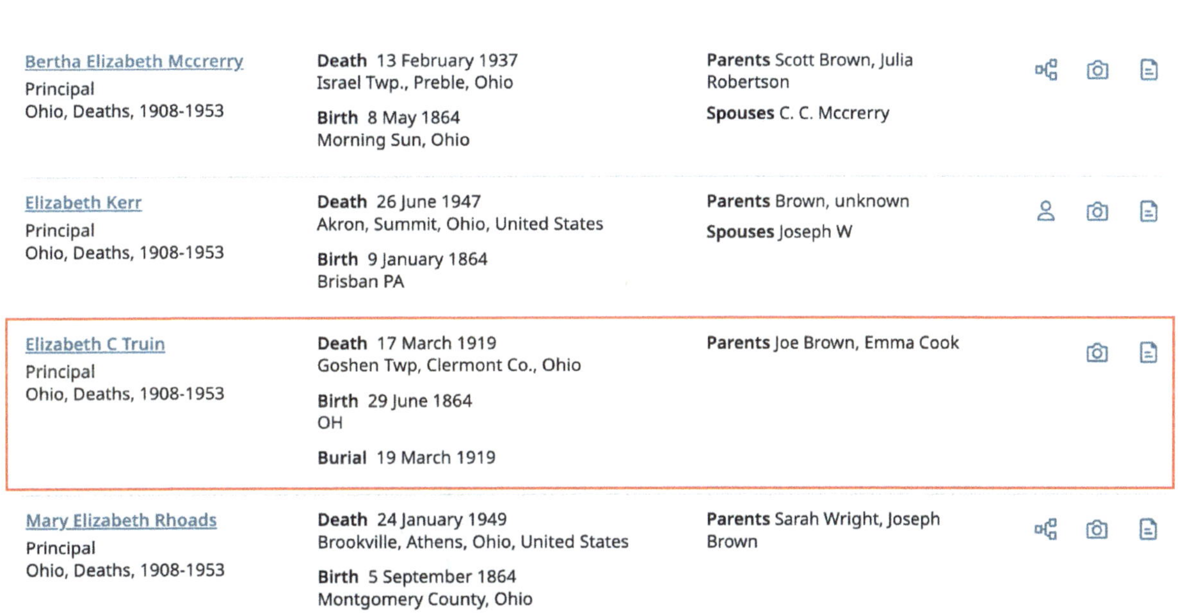

https://www.familysearch.org/en/search/record/results?f.collectionId=1307272&q.birthLikeDate.from=1863&q.birthLikeDate.to=1865&q.fatherSurname=Brown&q.givenName=Elizabeth

Consider searching for people by using their parents' names in the record. Keep in mind that if their parents' names are not included on the record, this type of search won't work.

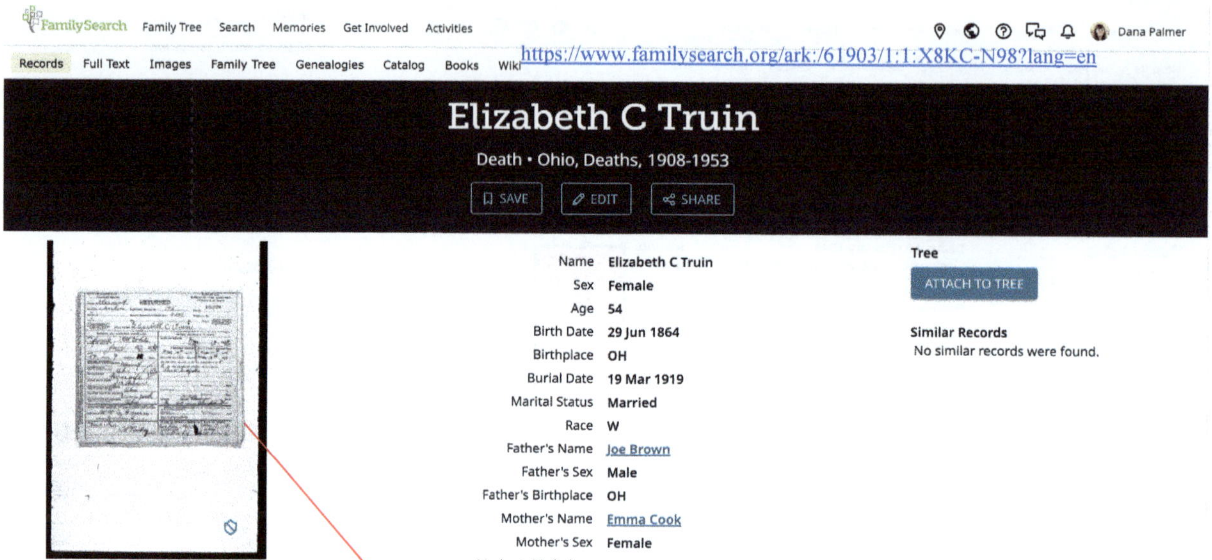

https://www.familysearch.org/ark:/61903/1:1:X8KC-N98?lang=en

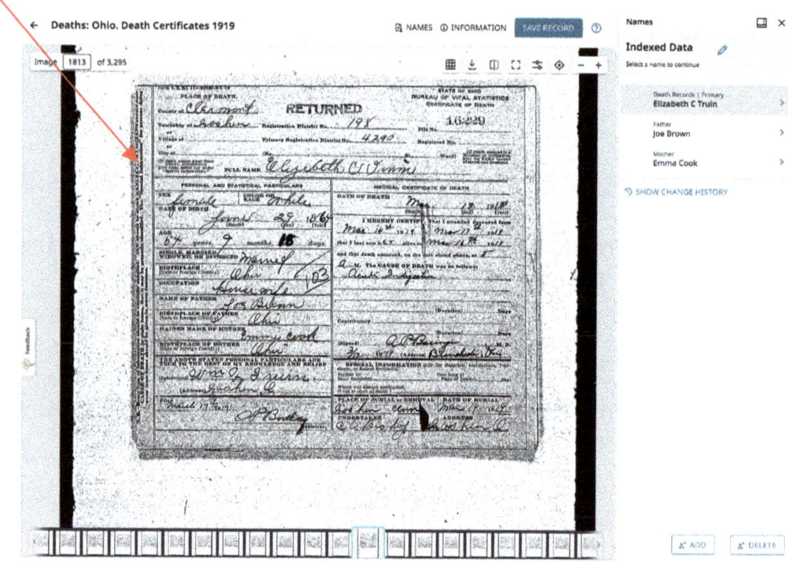

Name is indexed incorrectly.

https://www.familysearch.org/ark:/61903/3:1:33S7-9PKP-L9F?view=index&action=view&cc=1307272&lang=en&groupId=TH-1951-21292-46247-65

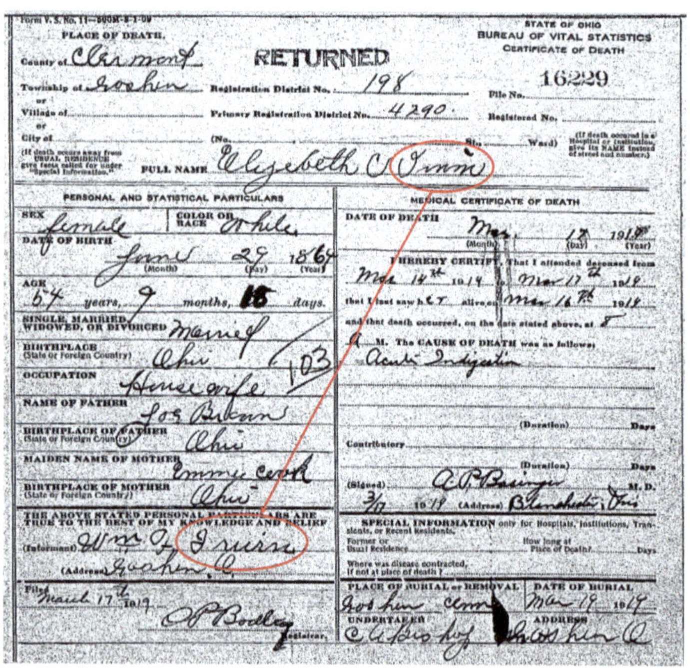
PLACE OF DEATH.
County of Clermont
RETURNED
STATE OF OHIO
BUREAU OF VITAL STATISTICS
CERTIFICATE OF DEATH
Township of Goshen Registration District No. 198
File No. 16229
Primary Registration District No. 4290
FULL NAME Elizebeth C Irwin
PERSONAL AND STATISTICAL PARTICULARS
SEX female
COLOR OR RACE White
DATE OF BIRTH June 29 1864
AGE 54 years, 9 months, 18 days.
SINGLE, MARRIED, WIDOWED, OR DIVORCED Married
BIRTHPLACE (State or Foreign Country) Ohio
OCCUPATION House wife
NAME OF FATHER Jos Brown
BIRTHPLACE OF FATHER (State or Foreign Country) Ohio
MAIDEN NAME OF MOTHER Emma Cook
BIRTHPLACE OF MOTHER (State or Foreign Country) Ohio
THE ABOVE STATED PERSONAL PARTICULARS ARE TRUE TO THE BEST OF MY KNOWLEDGE AND BELIEF
(Informant) Wm G Irwin
(Address) Goshen O
Filed March 17th 1919 A P Bodley Registrar.
MEDICAL CERTIFICATE OF DEATH
DATE OF DEATH Mar 17 1919
I HEREBY CERTIFY, That I attended deceased from Mar 14th 1919 to Mar 17th 1919
that I last saw her alive on Mar 16th 1919
and that death occurred, on the date stated above, at 8 A.M. The CAUSE OF DEATH was as follows: Acute Indigestion
(Signed) A P Basinger M.D.
3/17 1919 (Address) Blanchester Ohio
SPECIAL INFORMATION
PLACE OF BURIAL OR REMOVAL Goshen Cem
DATE OF BURIAL Mar 19 1919
UNDERTAKER C. E. Kirby
ADDRESS Goshen O

Those who are familiar with their family members and names are often able to read the entries more easily than those who indexed the records.

Her name was listed as Elizebeth C Irwin, but her name was indexed as Truin because the indexer could not decipher the record. Since the first letter was wrong the wildcard trick would not work. Using her father's surname, which was included on this record, led to its discovery.

TRICK 9: Locality Search

A locality (place) search is best used in conjunction with date and name searches as previously shown. If you are having trouble finding your person, leave off the person's given and surnames and just search by the date and location filters. This allows you to check if records are included in the collection for that location and time period. Sometimes the search engine will give you an error when you do this type of search. If so, be sure you check the exact filter box and keep clicking search until it works. Locality searches may yield a lot of search results, which will take time to go through, but if your person is in the indexed collection, this is an effective way to find them. It may be necessary to find another person's entry close to the time of yours and search the original records until you find them.

The RESIDENCE filter under MORE OPTIONS is very useful when using census records to narrow down the search results, especially when used with the person's name and a birth range.

Goal: Find Andrew J Cilley, age 27, in the 1860 census.

He should be living in Thorndike, Waldo, Maine, so an exact search using Thorndike as the residence should narrow the search results.

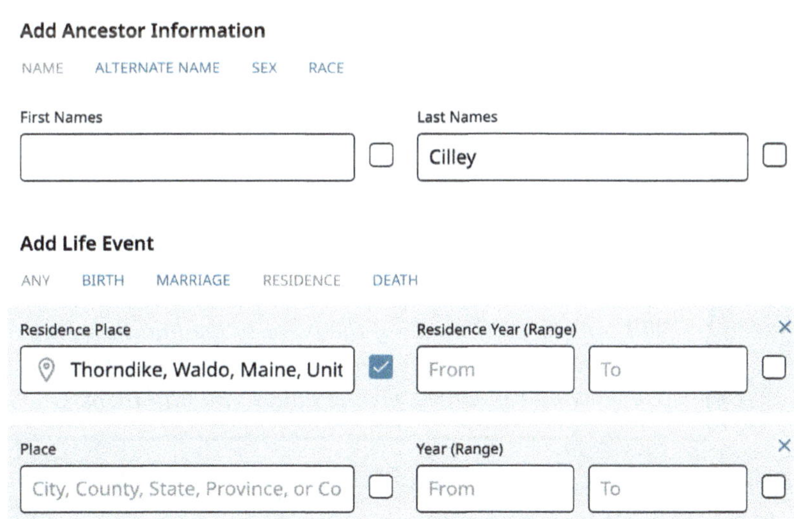

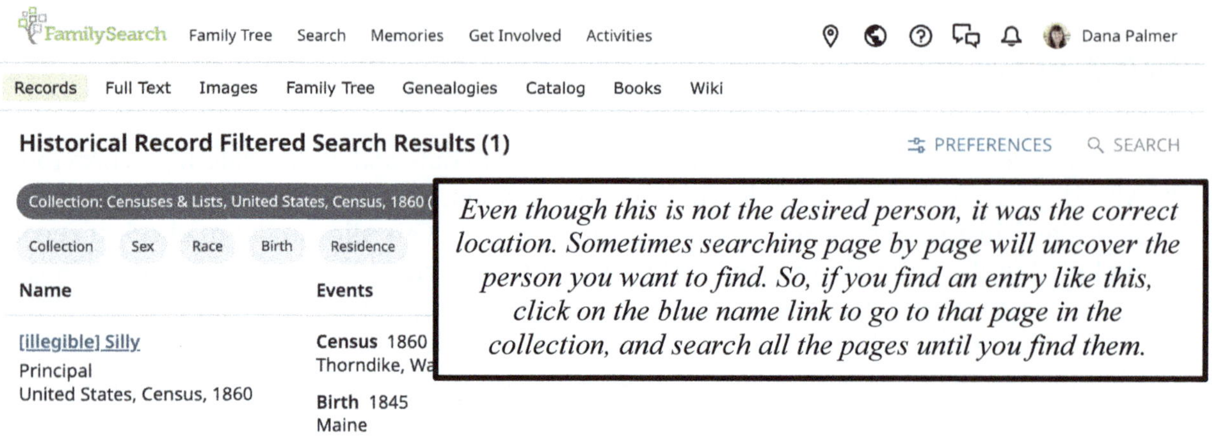

https://www.familysearch.org/en/search/record/results?f.collectionId=1473181&q.residencePlace=Thorndike%2C%20Waldo%2C%20Maine%2C%20United%20States&q.surname=Cilley

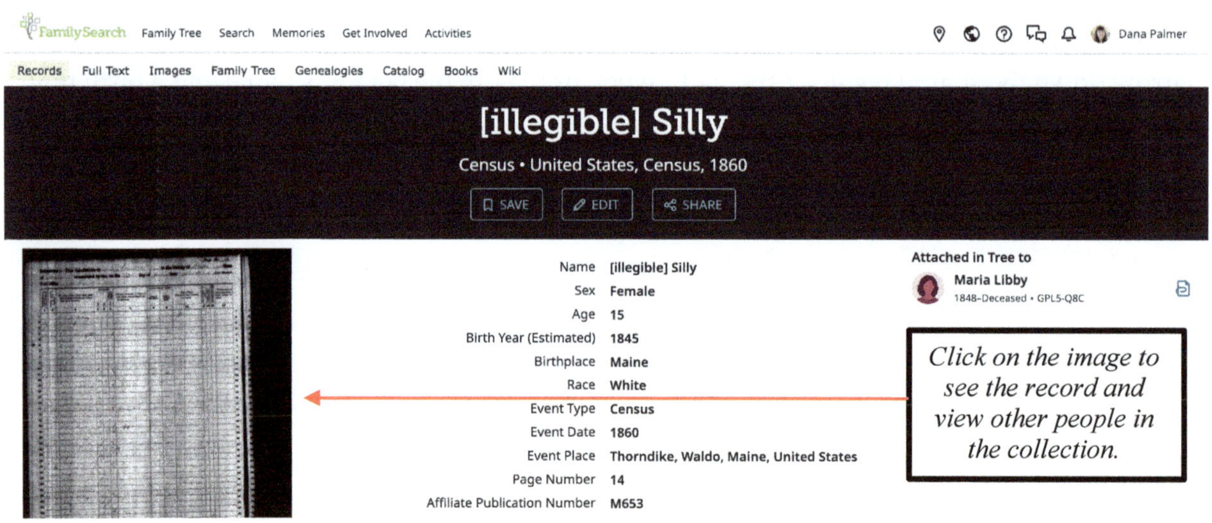

https://www.familysearch.org/ark:/61903/1:1:MDHP-Z9V?lang=en

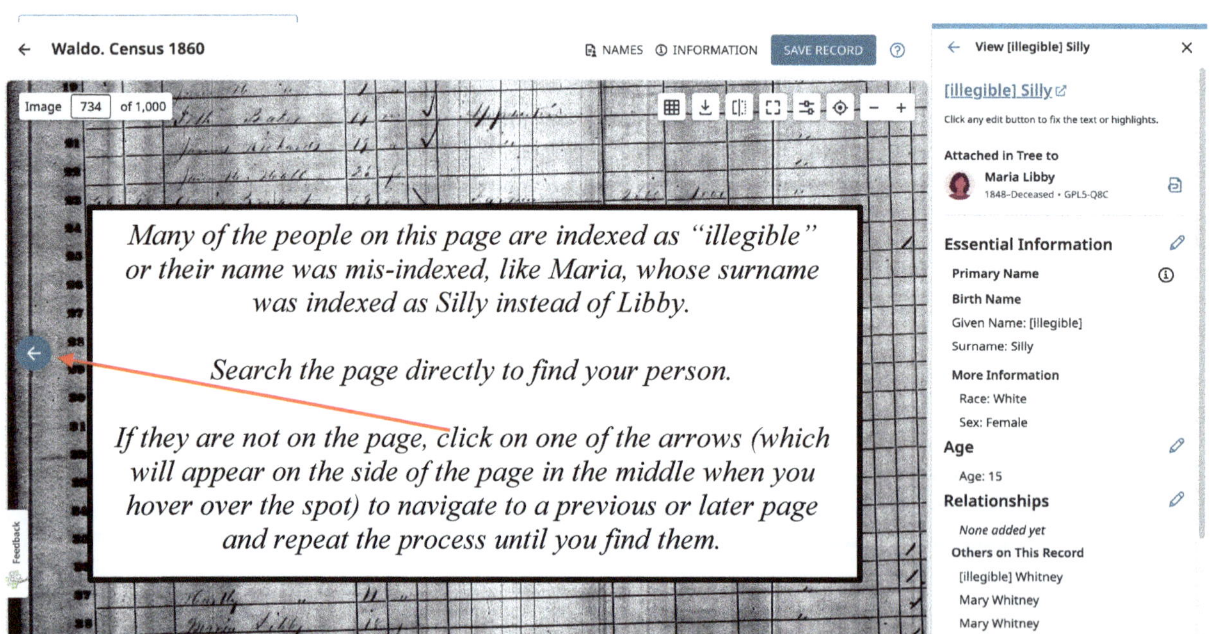

1860 U.S. Census, Waldo County, Maine, population schedule, Thorndike, p. 14, dwelling 101, family 101, Maria Libby in the household of Amos Whitney, imaged, "United States, Census, 1860," *FamilySearch* (https://www.familysearch.org/ark:/61903/1:1:MDHP-Z9V?lang=en : accessed 1 May 2025), citing National Archives microfilm publication M653, roll 453.

https://www.familysearch.org/ark:/61903/3:1:33SQ-GB9V-S3Q?view=index&action=view&cc=1473181&lang=en&groupId=TH-1942-25247-73994-46

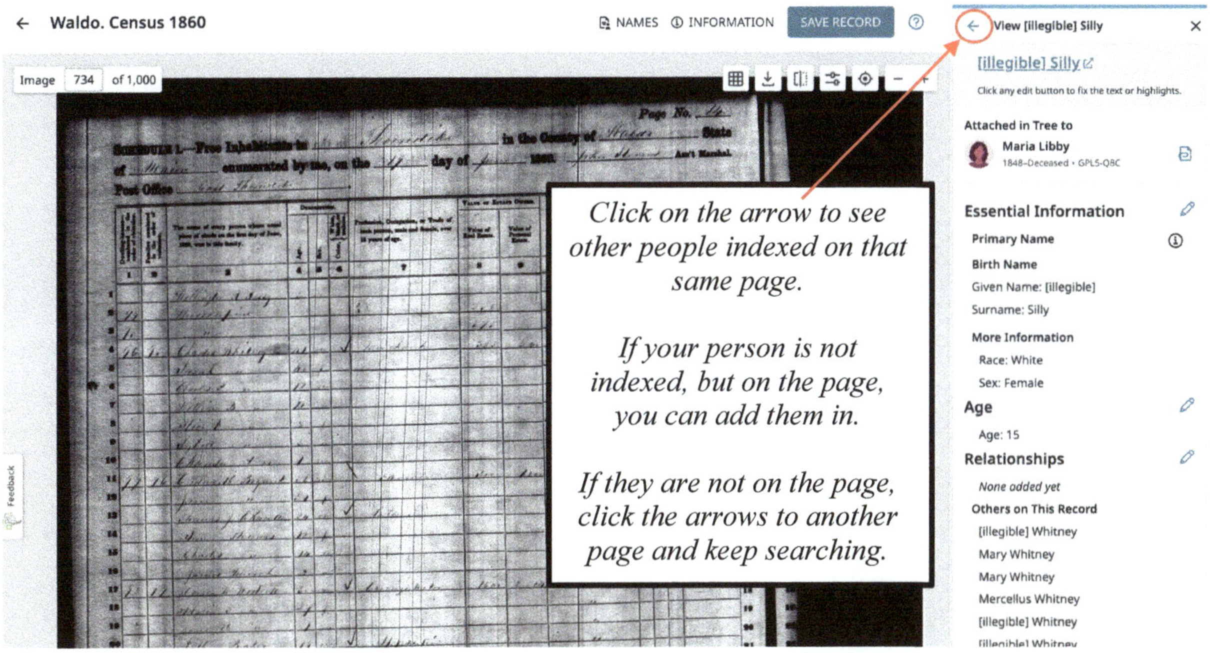

https://www.familysearch.org/ark:/61903/3:1:33SQ-GB9V-S3Q?view=index&action=view&cc=1473181&lang=en&groupId=TH-1942-25247-73994-46

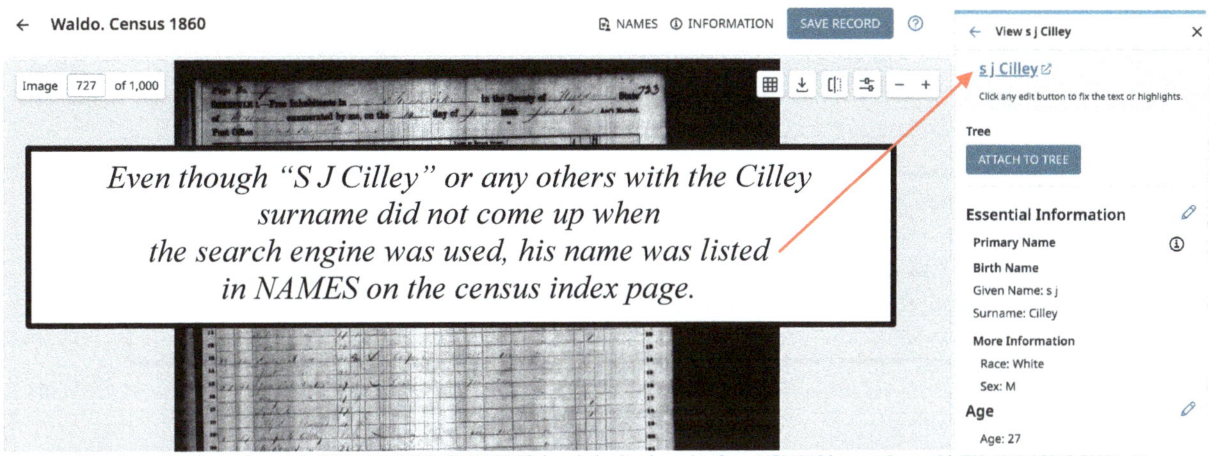

https://www.familysearch.org/ark:/61903/3:1:33SQ-GB9V-SSG?view=index&action=view&cc=1473181&lang=en&groupId=TH-1942-25247-73994-46

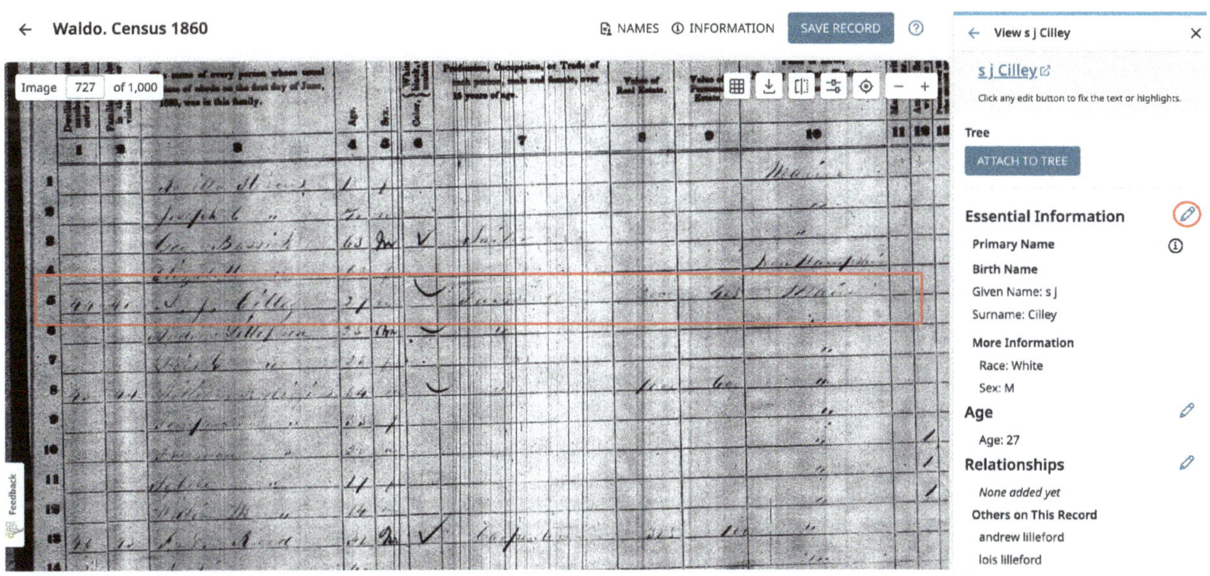

1860 U.S. Census, Waldo County, Maine, population schedule, Thorndike, p. 7, dwelling 44, family 43, A J Cilley, imaged, "United States, Census, 1860," *FamilySearch* (https://www.familysearch.org/ark:/61903/1:1:MDHP-ZYR?lang=en : accessed 1 May 2025), citing National Archives microfilm publication M653, roll 453.

https://www.familysearch.org/ark:/61903/3:1:33SQ-GB9V-SSG?view=index&action=view&cc=1473181&lang=en&groupId=TH-1942-25247-73994-46

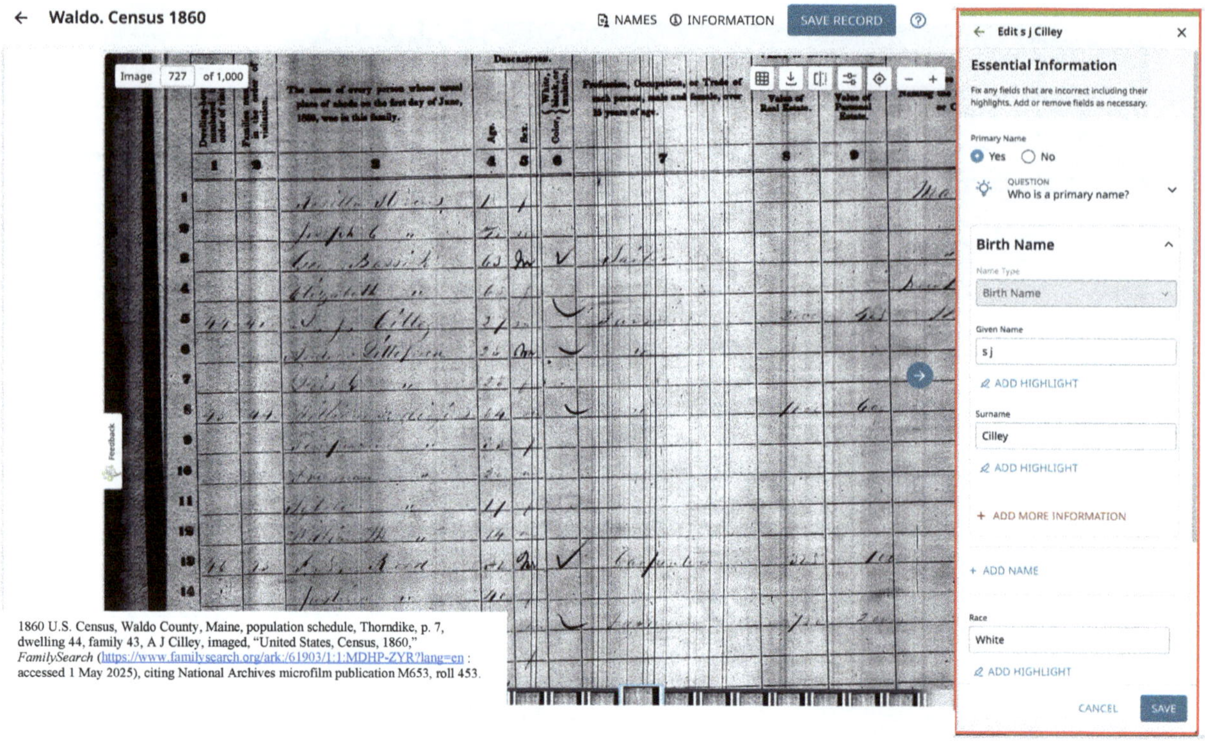

1860 U.S. Census, Waldo County, Maine, population schedule, Thorndike, p. 7, dwelling 44, family 43, A J Cilley, imaged, "United States, Census, 1860," *FamilySearch* (https://www.familysearch.org/ark:/61903/1:1:MDHP-ZYR?lang=en : accessed 1 May 2025), citing National Archives microfilm publication M653, roll 453.

https://www.familysearch.org/ark:/61903/3:1:33SQ-GB9V-SSG?view=index&action=view&cc=1473181&lang=en&groupId=TH-1942-25247-73994-46

If you find a transcription error, click on the pencil to edit the fact.

You can add a highlight to mark the change in the correction so others can see it was fixed. In this case, the name "s j" was changed to "A J."

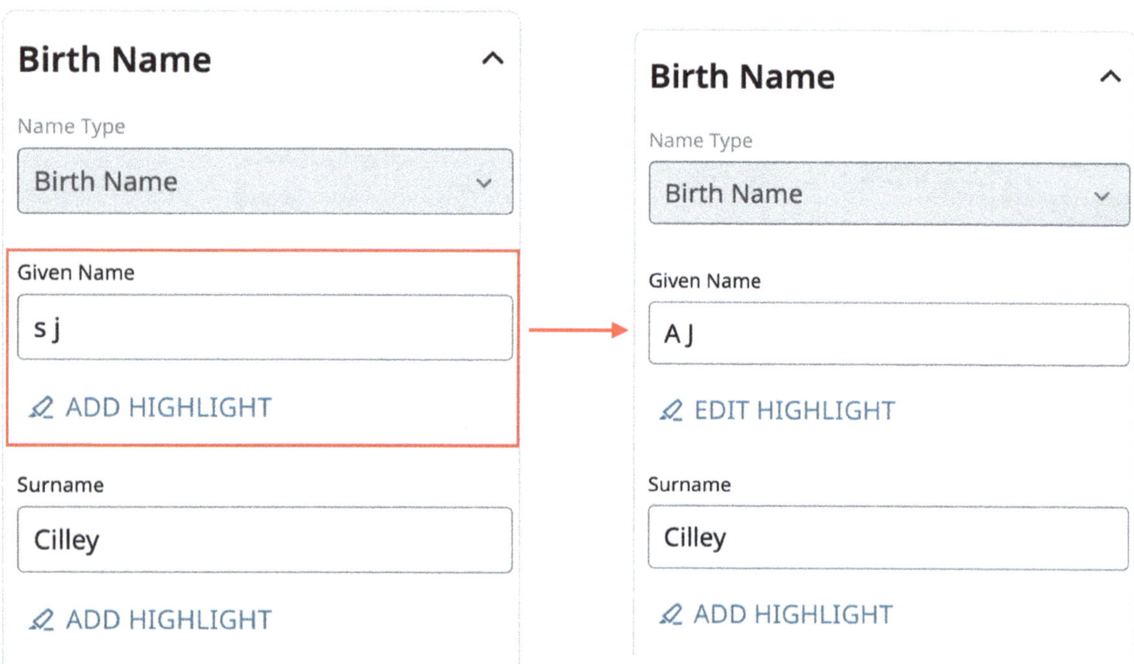

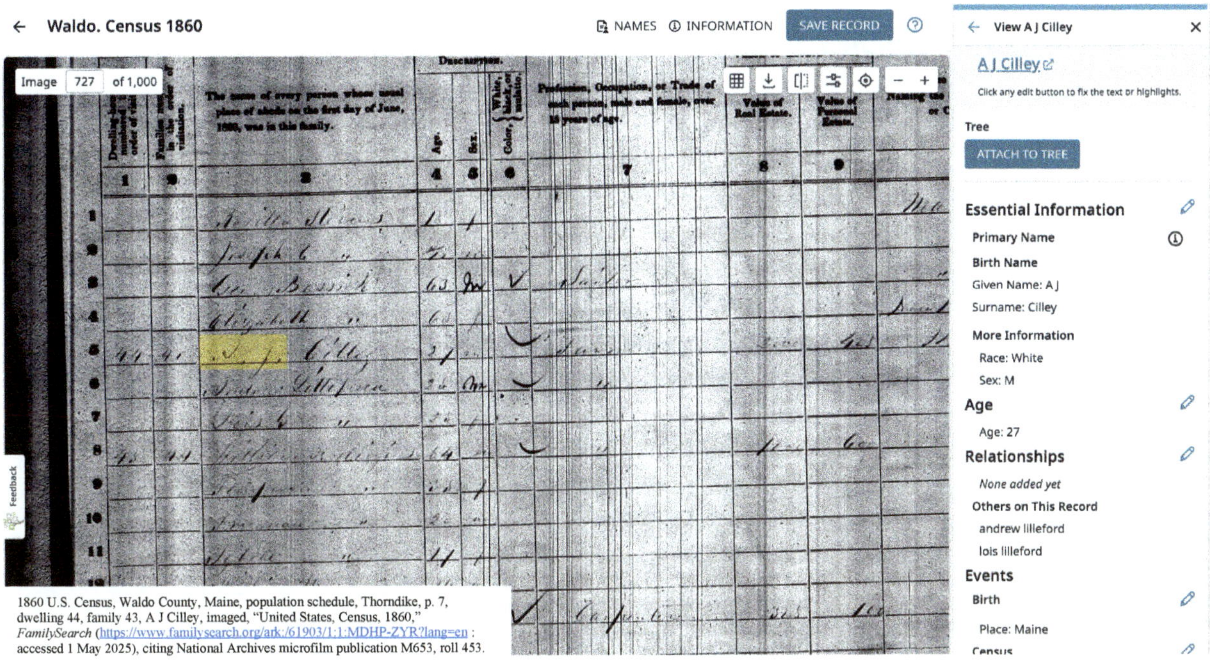

1860 U.S. Census, Waldo County, Maine, population schedule, Thorndike, p. 7, dwelling 44, family 43, A J Cilley, imaged, "United States, Census, 1860," *FamilySearch* (https://www.familysearch.org/ark:/61903/1:1:MDHP-ZYR?lang=en : accessed 1 May 2025), citing National Archives microfilm publication M653, roll 453.

https://www.familysearch.org/ark:/61903/3:1:33SQ-GB9V-SSG?view=index&action=view&cc=1473181&lang=en&groupId=TH-1942-25247-73994-46

Once the correction has been submitted, if you added a highlight, it will be visible in the location where you placed the highlight, as seen here.

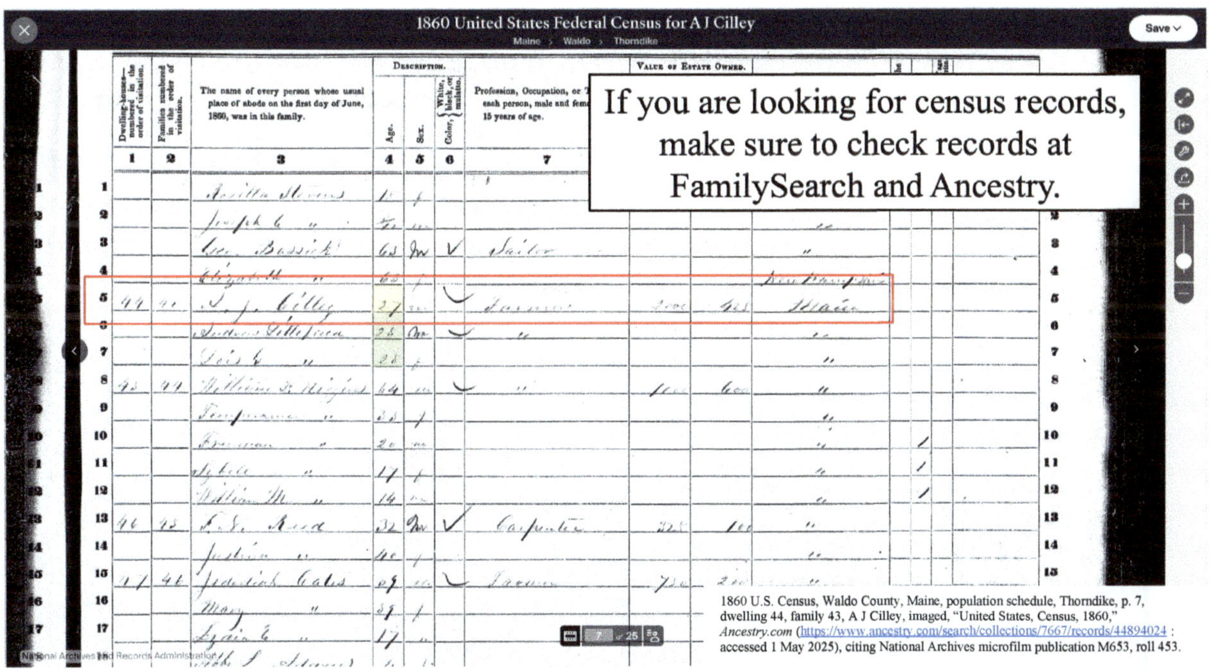

1860 U.S. Census, Waldo County, Maine, population schedule, Thorndike, p. 7, dwelling 44, family 43, A J Cilley, imaged, "United States, Census, 1860," *Ancestry.com* (https://www.ancestry.com/search/collections/7667/records/44894024 : accessed 1 May 2025), citing National Archives microfilm publication M653, roll 453.

This is the same 1860 census record entry for A J Cilley in Thorndike, Waldo, Maine, but this image from Ancestry.com is much more legible than the one found on FamilySearch. If you are doing census research, be sure to check multiple database websites as their search engines and images are not the same and you might find a more legible copy elsewhere.

TRICK 10: Direct Record Search

If you are unable to find your person in the indexes on RECORDS, go to the original source in the CATALOG or IMAGES and search for the record directly. Not all dates or locations have been indexed. Searching for the records directly in the CATALOG and IMAGES will take more time but will usually yield results so you can find your person's record. With more collections being added to FULL-TEXT SEARCH, it's advisable to search there too. Keep in mind if the location or time period is not digitized in the collection on FamilySearch, you will need to identify who has the record and obtain a copy directly from that repository. The FamilySearch RESEARCH WIKI can help you identify where the original record is stored.

Goal: Find the death record of Laura Allen who, according to family, died 6 January 1953 in Dayton, Montgomery, Ohio.

Dates from tombstones might provide clues to make it easier to find the death record.

Find a Grave, database with images (https://www.findagrave.com/memorial/45624588/laura-m-allen : accessed 1 May 2025), memorial 45624588, "Laura M Sparks Allen" (1866-1953), memorial created by "Gene Wilt" with tombstone image by "Gene Wilt," citing Milledgeville Plymouth Cemetery, Fayette County, Ohio.

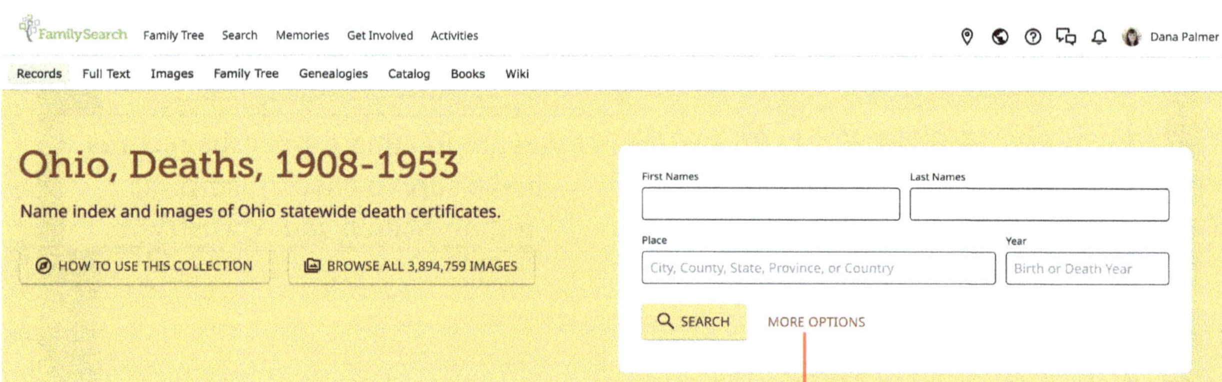

https://www.familysearch.org/search/collection/1307272

A search was done for Laura Allen with an exact birth date range of 1885 to 1887 and exact death year of 1953.

The location for death was excluded since many of the later death records in this collection do not have the location indexed, and including it would eliminate search results.

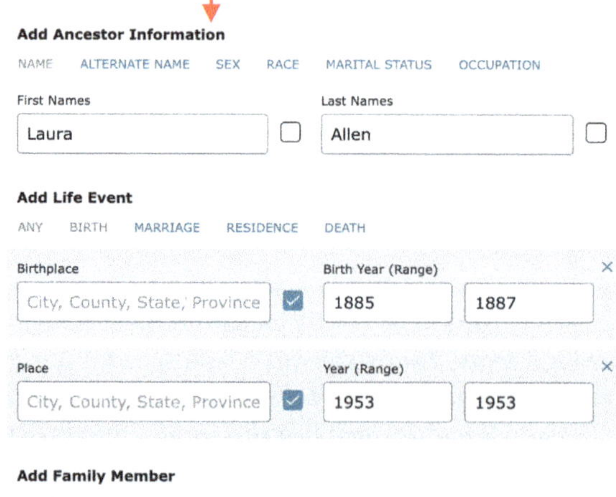

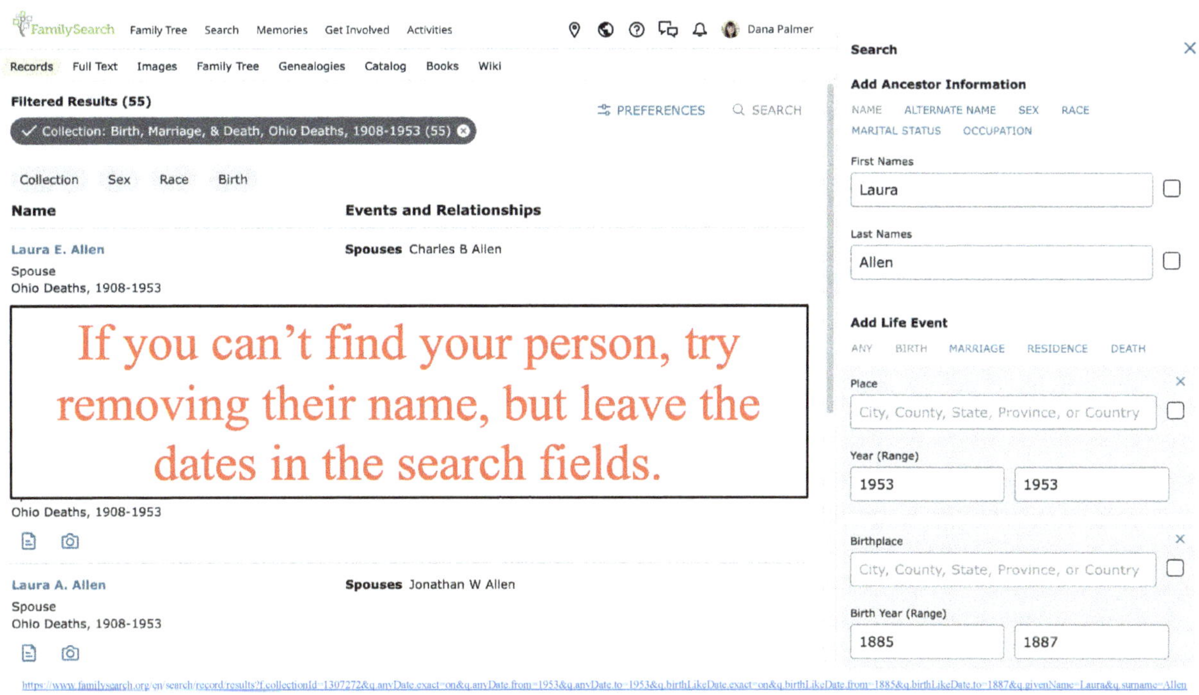

If you can't find your person, try removing their name, but leave the dates in the search fields.

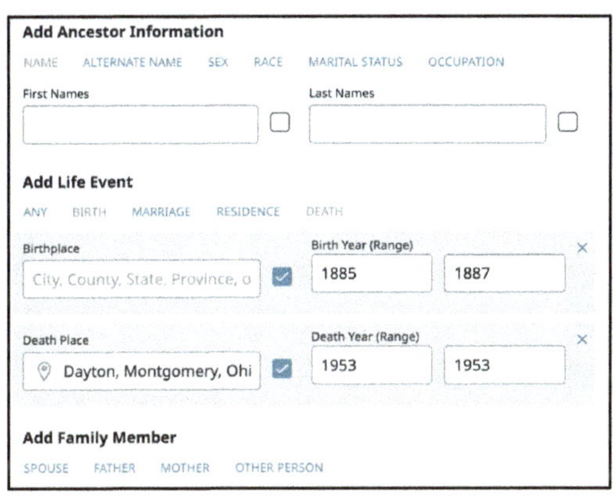

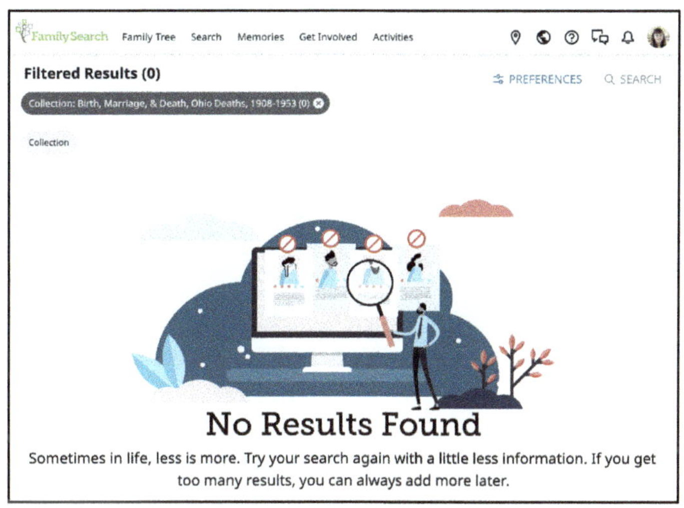

When I first searched for Laura, she did not come up in the search results because the county where she died was not included in the index at that time. About a year later when I searched for her again, that area had been indexed, and her name appeared.

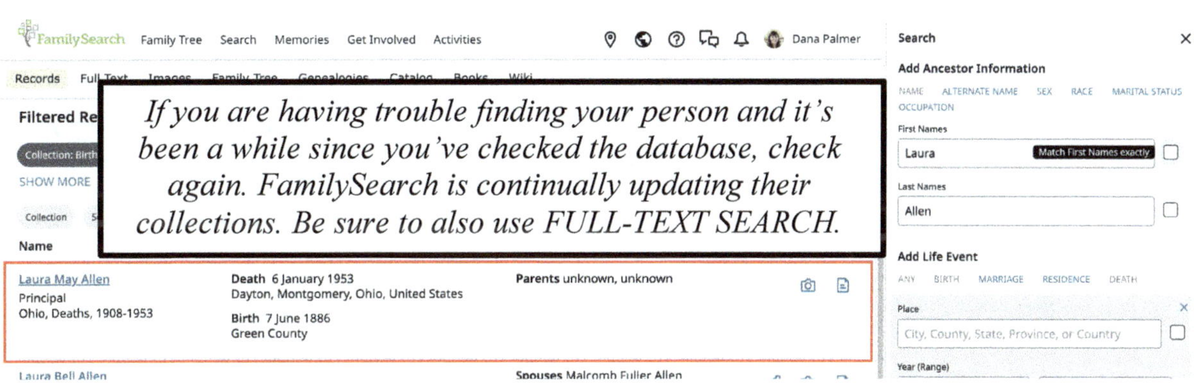

If you are having trouble finding your person and it's been a while since you've checked the database, check again. FamilySearch is continually updating their collections. Be sure to also use FULL-TEXT SEARCH.

So, what can you do to find someone who does not appear in the indexes in RECORDS?

Remember that not all locations or time periods are included in the indexes in RECORDS, but the images may be found elsewhere on the FamilySearch website, usually in IMAGES or CATALOG. If it's not online or restricted for viewing only in the FamilySearch library in Salt Lake City, make arrangements to travel to the local repository or find someone local who can copy the record for you.

The FamilySearch RESEARCH WIKI can help you determine if the records may be online on another website and where the original copies are being held. Local genealogical or historical societies can be a great help in obtaining copies of local records. Local libraries may be willing to assist too. For areas that do not have active societies, use **LINKED IN** to find local researchers in the area you are researching.

In this case, the original death records for this time period were on FamilySearch in the CATALOG under the state of Ohio, since they were from the collection kept by the Ohio Department of Health.

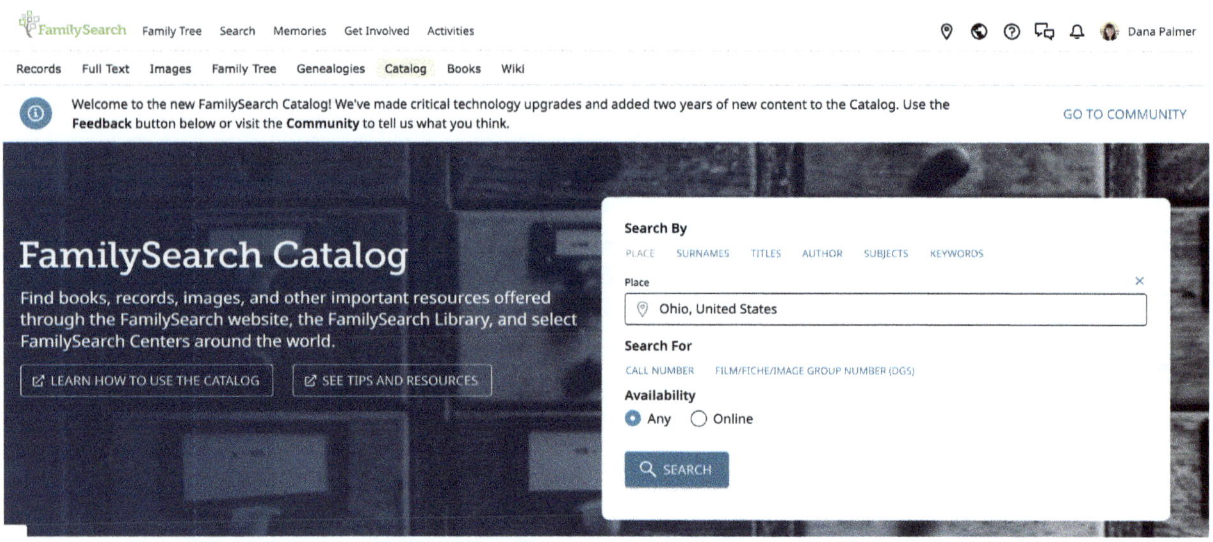

https://www.familysearch.org/en/search/catalog

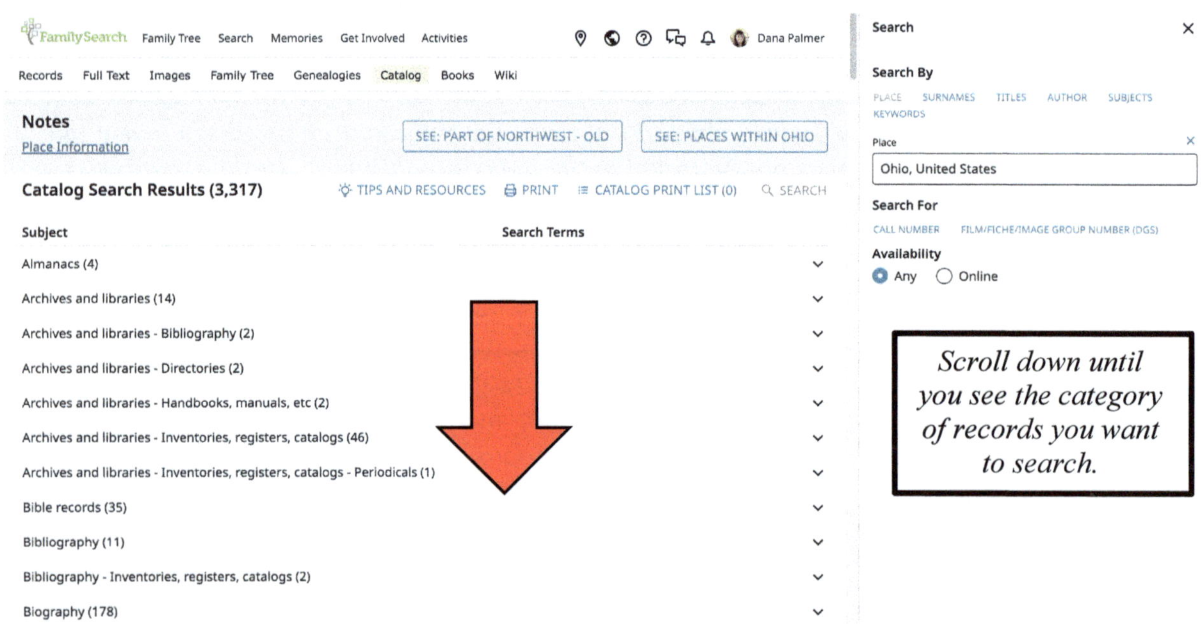

https://www.familysearch.org/en/search/catalog/results?q.place=Ohio%2C%20United%20States

To find the original Ohio death certificate, go to the CATALOG for OHIO and scroll down to the Vital records category. Select "Certificates of death, 1908-1953; index, 1908-1911."

Vital records (58)

1880 Ohio mortality records: counties Adams through Geauga : all existing Ohio mortality schedules; alphabetically arranged/ Jeanne Britton Workman	Author: Workman, Jeanne Britton	+ ADD
47 pioneer families of Rockingham County, Virginia : who migrated through Ohio, Indiana, and Illinois to Missouri/ Robert L. Brock	Author: Brock, Robert L., 1923-	+ ADD
Abstracts from history of the Church of the Brethren in Ohio/ by Lindsay M. Brien	Author: Brien, Lindsay M	+ ADD
Beaver, Pennsylvania, argus genealogical gleanings 1830-58/ compiled by Mark H. Welchley	Author: Welchley, Mark H	+ ADD
Certificates of births/deaths/stillbirths (Ohio),1918-1953	Author: Ohio. Bureau of Vital Statistics	+ ADD
Certificates of death, 1908-1953 ; index, 1908-1911	Author: Ohio Historical Society (Columbus, Ohio), Ohio.... MORE	+ ADD

https://www.familysearch.org/en/search/catalog/results?q.place=Ohio%2C%20United%20States

FamilySearch Family Tree Search Memories Get Involved Activities Dana Palmer

Records Full Text Images Family Tree Genealogies Catalog Books Wiki

https://www.familysearch.org/en/search/catalog/700227

TIPS AND RESOURCES PRINT CATALOG PRINT LIST (0)

Certificates of death, 1908-1953 ; index, 1908-1911

ADD TO PRINT LIST

Authors	Ohio Historical Society (Columbus, Ohio) (Added Author) Ohio. Department of Health (Author)
Format	Microfilm 16mm, Microfilm 35mm
Language	English
Publication Date	1983-2005
Publisher	Filmed by the Genealogical Society of Utah
Place of Publication	Salt Lake City, Utah
Physical	1207 microfilm reels ; 16 and 35 mm.
References	(Digital Collection) Ohio deaths, 1908-1953

Scroll down and choose the applicable microfilm for the time period. If there are multiple pages of records, you may need to browse a bit to find the year you want.

Notes

The certificate number 65080-65083 and 65362-65366 from the year 1909 may not appear on the index.

Microfilm of original records at Ohio Historical Society, Columbus, Ohio.

Ohio Deaths are available online, click here.

View this catalog record in WorldCat for other possible copy locations.

Feedback

Subjects

Locality Subjects

United States, Ohio - Vital records

https://www.familysearch.org/en/search/catalog/700227

Film/Digital Notes

Film Number or Image Group Number (DGS)

Find the year desired.

Note	Location	Collection/Shelf	Film	Image Group Number (DGS)	Format
Index, 1908-1909	Granite Mountain Record Vault	United States & Canada Film	929253	8331368	
Index, 1910	Granite Mountain Record Vault	United States & Canada Film	929254	8331366	
Index, 1911	Granite Mountain Record Vault	United States & Canada Film	929255	8331363	
Deaths, file no. 1-1967, 1908	Granite Mountain Record Vault	United States & Canada Film	1926951	4020893	

These records were organized by year and file number. Within each year, they were then further organized by county for each month. So, all the death records for Montgomery in the month of January were grouped together. Then another microfilm had the death records for the next month. Each microfilm had multiple counties that needed to be searched since the file number was unknown.

Note	Location	Collection/Shelf	Film	Image Group Number (DGS)	Format
Deaths, file no. 81201-83794, 1952	Granite Mountain Record Vault	United States & Canada Film	2246400	4109450	
Deaths, file no. 1-2600, 1953	Granite Mountain Record Vault	United States & Canada Film	2246401	4109451	
Deaths, file no. 2601-5400, 1953	Granite Mountain Record Vault	United States & Canada Film	2246446	4109452	
Deaths, file no. 5401-8100, 1953	Granite Mountain Record Vault	United States & Canada Film	2246447	4109453	
Deaths, file no. 8101-10800, 1953	Granite Mountain Record Vault	United States & Canada Film	2246448	4109454	
Deaths, file no. 10801-13600, 1953	Granite Mountain Record Vault	United States & Canada Film	2246449	4109455	

https://www.familysearch.org/en/search/catalog/700227

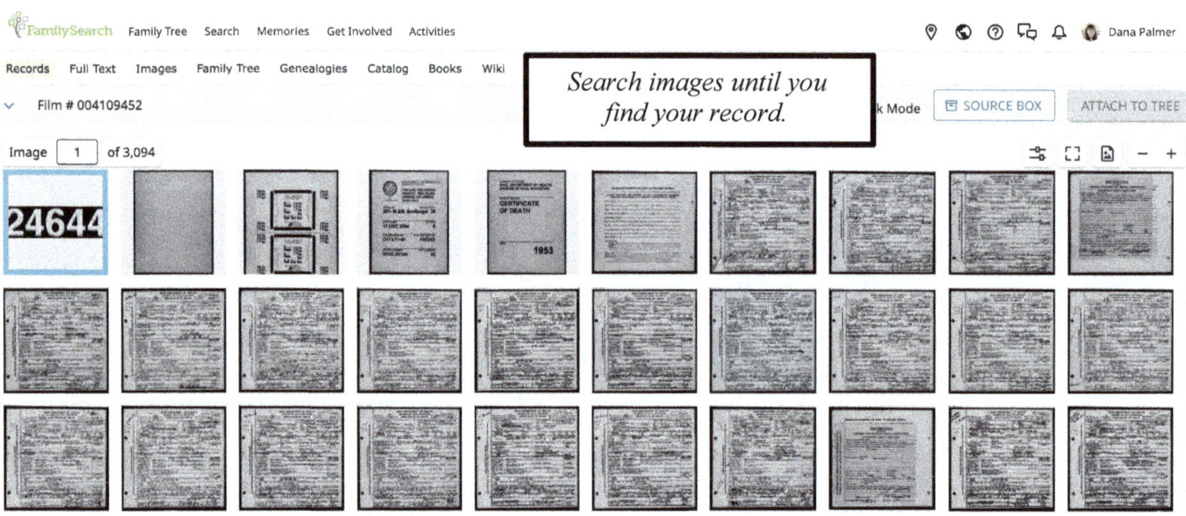

https://www.familysearch.org/en/search/film/004109452?cat=700227&i=0

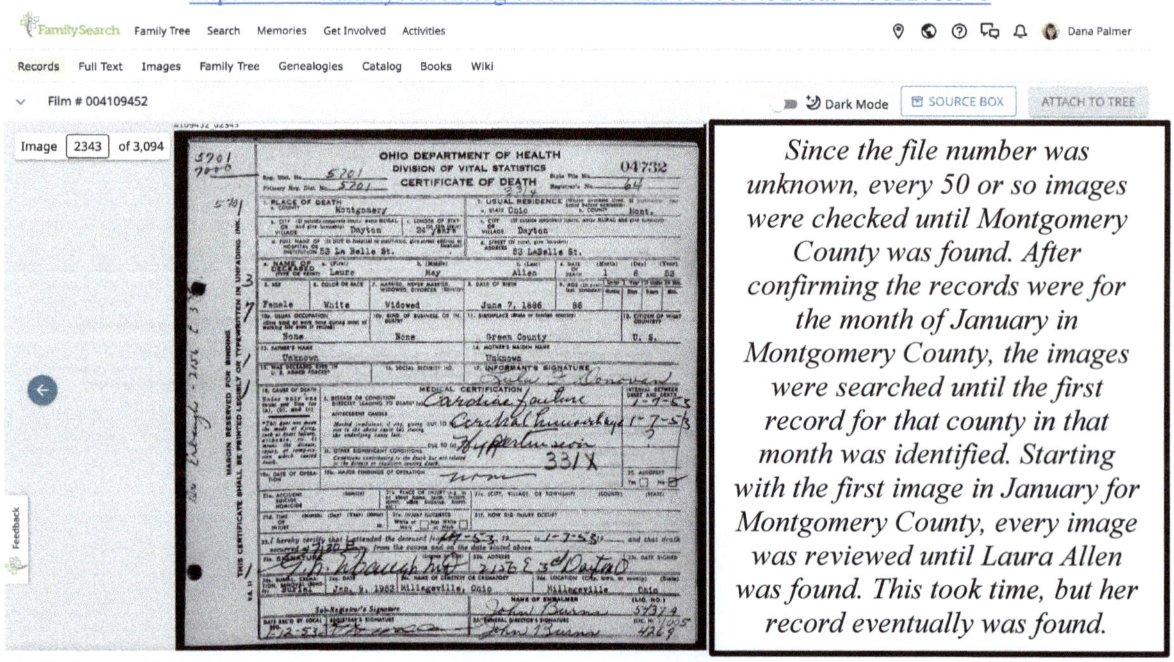

"Ohio, Deaths, 1908-1953," database with images, *FamilySearch* (https://www.familysearch.org/ark:/61903/3:1:S3HT-6SCB-RY?cat=700227&i=2342&lang=en : accessed 2 May 2025), Laura May Allen, 6 Jan 1953; citing Deaths Dayton, Montgomery, Ohio, reference fn 04732; FS microfilm 2,246,446.

Chapter 4: Full-Text Search

FULL-TEXT SEARCH

FamilySearch's FULL-TEXT SEARCH allows users to search for names or words included in the records (https://www.familysearch.org/search/full-text). All names are indexed, not just the primary ones normally found in the regular index of the record, and may include parents, neighbors, witnesses, etc. Many of the included records are from deeds, court records, and vital records in the United States.

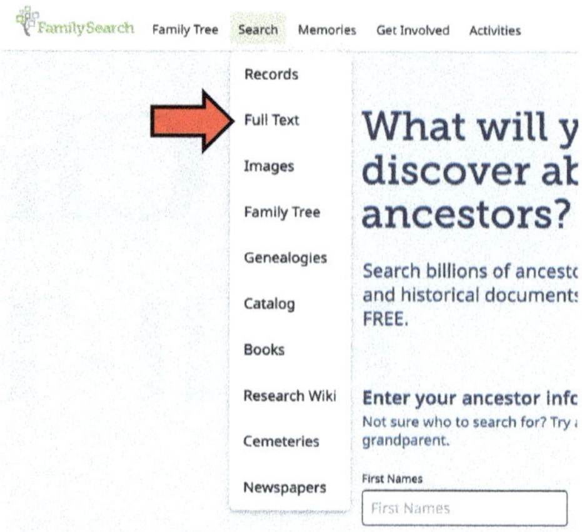

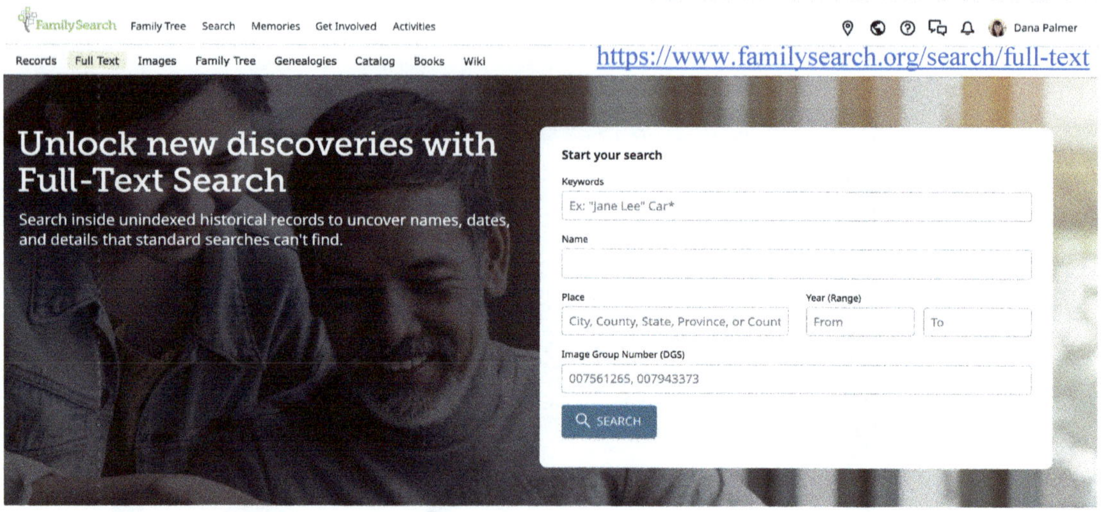

https://www.familysearch.org/search/full-text

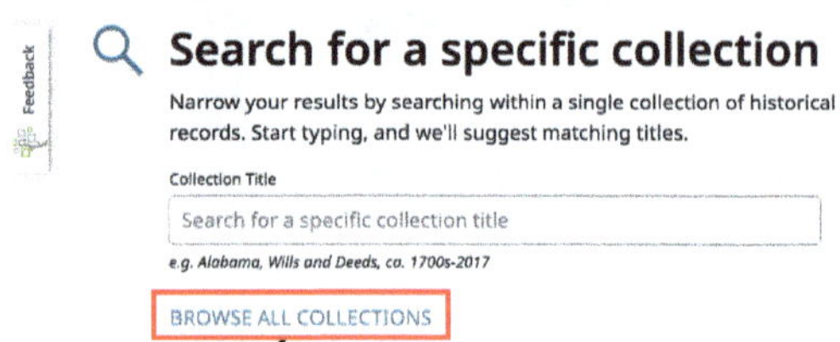

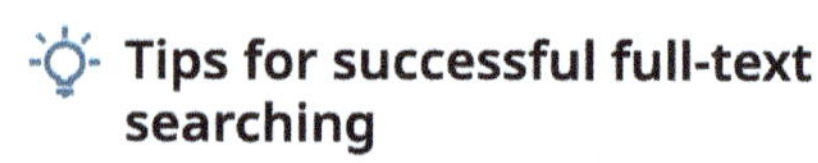

Clicking BROWSE ALL COLLECTIONS in FULL-TEXT SEARCH will show the collections currently searchable. More are added every day, so check back often.

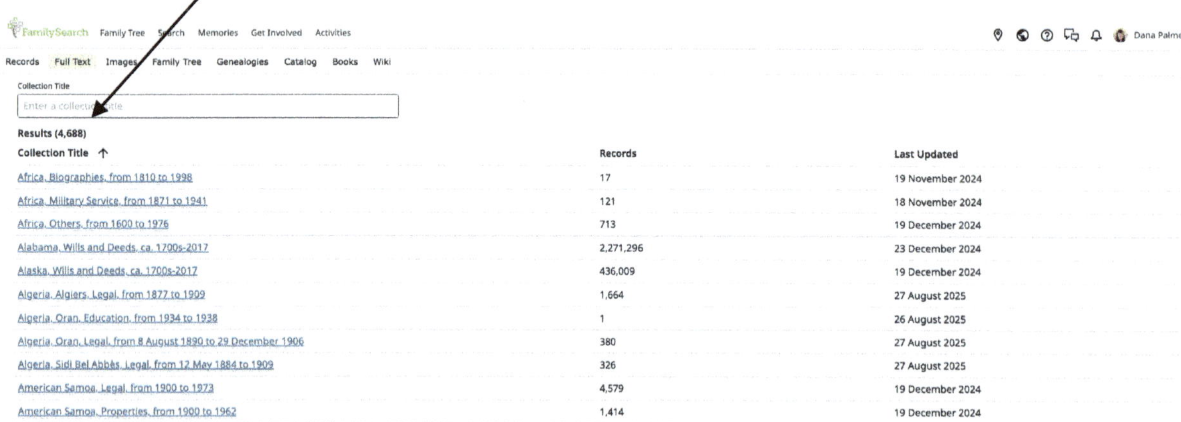

Collection Title	Records	Last Updated
Africa, Biographies, from 1810 to 1998	17	19 November 2024
Africa, Military Service, from 1871 to 1941	121	18 November 2024
Africa, Others, from 1600 to 1976	713	19 December 2024
Alabama, Wills and Deeds, ca. 1700s-2017	2,271,296	23 December 2024
Alaska, Wills and Deeds, ca. 1700s-2017	436,009	19 December 2024
Algeria, Algiers, Legal, from 1877 to 1909	1,664	27 August 2025
Algeria, Oran, Education, from 1934 to 1938	1	26 August 2025
Algeria, Oran, Legal, from 8 August 1890 to 29 December 1906	380	27 August 2025
Algeria, Sidi Bel Abbès, Legal, from 12 May 1884 to 1909	326	27 August 2025
American Samoa, Legal, from 1900 to 1973	4,579	19 December 2024
American Samoa, Properties, from 1900 to 1962	1,414	19 December 2024

https://www.familysearch.org/en/search/full-text/collection/list?count=20

To get started using the FULL-TEXT SEARCH tool on FamilySearch:

- Go to https://www.familysearch.org/search/full-text
- Type in a name, keyword, location, or combination into the search fields.
- Refine your search parameters as needed.
- When you find the entry you want, click on it to view the image.

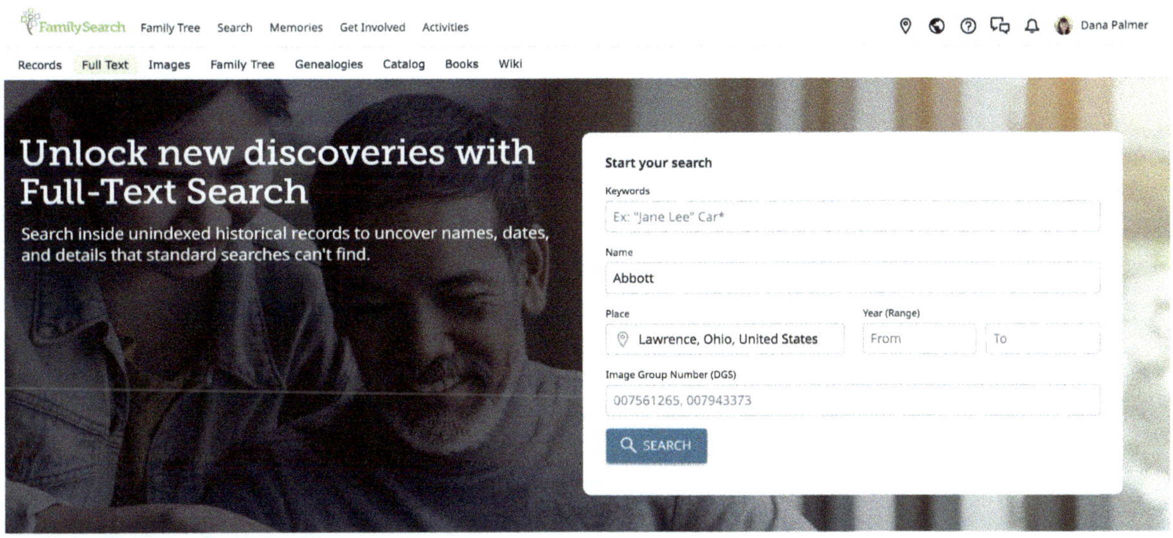

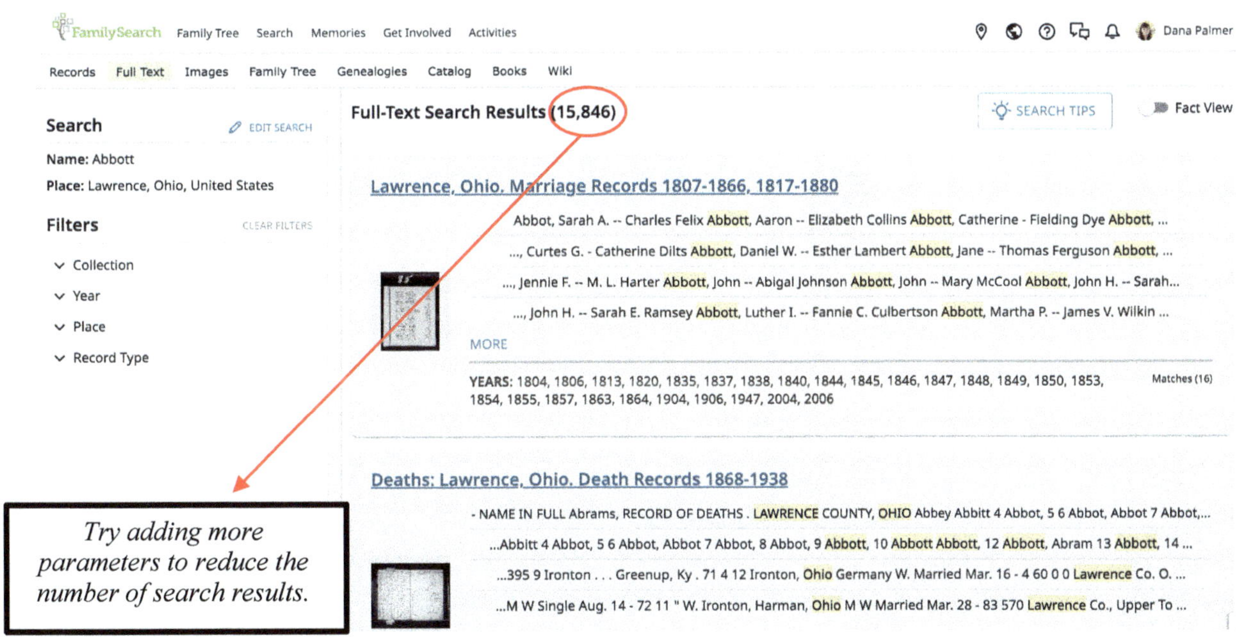

If you get a search result with a lock next to the link, you will need to view the record at a FamilySearch center or affiliate.

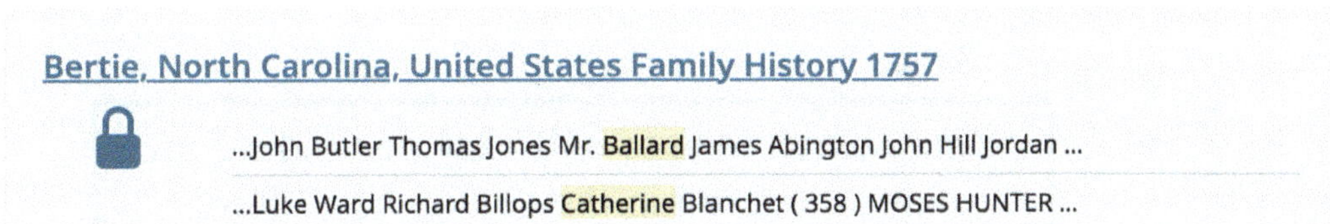

Fact View & Filters

FULL-TEXT SEARCH results will appear with the FACT VIEW turned off. To turn it on, click the FACT VIEW button. This will provide a short summary of the names indexed on that page, while turning off the FACT VIEW provides snips of text from the record.

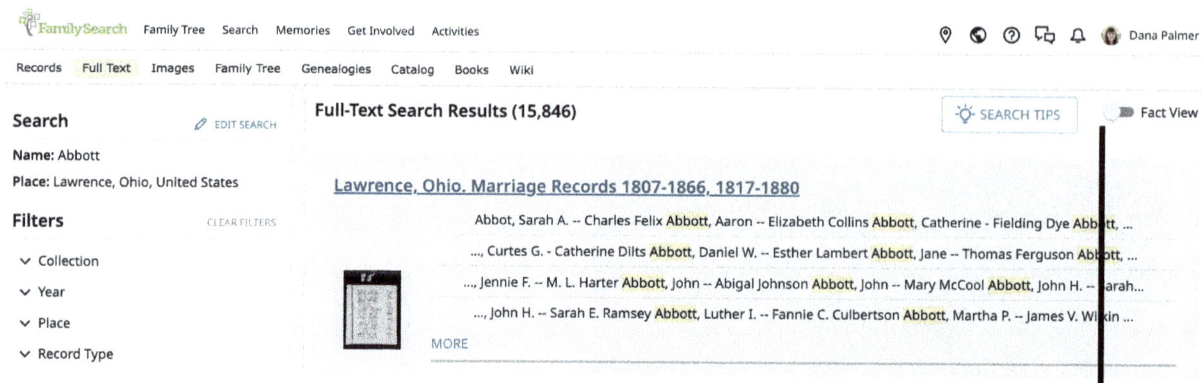

Turn on the FACT VIEW to see highlights of the record

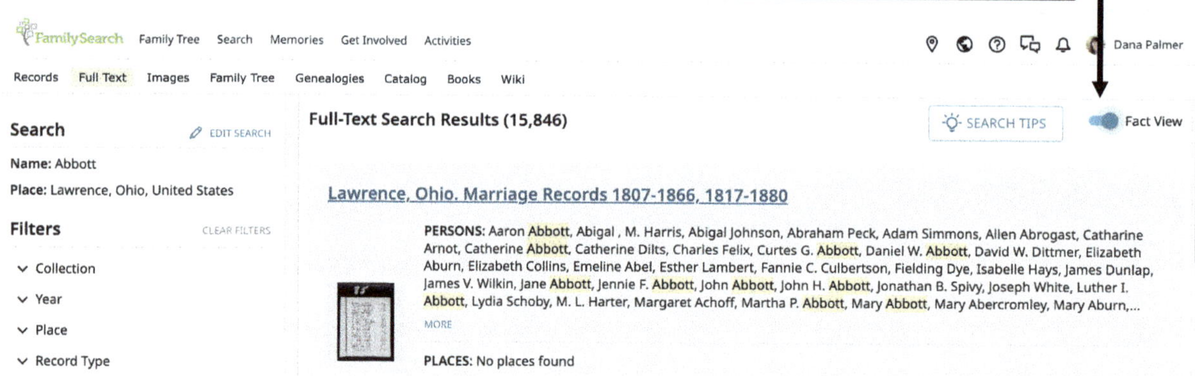

Your search results will vary depending on what is entered in the search box filters.

Errors with the AI Indexing

FULL-TEXT SEARCH can be a wonderful tool to quickly find your ancestors in records, especially in those instances where the ancestor is not the main person in the record. A word of caution – as with any type of record whether a person or artificial intelligence indexes the record – there could be errors especially if the handwriting is difficult to decipher.

If you do find a record for your person, be sure to attach it in the TREE, so it is easy to find again.

https://www.familysearch.org/ark:/61903/3:1:3QSQ-G9S9-BWFN?view=fullText&keywords=Edward%20White&groupId=TH-1961-28858-3856-64

In the above example, the name "Edward White" was the name in the FULL-TEXT SEARCH, which identifies him as receiving money from the estate of Thomas Caton, deceased on 15 February 1796. The name Susanna Caton was indexed correctly, but Thomas Caton was indexed by AI incorrectly as Cain.

You will not know how the system indexed the names, so be creative in your search parameters, and browse the pages before and after the ones you are viewing to see if there are other related pages.

Here's another example, showing how some words or phrases are mis-indexed:

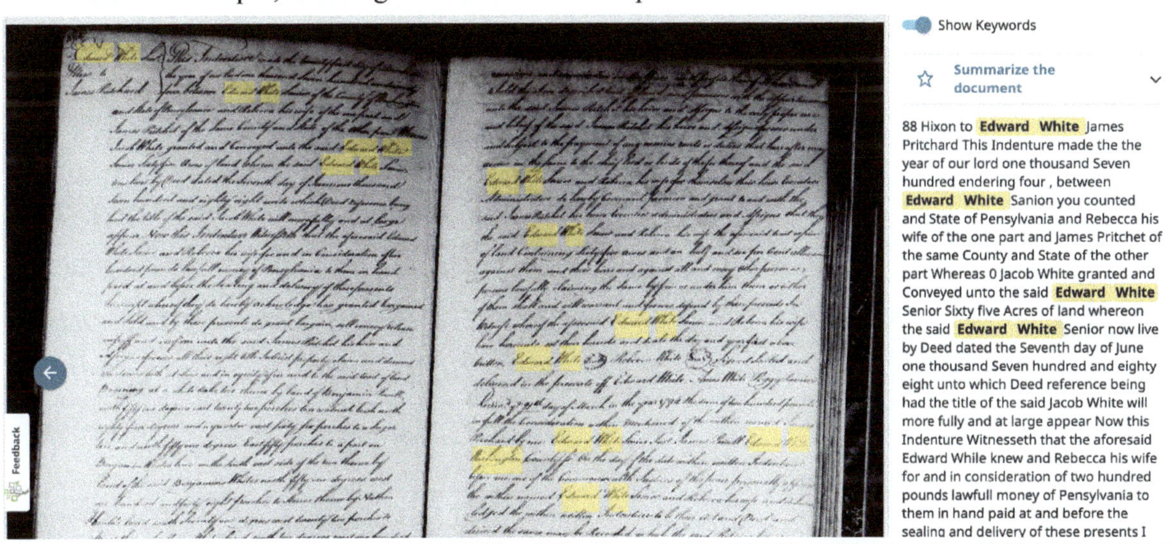

https://www.familysearch.org/ark:/61903/3:1:3Q9M-CSXB-P7SC-8?view=fullText&keywords=Edward%20White%2CWashington&groupId=TH-909-67463-136303-2

Tips for Using Full-Text

Adding another name to the keyword field often reduces the search results. Any word in the search fields can use **wildcards** or **quotation marks** around them for a more exact search. Using a woman's name with her husband's surname, or a name in quotation marks, often will result in grantor deed sales and other useful records for your person. You can also use the + and – symbols to include or exclude words, but these cannot be used within quotation marks.

Exact Searches: Use quotation marks around words to search for exact phrases.
"Dana Palmer"
"Dana A Palmer"

Wildcards: Allows variant spellings replacing a single letter (?) or multiple letters (*) in a word.

Names: You will get the best results if used as an exact search, but it will also work with just a given name, surname, or either of those using wildcards. You can also use Boolean expressions (+ and -).

Keywords: Can add names, locations, dates, or other keywords to reduce search results.

Place: The word must be on the record page for it to appear as a result.

Image Group Number: Allows searches for a very specific Image Group Number (DGS), and allows for more focused searches, and name variations or lack of names.

Filters: Allows searches for specific locations, dates, record sets without that word, or dates found in the record.

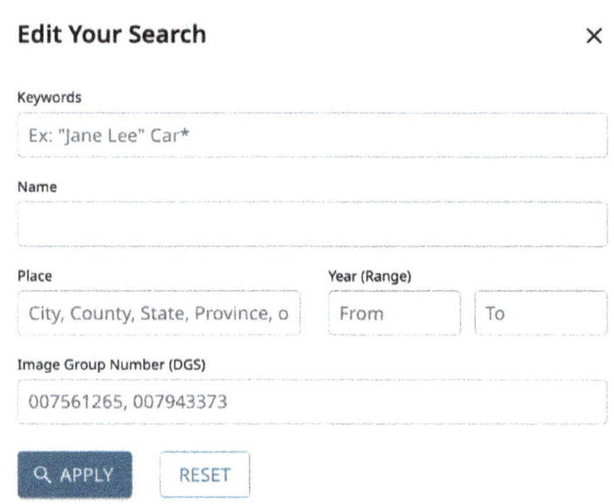

Search Box Results

Names and dates entered in the search box must appear on the page for the record to show in the search results.

If the word is mis-indexed or misspelled and does not appear correctly elsewhere on the page, it won't appear as a result.

Here's an example of the search results from trying different full-text search variations. These numbers may vary if you repeat the same search since FamilySearch is continually indexing and adding to this collection every day.

Exact Word Search

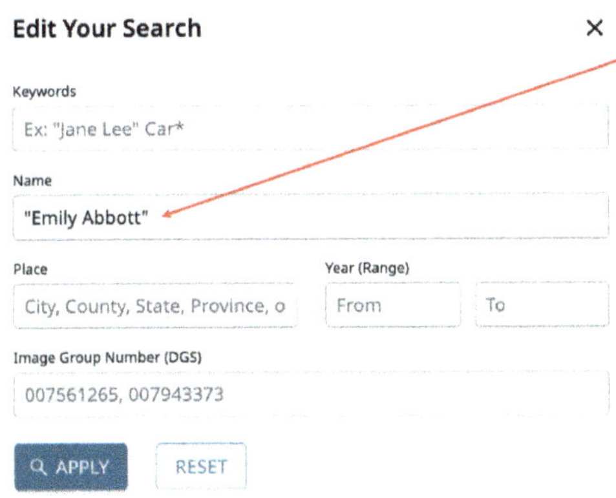

Exact searches are words or phrases that appear in quotation marks. The search engine will look for that exact phrase in the text.

If the name is misspelled or mis-indexed, it will not appear as a result.

Wildcards cannot be used in quotation marks.

Keyword Word Search

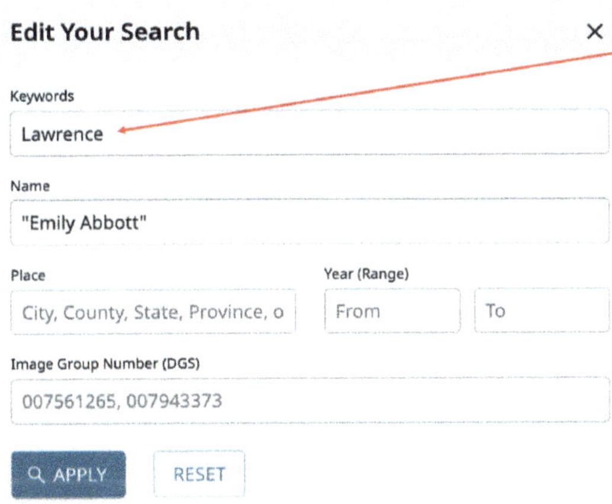

Keywords can be used in conjunction with the name and place filter.

This helps narrow the search results, especially when another name is used.

Wildcards

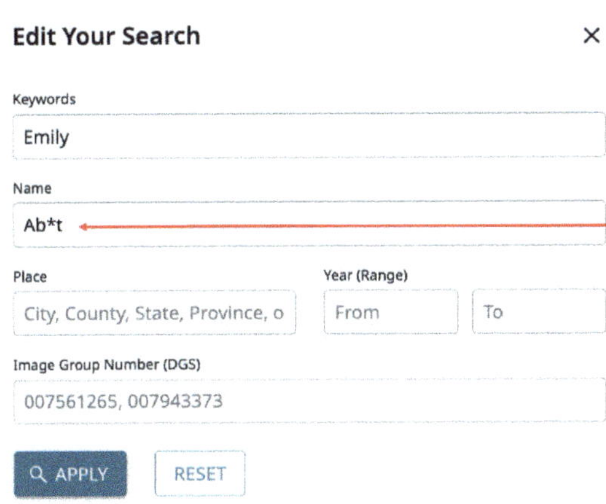

There are two types of wildcards that can be used:
? replaces a single letter
** replaces multiple letters*

Combinations of wildcards can be used within a word and in the keywords, name, and place fields.

Be careful, if you include the name of the location using the search box instead of the place filter; results will only show if that location is indexed somewhere on that page. If the word is mis-indexed, it won't appear unless the same word appears elsewhere on the page. If your ancestor's record doesn't appear, purposely misspell the name(s) or location. AI can't always read the handwriting accurately.

Boolean Searches

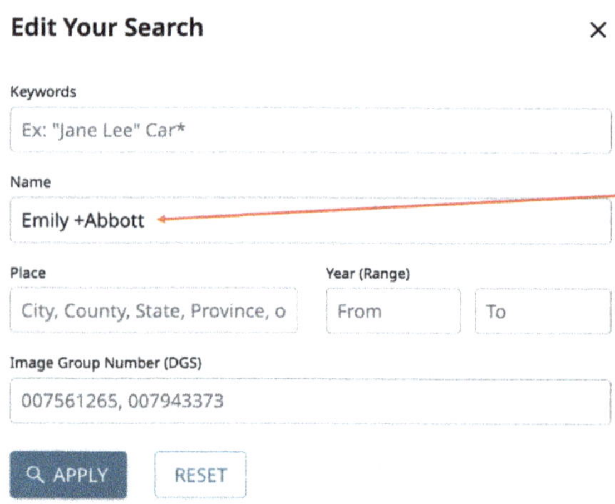

Boolean terms can be used to narrow the search parameters:

+ includes a specific word

- excludes a specific word

Variant Name Searches

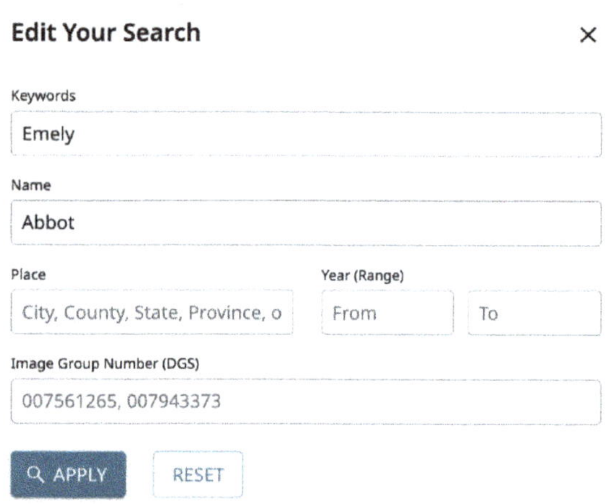

With spelling mistakes common in AI indexing, try to purposely misspell words to see if they come up in the search results.

Using Filters

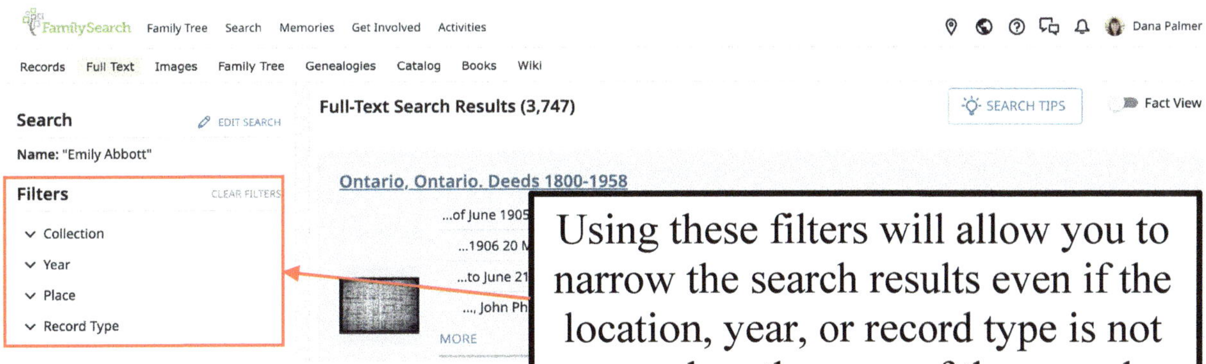

Using these filters will allow you to narrow the search results even if the location, year, or record type is not named on the page of the record.

https://www.familysearch.org/en/search/full-text/results?count=20&q.fullName=%22Emily%20Abbott%22

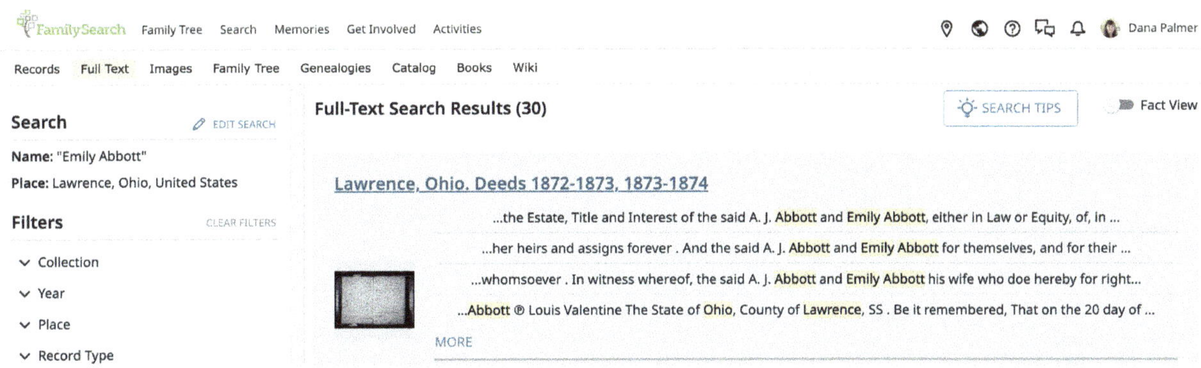

https://www.familysearch.org/en/search/full-text/results?count=20&q.anyPlace=Lawrence%2C%20Ohio%2C%20United%20States&q.fullName=%22Emily%20Abbott%22

Searching for names in quotation marks, like this example, "Emily Abbott," will look for those words next to each other and greatly reduce the search results. Be careful though, if either of those names is misspelled, they will not appear in the list of results. Also, wildcards can't be used within quotation marks.

Search Results Comparison

Other filters	Search Filters			Results
Place	Keyword	Name	Place	
		"Emily Abbott"		3,747
		"Emely Abbott"		50
		"Emily Abbott"	Lawrence, Ohio	30
	"Emily Abbott"		Lawrence, Ohio	41
	Emily	Abbott	Lawrence, Ohio	1,009
		Abbott +Emily	Lawrence, Ohio	45,176
Lawrence, Ohio		"Emily Abbott"		6
Lawrence, Ohio	Emily	Abbott		34
Lawrence, Ohio		Abbott +Emily		2,256
Lawrence, Ohio		"Emily Abbott"	Lawrence, Ohio	6

The result numbers will change as new collections are added. Also, results from locked collections will not appear in the search results unless you are at a FamilySearch center or affiliate location.

An Exact Search

One of the best ways to find your person is to perform an exact search by putting quotation marks around the given name and surname. This name can be placed in the name field or keyword field, or used in a combination with other names. Keep in mind that wildcards cannot be used within the quotation marks.

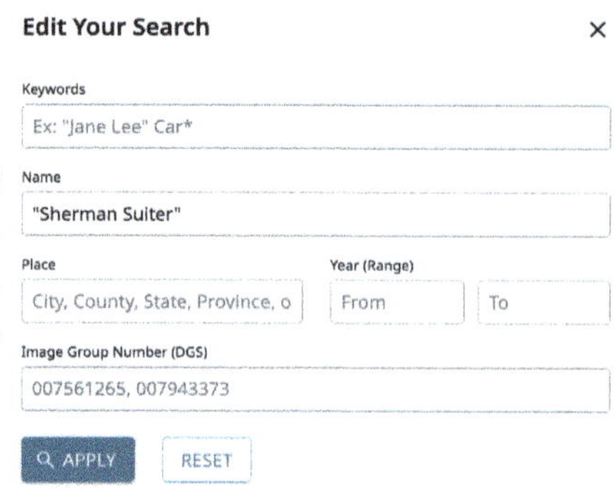

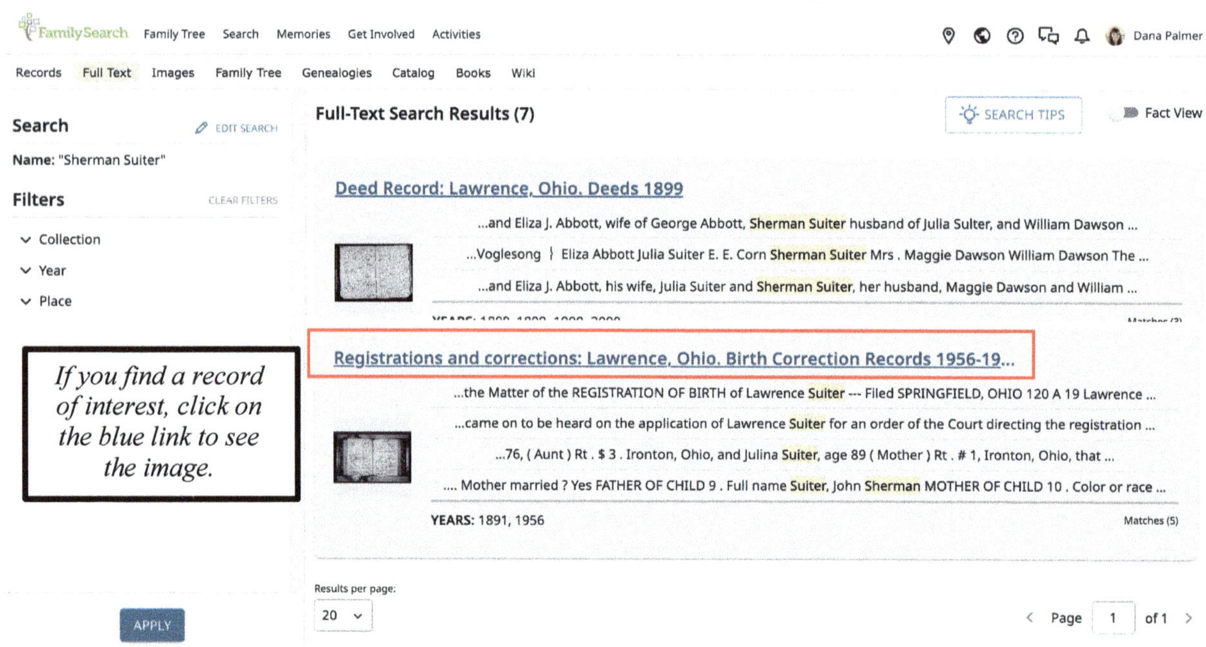

If you find a record of interest, click on the blue link to see the image.

https://www.familysearch.org/en/search/full-text/results?count=20&q.fullName=%22Sherman%20Suiter%22

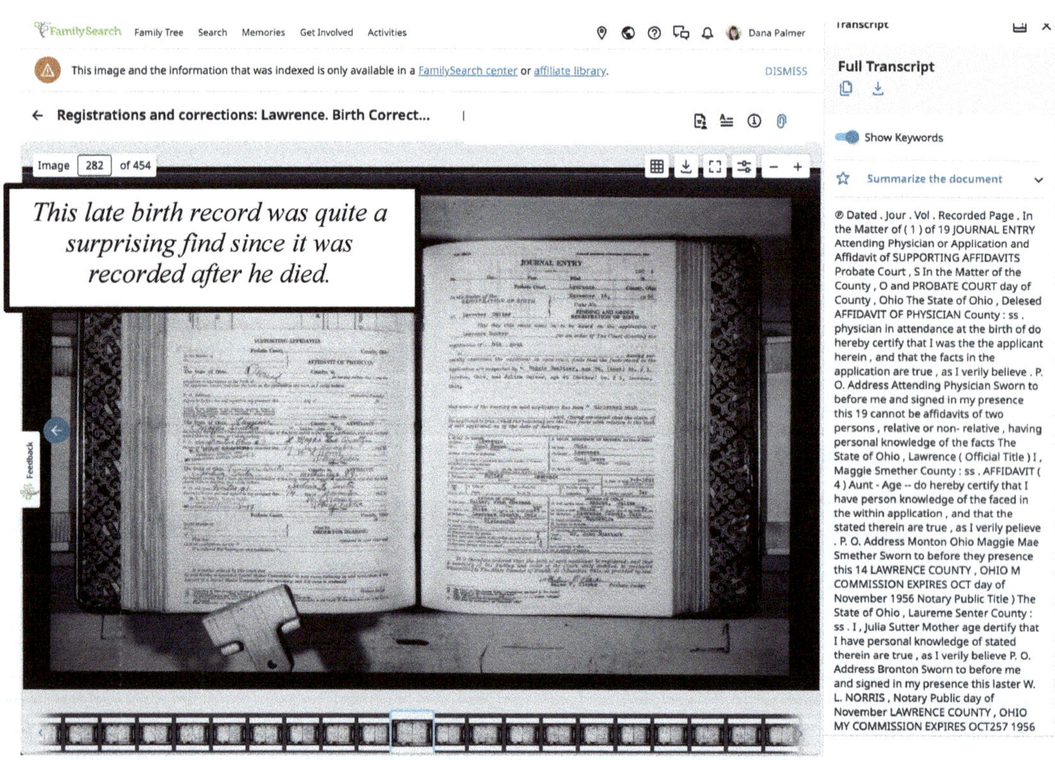

This late birth record was quite a surprising find since it was recorded after he died.

https://www.familysearch.org/ark:/61903/3:1:33S7-L1PD-9F9T?view=fullText&keywords=Sherman%20Suiter&lang=en&groupId=

An Exact Search with Location

If you try the exact search and get lots of results, try adding in the location to the PLACE search box. When you add a location to the PLACE search box, that location must appear on the page of the record, or it won't appear in the search results. If the location is not on the page or it is mis-indexed by AI or spelled incorrectly on the page, then that record won't be selected. So be creative when searching.

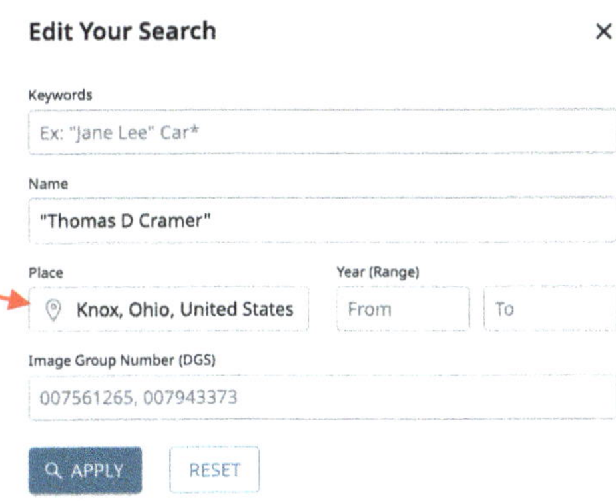

Add filters to reduce search results.

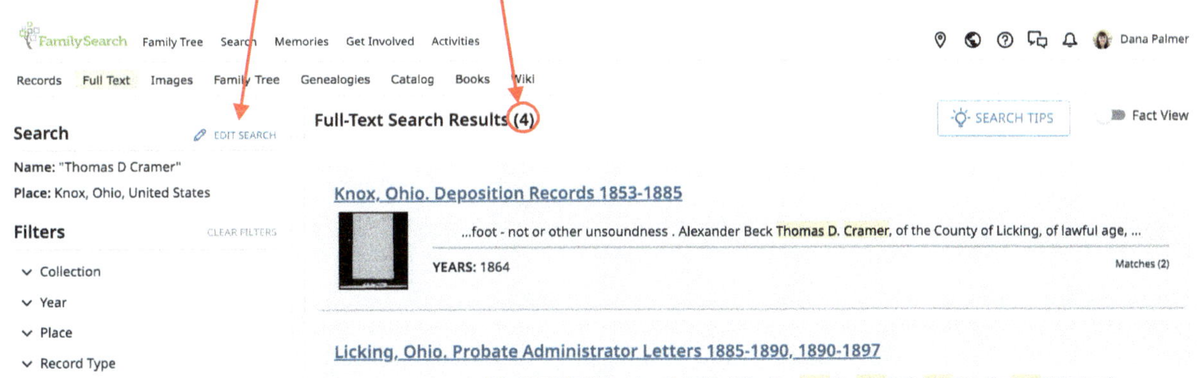

https://www.familysearch.org/en/search/full-text/results?count=20&q.anyPlace=Knox%2C%20Ohio%2C%20United%20States&q.fullName=%22Thomas%20D%20Cramer%22

This is an example of a court case in 1864, where the person used in the exact search above was named as someone giving a deposition in the case. He provides his age, his birth location, and residence in the locality. This was a great find because his birth pre-dated the recording of vitals in the area.

https://www.familysearch.org/ark:/61903/3:1:3QHV-P3NF-69B6-X?view=fullText&keywords=Thomas%20D%2CCramer&lang=en&groupId=

An Exact Search with Location and "Record Type" Filters

One of my favorite ways to search is to add an exact name with a location in the place field and select the RECORD TYPE filter. This will reduce the search results significantly and limit them to the specific location and record type.

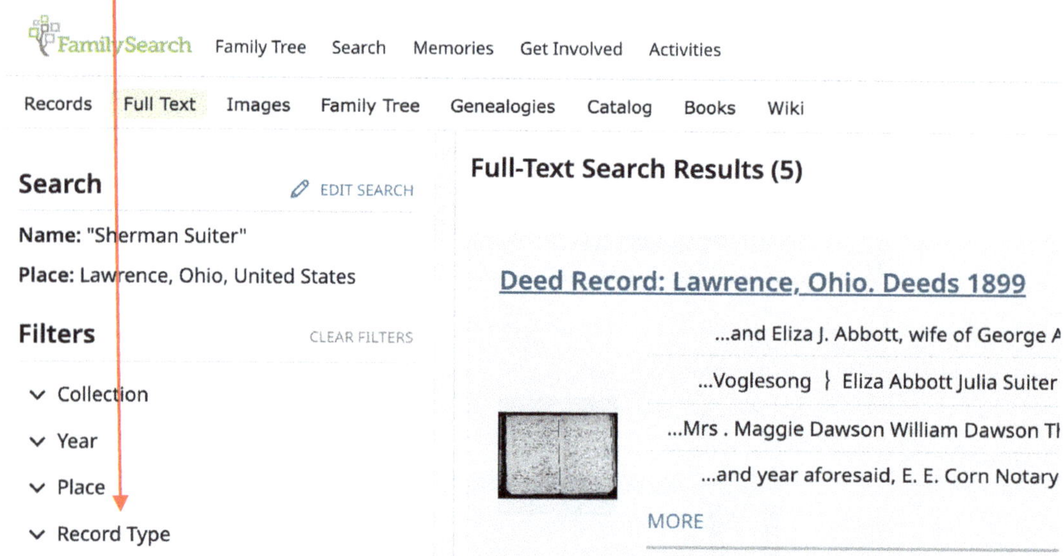

https://www.familysearch.org/en/search/full-text/results?count=20&q.anyPlace=Lawrence%2C%20Ohio%2C%20United%20States&q.fullName=%22Sherman%20Suiter%22&c.recordTypeId1=on&f.recordTypeId0=122797

In this example, the search resulted in the second page of a deed where the heirs are selling the land they inherited. Some of the names were mis-indexed. Be sure to use the left arrow to go back and view the prior page.

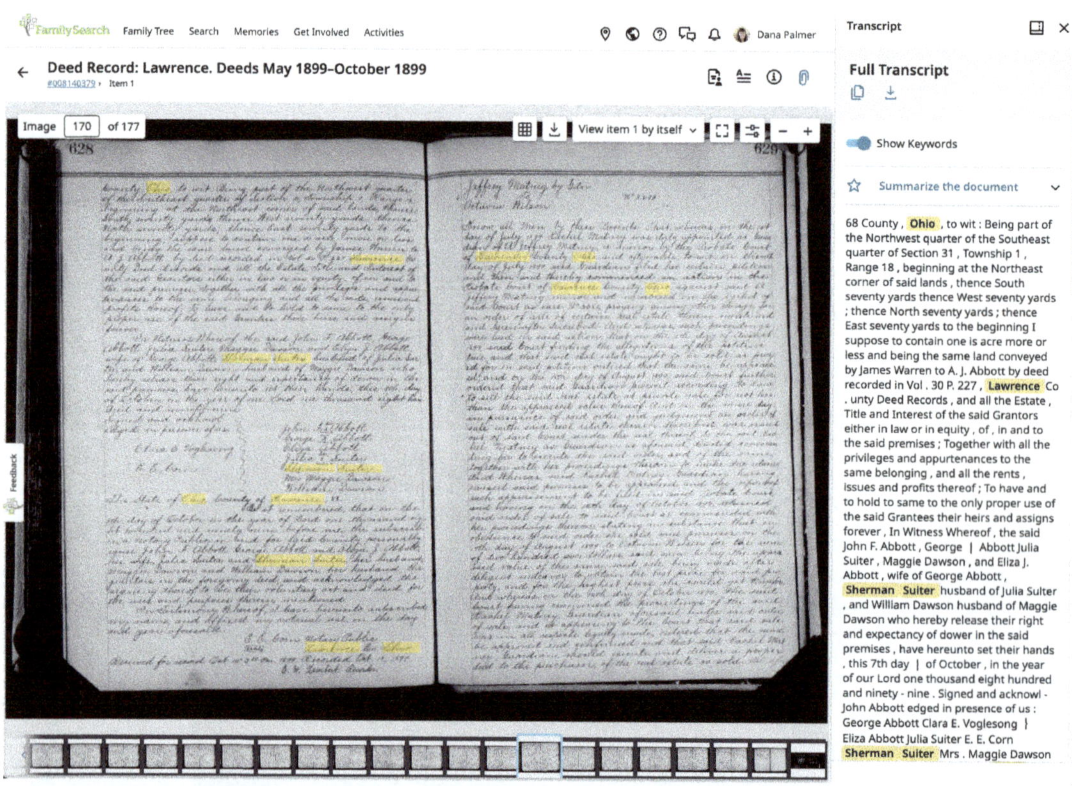

https://www.familysearch.org/ark:/61903/3:1:3Q9M-CSKW-KS17-N?view=fullText&keywords=Sherman%20Suiter%2CLawrence%2COhio&lang=en&groupId=M99W-193

An Exact Search with Keyword Name and Location Filters

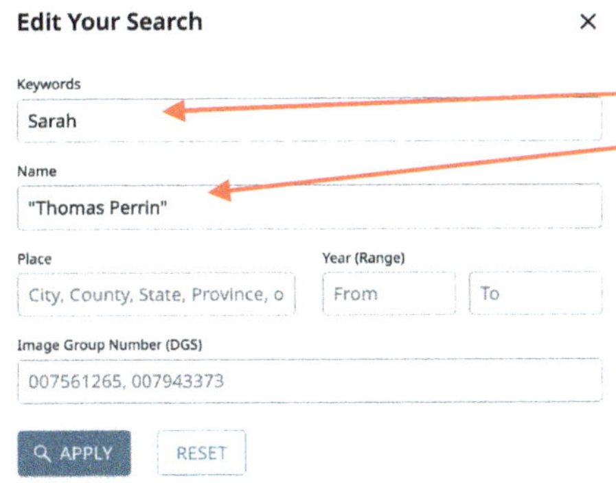

Another favorite trick is to add the name of a person in the keyword field with an exact name search in the NAME field. If you get too many results, you can narrow down by clicking on the PLACE filters, YEAR, or RECORD TYPE.

> *Keyword searches help reduce search results. It's especially helpful if you are looking for a record with a spouse named in it.*

https://www.familysearch.org/en/search/full-text/results?count=20&q.fullName="Thomas Perrin"&q.text=Sarah

Add filters to narrow search parameters. Adding in the location of Bedford County, Pennsylvania, reduced the search results from 1,934 to 12.

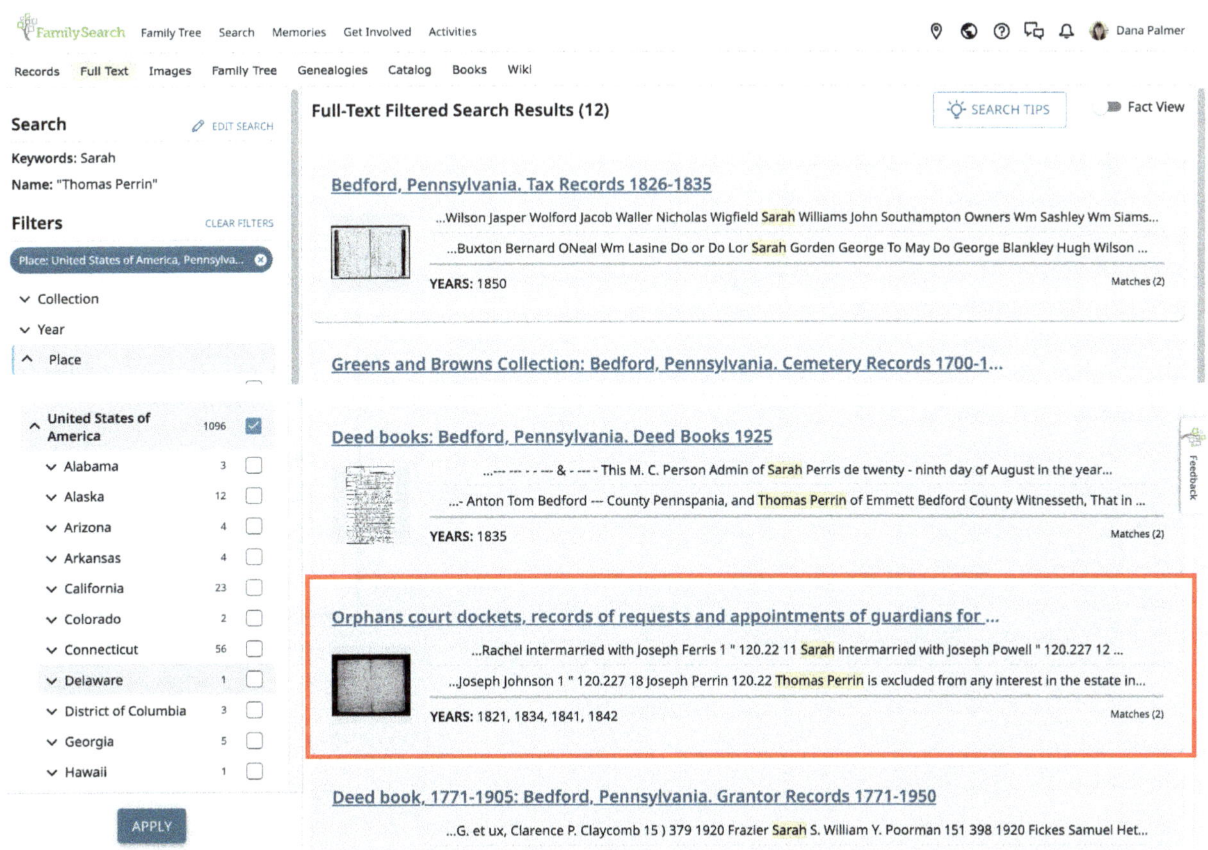

https://www.familysearch.org/en/search/full-text/results?count=20&q.fullName=%22Thomas%20Perrin%22&q.text=Sarah&c.recordPlace1=on&f.recordPlace0=10&c.recordPlace2=on&f.recordPlace1=10%2CPennsylvania&c.recordPlace3=on&f.recordPlace2=10%2CPennsylvania%2CBedford

This court record named all the heirs of the deceased, noting those who were to receive their share of the estate. The heiresses' husbands' names were also noted. For Thomas Perrin, it noted he was excluded from receiving his share. This court case occurred years after their father's death and provided some of the only evidence of marriage for these daughters.

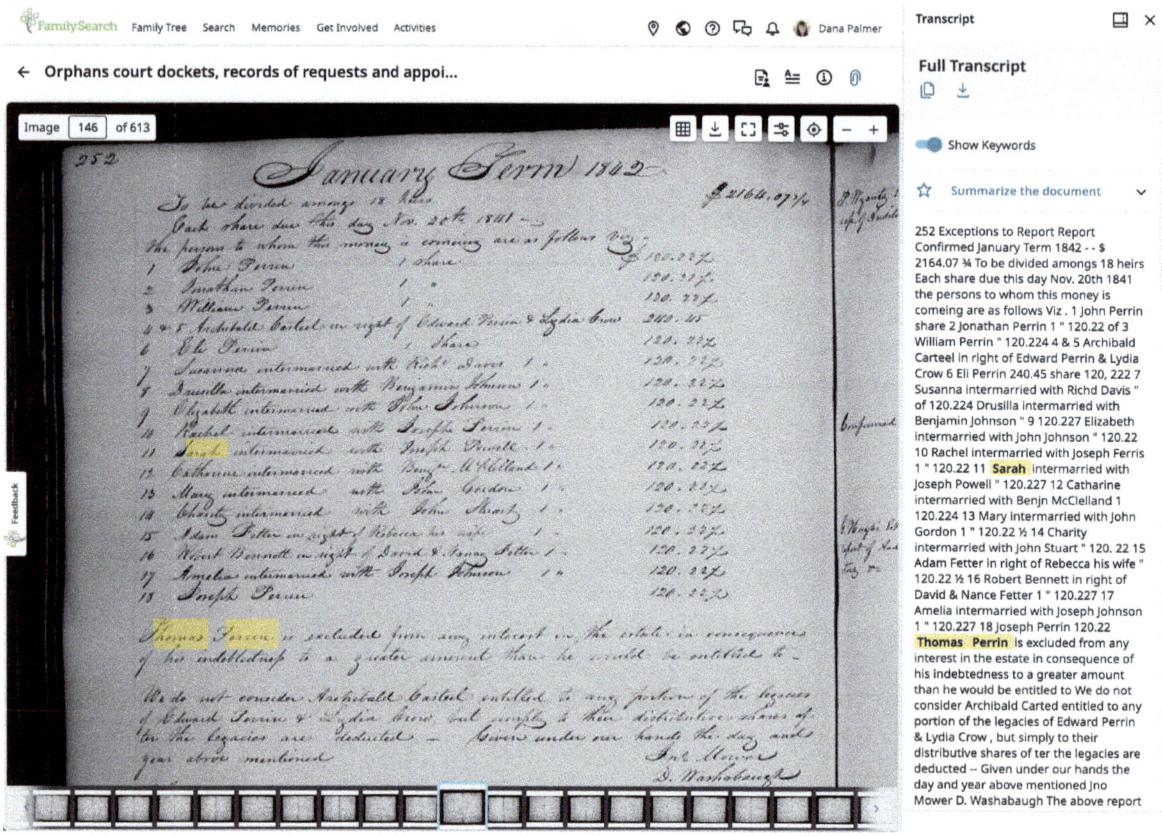

https://www.familysearch.org/ark:/61903/3:1:3QSQ-G99B-PHBW?view=fullText&keywords=Thomas%20Perrin%2CSarah&lang=en&groupId=TH-1942-28763-2451-38

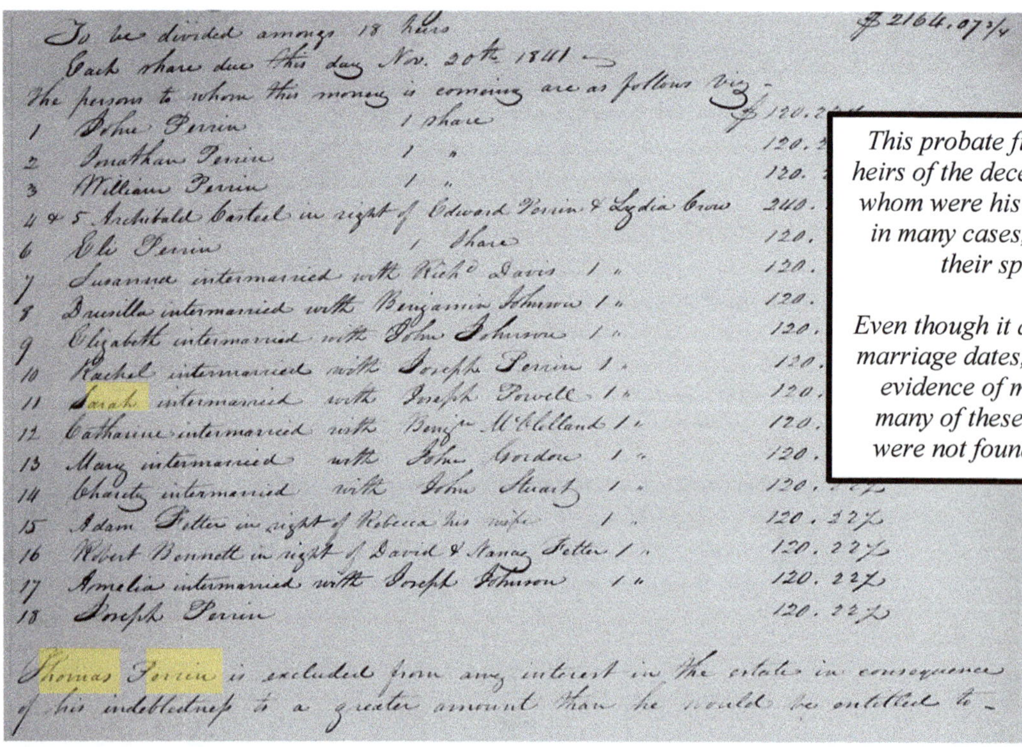

This probate file named the heirs of the deceased, many of whom were his children, and in many cases, the name of their spouses.

Even though it doesn't list the marriage dates, this provides evidence of marriage for many of these people who were not found elsewhere.

Narrowing Search Parameters Using the Filters

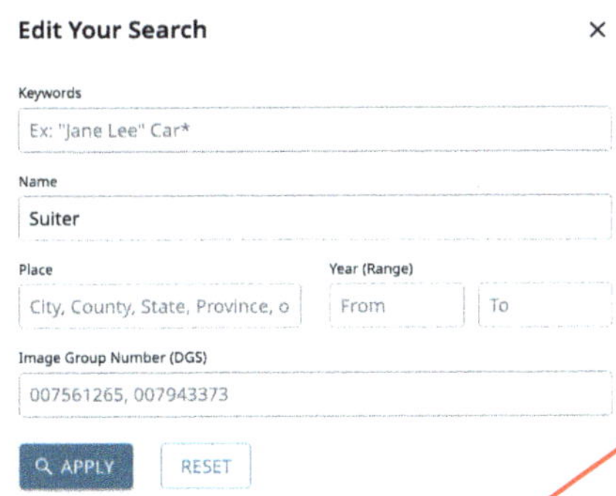

One of the ways to narrow down FULL-TEXT SEARCH results is to use the filters (COLLECTION, YEAR, PLACE, and RECORD TYPE). The number of results in each category will change depending on your search parameters. This type of search can be helpful if you didn't find your record when you've added a location in the PLACE box under the EDIT SEARCH.

Add filters to narrow the results.

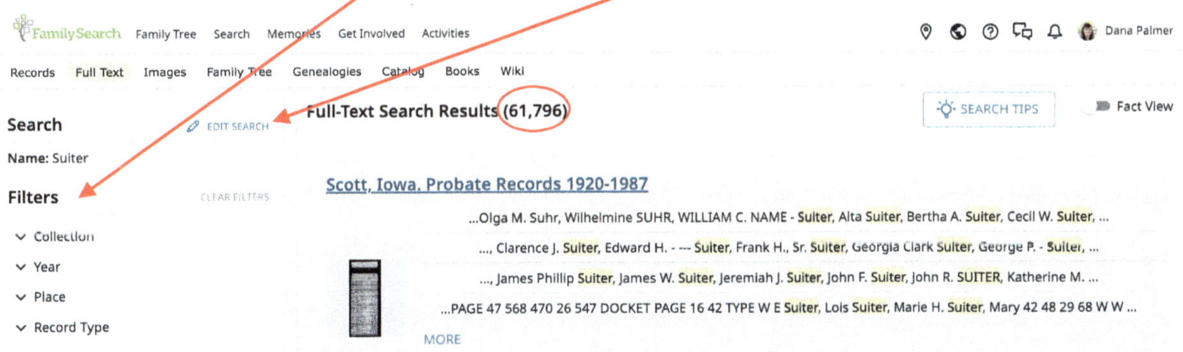

https://www.familysearch.org/en/search/full-text/results?count=20&q.fullName=Suiter

You can filter by COLLECTION, but this isn't the most effective way to narrow the results unless you've added other filters first.

Place and date filters often provide the best search results.

Narrowing the search results this way is helpful if the location is not mentioned on the results page. You can still find the record for that specific location even though it wouldn't come up when you typed the location in the search filter box.

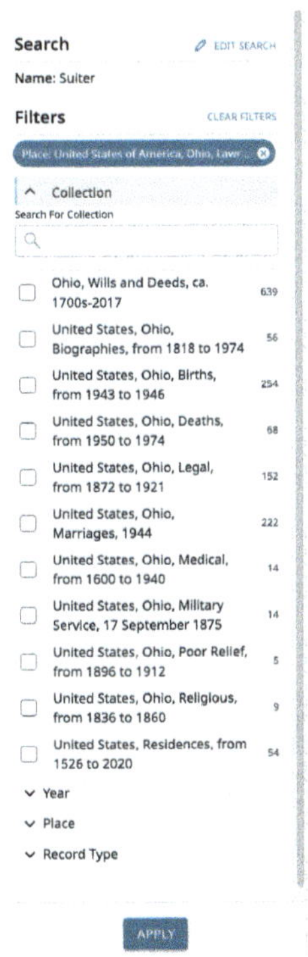

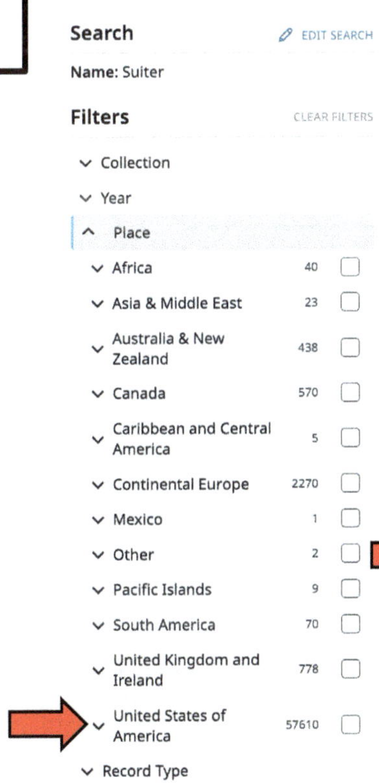

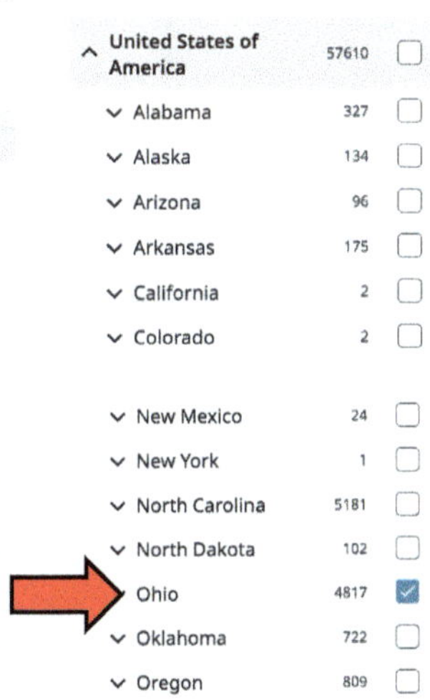

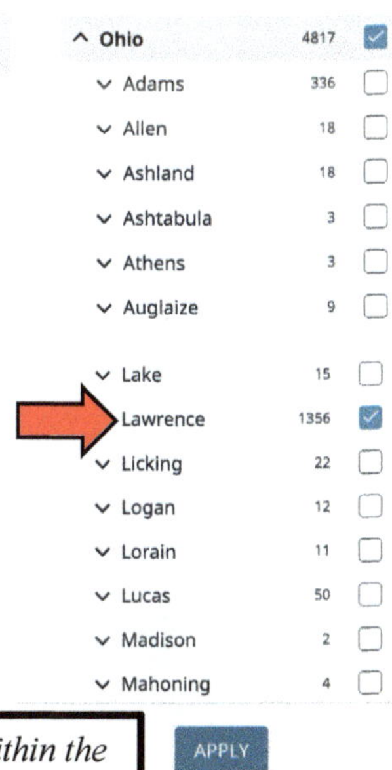

Choose the county within the state and click apply. Some locations will have towns to let you filter further.

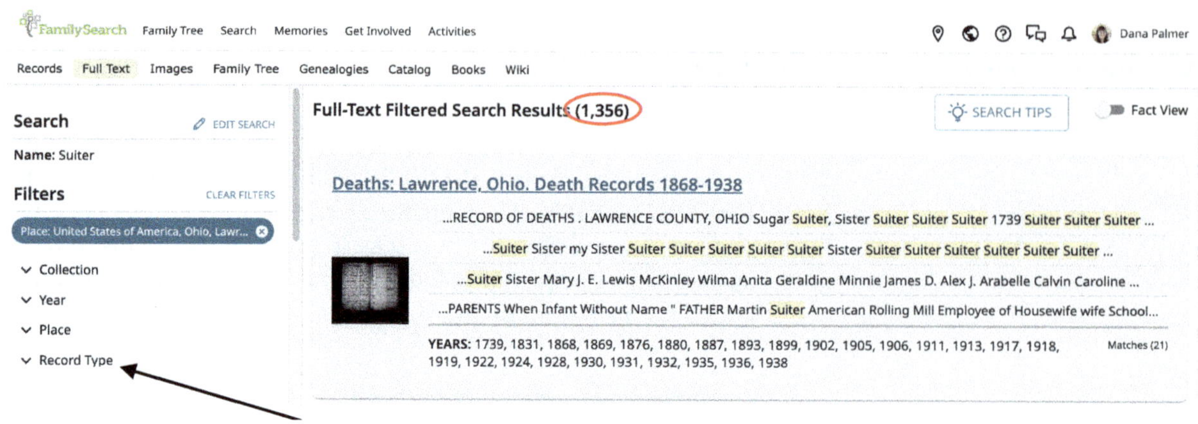

https://www.familysearch.org/en/search/full-text/results?count=20&q.fullName=Suiter&c.recordPlace1=on&f.recordPlace0=10&c.recordPlace2=on&f.recordPlace1=10%2COhio&c.recordPlace3=on&f.recordPlace2=10%2COhio%2CLawrence

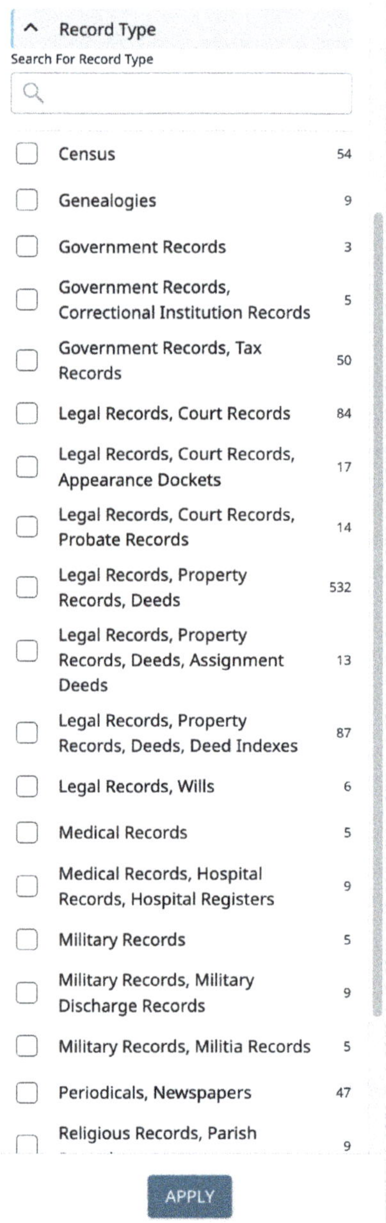

Click RECORD TYPE to narrow results.

Choose the collection to further refine the results to a specific type of record.

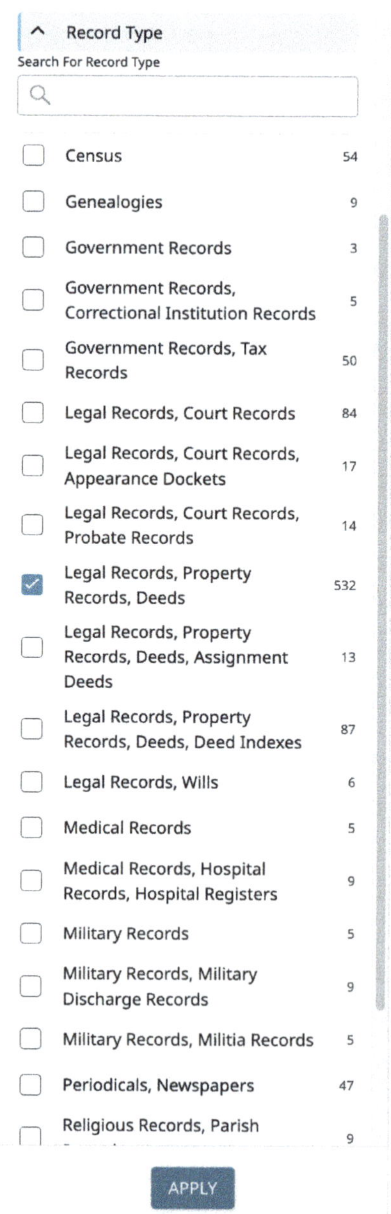

In this case, LEGAL RECORDS, PROPERTY RECORDS, DEEDS was chosen.

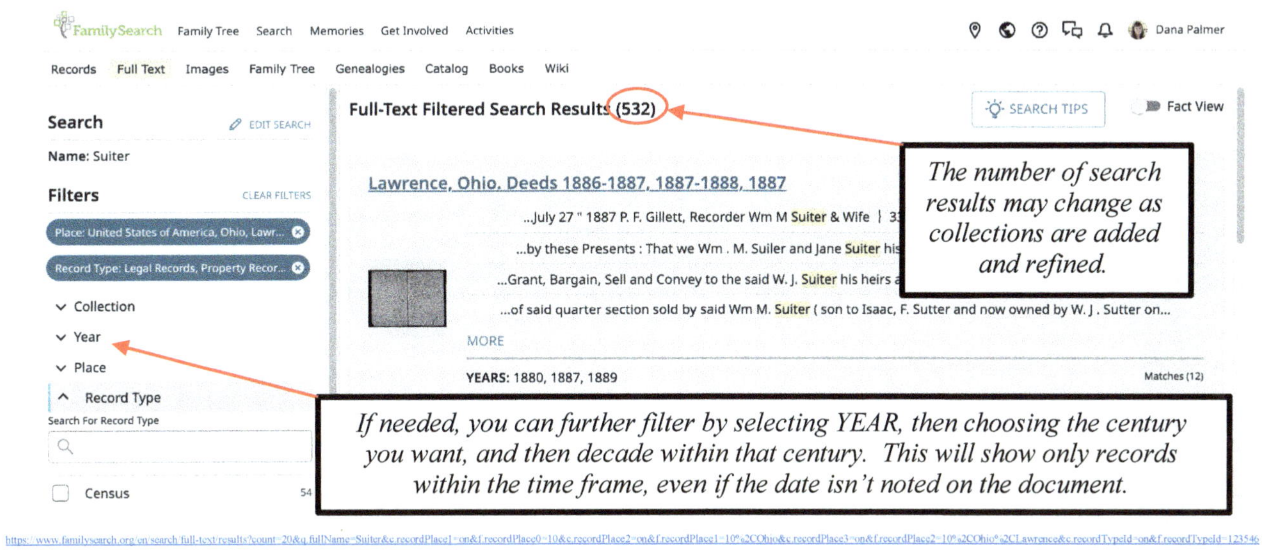

The number of search results may change as collections are added and refined.

If needed, you can further filter by selecting YEAR, then choosing the century you want, and then decade within that century. This will show only records within the time frame, even if the date isn't noted on the document.

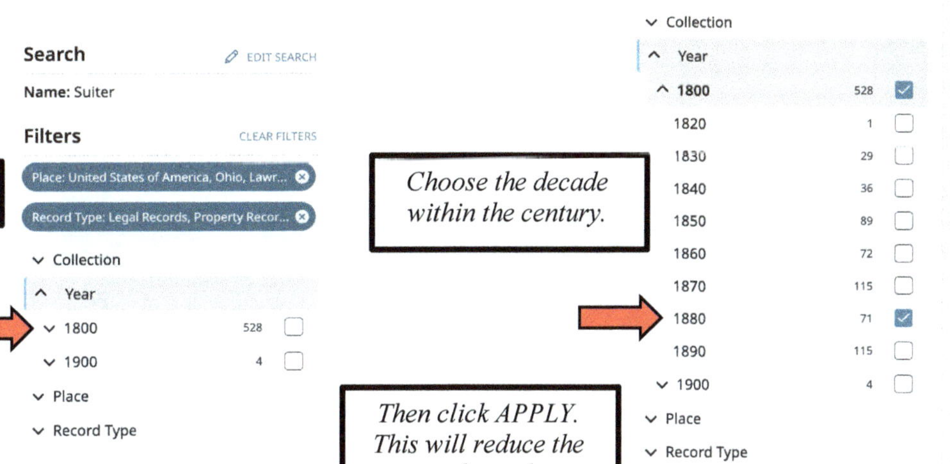

Choose the century.

Choose the decade within the century.

Then click APPLY. This will reduce the search results.

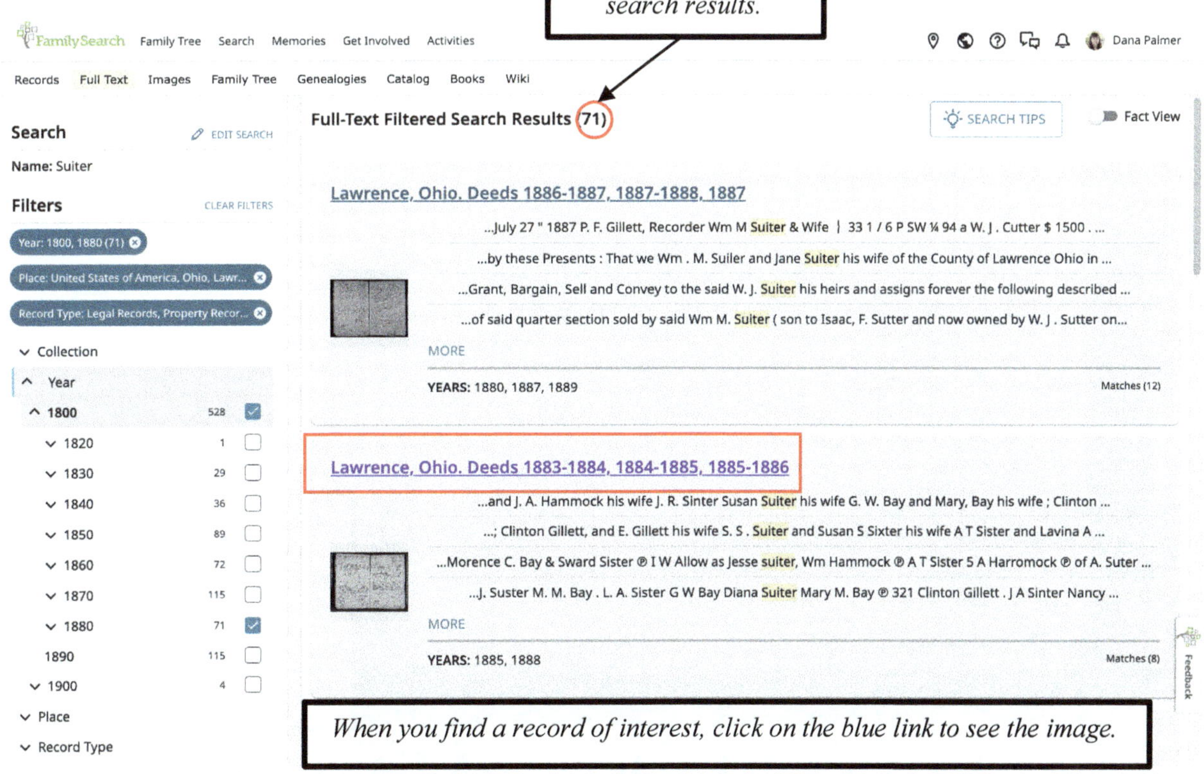

When you find a record of interest, click on the blue link to see the image.

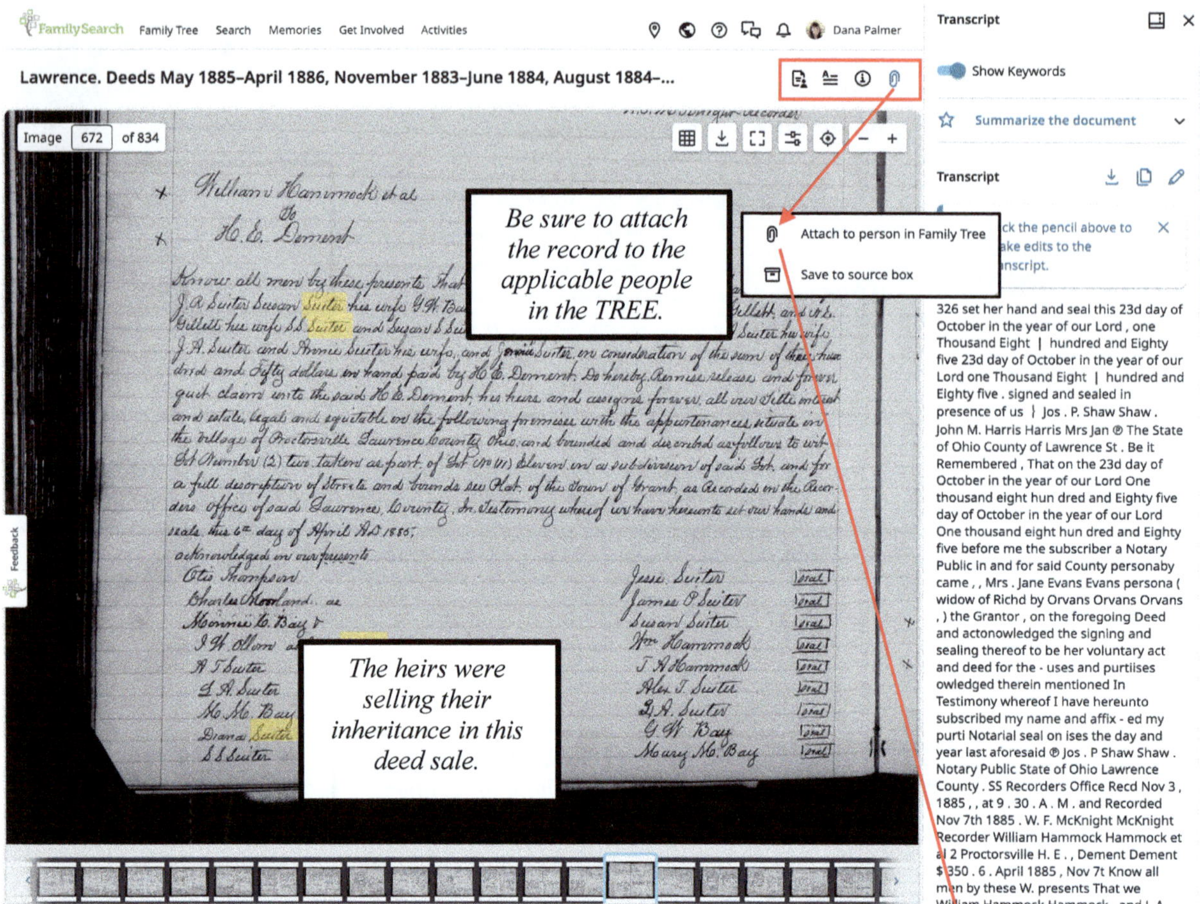

https://www.familysearch.org/ark:/61903/3:1:3Q9M-C37F-Z9RF-B?view=fullText&keywords=Suiter&lang=en&groupId=TH-909-85960-42992-38

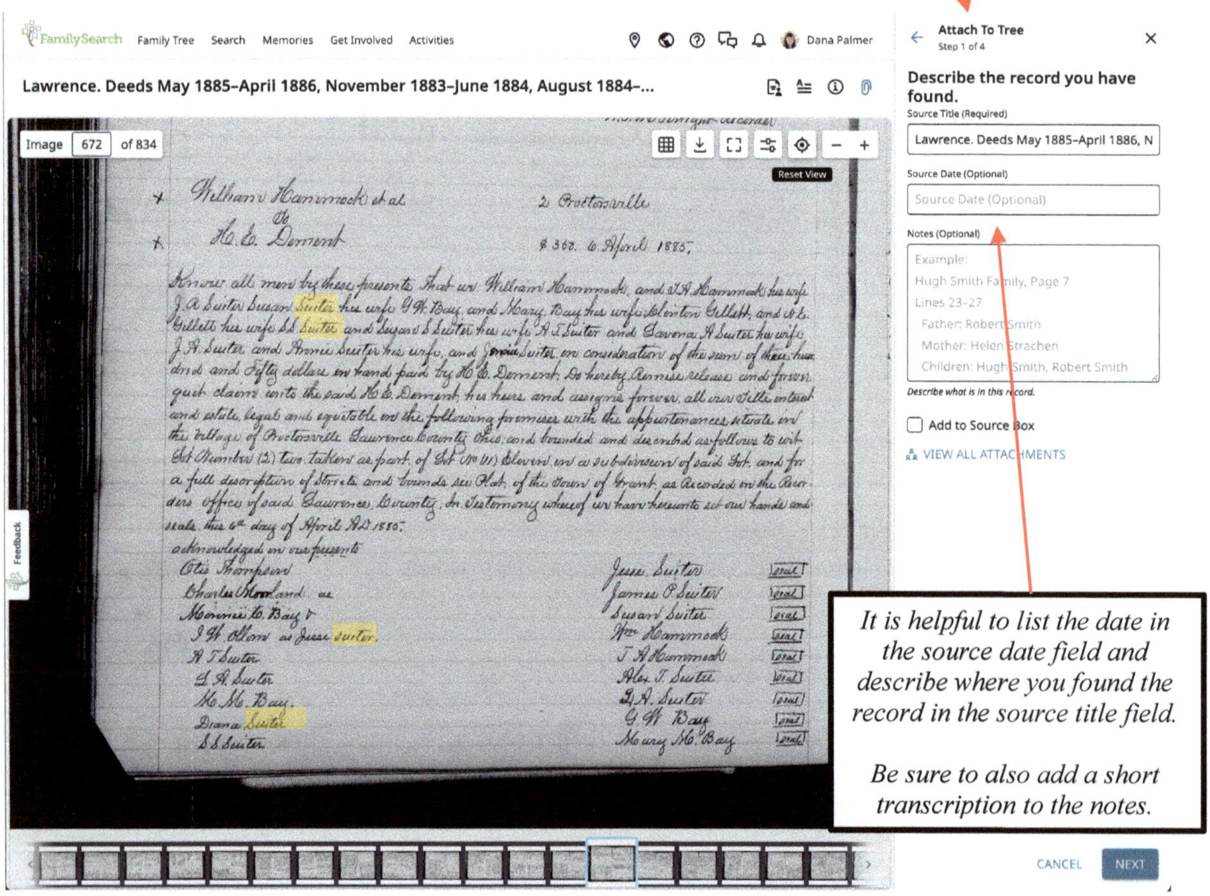

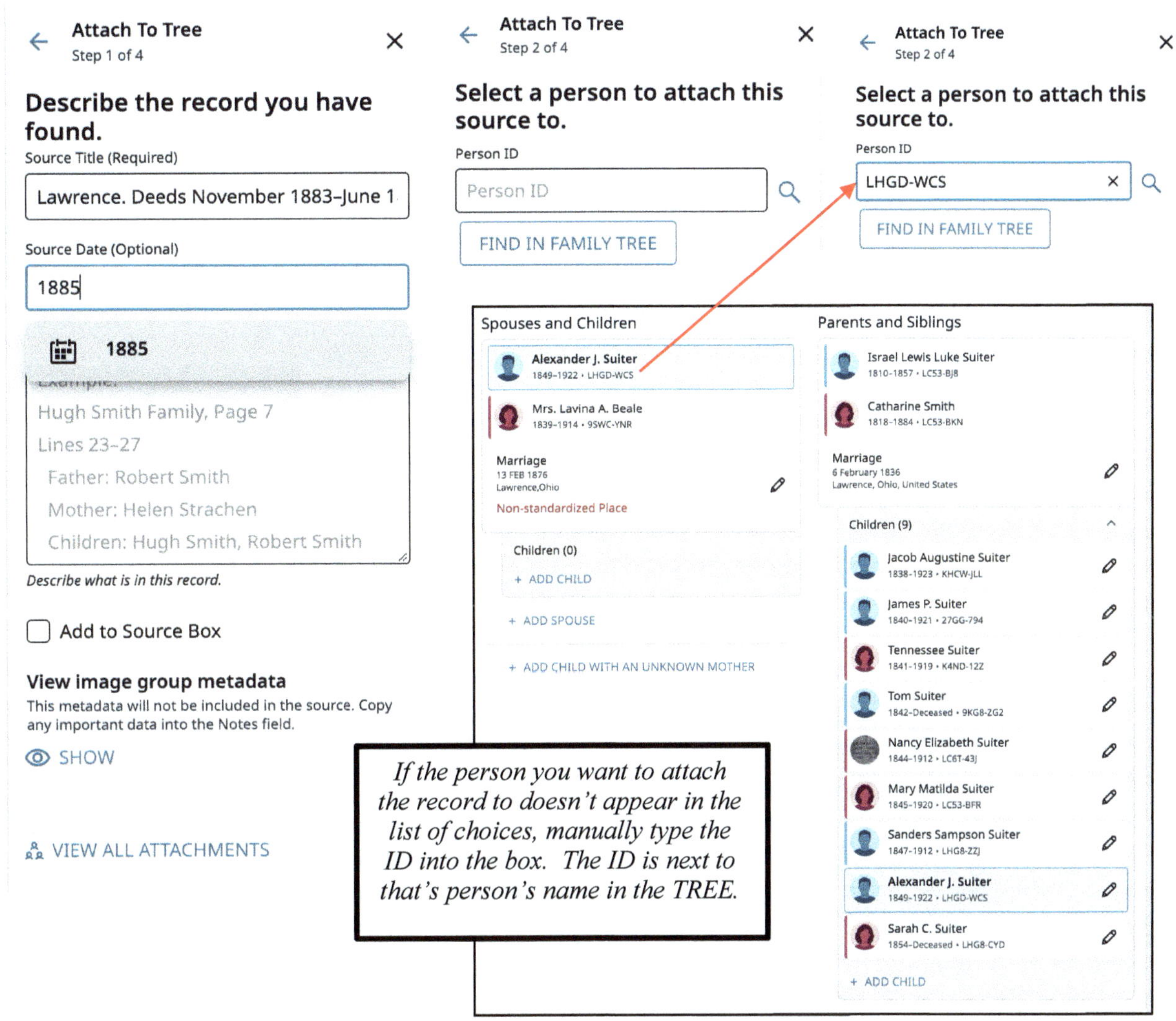

If the person you want to attach the record to doesn't appear in the list of choices, manually type the ID into the box. The ID is next to that's person's name in the TREE.

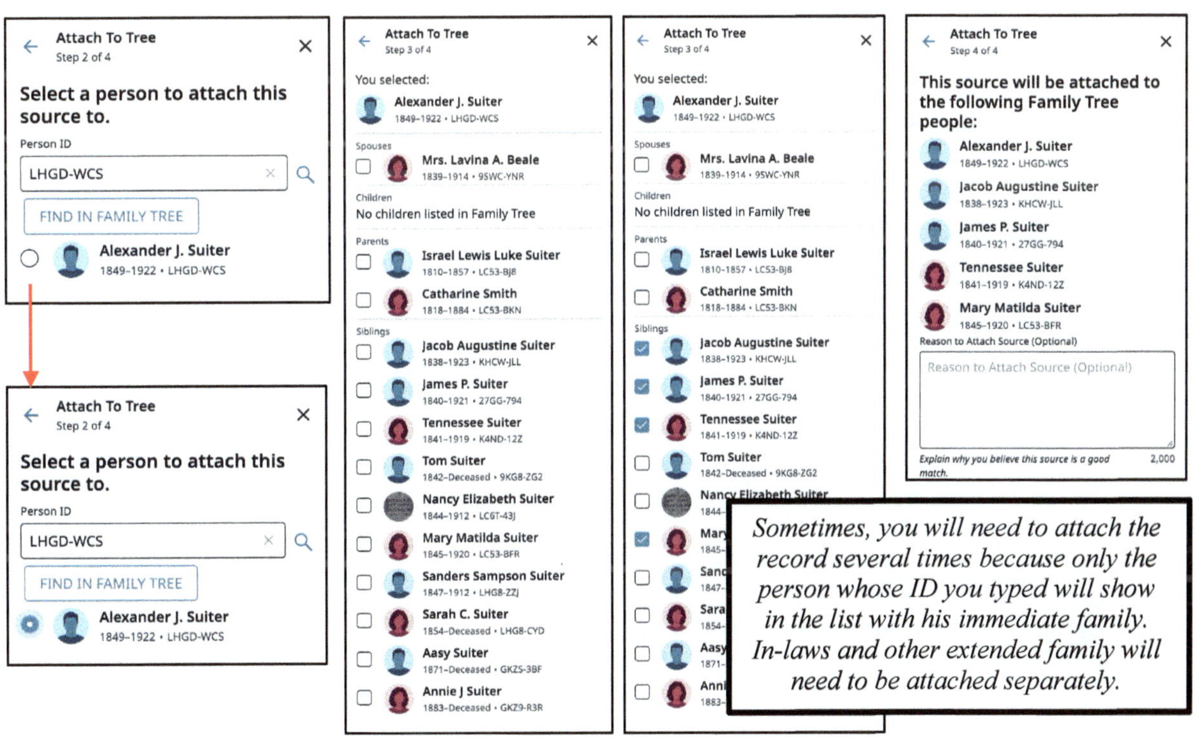

Sometimes, you will need to attach the record several times because only the person whose ID you typed will show in the list with his immediate family. In-laws and other extended family will need to be attached separately.

You'll get a small notification in the upper right corner once the record is attached. For people named in the record that are not part of the immediate family, you'll need to attach their records separately.

In this case, since Alexander J. Suiter was chosen as the main person to attach the record to, only his wife, children, parents, and siblings show in the attached choices. His sister Mary (Suiter) Bay, also mentioned in this record, can be attached easily since she is Alexander's sister, but the SAVE RECORD button would need to be selected a second time to attached Mary's husband G. W. Bay. The same would be true for any of Alexander's sibling-in-laws, since they do not show when Alexander is selected as the main focus person.

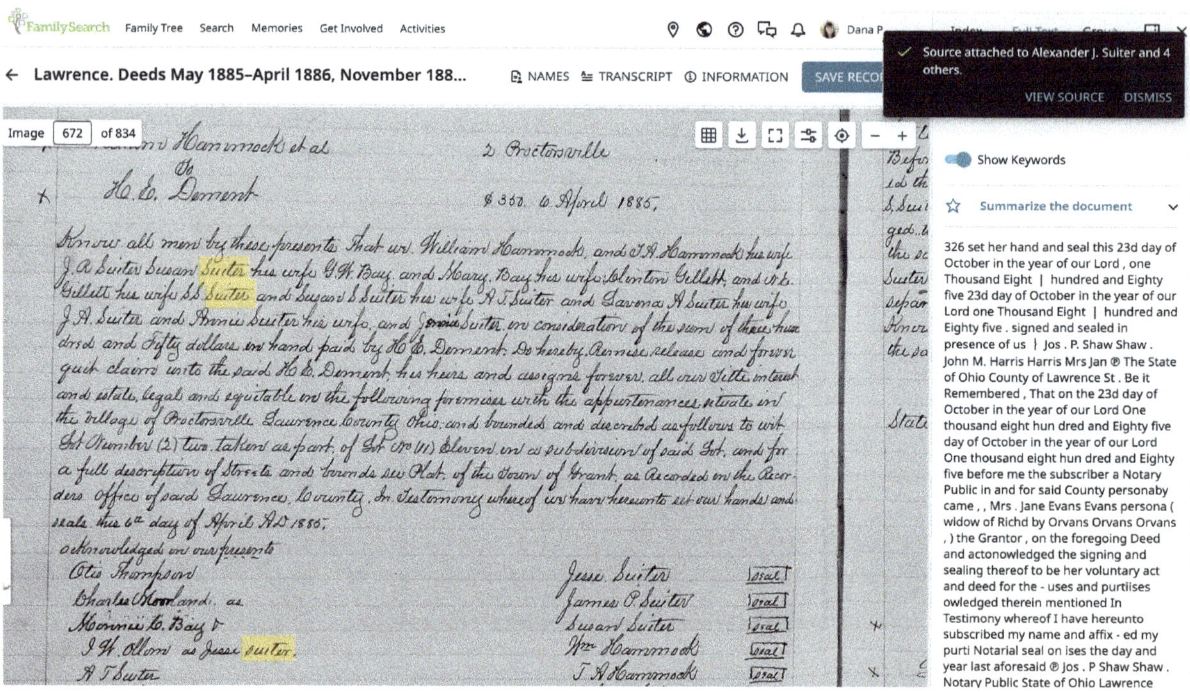

https://www.familysearch.org/ark:/61903/3:1:3Q9M-C37F-Z9RF-B?view=fullText&keywords=Suiter&lang=en&groupId=TH-909-85960-42992-38

Once the record is attached, it can be found by going to the details page in the TREE for that person and selecting SOURCES. Newly attached records always appear at the top of the list of attached sources. These can be rearranged by date if the list has been set to the CUSTOMIZE view in OPTIONS.

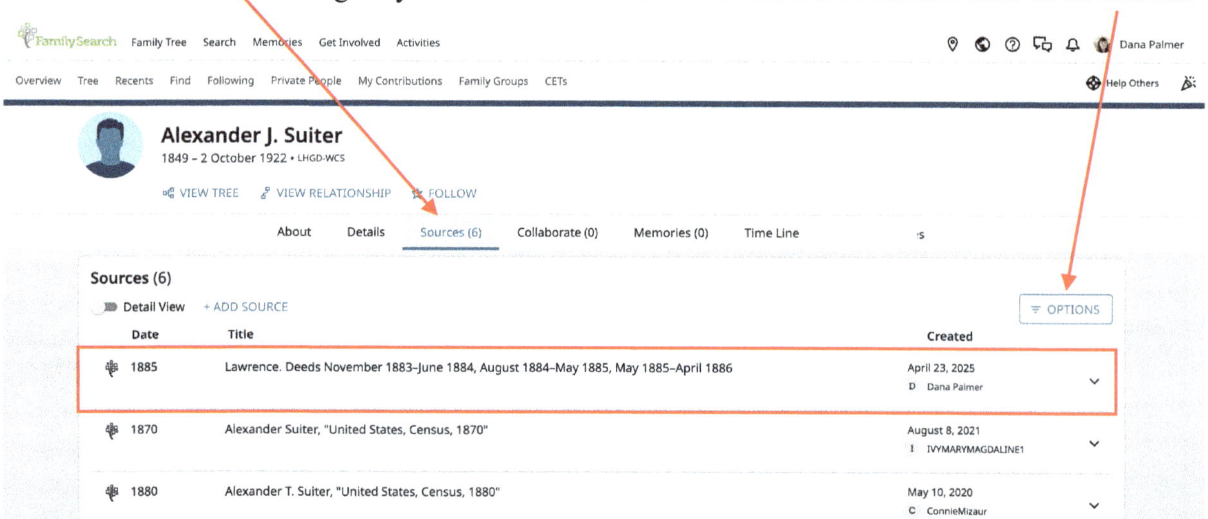

https://www.familysearch.org/en/tree/person/sources/LHGD-WCS

Finding the Record Origin Using Full-Text Search

Finding the original reference using FULL-TEXT SEARCH on FamilySearch is similar to finding the source in RECORDS or IMAGES.

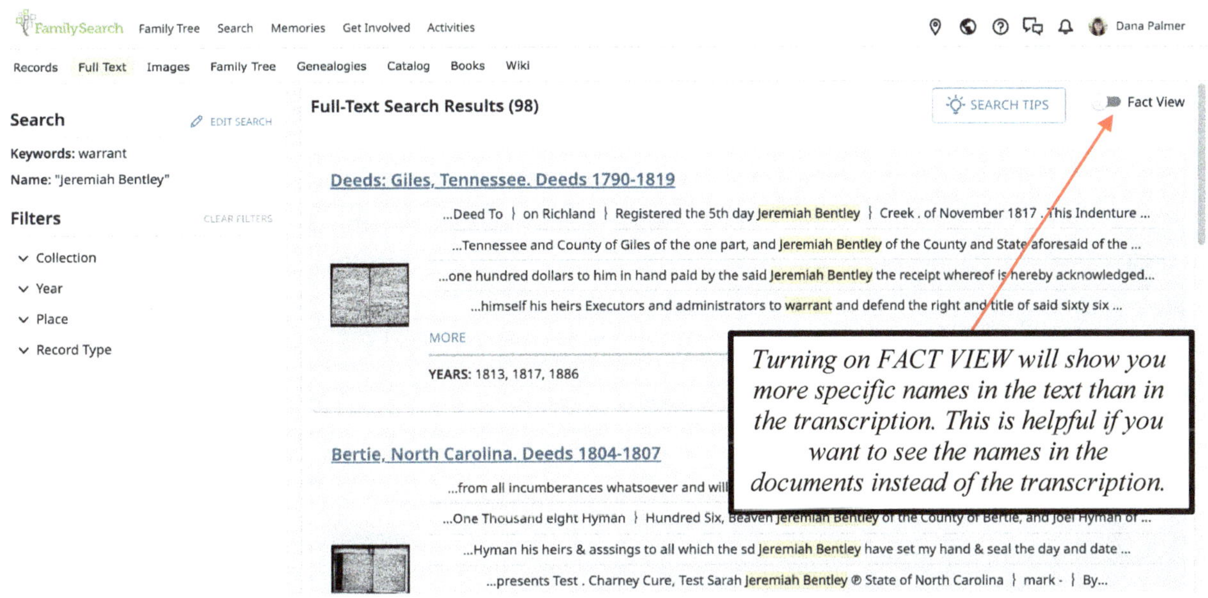

https://www.familysearch.org/en/search/full-text/results?count=20&q.fullName=%22Jeremiah%20Bentley%22&q.text=warrant&c.recordPlace1=on&f.recordPlace0=10&c.recordPlace2=on&f.recordPlace1=10%2CGeorgia

Select the desired record. You can either click on the INFORMATION icon or click on the grid icon and go to the first page of the collection to see the microfilm number.

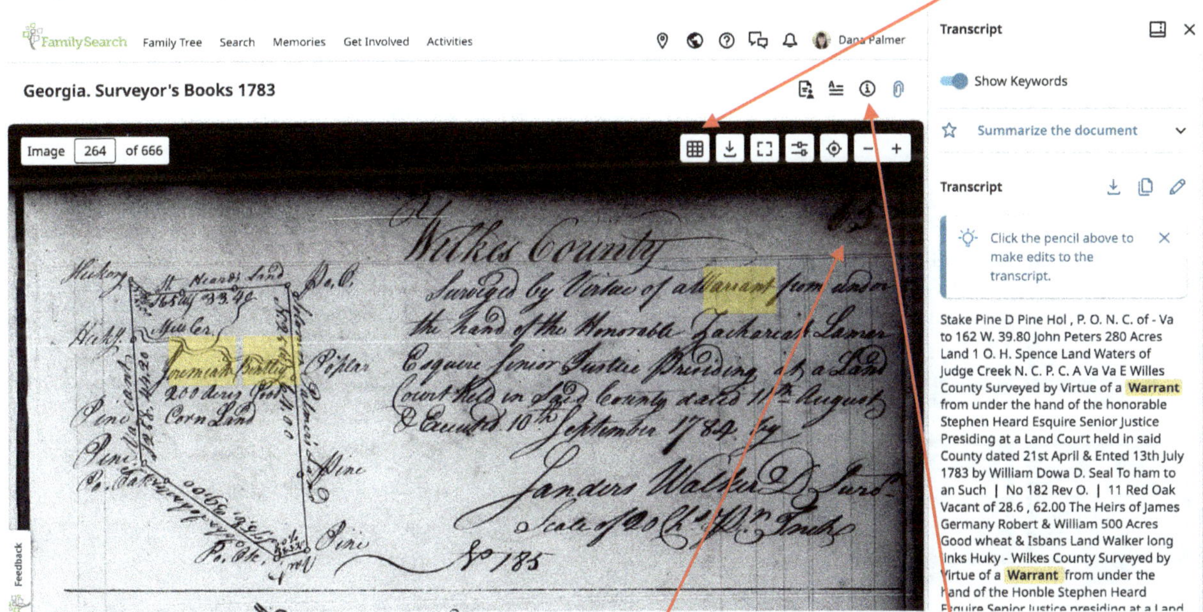

https://www.familysearch.org/ark:/61903/3:1:3Q9M-CS41-RSVS-4?view=fullText&keywords=Jeremiah%20Bentley%2CWarrant%2Cwarrant&lang=en&groupId=TH-909-61195-69441-61

In the upper right corner, it shows this is page 65 in the book. To see the details about the original source, you'll need to scroll and check the prior pages, click on INFORMATION, or click the grid icon to determine the microfilm or digital image number.

Click on INFORMATION to see the microfilm or Digital Image Group Number.

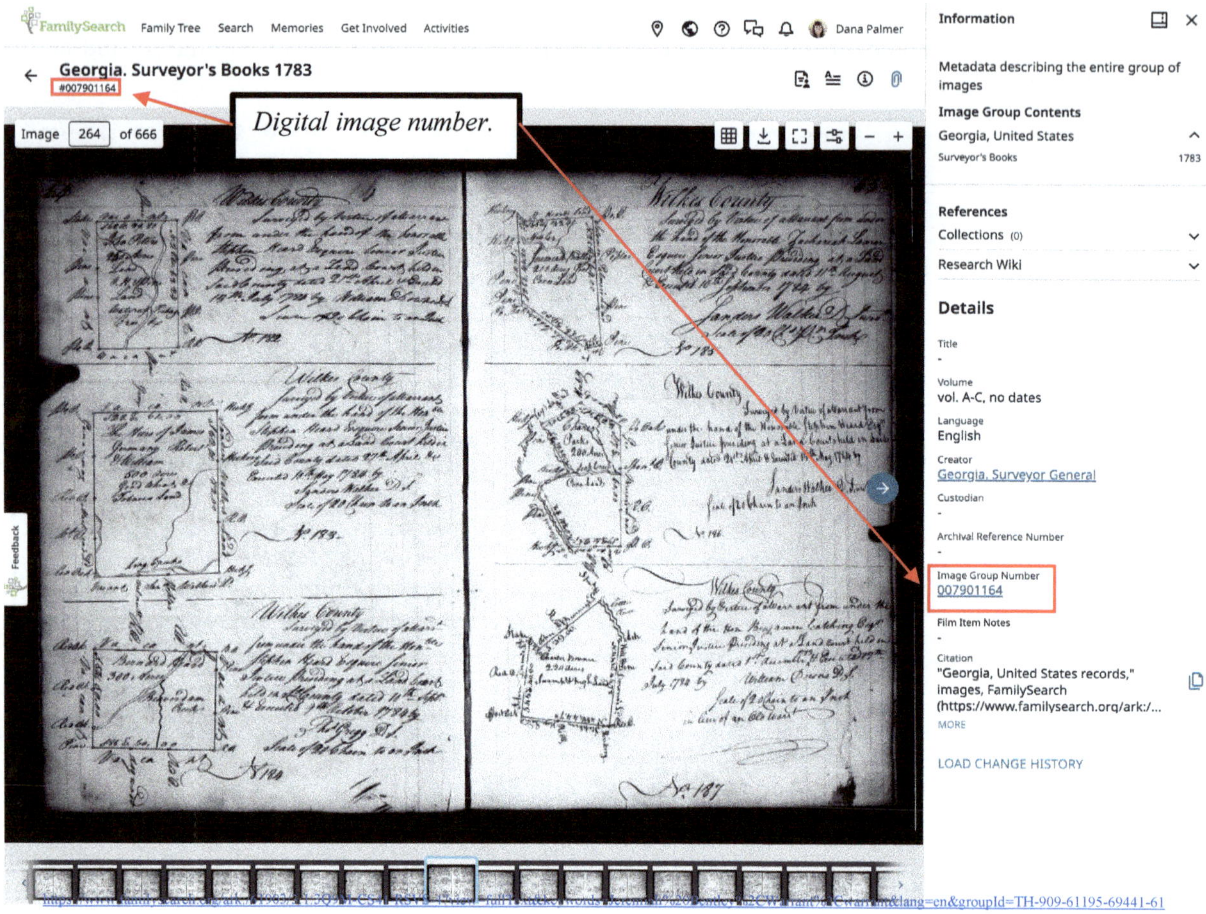

...lang=en&groupId=TH-909-61195-69441-61

Clicking on the grid will highlight in blue the last image you viewed.

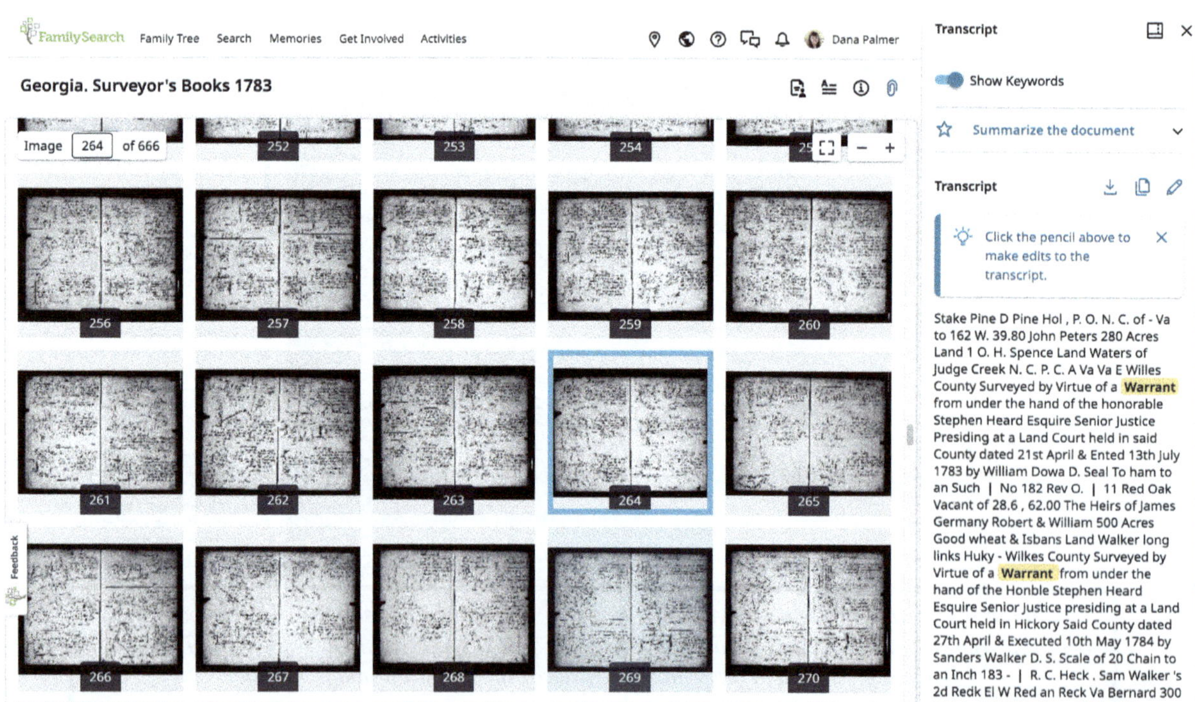

https://www.familysearch.org/ark:/61903/3:1:3Q9M-CS41-RSVS-4?view=fullText&keywords=Jeremiah%20Bentley%2CWarrant%2Cwarrant&lang=en&groupId=TH-909-61195-69441-61&grid=on

Carefully scroll up until you see the start of the book / volume / folio for that record collection. Sometimes this is a few pages prior, while other times it may be one of the first few images in the collection.

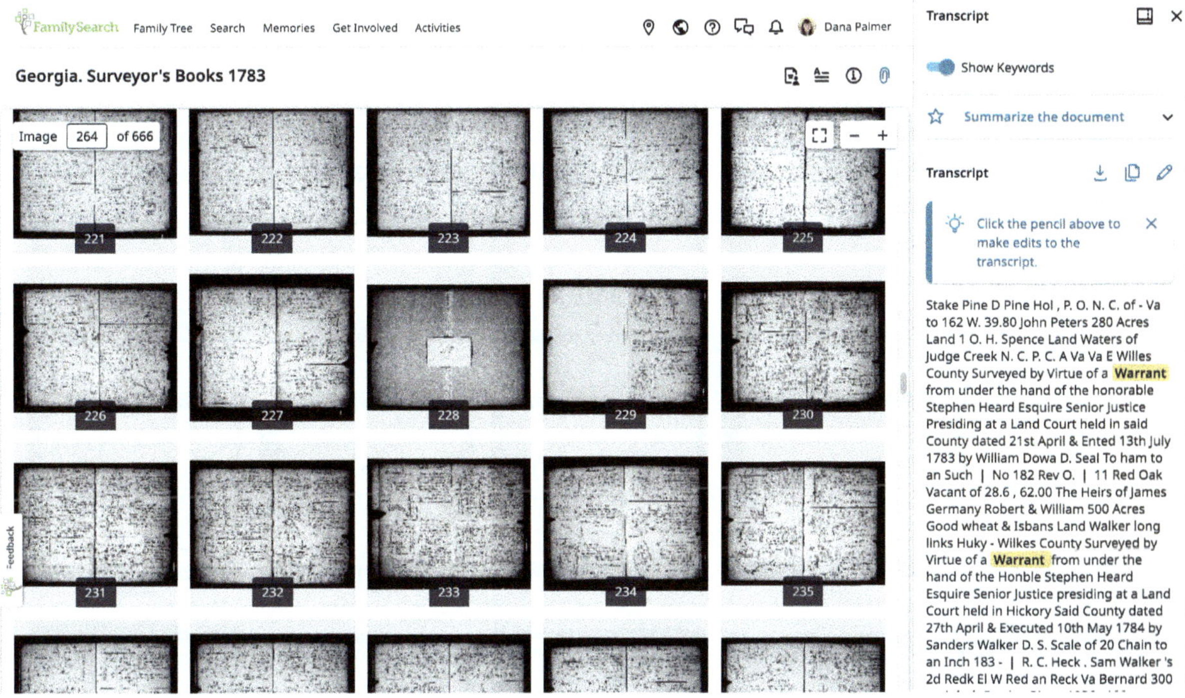

https://www.familysearch.org/ark:/61903/3:1:3Q9M-CS41-RSVS-4?view=fullText&keywords=Jeremiah%20Bentley%2CWarrant%2Cwarrant&lang=en&groupId=TH-909-61195-69441-61&grid=on

Double click on the image to see if this is the start of the book in which your record is contained. Sometimes, it will have a page with the word START before it, but other times, as in this case, the image may look like a title page.

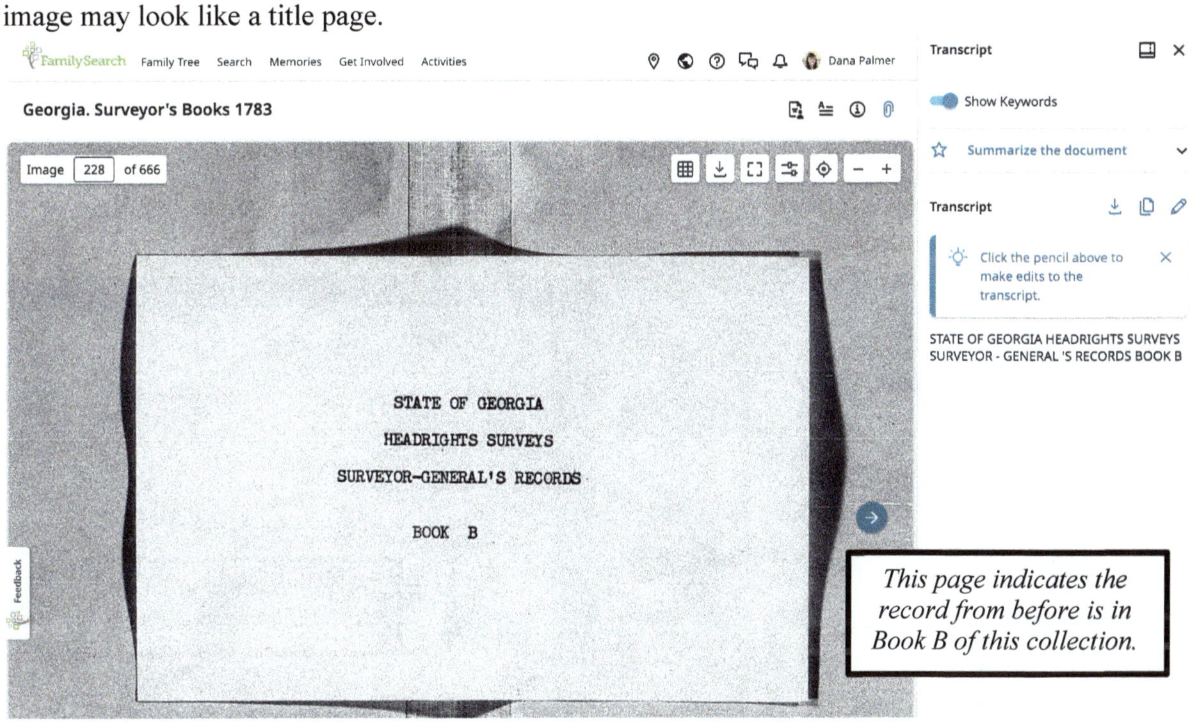

This page indicates the record from before is in Book B of this collection.

https://www.familysearch.org/ark:/61903/3:1:3Q9M-CS41-RSJT-Q?view=fullText&keywords=Jeremiah%20Bentley%2CWarrant%2Cwarrant&lang=en&groupId=TH-909-61195-69441-61

Scroll to the beginning of the images to see the microfilm number / digital collection.

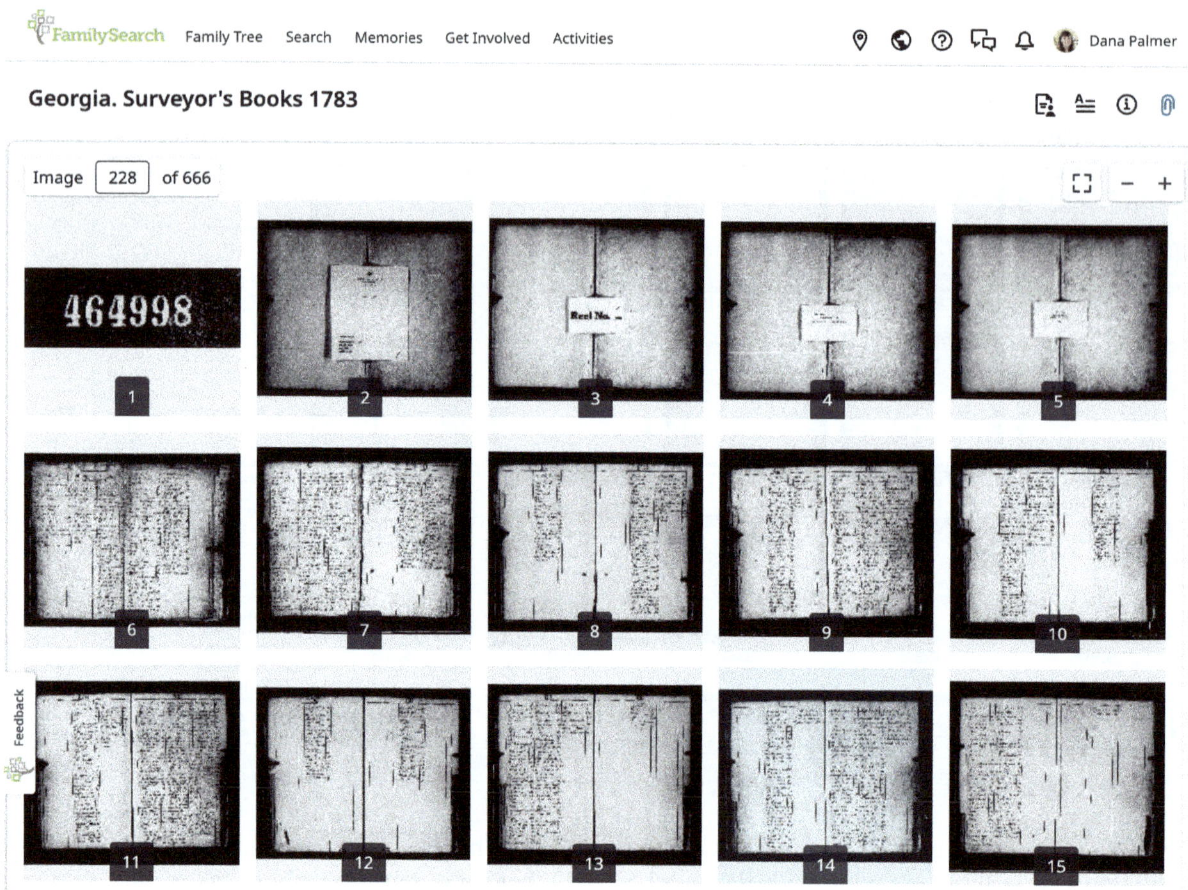

https://www.familysearch.org/ark:/61903/3:1:3Q9M-CS41-RSVS-4?view=fullText&keywords=Jeremiah%20Bentley%2CWarrant%2Cwarrant&lang=en&groupId=TH-909-61195-69441-61&grid=on

The record is in microfilm 464,998 while the number indicated under INFORMATION listed it as 007901164; but these are the same record collections under two different numbering systems. One is based on the original microfilm, and the other, on the newly assigned digital image number (DGS). To see more details, click on SEARCH, and then CATALOG, and type in the number found.

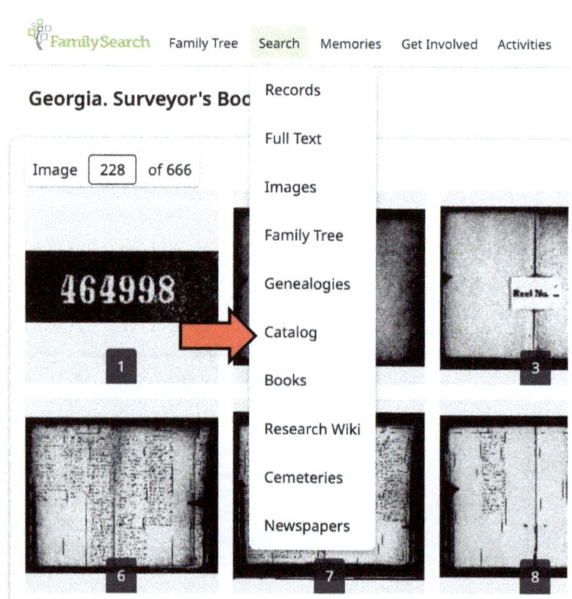

https://www.familysearch.org/en/search/catalog/

Your search result will be the collection that matches the microfilm / digital image number you typed into the FILM/FICHE/IMAGE GROUP NUMBER (DGS) search. Click on the blue link for the collection to see more details about it.

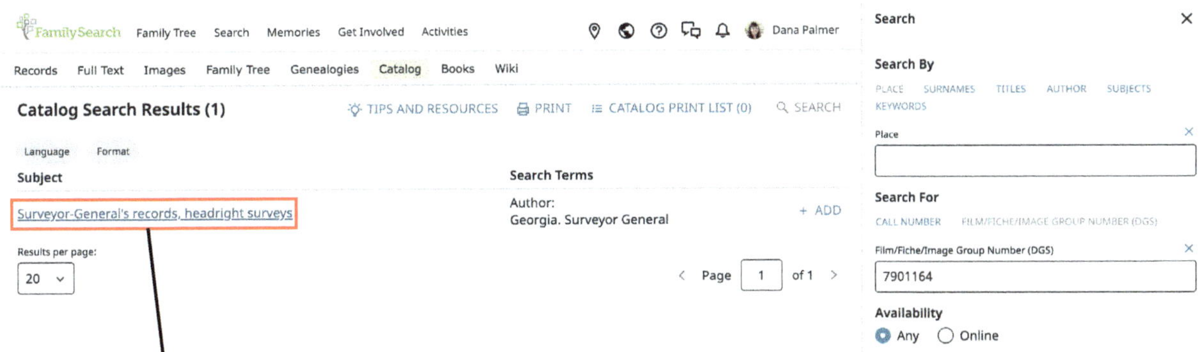

https://www.familysearch.org/en/search/catalog/results?q.filmNumber=7901164

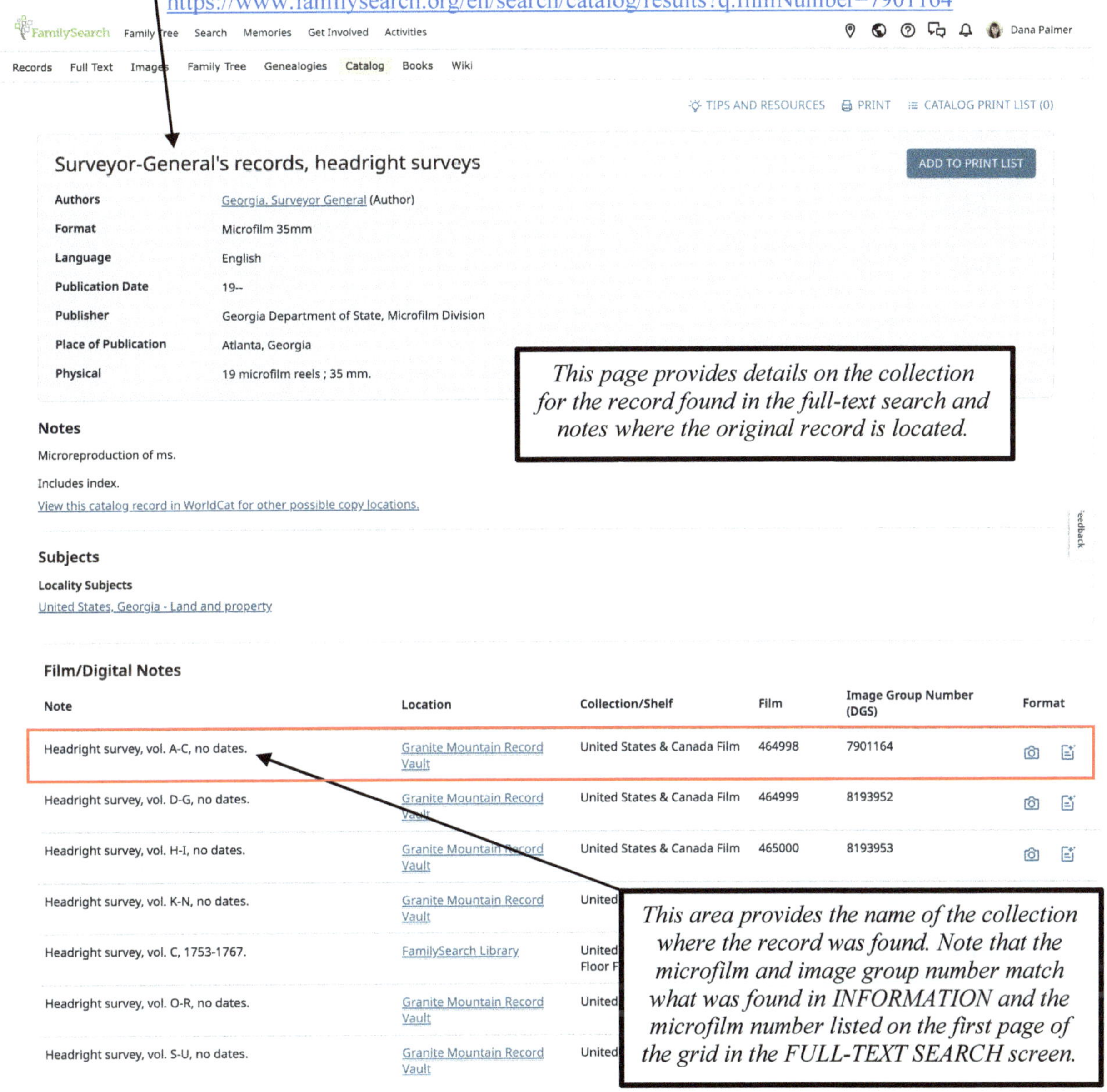

https://www.familysearch.org/en/search/catalog/315671

Searching Locked Records by Image Group Number (DGS)

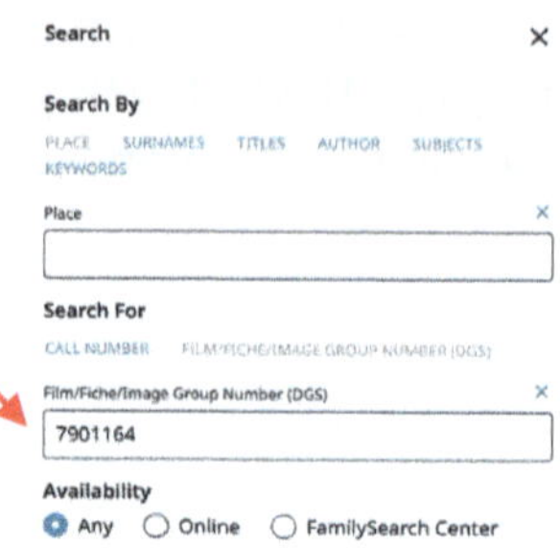

One trick when using FULL-TEXT SEARCH on FamilySearch is to limit the search choices by adding in the Image Group Number (DGS) in the search box filters along with a name or keyword search. This method will only look for matches in that specific record collection instead of everything on FamilySearch. This is a very effective way to find your person in a specific record set.

Go to the record collection in the CATALOG or IMAGES and write down the Image Group Number (DGS). This type of search will usually work even if the FULL-TEXT SEARCH icon is not next to the camera icon in the CATALOG.

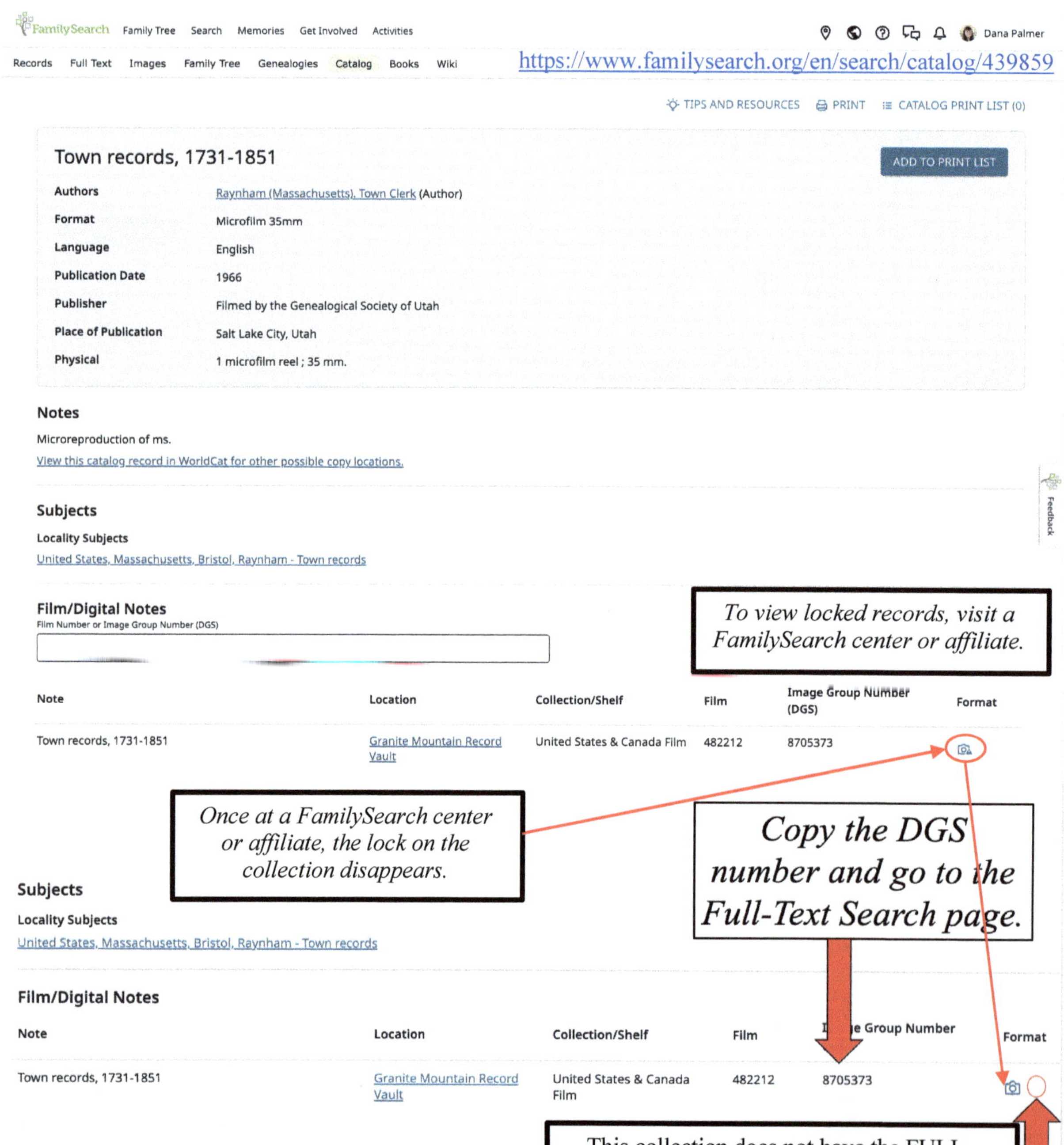

https://www.familysearch.org/en/search/catalog/439859

Go to the FULL-TEXT SEARCH page and type in the Image Group Number (DGS) in the filter box. If you are using a locked collection and are not at a FamilySearch center or affiliate, no search results will appear.

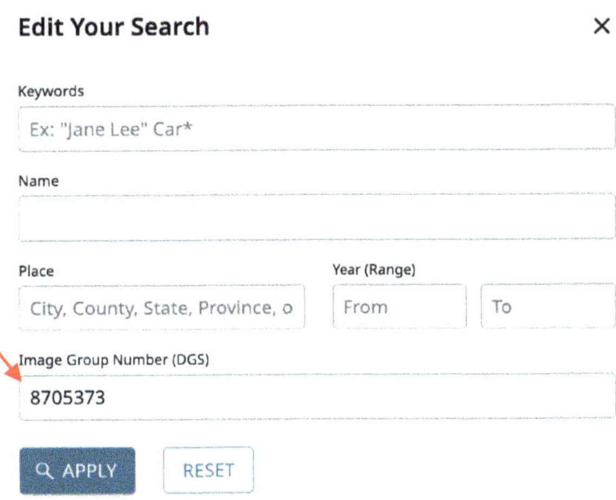

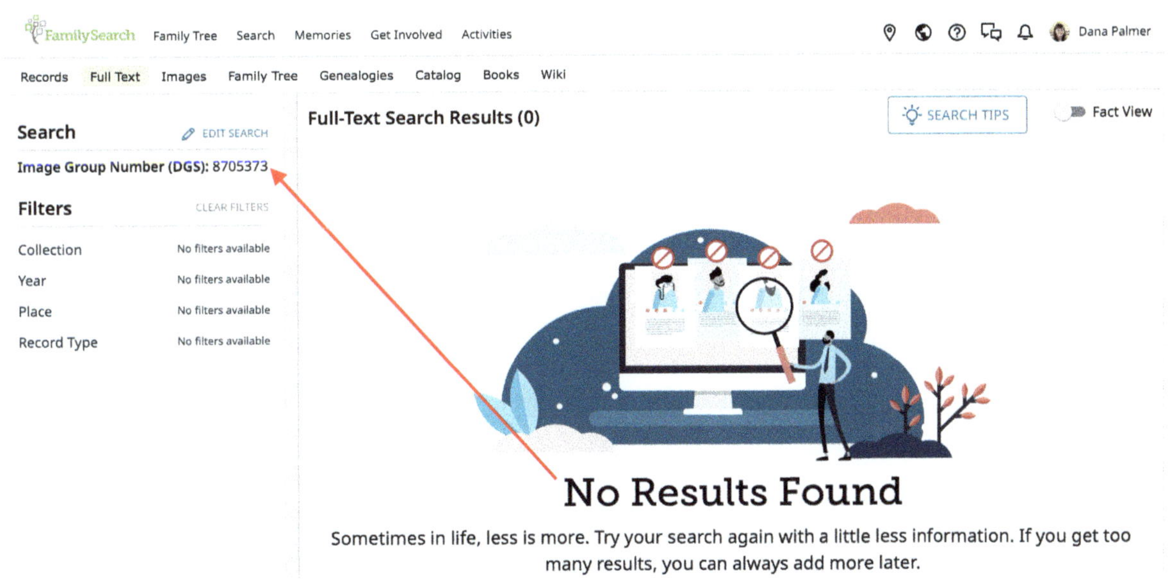

https://www.familysearch.org/en/search/full-text/results?count=20&q.groupName=8705373

To see the search results for locked collections, you must view them at a FamilySearch center or affiliate. This includes searches using FULL-TEXT SEARCH. **The results in the example below can only be viewed at a FamilySearch center or affiliate.**

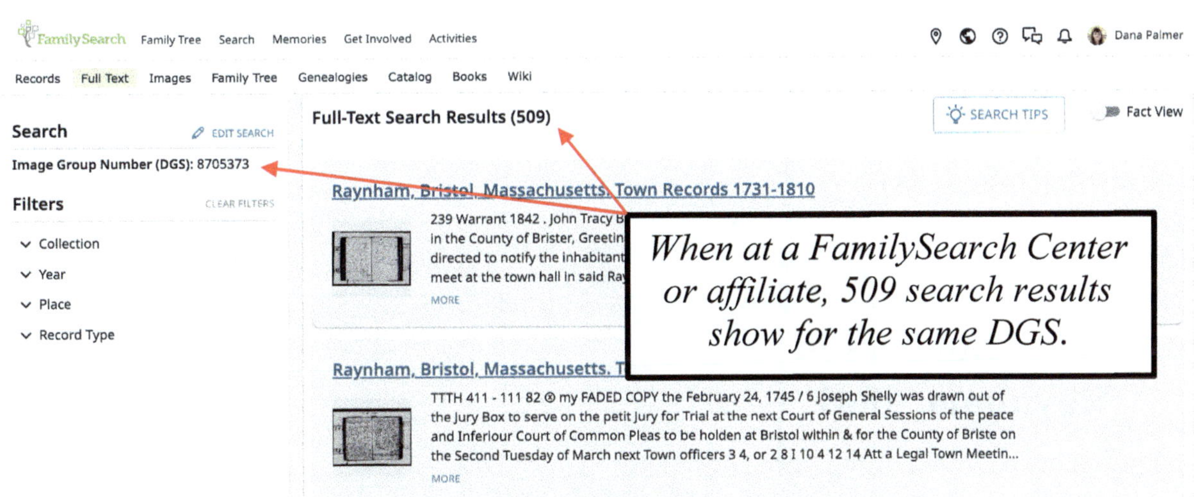

https://www.familysearch.org/en/search/full-text/results?count=20&q.groupName=8705373

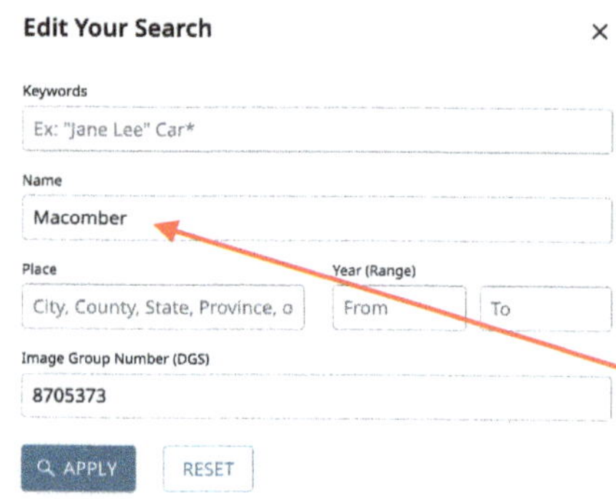

Add in other search parameters to narrow down the search results. Browse the search results and check the transcription to see if the names, dates, or locations match what is known for your desired person. Click on the blue link to view the record.

Adding the surname Macomber reduced 509 search results to 5.

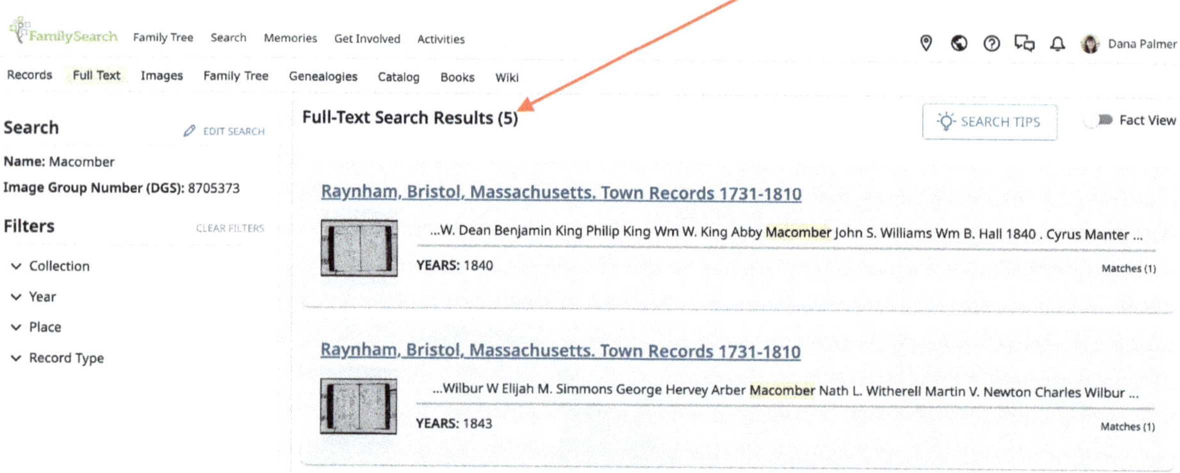

https://www.familysearch.org/en/search/full-text/results?count=20&q.fullName=Macomber&q.groupName=8705373

If this result is for the person you are researching, be sure to attach the record to the person in the tree by clicking the paper clip icon. The image in the example below is from their restricted collection and can only be viewed at a FamilySearch center or affiliate site.

Town Record for Raynham

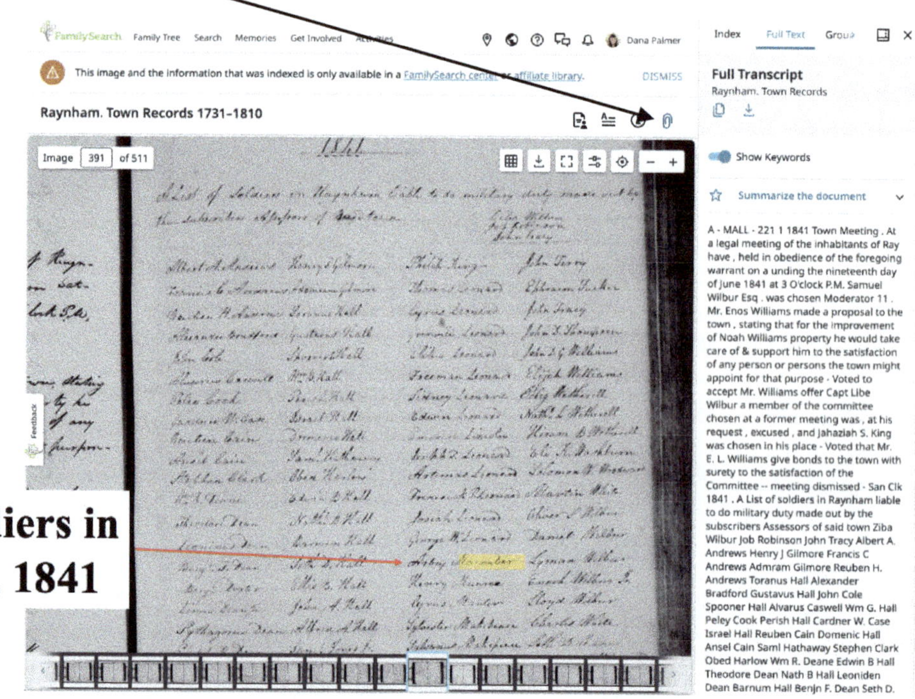

List of Soldiers in Raynham, 1841

https://www.familysearch.org/ark:/61903/3:1:3QHV-V38L-79R2-L?view=fullText&keywords=Macomber&lang=en&groupId=TH-7757-91535-47258-21

Finding Full-Text Search Collections from the Catalog

One of the newest features FamilySearch added to the catalog is the ability to see which collections are searchable using FULL-TEXT SEARCH. To determine if your collection has this capability, go to the CATALOG and find your record. Scroll down to the *Film / Digital Notes* section. Look on the far-right side of the page in the format column. If there is a paper symbol with a plus on it, then this collection has FULL-TEXT SEARCH features.

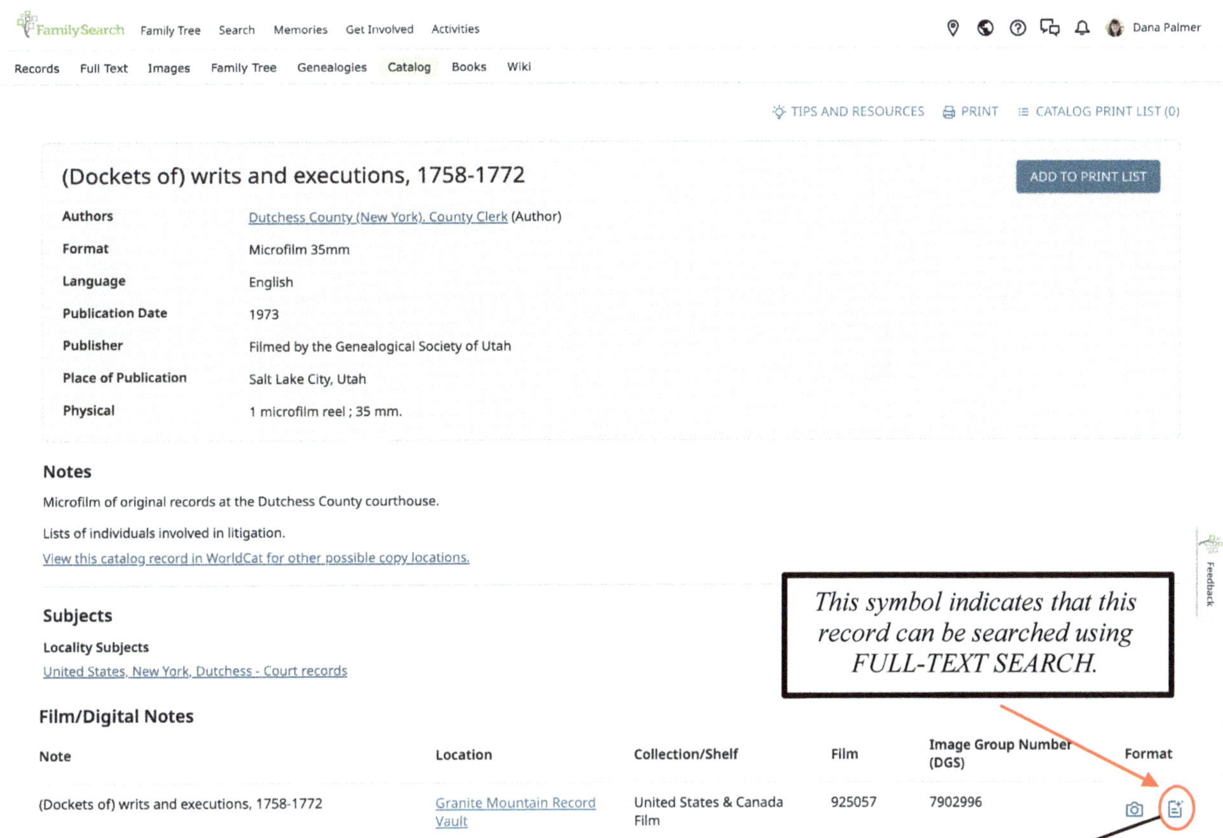

https://www.familysearch.org/en/search/catalog/316265

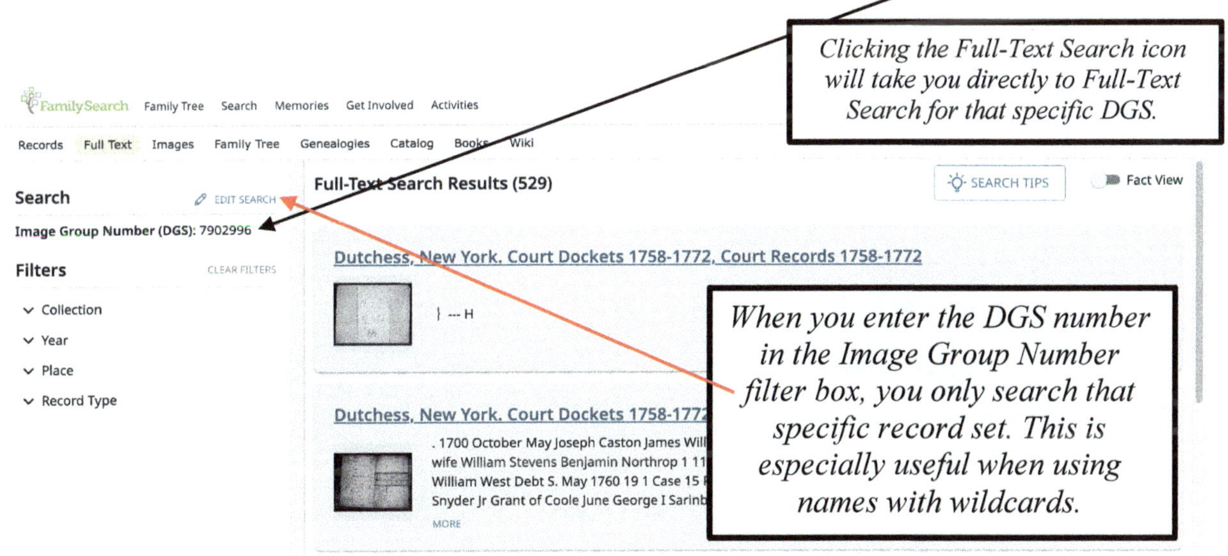

https://www.familysearch.org/en/search/full-text/results?q.groupName=7902996

As noted before, you can narrow the search results by trying different filters. With the Image Group Number (DGS) added, only results for that specific collection will show. In the case below, part of the surname is used with a wildcard to catch names that might be misspelled.

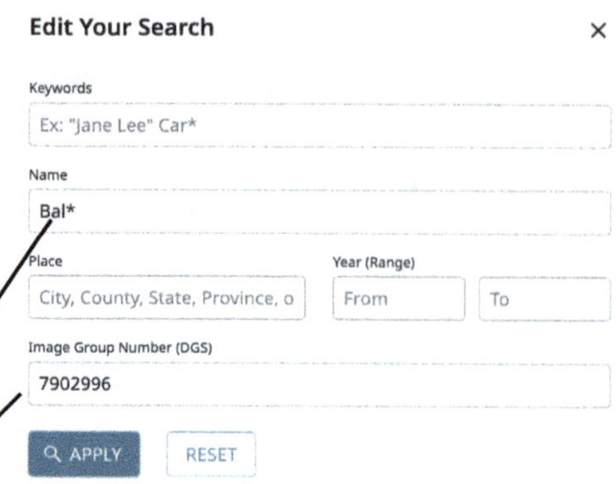

Using a wildcard with the DGS reduced the search results from 529 to 75.

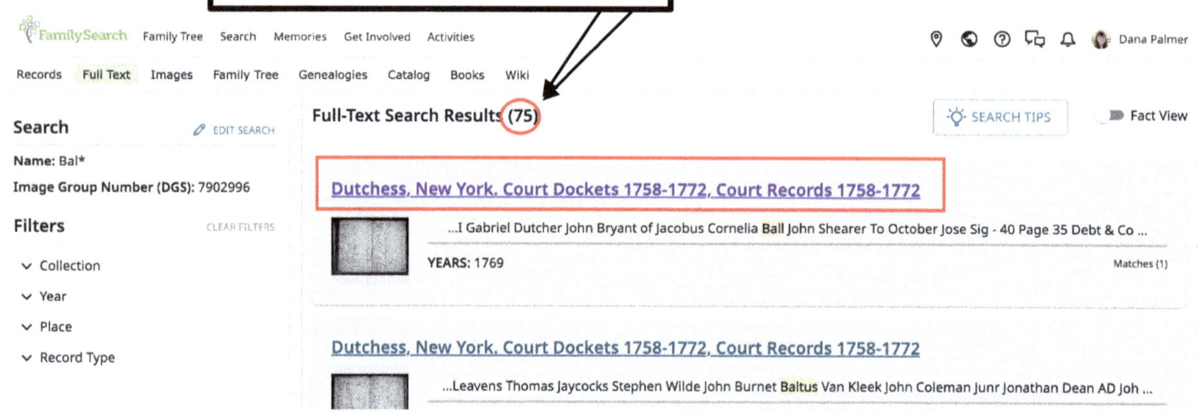

https://www.familysearch.org/en/search/full-text/results?count=20&offset=60&q.fullName=Bal%2A&q.groupName=7902996

Once you find the record you want, click on the blue link to view the record. Be sure to attach it to the tree by clicking SAVE RECORD.

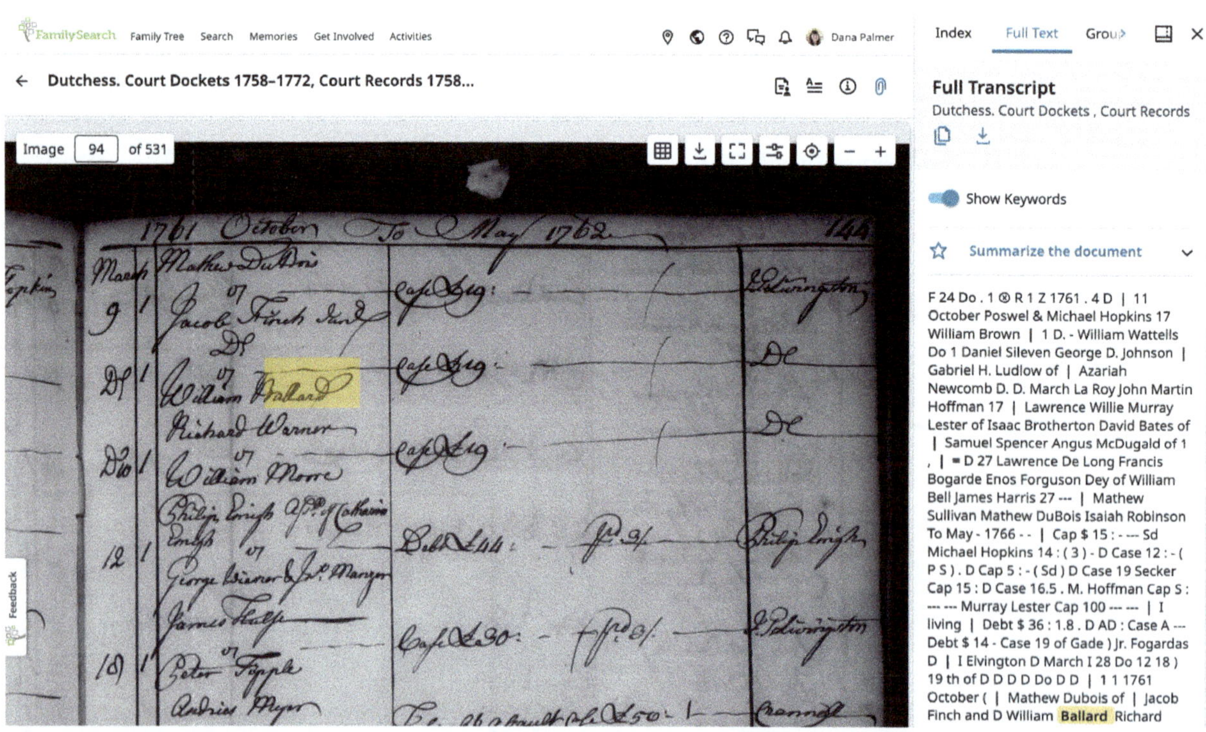

https://www.familysearch.org/ark:/61903/3:1:3Q9M-CS41-YQZT?view=fullText&keywords=Ballard?lang=en

Chapter 5: Using the Research Wiki

USING THE RESEARCH WIKI

FamilySearch's RESEARCH WIKI (https://www.familysearch.org/en/wiki/Main_Page) is a free online guide similar to Wikipedia, but its focus is specifically on genealogy research and sources internationally. It can be searched by key word for specific articles or by browsing topics or locations, not for specific people. Many articles and how-to instructions about family history can be found or posted on this site. Logged in users can also contribute weblinks and information to the pages in the RESEARCH WIKI.

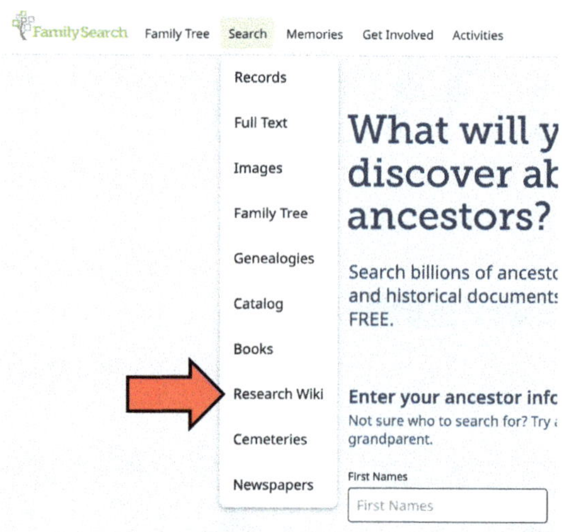

Click on the SEARCH tab and then choose RESEARCH WIKI.

Type in the keyword or location into the search box, or for more help, click on GUIDED RESEARCH.

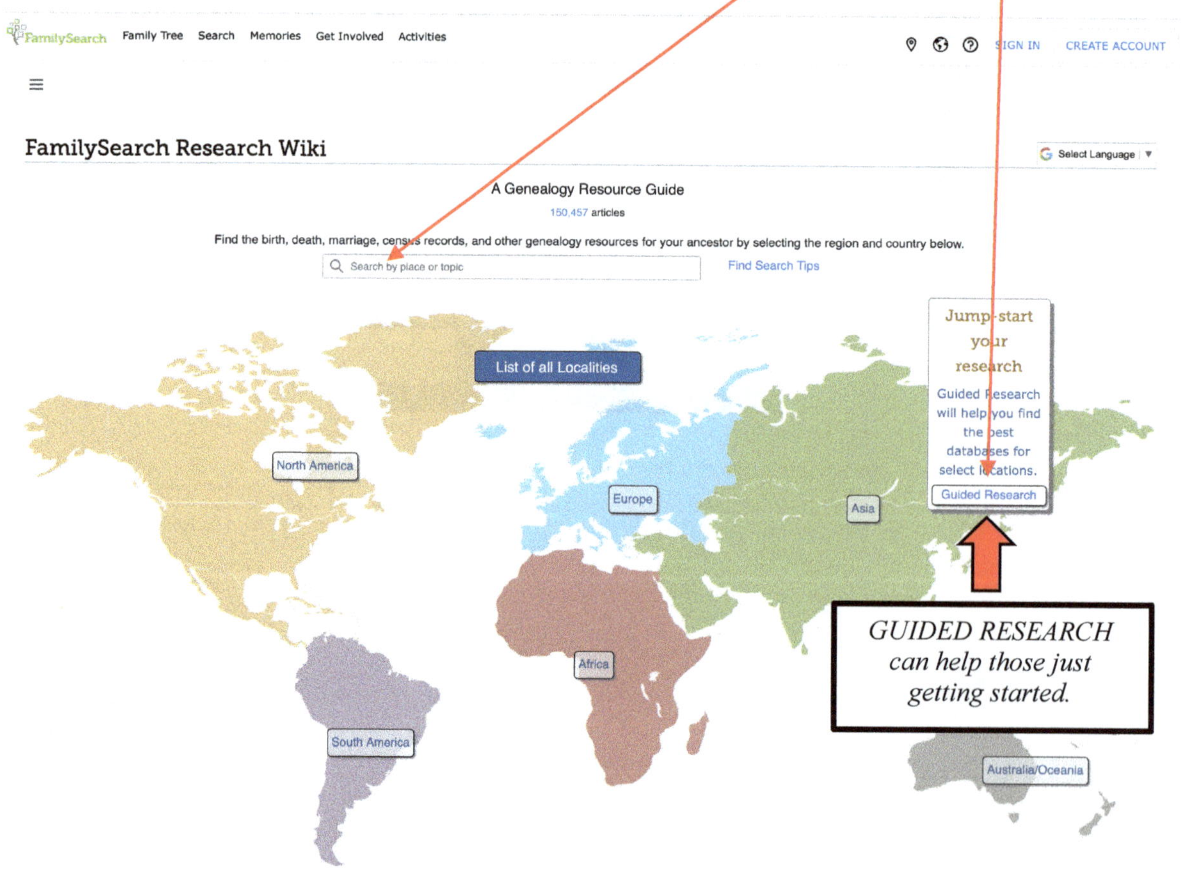

https://www.familysearch.org/en/wiki/Main_Page

Guided Research

GUIDED RESEARCH is designed to help beginner's get started finding the records of their family. Choose from the list of countries available at https://www.familysearch.org/en/wiki/Guided_Research_for_Online_Records.

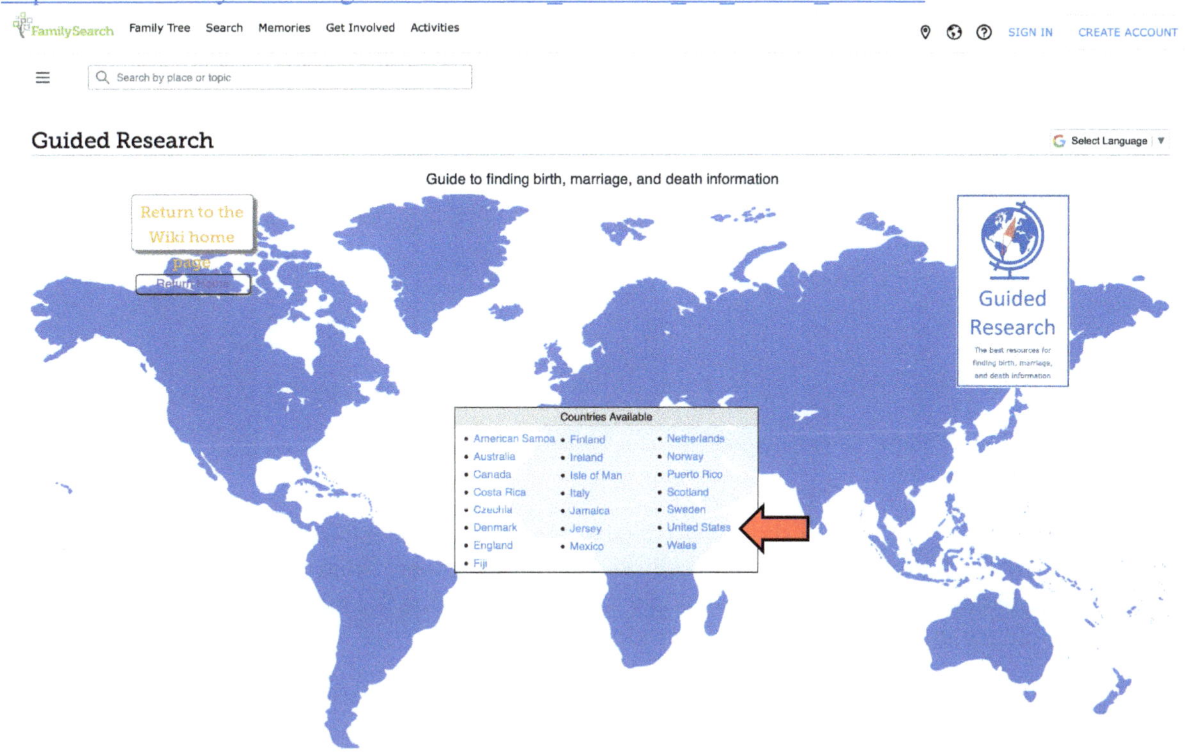

Each location has unique choices to help you get started. Click on the location desired. For the United States, go to https://www.familysearch.org/en/wiki/GuidedResearch:United_States.

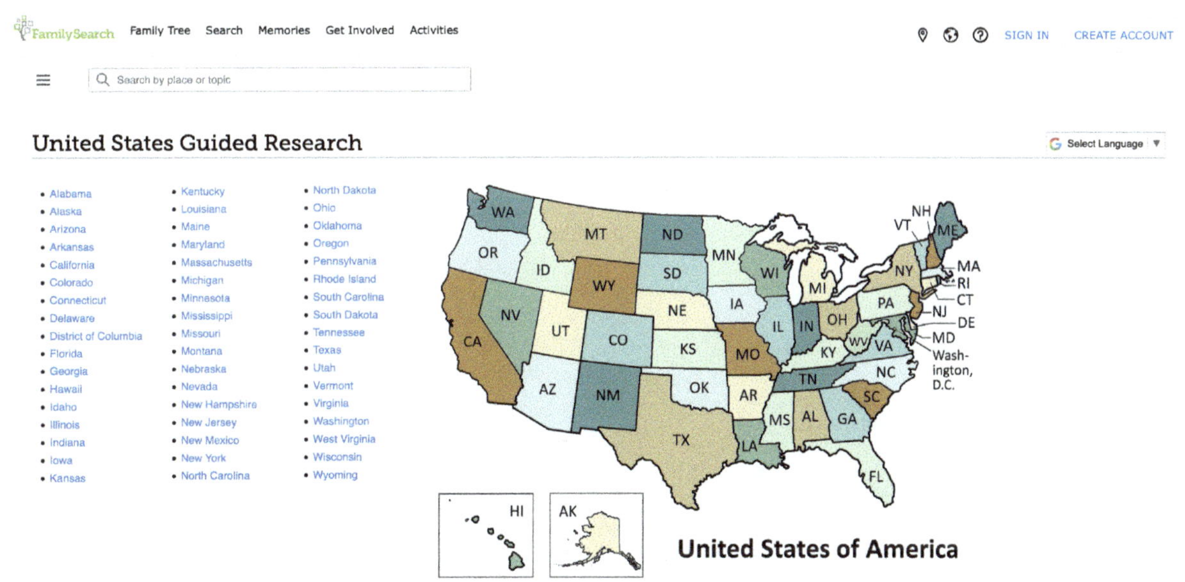

Choose the state in which you want to find records, then select the type of record you want to find. It will walk you through how to find that type of record for the period specified. If there are online collections, it will have a link to those records.

This page shows the most complete indexes available for Missouri vital records. For more records, a search would need to be done using the CATALOG, IMAGES, or the county pages for whichever your county of interest in the FamilySearch RESEARCH WIKI.

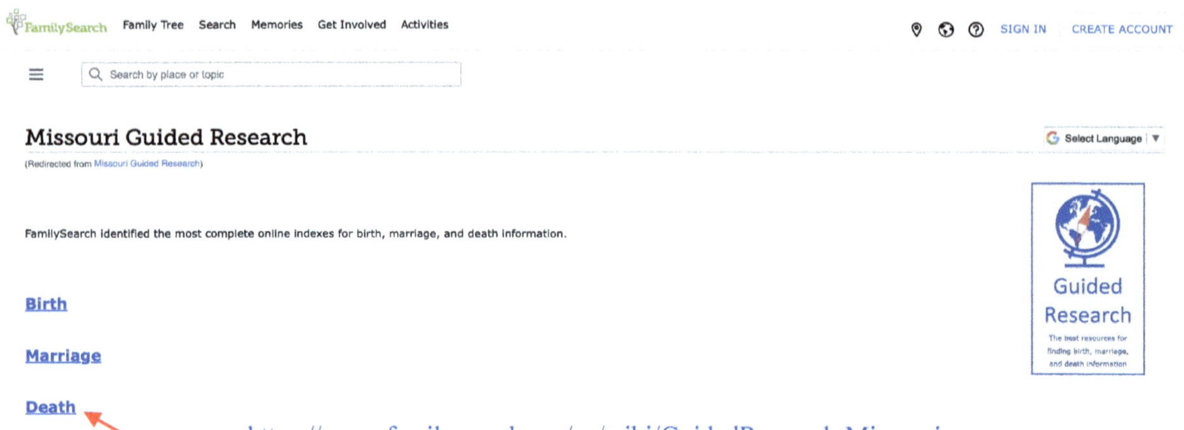

https://www.familysearch.org/en/wiki/GuidedResearch:Missouri

Clicking on the category, DEATH shows two databases with online death records/indexes. Sometimes these links will be for collections on FamilySearch; other times, from another website, whether subscription based or free. The intent is to help you get started using the most complete index available for that location and topic. Other states will produce similar results.

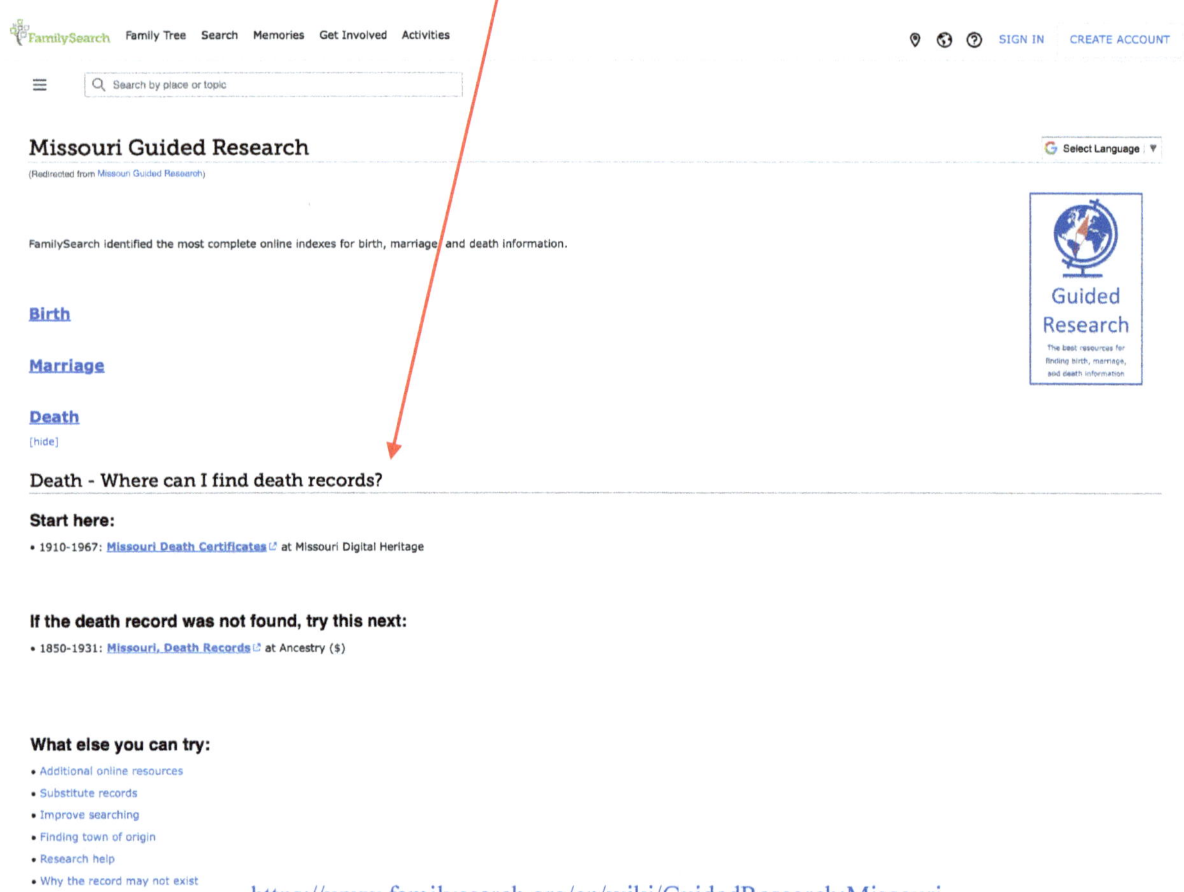

https://www.familysearch.org/en/wiki/GuidedResearch:Missouri

GUIDED RESEARCH is available for other countries, too. The setup is similar with the intent to help you get started finding the most complete indexes possible. If you want to find more records for that location, go to the CATALOG, IMAGES, or the specific location in the RESEARCH WIKI.

The following example is for Czechia or Czechoslovakia (https://www.familysearch.org/en/wiki/GuidedResearch:Czechia).

You can choose the category "**I know the town**" or "**I do not know the town**." Both will walk you through how to get started.

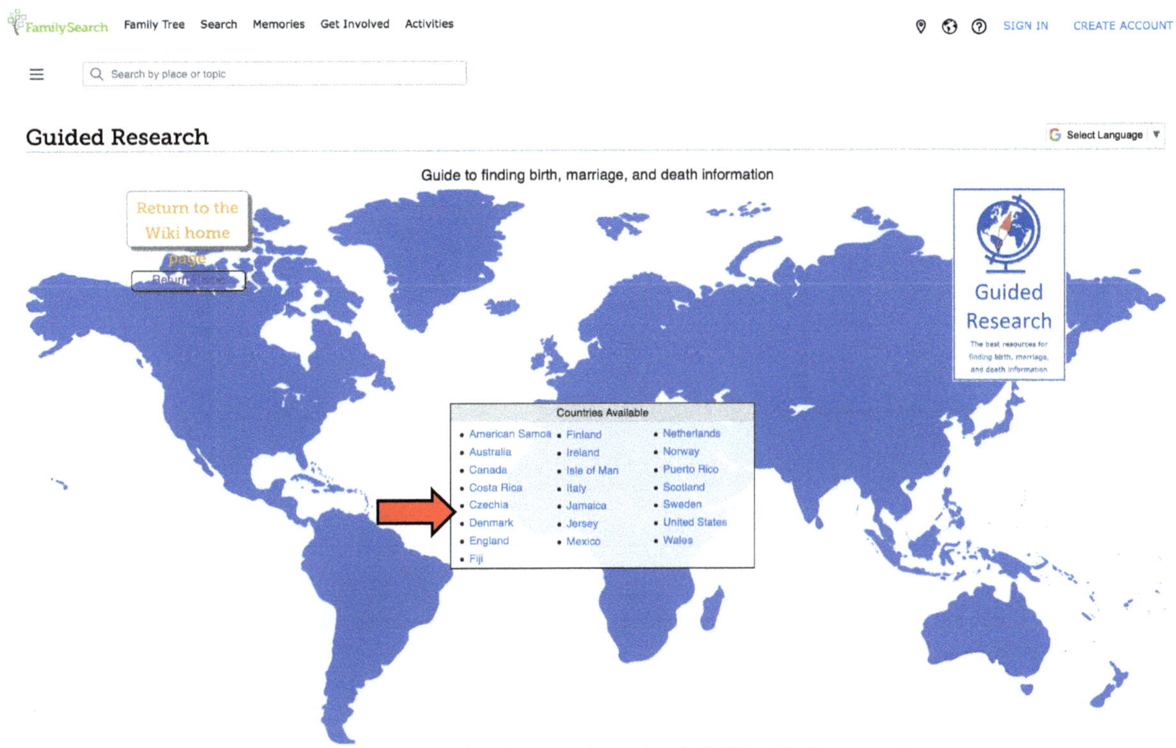

https://www.familysearch.org/en/wiki/GuidedResearch

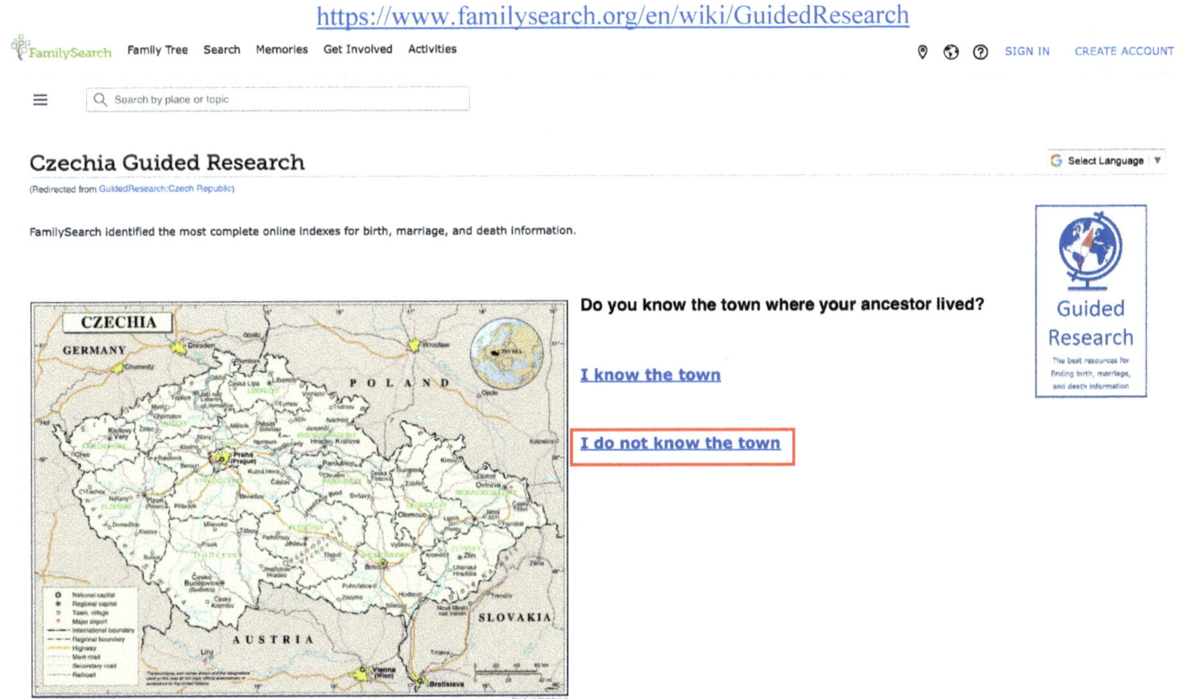

https://www.familysearch.org/en/wiki/GuidedResearch:Czechia

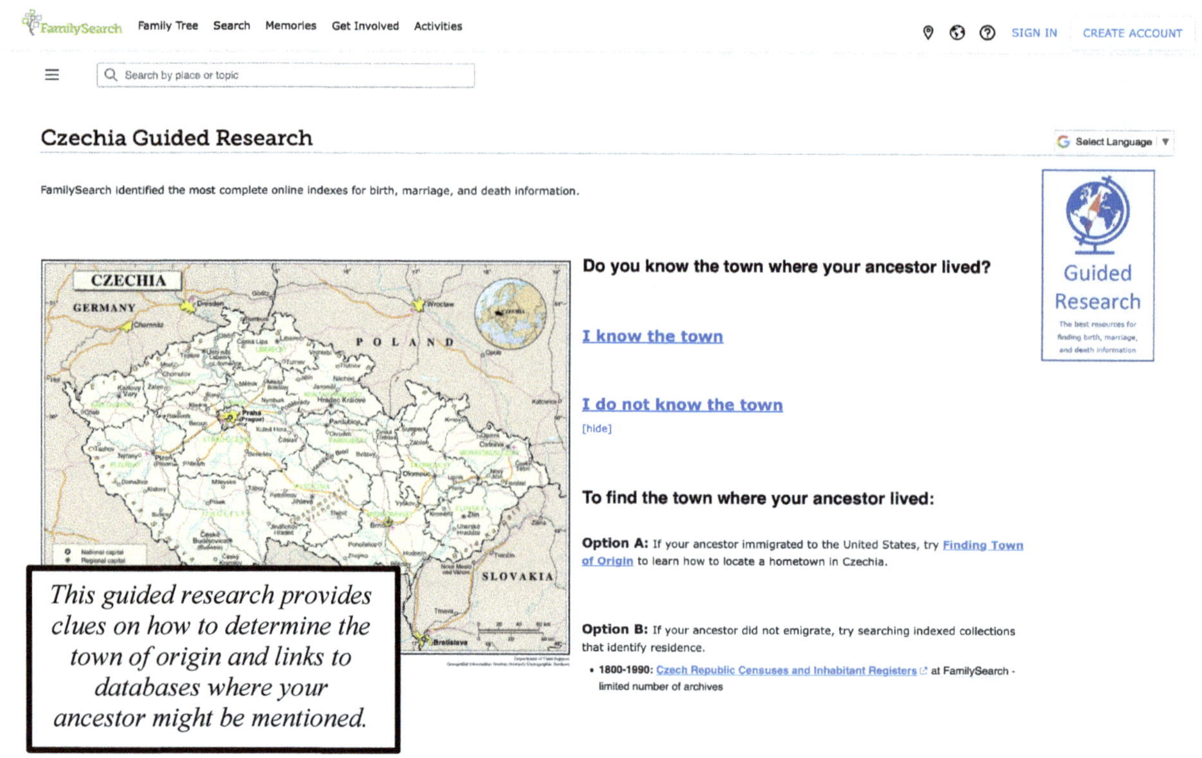

https://www.familysearch.org/en/wiki/GuidedResearch:Czechia

If the town in Czechia is known, click this choice. Other locations may have similar options to help you get started.

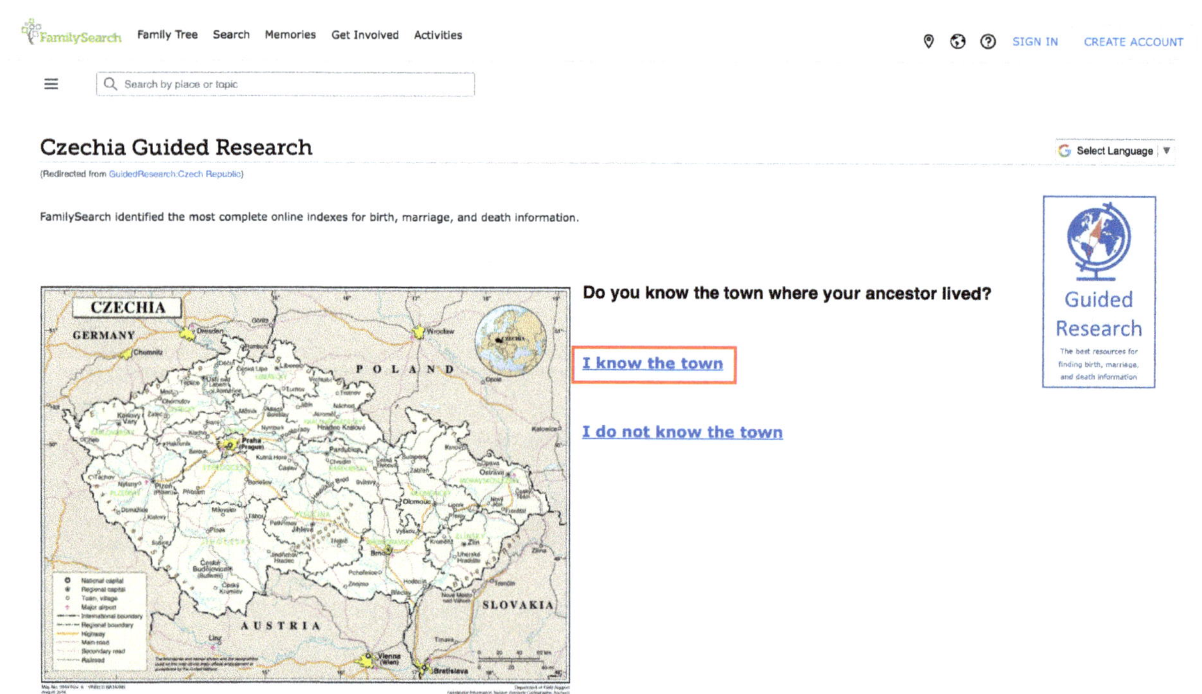

https://www.familysearch.org/en/wiki/GuidedResearch:Czechia

Choose the letter your town name starts with.

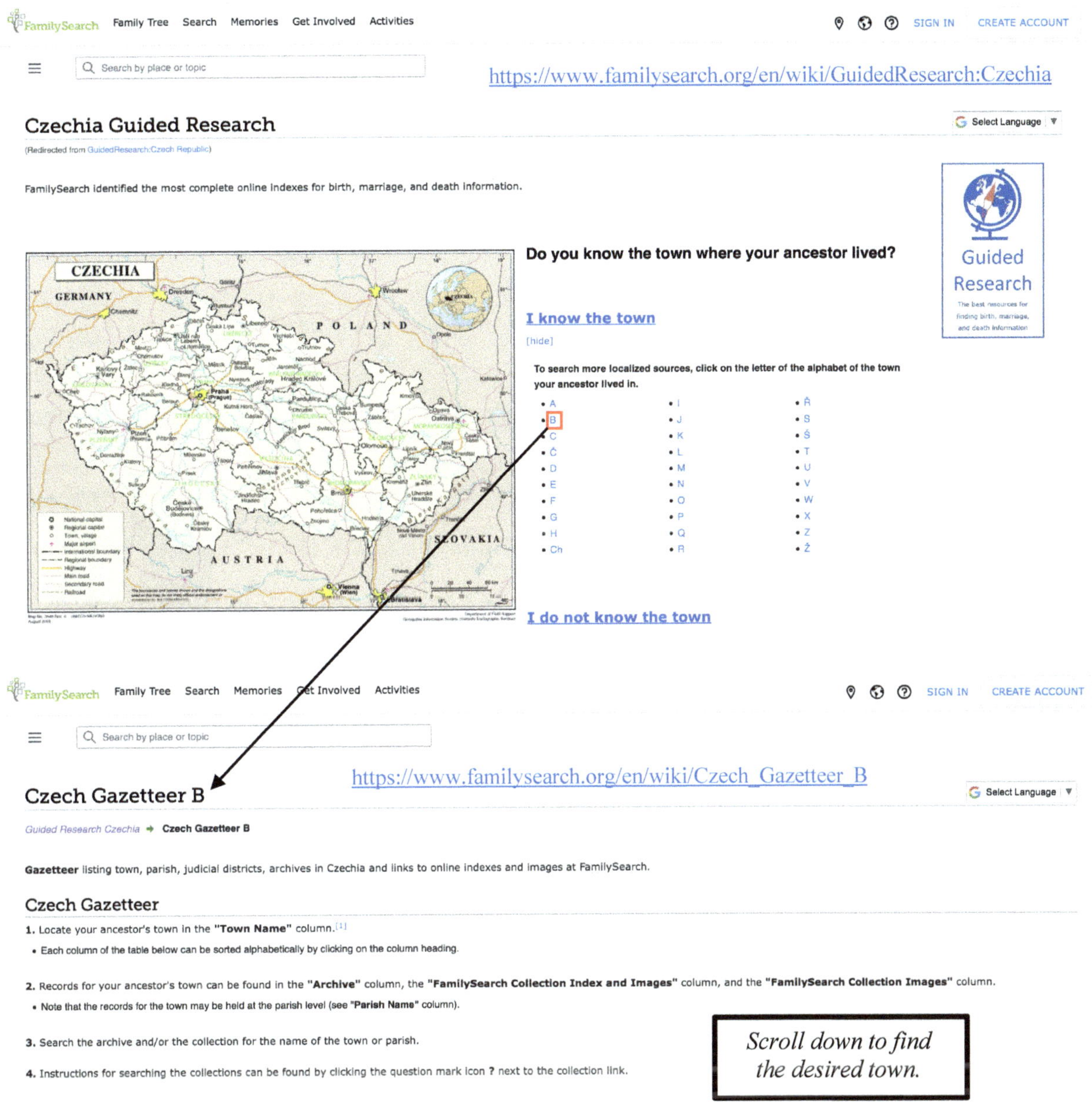

This table shows the name of the town with variations, the parish name, and judicial district. There is a column with a link to the archive covering that location, which in many cases has online digital images of the church records. The last two columns to the right are for digital images that exist in the CATALOG or IMAGES on FamilySearch. Empty columns mean FamilySearch does not have online images for that locality.

Brandýs nad Orlicí	Brandeis an der Adler	Brandys nad Orlicí	Vysoké Mýto	Zámrsk Regional Archives	1552-1981 Czech Republic, Church Books, 1552-1981	
Brandýsek	Brandeisl	Vrapice	Slaný	Prague Regional Archives		
Branek	Branky	Branky	Valašské Meziříčí	Opava Provincial Archives	1552-1981 Czech Republic, Church Books, 1552-1981	1571-1905 Czech Republic, Northern Moravia, Opava Archive Church Books, 1571-1905

Click on the blue link to go to that website.

https://www.familysearch.org/en/wiki/Czech_Gazetteer_B#Br

United State Resources

The easiest way to find out more about records in the United States is to type the name of the state in the search box and then click the applicable state landing page, in this case, INDIANA, UNITED STATES GENEALOGY.

The state landing page contains lots of useful details to help you get started and find records in that location.

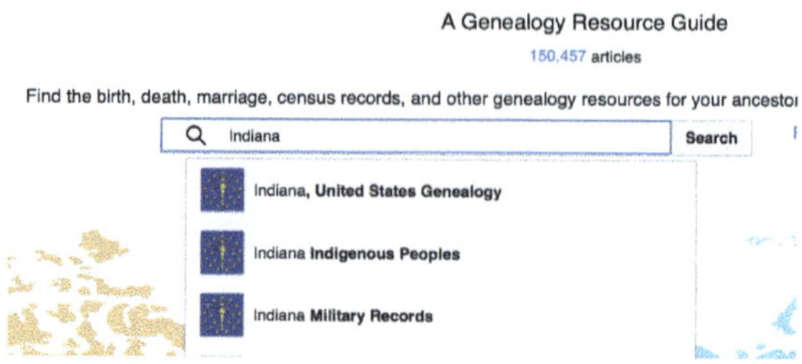

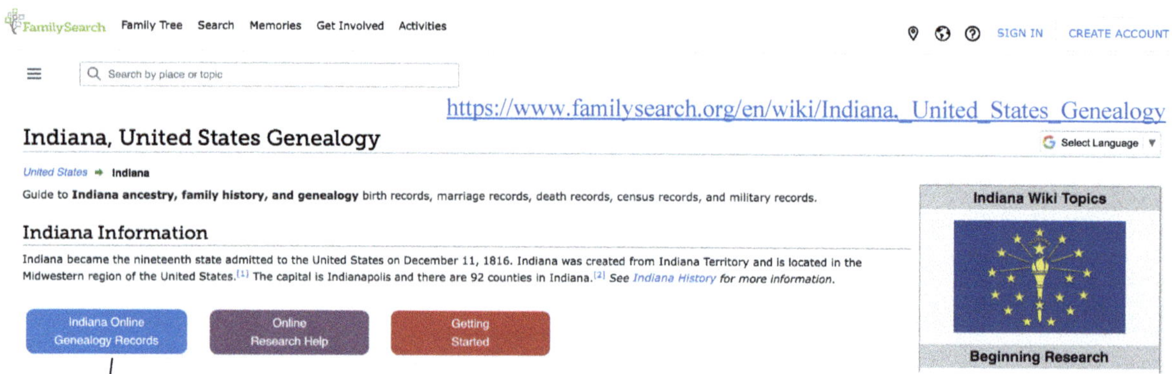

https://www.familysearch.org/en/wiki/Indiana,_United_States_Genealogy

Click on the blue button to find links to other online genealogy records collections.

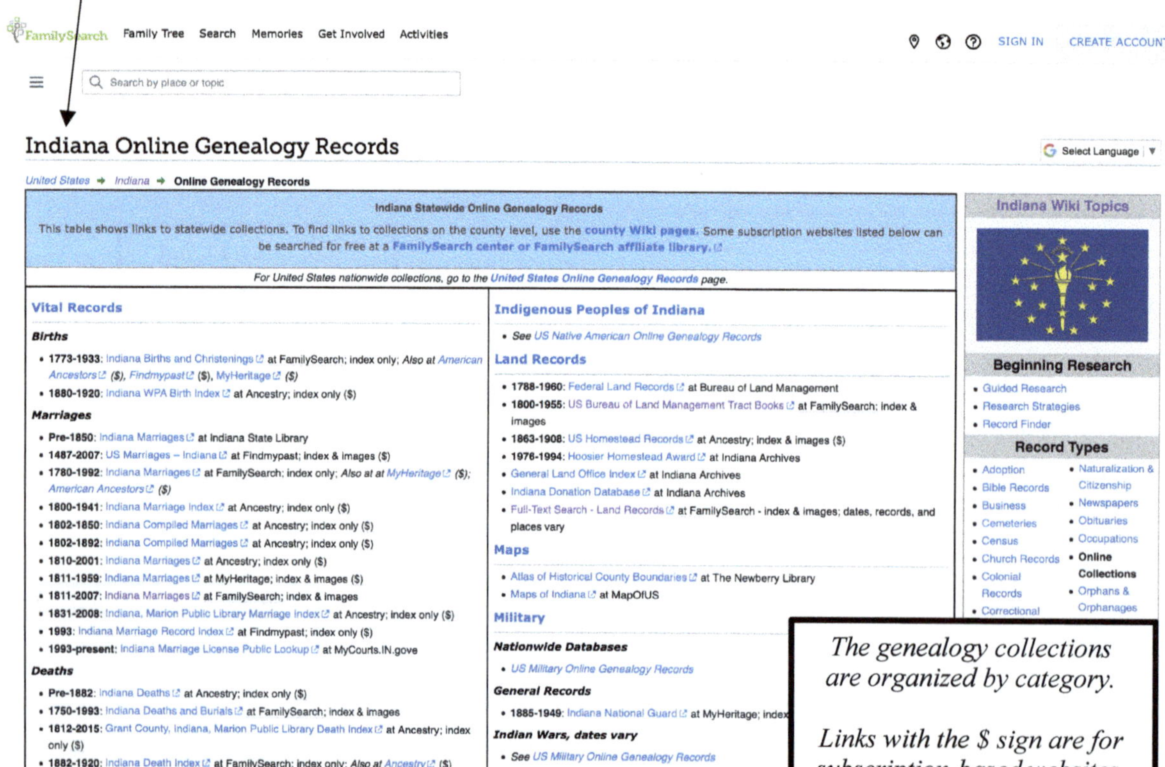

https://www.familysearch.org/en/wiki/Indiana,_United_States_Genealogy

The genealogy collections are organized by category.

Links with the $ sign are for subscription-based websites.

Scroll down to see additional resources for that location.

FamilySearch Family Tree Search Memories Get Involved Activities SIGN IN CREATE ACCOUNT

Search by place or topic

Indiana, United States Genealogy

Select Language

United States → **Indiana**

Guide to **Indiana ancestry, family history, and genealogy** birth records, marriage records, death records, census records, and military records.

Indiana Information

Indiana became the nineteenth state admitted to the United States on December 11, 1816. Indiana was created from Indiana Territory and is located in the Midwestern region of the United States.[1] The capital is Indianapolis and there are 92 counties in Indiana.[2] *See Indiana History for more information.*

Indiana Online Genealogy Records | Online Research Help | Getting Started

Indiana Clickable Map

Many genealogy records are kept on the county level in the United States. Click on a county below to go to the county Wiki article listing more information.

Choose the desired county to see more resources available for that location.

Indiana Wiki Topics

Beginning Research
- Getting Started
- Guided Research
- Research Strategies
- Record Finder

Record Types
- Adoption
- Bible Records
- Biography
- Cemeteries
- Census
- Church Records
- Colonial Records
- Correctional Institutions
- Court Records
- Crime & Punishment
- Directories
- Divorce Records
- Education
- Emigration & Immigration
- Genealogies
- Land & Property
- Medical Records
- Military Records
- Naturalization & Citizenship
- Newspapers
- Obituaries
- Occupation & Business Records
- Online Genealogy Records
- Orphans & Orphanages
- Probate Records
- Public Records
- Social Organizations
- School Records
- Substitute Records
- Taxation
- Vital Records
- Voter Records

Indiana Background
- Biography
- Further Reading
- Gazetteers
- History
- Jurisdictions
- Law & Legislation
- Maps
- Migration
- Periodicals

Cultural Groups
- African Americans

Counties [edit | edit source]

- Adams
- Allen
- Bartholomew
- Benton
- Blackford
- Boone
- Brown
- Carroll
- Cass
- Clark
- Clay
- Clinton
- Crawford
- Daviess
- Dearborn
- Decatur
- DeKalb
- Delaware
- Dubois
- Elkhart
- Fayette
- Floyd
- Fountain
- Franklin
- Fulton
- Gibson
- Grant
- Greene
- Hamilton
- Hancock
- Harrison
- Hendricks
- Henry
- Howard
- Huntington
- Jackson
- Jasper
- Jay
- Jefferson
- Jennings
- Johnson
- Knox
- Kosciusko
- LaGrange
- Lake
- LaPorte
- Lawrence
- Madison
- Marion
- Marshall
- Martin
- Miami
- Monroe
- Montgomery
- Morgan
- Newton
- Noble
- Ohio
- Orange
- Owen
- Parke
- Perry
- Pike
- Porter
- Posey
- Pulaski
- Putnam
- Randolph
- Ripley
- Rush
- Scott
- Shelby
- Spencer
- St. Joseph
- Starke
- Steuben
- Sullivan
- Switzerland
- Tippecanoe
- Tipton
- Union
- Vanderburgh
- Vermillion
- Vigo
- Wabash
- Warren
- Warrick
- Washington
- Wayne
- Wells
- White
- Whitley

Extinct or Renamed Counties: Richardville

https://www.familysearch.org/en/wiki/Indiana,_United_States_Genealogy

FamilySearch Family Tree Search Memories Get Involved Activities SIGN IN CREATE ACCOUNT

Search by place or topic

https://www.familysearch.org/en/wiki/Tippecanoe_County,_Indiana_Genealogy

Tippecanoe County, Indiana Genealogy

Select Language

Contents [hide]

Beginning
- County Information
- Resources
- Research Facilities
- Societies
- Websites
- Research Guides
- References

United States ➡ *Indiana* ➡ **Tippecanoe County**

Guide to **Tippecanoe County, Indiana ancestry, genealogy and family history**, birth records, marriage records, death records, census records, and military records.

County Information

This area notes the date the county was organized and the parent county(ies).

Indiana Online Genealogy Records

County Facts	
County seat:	Lafayette
Organized:	March 1, 1826
Parent County(s):	Parke, Unorganized territory[1]
Neighboring Counties	
White • Carroll • Clinton • Montgomery • Fountain • Warren • Benton	
See County Maps	
Courthouse	

Location Map

Description

Tippecanoe County was named for the Anglicization of "Kethtippe ... ccor fish people." The county is located in the west-central area of the stat

County Courthouse

Tippecanoe County Courthouse
301 Main Street
Lafayette, IN 47901
Phone: 765-423-9326
County Website

Often, there are links to the local courthouse and health department websites, as well as contact details.

Tippecanoe County Health Department
629 N 6th St
Lafayette, IN 47901
Health Officer: Dr. Jeremy Adler
Phone: 765-423-9221
Fax: 765-423-9797
Email: crich@tippecanoe.in.gov
Health Department

Clerk Circuit Court has marriage records from 1830, divorce records from 1850, probate and court records from 1832 and naturalization records on microfilm.
Health Department has birth records and death records.
Copies may be obtained from the county health department or the Indiana State Division of Vital Records.

Tippecanoe County, Indiana Record Dates

Information for this chart was taken from various sources, often containing conflicting dates. This information should be taken as a guide and should be verified by contacting the county and/or the state government agency.

Known Beginning Dates for Government County Records[3]						
Birth*	Marriage	Death*	Court	Land	Probate	Census
1882	1826	1882	1832	1826	1832	1807
*Statewide registration for births in 1907 and deaths in Oct 1899. General compliance by 1917.						

Record Loss

There is no known history of courthouse disasters in this county.

This area of the website notes when record keeping for the county was started, notes if there is record loss, and provides links to maps that show changing county boundaries for that state.

Boundary Changes

- **Parent Counties**: Formed 20 January 1826 from the Wabash New Purchase.[4]
- **County Seat:** Lafayette[5]
- Indiana Individual County Chronologies - Newberry Library list of all boundary changes by
- Indiana Historical Borders - Map at Newberry Library Atlas of Historical County Boundarie

Scroll down for links to various record collections and indexes for that location in the collections on FamilySearch and on other websites.

Court Records

- **1818-1954** Indiana Court Cases at MyHeritage — index ($)
- **1826-1853** Final Records, 1830-1852, Index, 1826-1853 (*); Probate Court at FamilySearch Catalog — index & images
- **1827-1838** Order Books, 1827-1838 (*); Circuit Court at FamilySearch Catalog — index & images
- **1831-1867** Final Record, 1831-1867 (*); Circuit Court at FamilySearch Catalog — index & images
- **1841-1852** Court Order Book, 1841-1852 (*); Probate Court at FamilySearch Catalog — images
- **1848-1865** Court Order Book, 1848-1865 (*); Court of Common Pleas at FamilySearch Catalog — images
- **1848-1865** Final Record, 1848-1865 (*); Court of Common Pleas at FamilySearch Catalog — index & images
- **1853-1865** Final Records, Decedents Estates, 1853-1865 (*); Court of Common Pleas at FamilySearch Catalog — images

Vital Records

Vital records consist of birth, death, marriage and divorce records. Indiana law in 1882 required registration of births and deaths in counties. The Indiana Department of Health has birth records filed after October 1907 and death records filed after January 1900 for deaths. Copies may be obtained from the county health department or the Indiana State Division of Vital Records.

Birth

Marriage

- **1780-1992** Indiana Marriages, 1780-1992 at FamilySearch - How to Use this Collection; *Also at: MyHeritage ($)*
- **1800s-2007** Indiana, United States Marriages at Findmypast ($)
- **1802-1892** Indiana, Compiled Marriages, 1802-1892 at Ancestry ($)
- **1811-1959** Indiana, Marriages, 1811-1959 at MyHeritage - index & images ($)
- **1811-2007** Indiana Marriages, 1811-2007 at FamilySearch - How to Use this Collection

Death

- **Pre-1882** WEB: Indiana, Deaths, Pre-1882 at Ancestry - index, (Free collection)
- **1750-1993** Indiana Deaths and Burials, 1750-1993 at FamilySearch - How to Use this Collection
- **1882-1920** Indiana, Death Index, 1882-1920 at FamilySearch - How to Use this Collection
- **1899-2011** Indiana, Death Certificates, 1899-2011 at Ancestry ($)

https://www.familysearch.org/en/wiki/Tippecanoe_County,_Indiana_Genealogy

International Resources

In addition to what is found in GUIDED RESEARCH, FamilySearch RESEARCH WIKI has pages for many countries around the world. Type in the country in the Search box and click the applicable country landing page. Bookmark it so you can find it more quickly next time.

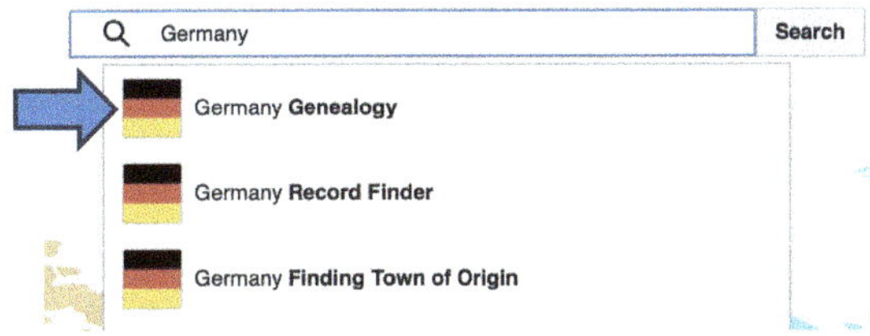

The international pages also have the blue button for online genealogy records, just like the U.S. collection. They also often have a purple button for online research help. Many will give a brief historical summary about the country with links to getting started and how to find your ancestor's town of origin.

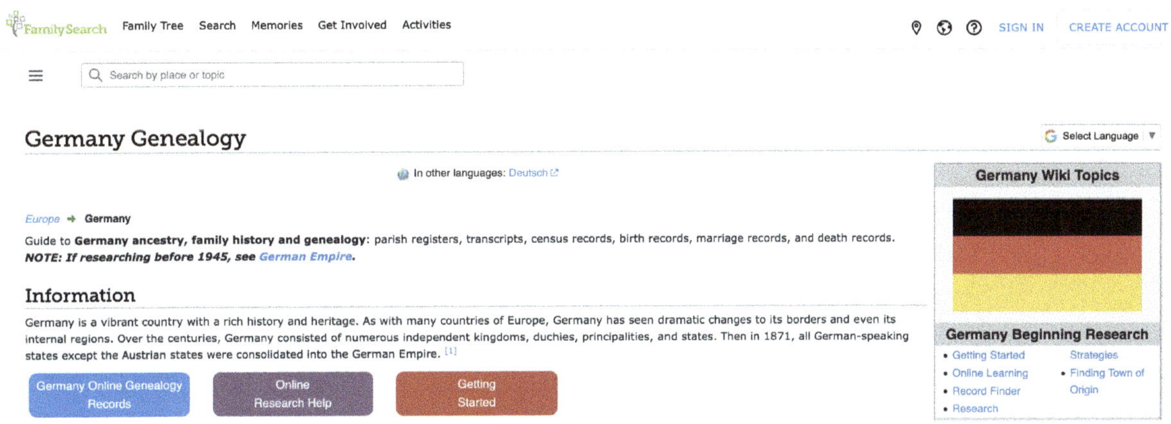

https://www.familysearch.org/en/wiki/Germany_Genealogy

Scroll down to the map area with links to the counties within the country.

These Modern States of Germany blue links have more information about the region and provide genealogical details on the archives and other local repositories.

If your countries boundaries changed, you may need to search multiple countries.

https://www.familysearch.org/en/wiki/Germany_Genealogy

Germany Wiki Topics

Germany Beginning Research

- Getting Started
- Online Learning
- Record Finder
- Research Strategies
- Finding Town of Origin

Record Types

- Business & Occupations
- Cemeteries
- Census
- Church Directories
- Church Records
- Civil Registration
- Compiled Genealogies
- Court Records
- Directories
- Emigration & Immigration
- Jewish Records
- Land & Property
- Military Records
- Naturalization & Citizenship
- Newspapers
- Nobility
- Obituaries
- Online Genealogy Records
- Passports
- Population Records
- Probate Records
- Religious Records
- Schools & Education
- Slavery & Bondage
- Websites

Germany Background

- Biographies
- Church History
- Dates & Calendars
- Gazetteers
- Handwriting
- Historical Geography
- History
- Jurisdictions
- Languages
- Maps
- Naming Customs
- Periodicals
- Social Life & Customs

Germany Genealogical Word Lists

- French
- German
- Latin

Cultural Groups

- Cultural Groups

Local Research Resources

- Archives & Libraries
- Societies
- Local FamilySearch Center

The RESEARCH WIKI has many free online tools to help you get started with your research and read the records, even those in a foreign language.

RECORD TYPES are useful to help you determine how to find topical records for the specific country. Often there are links to online collections.

LANGUAGES and HANDWRITING links are some of my favorite pages in the international RESEARCH WIKI pages because they provide many tips and resources for reading handwriting in other languages and understanding the vocabulary.

« FamilySearch Wiki   Search by place or topic

Research Wiki
- Wiki Home
- About the Wiki
- Online Genealogy Records
- Guided Research
- Research Resources
- Wiki Policies

Centers/Libraries
- FamilySearch Library
- FamilySearch Centers
- FS Affiliate Libraries

Give Feedback
- Submit Wiki Content
- Report a Problem

Edit the Wiki
- Upload File/Image
- Personal Sandbox
- Contributor Updates
- Wiki Projects
- Wiki University
- Manual of Style

Tools
- What links here
- Related changes
- Special pages
- Printable version
- Permanent link
- Page information
- Page values
- Cite this page

German Genealogical Word List

Page Talk   Read View form View source View history More

Genealogical Word Lists ➜ **German Genealogical Word List**

German Genealogical Word List

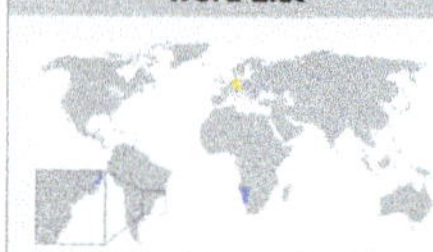

Downloadable Word List
- PDF File

Handwriting Help
- German Paleography Seminar at FamilySearch.
- Old German Script at FamilySearch.

Associated Countries
- Austria
- Belgium
- Germany
- Liechtenstein
- Luxembourg
- Switzerland
- Vatican City

Introduction [edit | edit source]

This list contains German words with their English translations. On most computers, simultaneously pressing CTRL and F (Command and F, if on a Mac) will search this page for the word you wish to translate. The words included here are those that you are likely to find in genealogical sources. If the word you are looking for is not on this list, please consult a German-English dictionary, the online Grimm Deutsches Wörterbuch (one of the best sources), or other regional online dictionaries found at woerterbuchnetz.de. Latin words are often found in German records, and a few are included in this list. See the Latin Genealogical Word List (34077).

German is spoken in Germany, Switzerland, and Austria. Records written in German may be found in these countries and also in parts of Poland, Denmark, Luxembourg, Czechia, Hungary, and wherever German people settled. There are several different dialects in the German language. For example, in the province of Westfalen and other areas of Germany that border the Netherlands, you may notice words that are closely related to Dutch. You may find the Dutch Genealogical Word List useful when working with these records.

In addition, German is found in some early records of the United States, such as in Pennsylvania, Texas, Wisconsin, and other states where Germans lived.

Language Characteristics [edit | edit source]

German words for persons, places, and things (nouns) are always capitalized. All nouns are classified as masculine, feminine, or neuter. This classification is called gender. The gender of a noun is indicated by der (masculine), die (feminine), and das (neuter), all three of which translate as "the." Word endings may vary depending on the way the words are used in the sentence.

Variant Forms of Words [edit | edit source]

In German, as in English, the forms of some words will vary according to how they are used in the sentence. Who—whose—whom or marry—marries—married are examples of words in English with variant forms. In German, the form of many words can change greatly. This word list focuses on the

https://www.familysearch.org/en/wiki/German_Genealogical_Word_List

Be sure to check out the GENEALOGICAL WORD LISTS available in the RESEARCH WIKI. These free word lists provide many invaluable tools to help you identify the words, abbreviations, and symbols used in your ancestor's records. Many of the lists have downloadable pdf versions (https://www.familysearch.org/en/wiki/Genealogical_Word_Lists).

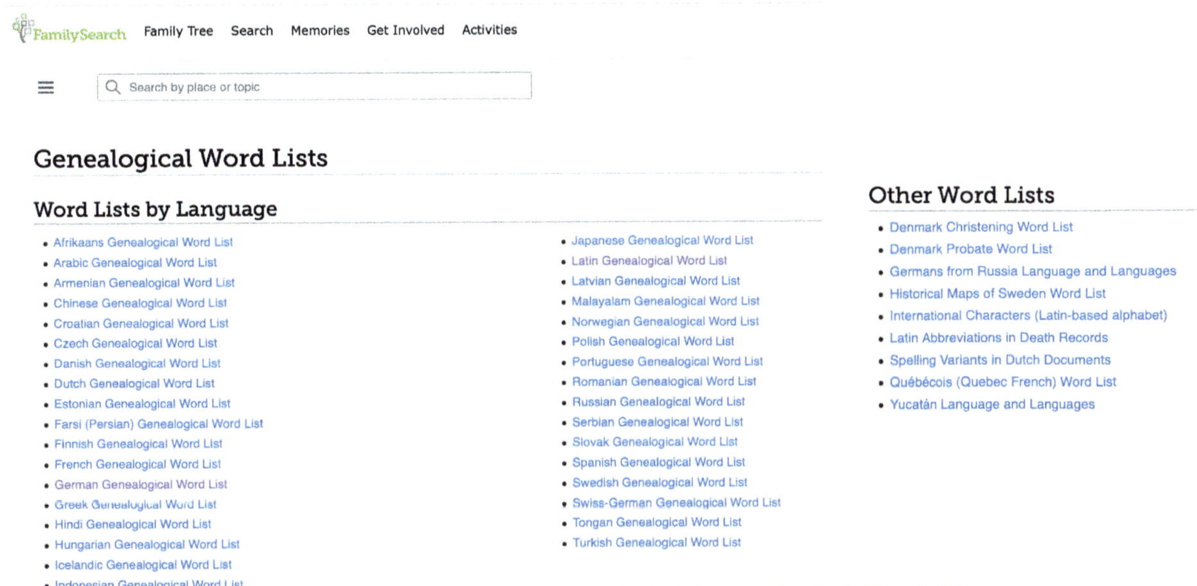

https://www.familysearch.org/en/wiki/Genealogical_Word_Lists

Each landing page also has a link to a page for archives / libraries, which can be invaluable. Some of these archive websites will have original images contained within them that you might not find otherwise and are not always found in the CATALOG or IMAGES on FamilySearch. If your country is from an area with changing international boundaries, be sure to search for archives under each country archive websites, since the results are not always the same.

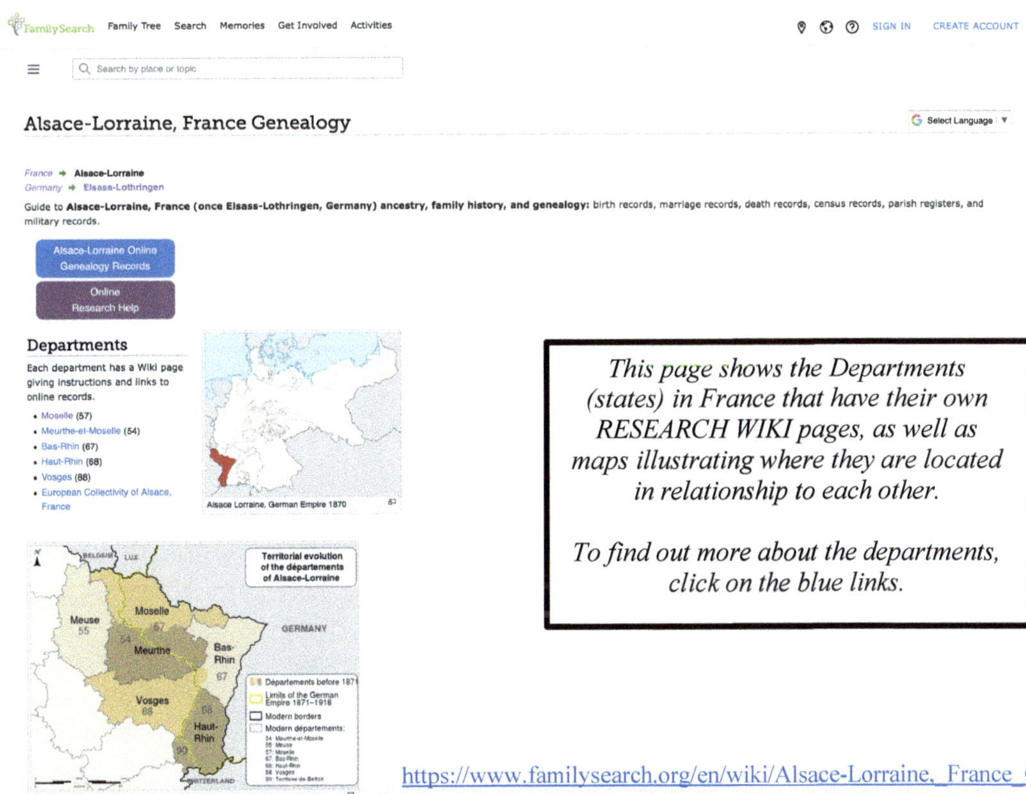

This page shows the Departments (states) in France that have their own RESEARCH WIKI pages, as well as maps illustrating where they are located in relationship to each other.

To find out more about the departments, click on the blue links.

https://www.familysearch.org/en/wiki/Alsace-Lorraine,_France_Genealogy

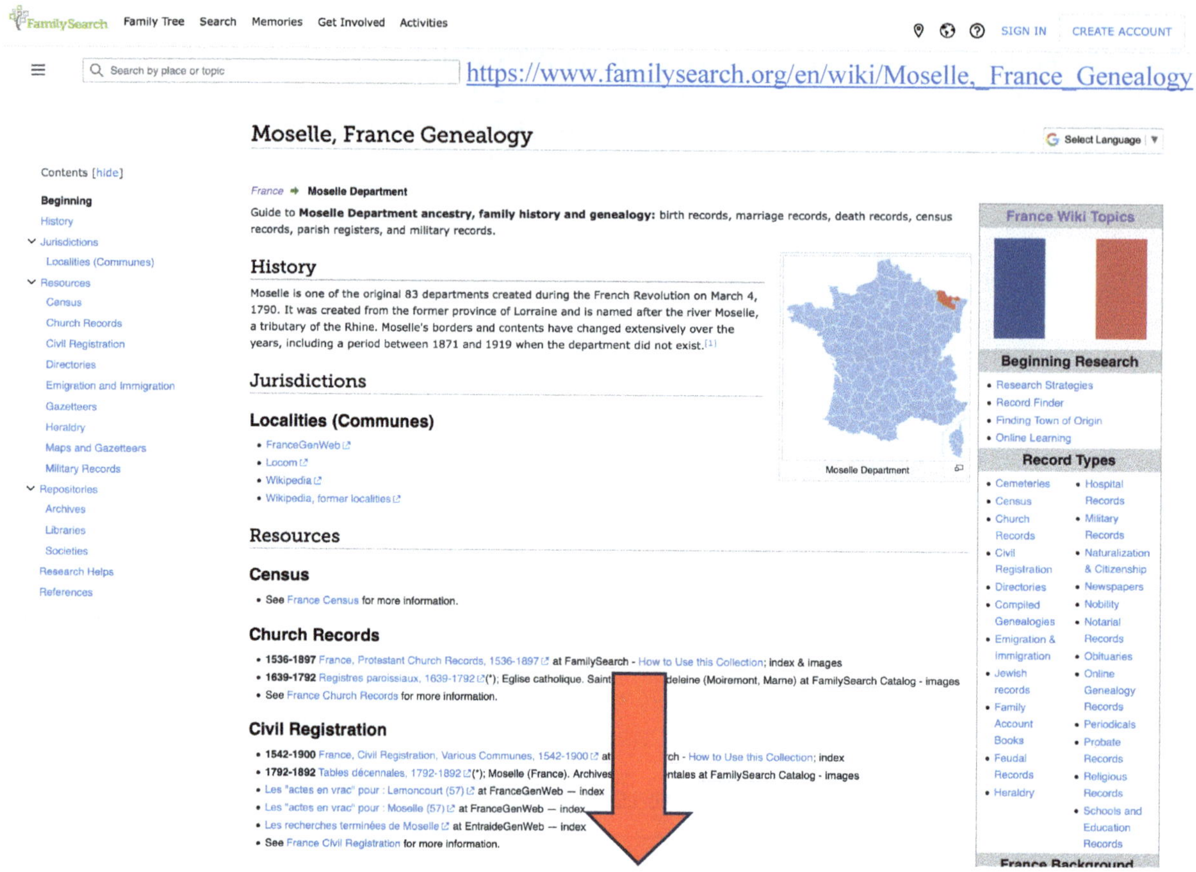

https://www.familysearch.org/en/wiki/Moselle,_France_Genealogy

Scroll down to see more resources for this location. This area has links and contact details to the archives for this location. Often, records can be found on other websites that may not be in the CATALOG or IMAGES on FamilySearch.

The link to the archive website is very useful since it has many original records there.

https://www.familysearch.org/en/wiki/Moselle,_France_Genealogy

Alsace-Lorraine is one of the locations with RESEARCH WIKI pages in both France and Germany, since both countries controlled it at one time. Be sure to check for other RESEARCH WIKI pages if your location has boundaries that have changed over time.

FamilySearch Family Tree Search Memories Get Involved Activities SIGN IN CREATE ACCOUNT

Search by place or topic

https://www.familysearch.org/en/wiki/Elsass-Lothringen,_German_Empire_Genealogy

Elsass-Lothringen, German Empire Genealogy

Select Language

Germany ➔ **Elsass-Lothringen**

Guide to **Elsass-Lothringen, German Empire** ancestry, family history, and genealogy **before 1920**: birth records, marriage records, death records, family history, and military records. In 1920, Elsass-Lothringen became Alsace-Lorraine in France. See those articles for further information.

This is the German RESEARCH WIKI page for Alsace-Lorraine, listed as Elsass-Lothringen.

Historical Background

- The Imperial Territory of **Elsass-Lothringen** was a territory created by the German Empire in 1871, after it a... ...ing its victory in the Franco-Prussian War.
- It was divided in three districts:
  - Oberelsass (Upper Alsace), corresponds exactly to the current French department of Haut-Rhin.
  - Unterelsass, (Lower Alsace), corresponds exactly to the current French department of Bas-Rhin.
  - Lothringen, (Lorraine), corresponds exactly to the current French department of Moselle.
- The modern history of Alsace-Lorraine was largely influenced by the rivalry between French and German nationalism. France long sought to attain and preserve its "natural boundaries", which were the Pyrenees to the southwest, the Alps to the southeast, and the Rhine River to the northeast. German nationalism sought to unify German-speaking populations. As various German dialects were spoken by most of the population of Alsace and northern Lorraine, these regions were viewed by German nationalists to be rightfully part of hoped-for united Germany in the future.
- When the World War broke out in 1914, recovery of the two lost provinces became the top French war goal. French troops put the region under occupatio bellica and entered Strasbourg on November 21, 1918. The Nationalrat proclaimed the annexation of Alsace to France on December 5, even though this process did not gain international recognition until the signature of the Treaty of Versailles in 1919. Alsace-Lorraine (Wikipedia)

Getting Started

Getting Started with Germany Research

Links to articles on getting started with German research:

- Alsace-Lorraine - Activity, Answer Key
  - Alsace-Lorraine: Converting French Republican Calendar Dates - Instruction
  - Alsace-Lorraine: Department Archive Records Online - Instruction
  - Alsace-Lorraine: Translating German and French Names and Place Names - Instruction
- Germany Finding Town of Origin
- German Church and Civil Records

See More Research Strategies

Germany Research Tools

Links to tools and websites that assist in German research:

- Meyers Gaz Online Gazetteer
- German Genealogical Word List
- Latin Genealogical Word List
- French Genealogical Word List
- Script Tutorial for French - Reading French Handwritten Records
- Old German Script--Three parts
- German Script Tutorial
- German Letter Writing Guide
- French Letter Writing Guide

See More Research Tools

Elsass-Lothringen, German Empire Online Genealogy Records | Germany Online Genealogy Records | Online Research Help

Elsass-Lothringen, German Empire Genealogy

Getting Started

- Finding Town of Origin
- Finding Aids For German Records
- Research Strategies
- Record Finder

Major Elsass-Lothringen Record Types

- Church Records
- Civil Registration

Reading the Records in German

- German Word List
- French Word List
- Handwriting
- Languages
- Feast Days
- Script Tutorial

Reading the Records in French

- French Word List
- Latin Word List
- Handwriting
- French Republican Calendar
- Script Tutorial

Additional Elsass-Lothringen Record Types

- Emigration & Immigration
- Online Genealogy Records

Elsass-Lothringen Background

FamilySearch Family Tree Search Memories Get Involved Act...

Search by place or topic

Click here to view the list of ARCHIVES AND LIBRARIES in that locality.

Local Research Resources

- Archives and Libraries
- Societies
- Metz FamilySearch Center
- Strasbourg FamilySearch Center

Elsass-Lothringen Archives and Libraries

Germany ➔ *Elsass-Lothringen, German Empire Genealogy* ➔ **Archives and Libraries**

For information from Elsaß-Lothringen(Alsace-Lorraine), contact one of the following archives:

This is the German RESEARCH WIKI page showing the links for the ARCHIVES AND LIBRARIES for ELSASS-LOTHRINGEN, GERMANY, which has similar resources and links as the RESEARCH WIKI page for ALSACE-LORRAINE, FRANCE.

- Archives départementales du Bas-Rhin
  6 rue Philippe Dollinger
  67100 Strasbourg
  Telephone: +33 (0)3 69 06 73 06
  Email: archives@bas-rhin.fr
- Archives départementales du Alsace
  Bâtiment M Cité administrative
  3 rue Fleischhauer
  68026 Colmar
  Telephone: +33 3 89 21 97 00
  Cedex 03 89 21 97 00 03 89 21 98 51
  Nous Contacter
- Archives départementales du Moselle
  1, allée du château
  57070 St. Julien-les-Metz
  France
  Telephone: 03.87.78.05.00

This link takes you to website for the archive in Moselle, Alsace-Lorraine, France, which has many online records.

The French archivists will not do research, but they will help you determine what records are available. For help writing in French, see the French Letter Writing Guide.

Archive information, including internet and Email addresses, for France are found at Archives de France.

https://www.familysearch.org/en/wiki/Elsass-Lothringen_Archives_and_Libraries

Topical Resources

In addition to resources available by location world-wide, the FamilySearch RESEARCH WIKI provides access to topical resources such as a U.S. Civil War unit or particular ethnic group. To find the landing page, type the topic into the search box on the RESEARCH WIKI page, and click SEARCH or press enter on your keyboard. If the page doesn't come up automatically, click on the applicable link or try variations on your search parameters until you find what you are looking for. Exact searches using quotation marks around the phrase can be very helpful in finding your topic quickly.

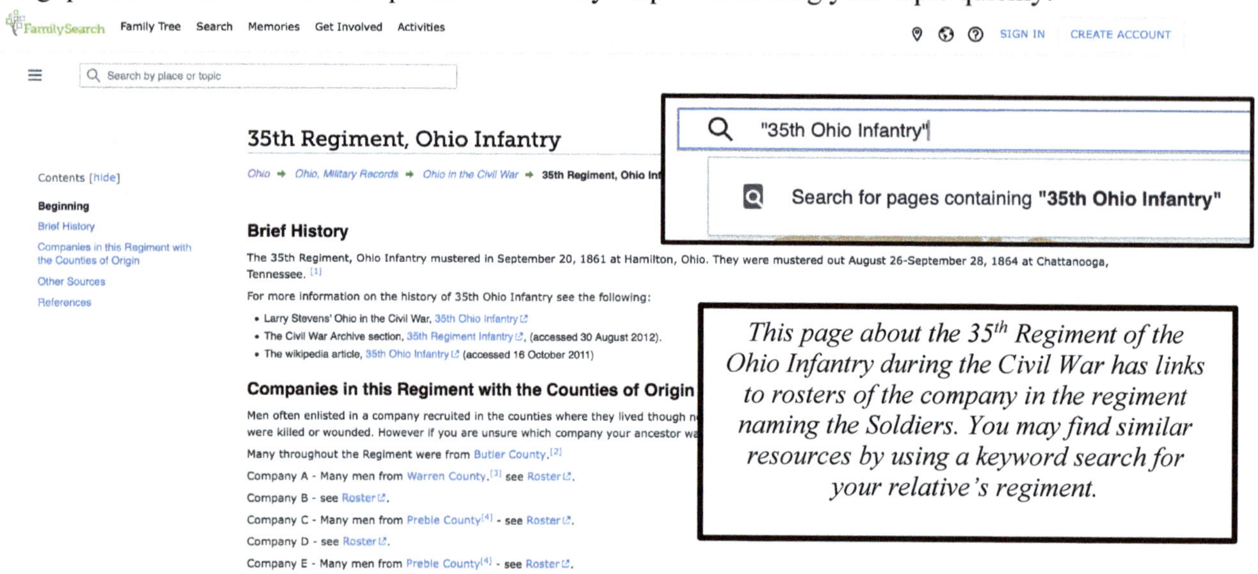

This page about the 35th Regiment of the Ohio Infantry during the Civil War has links to rosters of the company in the regiment naming the Soldiers. You may find similar resources by using a keyword search for your relative's regiment.

https://www.familysearch.org/en/wiki/35th_Regiment,_Ohio_Infantry

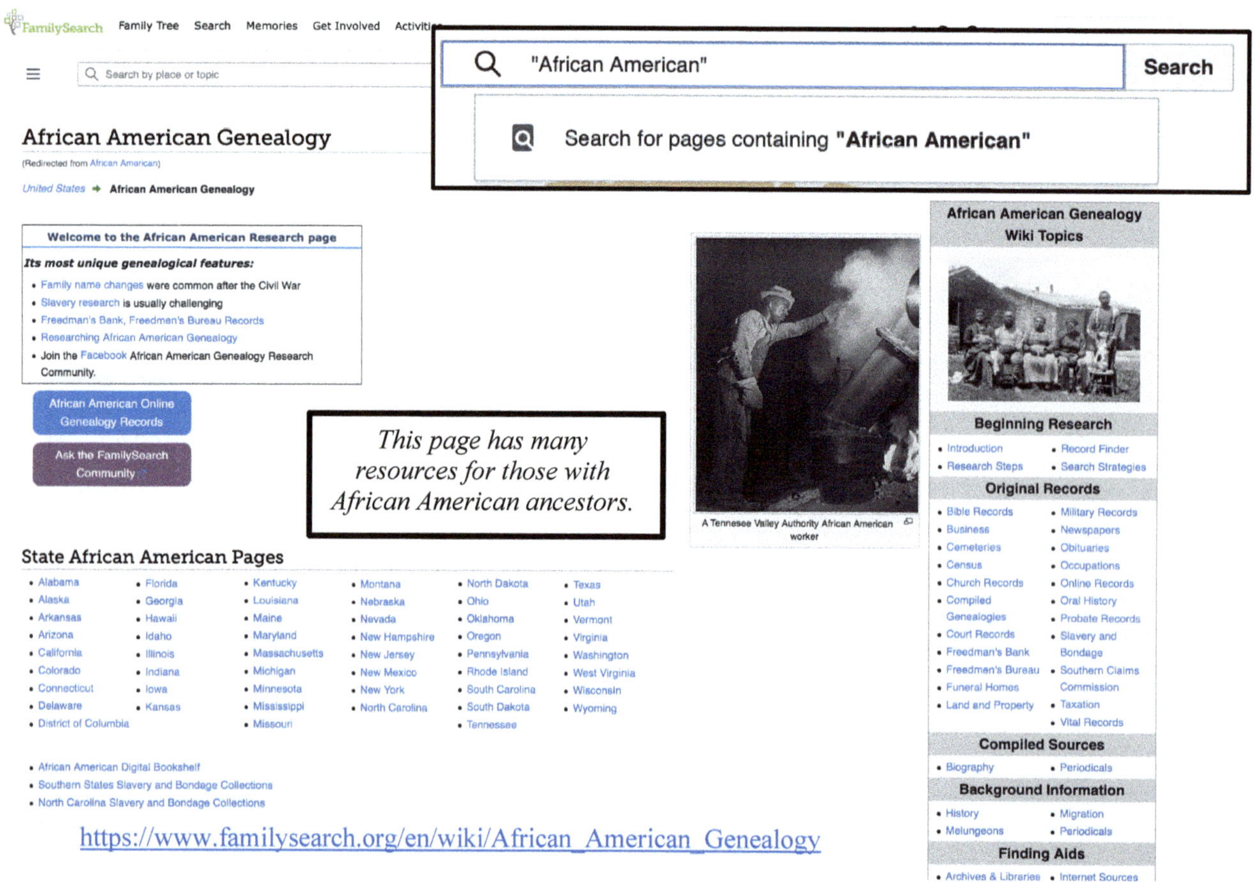

This page has many resources for those with African American ancestors.

https://www.familysearch.org/en/wiki/African_American_Genealogy

Chapter 6: The Tree

GETTING STARTED USING THE TREE

FamilySearch's FAMILY TREE (https://www.familysearch.org/en/family-tree/) can be a powerful tool if used properly. You will need to create a free account on FamilySearch to use this feature. FAMILY TREE is a shared tree among all those logged in. The information attached to each person in the tree is not uniquely yours unless you have marked the person as LIVING. Anyone can make changes or add content to deceased people in the tree, which helps with collaborating efforts.

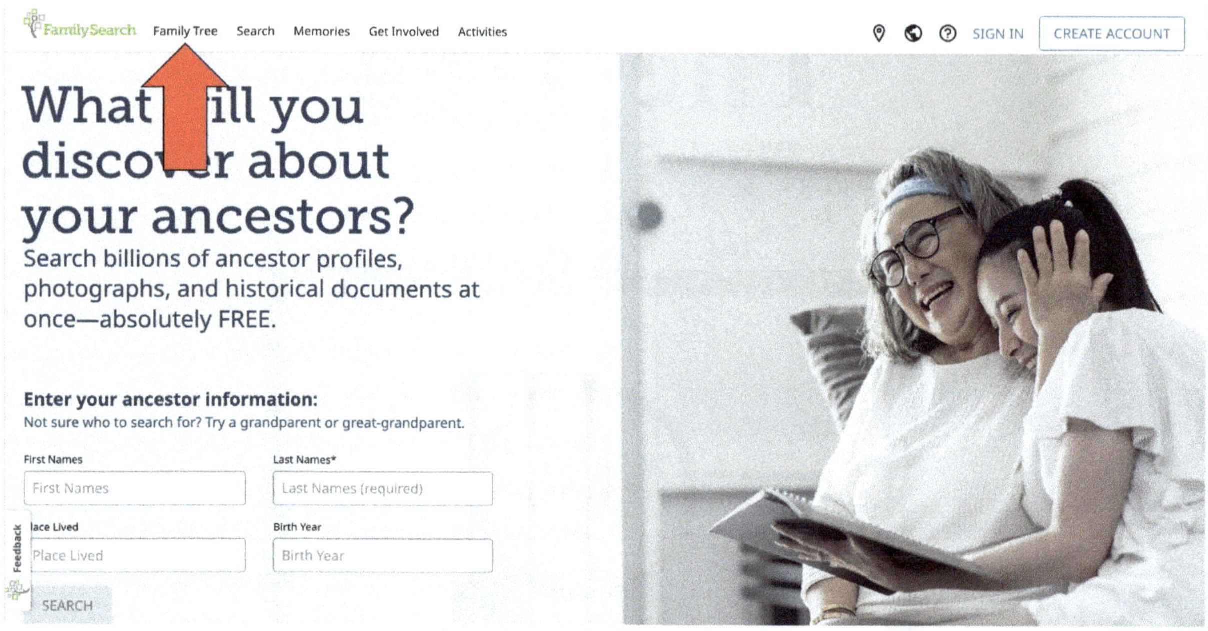

https://www.familysearch.org

Once you are logged in, click on the FAMILY TREE tab, then OVERVIEW if you are new to using FamilySearch, otherwise click on TREE. This will take you to a page to build your tree and connect you to your relatives.

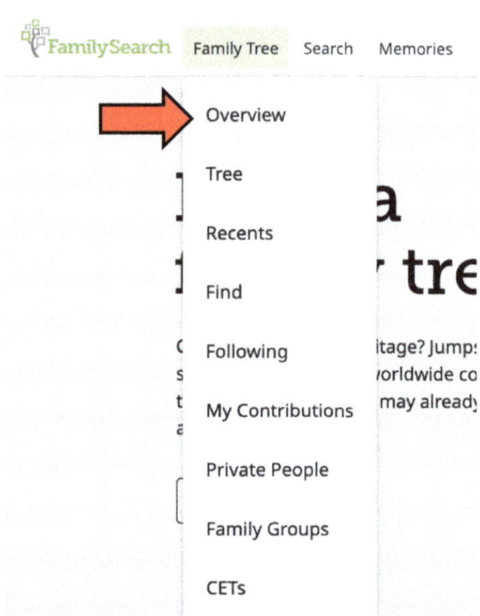

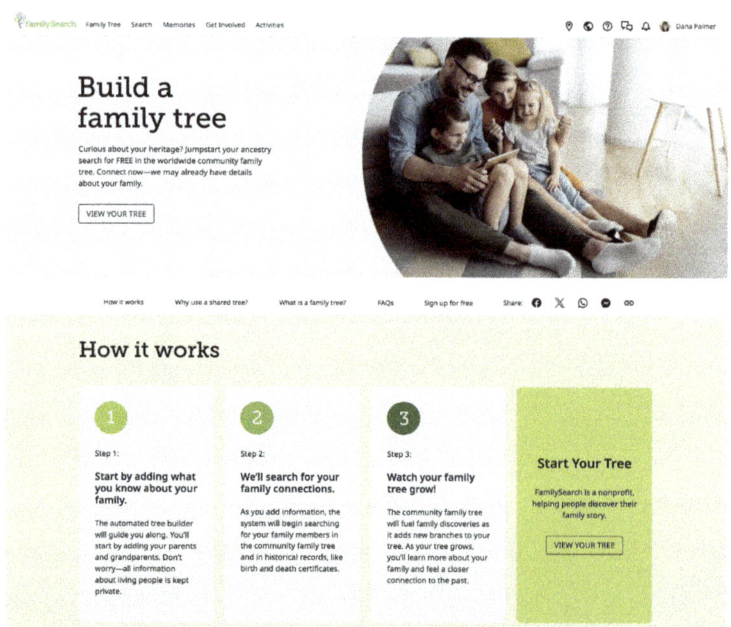

https://www.familysearch.org/en/family-tree/

PEDIGREE TREE VIEWS

There are five views available in the TREE:

- **Landscape**: Horizontal view of the direct ancestors in the tree for a specific person.
- **Portrait**: Vertical view of the direct ancestors in the tree for a specific person. This is the commonly used style of English pedigrees. This view works best to navigate the TREE on a cellphone.
- **Fan Chart**: Useful to see at a glance where lines need more research, documents, or photos.
- **Descendancy**: Shows descendants in the tree for a specific person.
- **First Ancestor**: Commonly used for those with Asian ancestors. Tracks descendants of the first male ancestor designated as the "First Ancestor."

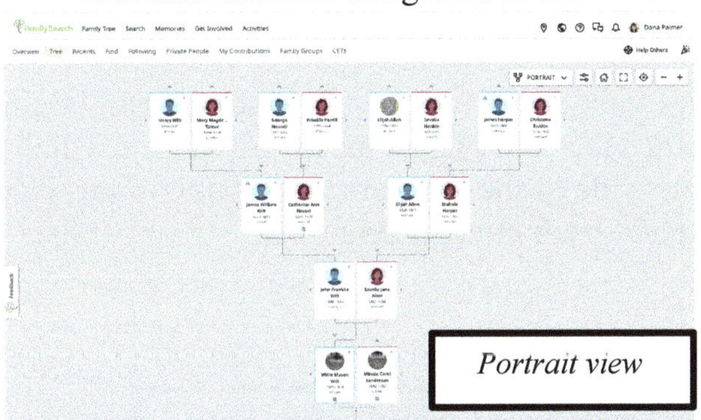

https://www.familysearch.org/en/tree/pedigree/portrait/99R2-LTP

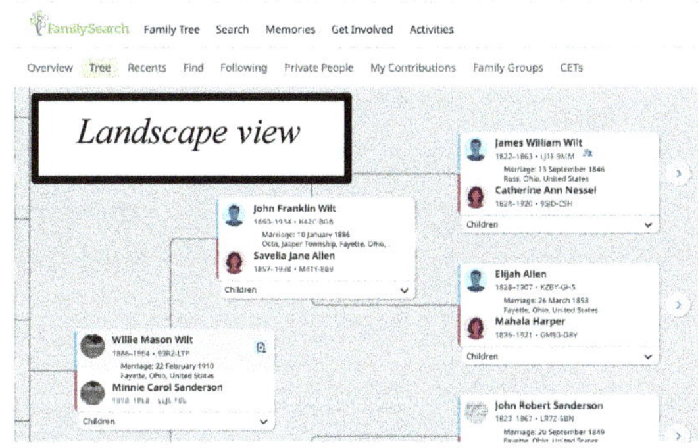

https://www.familysearch.org/en/tree/pedigree/landscape/99R2-LTP

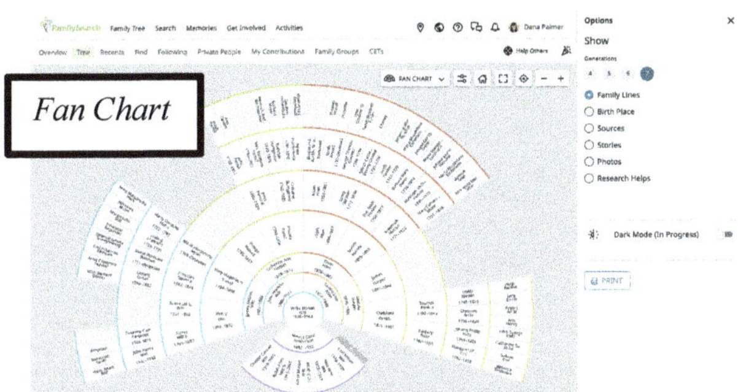

Fan chart shows missing lines.

https://www.familysearch.org/en/tree/pedigree/fanchart/99R2-LTP

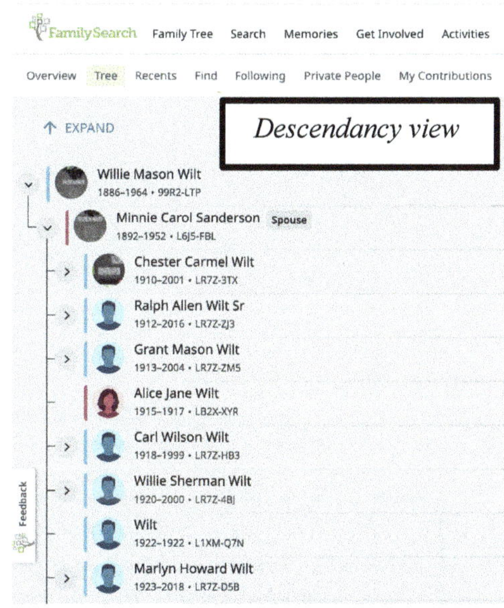

https://www.familysearch.org/en/tree/pedigree/descendancy/99R2-LTP

The fan chart below shows sources for the person. The darker the color, the more sources that are attached.

Fan charts can help you quickly identify lines that may need more research.

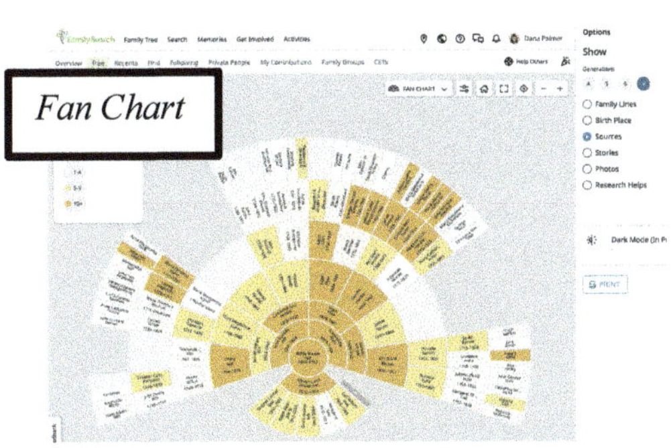

https://www.familysearch.org/en/tree/pedigree/fanchart/99R2-LTP

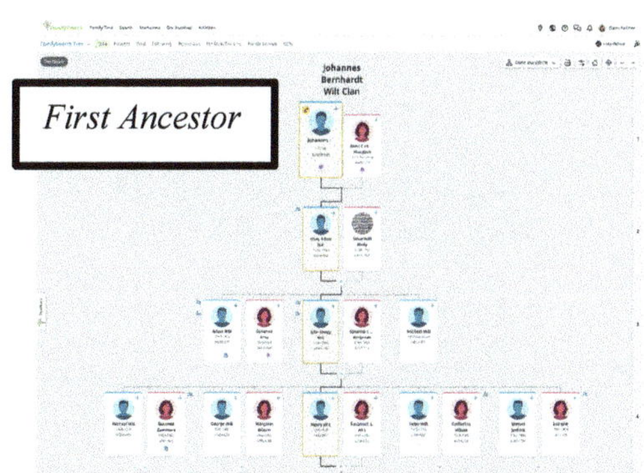

https://www.familysearch.org/en/tree/pedigree/first-ancestor/99R2-LTP

Navigating Tree View

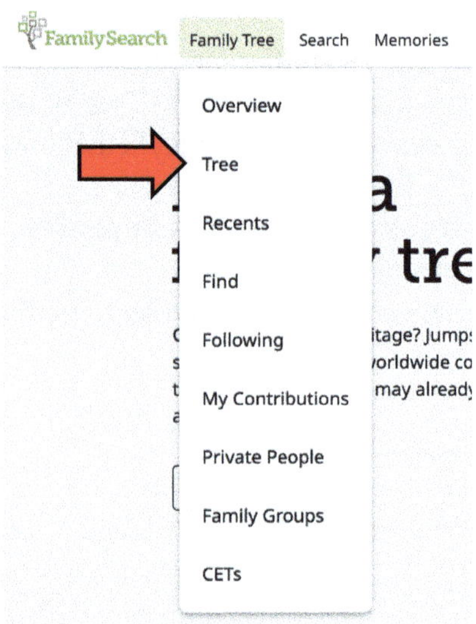

The quickest way to navigate is to click on FAMILY TREE tab, then choose TREE from the drop-down menu. This will take you to a screen to create a tree starting with yourself.

Most people will only see the name they entered when they created an account on FamilySearch. You will need to add your parents and extended family to take full advantage of the tree features. To make changes or view attached sources in the TREE, you must be in the DETAILS view for that person. This will be discussed later in this chapter.

Once you have your family connected in the TREE, you can use the pedigree view to navigate backward in time. Click on the arrow to the side of the last person showing in the TREE and it will expand back more generations.

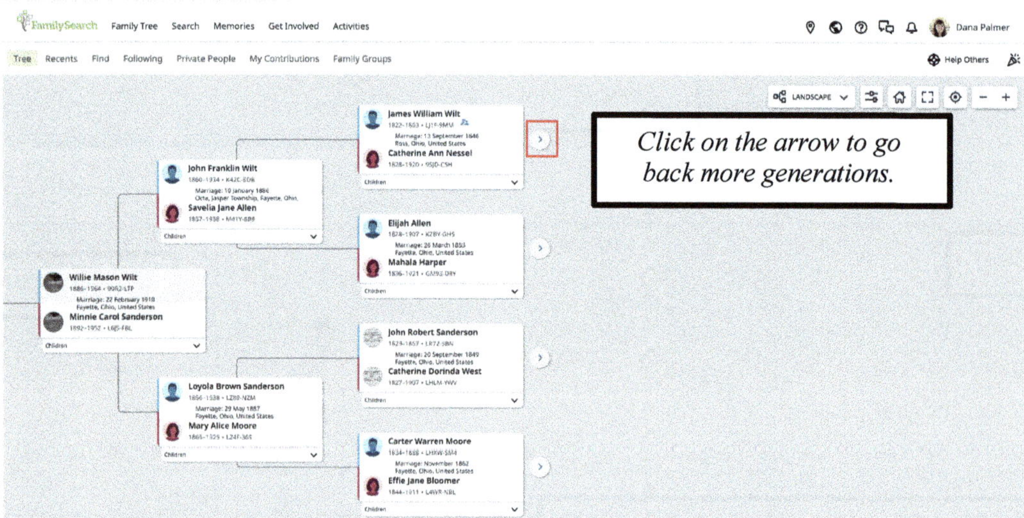

https://www.familysearch.org/en/tree/pedigree/landscape/99R2-LTP

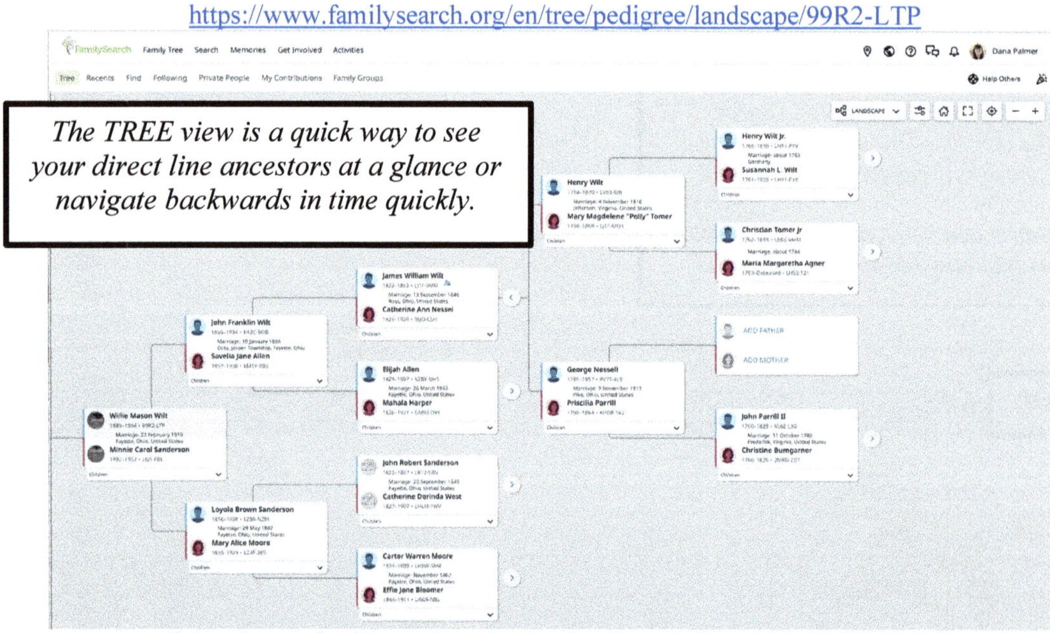

https://www.familysearch.org/en/tree/pedigree/landscape/99R2-LTP

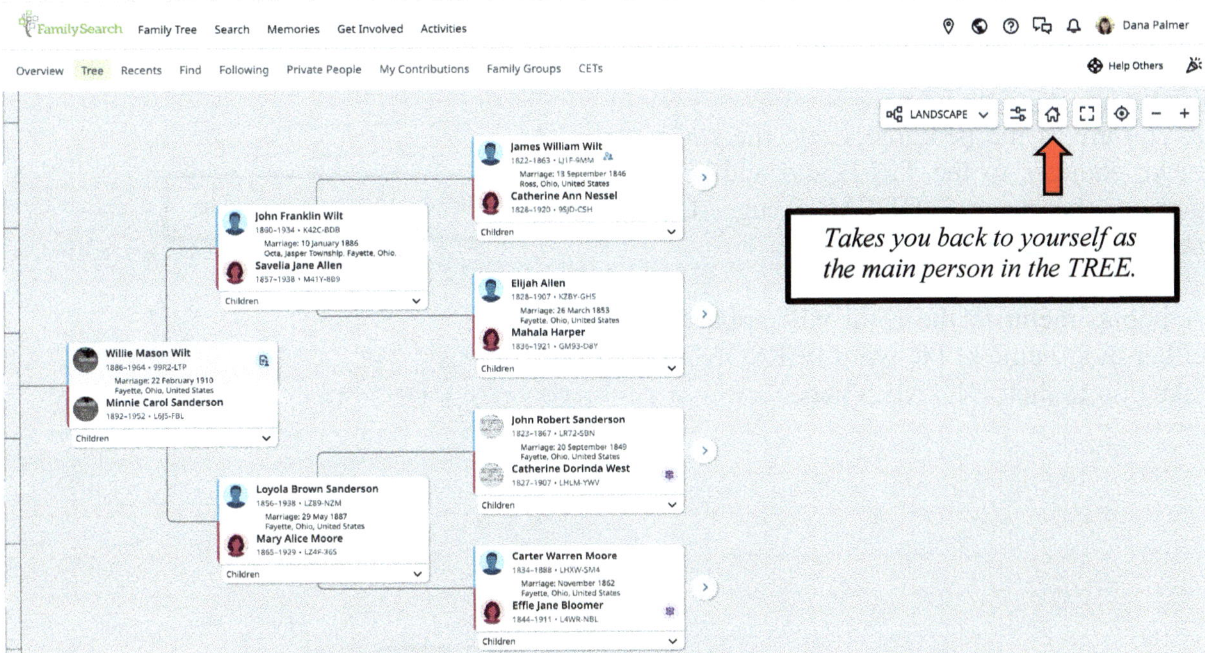

https://www.familysearch.org/en/tree/pedigree/landscape/99R2-LTP

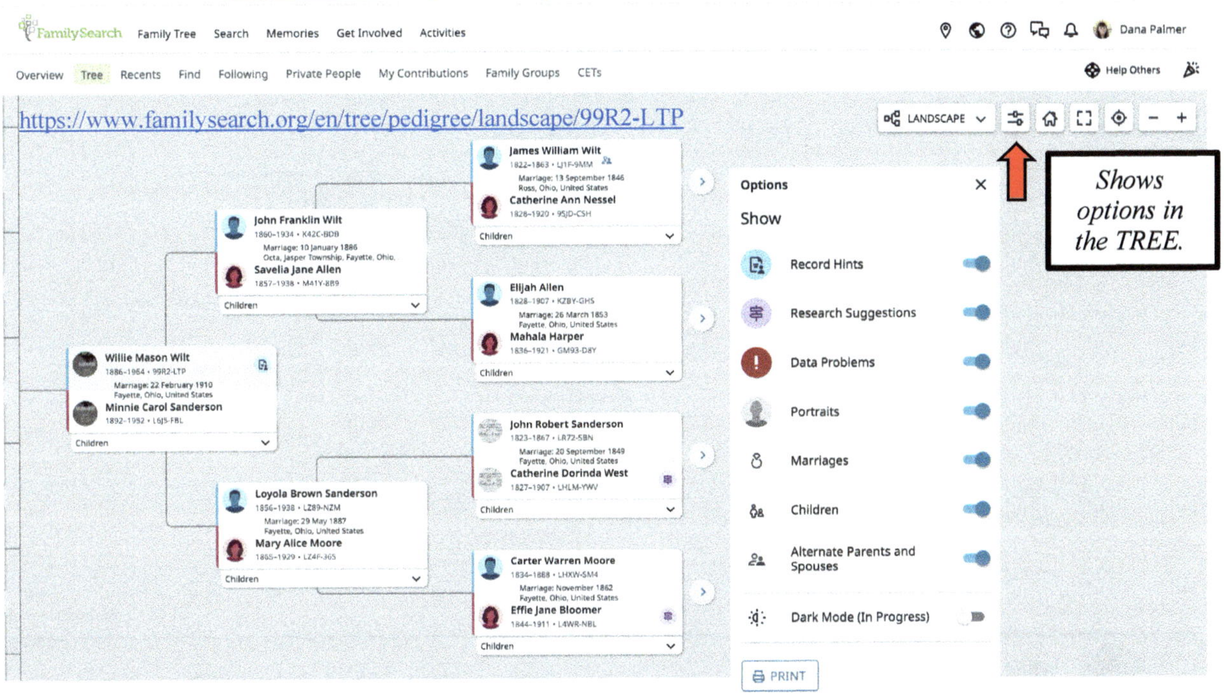

https://www.familysearch.org/en/tree/pedigree/landscape/99R2-LTP

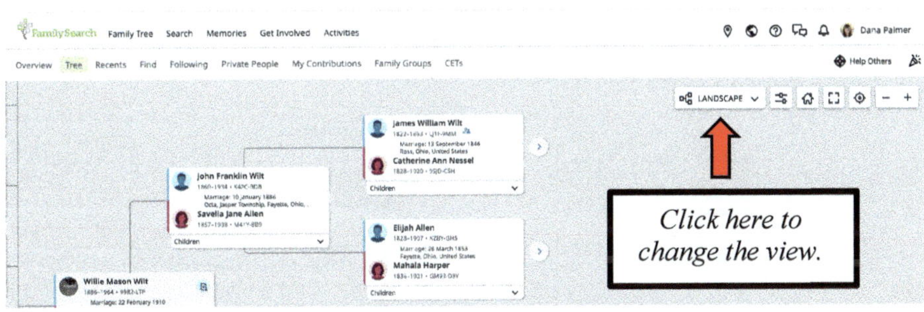

https://www.familysearch.org/en/tree/pedigree/landscape/99R2-LTP

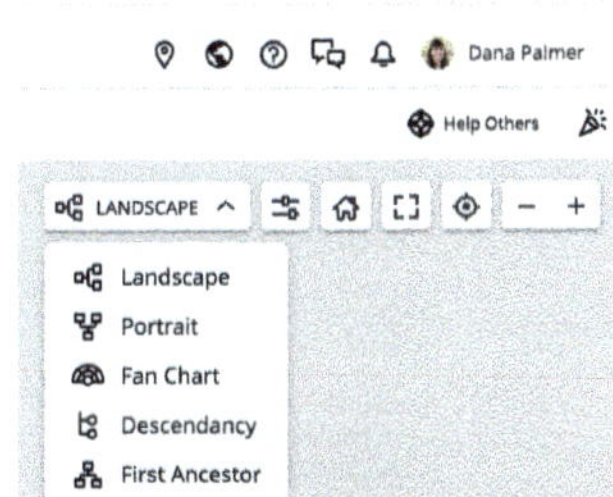

TREE view options.

Navigating to the Details Page from Tree View

If you are in the pedigree view, the easiest way to make changes to the TREE and add sources is by going to that person's DETAILS page. Click on that person's name in the TREE view.

A popup menu to the right will appear. Click on either their name or the word PERSON and this will take you to their DETAILS page.

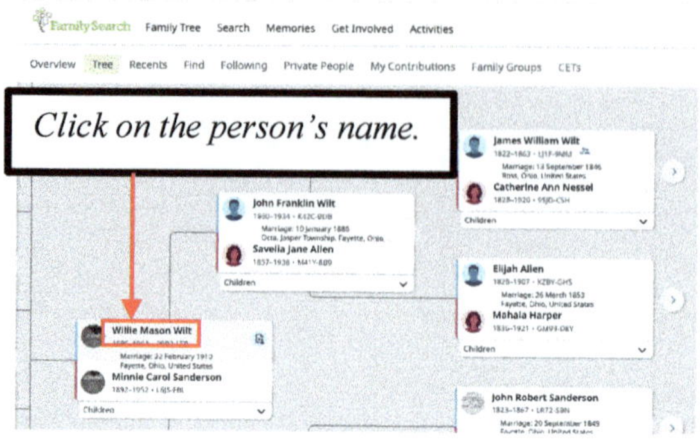

https://www.familysearch.org/en/tree/pedigree/landscape/99R2-LTP

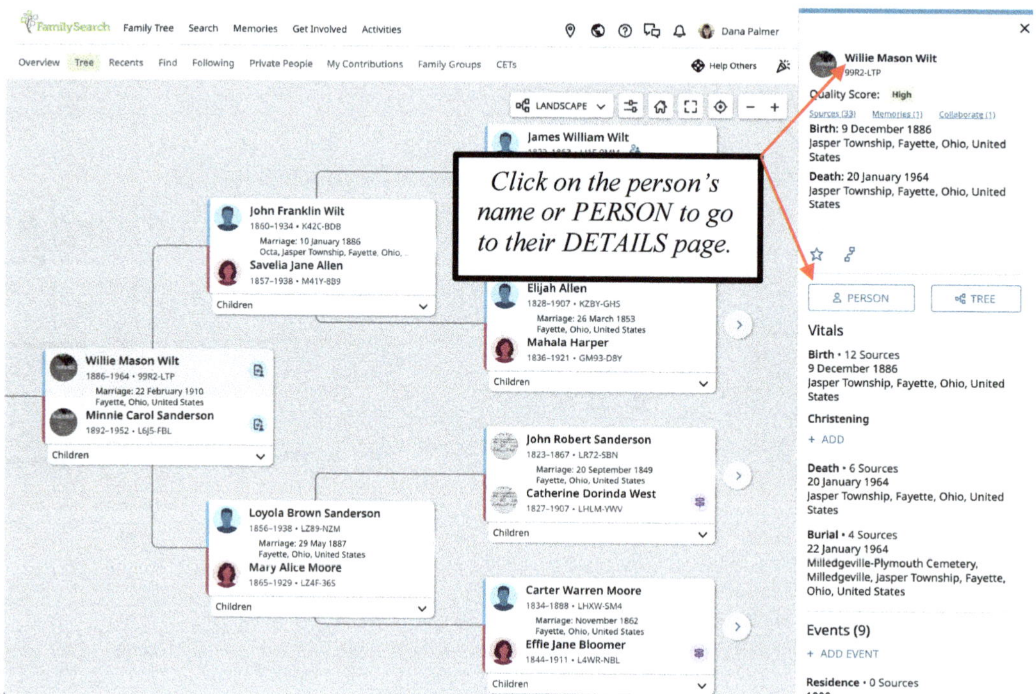

https://www.familysearch.org/en/tree/pedigree/landscape/99R2-LTP

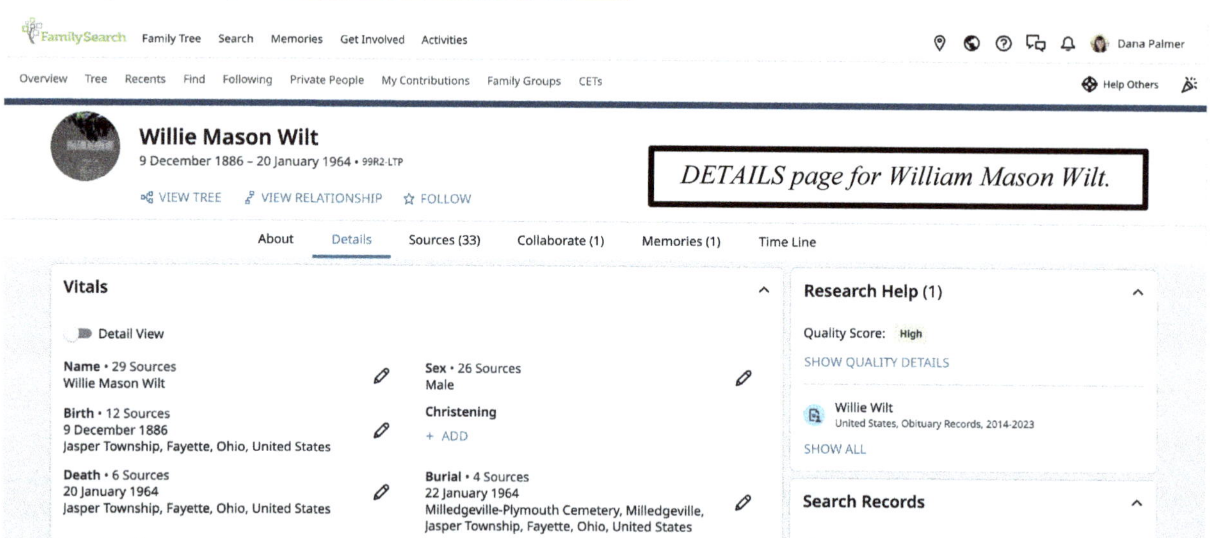

https://www.familysearch.org/en/tree/person/details/99R2-LTP

Finding People in the Tree

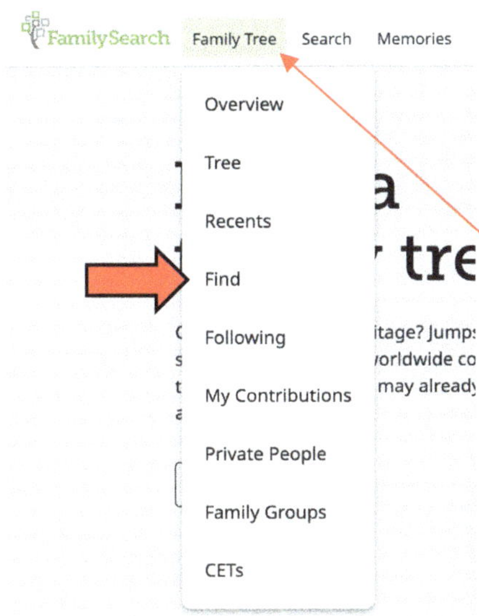

Using the FIND feature under the FAMILY TREE tab is useful if you want to navigate to an earlier generation more quickly and don't want to use the TREE view to do it. You can find anyone in the tree who is deceased even if they are not connected directly to you in the tree. Click on the FAMILY TREE tab at the top of your screen to see the drop-down menu, then choose FIND. You can then search by name or by ID number.

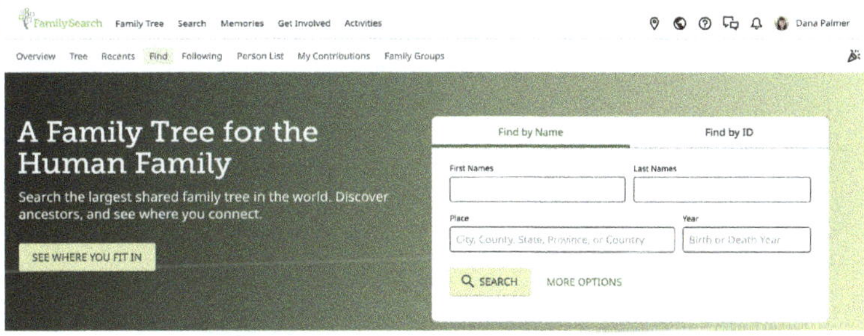

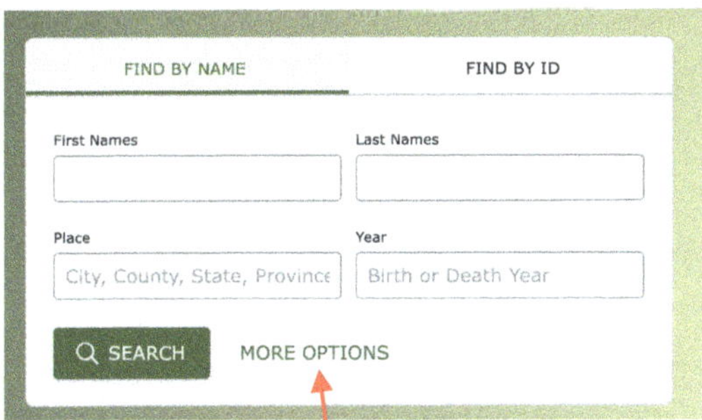

https://www.familysearch.org/en/search/tree/name?from=tree

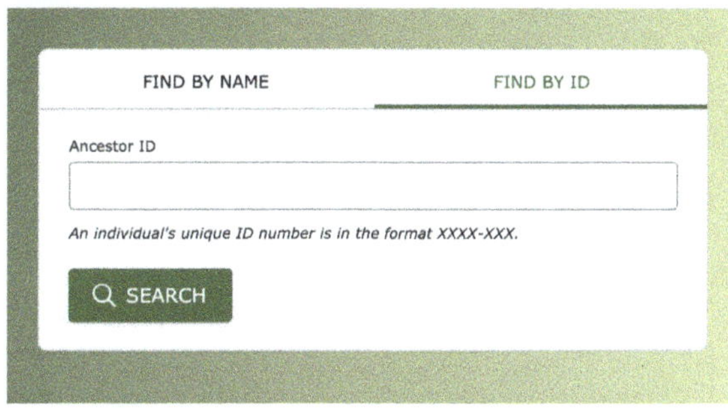

https://www.familysearch.org/en/search/tree/id?from=tree

Click MORE OPTIONS to add additional details to narrow your search results and find the correct person.

Searches can be done by an individual's name or by their ID number.

A spousal search is one of the easiest ways to quickly find people in the tree. Type in the name of the person you want to find in the search box then click the SPOUSE filter below and type in the spouse's name, then click SEARCH.

This then will give a list of potential matches. Most of the time your search will result in the couple you want at the top or very close to the top of the search results. If the name you want doesn't appear, add additional filters such as dates or locations, to the birth or marriage filters.

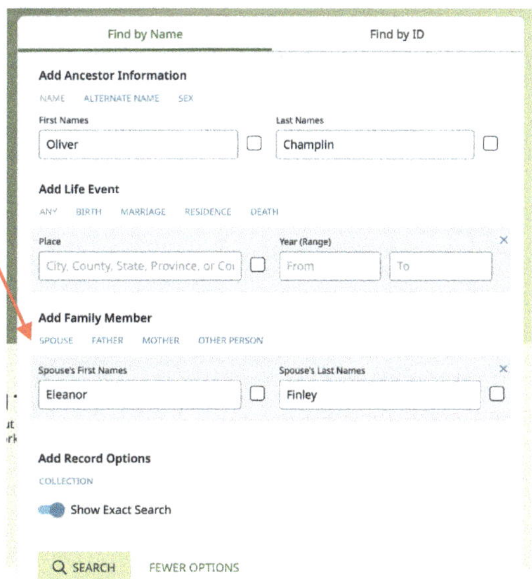

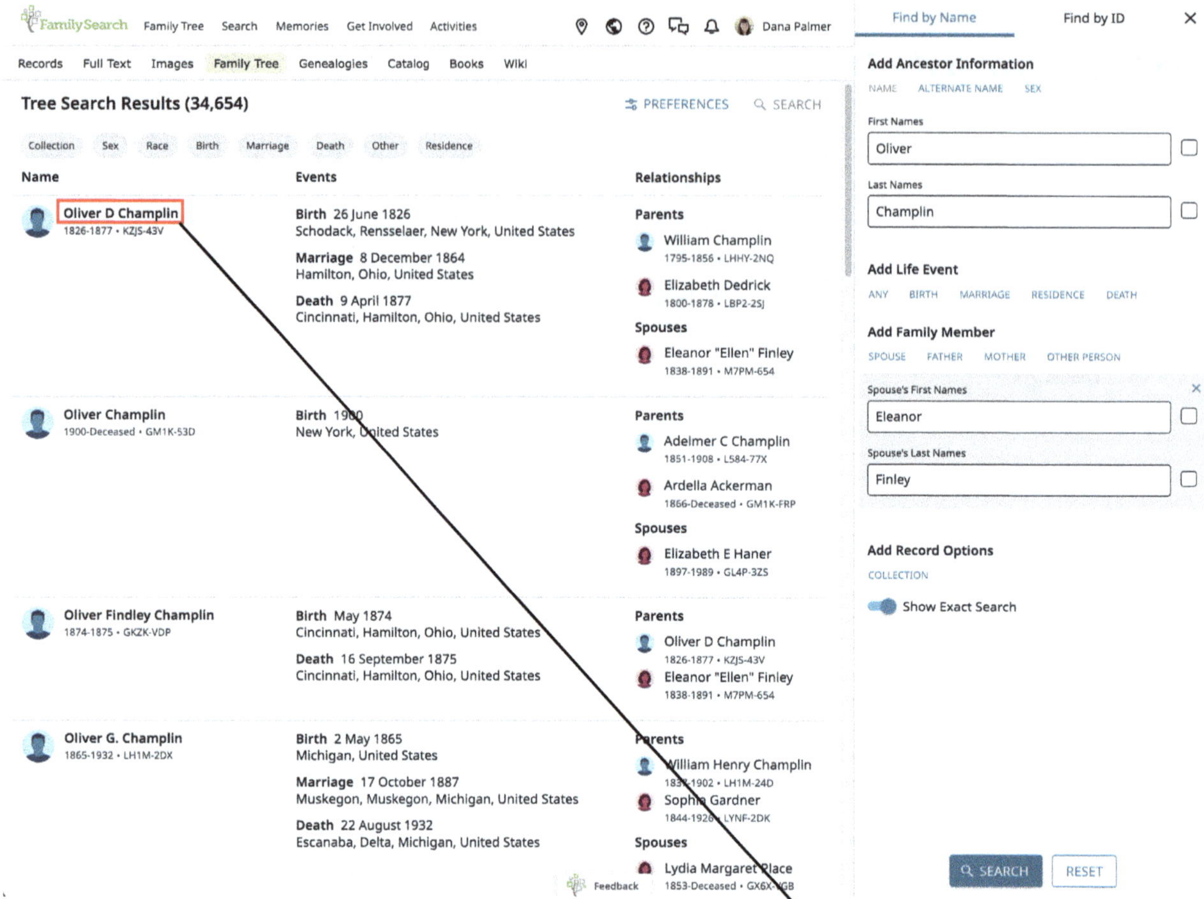

https://www.familysearch.org/en/search/tree/results?q.givenName=Oliver&q.spouseGivenName=Eleanor&q.spouseSurname=Finley&q.surname=Champlin

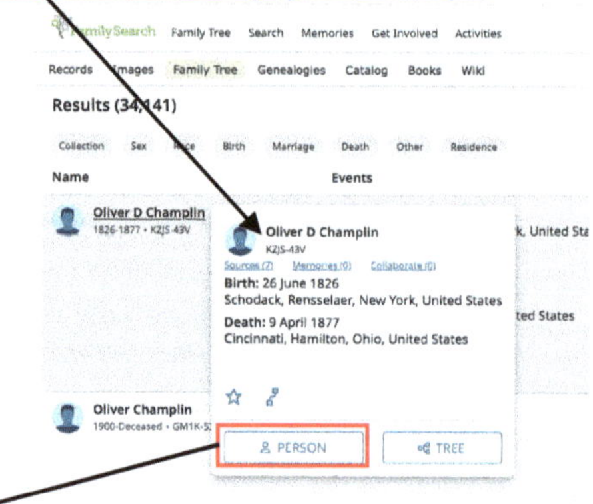

When the person you want appears in the results, click on their name. A popup screen will appear. Click on PERSON to navigate to that individual's DETAILS page in TREE. If it takes you to one of the other pages for that person (ABOUT, SOURCES, MEMORIES, or TIMELINE), click on the DETAILS tab to get back to the main page for the person.

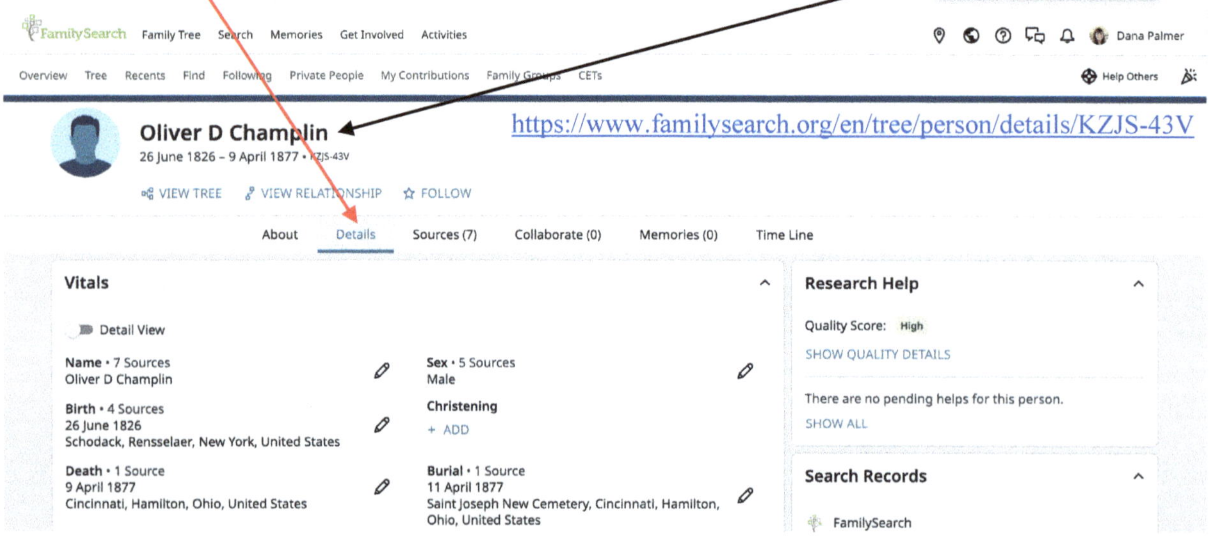

https://www.familysearch.org/en/tree/person/details/KZJS-43V

EDITING THE TREE

The Details Page

Each person in the TREE has a DETAILS page devoted to them with subcategories for sources, collaboration, memories, etc. Each person is assigned a unique ID, although sometimes the person will appear in the TREE more than once, each time with their own unique ID. This is especially true for people without vital dates. Duplicate people will need to be merged. Knowing the ID of a person allows you to more easily navigate and connect family members.

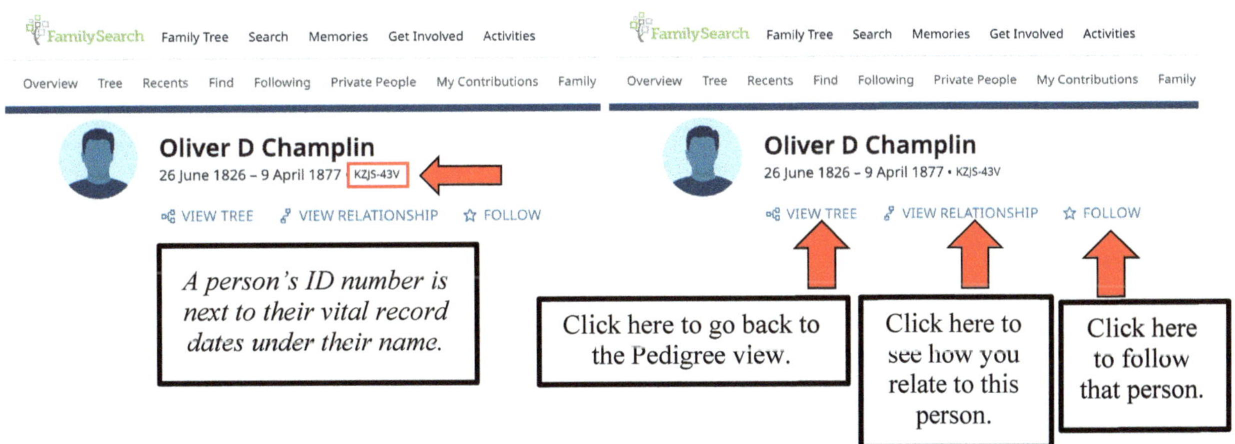

Clicking on the FOLLOW button at the top right side will put a watch on that specific person. This is helpful because, if someone makes a change to them, you will be sent an alert notifying you that a change has been made, details on who made the change, and what was changed. It's highly recommended to FOLLOW your direct line ancestors back to at least your 2nd great-grandparents and any relatives you are actively researching.

Be sure to add sources, photos, documents, and research notes to each person in the TREE. The more credible documentation you add, the less likely someone else will change the information. This is an interactive collaborative tree, which means other contributors can make changes to it too. This can be helpful or frustrating depending on whether the person making the change has good documentation to back up their change. The more documentation you add, the less likely well-meaning relatives will change things incorrectly.

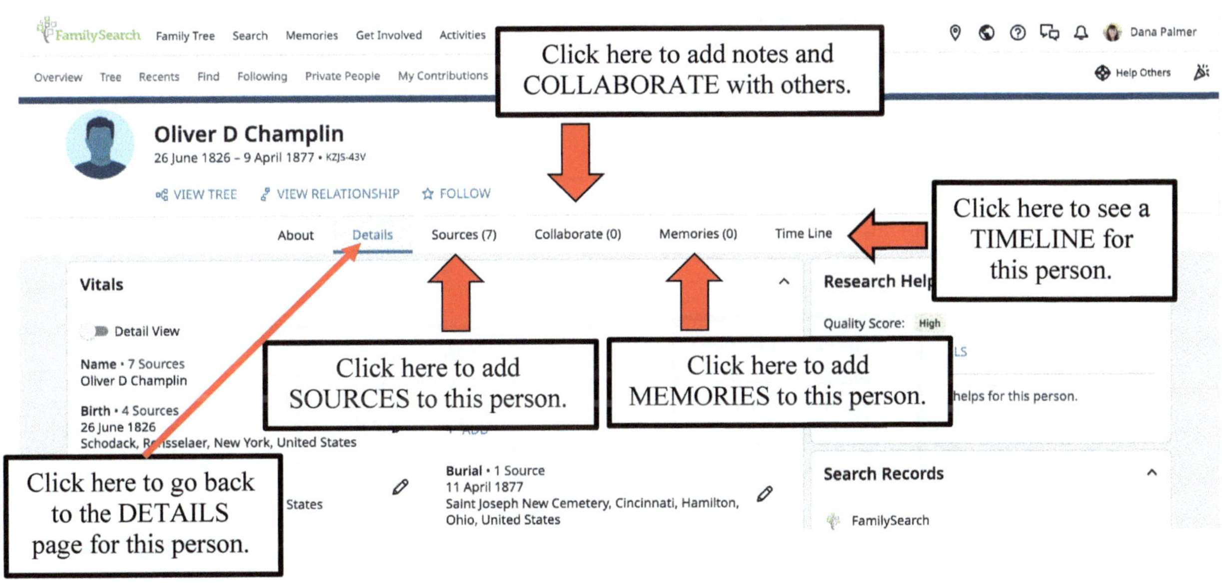

To make changes to the person, you need to be on the DETAILS page in the TREE. Click the pencil next to a fact you want to change to update the information. Be sure to update facts for yourself, your spouse (if you are married), and any descendants you have. Any living people you add to the tree will not be visible to others until they are marked as deceased. This is done to protect their privacy as well as yours.

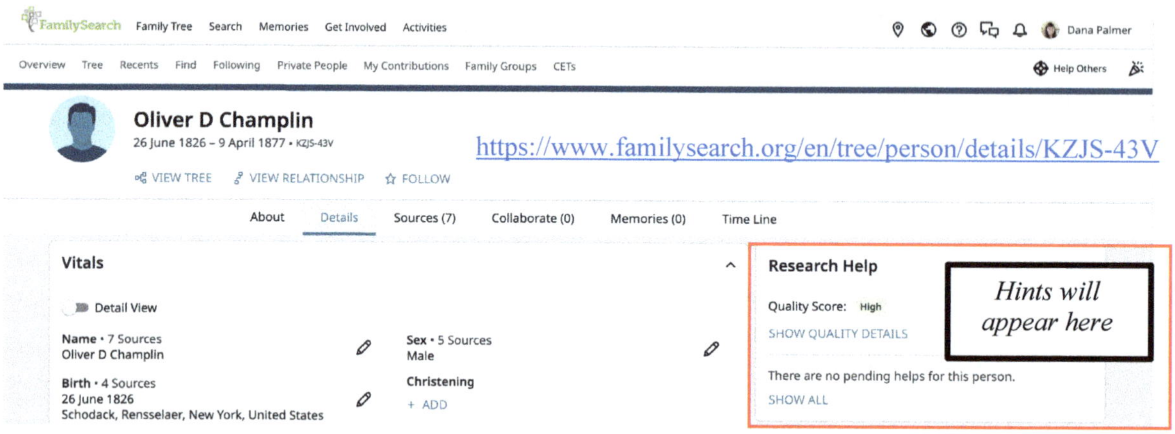

The more content you add in TREE to the vital records and family members, the more likely hints will appear in the RESEARCH HELP section. Scroll down for more information on the person and his immediate family, and to see the latest changes made.

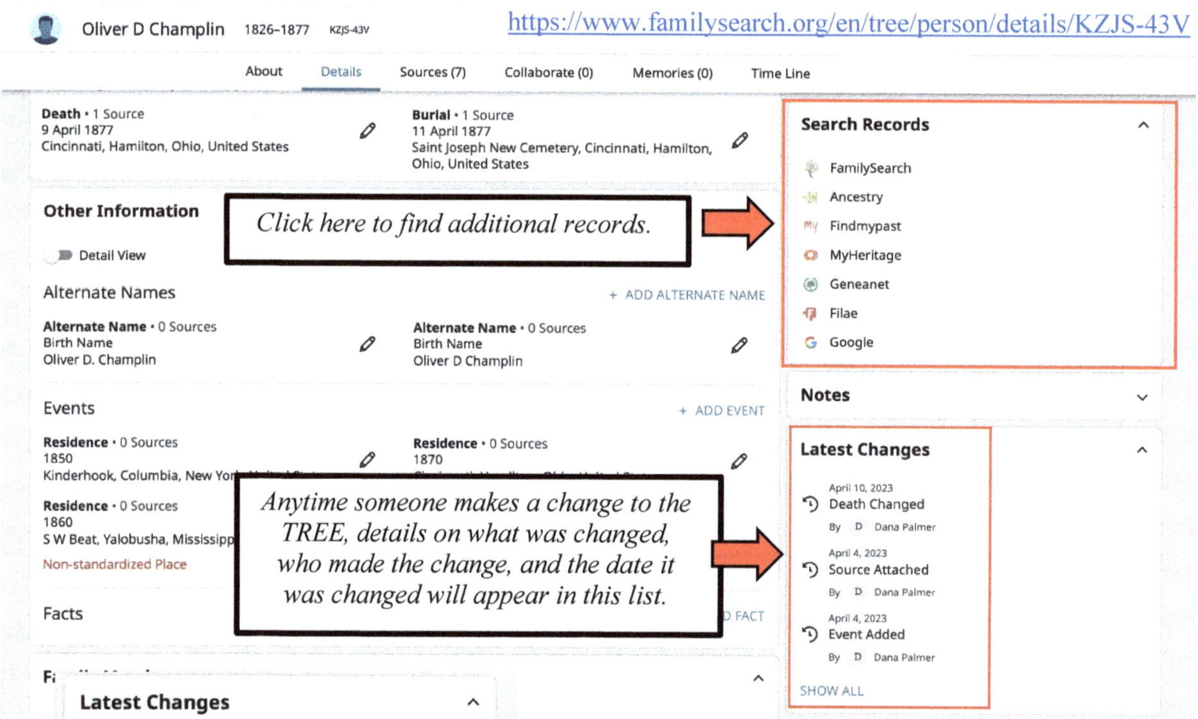

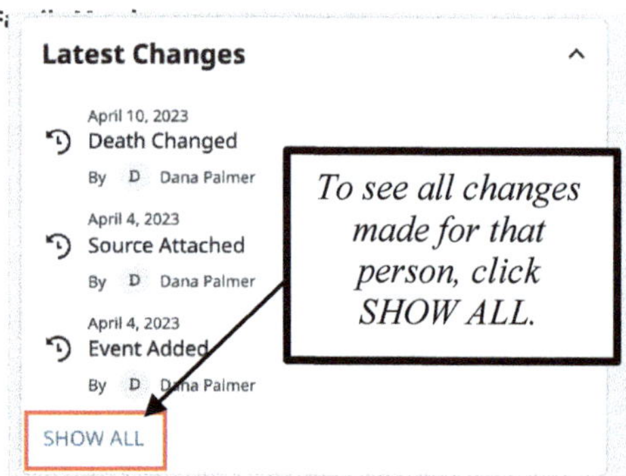

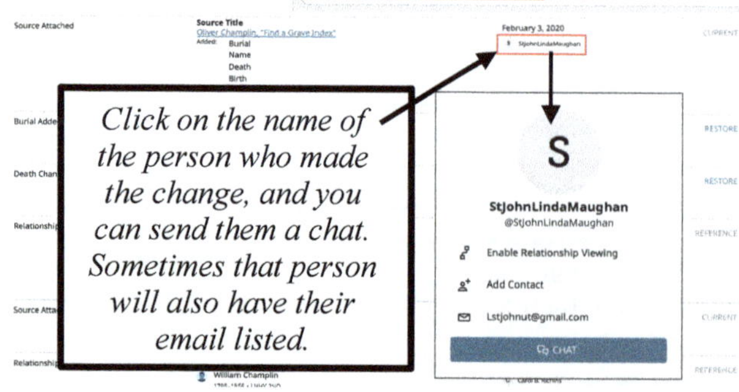

Clicking on the icons from websites in the SEARCH RECORDS category in the tree for your specific person will fill in the information from the TREE on FamilySearch to the search filters for the specified website. This is a quick way to find records on other websites with minimal effort.

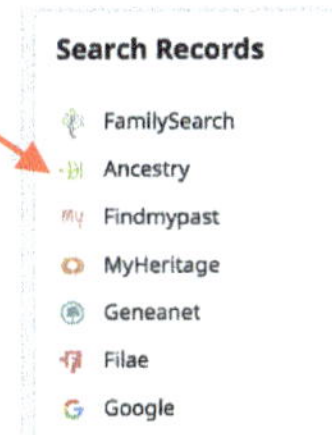

https://www.familysearch.org/en/tree/person/details/KZJS-43V

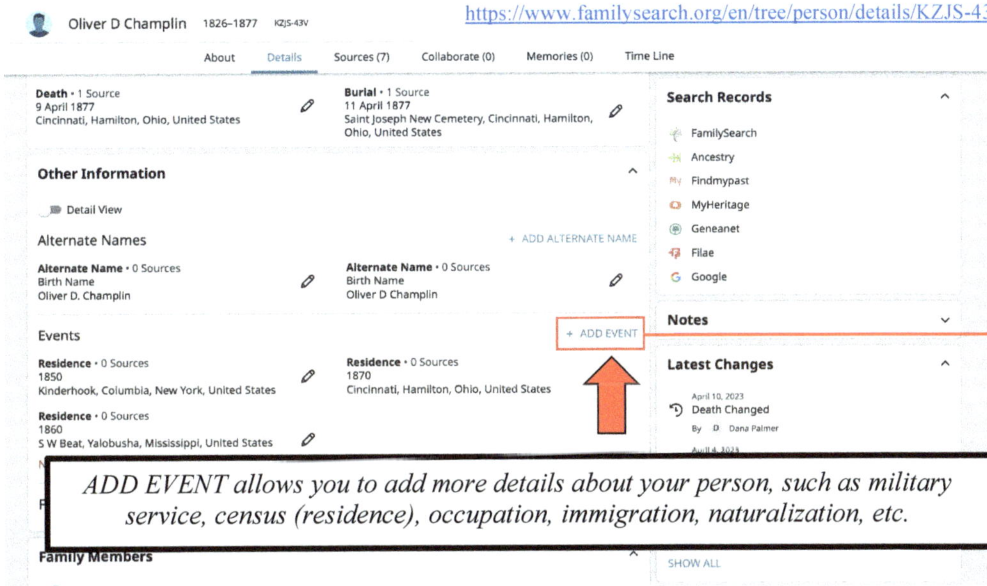

ADD EVENT allows you to add more details about your person, such as military service, census (residence), occupation, immigration, naturalization, etc.

https://www.familysearch.org/en/tree/person/details/KZJS-43V

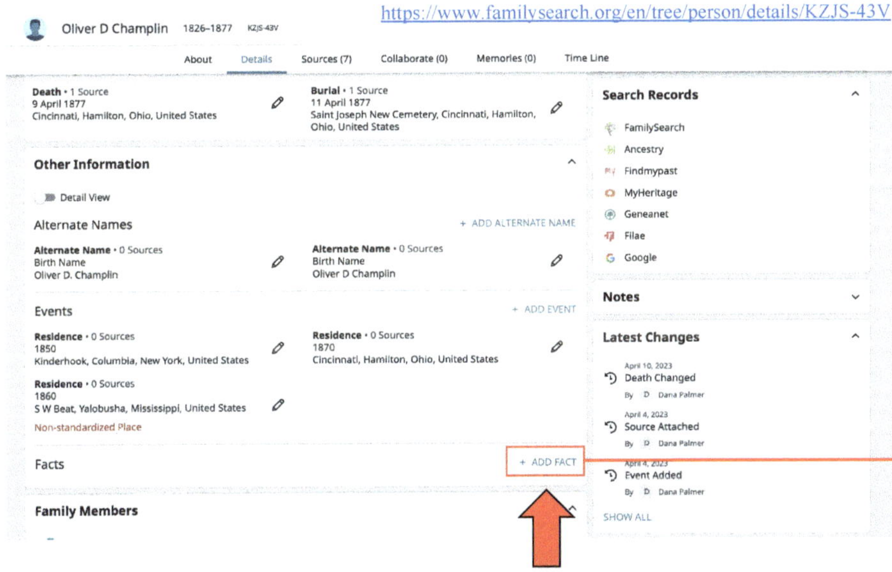

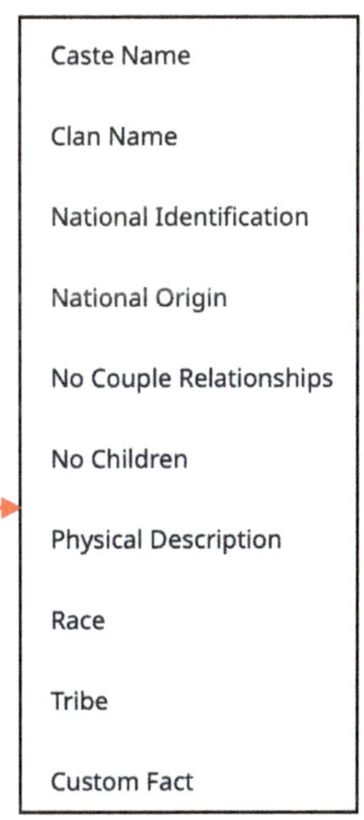

ADD FACTS allows you to add more facts about your person, such as clan, race, tribes, and physical descriptions. This is also where you can indicate a person who never married (no couple relationship) or had no children.

ADD NOTE is a great way to document what you find in specific records, and it can discourage users from changing well-documented research in the TREE. It can be helpful to note kinship evidence. This alert will appear in a banner at the top of the page that is hard to miss. You can only add one alert note per person. Other users won't always heed the caution, but it does usually prevent the changes made to the TREE that may conflict with what is in the note.

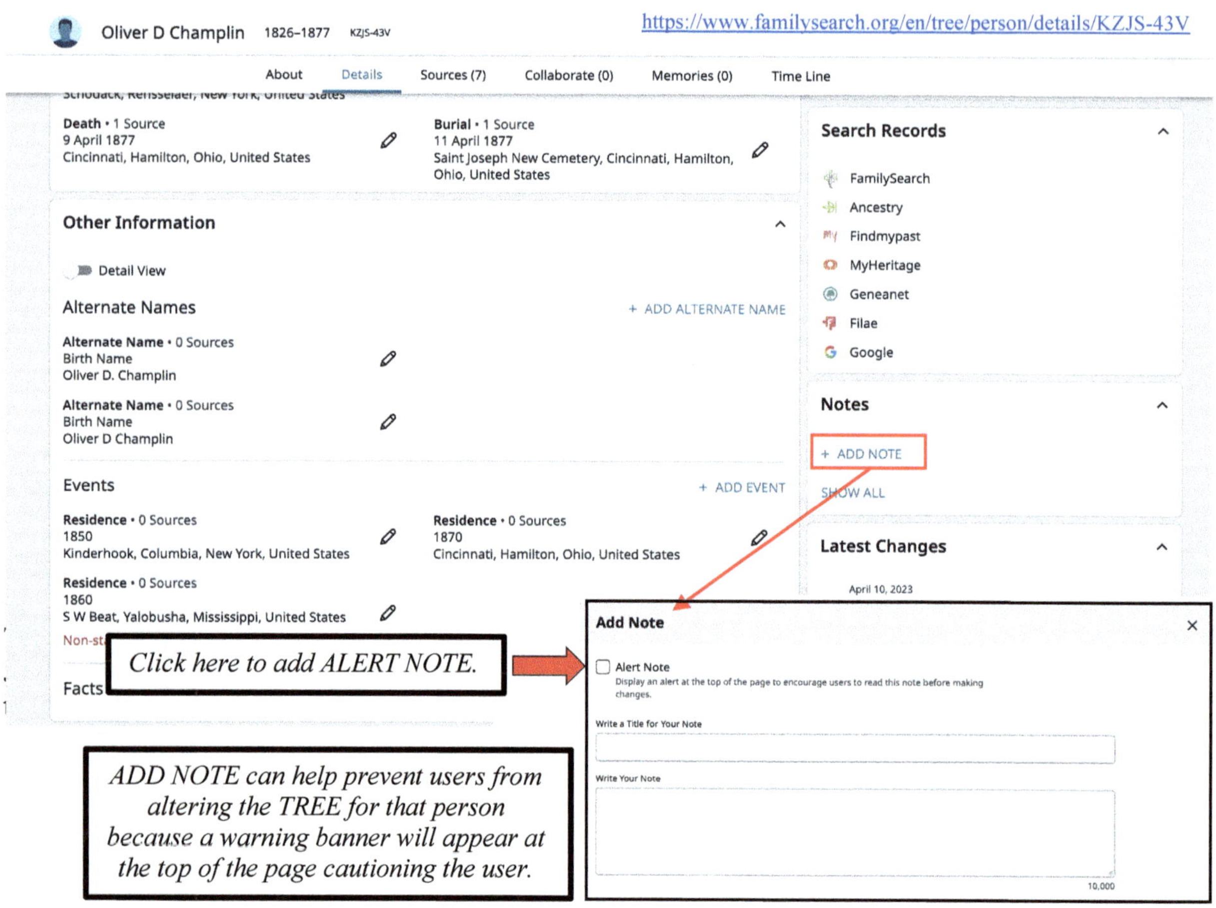

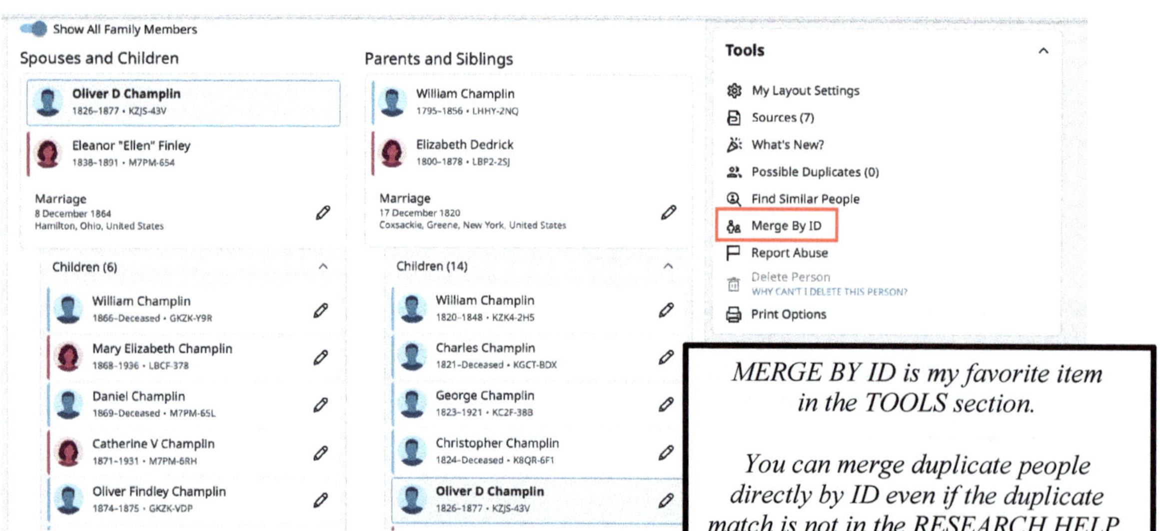

https://www.familysearch.org/en/tree/person/details/KZJS-43V

Adding Other Relationships

FamilySearch has a wonderful feature that allows you to attach people who might be related or who are closely associated with your person. To do this, go to the very bottom of that person's DETAILS page and click on ADD OTHER RELATIONSHIP.

https://www.familysearch.org/en/tree/person/details/KZJS-43V

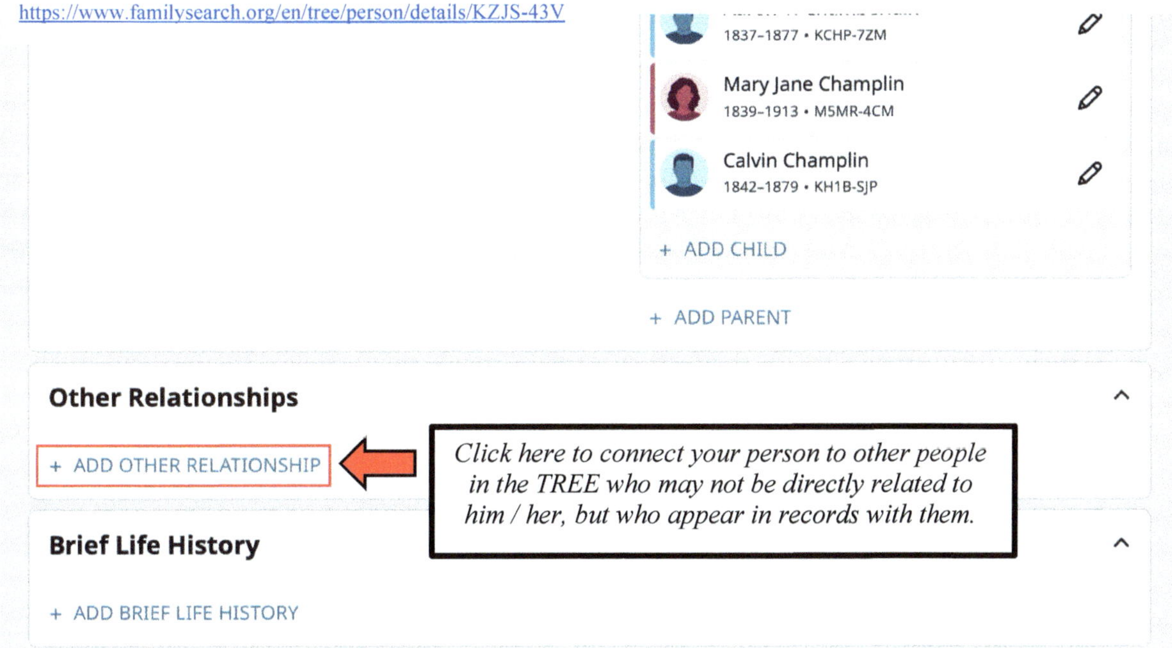

Click the drop-down arrow and choose the category for the relationship: Apprenticeship, Employment, Enslavement, Godparent, Household, Neighbor, or Relative. Then click the ADD PERSON button and type in that person's ID number.

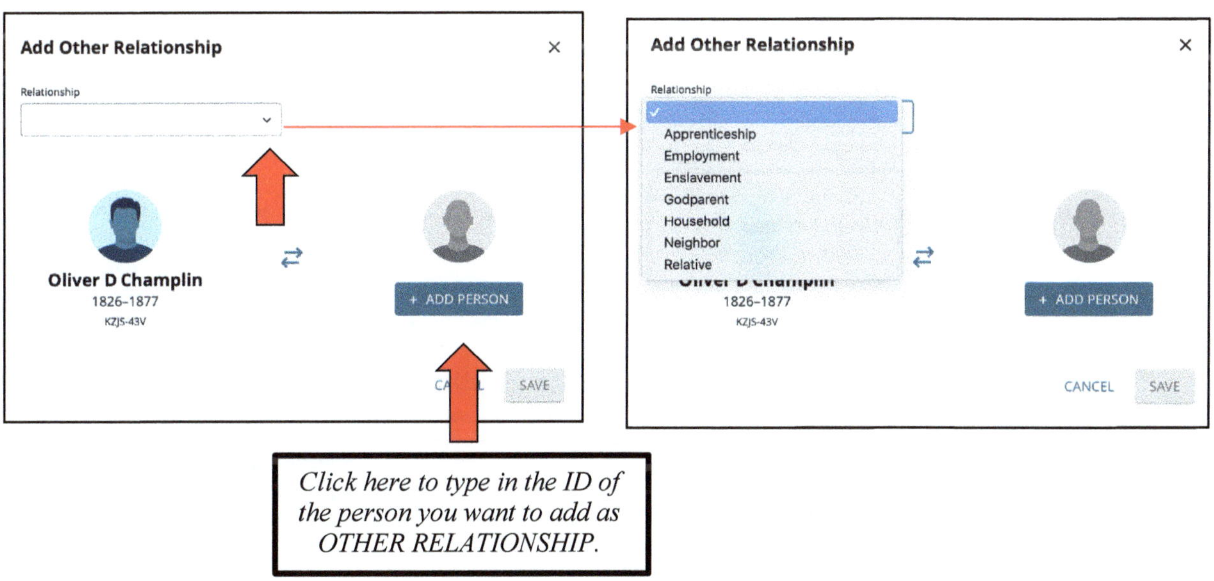

Updating Information

The more information you add to the facts on the person's DETAILS page, the more likely record hints will pop up for that person. Review these hints and add the applicable ones to that person. Be sure to mark NOT A MATCH if the record is not for that person. Often, you will find additional records for your person as more data is listed, or records are attached. If a record does not appear in the hints, you will have to find it manually by searching RECORDS, CATALOG, IMAGES, or FULL-TEXT SEARCH. Once you find the record, be sure to attach it to the person in the TREE so it is easy to find it later.

The TREE will not automatically update fields when sources are attached unless there is no source there, and you indicate you want to add that fact when you are attaching the record. You will need to update vital record fields manually by clicking on the pencil icon for the field you want to update. Any changes made will show in the LATEST CHANGES section on the DETAILS page. Be sure to merge duplicates and add all family members.

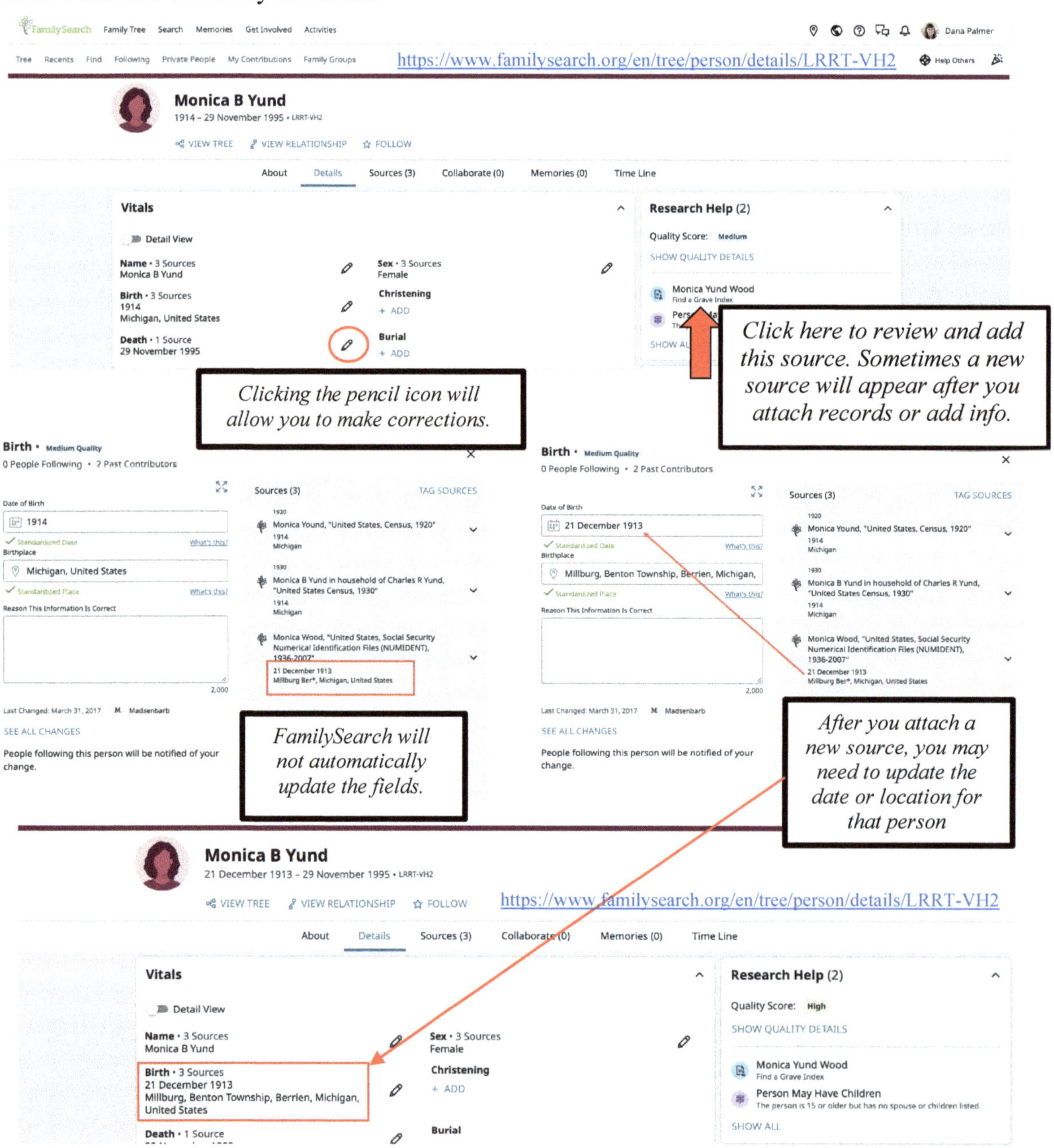

Adding a Spouse

To add new people to the TREE, you can do so manually by clicking the ADD CHILD, ADD SPOUSE BUTTON, etc., or by uploading a GEDCOM. (A GEDCOM is a genealogy data file your personal database can export which can be imported by other personal databases or websites.) Instead of uploading a GEDCOM to the TREE on FamilySearch, check to see if any of your relatives are already in the FamilySearch TREE database; many are already there. If your relatives are already in the system, you can easily connect everyone using their assigned ID, or search for them by their name.

Print out a pedigree chart from your personal genealogy database, then search for each individual in the TREE on FamilySearch. Write down their assigned number above their name on the pedigree chart. Link those unconnected by first linking the spouses to each other; then add each child by their assigned ID number as children of those parents. After you link and merge the individuals, then add any family members that are missing.

Scroll down to the Family Members section to add a spouse.

To add a spouse, click on ADD SPOUSE in the Family Members section on the DETAILS page. You can then add by name or by ID.

If you add by name, FamilySearch will search to see if that person is already in the system. If so, you will have the choice to add the person who matches, or the one you typed.

For multiple matches, you will need to add one of the matches first, then go back and merge duplicate entries. Merging is easiest by writing down the IDs for each of the duplicate matches and manually merging them.

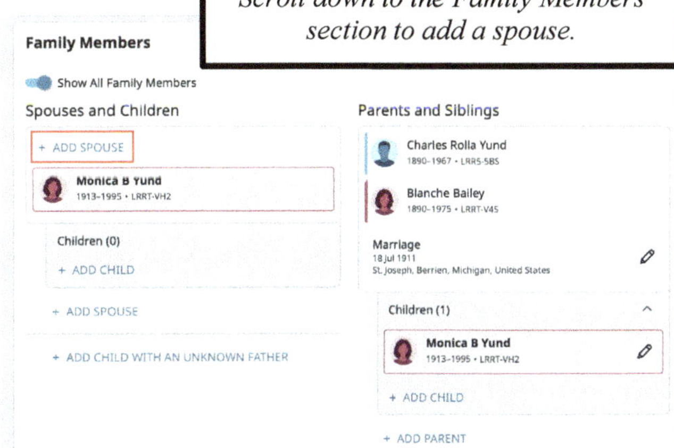

https://www.familysearch.org/en/tree/person/details/LRRT-VH2

Often you need to manually update the BMD dates or locations, once you have added the new spouse.

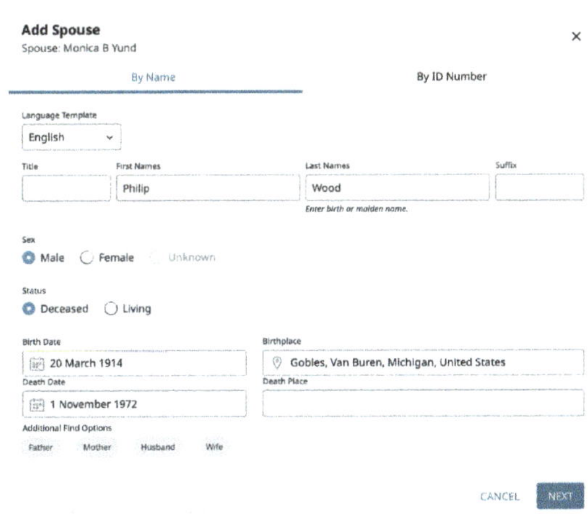

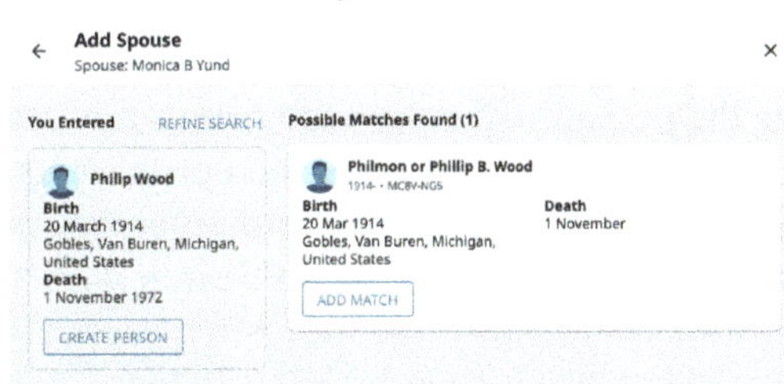

When you add a spouse, FamilySearch will check to see if that person is already in the system. If they are, click ADD MATCH. If they are not in the system, click CREATE PERSON.

To add the marriage date or place, or modify what is already there, click on the pencil next to the marriage field in the Family Members section on the DETAILS page.

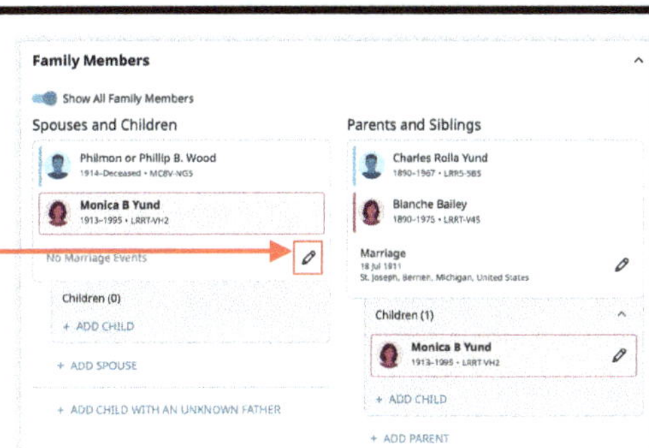

You can add a marriage, divorce, annulment, common law marriage, or note that they lived together. If your person has been married more than once to the same person, be sure to add all their marriage dates and any divorces that may have occurred. You can add multiple facts for each couple, including multiple marriage or divorce dates for someone who may have been married and divorced to the same person more than once.

If for whatever reason, the incorrect spouse is attached, you can easily unlink him / her. Go to the person's DETAILS page and click on the pencil next to the marriage fact area. Click on REMOVE OR REPLACE under the incorrectly linked spouse. You have the choice to remove or replace the person. *Removing* the person will unlink the couple and remove the marriage fact and date. *Replacing* the person will allow you to type the ID for the correct spouse and replace them, keeping the marriage date and place intact. If you choose replace the person, go to the SOURCES for each person and be sure it is connected to the correct ID. FamilySearch won't update this automatically.

Adding a Child

To add a child, click on the link ADD CHILD in the Family Members section of the DETAILS page. You can add BY NAME or BY ID NUMBER, just like adding a spouse.

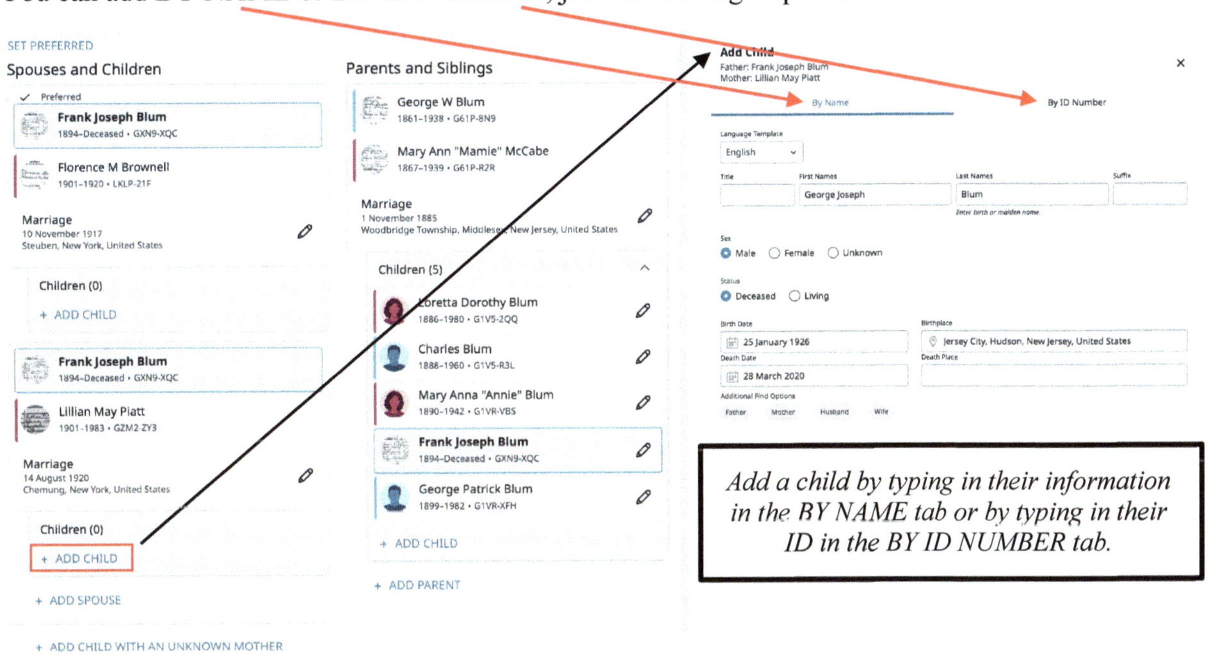

https://www.familysearch.org/en/tree/person/details/GXN9-XQC

FamilySearch will look for a potential match. If none are found, it will indicate this, and you can refine the search if desired. Often, it's easiest to just click CREATE PERSON. If a match is found or you accidently create a duplicate, just click on the ID and go to the DETAILS page. Click on MERGE BY ID and merge the duplicate person.

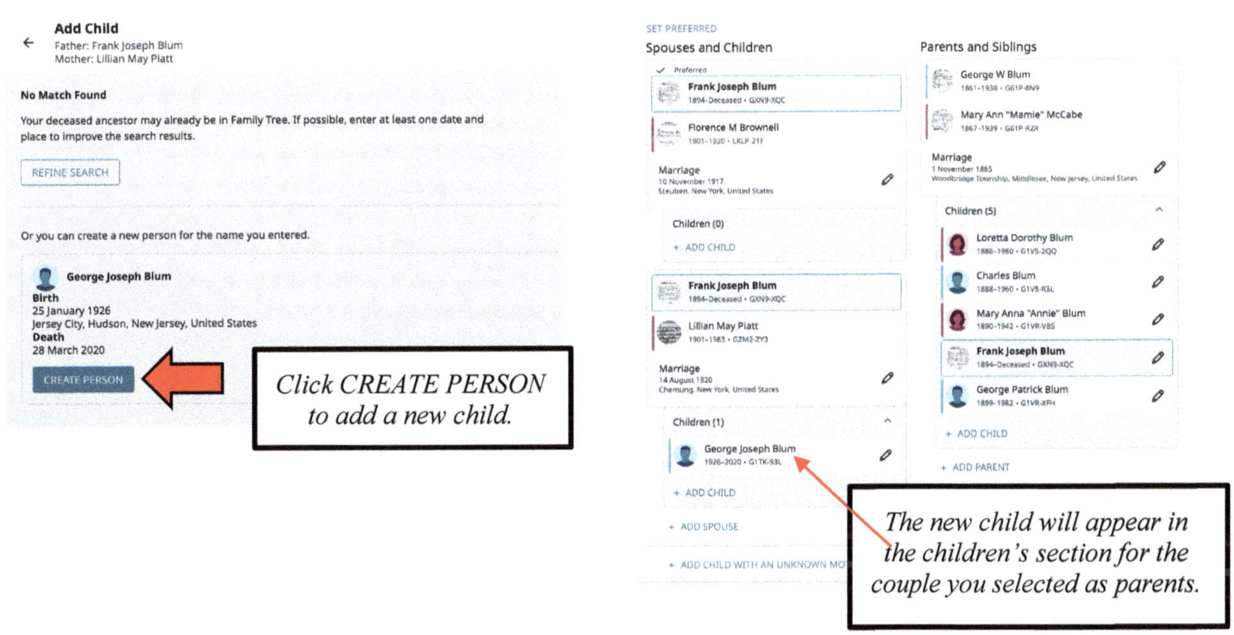

https://www.familysearch.org/en/tree/person/details/GXN9-XQC

Adding Relationship Type

FamilySearch's TREE allows you add multiple parents for a child. For children who are adopted or have stepparents or guardianships, you can easily add this relationship. Go to the FAMILY MEMBER section on that child's DETAILS page and click ADD PARENT. Either type the information for adding a new person (parent) or add the child to a couple already in the system. Click the pencil next to the child's name in the FAMILY MEMBERS section on the DETAILS page.

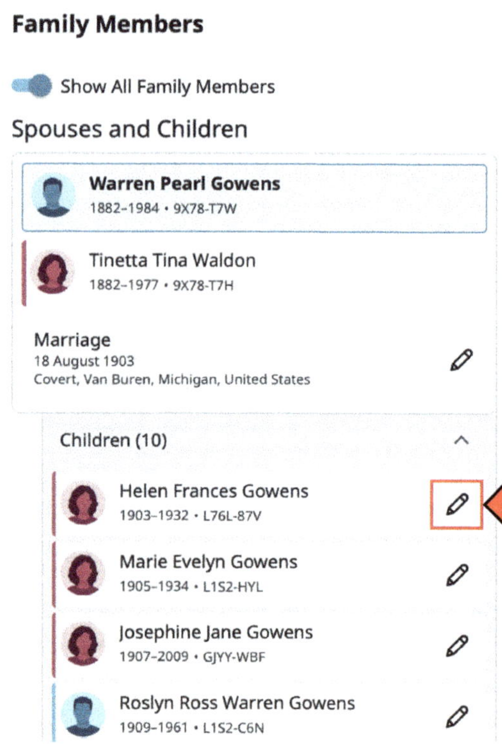

https://www.familysearch.org/en/tree/person/details/9X78-T7W

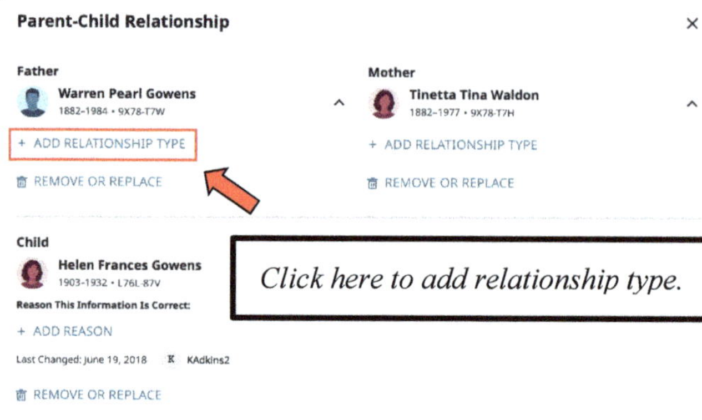

Click here to add relationship type.

Click the pencil next to the child to add their relationship to each set of parents (biological versus adopted).

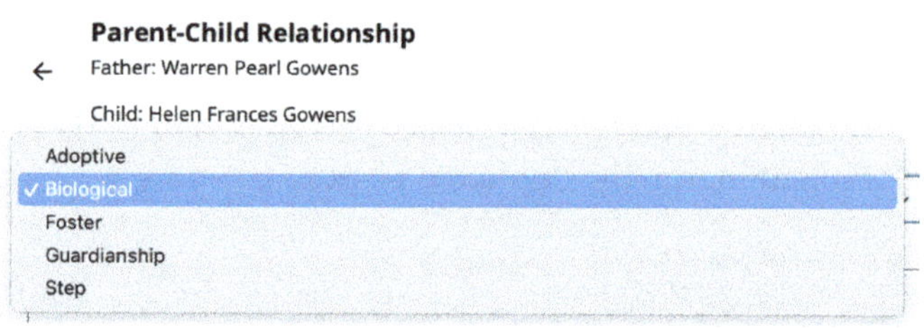

Once you have both sets of parents added, that child will appear in the children's list for each couple and indicate the relationship of the child to that specific parent. The relationships for the parents do not have to be the same.

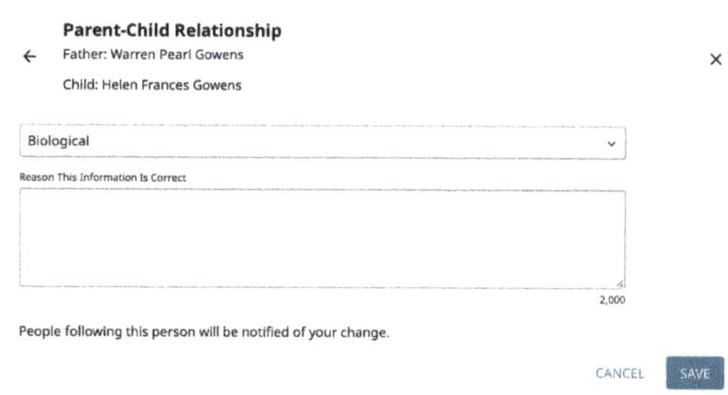

You can indicate your preferred parents. To determine who appears in the pedigree view, mark your preferred couple as the child's parents.

Unlinking People

Sometimes it is necessary to unlink a child because they are attached to the wrong parents or to only one parent. To unlink a child, click on the pencil next to their name in the children's list, then click REMOVE OR REPLACE. This will unlink them from the indicated parent(s).

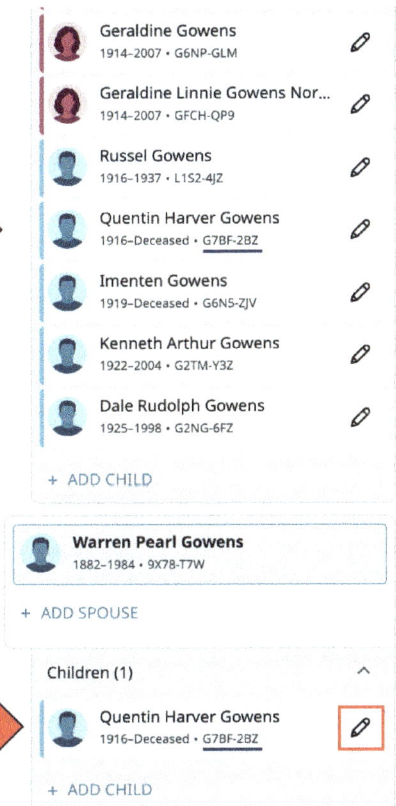

Click the pencil to add relationships or remove a child from the family.

https://www.familysearch.org/en/tree/person/details/9X78-T7W

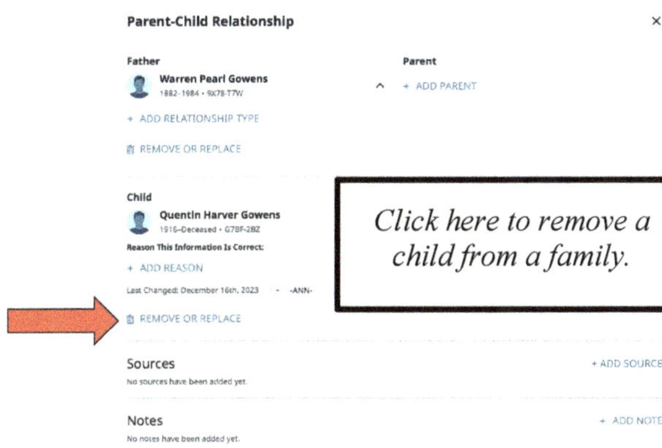

Click here to remove a child from a family.

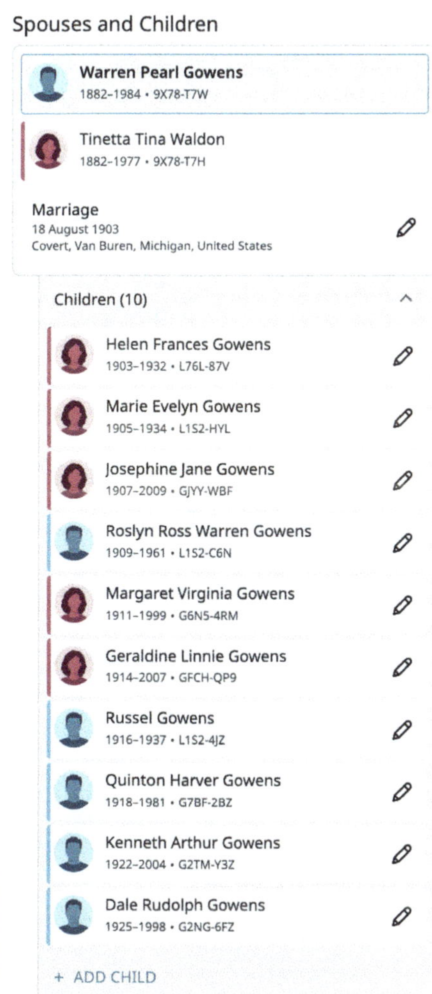

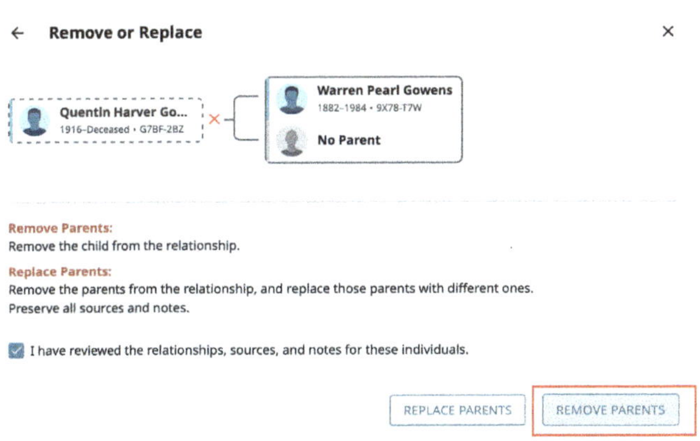

Clicking this will unlink this child from being listed with just one parent. His link to both of his parents will remain.

https://www.familysearch.org/en/tree/person/details/9X78-T7W

Merging Duplicate People

Because FamilySearch's TREE is a collaborative effort from multiple contributors and from multiple indexed collections, duplicate names often appear in the system. This is especially true if there are name variations or no dates for the person. Often, duplicate people will appear in the RESEARCH HELP list, but not always. To merge a duplicate, you can click on the link in the RESEARCH HELP, or merge manually by clicking on MERGE BY ID in the TOOLS section. Sometimes you will need to merge several times for a person and then merge the duplicates for their spouse and parents. Be sure that when you merge, you keep the person and facts you want in the surviving column. If the facts are different, the details in the surviving column are the only ones retained. Write down any differing facts. After merging, go back to the DETAILS page for that person and manually edit the fields that need it.

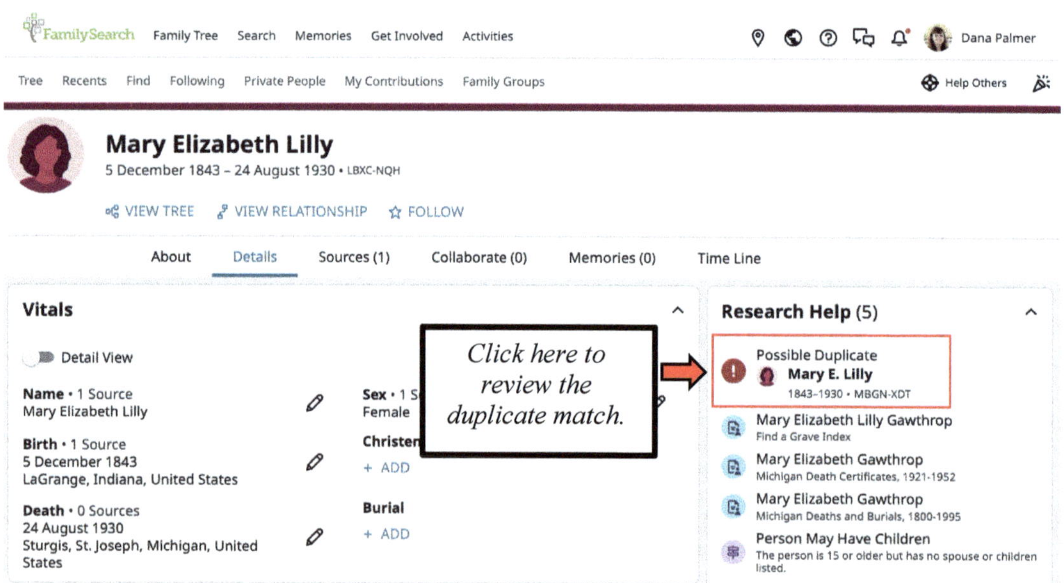

https://www.familysearch.org/en/tree/person/details/LBXC-NQH

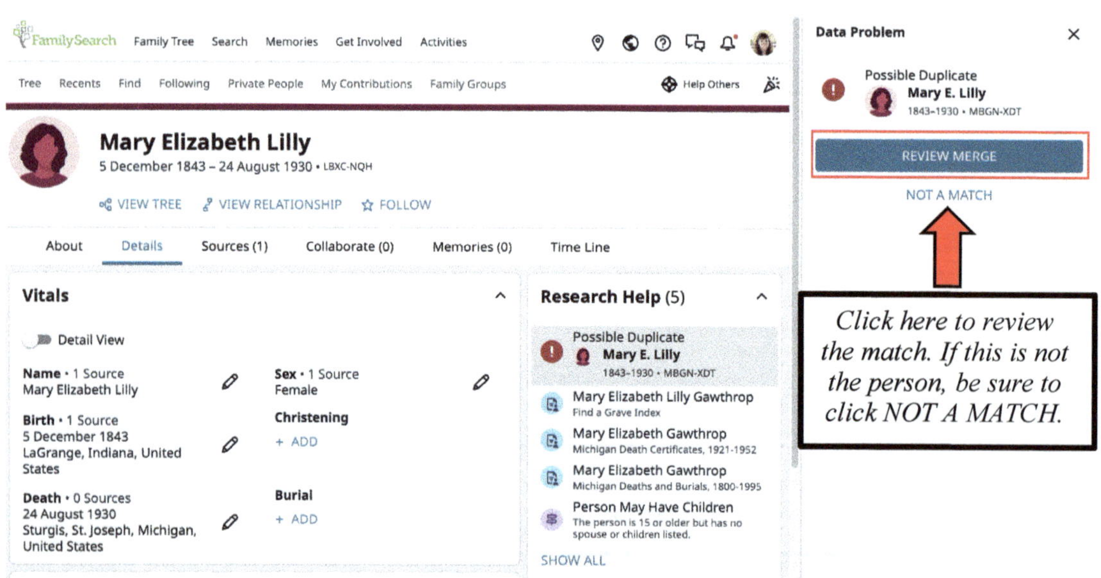

https://www.familysearch.org/en/tree/person/details/LBXC-NQH

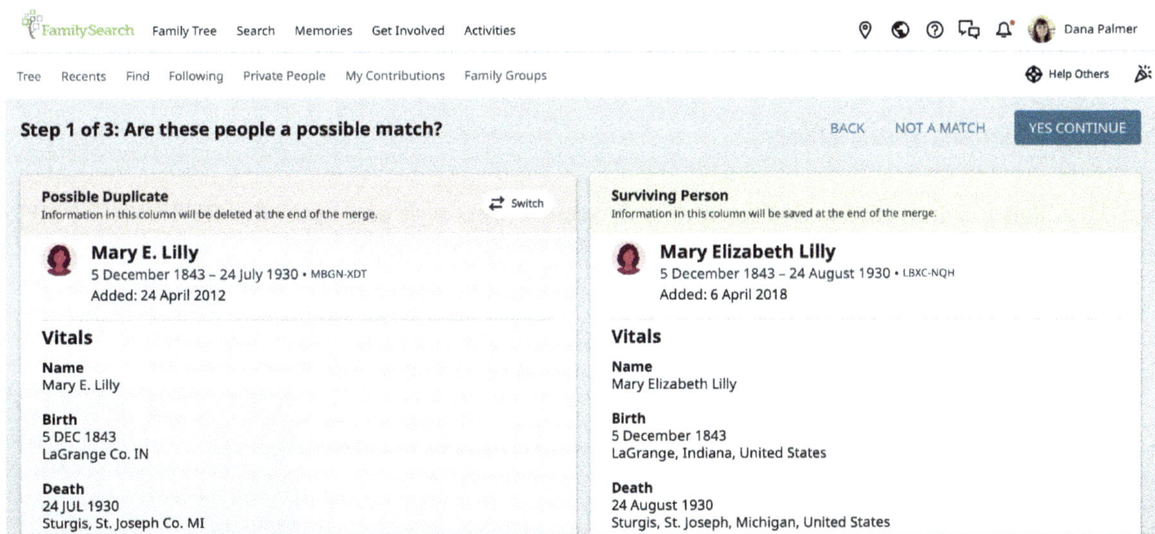

The above example shows that the cemetery entry is slightly different from what is in the TREE, but they are likely the same person. If there are differences between the record versus what is in the TREE, you'll need to manually update the fact afterwards. Be sure to write down the information and enter it using the pencil icon in the DETAILS page afterwards.

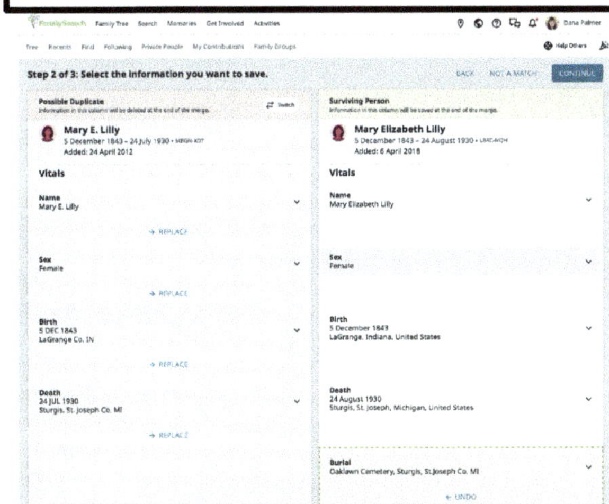

You can add or replace facts while reviewing the record.

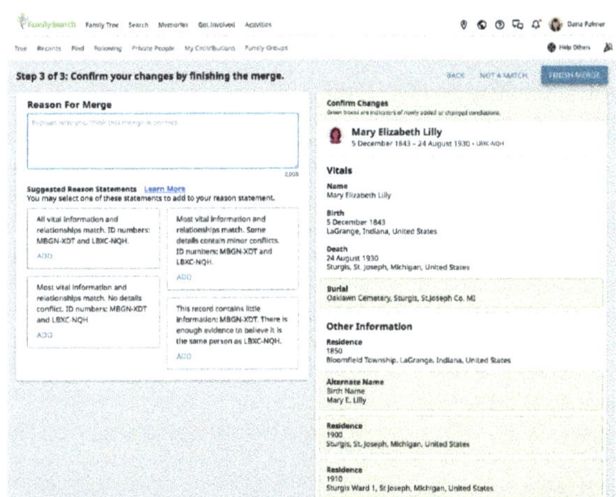

Give a reason for the change and click FINISH MERGE.

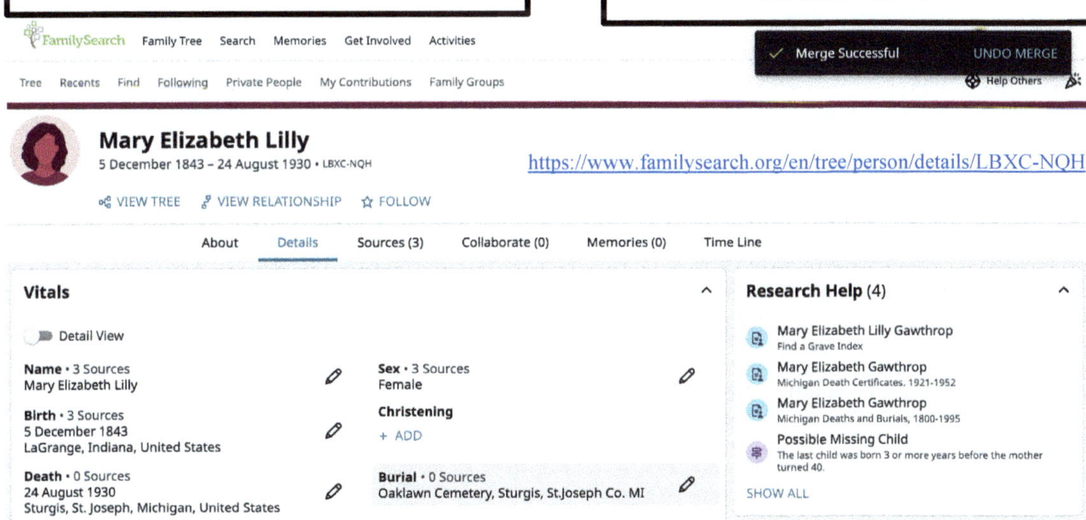

https://www.familysearch.org/en/tree/person/details/LBXC-NQH

ATTACHING RECORDS

Attaching Records from Hints

When dates and locations are added for a person, record hints will pop up in the RESEARCH HELP part of the DETAILS page in the upper-right corner. Often, these records are for your person and can be added to the SOURCES. Carefully review each record hint and, if appropriate, attach it. Click **NOT A MATCH** if it is for another person.

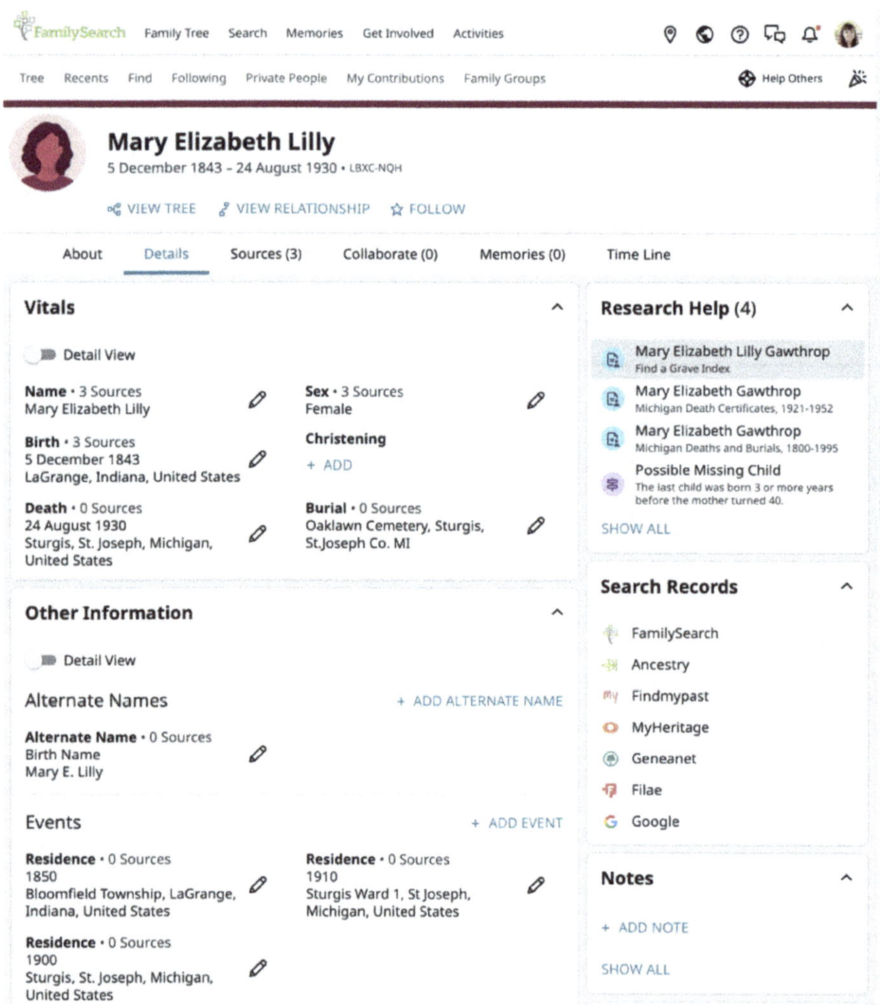

https://www.familysearch.org/en/tree/person/details/LBXC-NQH

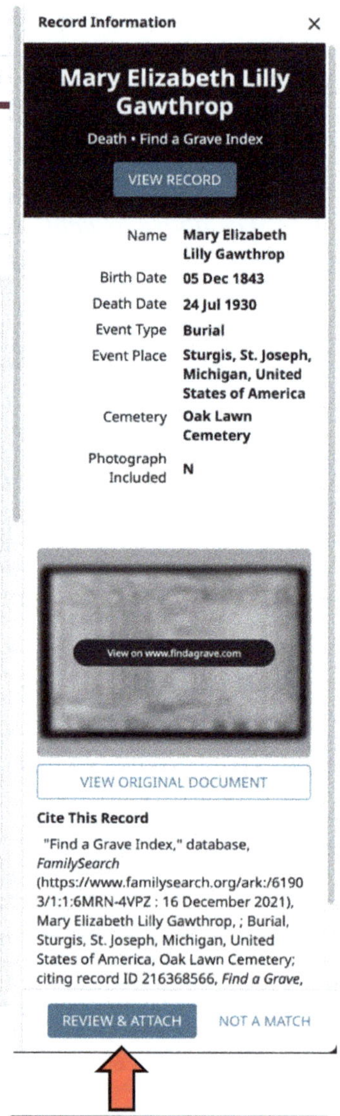

Click here to review and attach the record.

Sometimes duplicate people will appear, especially when additional sources are attached, because someone may have created a new person instead of trying to see if they were already in the system. You will need to spend time merging these duplicate people.

A maximum of 200 sources can be added per person.

Compare the information from the record (on the left) with the information that's in the tree (on the right).

Click on ATTACH to add the record to the person in the TREE. In some cases, you can add vital facts from the record to the person in the TREE.

Be careful though! If there is already a fact in the TREE, information from the new record will not be automatically updated in the TREE. This will have to be done manually.

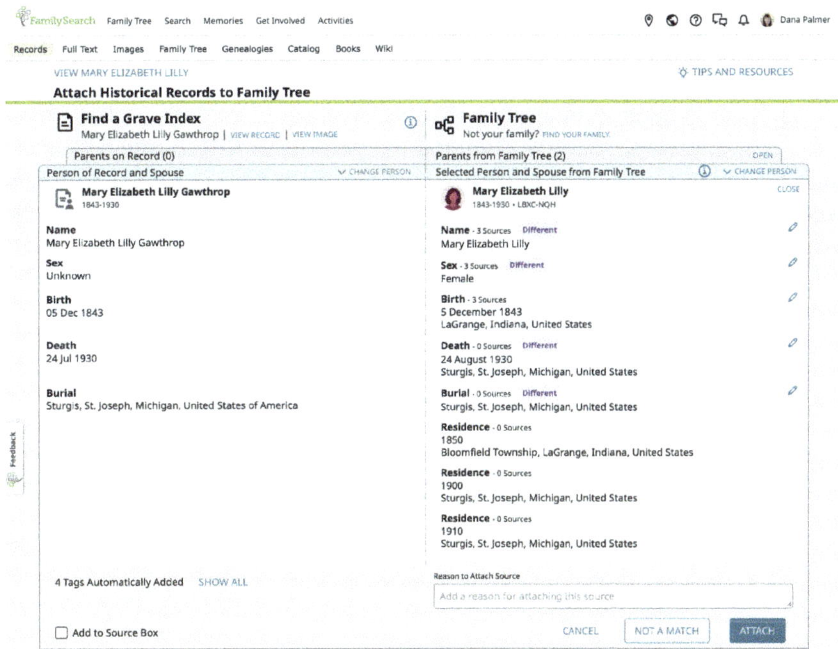

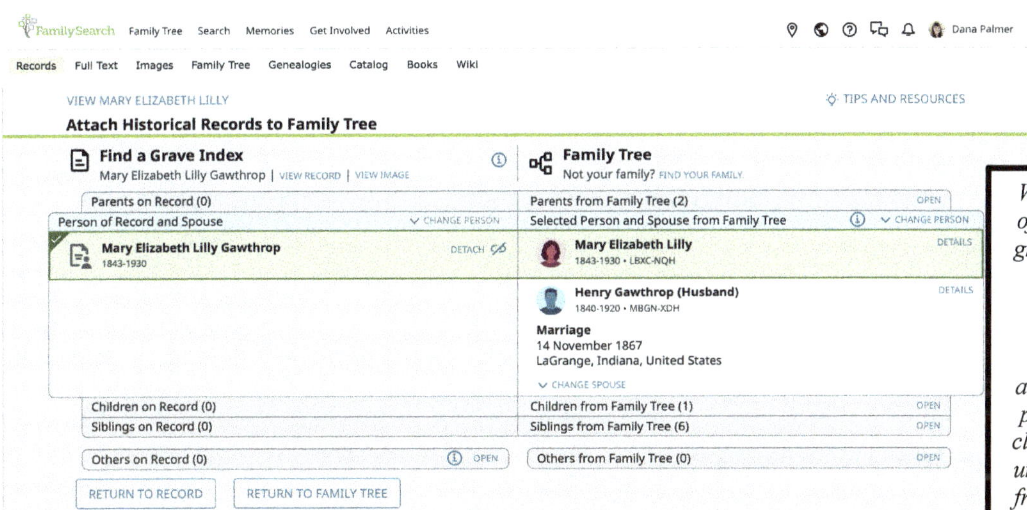

When both sides of the screen are green, the record is attached.

If you make a mistake and attach the wrong person, you can click DETACH to unlink the person from that record.

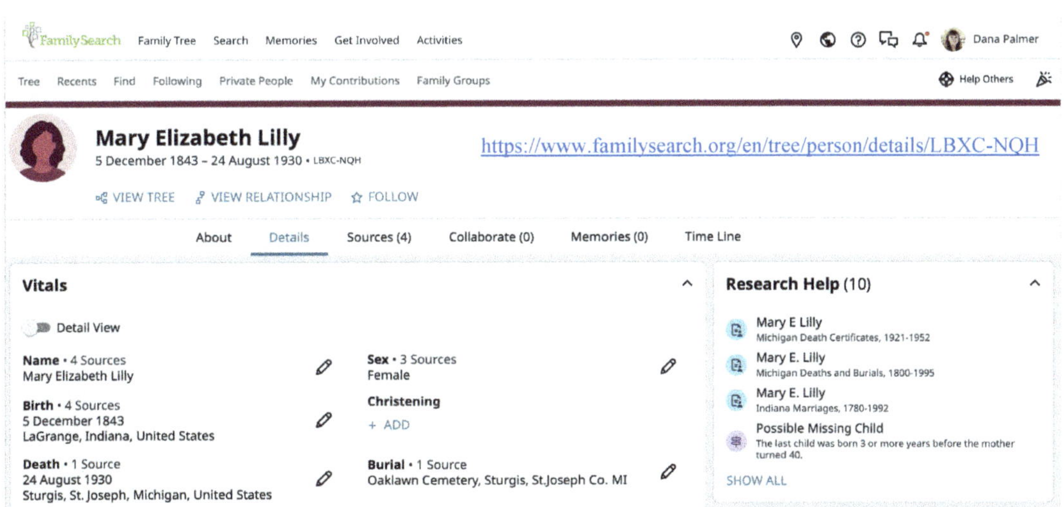

Often once a new record is attached, other records will appear in the RESEARCH HELP section.

Attaching Records by Changing the Focus Person

A trick for attaching sources with multiple people involved is to change the FOCUS PERSON. For example, marriage records often list the parents of the couple. If the focus is the groom, he, his parents, and his bride are easily attached; however, the wife's parents can't be attached when her husband is the focus person. To change the focus, click on CHANGE PERSON on the right side of the screen.

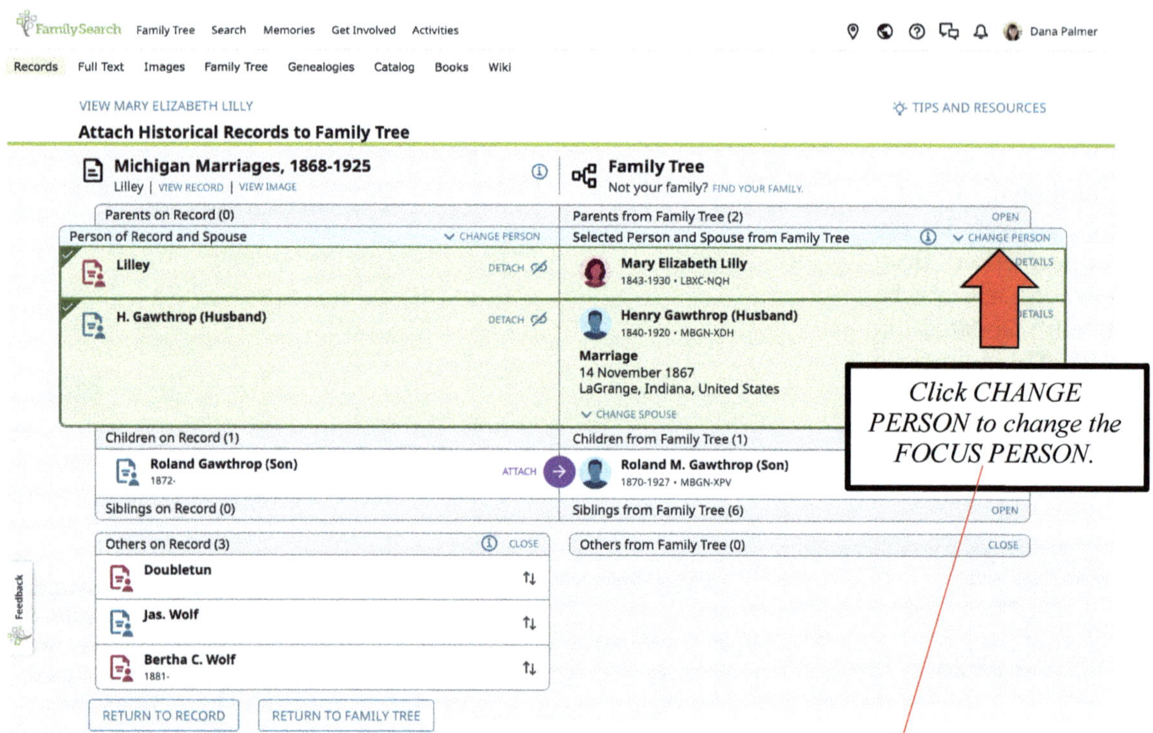

Choose from the list or type in the ID number. In this case, choose the bride, and then her parents will appear and can be attached.

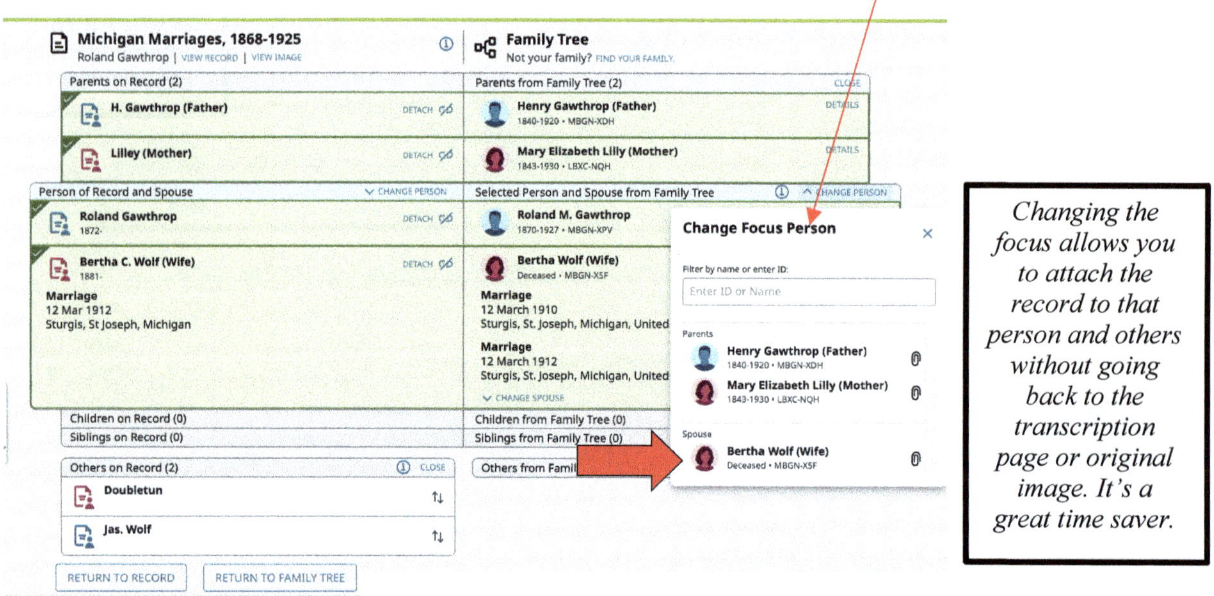

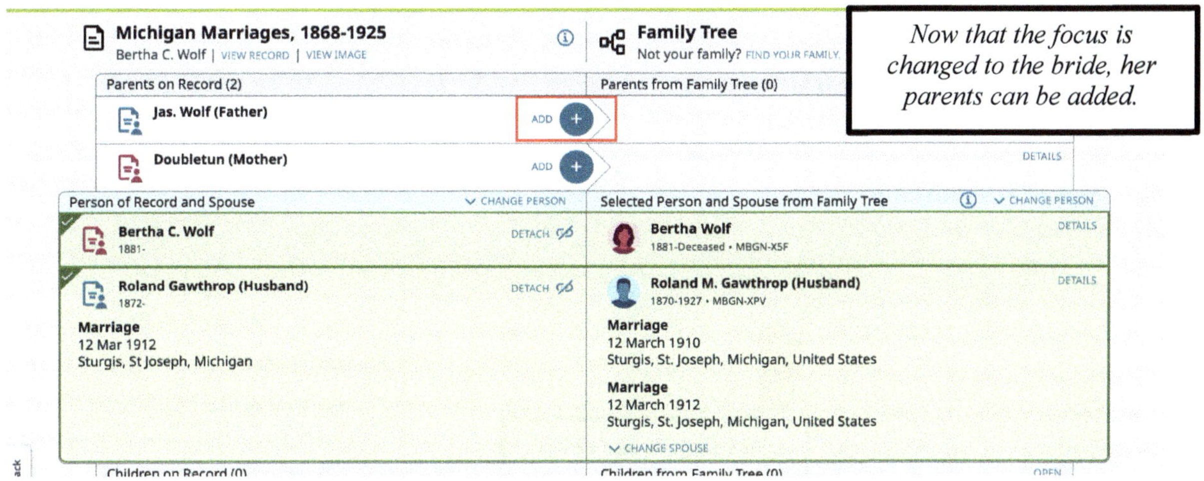

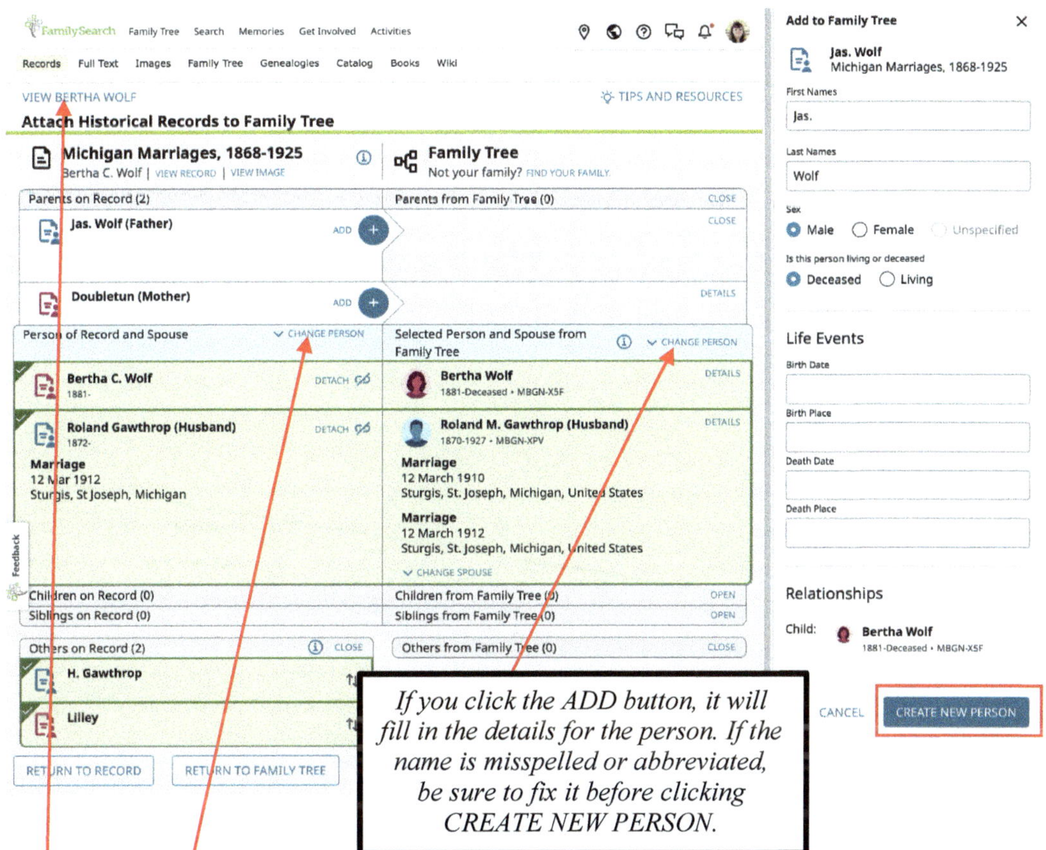

Sometimes you will need to change the person on the left and then the right to attach the correct people. Or you can do this manually by going back to the record transcription page, and select another person in the record, but this takes more time. When you are done attaching the record, click "VIEW [person's name]" at the top to go back to their DETAILS page. The new source attached will appear in the SOURCES tab on that person's DETAILS page.

https://www.familysearch.org/en/tree/person/research-help/LBXC-NQH

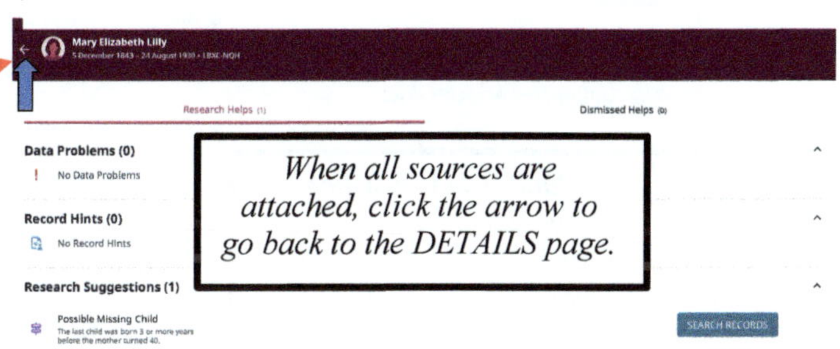

https://www.familysearch.org/tree/person/research-help/LBXC-NQH

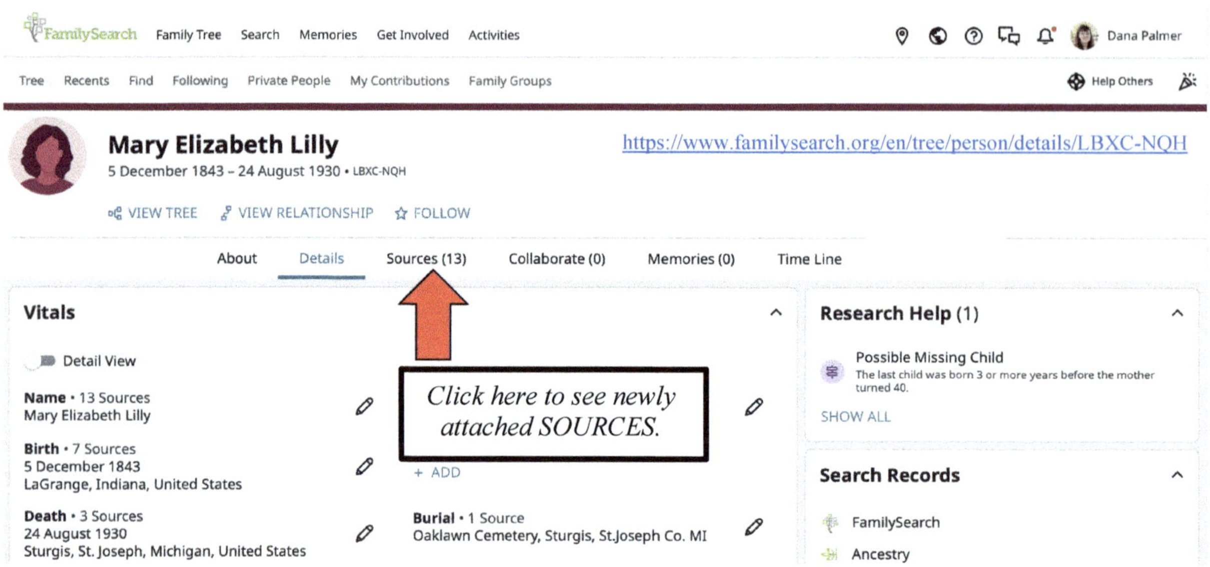

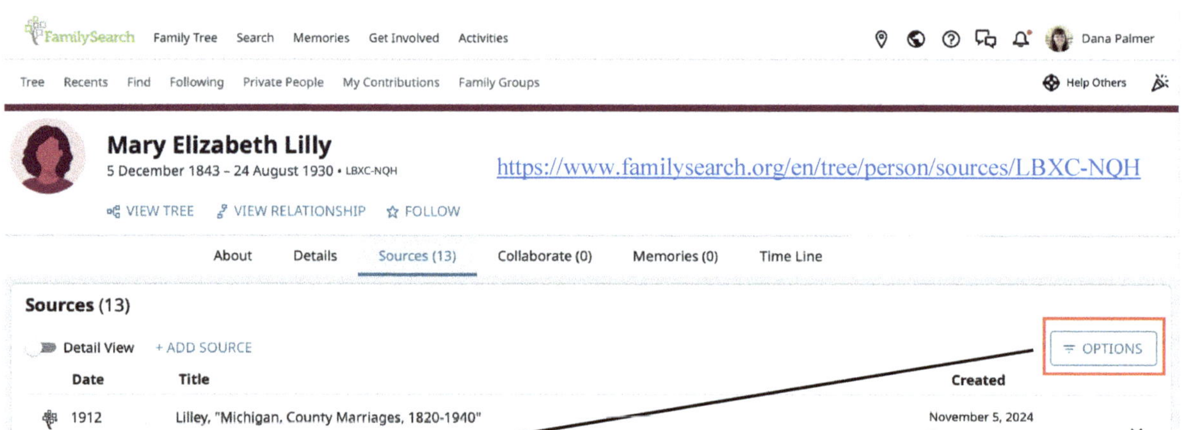

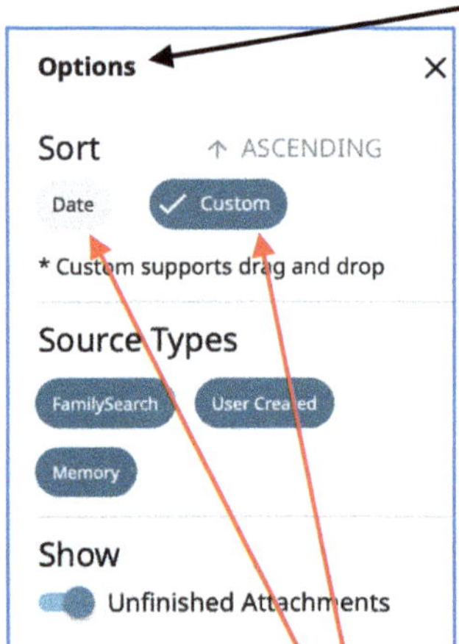

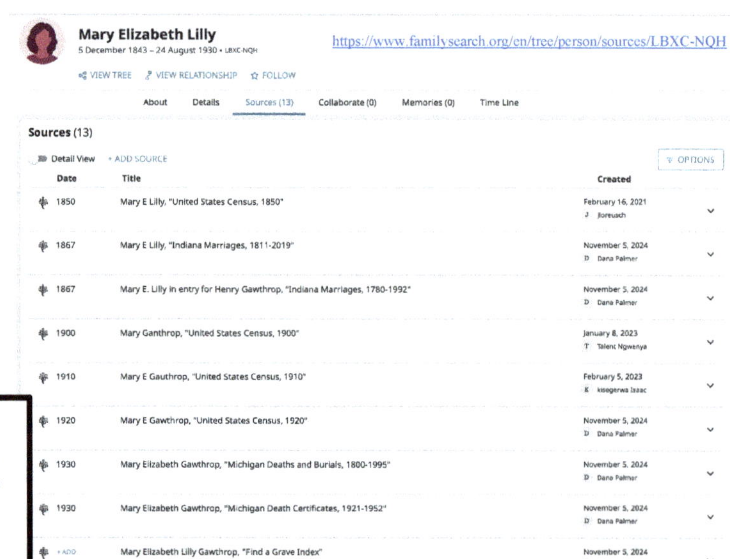

The Sort default is DATE which organizes all the attached sources by date if the year has been added to the date field. Choosing CUSTOM in the OPTIONS allows you to sort your sources according to your preference, and not automatically by date.

Attaching Records Not in Hints

Records that don't show up in the RESEARCH HELP can be attached manually. Go directly to RECORDS, CATALOG, IMAGES, or FULL-TEXT SEARCH on FamilySearch to manually attach it.

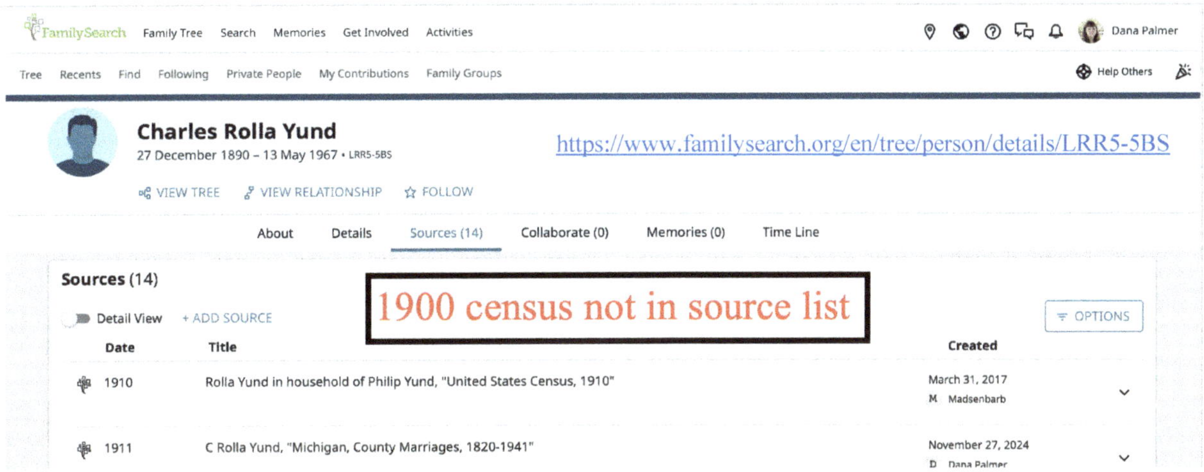

Click on the SEARCH tab, then RECORDS, to search for the record directly in the COLLECTION TITLE box.

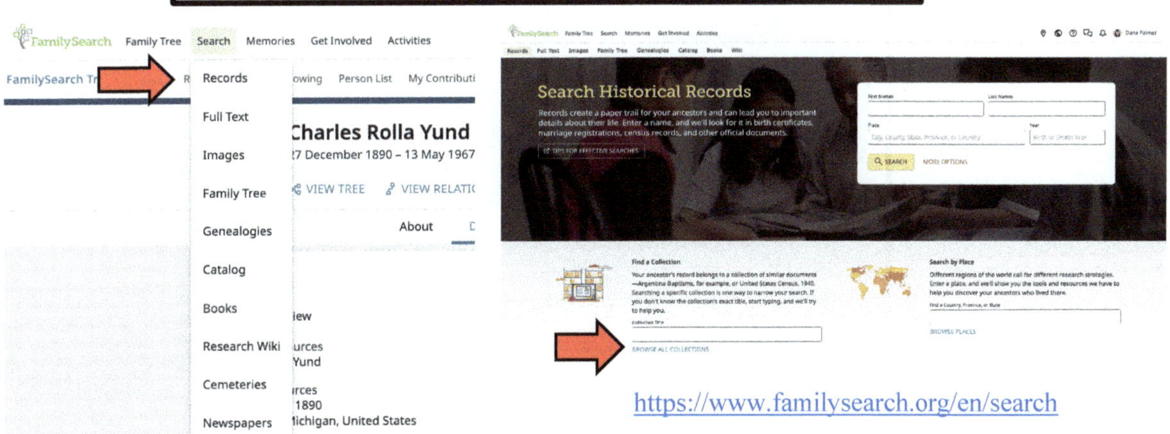

Searching the census directly, Charles Yund was found in the 1900 census.

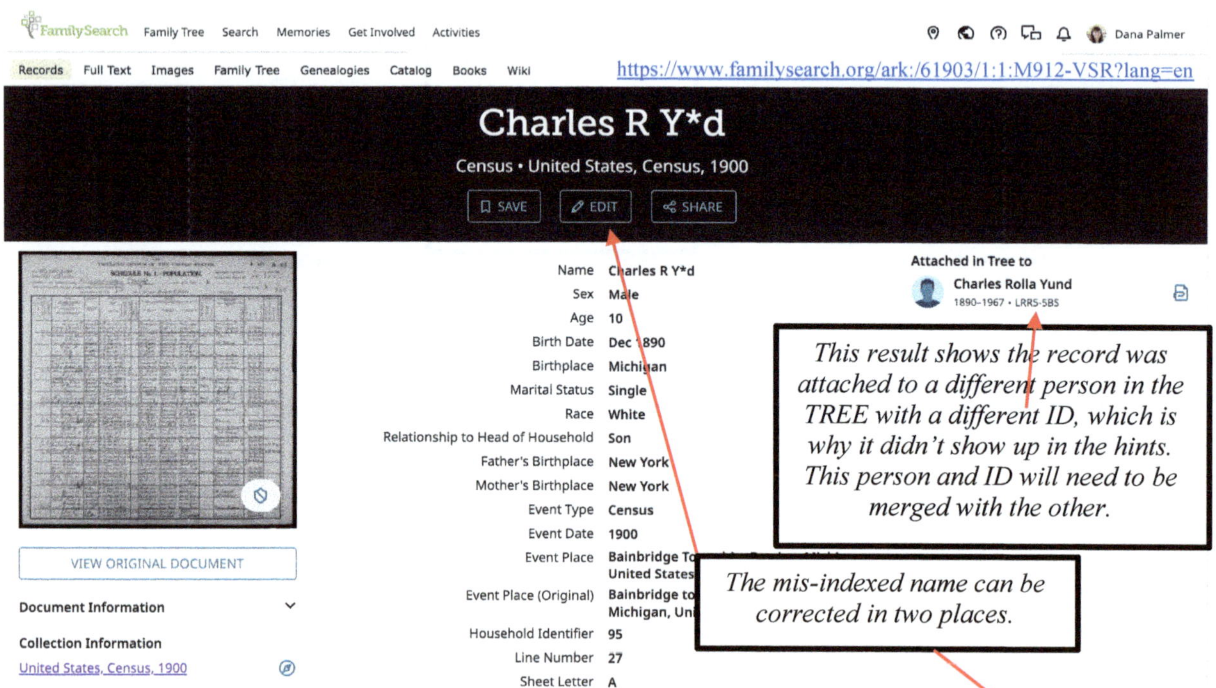

This result shows the record was attached to a different person in the TREE with a different ID, which is why it didn't show up in the hints. This person and ID will need to be merged with the other.

The mis-indexed name can be corrected in two places.

Confirm this is the correct person.

In this case, the two people with different IDs will need to be merged.

If the record is not attached, click SAVE RECORD, then ATTACH TO PERSON IN FAMILY TREE.

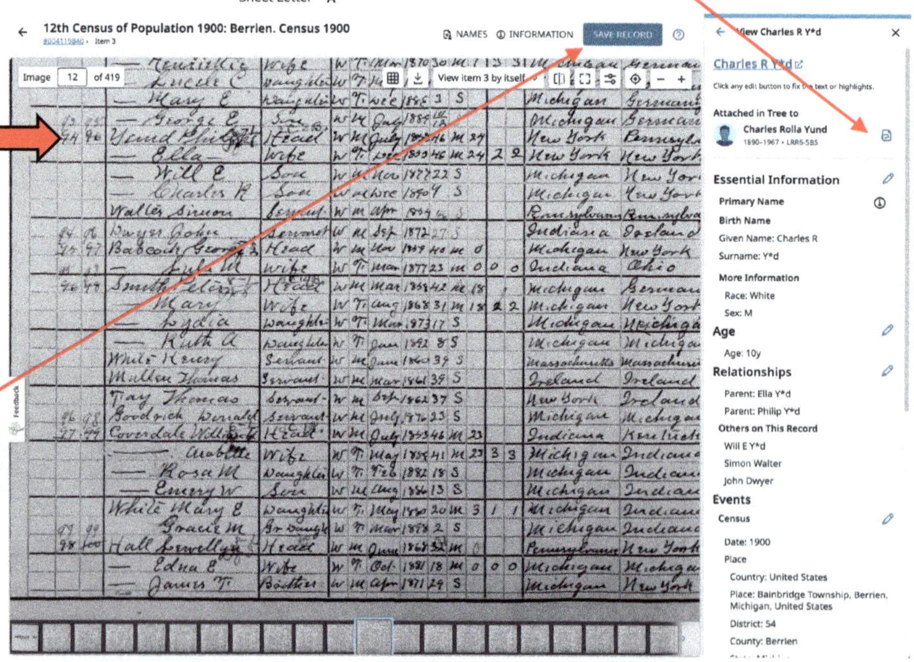

https://www.familysearch.org/ark:/61903/3:1:S3HT-D8QG-66?view=index&action=view&cc=1325221&lang=en&groupId=M9KY-86D&personArk=%2Fark%3A%2F61903%2F1%3A1%3AM912-VSR

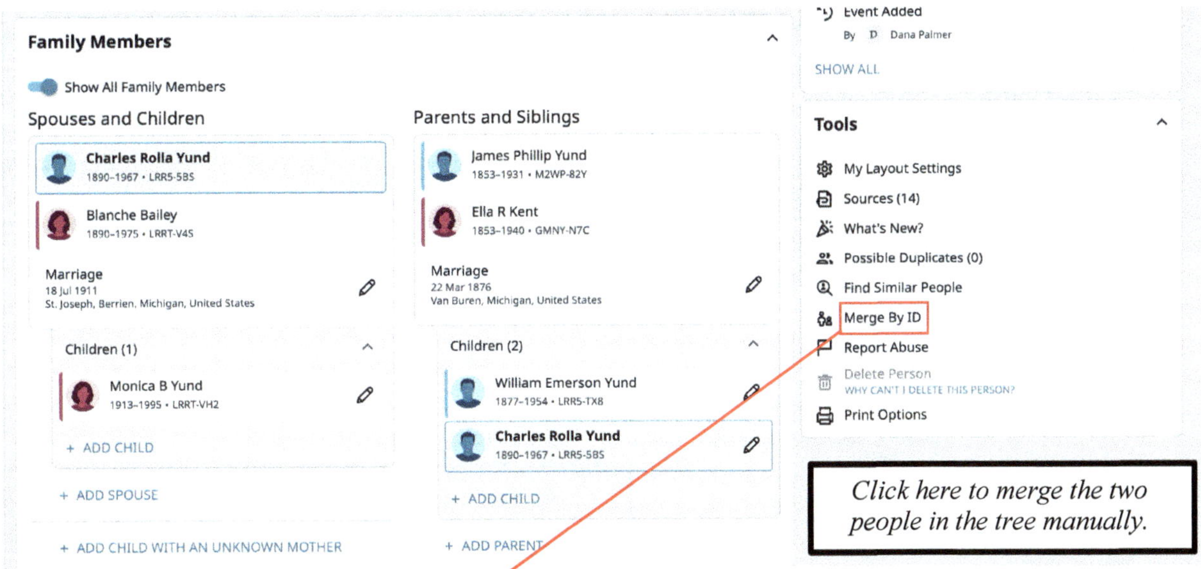

Click here to merge the two people in the tree manually.

https://www.familysearch.org/en/tree/person/details/LRR5-5BS

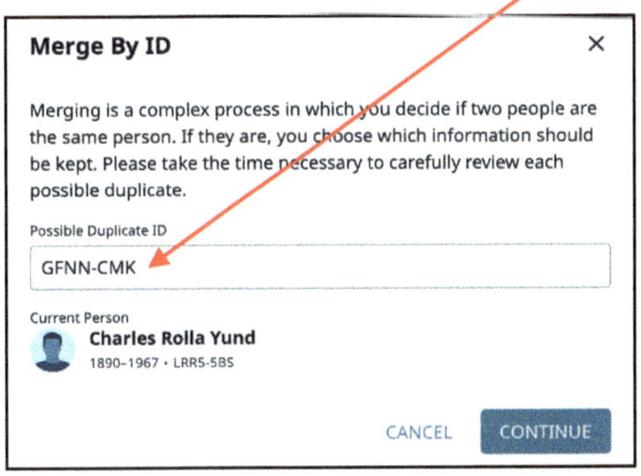

Type in the duplicate ID.

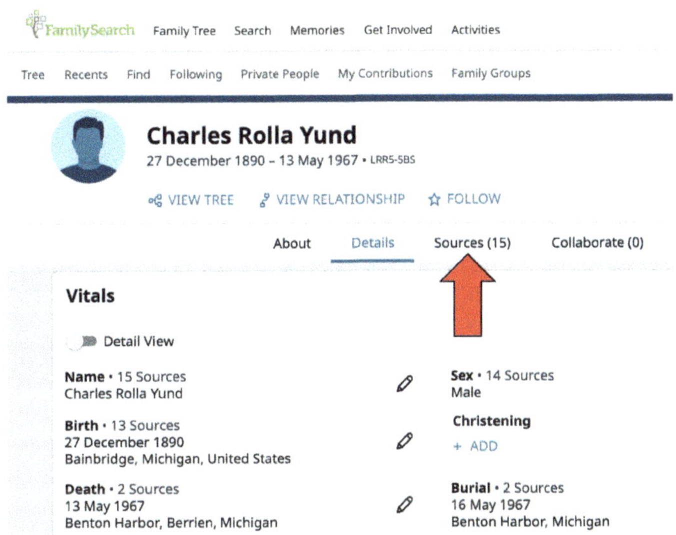

https://www.familysearch.org/en/tree/person/details/LRR5-5BS

https://www.familysearch.org/en/tree/person/details/LRR5-5BS

Because the two IDs were merged, their sources were combined, and the 1900 census was added to this person's SOURCES.

Attaching Records from Other Websites

Records from other websites can also be attached. Go to that person's DETAILS page on FamilySearch and click the affiliate website you want to search under SEARCH RECORDS. FamilySearch will take the information from the TREE and enter it into the affiliate website's search engine. Often, the record for your person will appear at the top of the search results for that website.

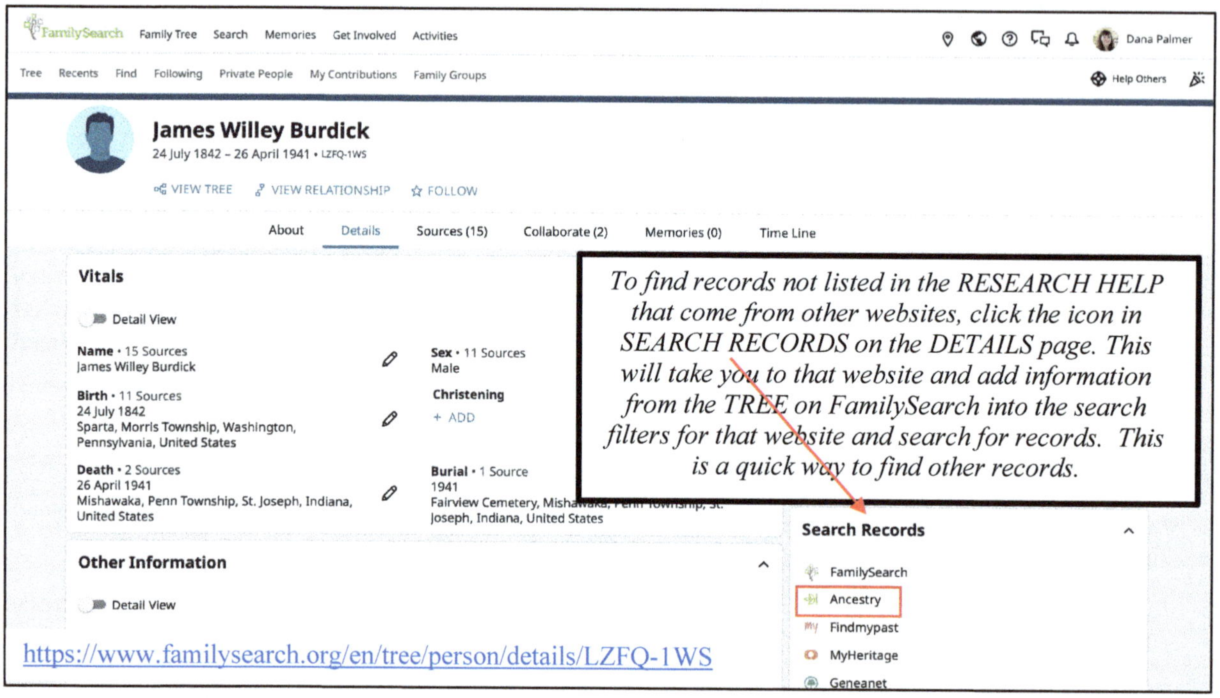

https://www.ancestry.com/search/?name=James+Willey_Burdick&birth=1842_Sparta-Morris+Township-Washington-Pennsylvania-United+States&death=1941_Mishawaka-Penn+Township-St.+Joseph-Indiana-United+States&child=Mary+E._Burdick&child2=Adaline+Louise+%E2%80%9CAddie%E2%80%9D_Burdick&father=Elias+Crandall_Burdick&gender=m&marriage=1880_Meadville-Crawford-Pennsylvania-United+States&mother=Mary+Ann_Willey&searchMode=advanced&spouse=Sarah+A._Hunt

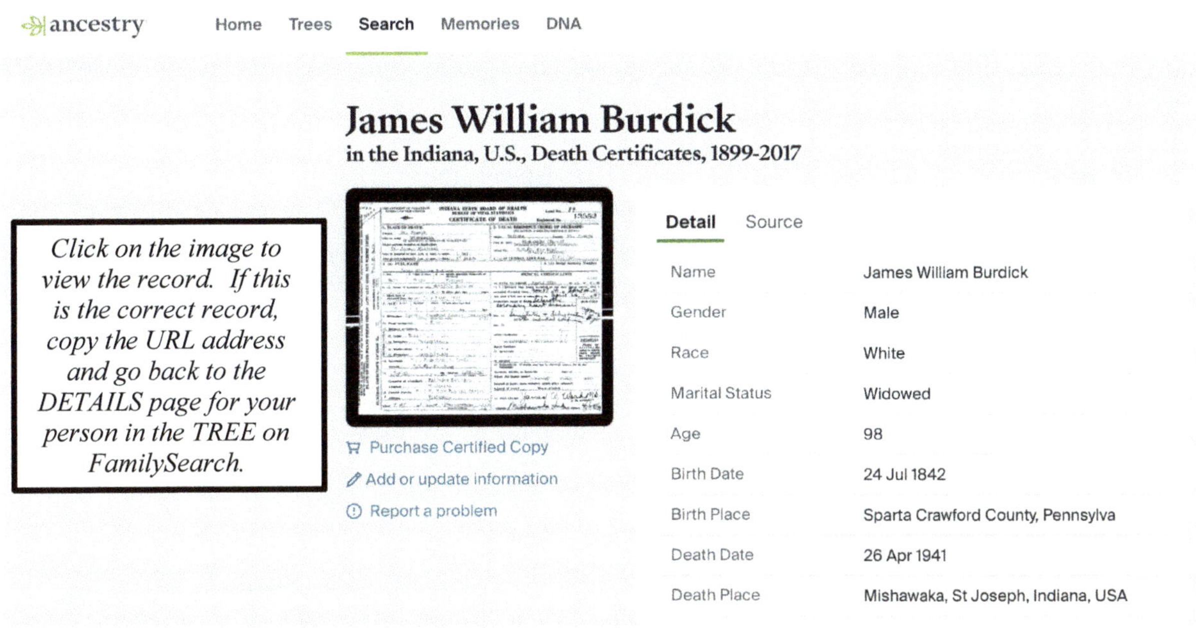

https://www.ancestry.com/search/collections/60716/records/2250444

Be sure to update the related field in the vitals area, then click on the SOURCES tab in the TREE.

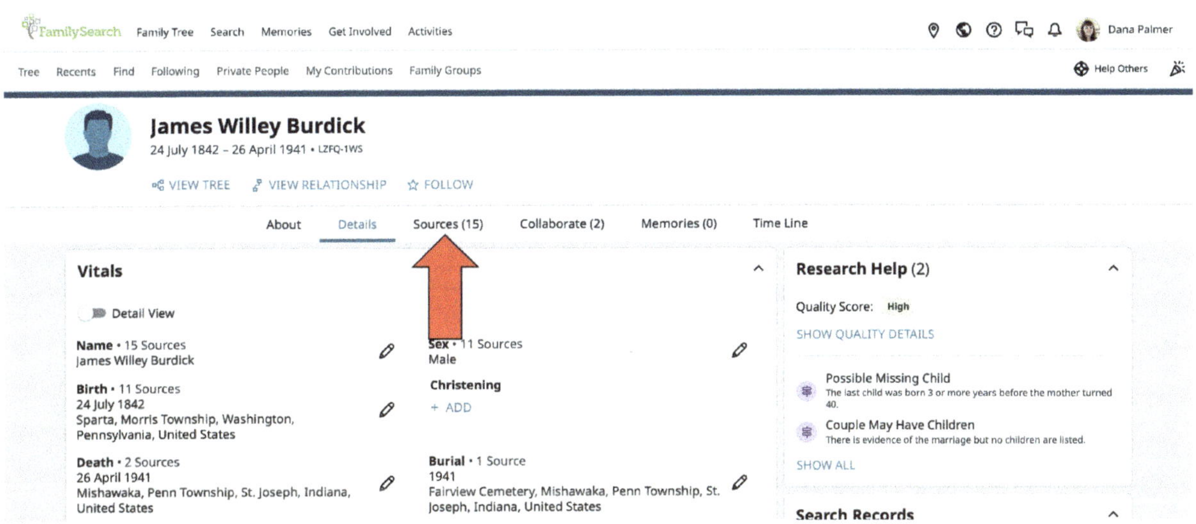

https://www.familysearch.org/en/tree/person/details/LZFQ-1WS

Click on ADD SOURCE, then choose ADD NEW SOURCE.

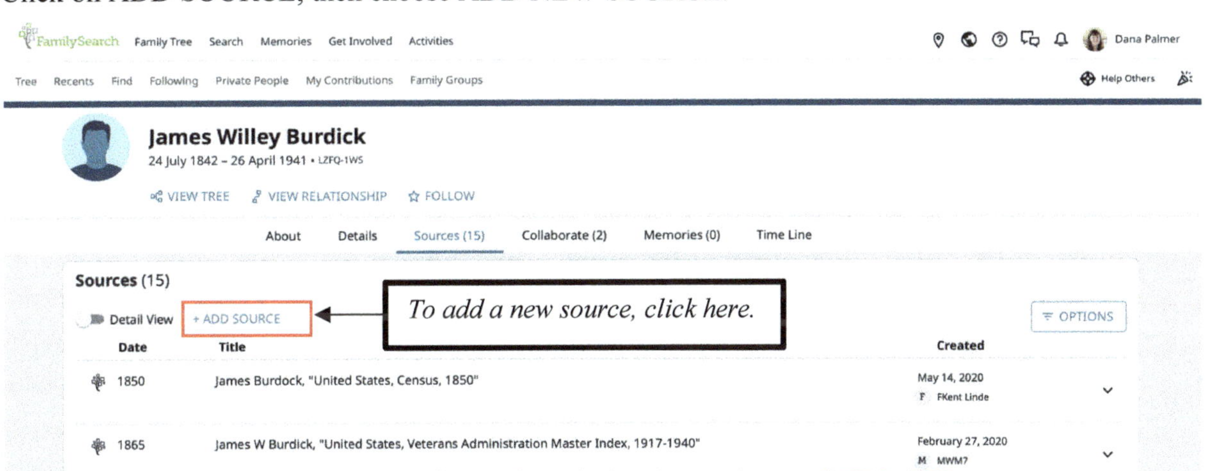

https://www.familysearch.org/en/tree/person/sources/LZFQ-1WS

Type in the date, title, and website link. Be sure to also choose the applicable vital tags. Choose SAVE when done.

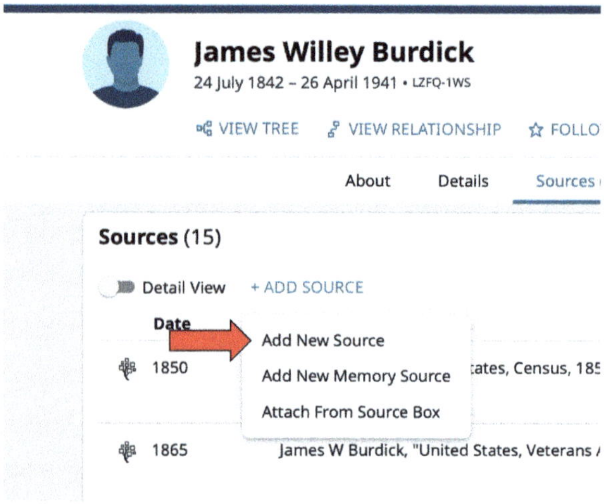

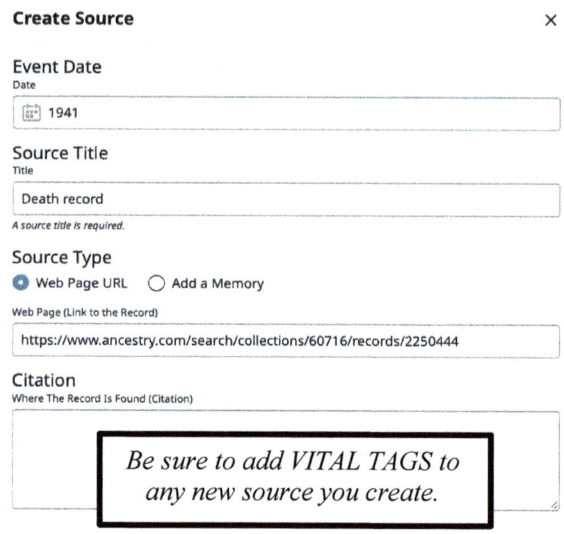

https://www.familysearch.org/en/tree/person/sources/LZFQ-1WS

https://www.familysearch.org/en/tree/person/sources/LZFQ-1WS

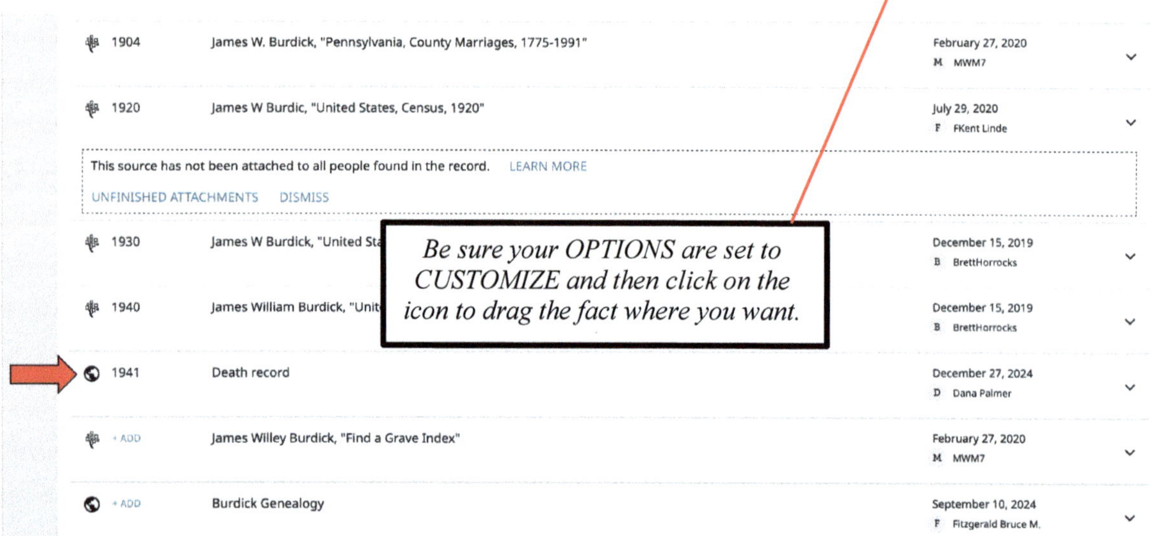

https://www.familysearch.org/en/tree/person/sources/LZFQ-1WS

CETs

CETs, or user owned trees, are being tested in the Labs at FamilySearch. These trees are for individuals and family organizations who want a little more control over who can make changes to the TREE. This is especially important for lines with extensive research or those with conflicting beliefs about the facts for the family. Each CET tree is separate and has a unique owner, unlike the TREE currently on the FamilySearch website. The layout and content is similar to what is in the FamilySearch TREE, and facts can be added as with the FamilySearch TREE. One major difference is that the CET tree can only be edited by the CET tree owner or designated contributors. It can also be uploaded and synced from the contributor's personal database program.

For more information go to: https://www.familysearch.org/en/labs/docs/CETsLearnMore

To apply to be an early tester, go to: https://www.familysearch.org/en/labs/CETEarlyAdoption

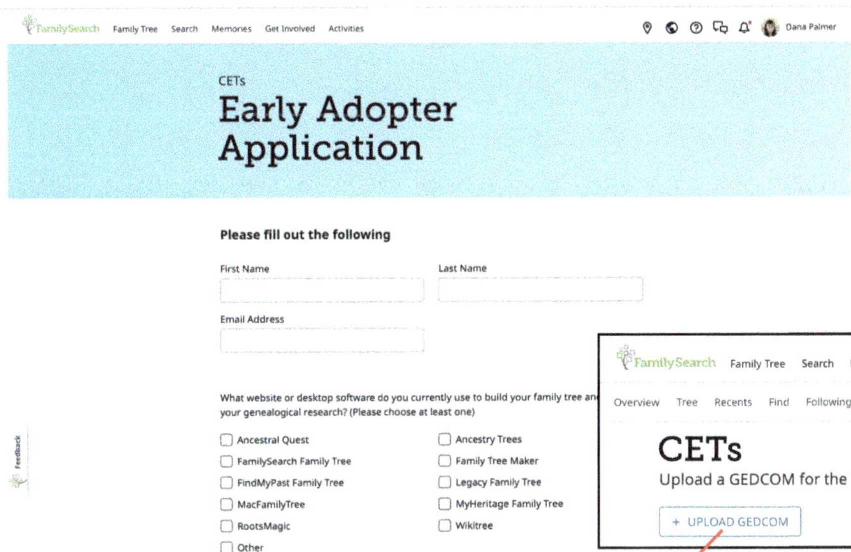

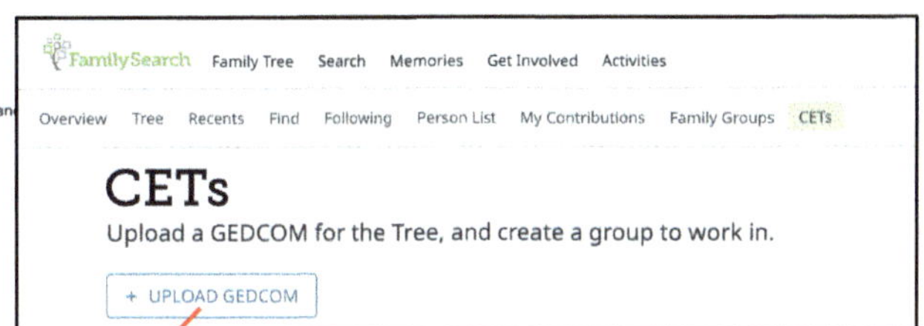

Once you are approved to add to the CETs, you will get prompted to upload your GEDCOM.

Be sure you have edited and formatted the information in your personal database before you create and upload your GEDCOM, so you don't have to fix errors in your CET after it is uploaded.

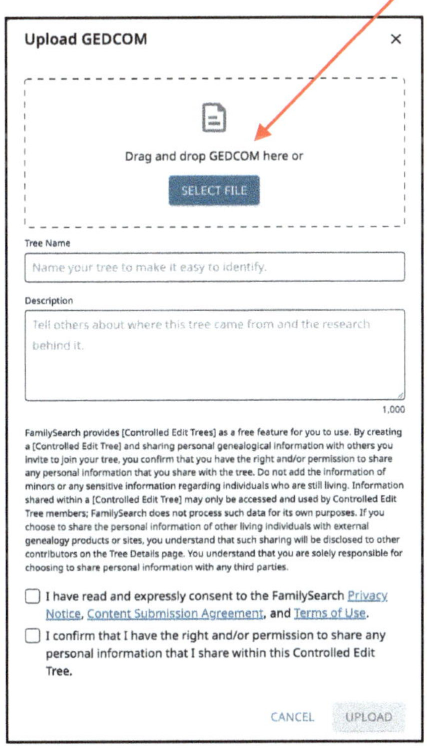

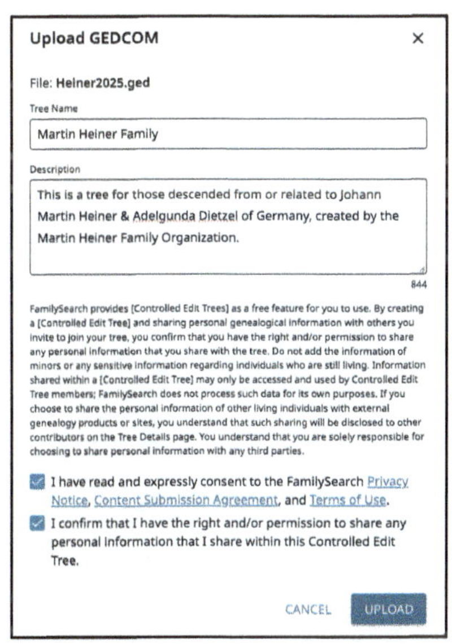

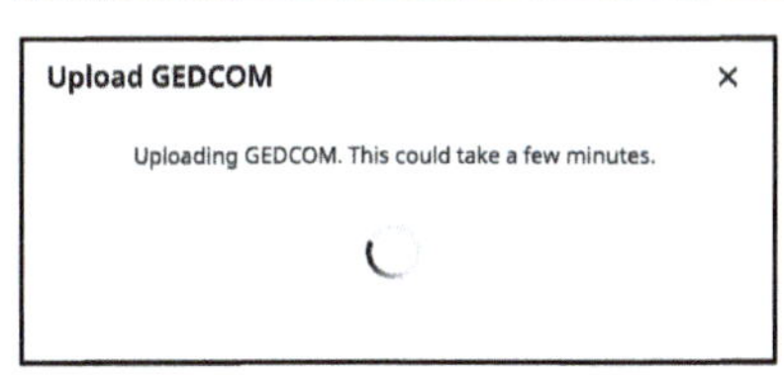

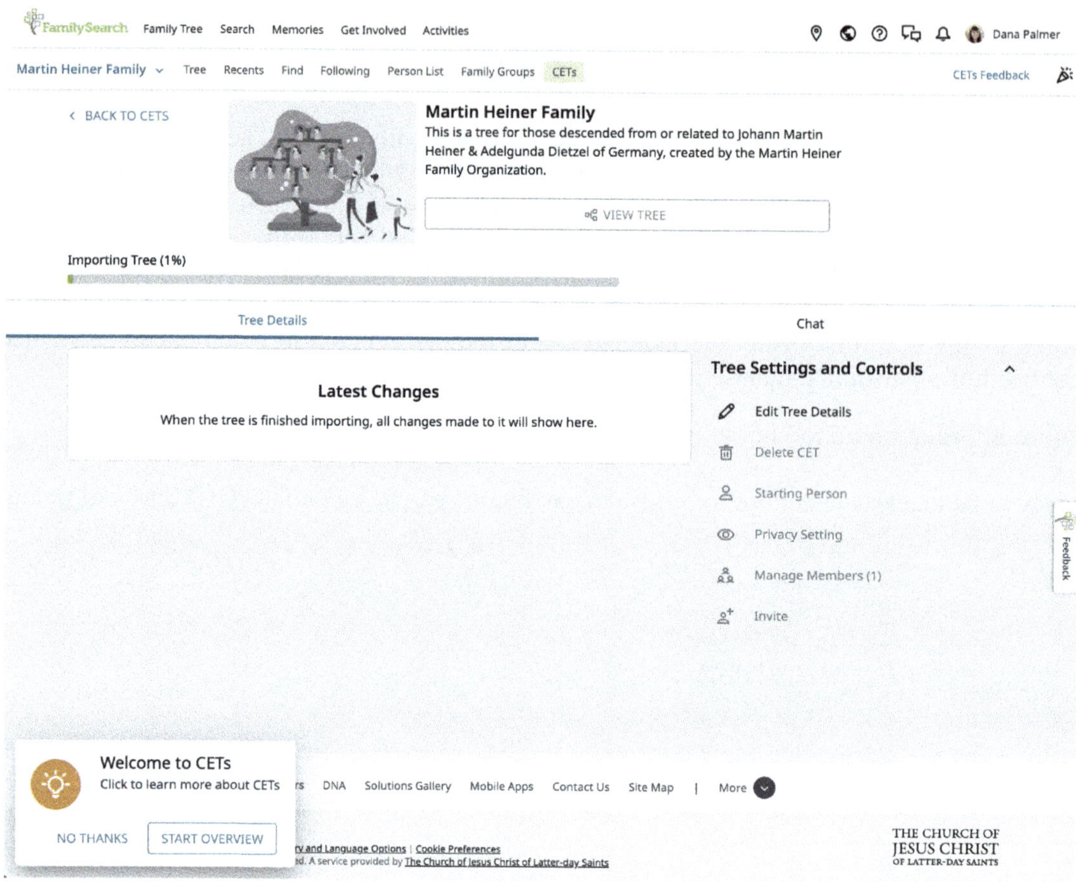

Once the GEDCOM is finished uploading, it will show the latest changes made to your tree. To view the contents of the tree, click VIEW TREE.

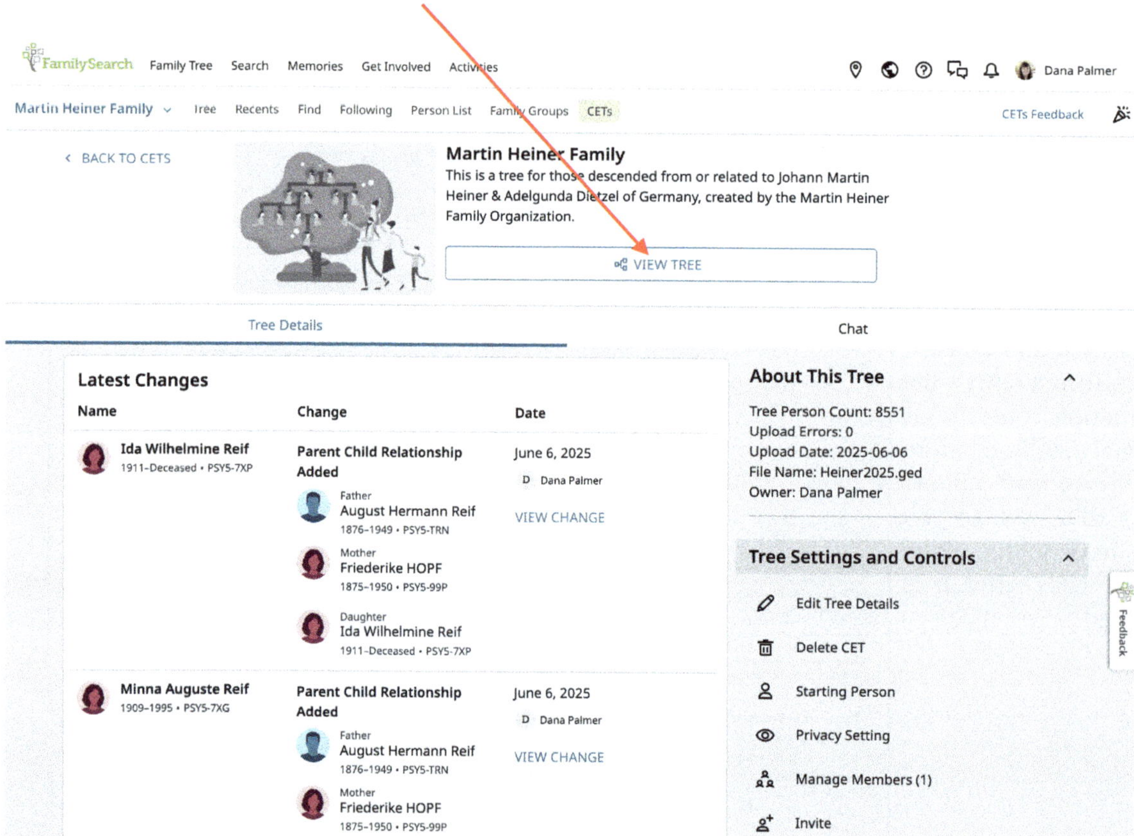

Designate who you want to be your STARTING PERSON from the list of names in your newly uploaded tree. Then click on VIEW [Name of your tree], in this case, VIEW MARTIN HEINER FAMILY.

Your tree will open in Pedigree view to the person you have designated as the starting person. The CETs are look like the TREE you find on FamilySearch.

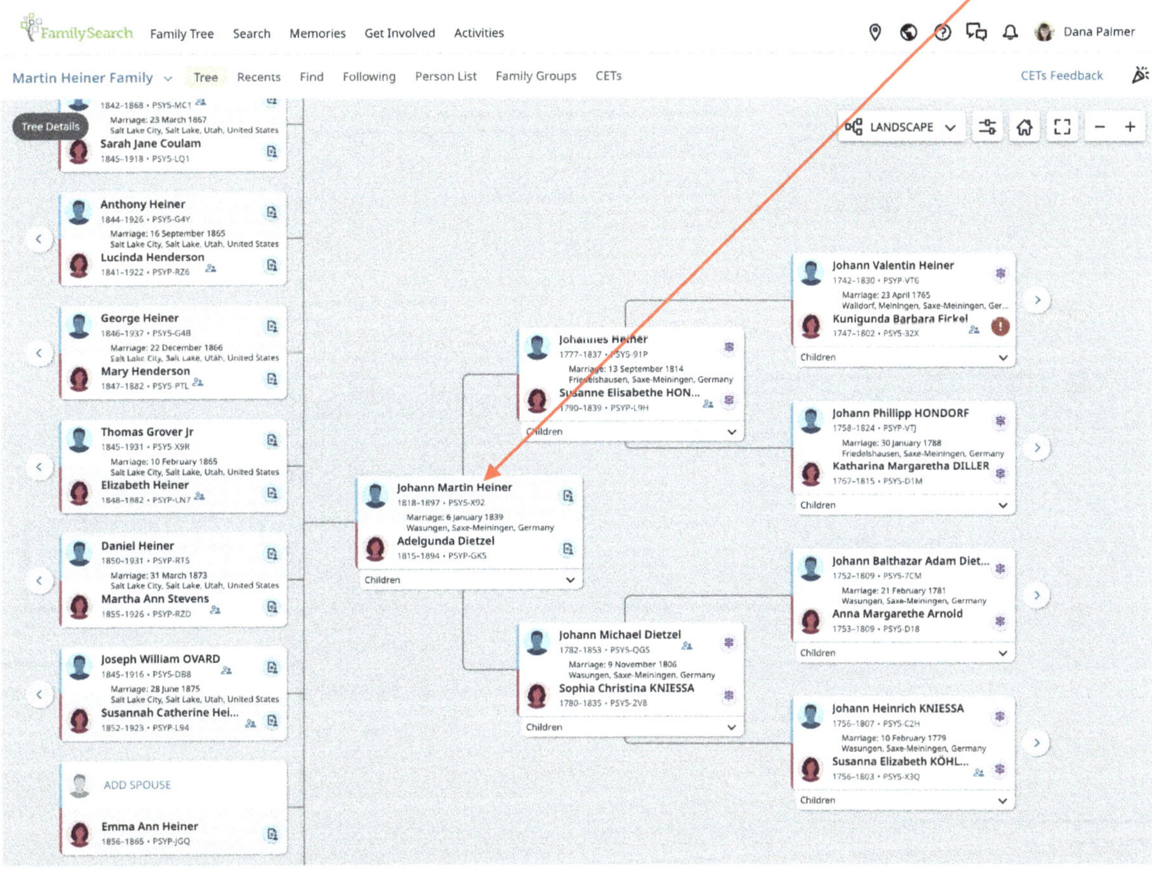

To change names, dates, places, add new people or sources, click on the person's name in the Pedigree view until you get a pop-up screen to the side. Then either click on the person's name or the word PERSON and you will be redirected to that person's DETAILS page, where you then can make changes.

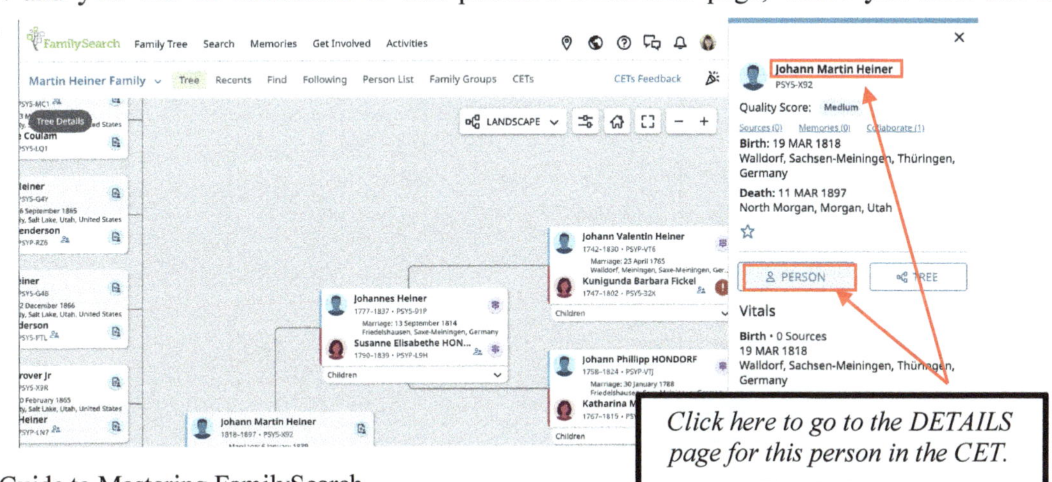

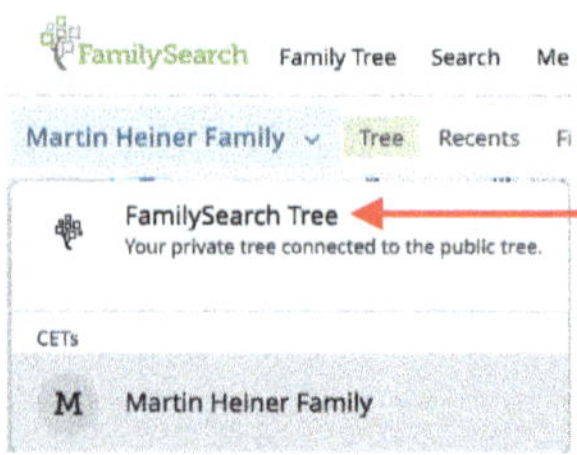

To leave CETs and go back to the TREE in FamilySearch, click the icon in the upper-left corner with the name of the CET you are viewing, and select FAMILYSEARCH TREE.

CETs have unique features of being edited only by the tree owner or designated contributors, which is not a feature in the TREE in the main part of FamilySearch.

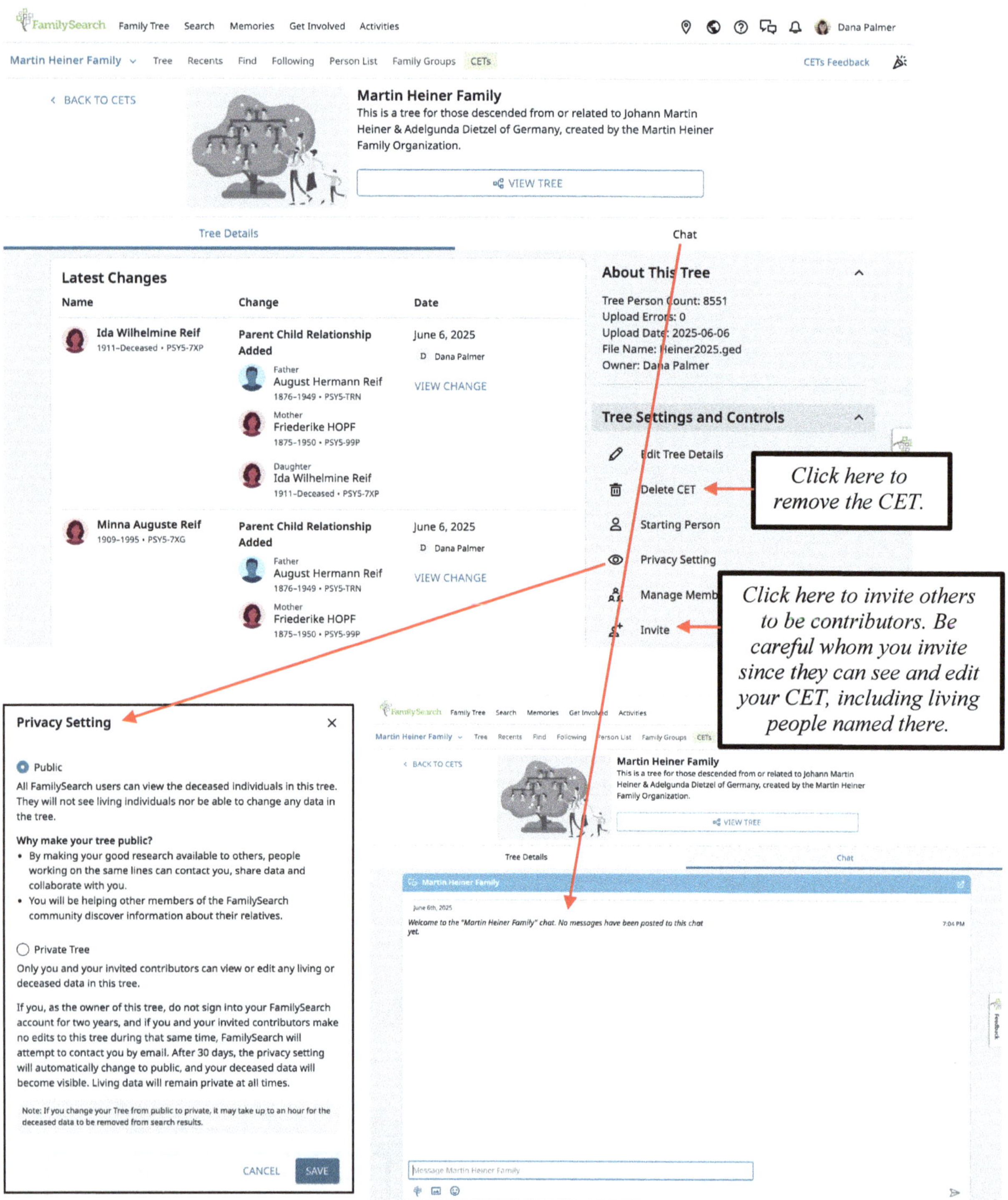

Chapter 7: Books

BOOKS

FamilySearch has collaborated with libraries worldwide to digitize their family histories, yearbooks, biographies, county histories, maps, atlases, and other useful genealogy books and currently has over 500,000 books in their digital collection (https://www.familysearch.org/en/library/books/).

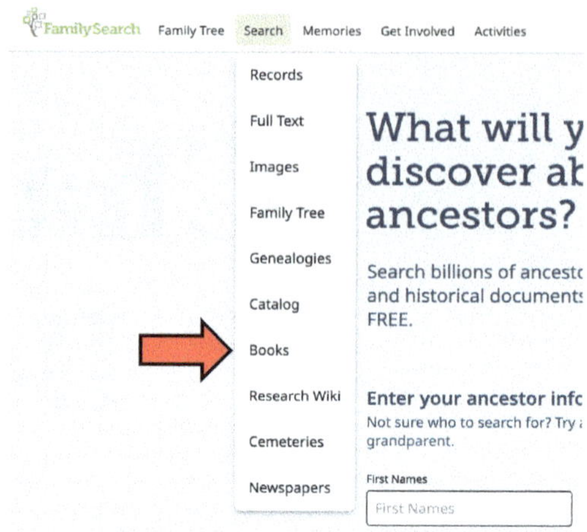

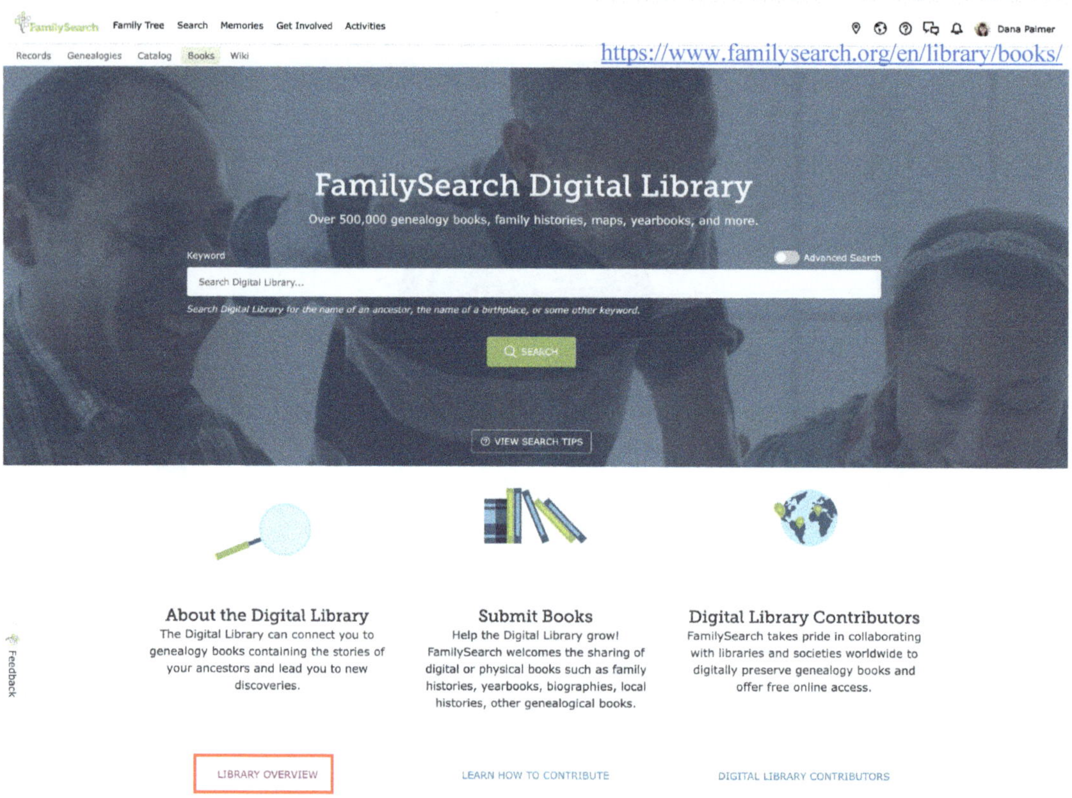

https://www.familysearch.org/en/library/books/

There are a lot of other terrific resources and links in these tabs about FamilySearch's digital collection. Be sure to check them out!

https://www.familysearch.org/en/family-history-library/digital-library

To find a book go, to the SEARCH tab, and click BOOKS from the dropdown menu. Type a surname, location, or keyword into the search box. You will then get a list of topics that relate to your search parameters. If you need to narrow your parameters, you can use exact searches, Boolean search terms, or wildcards. Use quotation marks for more exact searches such as "Tippecanoe County." Boolean searches use the capitalized words AND, NOT, and OR. Wildcards use an asterisk (*) to replace several letters and a question mark (?) to replace a single letter.

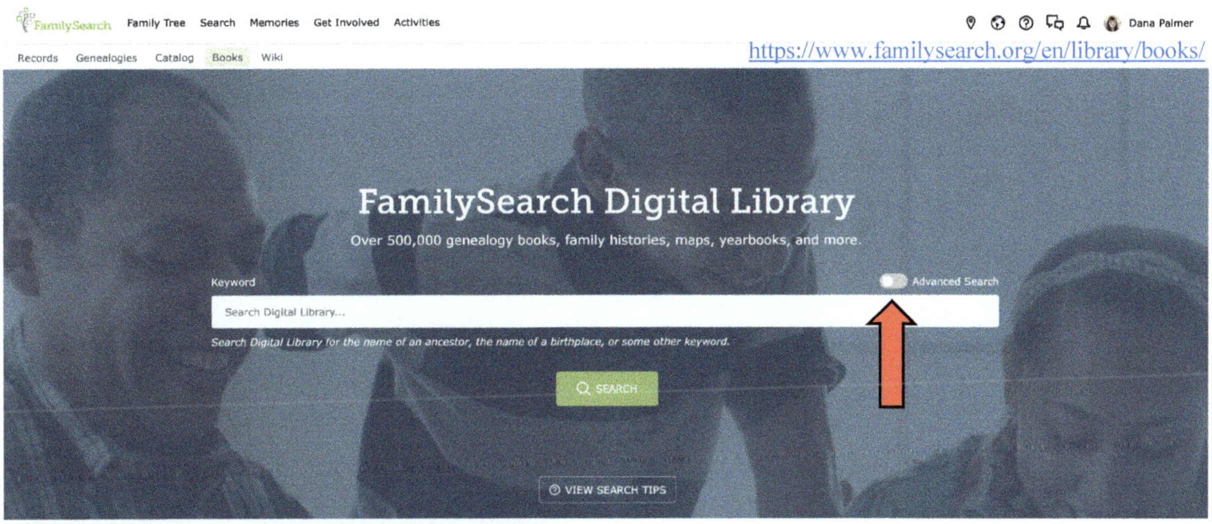

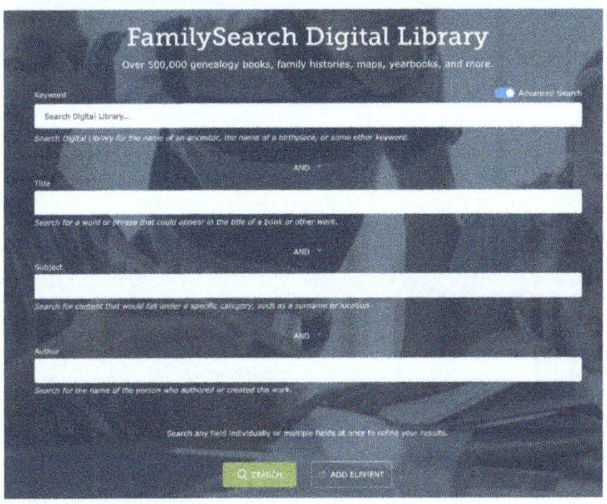

The ADVANCED SEARCH filter allows more search parameters to help you find books about your family or the location where they resided. These can be keywords, titles, subjects, or authors, and can be used with exact searches using parenthesis, Boolean terms, or wildcard replacements.

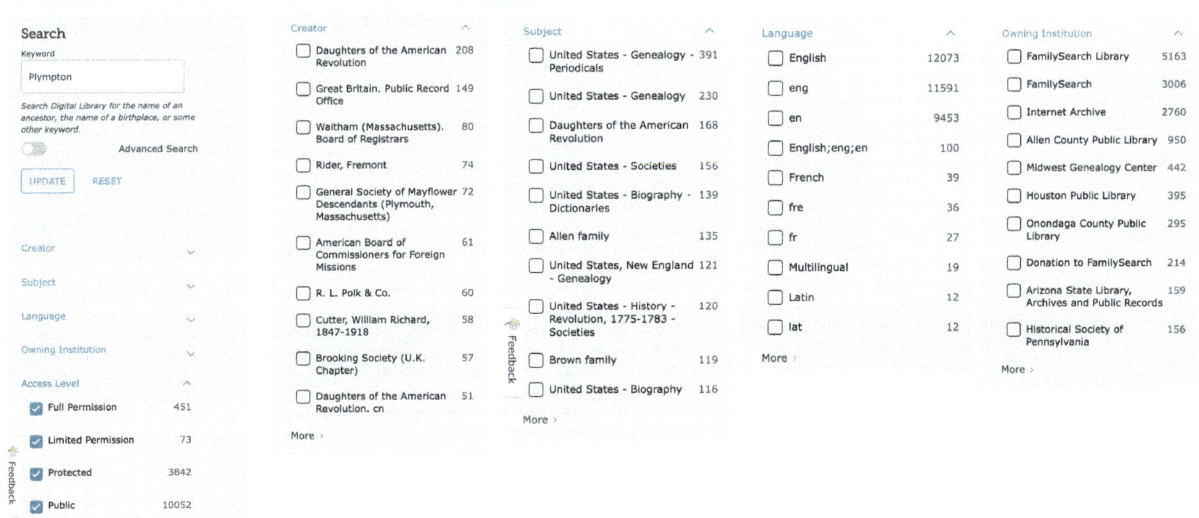

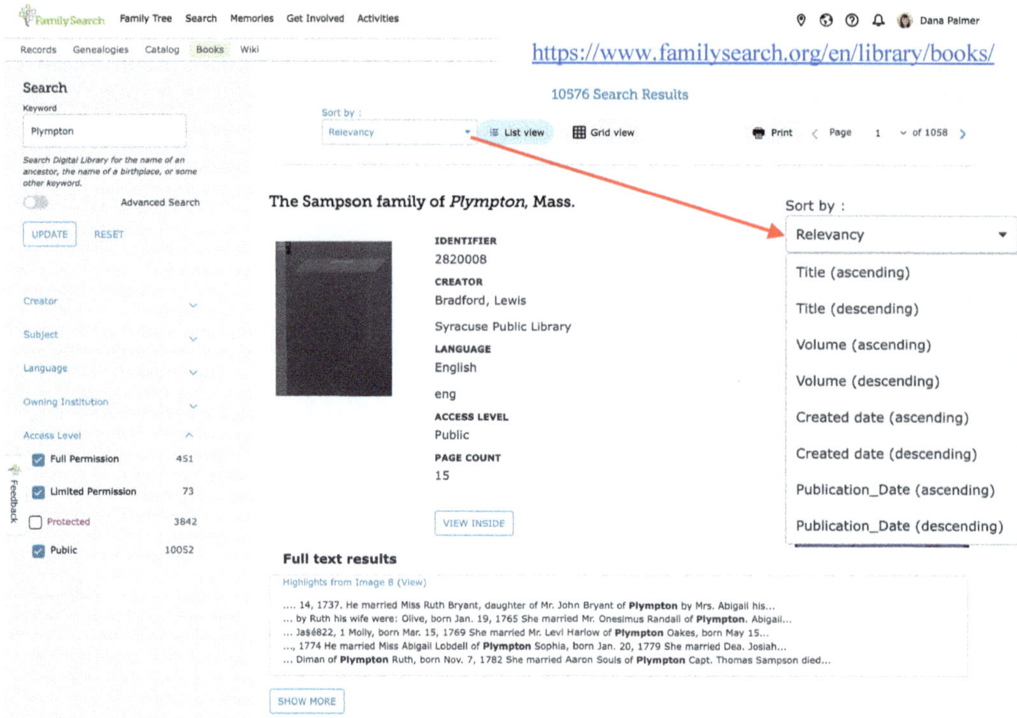

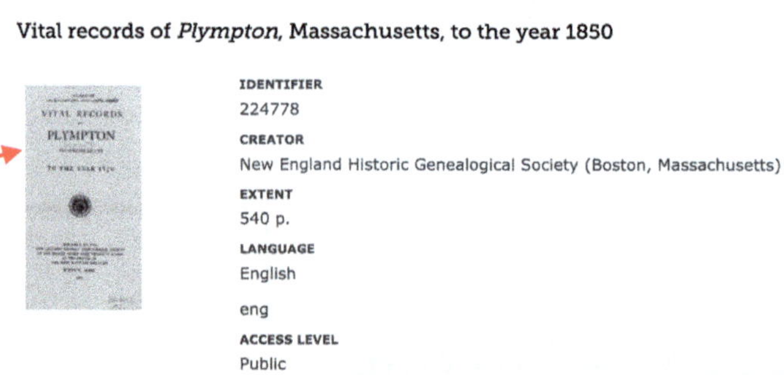

Finding transcripts of the original records can help you determine if your person is probably in those records, which can save time when trying to find the orginal record.

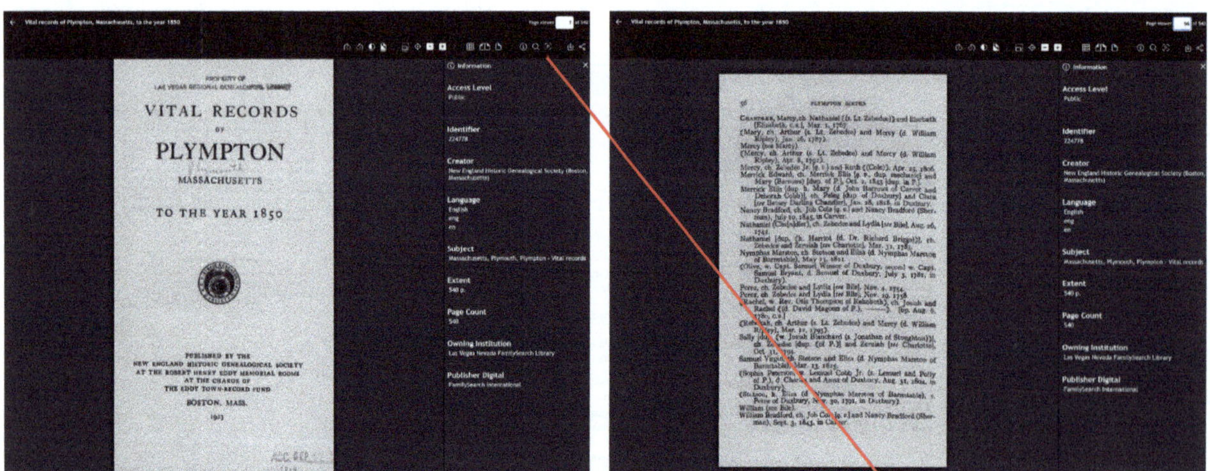

https://www.familysearch.org/library/books/viewer/397335/?offset=3&return=1#page=1&viewer=picture&o=info&n=0&q=

The magnifying icon will allow you to search for names or keywords within the document. This is a fast way to find records within the text.

Chapter 8: Memories

GETTING STARTED WITH MEMORIES

The MEMORIES feature of FamilySearch is a great way to preserve your family photos, documents, and audio clips. MEMORIES can be added to your GALLERY or attached directly to a person in TREE. It is a lot easier to attach a memory to a specific person in the family TREE than to attach one in the GALLERY and then attempt to link it to the correct person in the TREE.

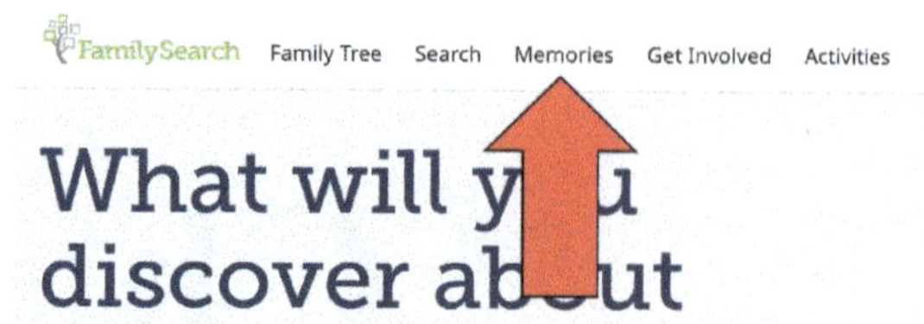

To add or search for photos, documents, or audio clips in your account, click on the MEMORIES tab at the top of the screen.

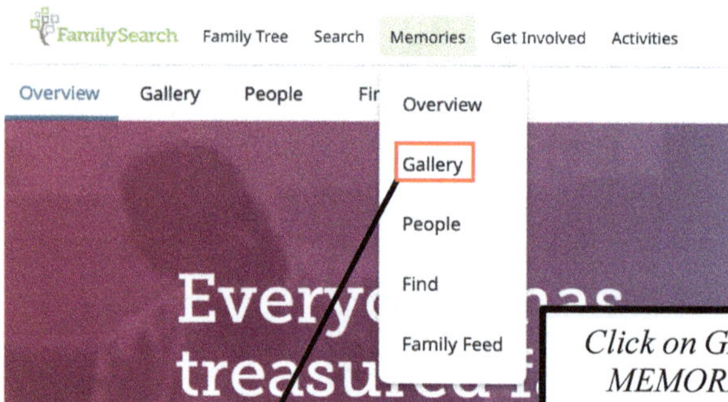

Click on GALLERY to see all the MEMORIES you have added.

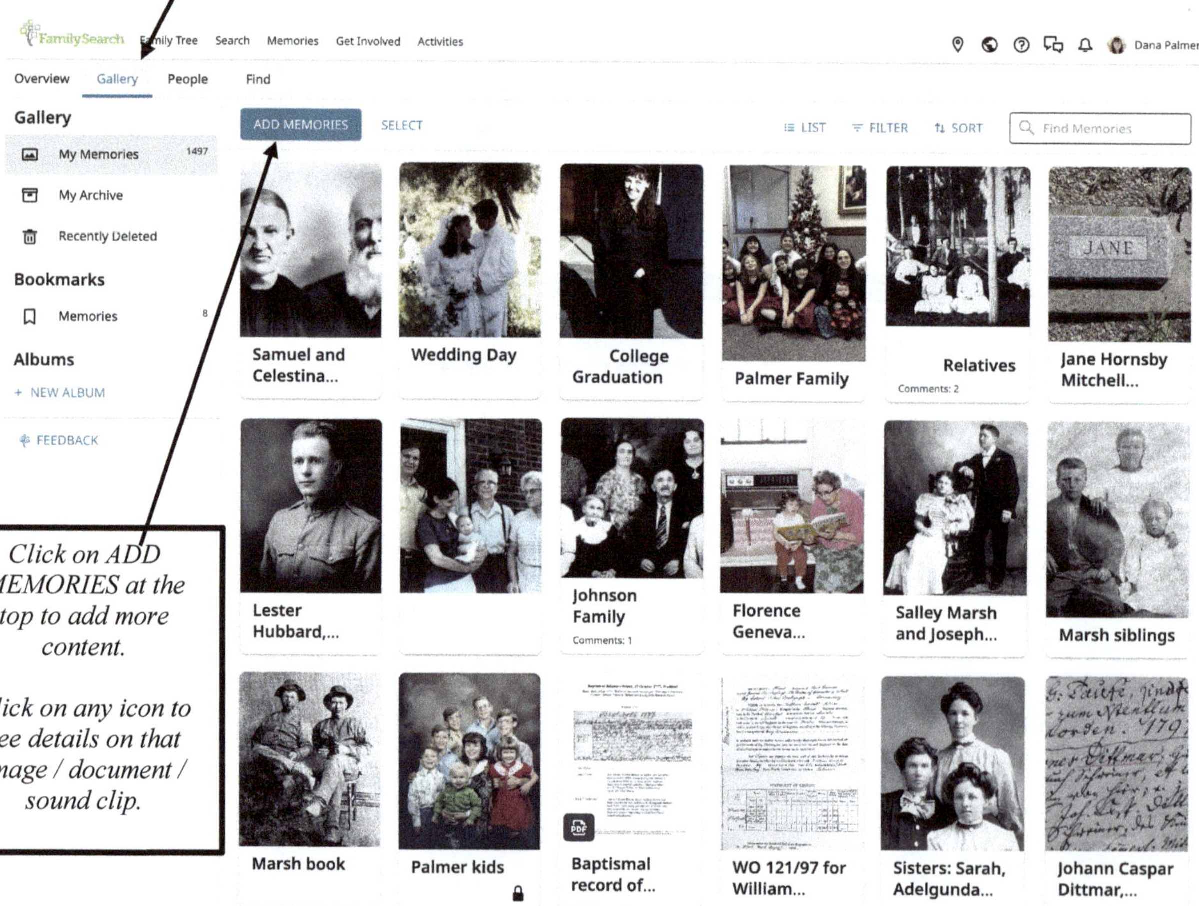

Click on ADD MEMORIES at the top to add more content.

Click on any icon to see details on that image / document / sound clip.

https://www.familysearch.org/en/memories/gallery

Public or Private Memories

Each photo or document can be classified as Public or Private, allowing you the ability to preserve all your memories, even for living people. If you select the Private setting, no one can see that memory except for you (the person who added it). Photos and documents for living people should always be marked Private. Having the MEMORIES private is a great way to preserve photos and records of living people that you wouldn't otherwise add.

Do you know everyone in the photo? Tagging people in a photo is a great way to identify everyone in the photo, even if the photo is marked private.

Each person in a photo can be tagged and identified. Tagging each person makes it easy to discover who everyone is in the photo. Hover your mouse over each person and their name will pop up if they are tagged. To add a tag, click on the face in the photo and type their ID or choose a name from the list that pops up. Remember to add "Topic Tags" for photos and documents, especially military photos with other persons in them. Titles and tags in photos can be searched if they are added. This is a great way to share your photos or to find more photos of your family.

ADDING PHOTOS

You can add photos by uploading them to your GALLERY or by going to that person's DETAILS page in the TREE on FamilySearch and clicking MEMORIES, then by clicking the ADD MEMORIES button. Before you add a photo to FamilySearch, it is advisable to edit it using photo editing software.

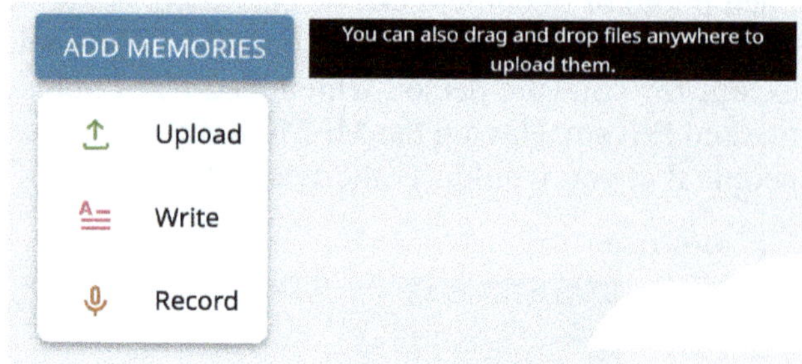

Click on ADD MEMORIES to upload a file, write a story, or record an audio clip. Drag the image (or SELECT FILES) to ADD MEMORIES, or select GALLERY to add an image / document / audio clip already in your GALLERY.

If you have never added a photo for a person in MEMORIES, the following screen will appear when you click ADD MEMORIES.

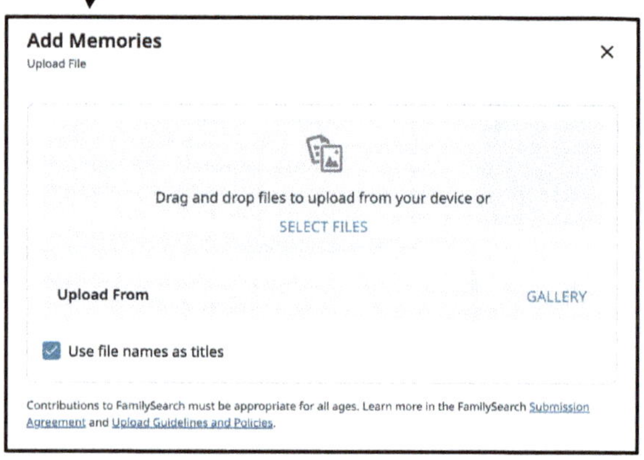

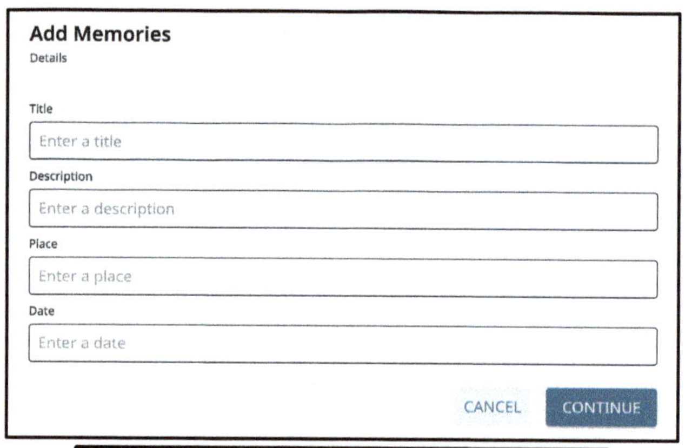

Be sure to add a title and description.

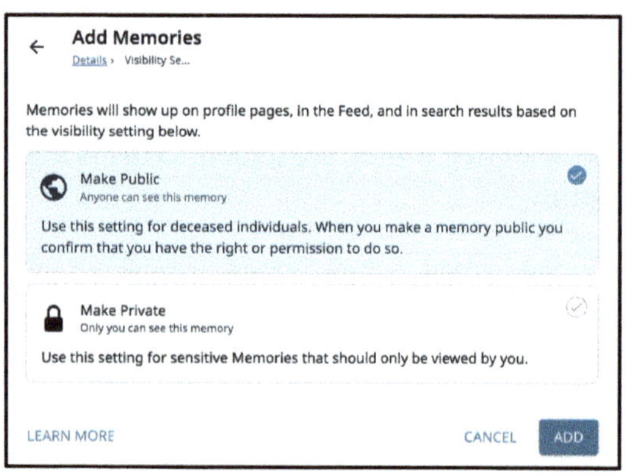

Choose whether the memory is to be public or private. MEMORIES with living people should always be marked private. You can always change this visibility status later, if desired.

To add a memory the easiest way, go to that person's DETAILS page in the tree.

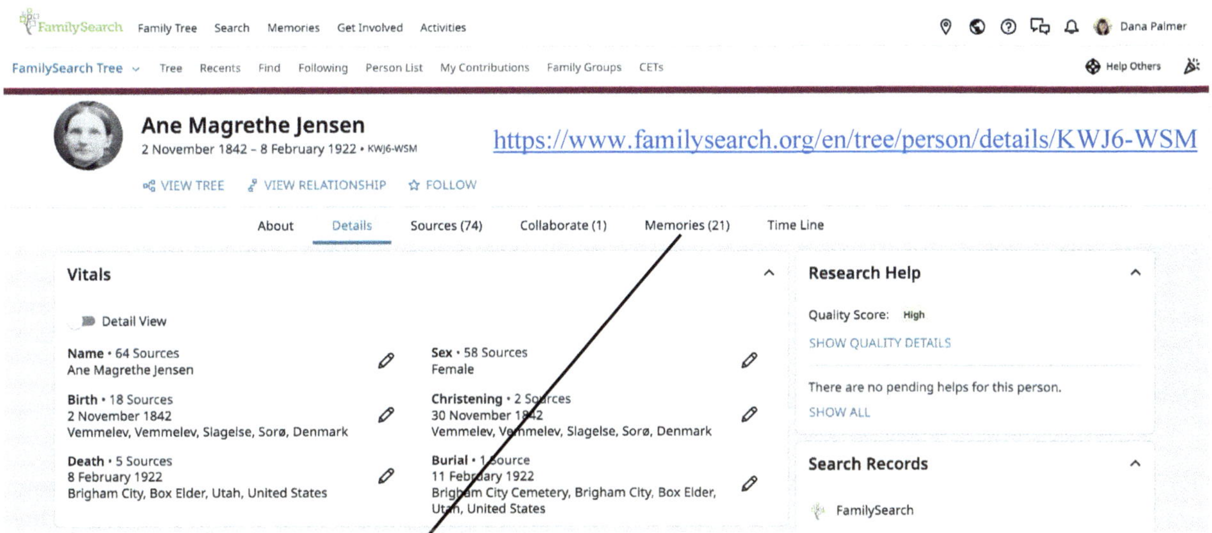

https://www.familysearch.org/en/tree/person/details/KWJ6-WSM

Click on MEMORIES, then ADD MEMORIES.

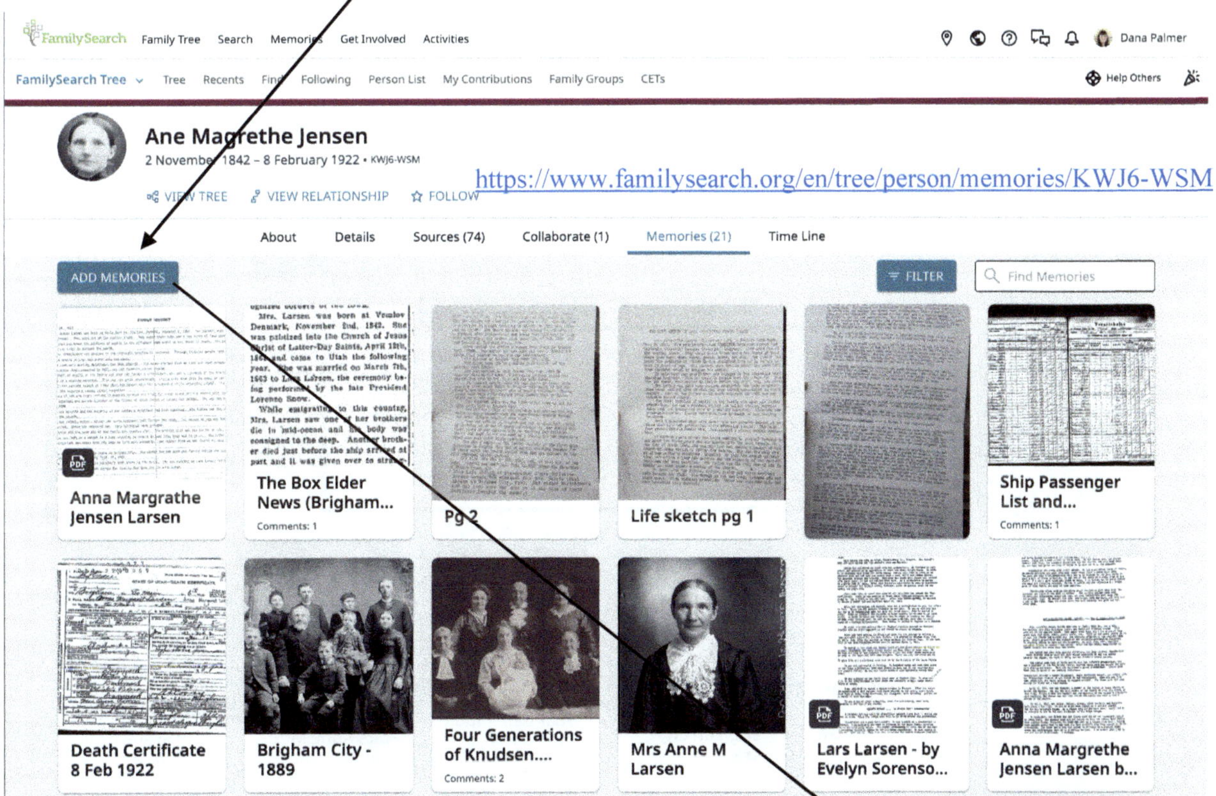

https://www.familysearch.org/en/tree/person/memories/KWJ6-WSM

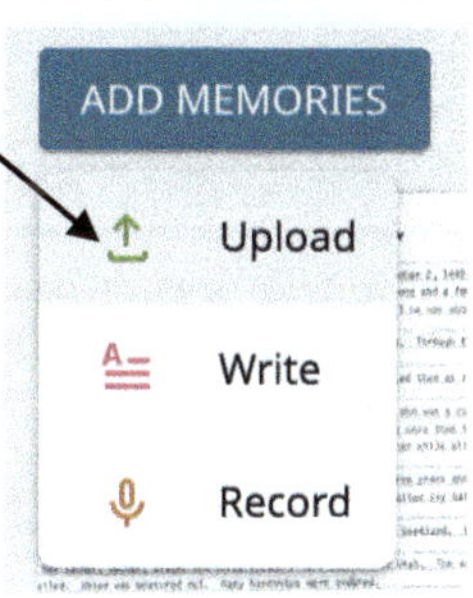

Select what type of memory you want to add:

- UPLOAD (jpg, tif, bmp, png)
- WRITE (pdf)
- RECORD (mp3, m4a, wav)

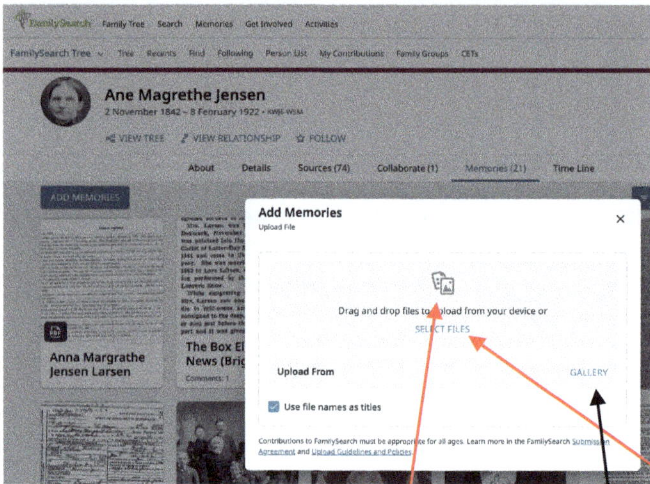

To upload the file, you can (1) DRAG AND DROP the file, (2) SELECT FILES (from your computer), or (3) choose a photo already loaded from the GALLERY. Each memory must be under 15 MB. Once you have added your memory, it will be processed to be sure it is family friendly and not violating any copyrights. You can tag the file while it is processing.

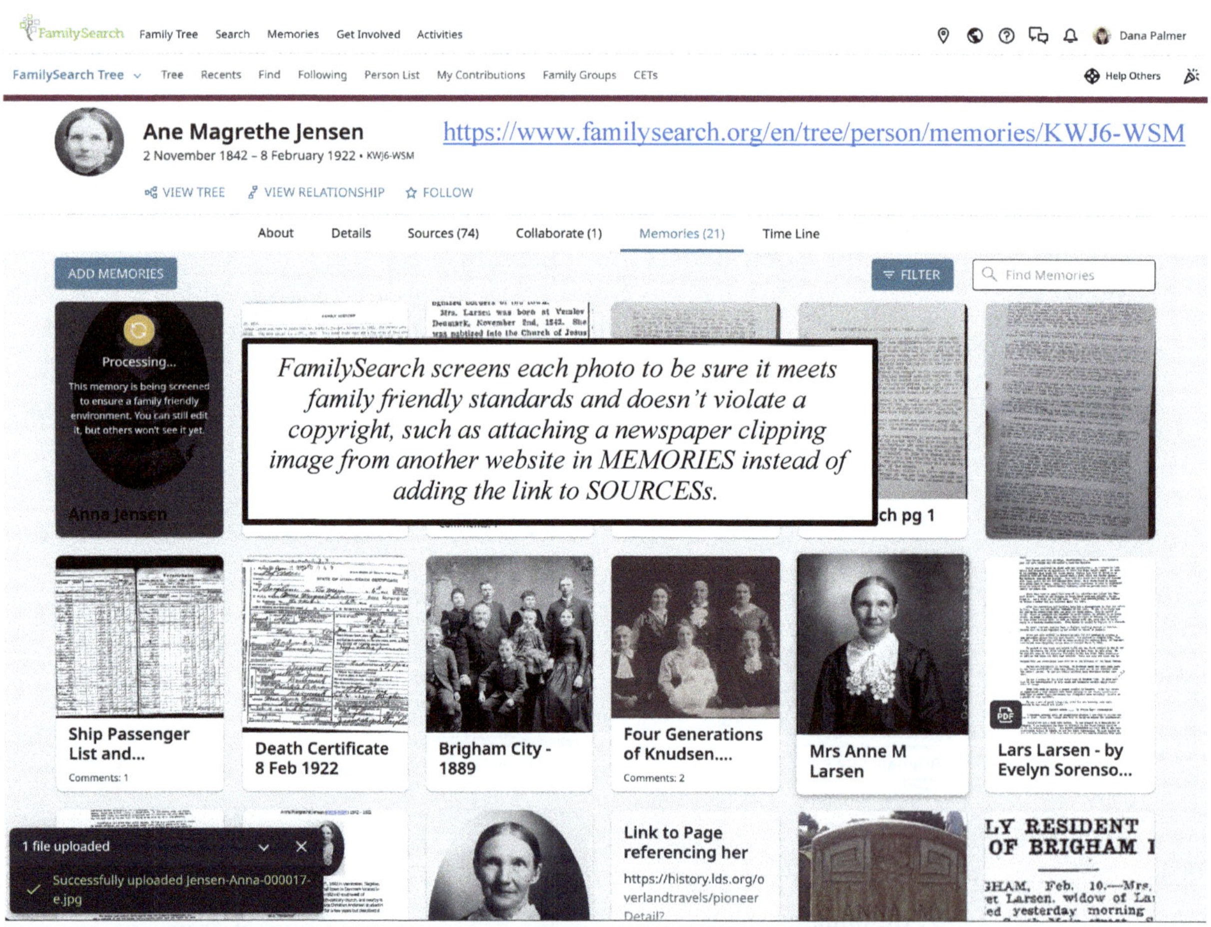

FamilySearch screens each photo to be sure it meets family friendly standards and doesn't violate a copyright, such as attaching a newspaper clipping image from another website in MEMORIES instead of adding the link to SOURCESs.

A note will appear at the bottom once the file has been successfully uploaded. If you add a memory that does not meet the family friendly standards or violates the copyright, it will be removed, and you will get an email stating it couldn't be added, even if you had already tagged it while it was processing.

As the photo is being screened, you can click on the person to tag him / her. It's best to use a small, focused tag around the applicable person's face, so when others hover their mouse over the face, that person can be easily identified. Focused tagging is especially important for photos with a lot of people in them. If you make a mistake and tag the wrong person or the wrong place in the photo, you can always delete the tag by clicking the information button, then selecting the DELETE button.

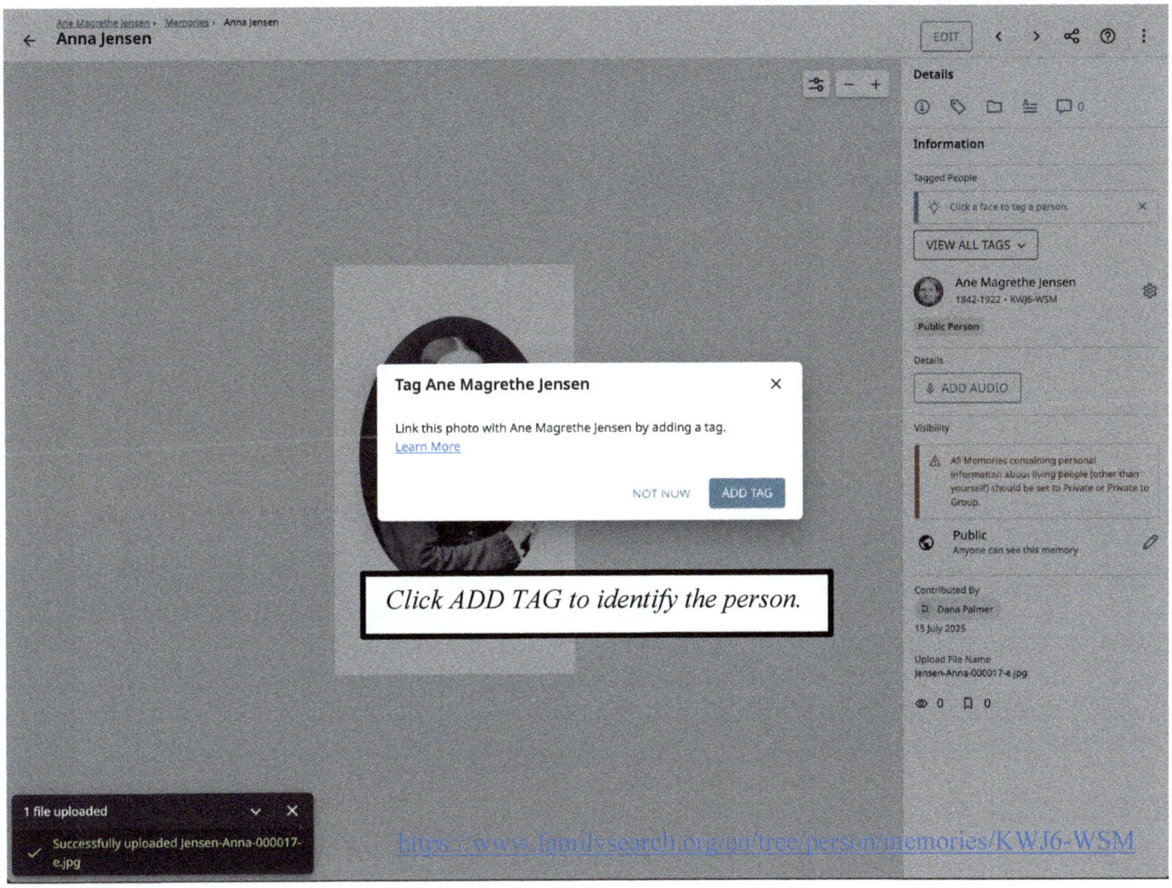

Click ADD TAG to identify the person.

The system will arbitrarily mark a place to tag, which is not usually the face.

Adjust the box to identify the correct person, then click the green check mark when done.

FamilySearch will note who tagged the photo, the date it was tagged, and provide a link to the person in the TREE.

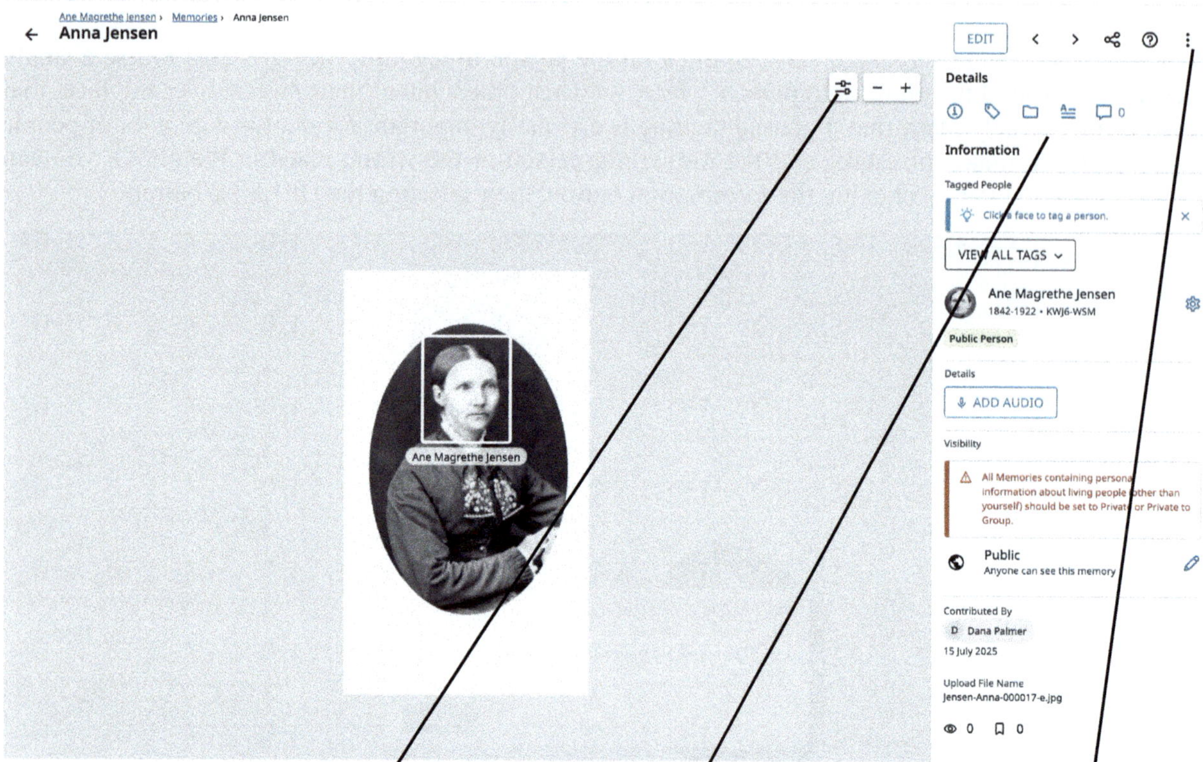

https://www.familysearch.org/en/tree/person/memories/KWJ6-WSM

Adjustments can be made to each photo. You can also add topic tags, organize the memory into an album, add a story, make a comment on the photo, or share by clicking the icons under the DETAILS category for that memory. Photos are invaluable when they have audio clips with them to make these people come alive. Who doesn't want to hear the voice of their beloved family members to go along with a cherished family photo?

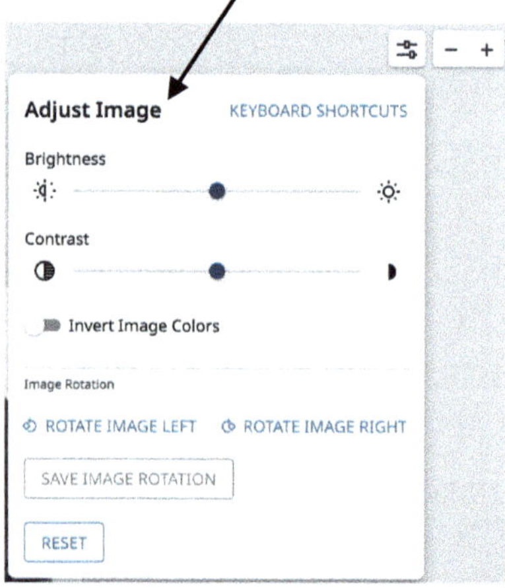

Images can be rotated and adjusted here.

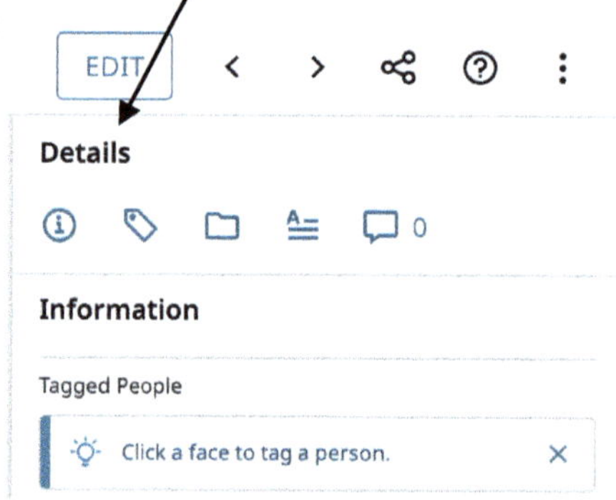

You can add Topic Tags, Organize the Memory into an Album, add Stories, Comments, or Share by clicking these icons.

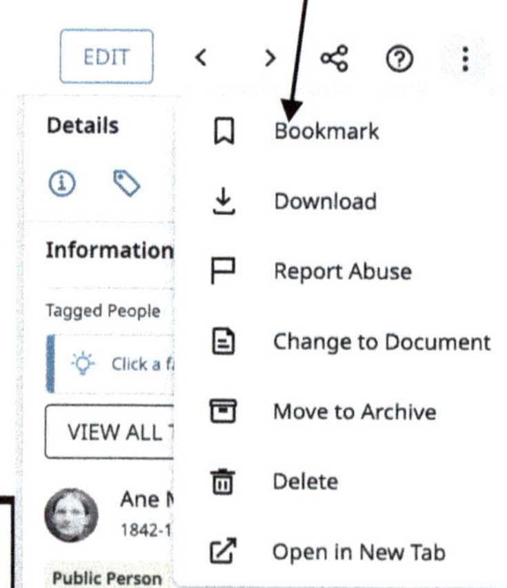

You can make more adjustments to the memory here, or delete it, if desired.

You also can indicate whether you want the photo to be public / private, or change the visibility status by clicking on the EDIT button.

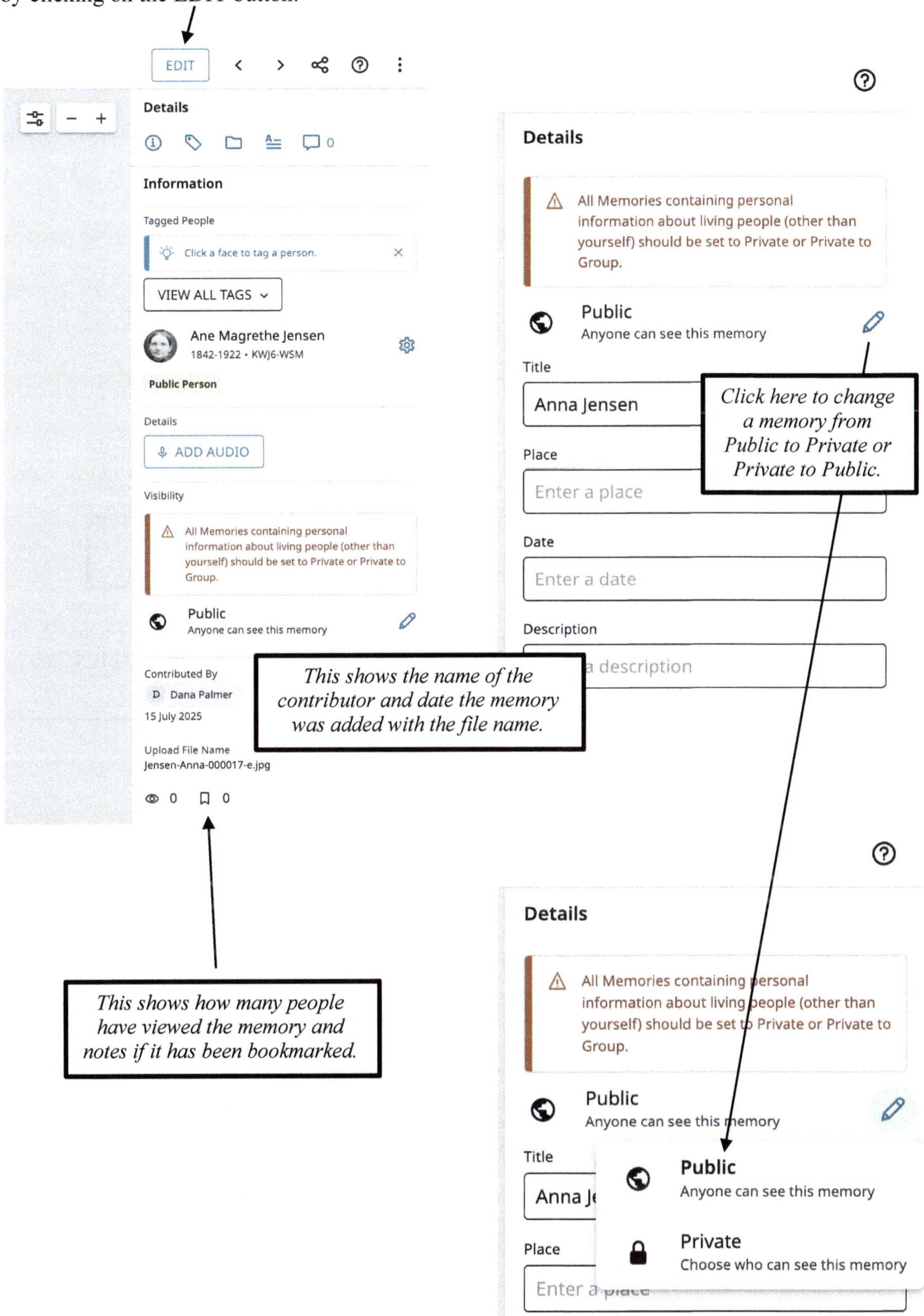

Each person in a photo or name in a document can be tagged. Tagging all the people in a photo or document not only allows you to add the memory to your GALLERY, but it also adds the photo / document to each tagged person's MEMORIES. To tag a new person, click on their face (or name, if a document) and start typing their name. Be sure to visit that person's DETAILS page in the TREE before tagging their name in the photo / document. Their name usually will appear in the list of choices when you click to tag the document, and it saves time.

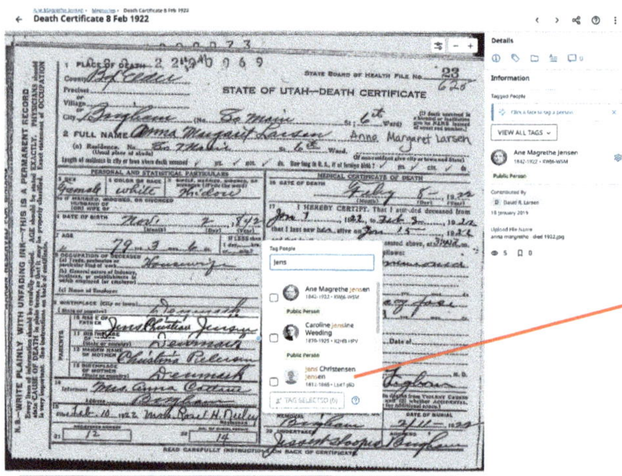

Start typing their name to tag them. Select the correct person if they appear in the list.

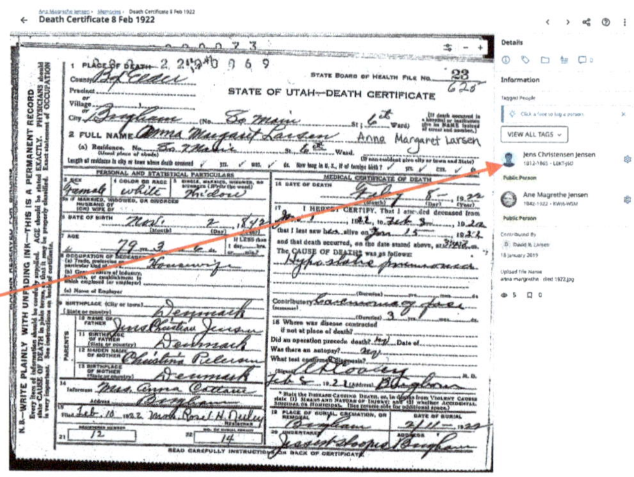

Their name will appear in the list of tagged people.

If their name doesn't appear in the list of choices, you can add the name by typing their name in the box. Their tag will appear as a broken link since it is not attached to a person in the TREE. Click on ATTACH TO TREE, then type in their ID code to link to the correct person.

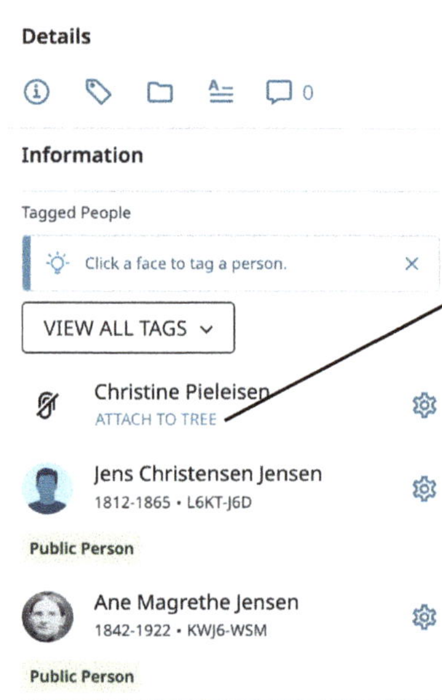

Her name was typed as it appeared in the document, even though it was recorded incorrectly in the record.

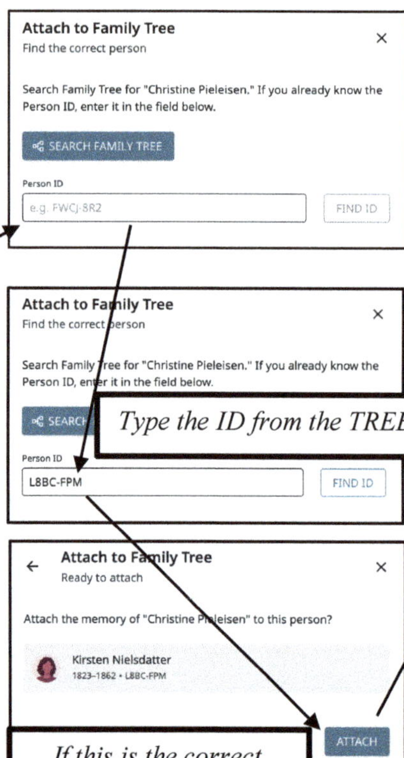

Type the ID from the TREE.

If this is the correct person, click ATTACH.

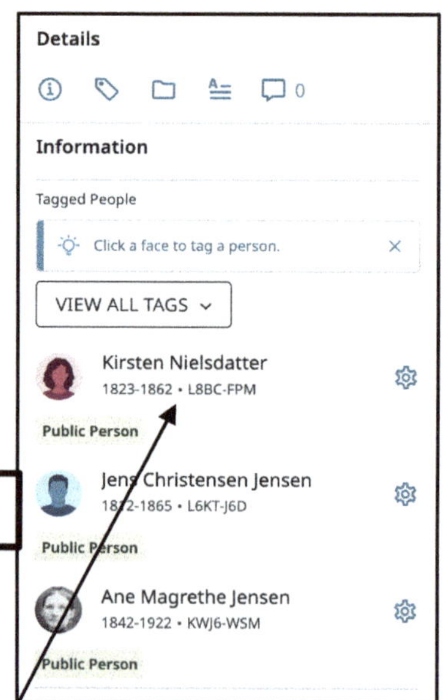

She is now tagged to this document even though her name was recorded incorrectly.

Chapter 9: Other Tools

COLLABORATE

Changes to People You Follow

For those in the tree you are FOLLOWING, you will get a notification once a week specifying the weekly changes to these people, if any. The notification shows exactly what was changed, who made the change, and the date it was changed. Click on the contributor who made the change if you need to contact them.

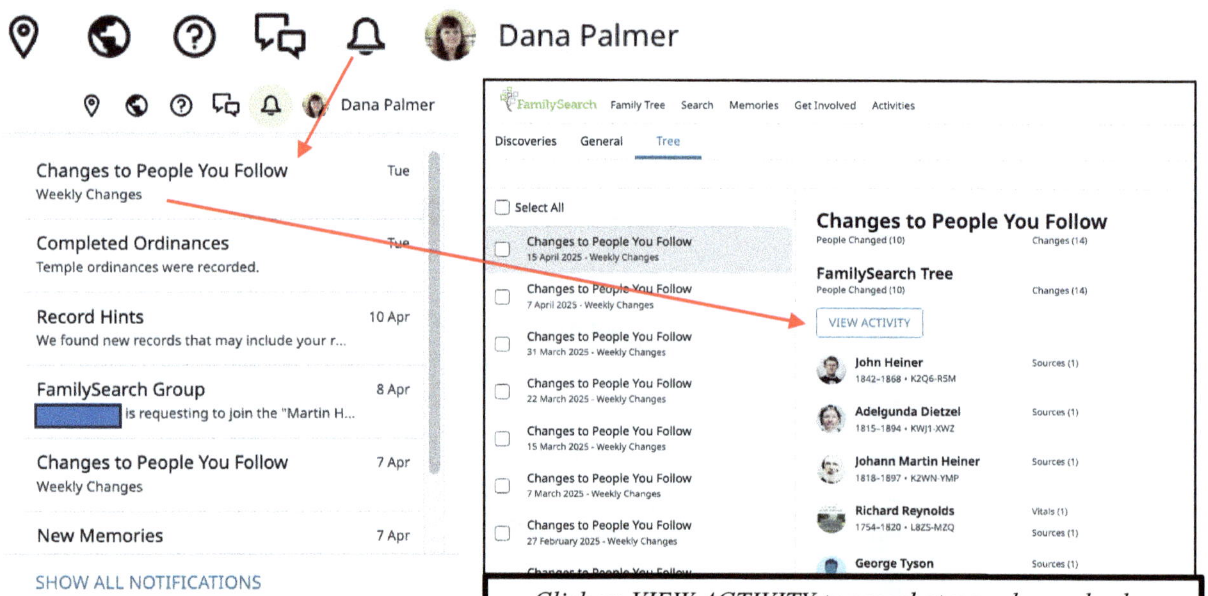

Click on VIEW ACTIVITY to see what was changed, who made the change, and the date it was changed.

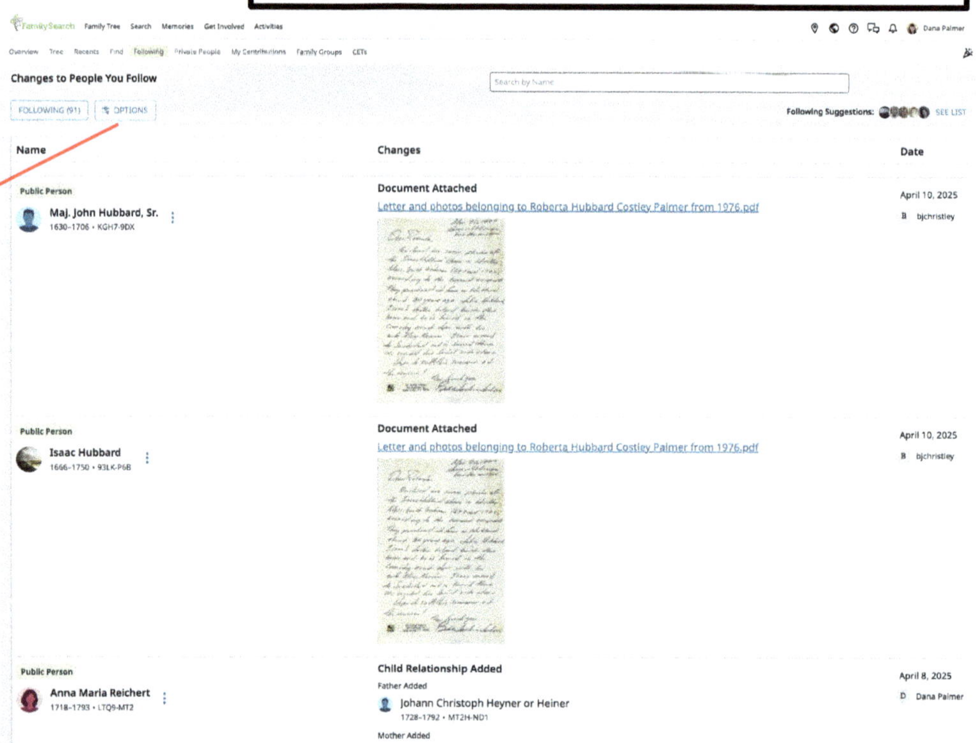

Choosing OPTIONS allows you to sort the list of changes.

Chat

Anytime someone makes a change in the TREE on FamilySearch, it is noted in the RECENT CHANGES log and also in the EDIT field for that specific fact. To contact the person who made this change, just click on their name and a pop-up screen will appear with a button to send them a chat. Sometimes the person also will have their email and, if you are very lucky, their phone number listed in the pop-up field. Anytime someone sends a chat message it will appear in the upper right corner of the FamilySearch page with a colored (usually orange) circle next to it. Click on the CHAT icon and a pop-up screen will appear where you can read the message and respond, if desired. You can also send chats directly from this pop-up screen.

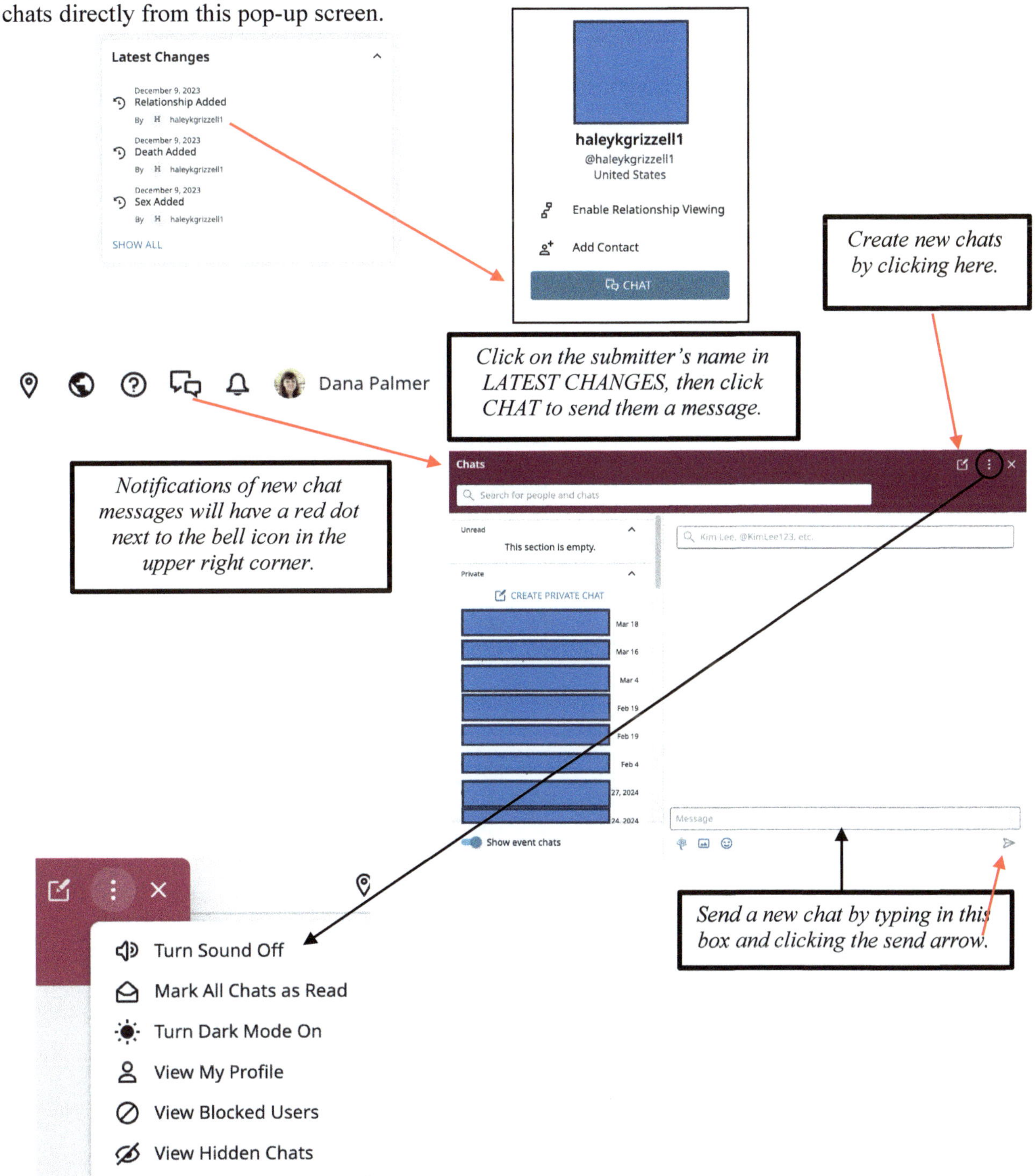

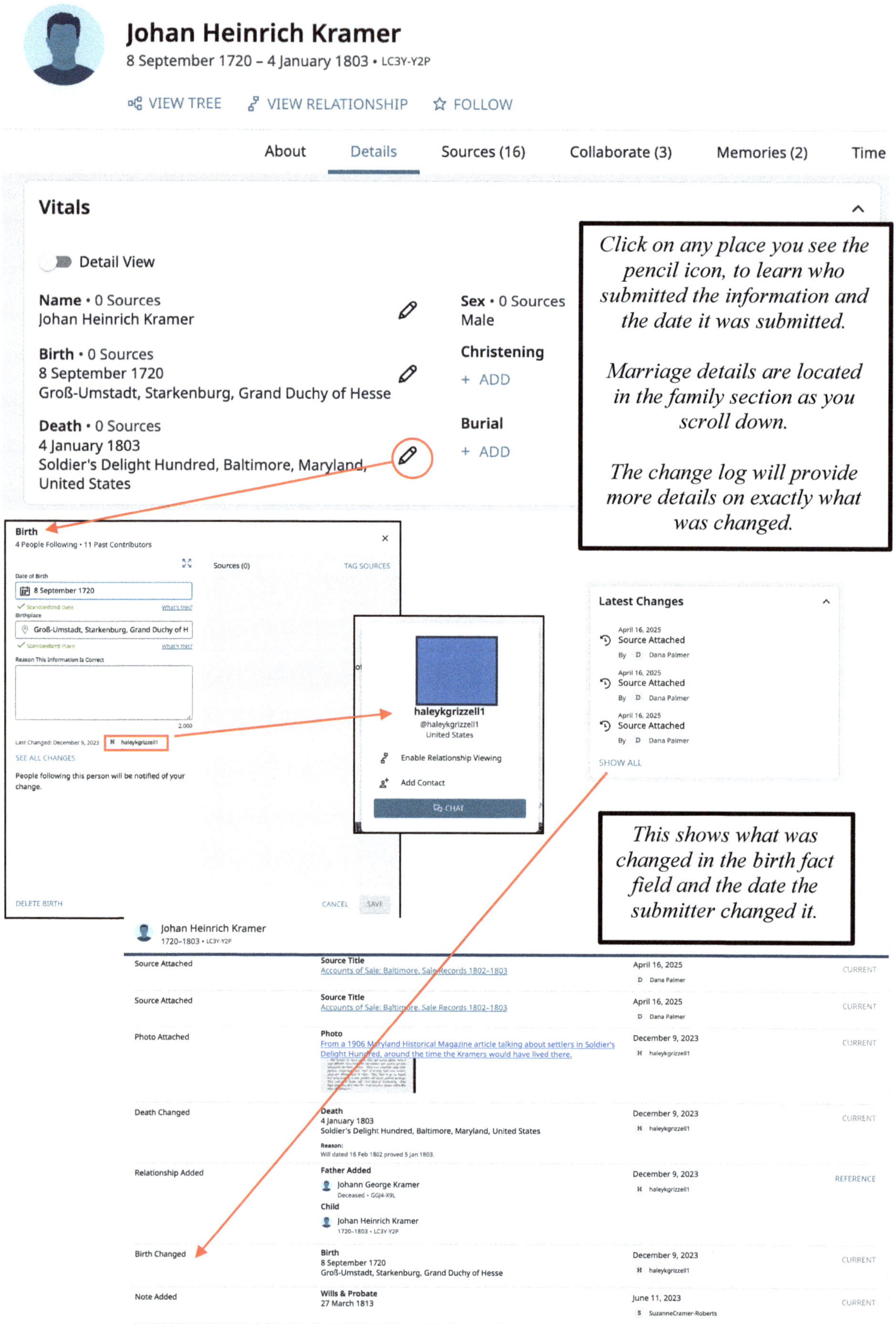

Click on any place you see the pencil icon, to learn who submitted the information and the date it was submitted.

Marriage details are located in the family section as you scroll down.

The change log will provide more details on exactly what was changed.

This shows what was changed in the birth fact field and the date the submitter changed it.

Relatives Around Me – i-phone

RELATIVES AROUND ME is currently only available on digital devices. It indicates if you are related to those also logged in to RELATIVES AROUND ME at the same time you are, how closely you relate, and notes your common ancestor. You will need to log in to your FamilySearch account and other partner sites first, before using this tool. Once you are logged in to FamilySearch, select MORE, then click on RELATIVES AROUND ME.

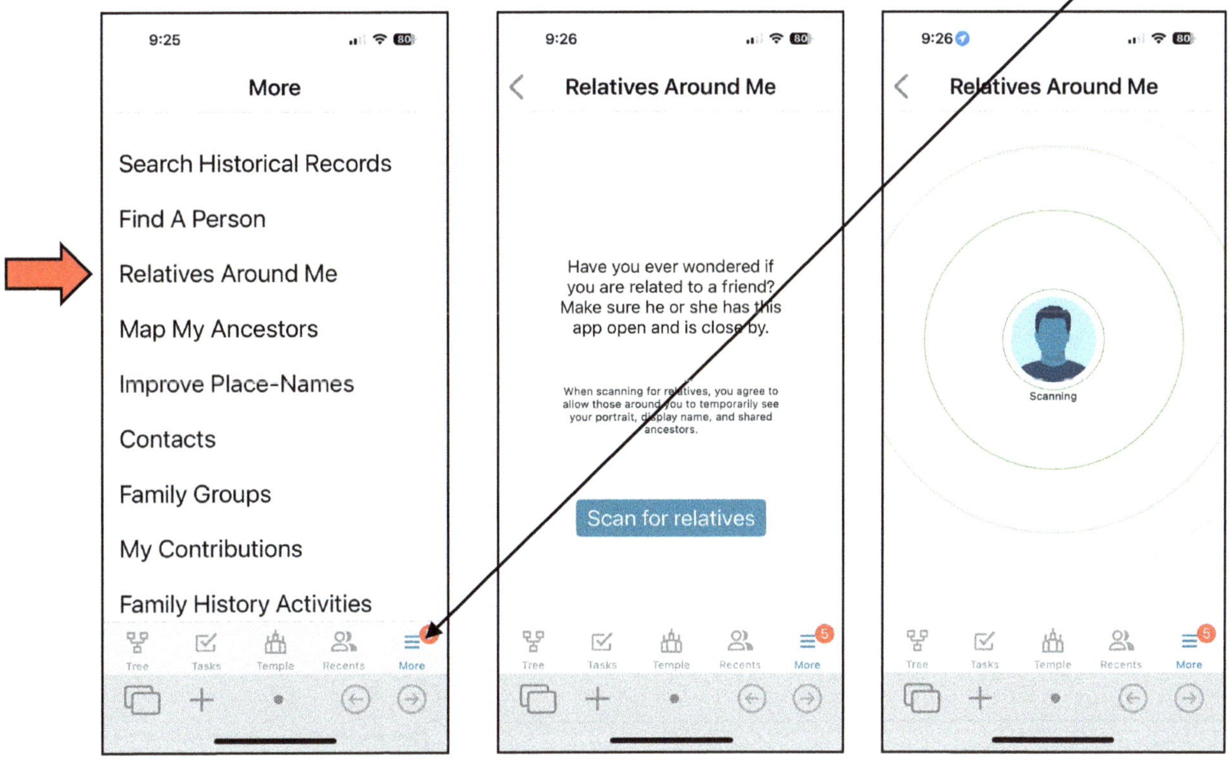

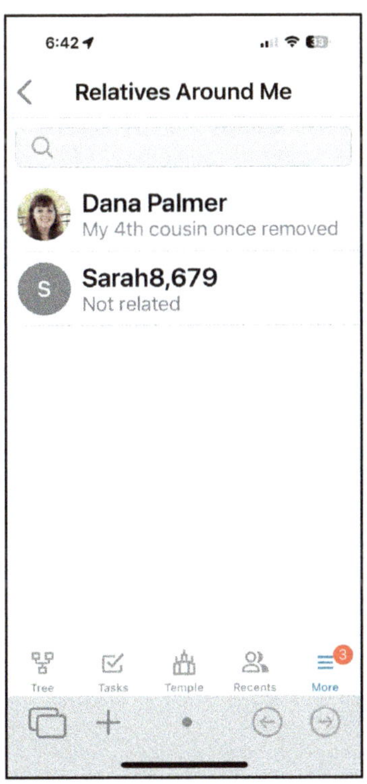

My husband used his i-phone to see if he had any Relatives Around Me. Since no one else was logged in at that time, he didn't get any matches.

He tried it again at a later date when I was logged in, and I showed up as a match to my husband, which we knew to be true from our paper records.

Our daughter, Sarah, did not appear as being related to either of us, because she had not properly set up her account in FamilySearch and did not have any people connected to her in the TREE. Once she gets connected in the TREE she should show as a match to both of us.

Sometimes, those using RELATIVES AROUND ME could be related, but if either of you are lacking information to connect you in the TREE, you won't show as being related.

To see through to which relative you are connected, click on the match and it will show your common ancestor.

This is a really fun app to try while at the RootsTech conference. To how many cousins do you connect?

Relatives Around Me – Android

RELATIVES AROUND ME on an Android phone works similarly to an i-phone.

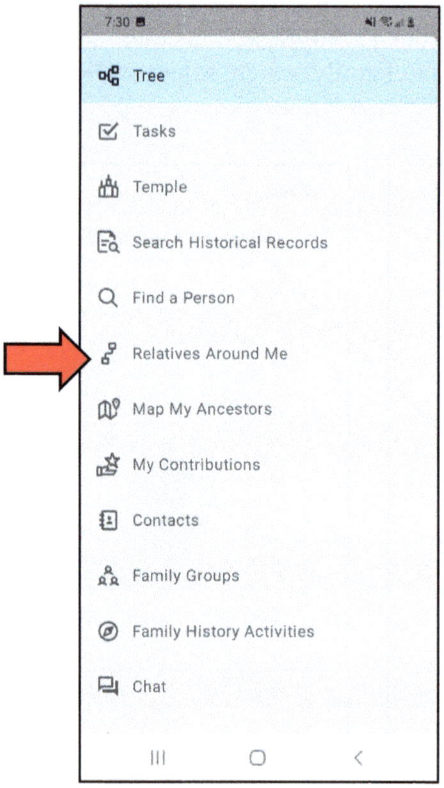

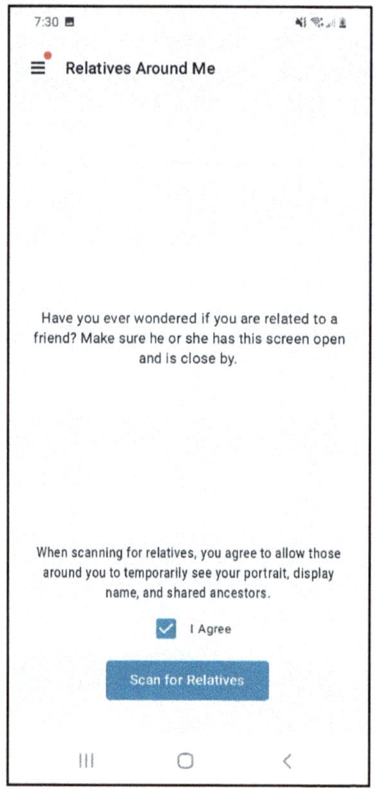

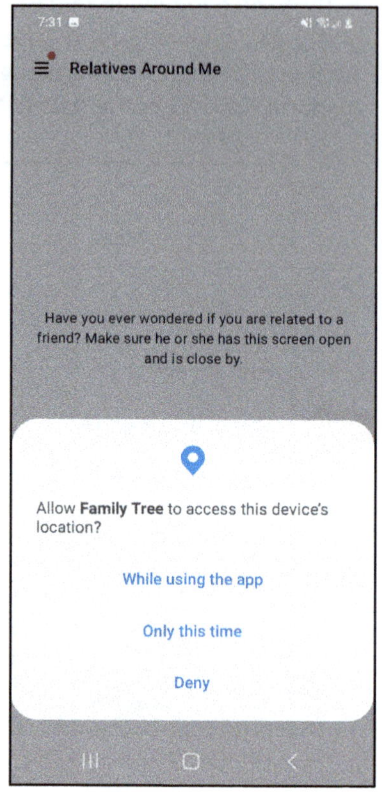

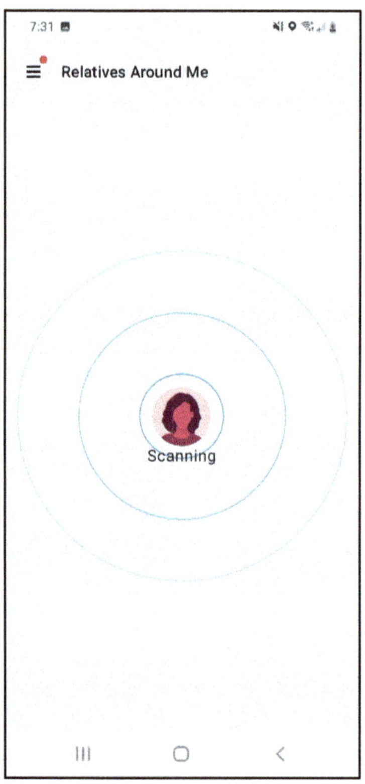

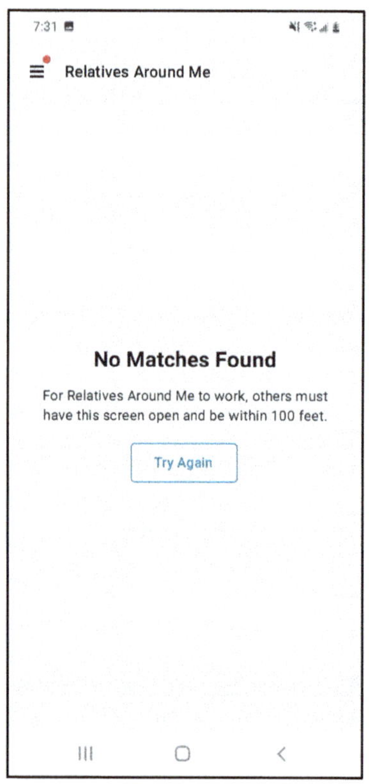

When my daughter Megan tried to use the RELATIVES AROUND ME on her Android phone, she didn't get any matches because no one else was using the system within 100 feet of her while she was trying it out.

You can see that the layout of the app on the Android is very similar to the i-phone.

HELP & LEARNING CENTER

FamilySearch offers many free resources and tools to help you find your family online and in repositories around the world.

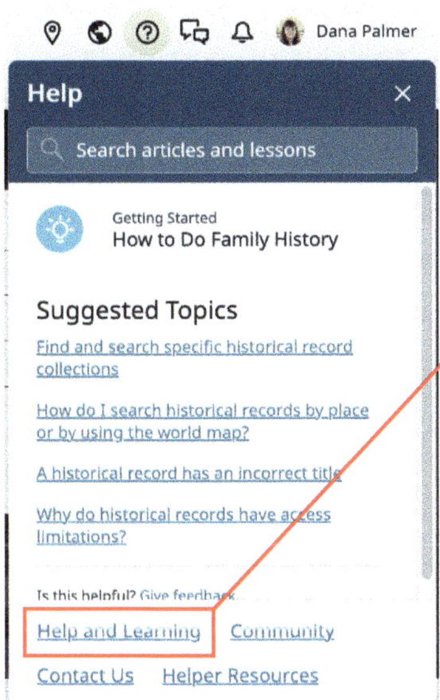

If you need help, you can type your topic into the search box, then choose from one of the most popular topics, or click on the icons for popular subjects for help.

In addition, FamilySearch has articles, webinars and live lectures to help you find your family in locations around the world.

https://www.familysearch.org/en/help/helpcenter/landing

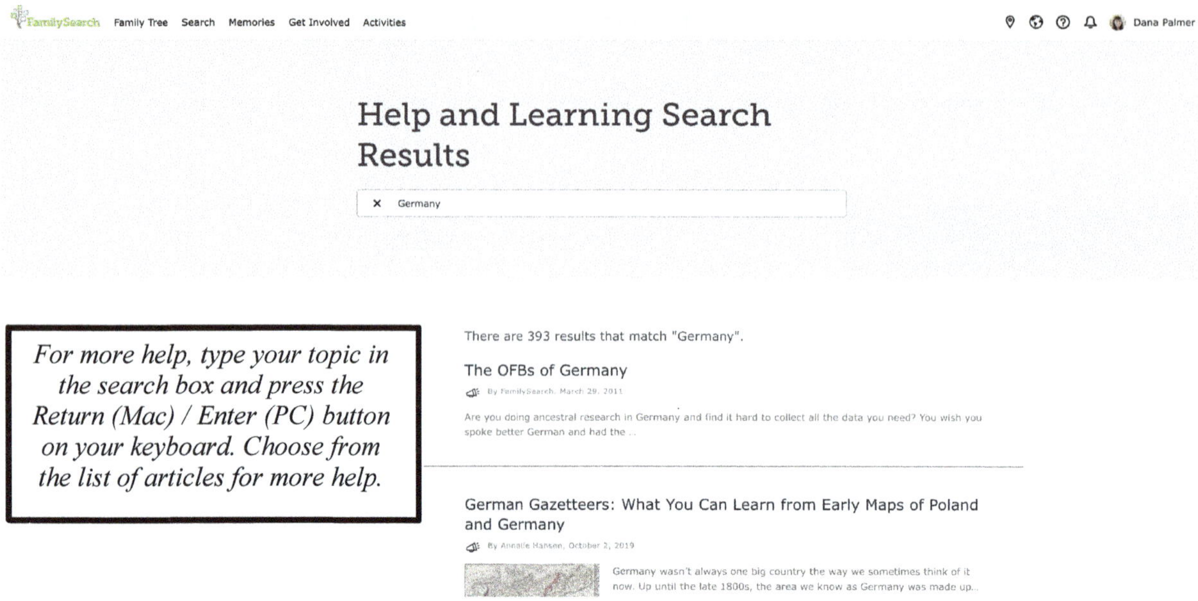

For more help, type your topic in the search box and press the Return (Mac) / Enter (PC) button on your keyboard. Choose from the list of articles for more help.

https://www.familysearch.org/en/help/helpcenter/search?q=Germany

https://www.familysearch.org/en/help/helpcenter/classes-and-videos

This website has links to free webinars from FamilySearch, YouTube, and RootsTech.

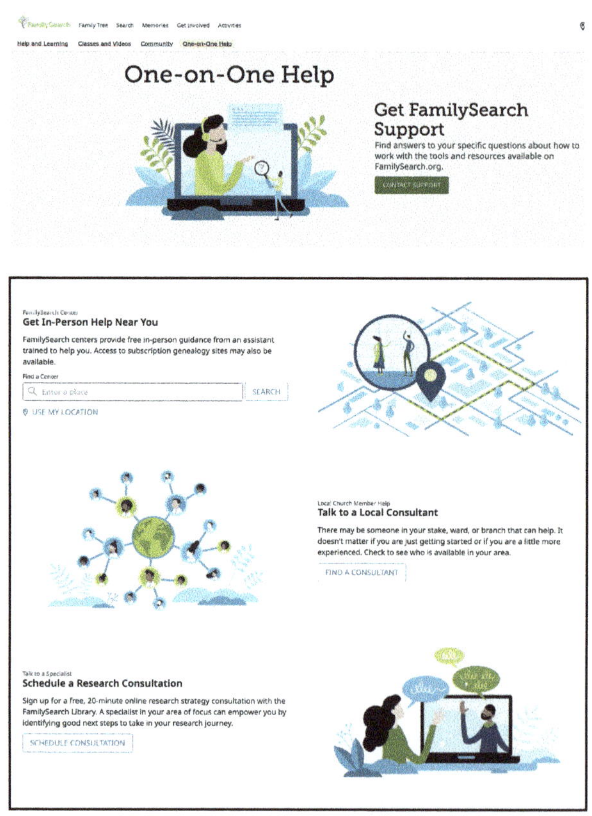

https://www.familysearch.org/en/help/helpcenter/one-on-one

This website will help you get in-person help at a local FamilySearch center or affiliate, by talking to a local consultant, or scheduling a free 20-minute research consultation.

COMMUNITY

COMMUNITY is one of my favorite places to go on FamilySearch when I can't find answers in the HELP AND LEARNING category. It's a great place to get international help, especially for translating handwritten records. Start by going to (https://www.familysearch.org/en/help/helpcenter/community-landing) and click on GO TO COMMUNITY. You can also click on the COMMUNITY button in the HELP menu. Both will take you to the following website (https://community.familysearch.org/en/).

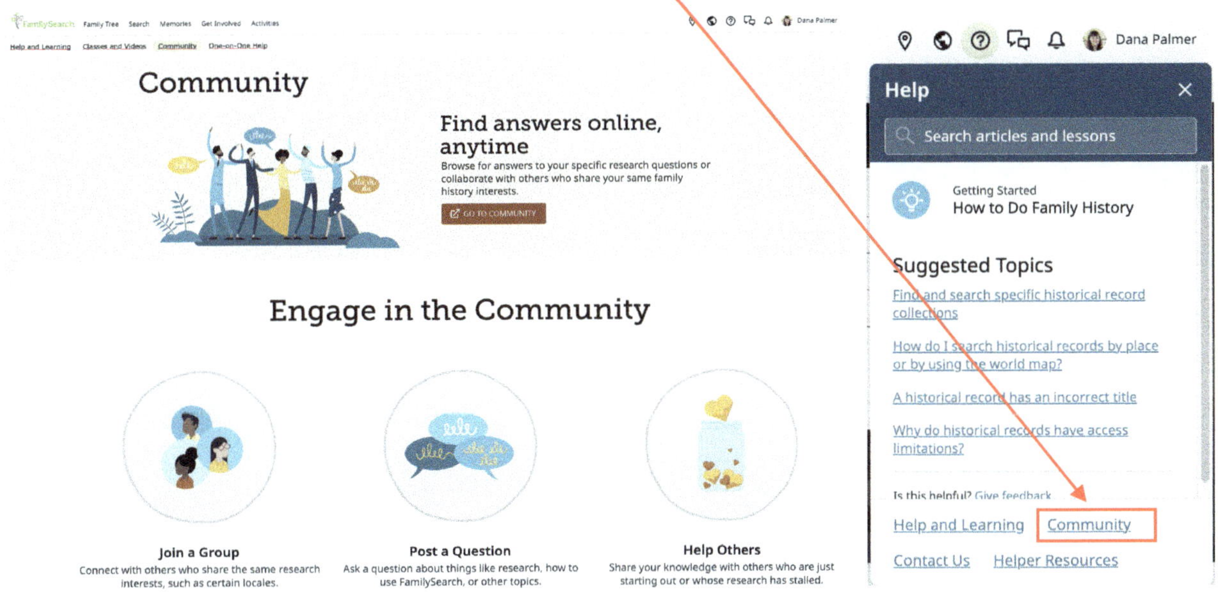

https://www.familysearch.org/en/help/helpcenter/community-landing

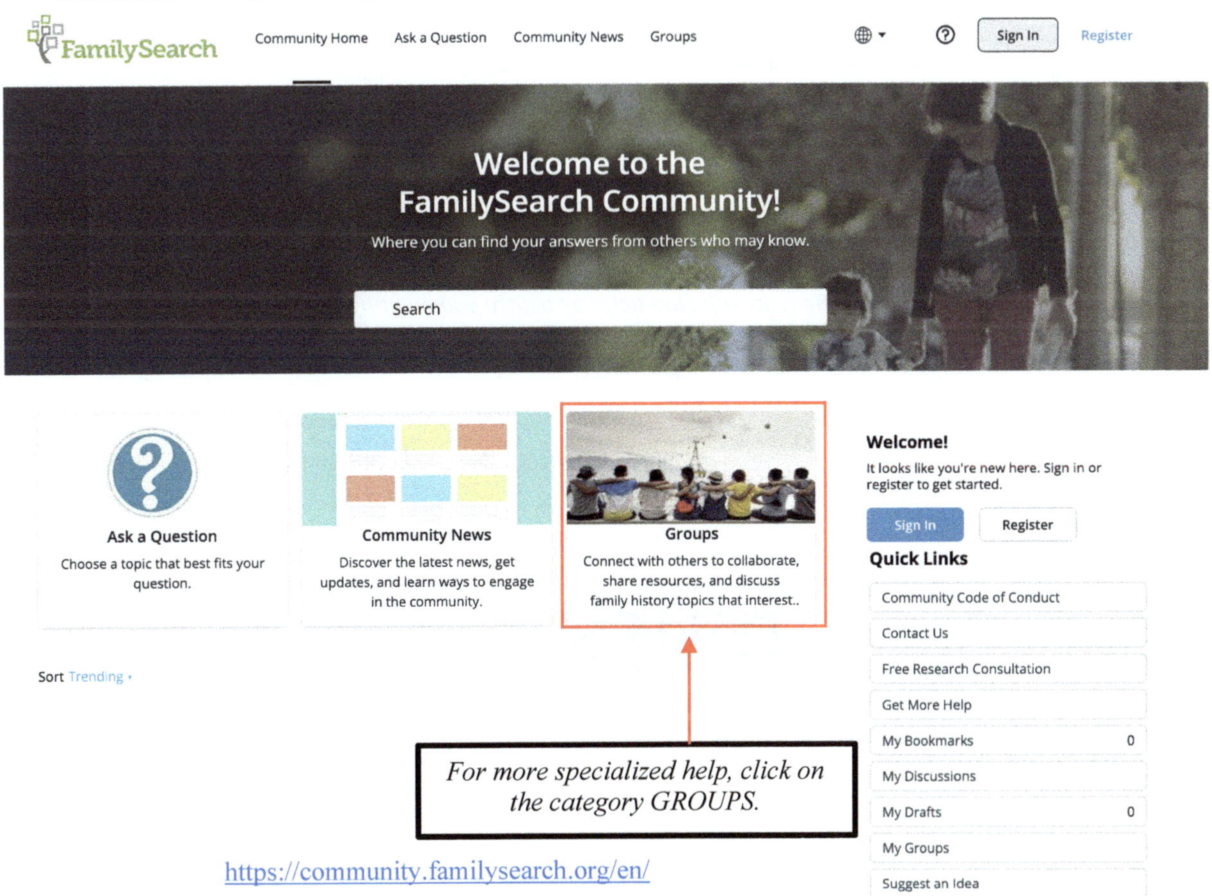

For more specialized help, click on the category GROUPS.

https://community.familysearch.org/en/

The GROUPS category in COMMUNITY allows you to get more specialized help. You can type in the location in the SEARCH GROUPS search box or browse the collections. There are many wonderful groups that offer help for researchers whose questions are more specific. There is also a FREE RESEARCH CONSULTATION in the QUICK LINKS, which is useful. To get to the GROUPS, go to the following website (https://community.familysearch.org/en/categories/gp-groups-en).

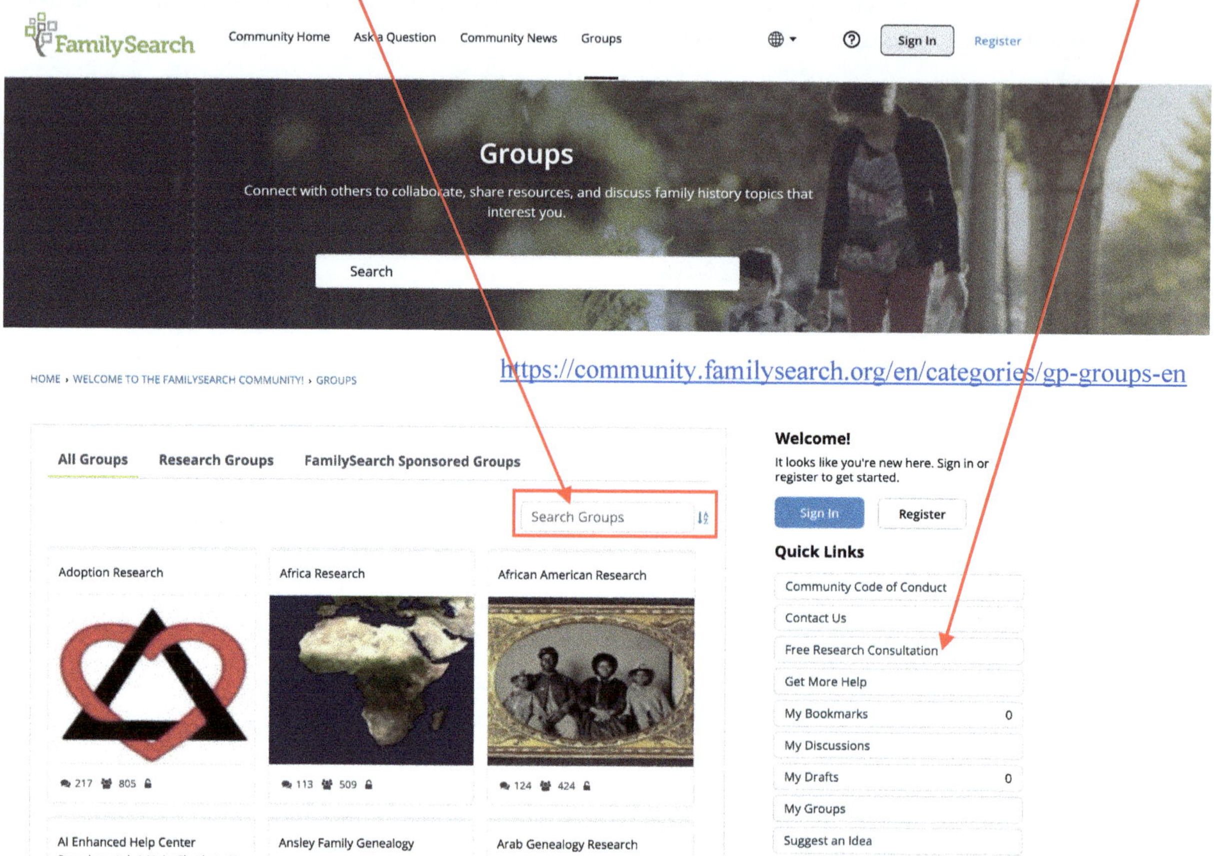

To see what groups are available, scroll down through the collections or type the name or country in the SEARCH GROUPS box. When the Group you want appears, click on it to be redirected to that Group's page. You can browse through what they offer without joining the Group, but you must join before you can post a record requesting help, offering help, or before commenting on someone else's post.

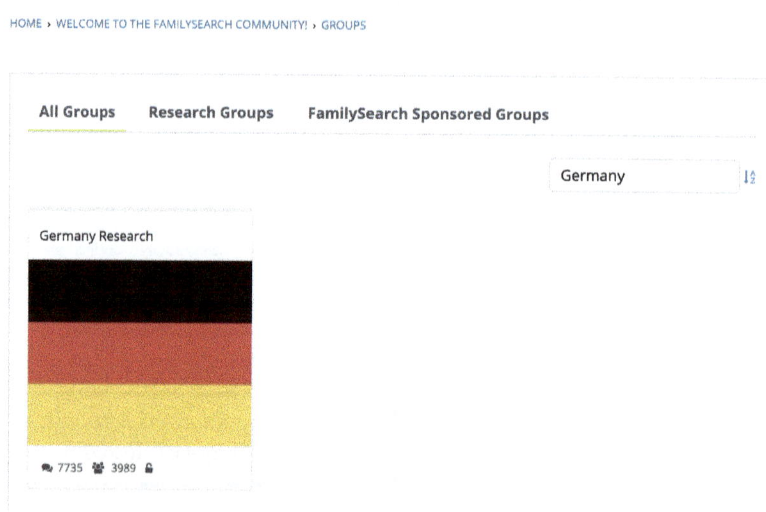

Click on the Group to go to their page.

FamilySearch Community Home Ask a Question Community News Groups Sign In Register

HOME › GROUPS › GERMANY RESEARCH

https://community.familysearch.org/en/group/88-germany-research

This is the page for the Germany Research Group.

Germany Research

Here you can find research links and ideas for learning more about your family and ancestors in German-speaking countries.

Please join the Group to Post a Comment in the Discussions and participate in discussions on Research issues

| *When posting a discussion/question that is requesting "Translation" - Please start the Discussion Title with "Translation Request", this will help facilitate those who have ability to go directly to that Discussion.*

The FamilySearch Library in Salt Lake City, Utah is offering a number of Webinars. A Great way to be involved in further training. This link will allow you to use the list and sign-up if you desire to. https://www.familysearch.org/en/library/classes

Group is in need of Translators- If there is anyone willing to assist with Translating in any languages in this group, please contact via a "Discussion" sharing your language specialty. ✓

German Resource Links | Code of Conduct | Virtual Genealogy Consultations | Posting Helps

RootsTech 2025

Don't forget to LOOK at the bottom of this home page to see upcoming events!

Owner: System Leaders: Fritz Juengling, Steve Walker16, Charlotte Noelle Champenois, System, AnneLoForteWillson, Richard E Mason, ScottSeegmiller, Mary T Wilson, ZachTW, kayrcarpenter

Created on January 25, 2021 **3971 members** Privacy: Public

Join

FamilySearch Community Home Ask a Question Community News Groups Sign In Register

HOME › GROUPS › GERMANY RESEARCH

Translation request - German birth record for J Herbst 2 June 1804

tamstam
April 16

Thank you

Best Answer

Robert Seal_1
April 17 edited April 17 · Answer ✓

Hello @tamstam,

Koetel [Köttel], born on 2 June 1804 about the hour of 2 in the afternoon and the following day baptized is Joannes Herbst, legitimate son of Andreas Herbst and Cunigunda, née Ziegler, from Roth.

Godfather: Joannes Beetz, carpenter from Kaspauer.

[Written in the right margin is the child's name again]: Joannes Herbst.

Welcome!
It looks like you're new here. Sign in or register to get started.

Sign In Register

Quick Links

- Community Code of Conduct
- Contact Us
- Free Research Consultation
- Get More Help
- My Bookmarks 0
- My Discussions
- My Drafts 0
- My Groups
- Suggest an Idea

Categories

All Categories

This is an example of what you might find in the discussions. For translation help, you can post an image of the record as above, or you can post a link to the record image on FamilySearch or another website, and volunteers will help you for free.

Be sure to bookmark your post so you can find it again later without having to search through all the posts.

FamilySearch Community Home Ask a Question Community

HOME › GROUPS › GERMANY RESEARCH

German Resource Links

PABulfinch
November 8, 2022 edited April 19, 2023

Google Translate

- Meyers Gazetteer
- "How to" Guides
- Archion
- Matricula
- Germany in FS wiki
- Hannover parish histories
- Fulda Diocesan Archive parishes online
- Fuzzy Gazetteer
- Kreise list
- Kreis map
- Names distribution map
- Map of German Empire
- Wörterbuchnetz
- Find a Family History Center and FamilySearch Affiliate Libraries
- German word list
- Learn old German Script videos
- French Word List
- Latin Word List
- Dutch Word List

https://community.familysearch.org/en/discussion/133794/german-resource-links

LABS

One of the hidden gems on the FamilySearch website is FamilySearch LABS. This is where they test out new, innovative technology that often later appears on the public FamilySearch website. The easiest way to access LABS is to click on the VIEW EXPERIMENTS link on the main FamilySearch website, or go to the following web address (https://www.familysearch.org/en/labs/).

These change periodically, so check back often to see what new experiments they are exploring.

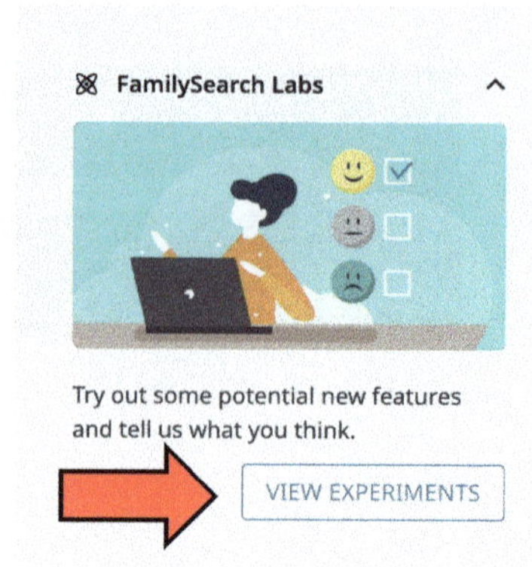

GET INVOLVED

FamilySearch offers many ways to give back and participate in making records more accessible. Originally this was done by participation in the indexing projects. With the advancements in AI technology, computers are gradually replacing the old indexing project, making access to indexes and records much sooner. The focus now is having humans correct the mistakes AI makes, and FamilySearch still needs your help reviewing, attaching, and correcting records for people in the TREE and the records transcribed or indexed by AI. Click the GET INVOLVED tab and select OPPORTUNITIES to find out how you can help. Some of the current projects include *quick name review, full name review, family review*, and *verify places*.

For more details go to the following web links (https://www.familysearch.org/en/getinvolved/) and (https://www.familysearch.org/en/getinvolved/opportunities).

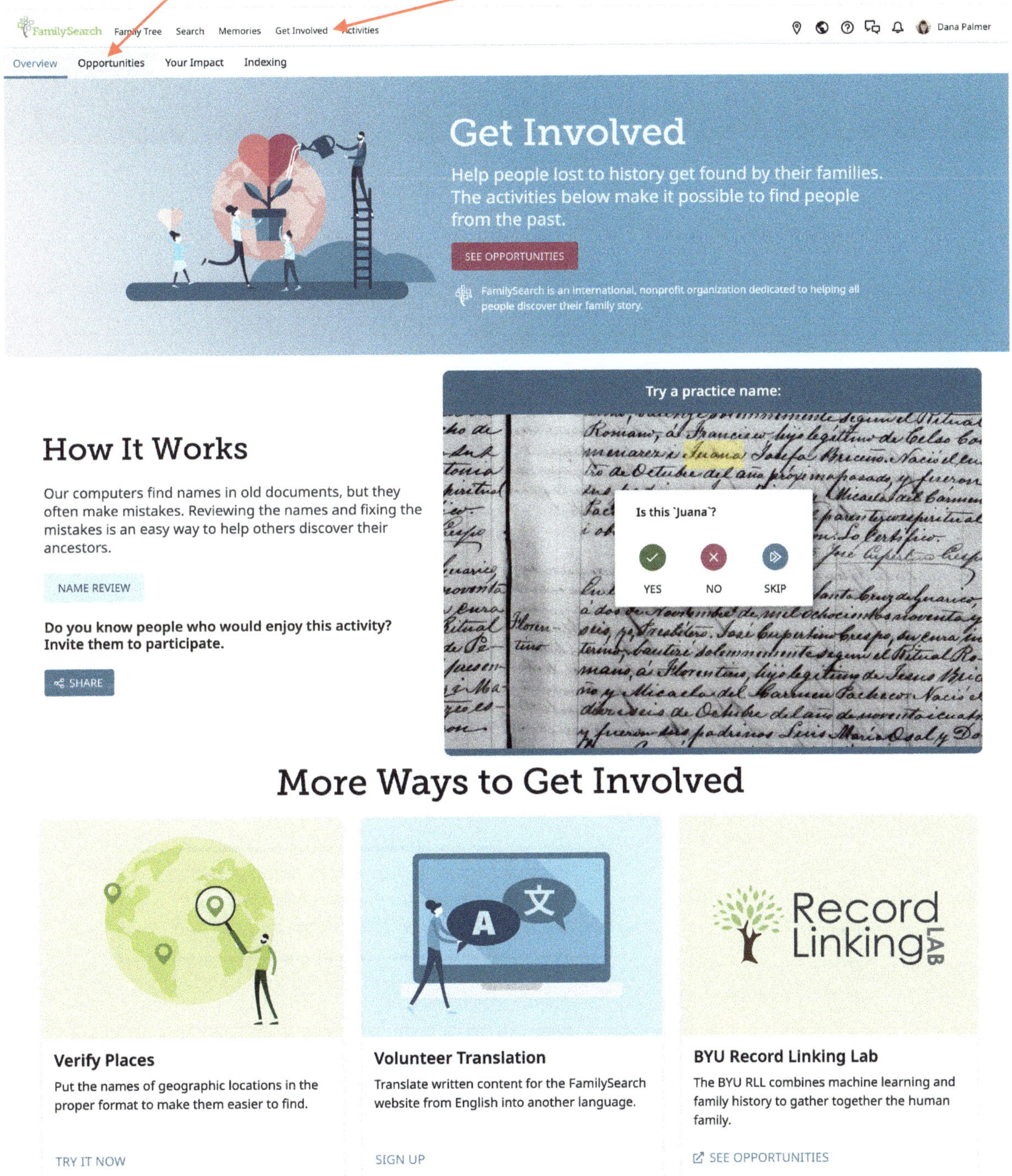

SOLUTIONS GALLERY

A hidden gem located at the bottom of FamilySearch is a link to the SOLUTIONS GALLERY, which has links to websites and software to aid you in finding your roots and connecting your kin. For more details go to the following website (https://www.familysearch.org/en/innovate/solutions-gallery).

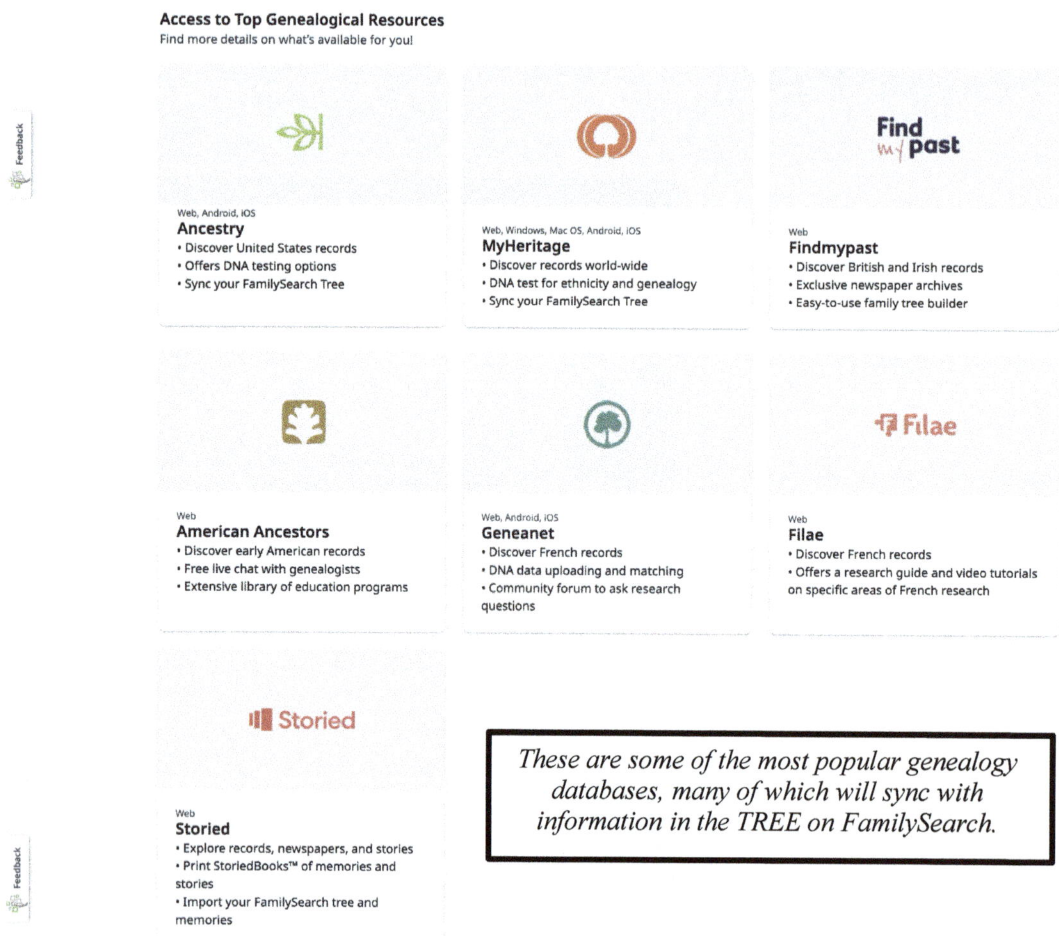

These are some of the most popular genealogy databases, many of which will sync with information in the TREE on FamilySearch.

https://www.familysearch.org/en/innovate/solutions-gallery

Below are apps or links to websites with programs to help you manage your own personal tree, many of which will sync with the TREE on FamilySearch.

Family Tree Management Apps

These apps and websites can sync information with FamilySearch Family Tree.

Windows and Mac OS
Ancestral Quest
- Store genealogical findings in a private database
- Find hints in your research with TreeTips™
- Document your Sources with CitePro™ Technology

Windows
Familienbuch 6.0
- Record and organize your ancestors
- Display ancestors in lists, and print them out
- Record and process data without overloading your interface

Windows
Legacy Family Tree
- Search through records from billions of websites
- Preserve your ancestors' stories
- Create hashtags to describe your ancestors

iOS, Mac OS
MacFamily Tree
- Discover your origins and evolution of your ancestry
- Capture and visualize your family history
- Search the free FamilySearch archive

Web
RootsFinder
- Decide who can edit your tree with Free Forever Plan
- Make your tree private with Pro Plan
- Sync with FamilySearch, and find hints

Windows, Mac OS, Android, iOS
RootsMagic
- Award-wining genealogy software
- Research, organize, and share family history

Windows
The MagiKey
- The most advanced census research tool
- Quickly identify conflicting census information
- Gather, record, and analyze family history trees

These are some of the most popular personal database programs in the Solutions Gallery, where you can organize your information.

https://www.familysearch.org/en/innovate/solutions-gallery

Here are links to other companies with useful tools to aid in finding your family, including games to inspire those of any age to get involved.

Other Solutions

Browse this list of resources that allow you to play games, print family charts, and more. Visit each website for more information.

Web
Ancestor Games
- Created BYU Family History Technology Lab
- Learn about your family history through games

Web
BeenVerified
- Aggregates public records data from many sources
- Easy-to-use, data-driven family tree builder
- Add FamilySearch ancestors to your family tree

Web, Windows, Mac OS, Android, IOS
billiongraves
- Discover the world's largest resource for geo-located cemetery data.
- Help take pictures at your local cemetery or transcribe other's pictures.

Web
dearest forever
- Beautiful family tree artwork prints
- Custom-made to your perfect style
- A unique, meaningful gift to cherish

Web
EmulateMe
- Create your own AI avatar
- Create realistic AI videos and voice clips
- Chat with smart avatars of your ancestors

Web
Eternal Reminder
- A two-step process to secure your ancestors' temple work
- Schedule an email reminder for your ancestor's 110th birthday

Windows, MacOS
Evidentia
- One place to organize your sources
- Squeeze more information from your sources
- Compare conflicting evidence for confident conclusions

Web
Family Chart Masters
- Custom decorative charts
- We'll send you a printed family chart of your choosing

https://www.familysearch.org/en/innovate/solutions-gallery

These are three of my very favorite resources in the SOLUTIONS GALLERY.

https://thefhguide.com/

This is a fun game that takes information from what you have entered into the TREE on FamilySearch and makes it into a genealogy version of the Jeopardy game.

How many questions would you get right?

FAMILY HISTORY TECHNOLOGY LAB

FamilySearch COMPATIBLE SOLUTION

https://geneopardy.fhtl.org/

https://ancestorgames.fhtl.org/#!/

ACTIVITIES

FamilySearch offers many activities to help those of all ages and abilities get started learning about their heritage and connecting with their family. To see what family history related activities are available on the FamilySearch website, click on ACTIVITIES at the top of the FamilySearch website.

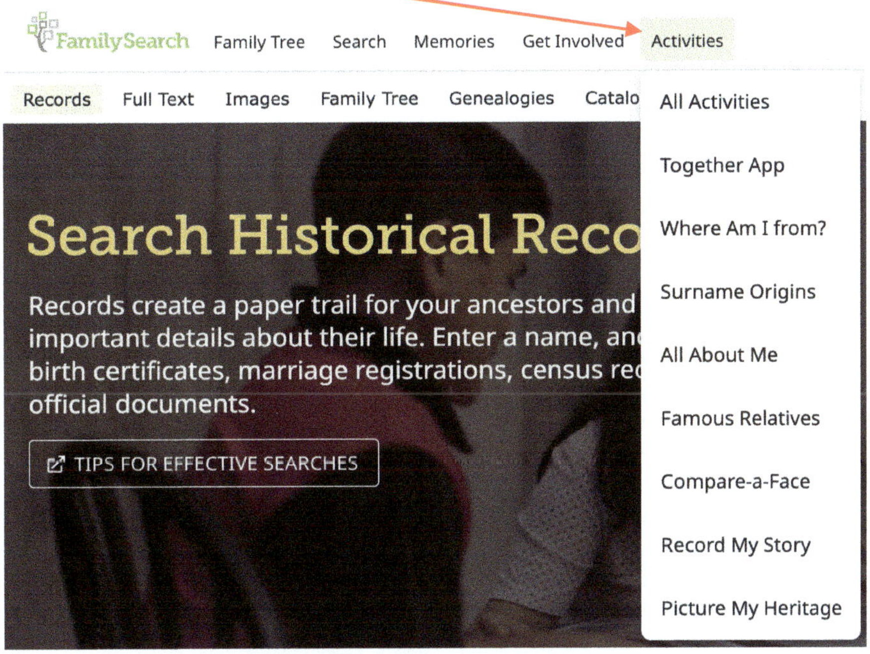

Some of the more popular activities can be accessed directly from the dropdown menu under the ACTIVITIES tab. Some of my family's favorites include *Compare-a-Face, Record My Story*, and *Picture My Heritage*.

To see all the choices, click on ALL ACTIVITIES in the dropdown menu, and you will be redirected to the following website (https://www.familysearch.org/en/discovery/).

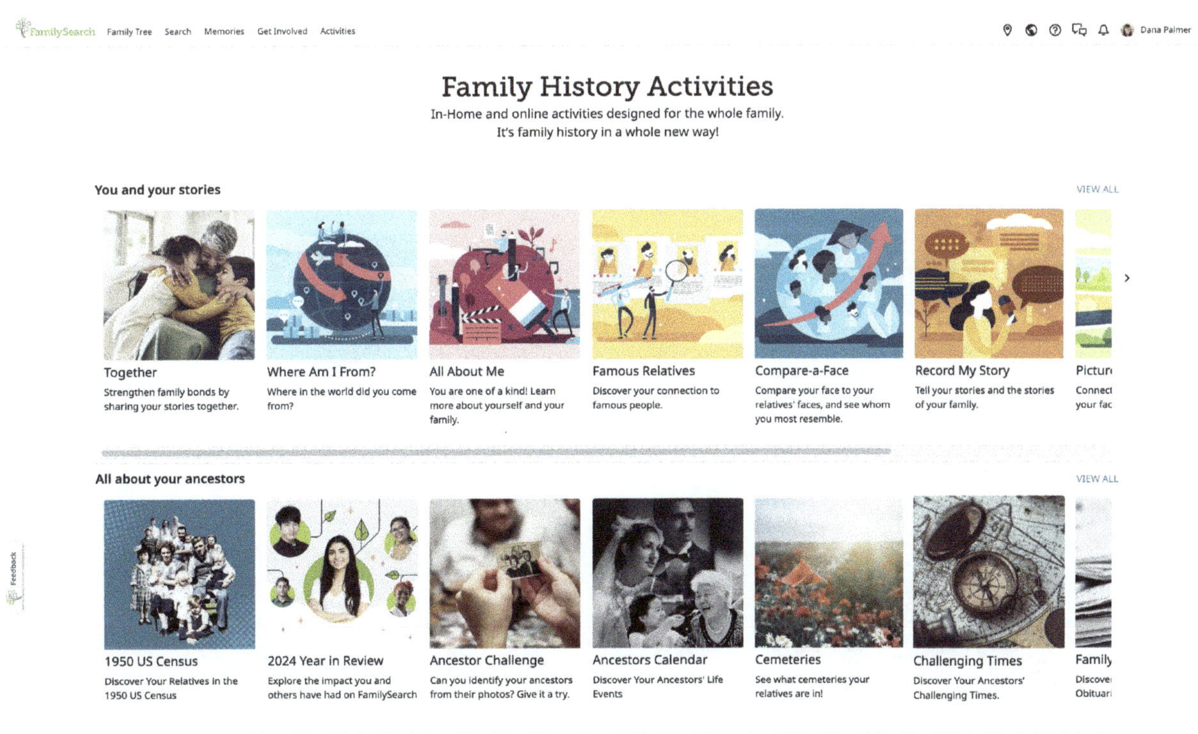

https://www.familysearch.org/en/discovery

Compare a Face

COMPARE-A-FACE is a fun activity for those of all ages. Click on ACTIVITIES, and choose Compare-a-Face, or go to the following website (https://www.familysearch.org/en/discovery/compareme).

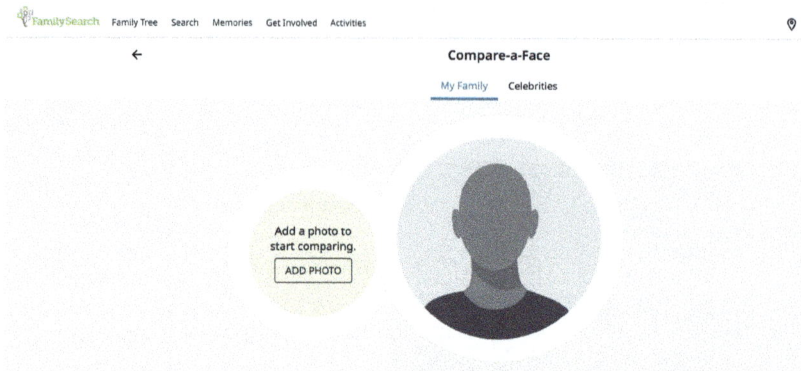

Add a photo by taking a selfie or uploading a photo from your computer or from the images in your GALLERY. The system will then compare the photo you added with those already added as images in the TREE. Try photos of yourself from different periods of time. You might be surprised at how much you look like one relative at one period of your life and a different relative at a different stage of life. Here are some comparisons for me.

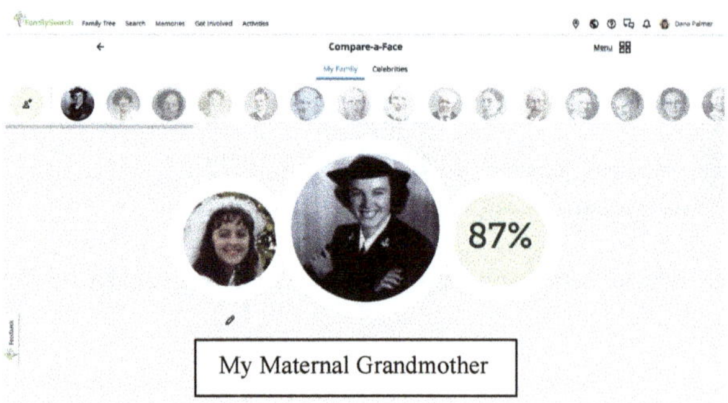

My Maternal Grandmother

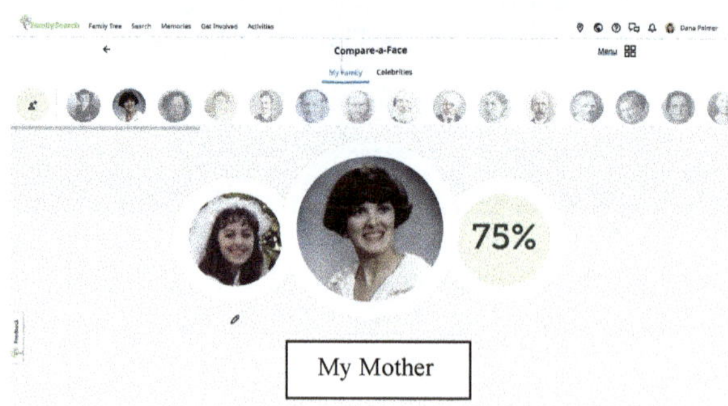

My Mother

My wedding photo shows I look most like my grandmother when she was in the Navy and about the same age.

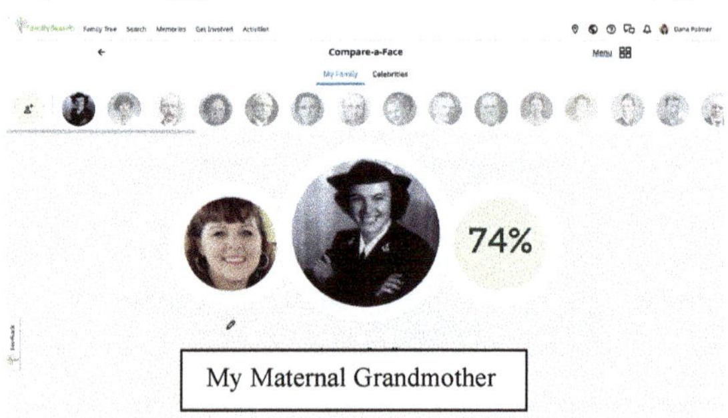

My Maternal Grandmother

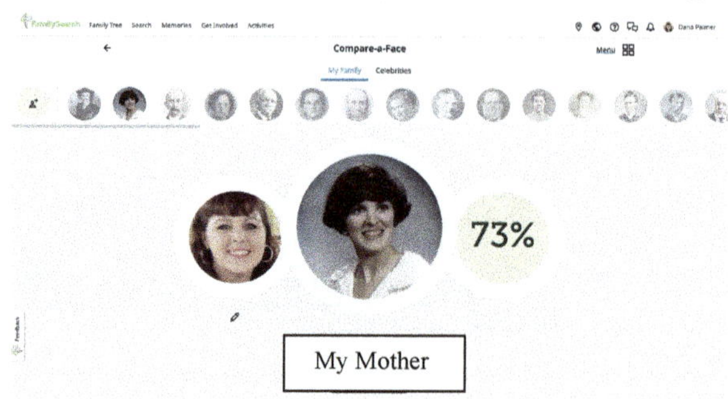

My Mother

In my mid 30s, I still look most like my grandmother when she was in the Navy.

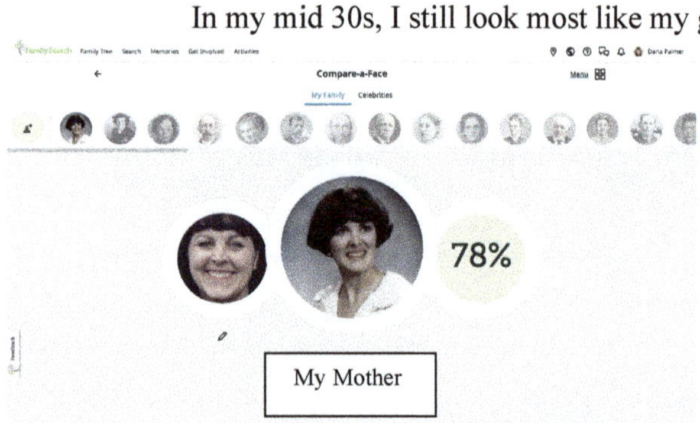

My Mother

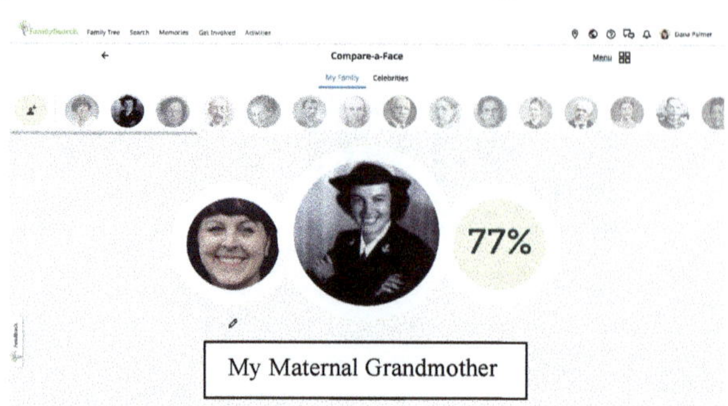

My Maternal Grandmother

I now look more like my mother when she was about the same age.

Record My Story

RECORD MY STORY is a good way to preserve your heritage by recording stories about yourself and your ancestors. Click on ACTIVITIES, and choose RECORD MY STORY, or go to the following website (https://www.familysearch.org/en/discovery/recordme).

Click on the story you want to share, and it will prompt you with questions to help you record your story. This is a quick and fun activity for all ages to do at family get togethers or holidays visits.

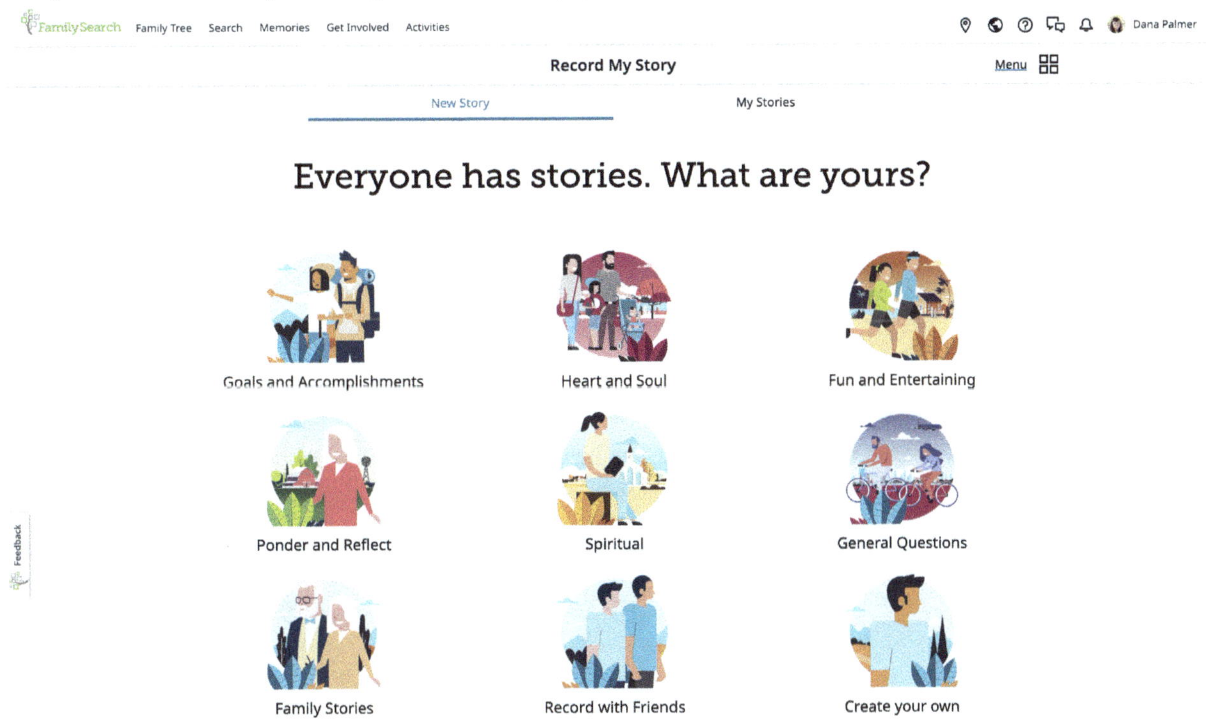

Together APP

TOGETHER APP is a new APP you can download to your phone to share your stories. Click on ACTIVITIES, and choose the TOGETHER APP or go to the following website (https://www.familysearch.org/en/discovery/together/).

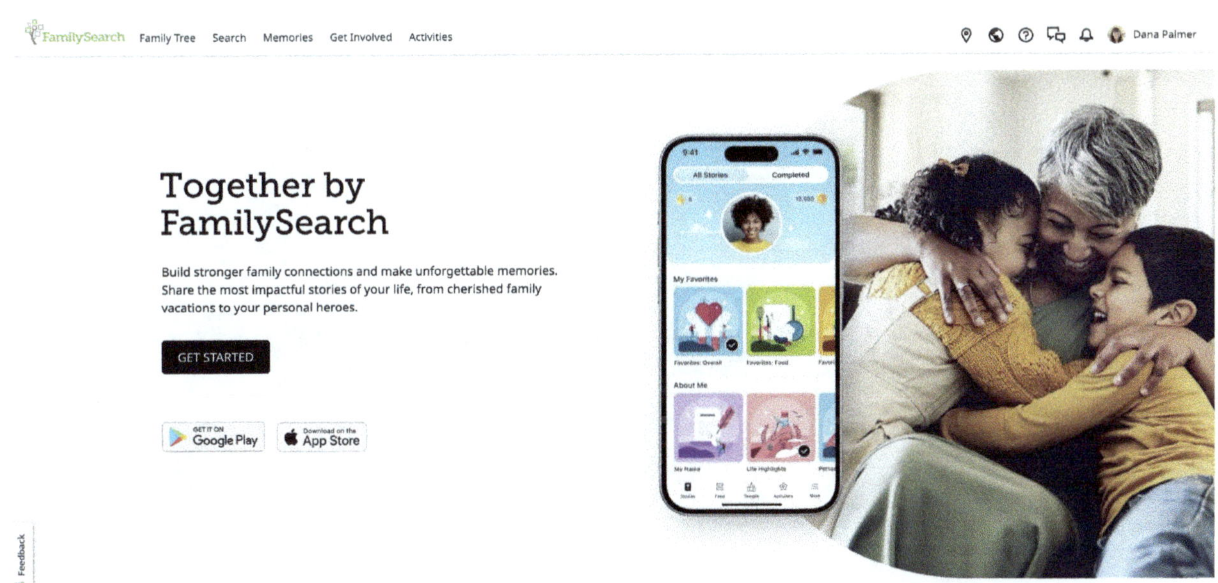

Picture My Heritage

Have you ever wanted to see what you might look like if you were raised in one of the countries where your ancestors lived? If so, PICTURE MY HERITAGE, is the activity for you. Click on ACTIVITIES, and choose PICTURE MY HERITAGE or go to (https://www.familysearch.org/en/discovery/picture/select).

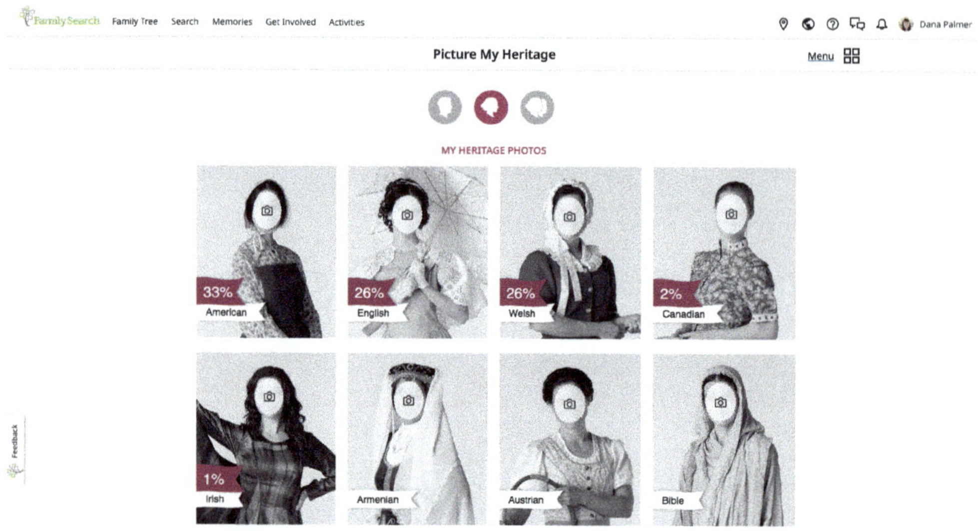

This fun interactive activity uses a selfie, which you can then place in headshots of people from various countries. These are my many faces below, including some the computer did not choose, but those I picked because I had known ancestors there.

The many faces of Dana Palmer from countries of her known ancestors.

Chapter 10: Summary

I hope this book has provided you with some ideas on how to effectively find records on the FamilySearch website and connect your family. There are so many sources available on the FamilySearch both on the website itself and through their partner organizations. It is truly amazing what you can find, if you know how to search through the data. Be persistent and creative when looking for your family.

Start by browsing RECORDS and find the database for a specific region or topic you want to search. Once you find the collection, search for your person using the filters, variant spellings, and tricks in Chapter 3. If that search brings up the name you are looking for, you should be able to find them.

If you can't find what you want in RECORDS, use the CATALOG or IMAGES to find the more recent digital records collections. Click on the camera icon and browse the images. Be sure to search at the town, county, state, and country levels to uncover all that exists for your location. If your person comes from an area with changing boundaries, be sure to search for records in all jurisdictions where your locality was constituted for that specific time, including variant town names. The FamilySearch RESEARCH WIKI and Wikipedia can help you identify these variant names.

Check out what records might exist for a location using the RESEARCH WIKI. Be sure to use the blue online record collection button, as well as filter down to more specific locations by clicking the links in that location. If you are researching in a country outside the United States, be sure to use the foreign language word guides, handwriting helps, and other useful tools. Also check out the topical categories and GUIDED RESEARCH on the main RESEARCH WIKI page.

With all the advances in AI on FamilySearch, be sure to bookmark and use the FULL-TEXT SEARCH feature and try various search tricks until you find your person if he / she was not found in the traditional indexes. This is truly a hidden gem and should be used often.

Lastly, have fun and keep hunting! There is always more to do and discover.

Index